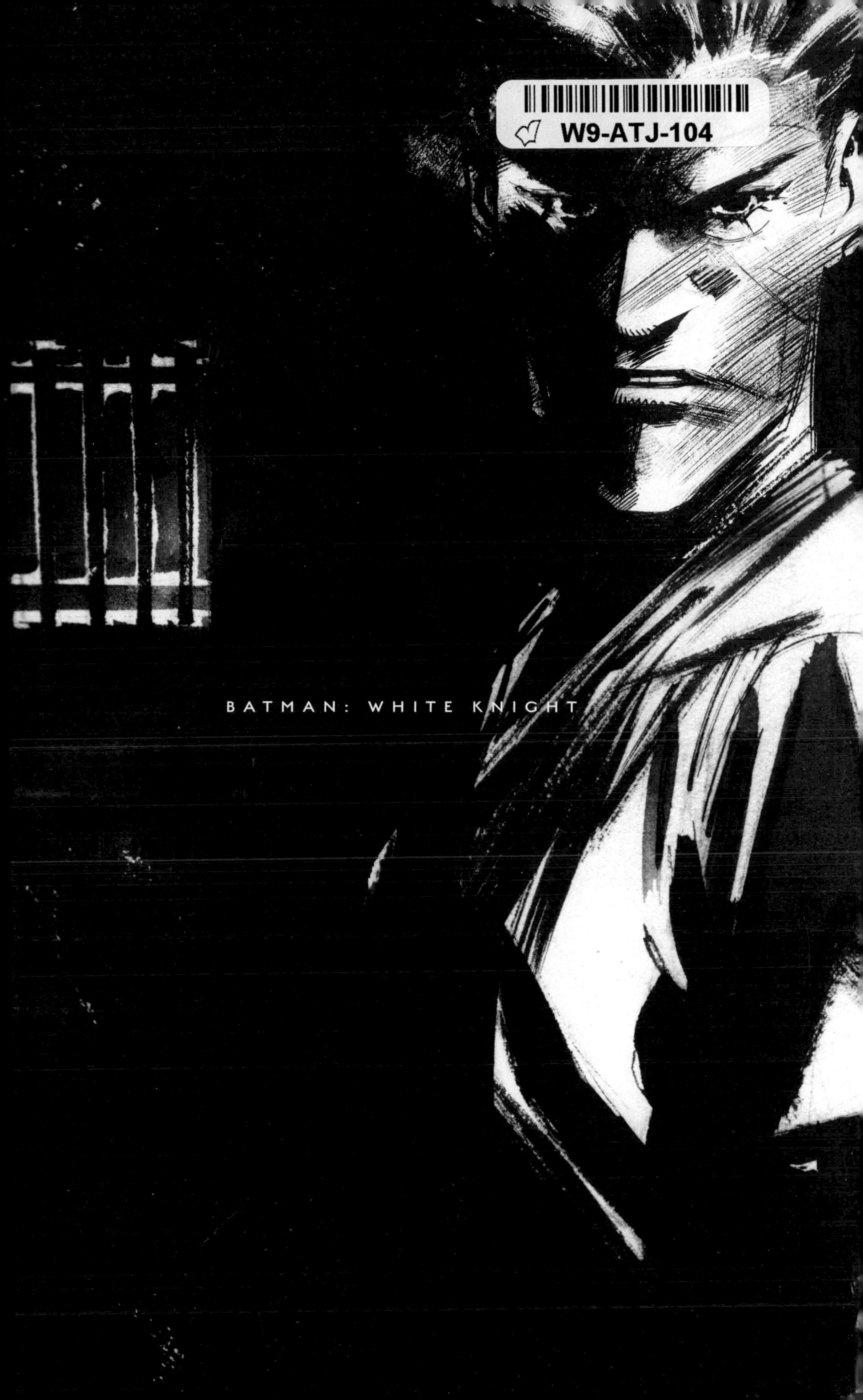
BATMAN: WHITE KNIGHT

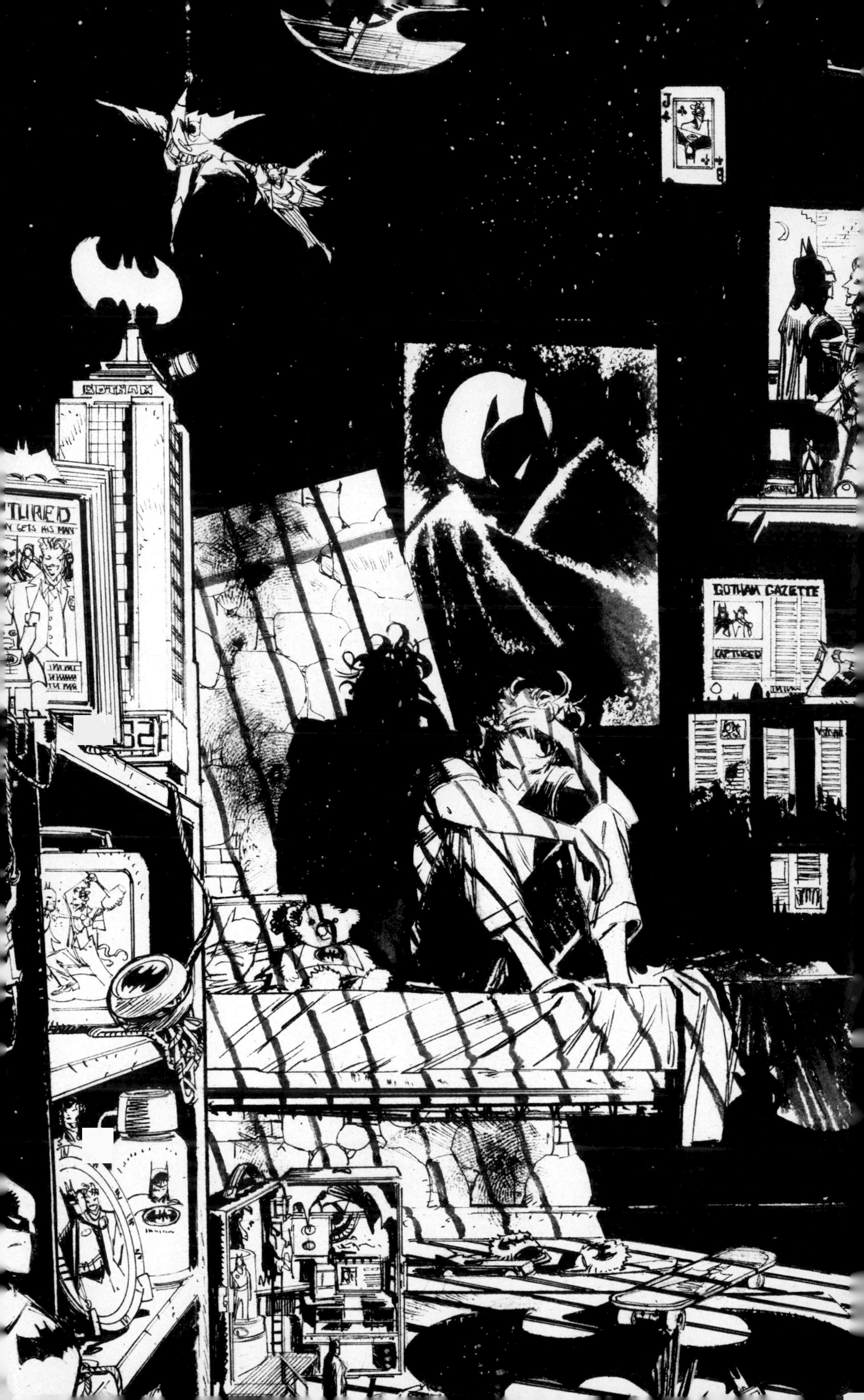
GOTHAM GAZETTE
CAPTURED

BATMAN
WHITE KNIGHT

SEAN MURPHY
writer and artist

MATT HOLLINGSWORTH
colorist

TODD KLEIN
letterer

**SEAN MURPHY
& MATT HOLLINGSWORTH**
cover art and original series covers

BATMAN created by BOB KANE
with BILL FINGER

MARK DOYLE Editor – Original Series
MAGGIE HOWELL Assistant Editor – Original Series
JEB WOODARD Group Editor – Collected Editions
SCOTT NYBAKKEN Editor – Collected Edition
STEVE COOK Design Director – Books
MONIQUE NARBONETA Publication Design

BOB HARRAS Senior VP – Editor-in-Chief, DC Comics
MARK DOYLE Executive Editor, Vertigo & Black Label

DAN DiDIO Publisher
JIM LEE Publisher & Chief Creative Officer
AMIT DESAI Executive VP – Business & Marketing Strategy,
Direct to Consumer & Global Franchise Management
BOBBIE CHASE VP & Executive Editor, Young Reader & Talent Development
MARK CHIARELLO Senior VP – Art, Design & Collected Editions
JOHN CUNNINGHAM Senior VP – Sales & Trade Marketing
BRIAR DARDEN VP – Business Affairs
ANNE DePIES Senior VP – Business Strategy, Finance & Administration
DON FALLETTI VP – Manufacturing Operations
LAWRENCE GANEM VP – Editorial Administration & Talent Relations
ALISON GILL Senior VP – Manufacturing & Operations
JASON GREENBERG VP – Business Strategy & Finance
HANK KANALZ Senior VP – Editorial Strategy & Administration
JAY KOGAN VP – Legal Affairs
NICK J. NAPOLITANO VP – Manufacturing Administration
LISETTE OSTERLOH VP – Digital Marketing & Events
EDDIE SCANNELL VP – Consumer Marketing
COURTNEY SIMMONS Senior VP – Publicity & Communications
JIM (SKI) SOKOLOWSKI VP – Comic Book Specialty Sales & Trade Marketing
NANCY SPEARS VP – Mass, Book, Digital Sales & Trade Marketing
MICHELE R. WELLS VP – Content Strategy

*Dedicated to Clay McCormack,
whose help was invaluable.*
—Sean Murphy

BATMAN: WHITE KNIGHT

Published by DC Comics. Compilation and all new material Copyright © 2018
DC Comics. All Rights Reserved. Originally published in single magazine
form in BATMAN: WHITE KNIGHT 1-8. Copyright © 2017, 2018 DC Comics.
All Rights Reserved. All characters, their distinctive likenesses and related
elements featured in this publication are trademarks of DC Comics.
The stories, characters and incidents featured in this publication are entirely
fictional. DC Comics does not read or accept unsolicited submissions
of ideas, stories or artwork.

DC Comics, 2900 West Alameda Ave., Burbank, CA 91505
Printed by LSC Communications, Kendallville, IN, USA. 8/31/18. First Printing.
ISBN: 978-1-4012-7959-2

Library of Congress Cataloging-in-Publication Data is available.

PEFC Certified

This product is from
sustainably managed
forests and controlled
sources

PEFC

PEFC/29-31-337   www.pefc.org

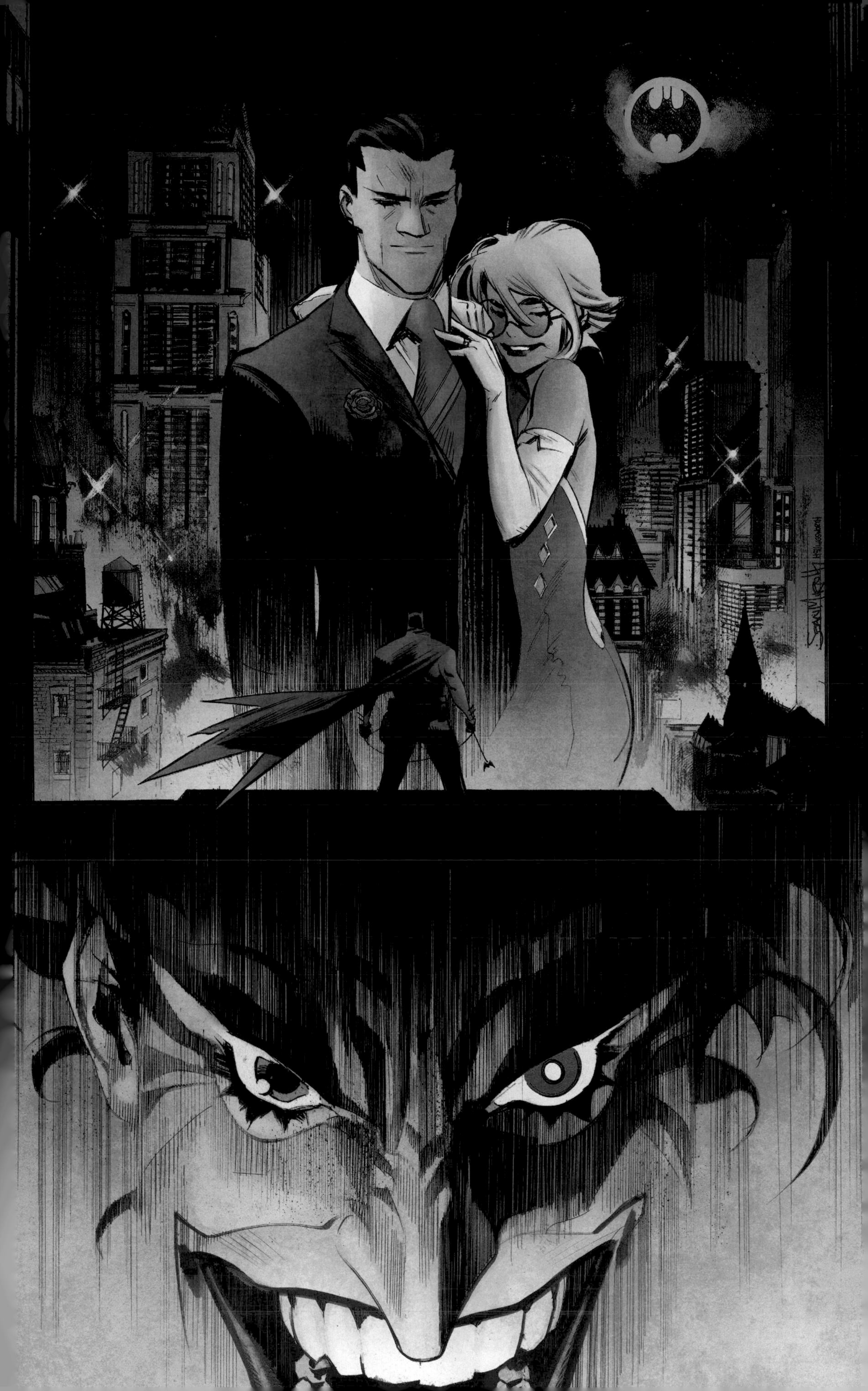

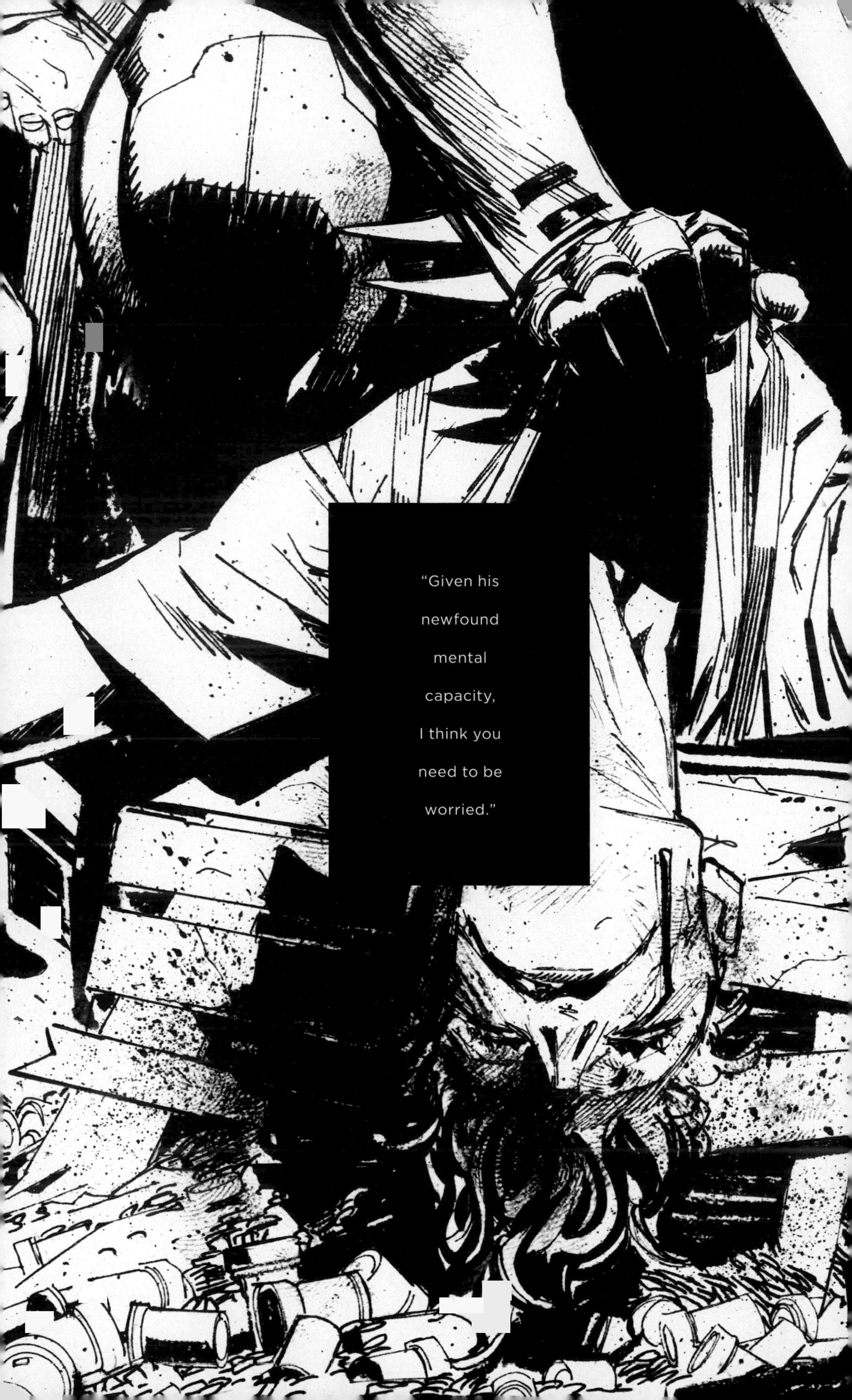

"Given his newfound mental capacity, I think you need to be worried."

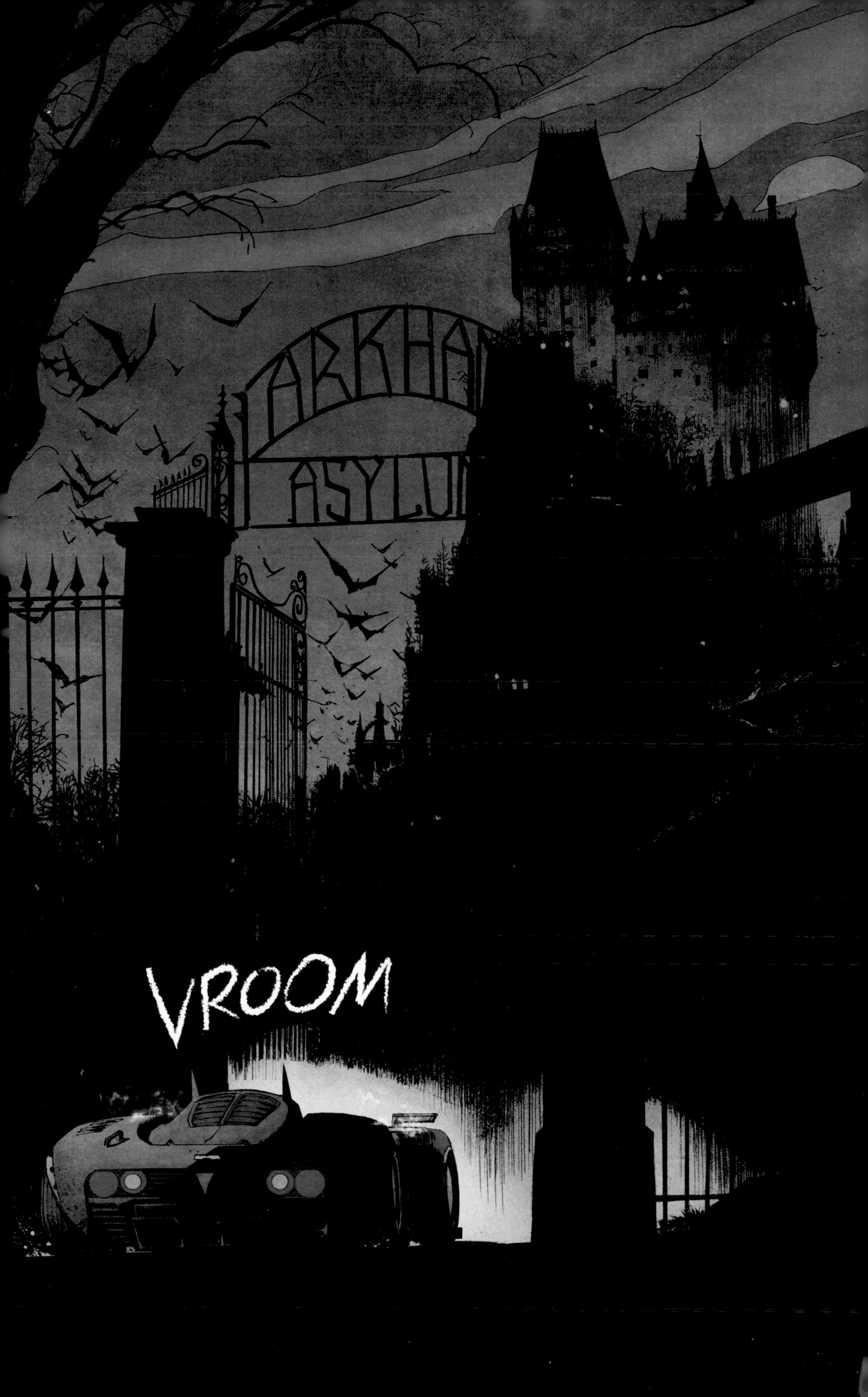
VROOM

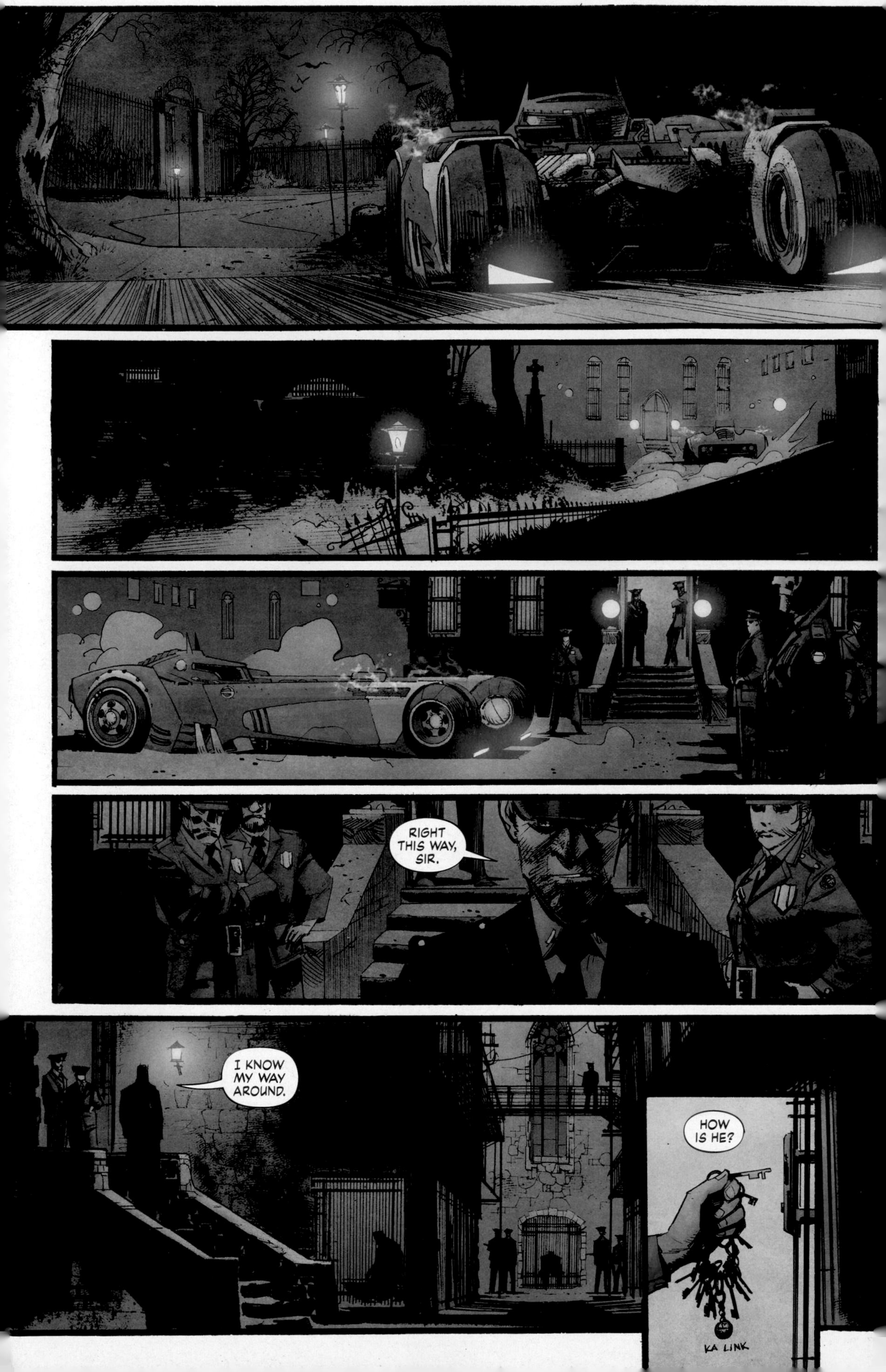
RIGHT THIS WAY, SIR.
I KNOW MY WAY AROUND.
HOW IS HE?
KA LINK

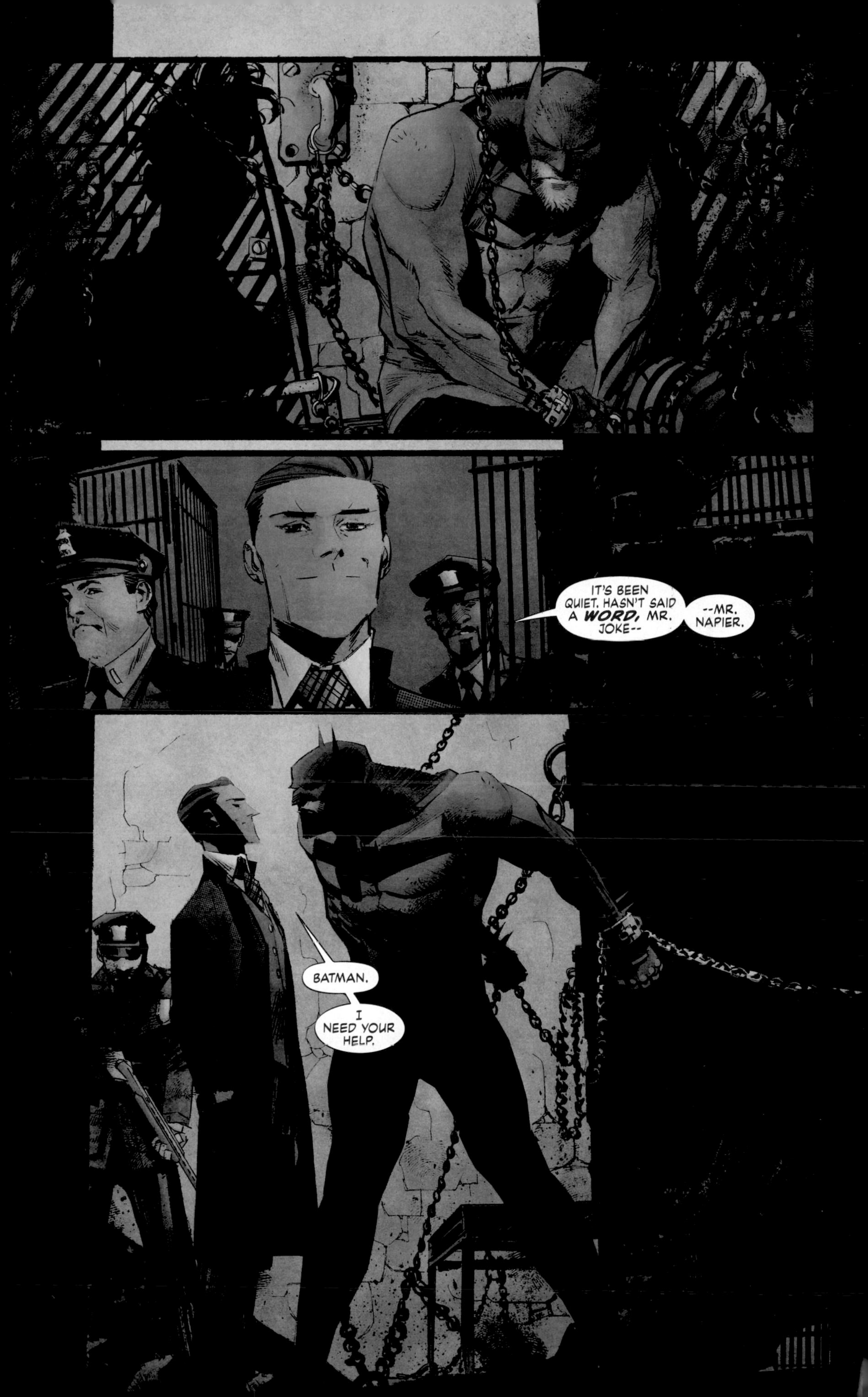
IT'S BEEN QUIET. HASN'T SAID A WORD, MR. JOKE--
--MR. NAPIER.
BATMAN.
I NEED YOUR HELP.

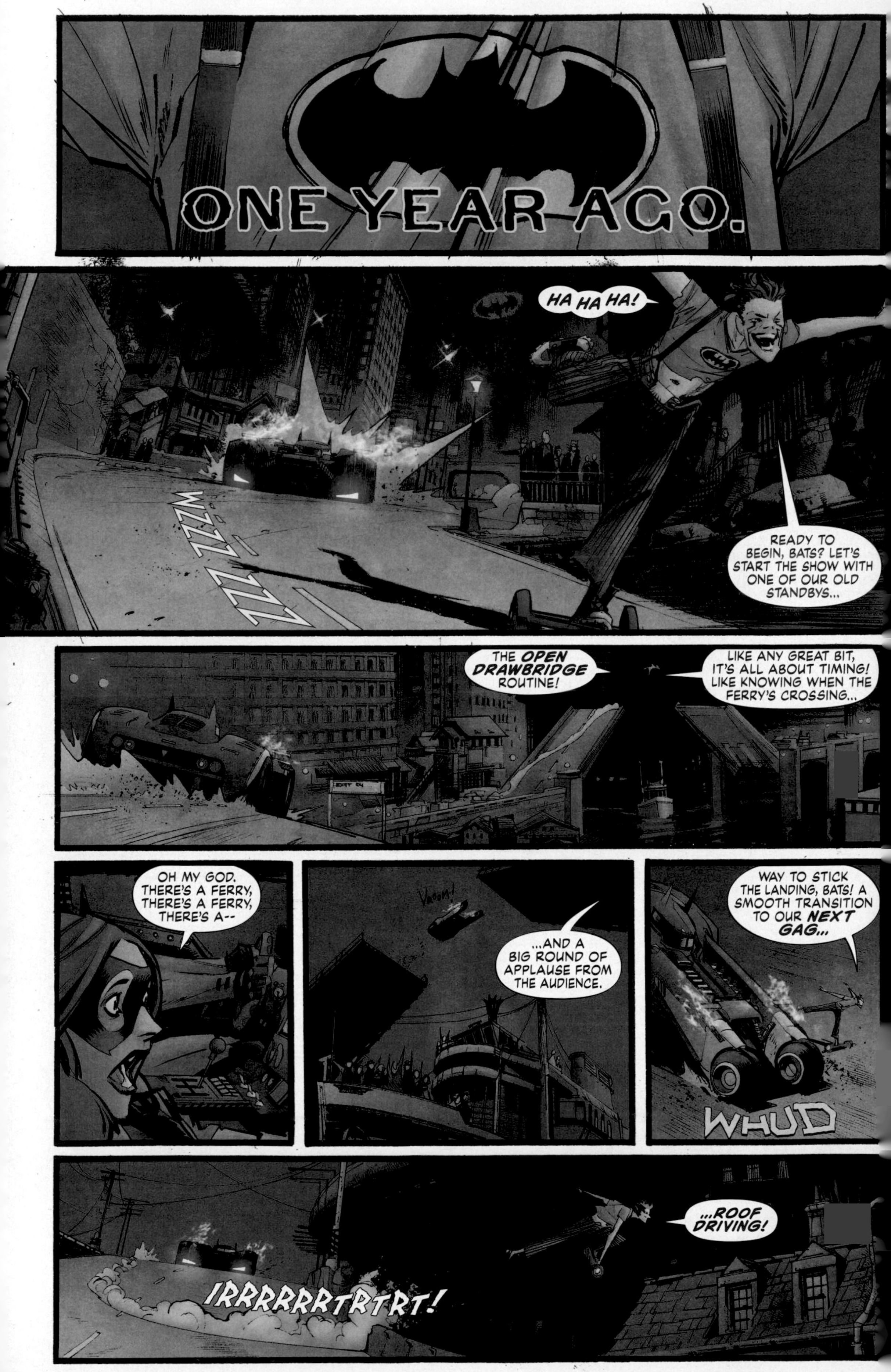
ONE YEAR AGO.
HA HA HA!
READY TO BEGIN, BATS? LET'S START THE SHOW WITH ONE OF OUR OLD STANDBYS...
WZZZ ZZZ ZZZ
THE OPEN DRAWBRIDGE ROUTINE!
LIKE ANY GREAT BIT, IT'S ALL ABOUT TIMING! LIKE KNOWING WHEN THE FERRY'S CROSSING...
OH MY GOD. THERE'S A FERRY, THERE'S A FERRY, THERE'S A--
...AND A BIG ROUND OF APPLAUSE FROM THE AUDIENCE.
WAY TO STICK THE LANDING, BATS! A SMOOTH TRANSITION TO OUR NEXT GAG...
WHUD
...ROOF DRIVING!
IRRRRRRTRTRT!

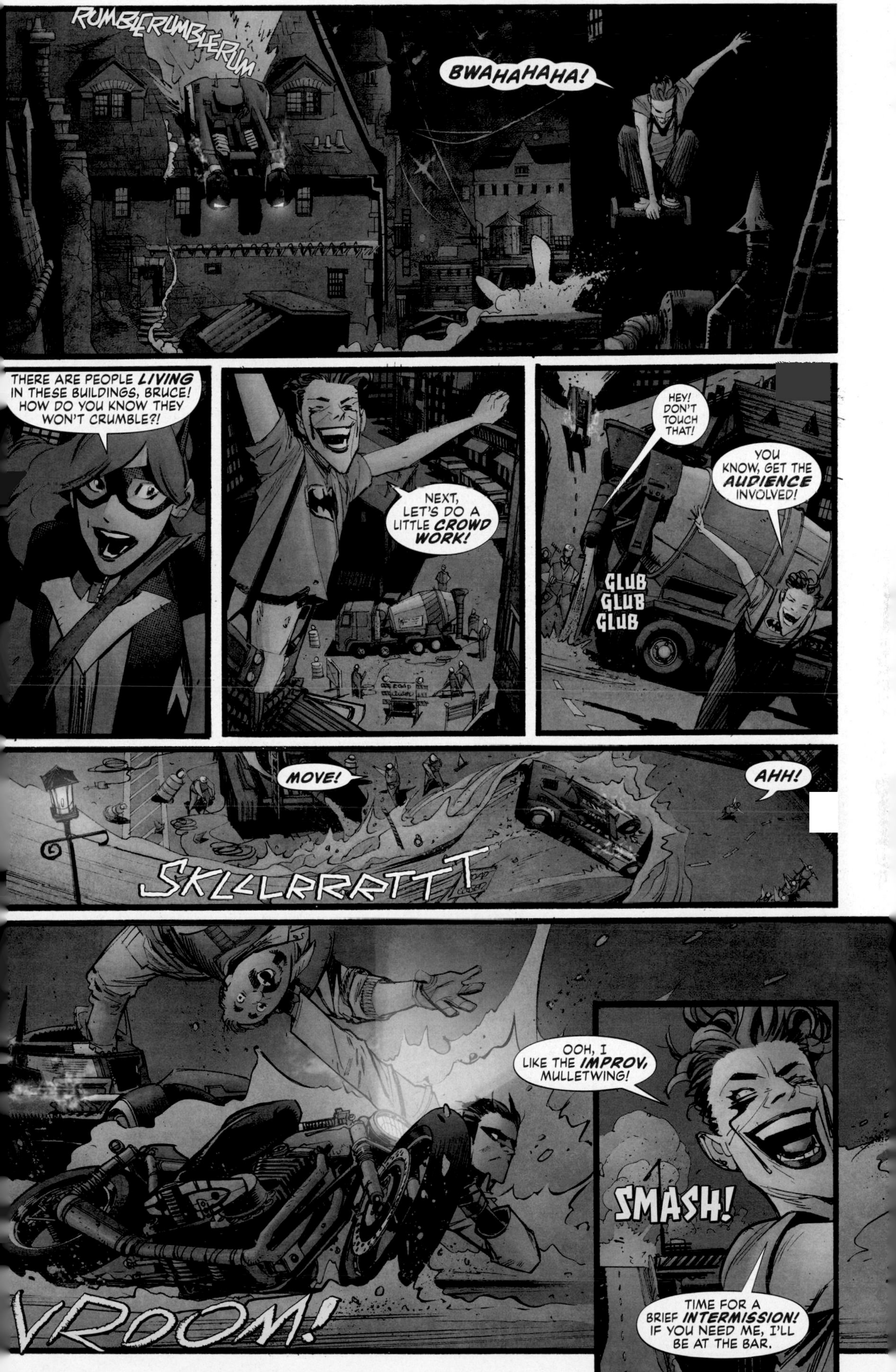
RUMBLERUMBLERUM
BWAHAHAHA!
THERE ARE PEOPLE LIVING IN THESE BUILDINGS, BRUCE! HOW DO YOU KNOW THEY WON'T CRUMBLE?!
NEXT, LET'S DO A LITTLE CROWD WORK!
HEY! DON'T TOUCH THAT!
YOU KNOW, GET THE AUDIENCE INVOLVED!
GLUB GLUB GLUB
MOVE!
AHH!
SKLLLRRRRTTT
OOH, I LIKE THE IMPROV, MULLETWING!
SMASH!
TIME FOR A BRIEF INTERMISSION! IF YOU NEED ME, I'LL BE AT THE BAR.
VROOM!

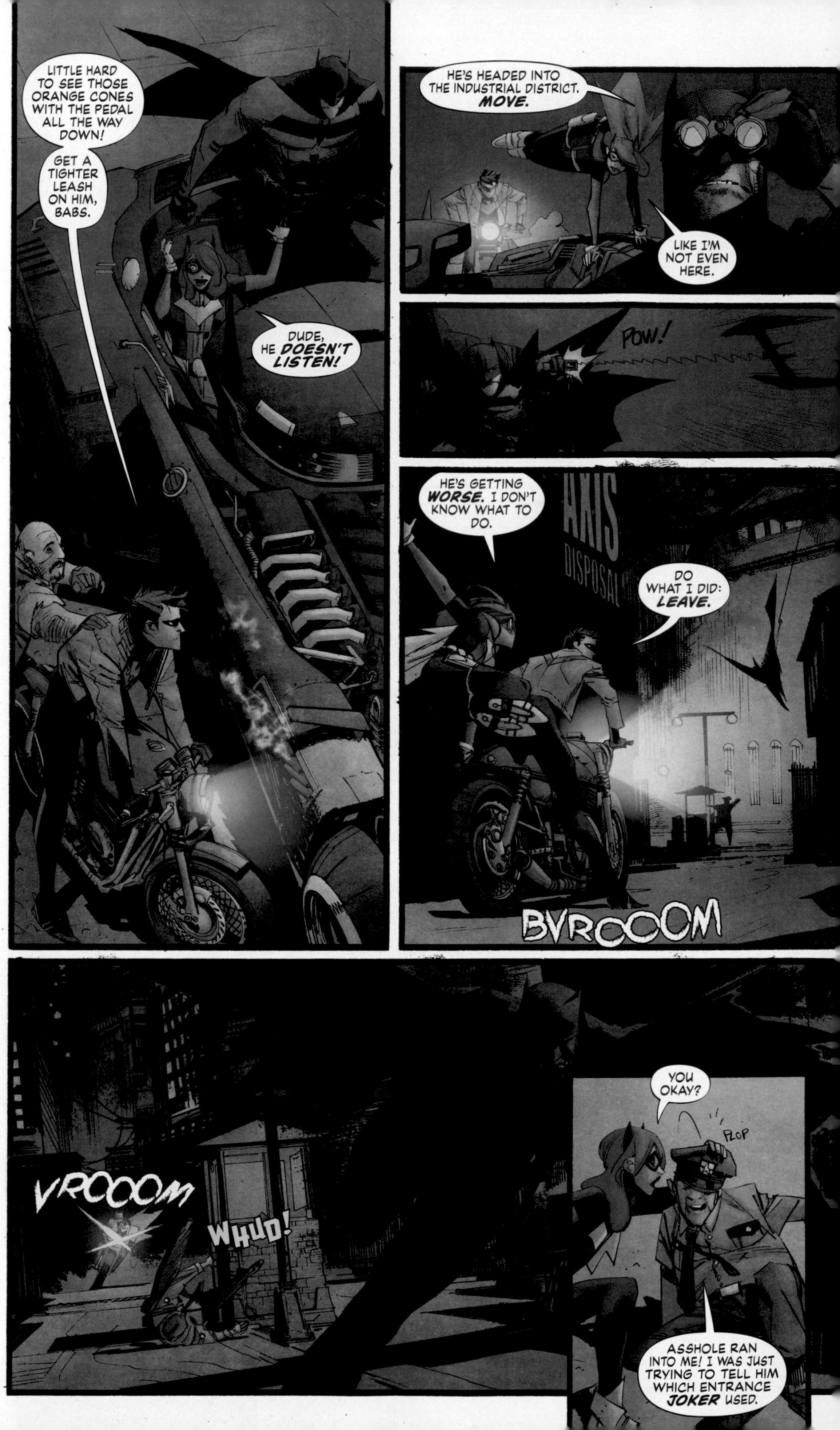

LITTLE HARD TO SEE THOSE ORANGE CONES WITH THE PEDAL ALL THE WAY DOWN!
GET A TIGHTER LEASH ON HIM, BABS.
DUDE, HE **DOESN'T LISTEN!**
HE'S HEADED INTO THE INDUSTRIAL DISTRICT. **MOVE.**
LIKE I'M NOT EVEN HERE.
POW!
HE'S GETTING **WORSE.** I DON'T KNOW WHAT TO DO.
AXIS DISPOSAL
DO WHAT I DID: **LEAVE.**
BVROOOM
VROOOM
WHUD!
YOU OKAY?
FLOP
ASSHOLE RAN INTO ME! I WAS JUST TRYING TO TELL HIM WHICH ENTRANCE **JOKER** USED.

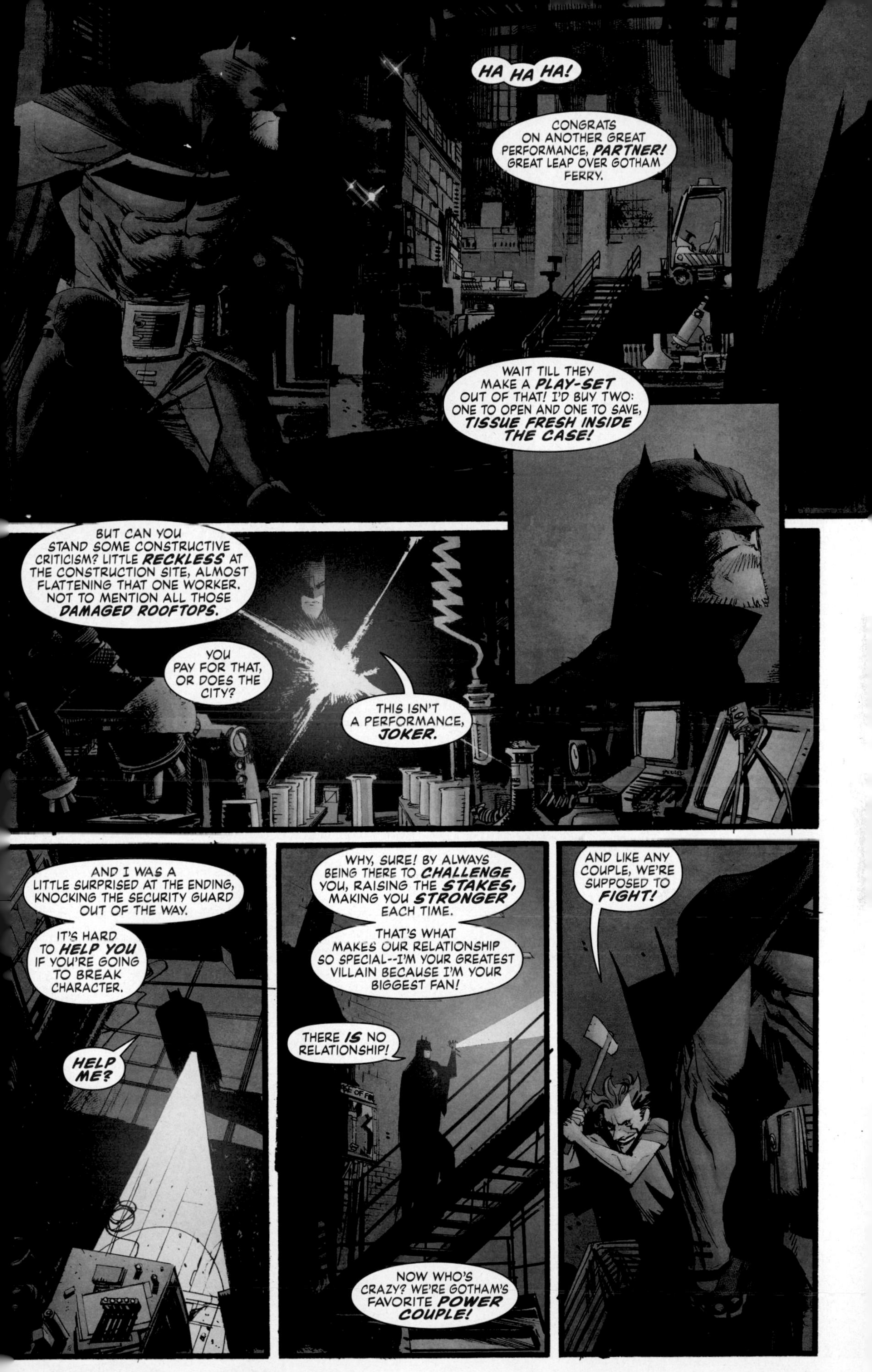
HA HA HA!
CONGRATS ON ANOTHER GREAT PERFORMANCE, PARTNER! GREAT LEAP OVER GOTHAM FERRY.
WAIT TILL THEY MAKE A PLAY-SET OUT OF THAT! I'D BUY TWO: ONE TO OPEN AND ONE TO SAVE, TISSUE FRESH INSIDE THE CASE!
BUT CAN YOU STAND SOME CONSTRUCTIVE CRITICISM? LITTLE RECKLESS AT THE CONSTRUCTION SITE, ALMOST FLATTENING THAT ONE WORKER. NOT TO MENTION ALL THOSE DAMAGED ROOFTOPS.
YOU PAY FOR THAT, OR DOES THE CITY?
THIS ISN'T A PERFORMANCE, JOKER.
AND I WAS A LITTLE SURPRISED AT THE ENDING, KNOCKING THE SECURITY GUARD OUT OF THE WAY.
IT'S HARD TO HELP YOU IF YOU'RE GOING TO BREAK CHARACTER.
HELP ME?
WHY, SURE! BY ALWAYS BEING THERE TO CHALLENGE YOU, RAISING THE STAKES, MAKING YOU STRONGER EACH TIME.
THAT'S WHAT MAKES OUR RELATIONSHIP SO SPECIAL--I'M YOUR GREATEST VILLAIN BECAUSE I'M YOUR BIGGEST FAN!
THERE IS NO RELATIONSHIP!
NOW WHO'S CRAZY? WE'RE GOTHAM'S FAVORITE POWER COUPLE!
AND LIKE ANY COUPLE, WE'RE SUPPOSED TO FIGHT!

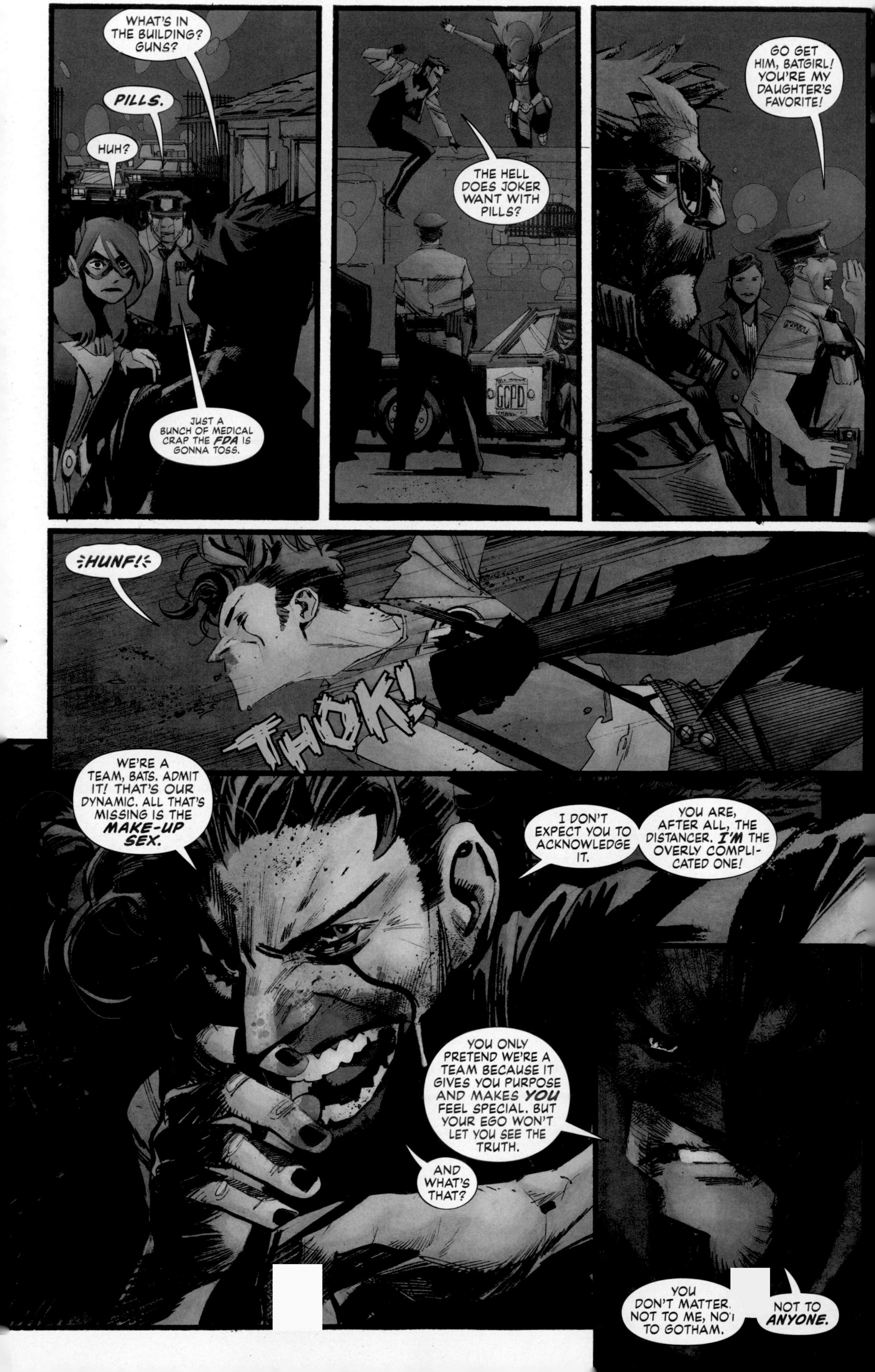
WHAT'S IN THE BUILDING? GUNS?
PILLS.
HUH?
JUST A BUNCH OF MEDICAL CRAP THE FDA IS GONNA TOSS.
THE HELL DOES JOKER WANT WITH PILLS?
GO GET HIM, BATGIRL! YOU'RE MY DAUGHTER'S FAVORITE!
HUNF!
THOK!
WE'RE A TEAM, BATS. ADMIT IT! THAT'S OUR DYNAMIC. ALL THAT'S MISSING IS THE MAKE-UP SEX.
I DON'T EXPECT YOU TO ACKNOWLEDGE IT.
YOU ARE, AFTER ALL, THE DISTANCER. I'M THE OVERLY COMPLI-CATED ONE!
YOU ONLY PRETEND WE'RE A TEAM BECAUSE IT GIVES YOU PURPOSE AND MAKES YOU FEEL SPECIAL. BUT YOUR EGO WON'T LET YOU SEE THE TRUTH.
AND WHAT'S THAT?
YOU DON'T MATTER. NOT TO ME, NOT TO GOTHAM.
NOT TO ANYONE.

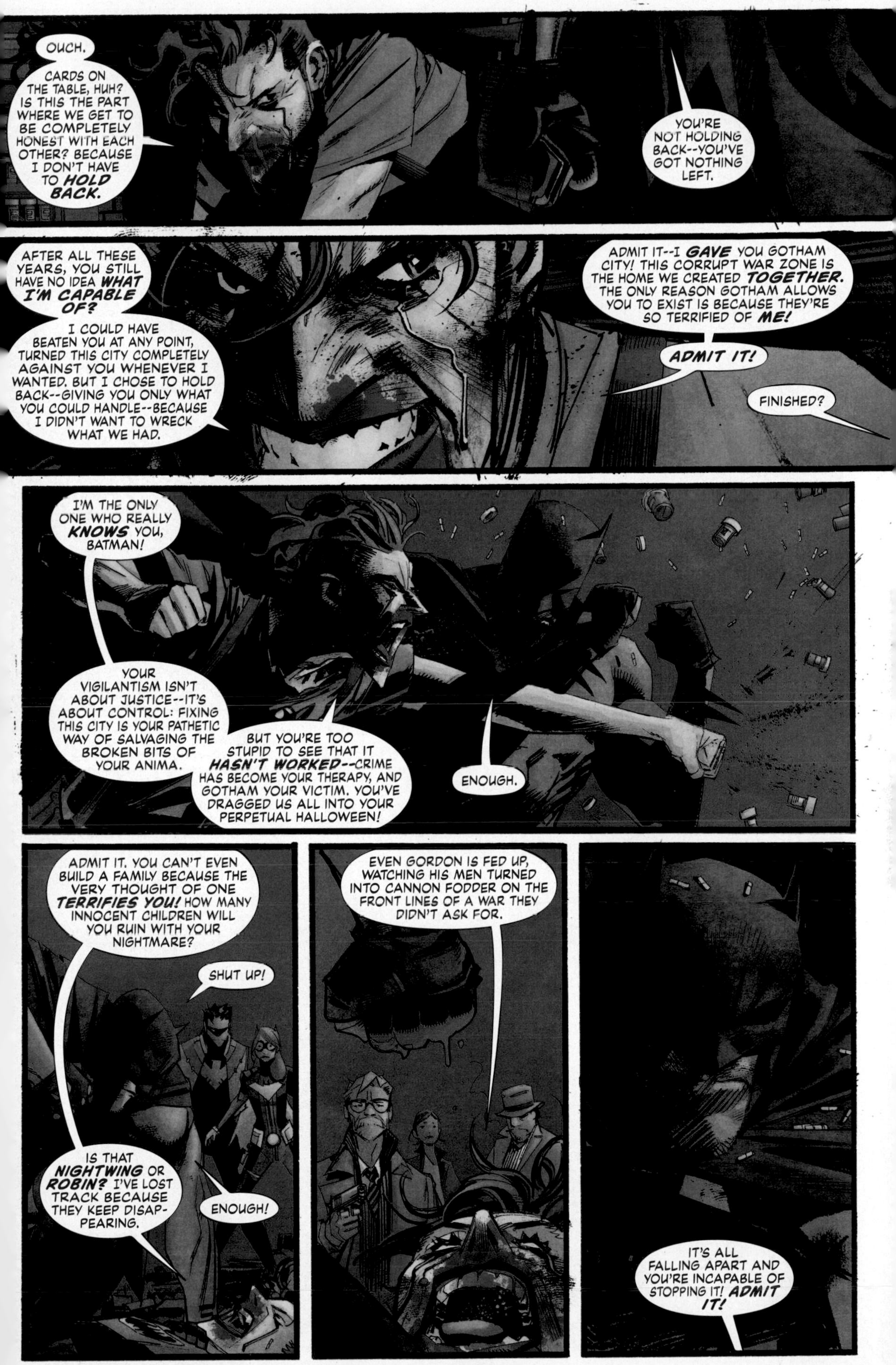
OUCH.
CARDS ON THE TABLE, HUH? IS THIS THE PART WHERE WE GET TO BE COMPLETELY HONEST WITH EACH OTHER? BECAUSE I DON'T HAVE TO HOLD BACK.
YOU'RE NOT HOLDING BACK--YOU'VE GOT NOTHING LEFT.
AFTER ALL THESE YEARS, YOU STILL HAVE NO IDEA WHAT I'M CAPABLE OF?
I COULD HAVE BEATEN YOU AT ANY POINT, TURNED THIS CITY COMPLETELY AGAINST YOU WHENEVER I WANTED. BUT I CHOSE TO HOLD BACK--GIVING YOU ONLY WHAT YOU COULD HANDLE--BECAUSE I DIDN'T WANT TO WRECK WHAT WE HAD.
ADMIT IT--I GAVE YOU GOTHAM CITY! THIS CORRUPT WAR ZONE IS THE HOME WE CREATED TOGETHER. THE ONLY REASON GOTHAM ALLOWS YOU TO EXIST IS BECAUSE THEY'RE SO TERRIFIED OF ME!
ADMIT IT!
FINISHED?
I'M THE ONLY ONE WHO REALLY KNOWS YOU, BATMAN!
YOUR VIGILANTISM ISN'T ABOUT JUSTICE--IT'S ABOUT CONTROL: FIXING THIS CITY IS YOUR PATHETIC WAY OF SALVAGING THE BROKEN BITS OF YOUR ANIMA.
BUT YOU'RE TOO STUPID TO SEE THAT IT HASN'T WORKED--CRIME HAS BECOME YOUR THERAPY, AND GOTHAM YOUR VICTIM. YOU'VE DRAGGED US ALL INTO YOUR PERPETUAL HALLOWEEN!
ENOUGH.
ADMIT IT. YOU CAN'T EVEN BUILD A FAMILY BECAUSE THE VERY THOUGHT OF ONE TERRIFIES YOU! HOW MANY INNOCENT CHILDREN WILL YOU RUIN WITH YOUR NIGHTMARE?
SHUT UP!
IS THAT NIGHTWING OR ROBIN? I'VE LOST TRACK BECAUSE THEY KEEP DISAP-PEARING.
ENOUGH!
EVEN GORDON IS FED UP, WATCHING HIS MEN TURNED INTO CANNON FODDER ON THE FRONT LINES OF A WAR THEY DIDN'T ASK FOR.
IT'S ALL FALLING APART AND YOU'RE INCAPABLE OF STOPPING IT! ADMIT IT!

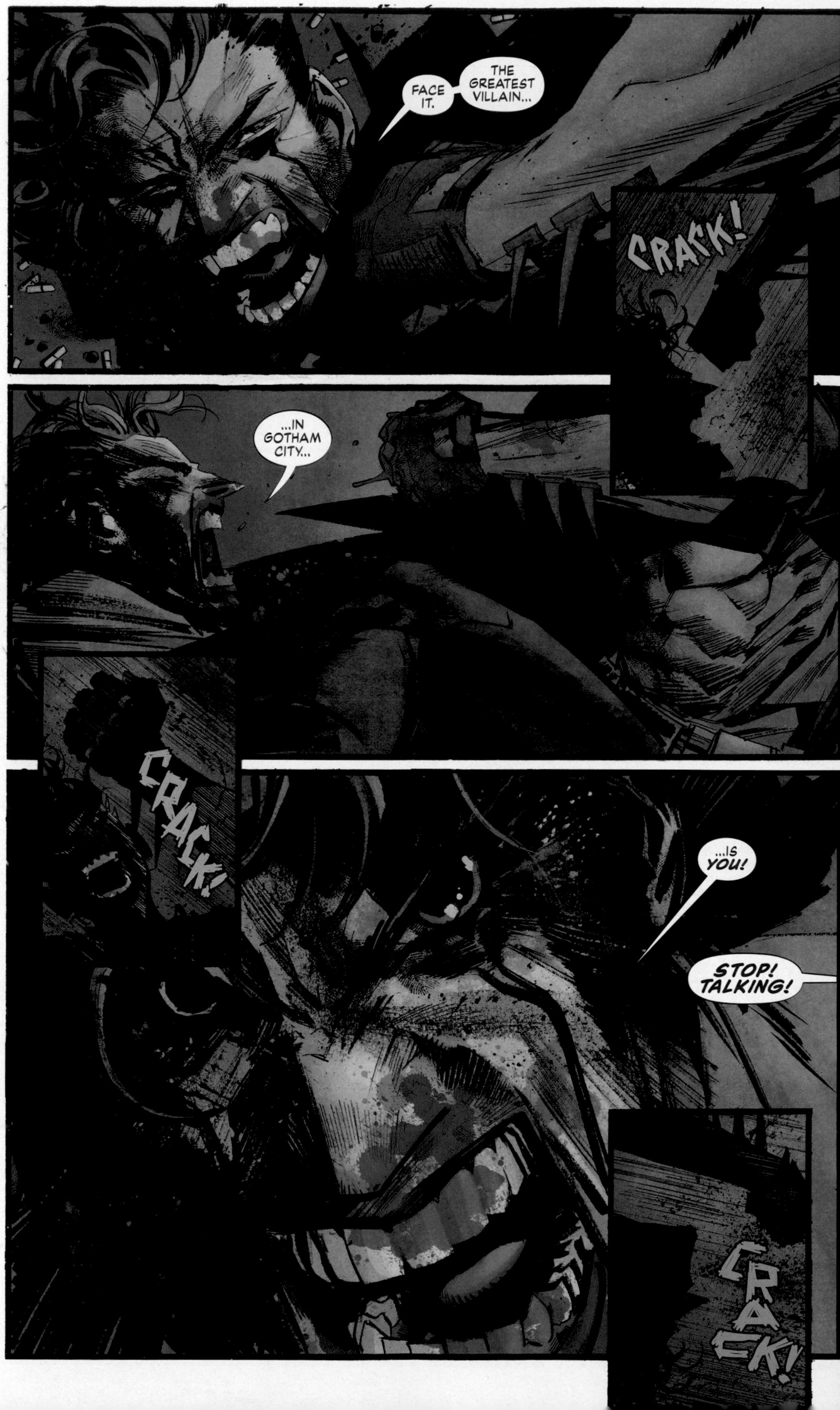

FACE IT.
THE GREATEST VILLAIN...
CRACK!
...IN GOTHAM CITY...
CRACK!
...IS YOU!
STOP! TALKING!
CRACK!

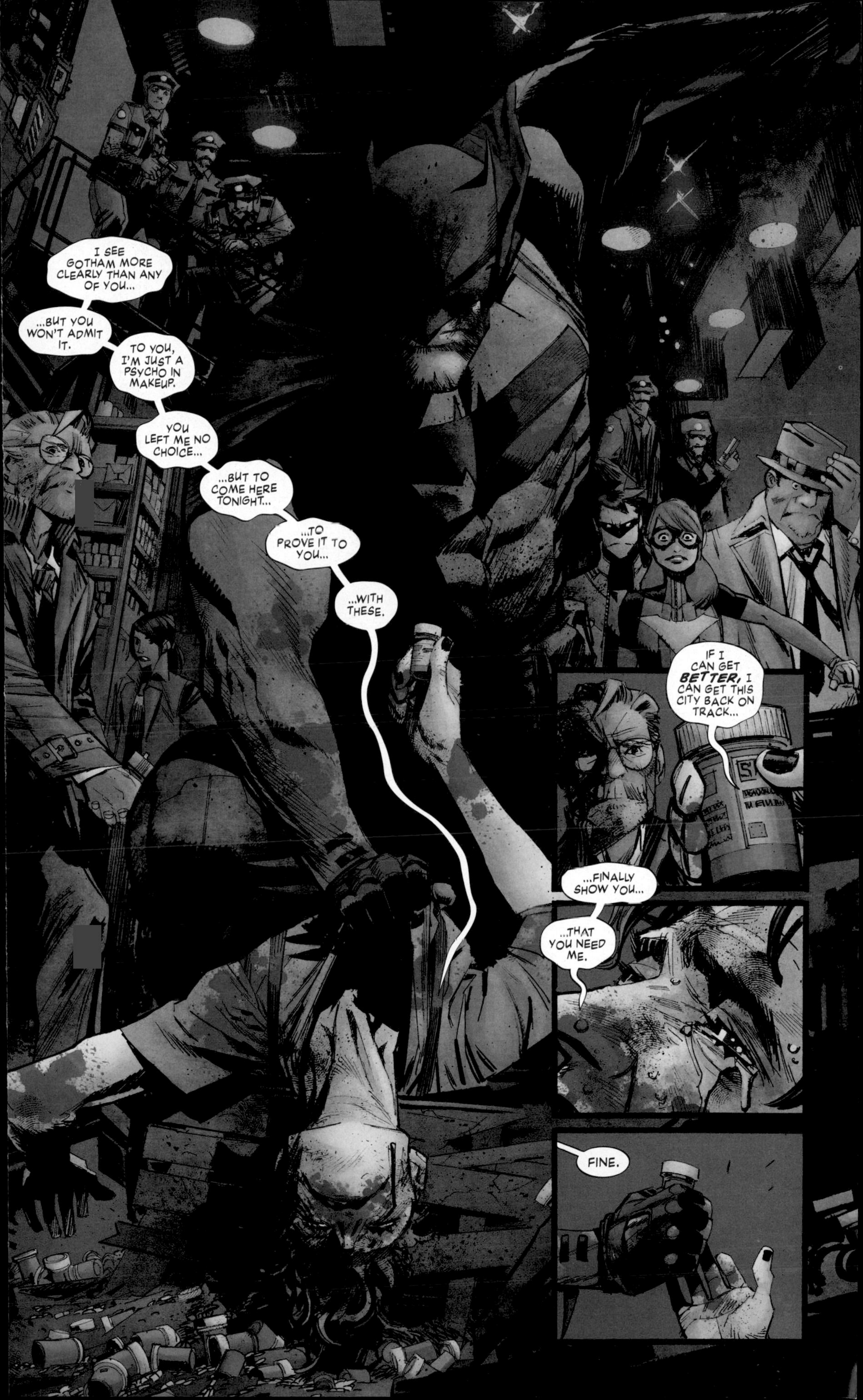
I SEE GOTHAM MORE CLEARLY THAN ANY OF YOU...
...BUT YOU WON'T ADMIT IT.
TO YOU, I'M JUST A PSYCHO IN MAKEUP.
YOU LEFT ME NO CHOICE...
...BUT TO COME HERE TONIGHT...
...TO PROVE IT TO YOU...
...WITH THESE.
IF I CAN GET **BETTER,** I CAN GET THIS CITY BACK ON TRACK...
...FINALLY SHOW YOU...
...THAT YOU NEED ME.
FINE.

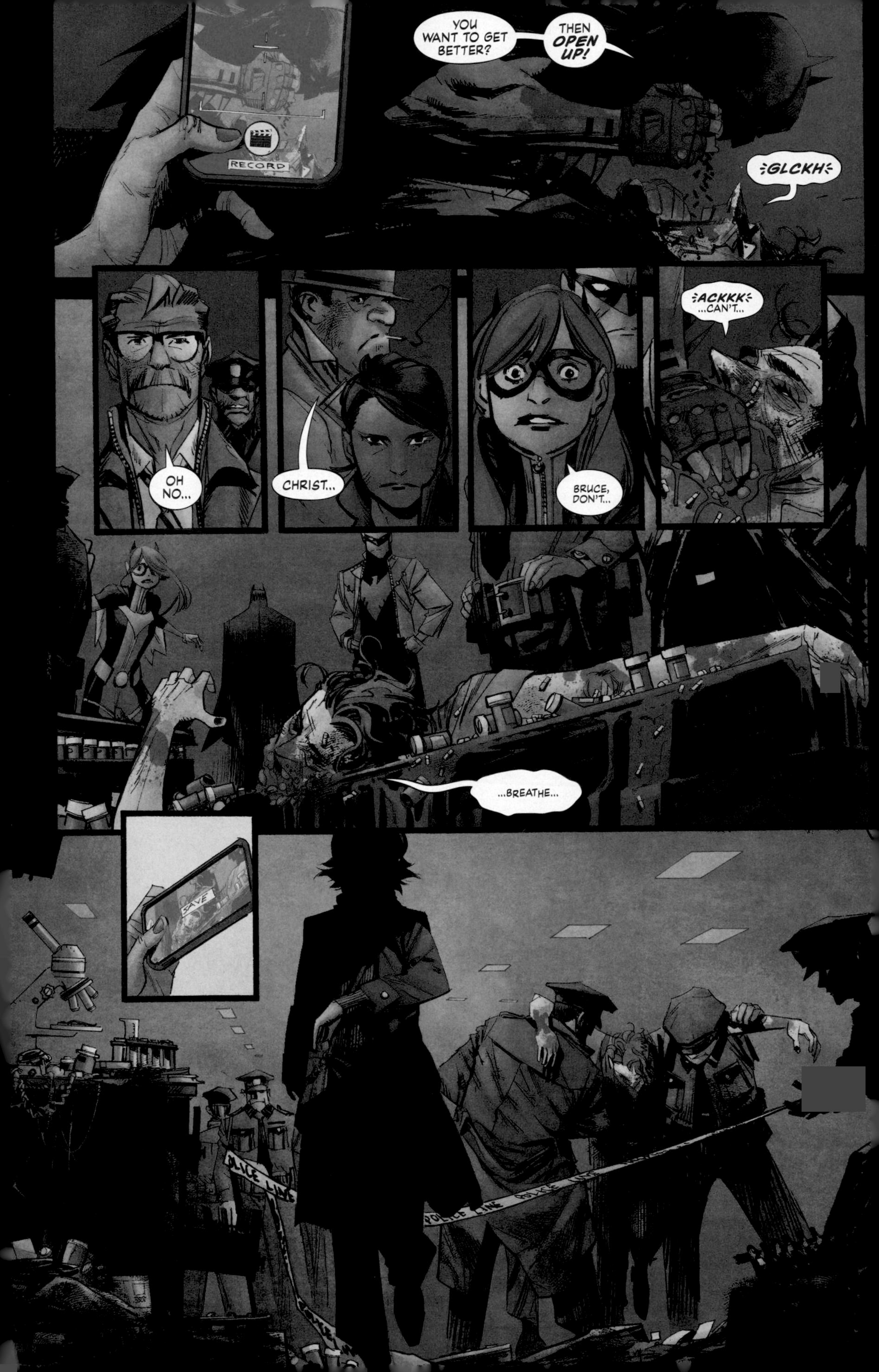
RECORD
YOU WANT TO GET BETTER?
THEN OPEN UP!
GLCKH
OH NO...
CHRIST...
BRUCE, DON'T...
ACKKK ...CAN'T...
...BREATHE...
SAVE
POLICE LINE

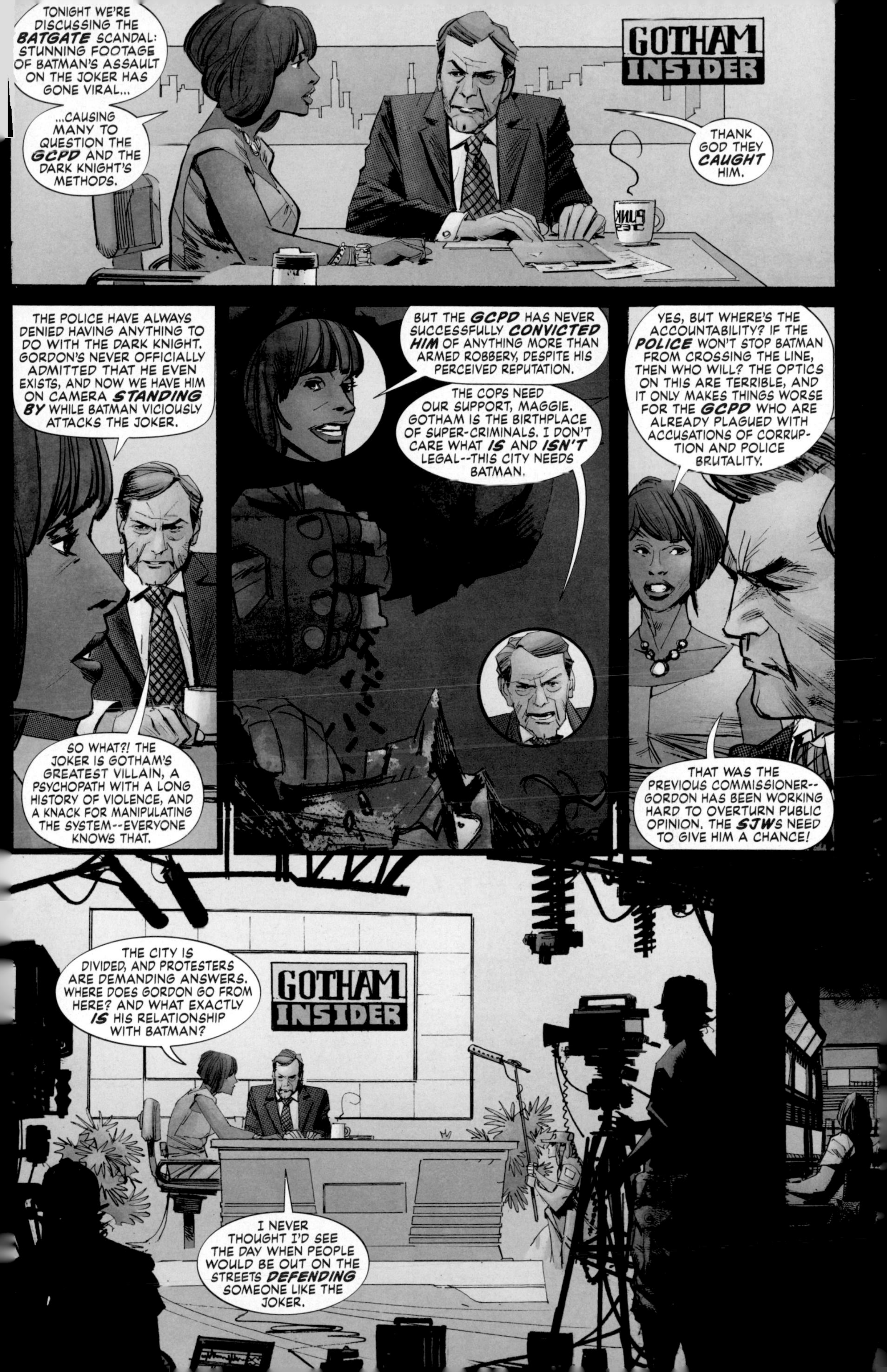
GOTHAM INSIDER
TONIGHT WE'RE DISCUSSING THE BATGATE SCANDAL: STUNNING FOOTAGE OF BATMAN'S ASSAULT ON THE JOKER HAS GONE VIRAL...
...CAUSING MANY TO QUESTION THE GCPD AND THE DARK KNIGHT'S METHODS.
THANK GOD THEY CAUGHT HIM.
THE POLICE HAVE ALWAYS DENIED HAVING ANYTHING TO DO WITH THE DARK KNIGHT. GORDON'S NEVER OFFICIALLY ADMITTED THAT HE EVEN EXISTS, AND NOW WE HAVE HIM ON CAMERA STANDING BY WHILE BATMAN VICIOUSLY ATTACKS THE JOKER.
SO WHAT?! THE JOKER IS GOTHAM'S GREATEST VILLAIN, A PSYCHOPATH WITH A LONG HISTORY OF VIOLENCE, AND A KNACK FOR MANIPULATING THE SYSTEM--EVERYONE KNOWS THAT.
BUT THE GCPD HAS NEVER SUCCESSFULLY CONVICTED HIM OF ANYTHING MORE THAN ARMED ROBBERY, DESPITE HIS PERCEIVED REPUTATION.
THE COPS NEED OUR SUPPORT, MAGGIE. GOTHAM IS THE BIRTHPLACE OF SUPER-CRIMINALS. I DON'T CARE WHAT IS AND ISN'T LEGAL--THIS CITY NEEDS BATMAN.
YES, BUT WHERE'S THE ACCOUNTABILITY? IF THE POLICE WON'T STOP BATMAN FROM CROSSING THE LINE, THEN WHO WILL? THE OPTICS ON THIS ARE TERRIBLE, AND IT ONLY MAKES THINGS WORSE FOR THE GCPD WHO ARE ALREADY PLAGUED WITH ACCUSATIONS OF CORRUPTION AND POLICE BRUTALITY.
THAT WAS THE PREVIOUS COMMISSIONER--GORDON HAS BEEN WORKING HARD TO OVERTURN PUBLIC OPINION. THE SJWS NEED TO GIVE HIM A CHANCE!
GOTHAM INSIDER
THE CITY IS DIVIDED, AND PROTESTERS ARE DEMANDING ANSWERS. WHERE DOES GORDON GO FROM HERE? AND WHAT EXACTLY IS HIS RELATIONSHIP WITH BATMAN?
I NEVER THOUGHT I'D SEE THE DAY WHEN PEOPLE WOULD BE OUT ON THE STREETS DEFENDING SOMEONE LIKE THE JOKER.

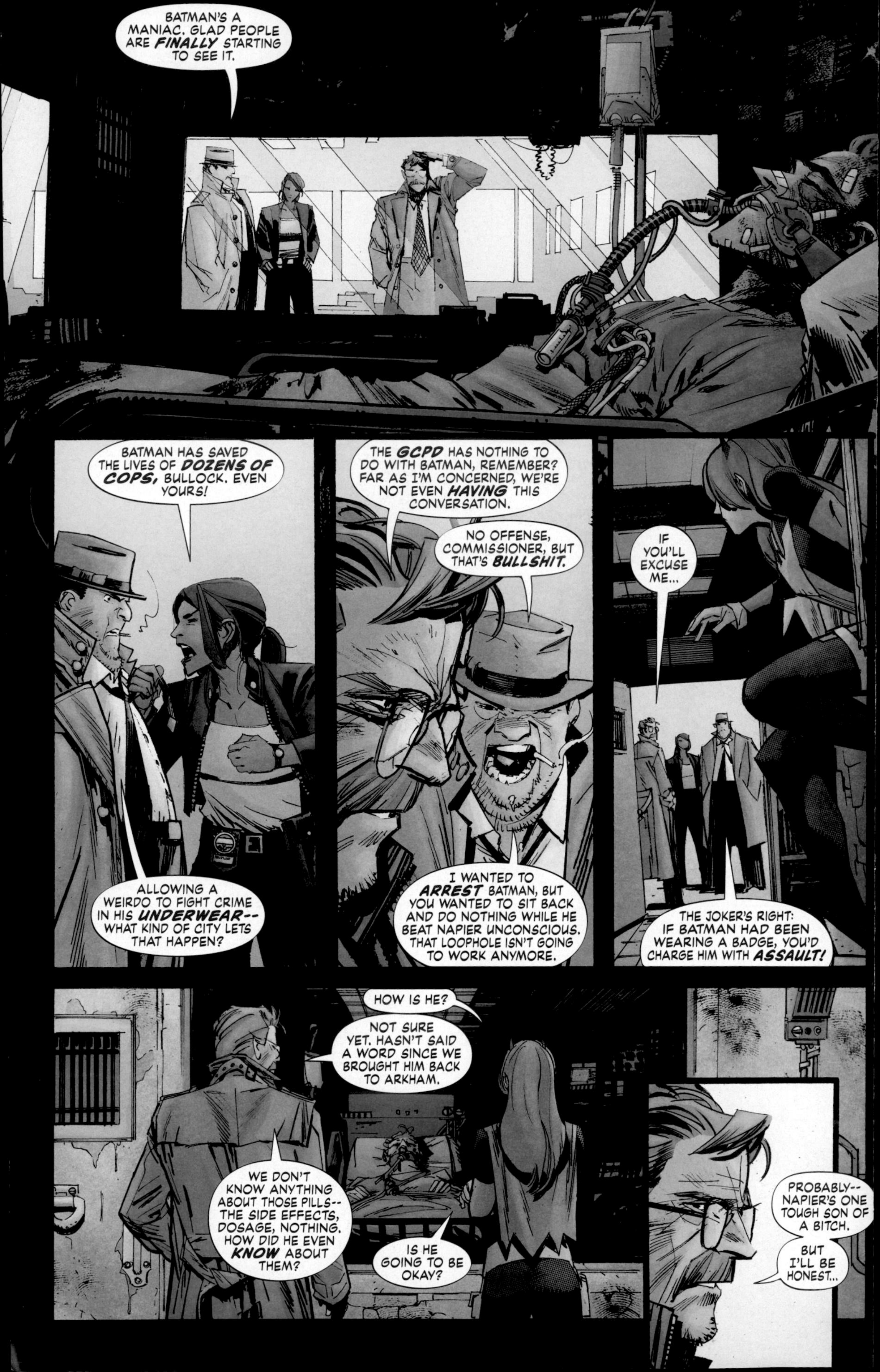

BATMAN'S A MANIAC. GLAD PEOPLE ARE FINALLY STARTING TO SEE IT.
BATMAN HAS SAVED THE LIVES OF DOZENS OF COPS, BULLOCK. EVEN YOURS!
ALLOWING A WEIRDO TO FIGHT CRIME IN HIS UNDERWEAR-- WHAT KIND OF CITY LETS THAT HAPPEN?
THE GCPD HAS NOTHING TO DO WITH BATMAN, REMEMBER? FAR AS I'M CONCERNED, WE'RE NOT EVEN HAVING THIS CONVERSATION.
NO OFFENSE, COMMISSIONER, BUT THAT'S BULLSHIT.
I WANTED TO ARREST BATMAN, BUT YOU WANTED TO SIT BACK AND DO NOTHING WHILE HE BEAT NAPIER UNCONSCIOUS. THAT LOOPHOLE ISN'T GOING TO WORK ANYMORE.
IF YOU'LL EXCUSE ME...
THE JOKER'S RIGHT: IF BATMAN HAD BEEN WEARING A BADGE, YOU'D CHARGE HIM WITH ASSAULT!
HOW IS HE?
NOT SURE YET. HASN'T SAID A WORD SINCE WE BROUGHT HIM BACK TO ARKHAM.
WE DON'T KNOW ANYTHING ABOUT THOSE PILLS-- THE SIDE EFFECTS, DOSAGE, NOTHING. HOW DID HE EVEN KNOW ABOUT THEM?
IS HE GOING TO BE OKAY?
PROBABLY-- NAPIER'S ONE TOUGH SON OF A BITCH.
BUT I'LL BE HONEST...

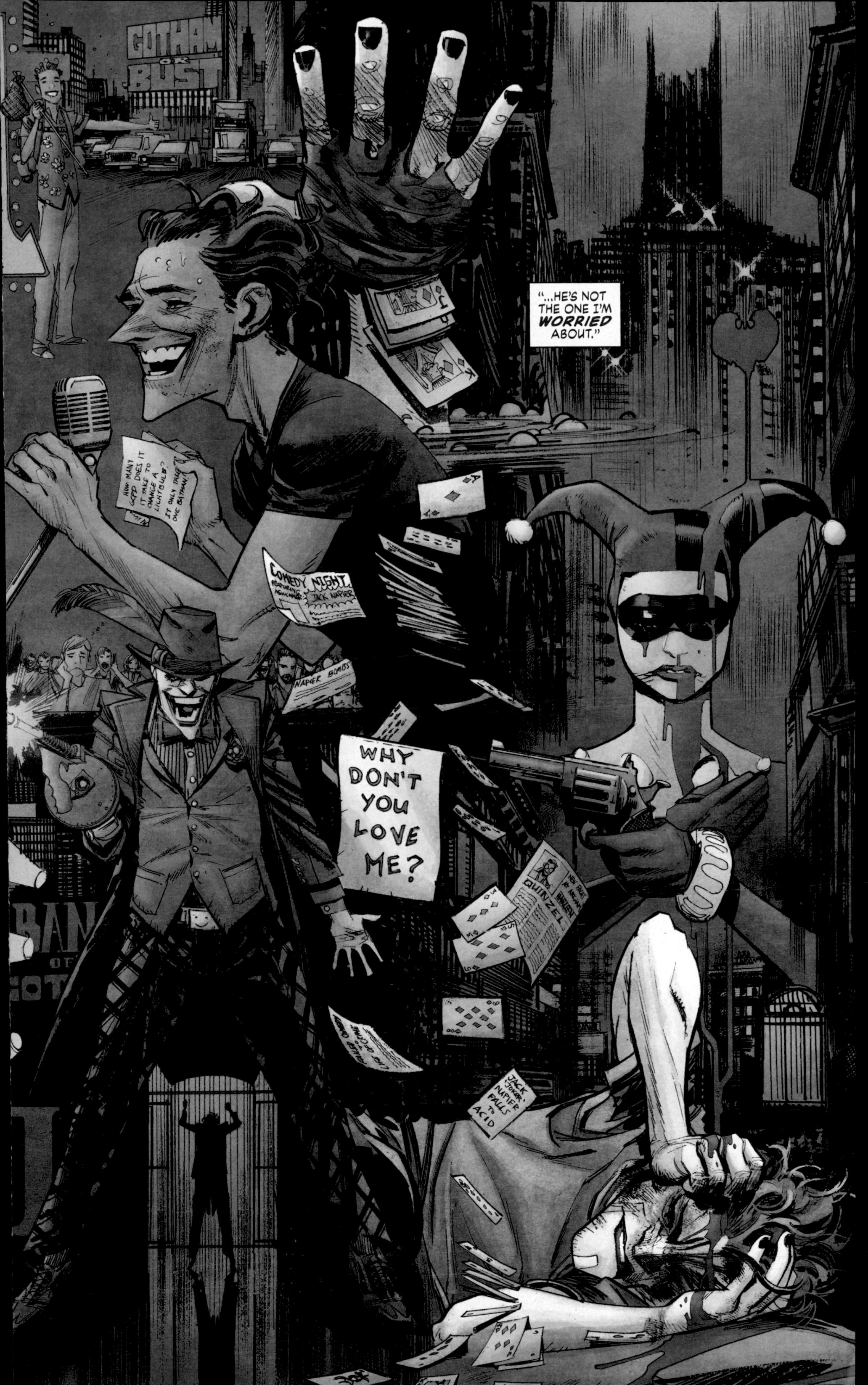
GOTHAM OR BUST
"...HE'S NOT THE ONE I'M ***WORRIED*** ABOUT."
HOW MANY GCPD DOES IT TAKE TO CHANGE A LIGHTBULB? IT ONLY TAKES ONE BATMAN!
COMEDY NIGHT FEATURING NEWCOMER JACK NAPIER
NAPIER BOMBS
WHY DON'T YOU LOVE ME?
QUINZEL
NEW FACES AT ARKHAM
HARLEEN
JACK 'JOKER' NAPIER FALLS TO ACID

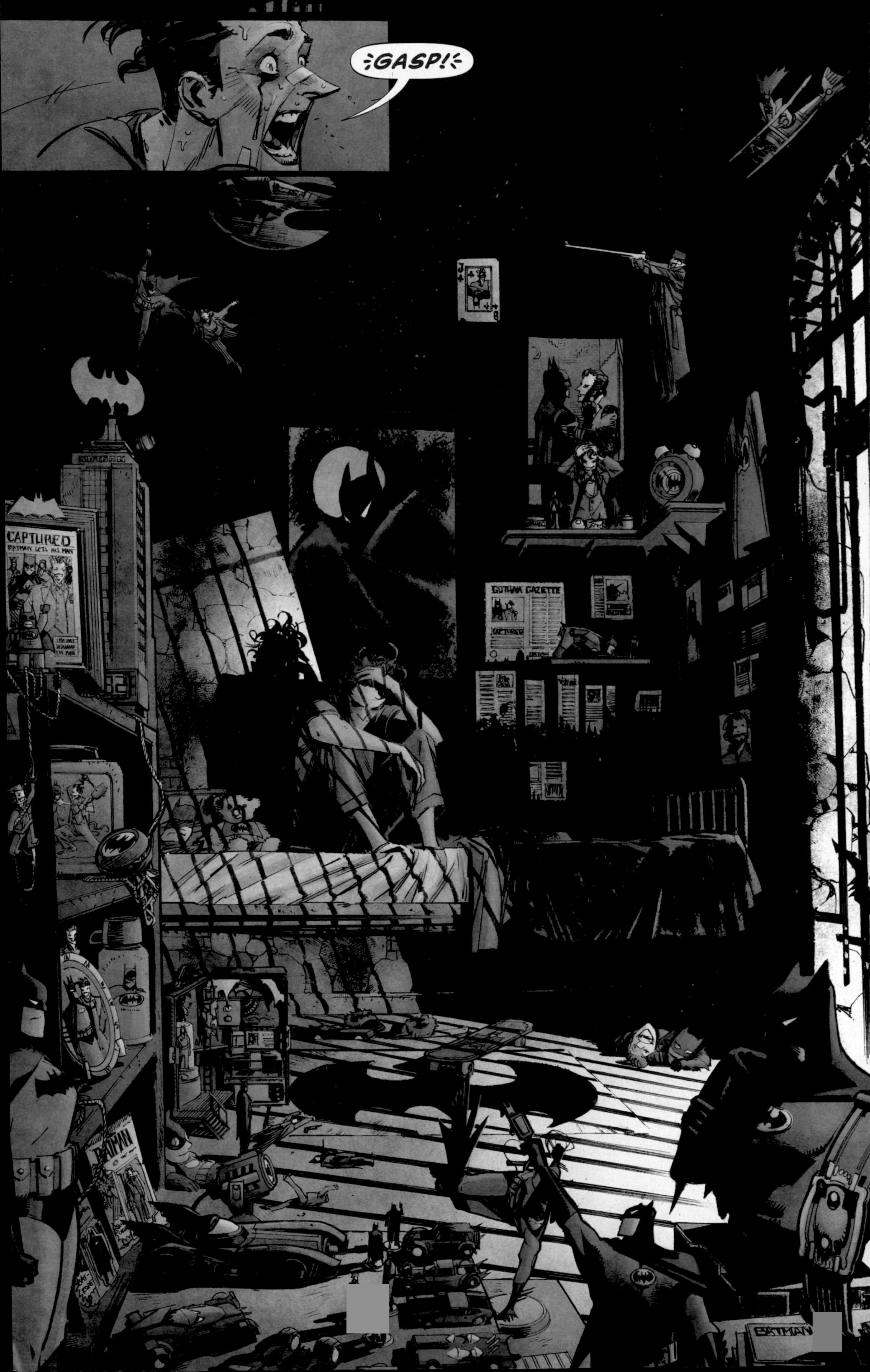
GASP!
CAPTURED
BATMAN GETS HIS MAN
GOTHAM GAZETTE
CAPTURED
BATMAN

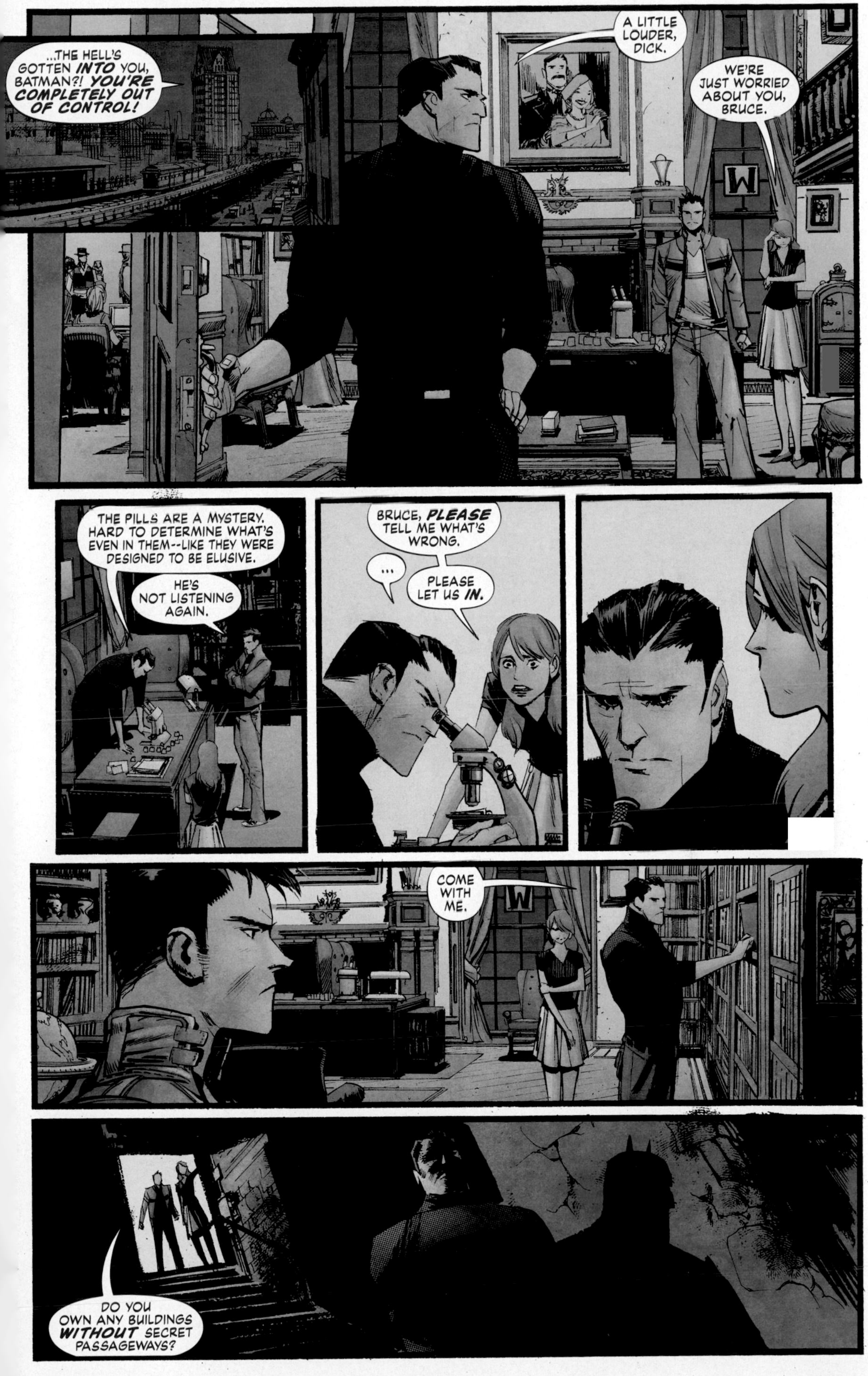
...THE HELL'S GOTTEN INTO YOU, BATMAN?! YOU'RE COMPLETELY OUT OF CONTROL!
A LITTLE LOUDER, DICK.
WE'RE JUST WORRIED ABOUT YOU, BRUCE.
THE PILLS ARE A MYSTERY. HARD TO DETERMINE WHAT'S EVEN IN THEM--LIKE THEY WERE DESIGNED TO BE ELUSIVE.
HE'S NOT LISTENING AGAIN.
BRUCE, PLEASE TELL ME WHAT'S WRONG.
...
PLEASE LET US IN.
COME WITH ME.
DO YOU OWN ANY BUILDINGS WITHOUT SECRET PASSAGEWAYS?

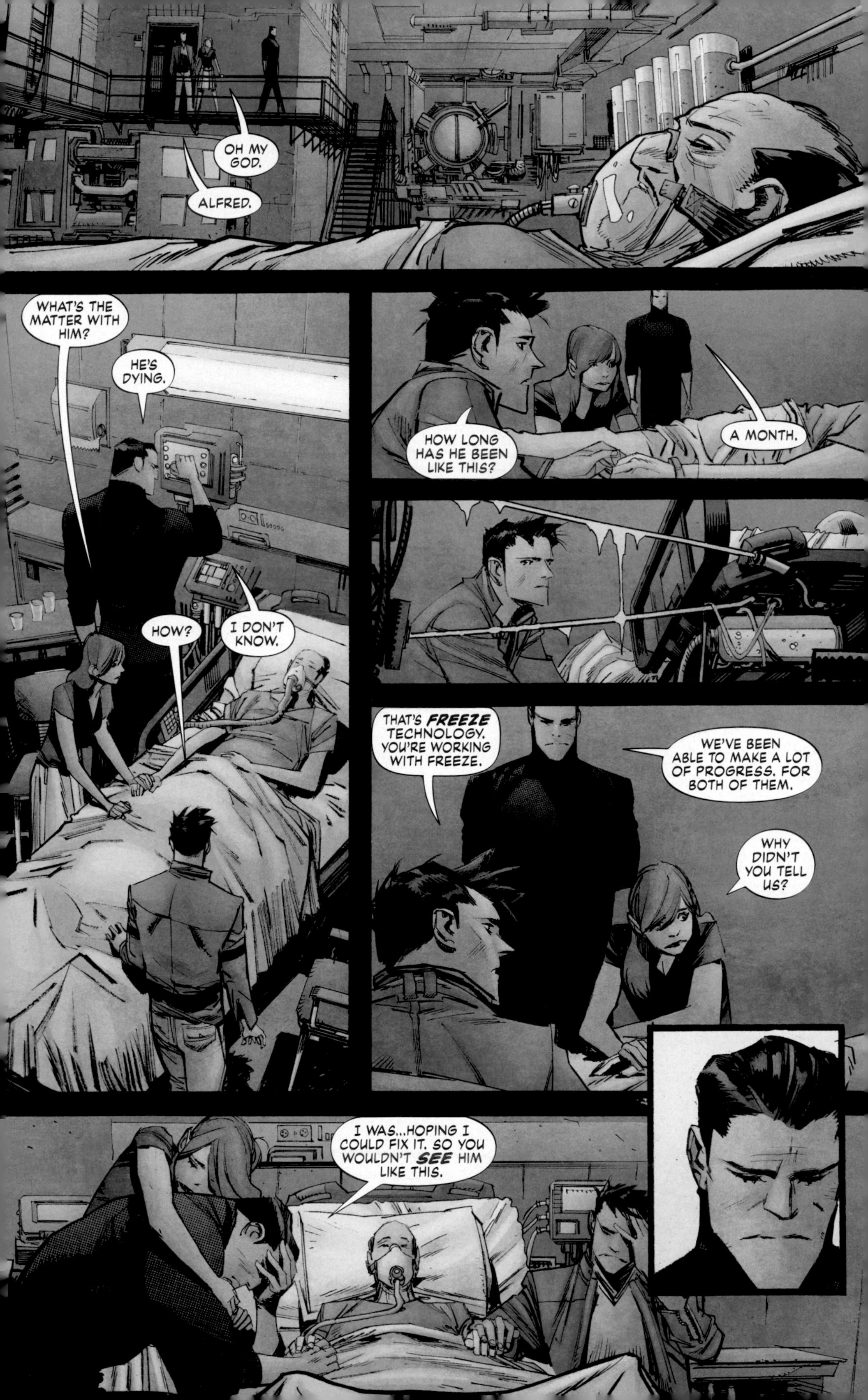
OH MY GOD.
ALFRED.
WHAT'S THE MATTER WITH HIM?
HE'S DYING.
HOW?
I DON'T KNOW.
HOW LONG HAS HE BEEN LIKE THIS?
A MONTH.
THAT'S FREEZE TECHNOLOGY. YOU'RE WORKING WITH FREEZE.
WE'VE BEEN ABLE TO MAKE A LOT OF PROGRESS. FOR BOTH OF THEM.
WHY DIDN'T YOU TELL US?
I WAS...HOPING I COULD FIX IT. SO YOU WOULDN'T SEE HIM LIKE THIS.

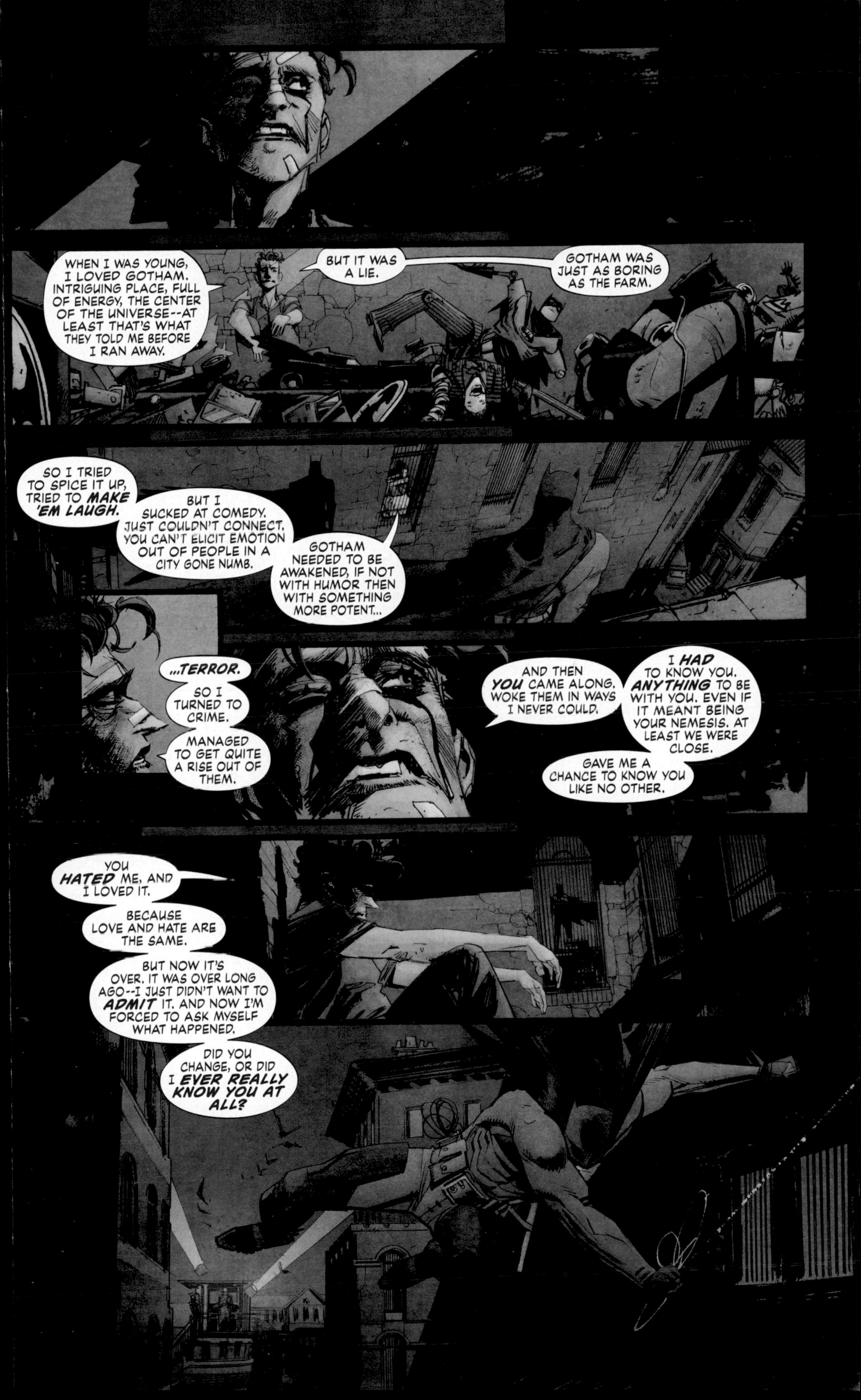
WHEN I WAS YOUNG, I LOVED GOTHAM. INTRIGUING PLACE, FULL OF ENERGY, THE CENTER OF THE UNIVERSE--AT LEAST THAT'S WHAT THEY TOLD ME BEFORE I RAN AWAY.
BUT IT WAS A LIE.
GOTHAM WAS JUST AS BORING AS THE FARM.
SO I TRIED TO SPICE IT UP, TRIED TO MAKE 'EM LAUGH.
BUT I SUCKED AT COMEDY. JUST COULDN'T CONNECT. YOU CAN'T ELICIT EMOTION OUT OF PEOPLE IN A CITY GONE NUMB.
GOTHAM NEEDED TO BE AWAKENED, IF NOT WITH HUMOR THEN WITH SOMETHING MORE POTENT...
...TERROR.
SO I TURNED TO CRIME.
MANAGED TO GET QUITE A RISE OUT OF THEM.
AND THEN YOU CAME ALONG. WOKE THEM IN WAYS I NEVER COULD.
I HAD TO KNOW YOU. ANYTHING TO BE WITH YOU. EVEN IF IT MEANT BEING YOUR NEMESIS. AT LEAST WE WERE CLOSE.
GAVE ME A CHANCE TO KNOW YOU LIKE NO OTHER.
YOU HATED ME, AND I LOVED IT.
BECAUSE LOVE AND HATE ARE THE SAME.
BUT NOW IT'S OVER. IT WAS OVER LONG AGO--I JUST DIDN'T WANT TO ADMIT IT. AND NOW I'M FORCED TO ASK MYSELF WHAT HAPPENED.
DID YOU CHANGE, OR DID I EVER REALLY KNOW YOU AT ALL?

NAPIER HAS BEEN TERRORIZING GOTHAM FOR YEARS. ARE THEIR MEMORIES *THAT* SHORT?! WHY THE HELL IS ANYONE DEFENDING HIM?

THIS ISN'T JUST ABOUT THE JOKER. THEY SEE THIS AS ANOTHER POLICE BRUTALITY ISSUE.

I MADE YOU COMMIS-SIONER HOPING YOU'D *FIX* THE DEPARTMENT, JIM!

I SPENT THE LAST YEAR CLEANING UP, CRACKED DOWN ON CORRUPTION AND SUSPENDED THE OFFICERS WHO SPARKED THE RACE RIOTS!

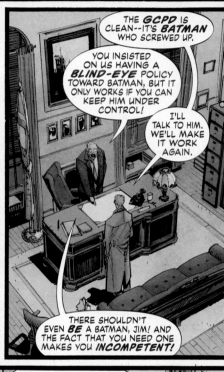

THE GCPD IS CLEAN--IT'S *BATMAN* WHO SCREWED UP.

YOU INSISTED ON US HAVING A *BLIND-EYE* POLICY TOWARD BATMAN, BUT IT ONLY WORKS IF YOU CAN KEEP HIM UNDER CONTROL!

I'LL TALK TO HIM. WE'LL MAKE IT WORK AGAIN.

THERE SHOULDN'T EVEN *BE* A BATMAN, JIM! AND THE FACT THAT YOU NEED ONE MAKES YOU *INCOMPETENT!*

I DON'T CARE HOW REPUTABLE YOU THINK THE GCPD IS. IF IT CONDONES VIGILANTISM, THEN IT'S *STILL* CORRUPT!

DR. LESLIE THOMPKINS IS HERE TO SEE YOU, SIR.

SEND HER IN.

HOW IS HE?

JACK NAPIER HAS MADE A *FULL* RECOVERY, SIR. IT TOOK SOME PLASTIC SURGERY AND A LOT OF STITCHES, BUT PHYSICALLY HE'S GOING TO BE FINE.

THANK GOD. MAYBE NOW HE WON'T *SUE* US.

PHYSICALLY HE'S HEALED, BUT I'M EXTREMELY WORRIED ABOUT HIS *MENTAL* CONDITION.

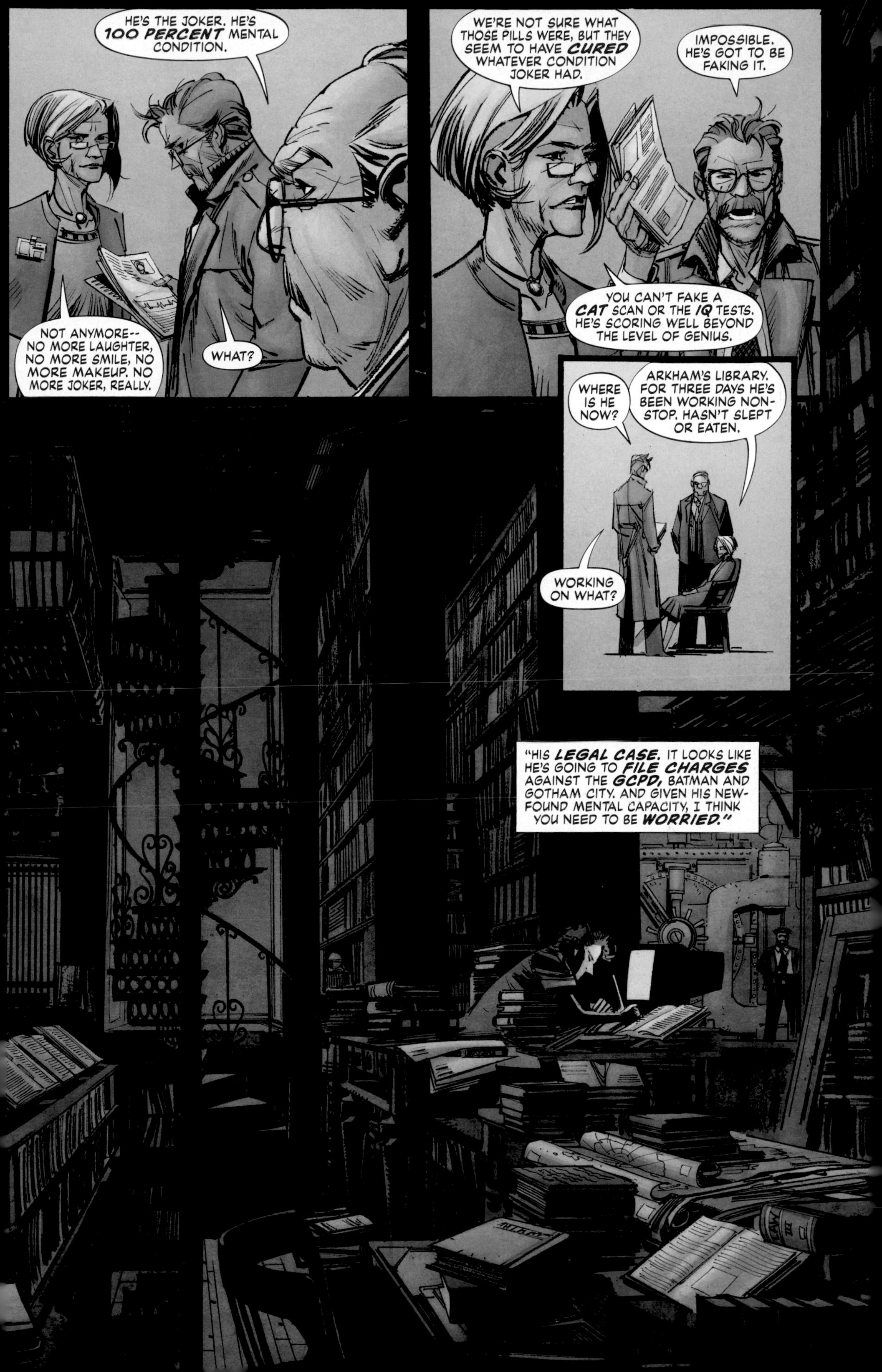

HE'S THE JOKER. HE'S 100 PERCENT MENTAL CONDITION.
NOT ANYMORE-- NO MORE LAUGHTER, NO MORE SMILE, NO MORE MAKEUP. NO MORE JOKER, REALLY.
WHAT?
WE'RE NOT SURE WHAT THOSE PILLS WERE, BUT THEY SEEM TO HAVE CURED WHATEVER CONDITION JOKER HAD.
IMPOSSIBLE. HE'S GOT TO BE FAKING IT.
YOU CAN'T FAKE A CAT SCAN OR THE IQ TESTS. HE'S SCORING WELL BEYOND THE LEVEL OF GENIUS.
WHERE IS HE NOW?
ARKHAM'S LIBRARY. FOR THREE DAYS HE'S BEEN WORKING NON-STOP. HASN'T SLEPT OR EATEN.
WORKING ON WHAT?
"HIS LEGAL CASE. IT LOOKS LIKE HE'S GOING TO FILE CHARGES AGAINST THE GCPD, BATMAN AND GOTHAM CITY. AND GIVEN HIS NEW-FOUND MENTAL CAPACITY, I THINK YOU NEED TO BE WORRIED."

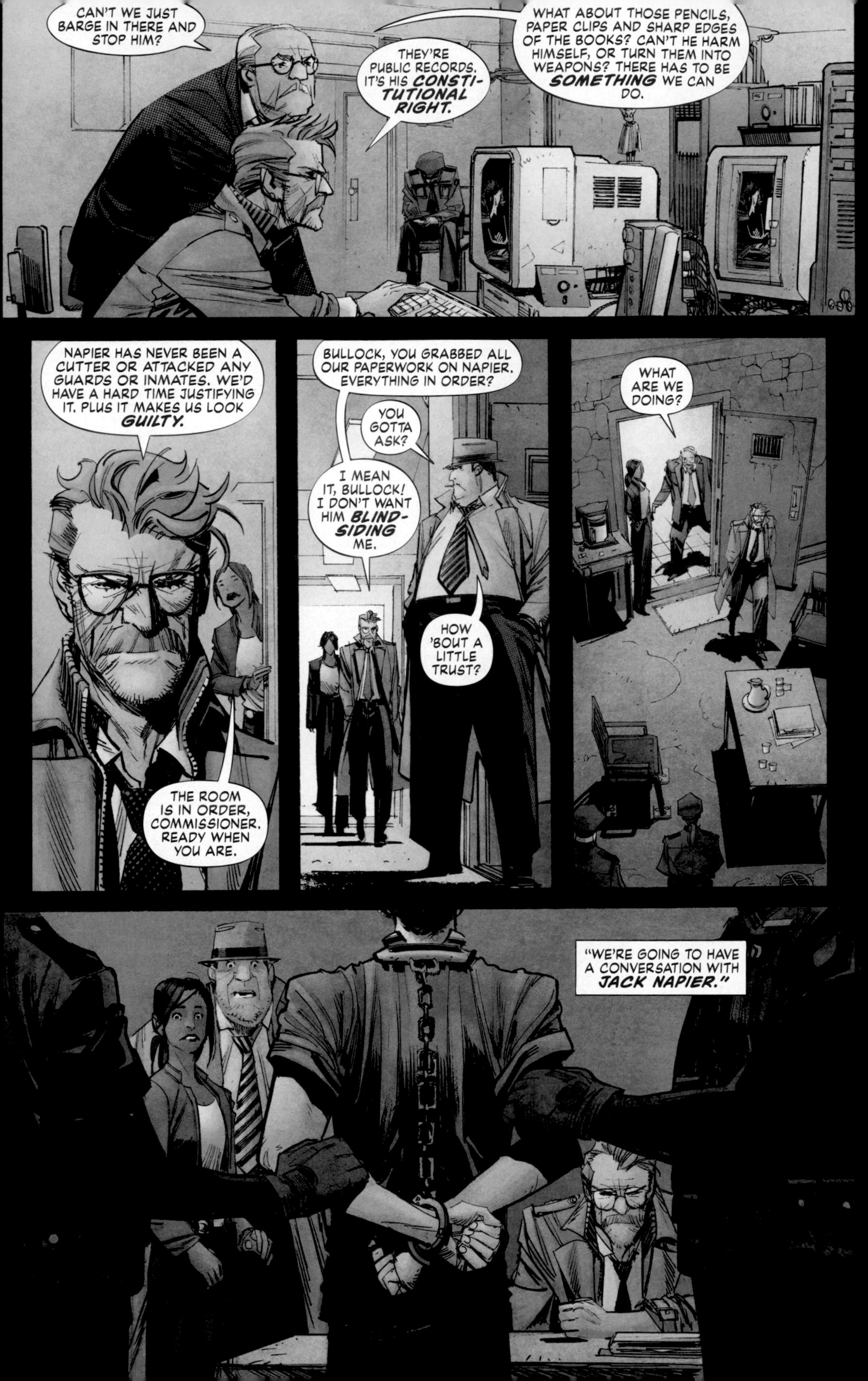
CAN'T WE JUST BARGE IN THERE AND STOP HIM?
THEY'RE PUBLIC RECORDS. IT'S HIS CONSTITUTIONAL RIGHT.
WHAT ABOUT THOSE PENCILS, PAPER CLIPS AND SHARP EDGES OF THE BOOKS? CAN'T HE HARM HIMSELF, OR TURN THEM INTO WEAPONS? THERE HAS TO BE SOMETHING WE CAN DO.
NAPIER HAS NEVER BEEN A CUTTER OR ATTACKED ANY GUARDS OR INMATES. WE'D HAVE A HARD TIME JUSTIFYING IT. PLUS IT MAKES US LOOK GUILTY.
THE ROOM IS IN ORDER, COMMISSIONER. READY WHEN YOU ARE.
BULLOCK, YOU GRABBED ALL OUR PAPERWORK ON NAPIER. EVERYTHING IN ORDER?
YOU GOTTA ASK?
I MEAN IT, BULLOCK! I DON'T WANT HIM BLINDSIDING ME.
HOW 'BOUT A LITTLE TRUST?
WHAT ARE WE DOING?
"WE'RE GOING TO HAVE A CONVERSATION WITH JACK NAPIER."

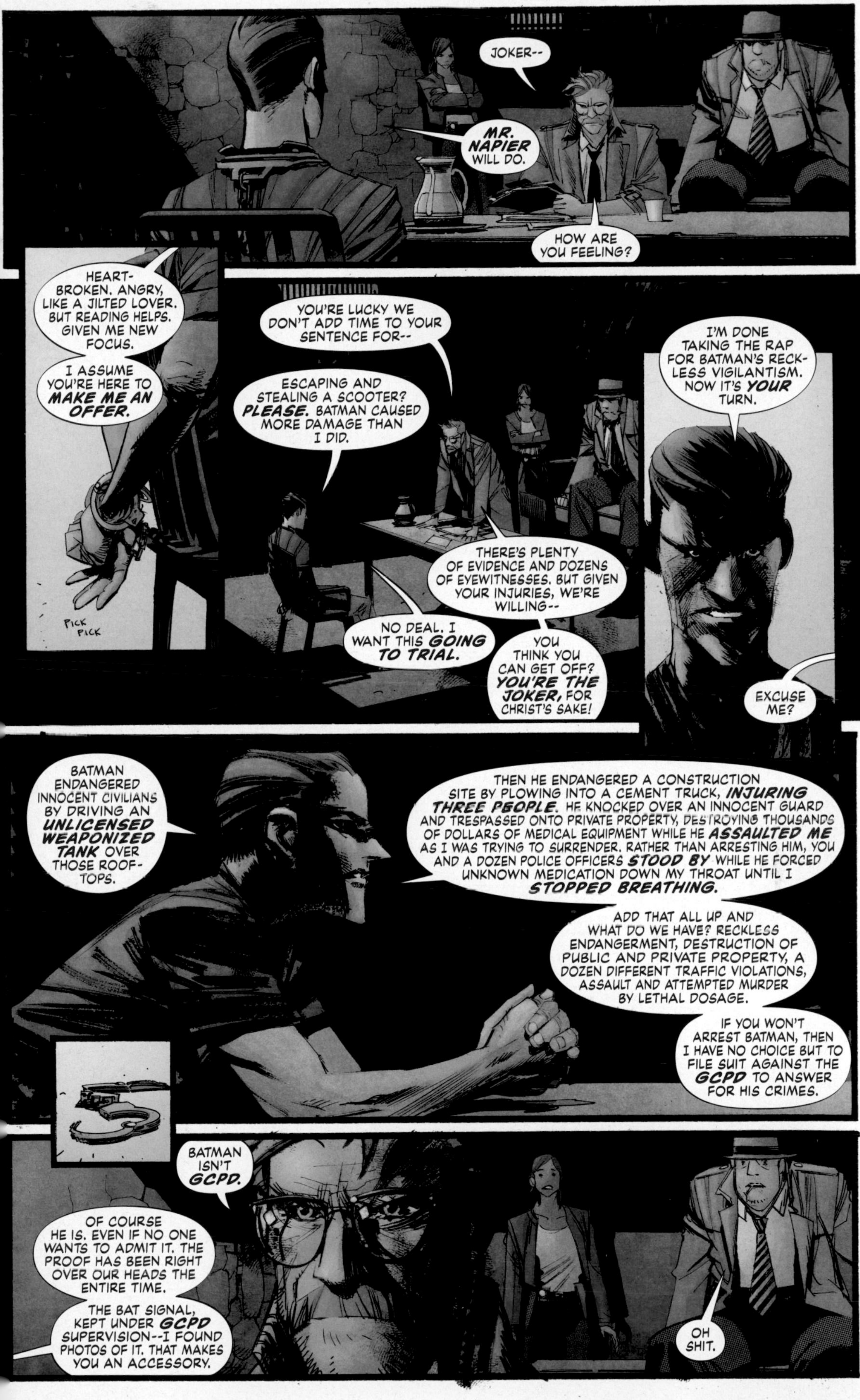
JOKER--
MR. NAPIER WILL DO.
HOW ARE YOU FEELING?
HEART-BROKEN. ANGRY, LIKE A JILTED LOVER. BUT READING HELPS. GIVEN ME NEW FOCUS.
I ASSUME YOU'RE HERE TO MAKE ME AN OFFER.
PICK PICK
YOU'RE LUCKY WE DON'T ADD TIME TO YOUR SENTENCE FOR--
ESCAPING AND STEALING A SCOOTER? PLEASE. BATMAN CAUSED MORE DAMAGE THAN I DID.
THERE'S PLENTY OF EVIDENCE AND DOZENS OF EYEWITNESSES. BUT GIVEN YOUR INJURIES, WE'RE WILLING--
NO DEAL. I WANT THIS GOING TO TRIAL.
YOU THINK YOU CAN GET OFF? YOU'RE THE JOKER, FOR CHRIST'S SAKE!
I'M DONE TAKING THE RAP FOR BATMAN'S RECK-LESS VIGILANTISM. NOW IT'S YOUR TURN.
EXCUSE ME?
BATMAN ENDANGERED INNOCENT CIVILIANS BY DRIVING AN UNLICENSED WEAPONIZED TANK OVER THOSE ROOF-TOPS.
THEN HE ENDANGERED A CONSTRUCTION SITE BY PLOWING INTO A CEMENT TRUCK, INJURING THREE PEOPLE. HE KNOCKED OVER AN INNOCENT GUARD AND TRESPASSED ONTO PRIVATE PROPERTY, DESTROYING THOUSANDS OF DOLLARS OF MEDICAL EQUIPMENT WHILE HE ASSAULTED ME AS I WAS TRYING TO SURRENDER. RATHER THAN ARRESTING HIM, YOU AND A DOZEN POLICE OFFICERS STOOD BY WHILE HE FORCED UNKNOWN MEDICATION DOWN MY THROAT UNTIL I STOPPED BREATHING.
ADD THAT ALL UP AND WHAT DO WE HAVE? RECKLESS ENDANGERMENT, DESTRUCTION OF PUBLIC AND PRIVATE PROPERTY, A DOZEN DIFFERENT TRAFFIC VIOLATIONS, ASSAULT AND ATTEMPTED MURDER BY LETHAL DOSAGE.
IF YOU WON'T ARREST BATMAN, THEN I HAVE NO CHOICE BUT TO FILE SUIT AGAINST THE GCPD TO ANSWER FOR HIS CRIMES.
BATMAN ISN'T GCPD.
OF COURSE HE IS. EVEN IF NO ONE WANTS TO ADMIT IT. THE PROOF HAS BEEN RIGHT OVER OUR HEADS THE ENTIRE TIME.
THE BAT SIGNAL, KEPT UNDER GCPD SUPERVISION--I FOUND PHOTOS OF IT. THAT MAKES YOU AN ACCESSORY.
OH SHIT.

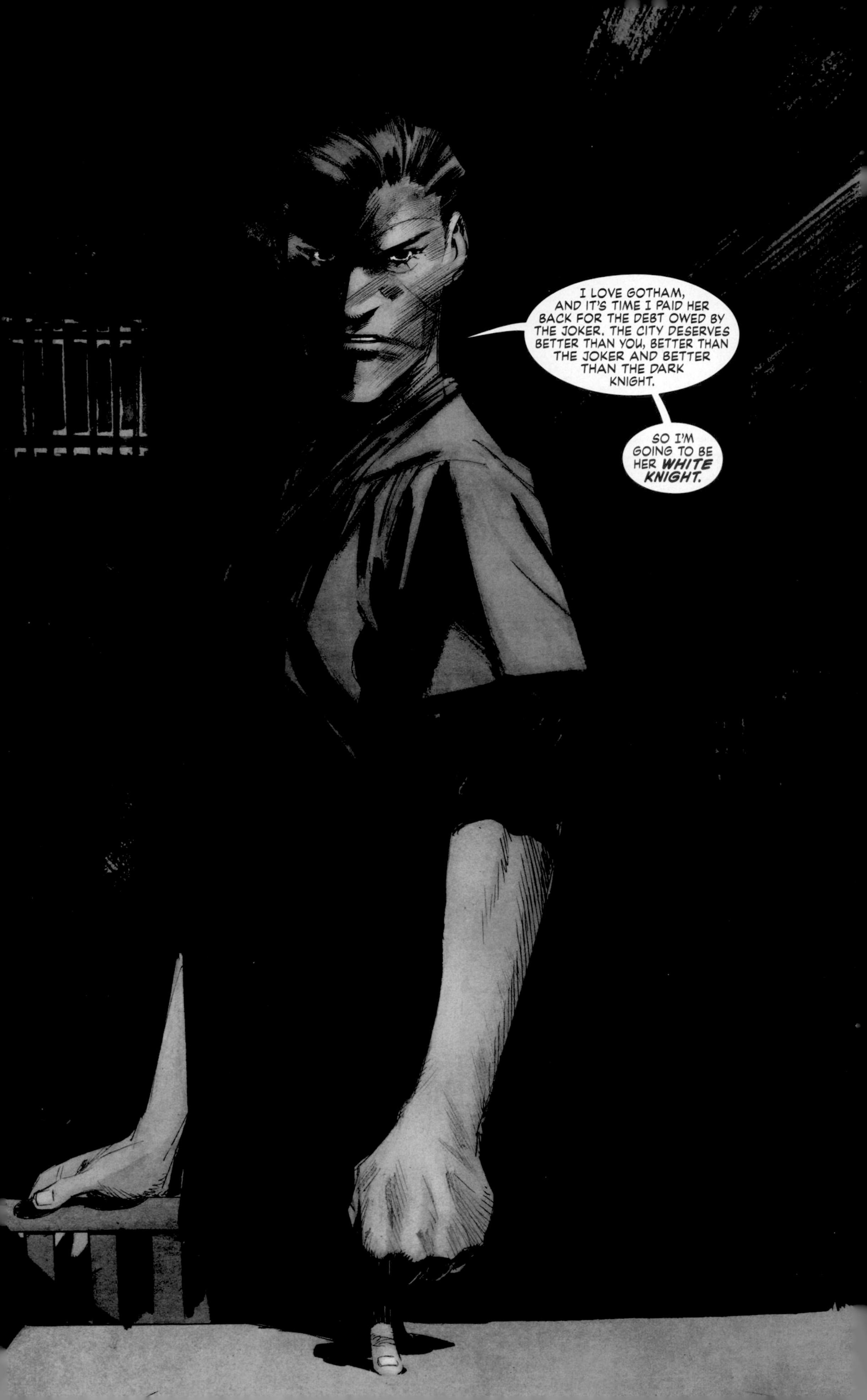
I LOVE GOTHAM, AND IT'S TIME I PAID HER BACK FOR THE DEBT OWED BY THE JOKER. THE CITY DESERVES BETTER THAN YOU, BETTER THAN THE JOKER AND BETTER THAN THE DARK KNIGHT.
SO I'M GOING TO BE HER *WHITE KNIGHT.*

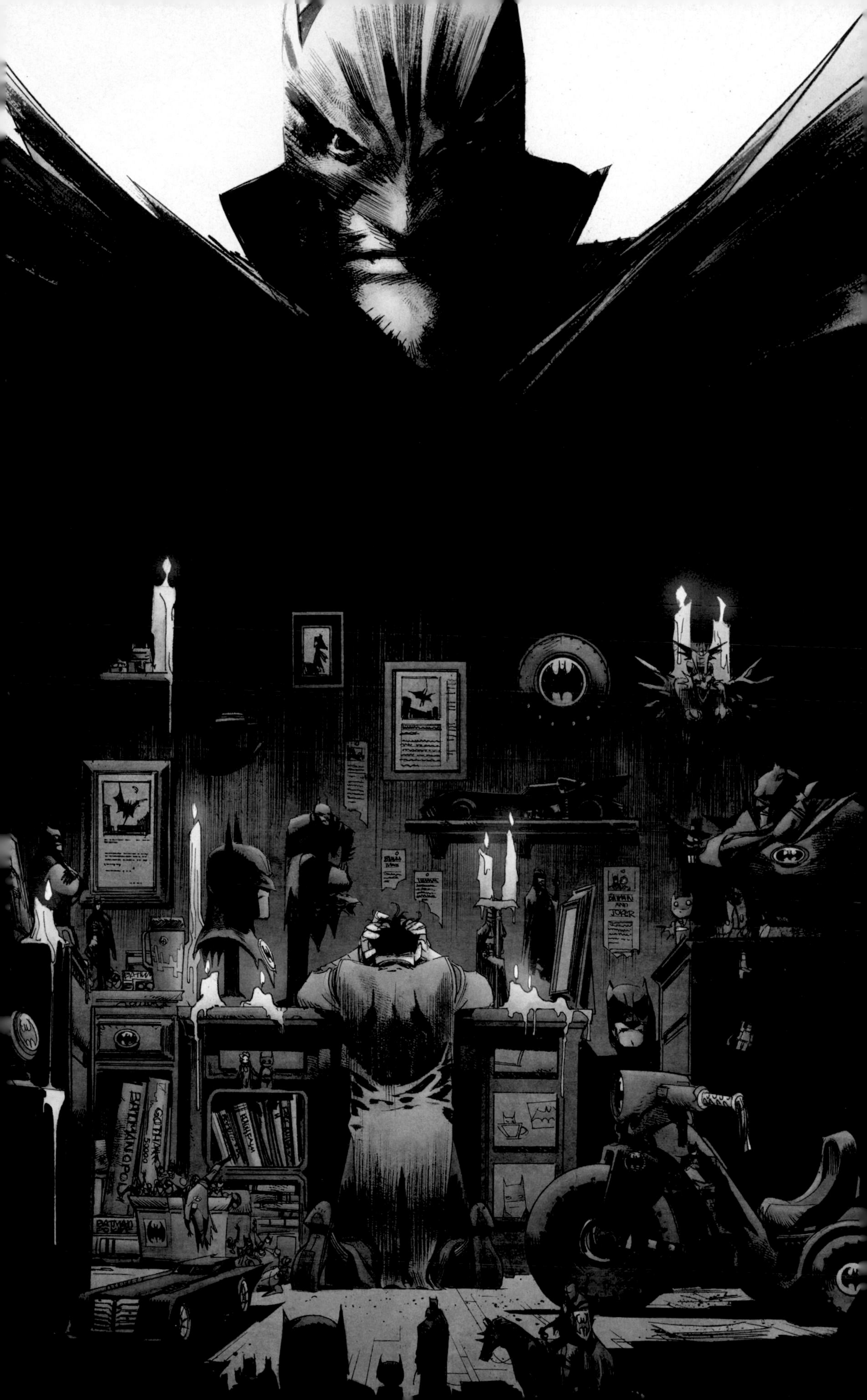
BATMAN AND JOKER
BATMANOPOLY
GOTHAM 50000

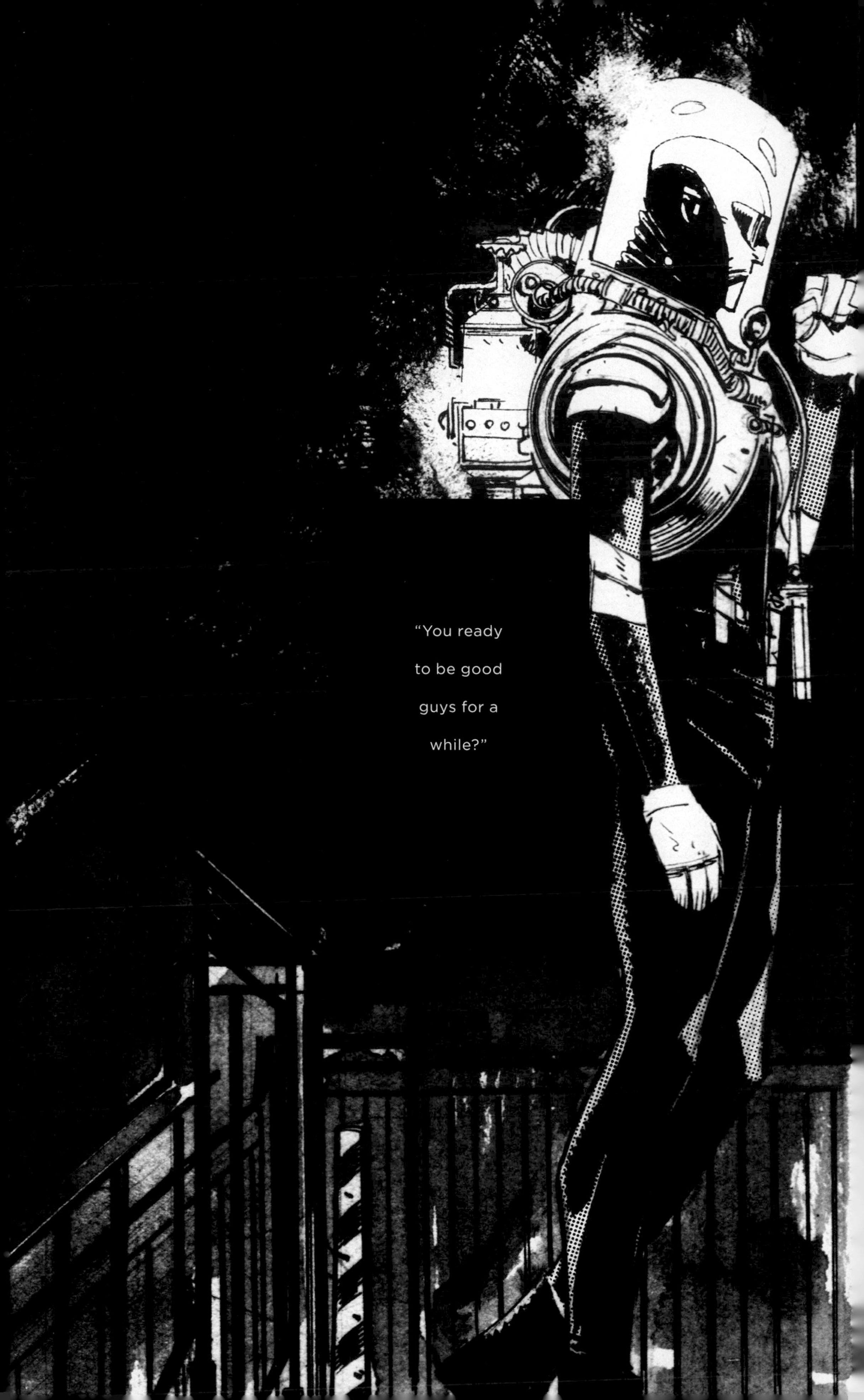
"You ready to be good guys for a while?"

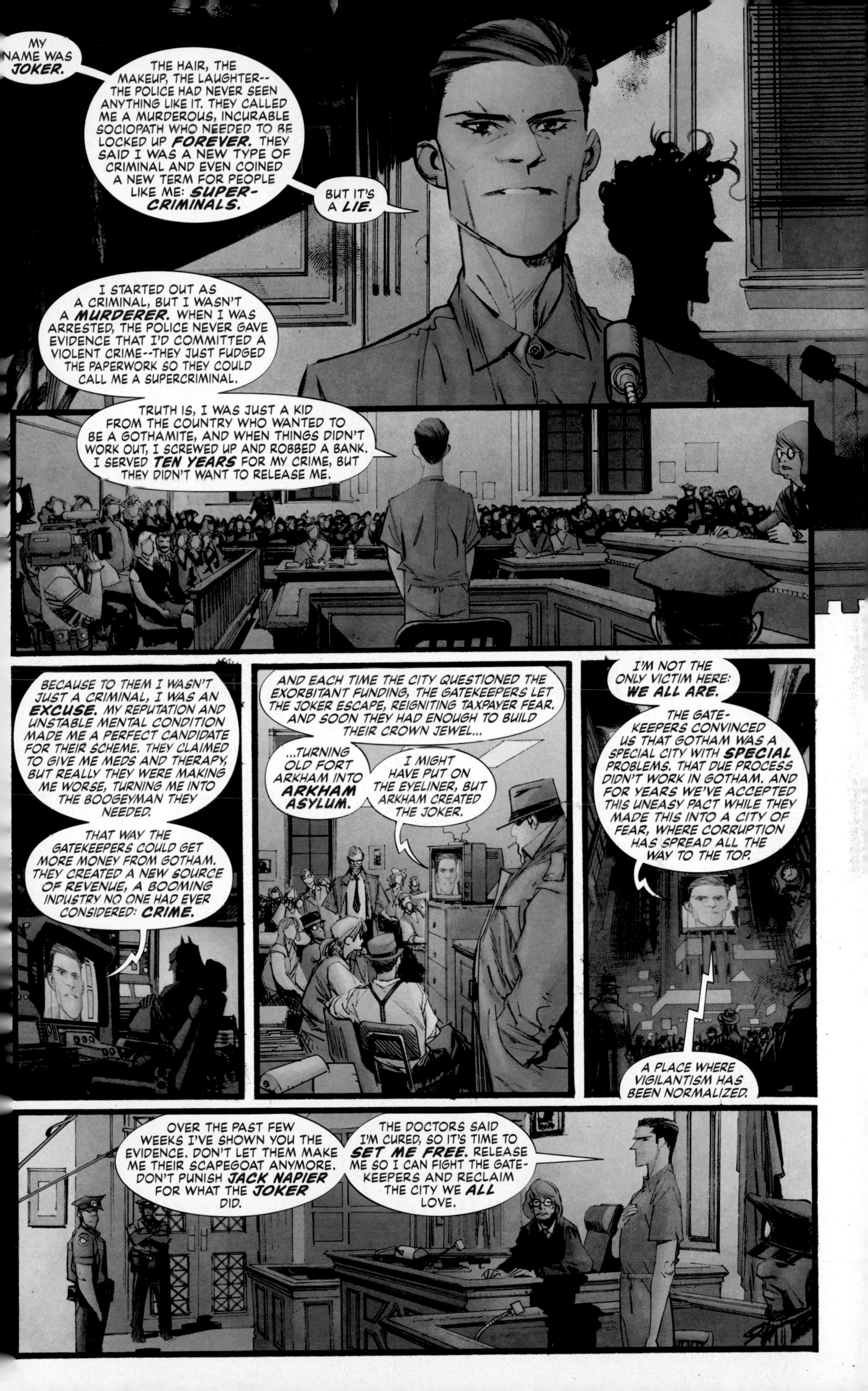
MY NAME WAS JOKER.
THE HAIR, THE MAKEUP, THE LAUGHTER-- THE POLICE HAD NEVER SEEN ANYTHING LIKE IT. THEY CALLED ME A MURDEROUS, INCURABLE SOCIOPATH WHO NEEDED TO BE LOCKED UP FOREVER. THEY SAID I WAS A NEW TYPE OF CRIMINAL AND EVEN COINED A NEW TERM FOR PEOPLE LIKE ME: SUPER-CRIMINALS.
BUT IT'S A LIE.
I STARTED OUT AS A CRIMINAL, BUT I WASN'T A MURDERER. WHEN I WAS ARRESTED, THE POLICE NEVER GAVE EVIDENCE THAT I'D COMMITTED A VIOLENT CRIME--THEY JUST FUDGED THE PAPERWORK SO THEY COULD CALL ME A SUPERCRIMINAL.
TRUTH IS, I WAS JUST A KID FROM THE COUNTRY WHO WANTED TO BE A GOTHAMITE, AND WHEN THINGS DIDN'T WORK OUT, I SCREWED UP AND ROBBED A BANK. I SERVED TEN YEARS FOR MY CRIME, BUT THEY DIDN'T WANT TO RELEASE ME.
BECAUSE TO THEM I WASN'T JUST A CRIMINAL, I WAS AN EXCUSE. MY REPUTATION AND UNSTABLE MENTAL CONDITION MADE ME A PERFECT CANDIDATE FOR THEIR SCHEME. THEY CLAIMED TO GIVE ME MEDS AND THERAPY, BUT REALLY THEY WERE MAKING ME WORSE, TURNING ME INTO THE BOOGEYMAN THEY NEEDED.
THAT WAY THE GATEKEEPERS COULD GET MORE MONEY FROM GOTHAM. THEY CREATED A NEW SOURCE OF REVENUE, A BOOMING INDUSTRY NO ONE HAD EVER CONSIDERED: CRIME.
AND EACH TIME THE CITY QUESTIONED THE EXORBITANT FUNDING, THE GATEKEEPERS LET THE JOKER ESCAPE, REIGNITING TAXPAYER FEAR. AND SOON THEY HAD ENOUGH TO BUILD THEIR CROWN JEWEL...
...TURNING OLD FORT ARKHAM INTO ARKHAM ASYLUM.
I MIGHT HAVE PUT ON THE EYELINER, BUT ARKHAM CREATED THE JOKER.
I'M NOT THE ONLY VICTIM HERE: WE ALL ARE.
THE GATE-KEEPERS CONVINCED US THAT GOTHAM WAS A SPECIAL CITY WITH SPECIAL PROBLEMS. THAT DUE PROCESS DIDN'T WORK IN GOTHAM. AND FOR YEARS WE'VE ACCEPTED THIS UNEASY PACT WHILE THEY MADE THIS INTO A CITY OF FEAR, WHERE CORRUPTION HAS SPREAD ALL THE WAY TO THE TOP.
A PLACE WHERE VIGILANTISM HAS BEEN NORMALIZED.
OVER THE PAST FEW WEEKS I'VE SHOWN YOU THE EVIDENCE. DON'T LET THEM MAKE ME THEIR SCAPEGOAT ANYMORE. DON'T PUNISH JACK NAPIER FOR WHAT THE JOKER DID.
THE DOCTORS SAID I'M CURED, SO IT'S TIME TO SET ME FREE. RELEASE ME SO I CAN FIGHT THE GATE-KEEPERS AND RECLAIM THE CITY WE ALL LOVE.

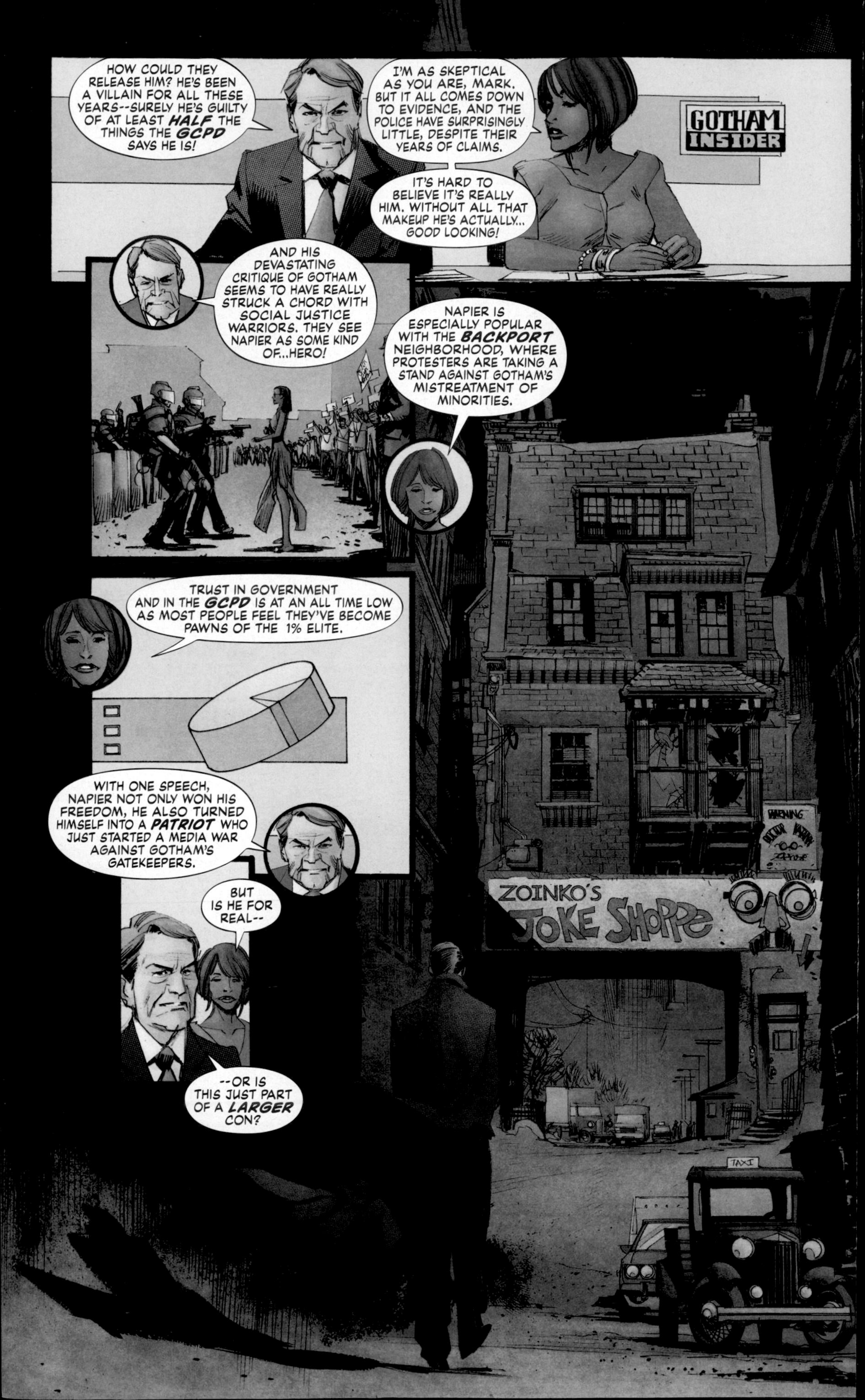
HOW COULD THEY RELEASE HIM? HE'S BEEN A VILLAIN FOR ALL THESE YEARS--SURELY HE'S GUILTY OF AT LEAST HALF THE THINGS THE GCPD SAYS HE IS!
I'M AS SKEPTICAL AS YOU ARE, MARK. BUT IT ALL COMES DOWN TO EVIDENCE, AND THE POLICE HAVE SURPRISINGLY LITTLE, DESPITE THEIR YEARS OF CLAIMS.
GOTHAM INSIDER
IT'S HARD TO BELIEVE IT'S REALLY HIM. WITHOUT ALL THAT MAKEUP HE'S ACTUALLY... GOOD LOOKING!
AND HIS DEVASTATING CRITIQUE OF GOTHAM SEEMS TO HAVE REALLY STRUCK A CHORD WITH SOCIAL JUSTICE WARRIORS. THEY SEE NAPIER AS SOME KIND OF...HERO!
NAPIER IS ESPECIALLY POPULAR WITH THE BACKPORT NEIGHBORHOOD, WHERE PROTESTERS ARE TAKING A STAND AGAINST GOTHAM'S MISTREATMENT OF MINORITIES.
TRUST IN GOVERNMENT AND IN THE GCPD IS AT AN ALL TIME LOW AS MOST PEOPLE FEEL THEY'VE BECOME PAWNS OF THE 1% ELITE.
WITH ONE SPEECH, NAPIER NOT ONLY WON HIS FREEDOM, HE ALSO TURNED HIMSELF INTO A PATRIOT WHO JUST STARTED A MEDIA WAR AGAINST GOTHAM'S GATEKEEPERS.
BUT IS HE FOR REAL--
--OR IS THIS JUST PART OF A LARGER CON?
WARNING
ZOINKO'S JOKE SHOPPE
TAXI

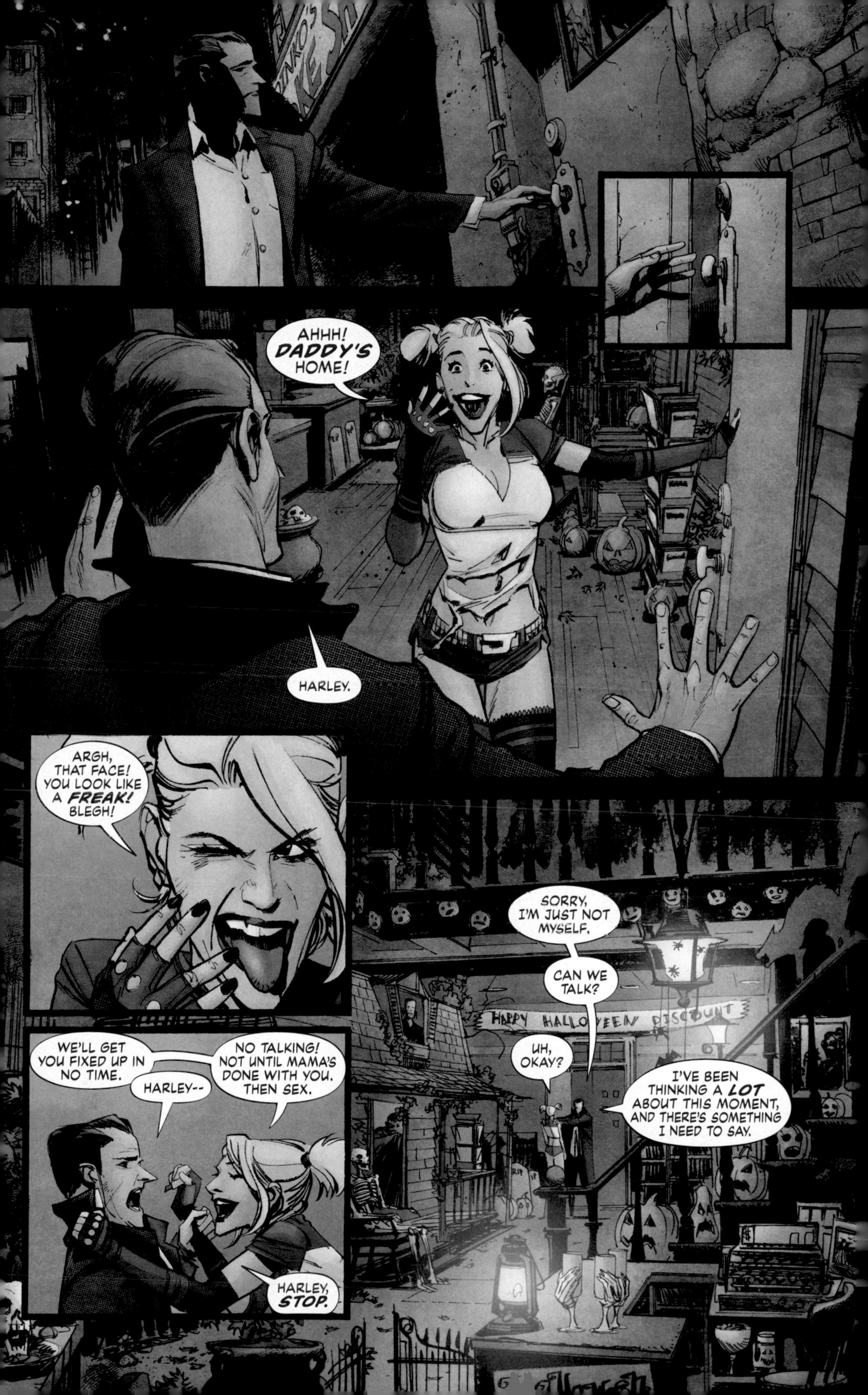
AHHH! DADDY'S HOME!
HARLEY.
ARGH, THAT FACE! YOU LOOK LIKE A FREAK! BLEGH!
WE'LL GET YOU FIXED UP IN NO TIME.
NO TALKING! NOT UNTIL MAMA'S DONE WITH YOU. THEN SEX.
HARLEY--
HARLEY, STOP.
SORRY, I'M JUST NOT MYSELF.
CAN WE TALK?
UH, OKAY?
I'VE BEEN THINKING A LOT ABOUT THIS MOMENT, AND THERE'S SOMETHING I NEED TO SAY.
HAPPY HALLOWEEN DISCOUNT

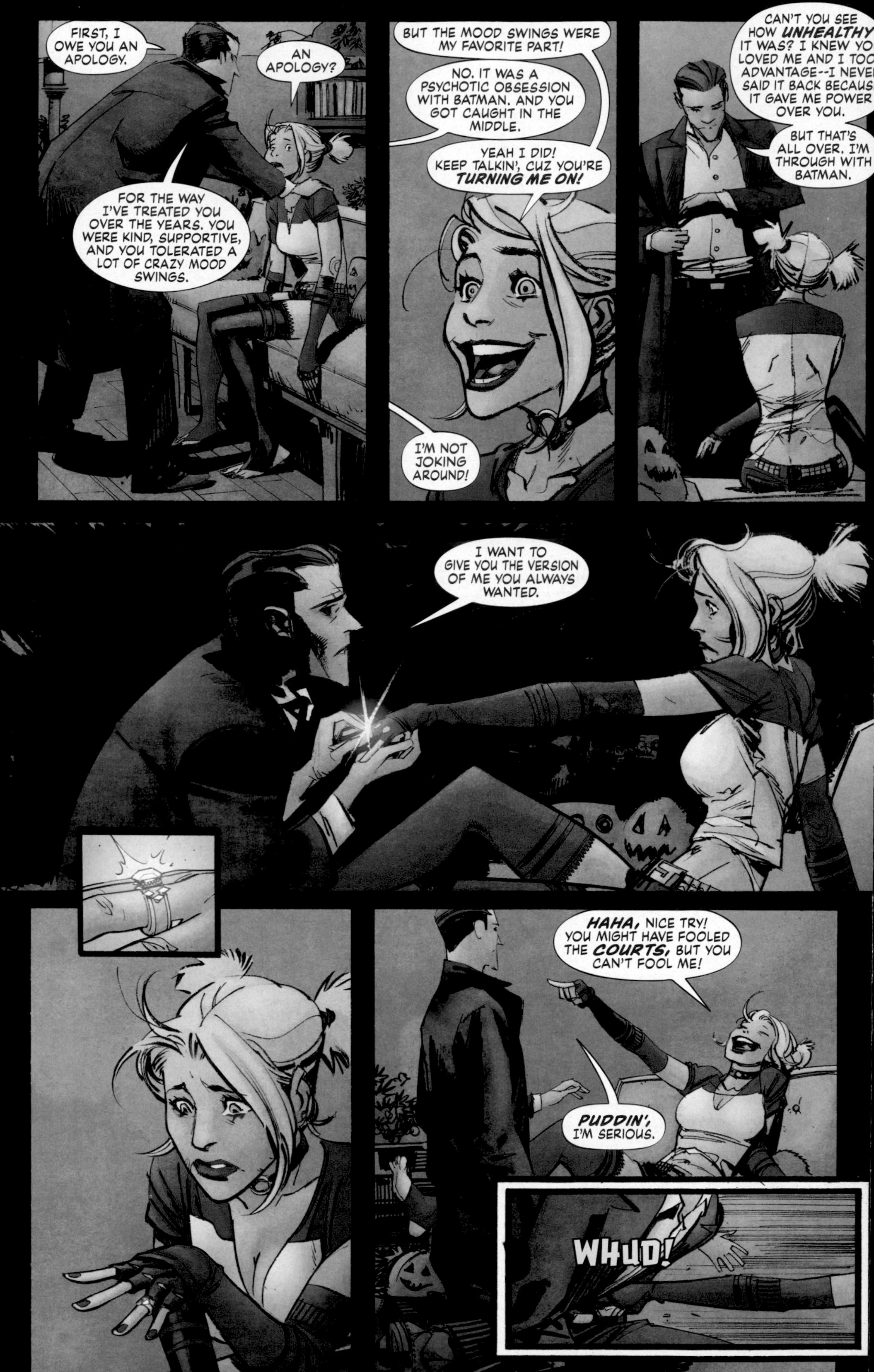
FIRST, I OWE YOU AN APOLOGY.
AN APOLOGY?
FOR THE WAY I'VE TREATED YOU OVER THE YEARS. YOU WERE KIND, SUPPORTIVE, AND YOU TOLERATED A LOT OF CRAZY MOOD SWINGS.
BUT THE MOOD SWINGS WERE MY FAVORITE PART!
NO. IT WAS A PSYCHOTIC OBSESSION WITH BATMAN. AND YOU GOT CAUGHT IN THE MIDDLE.
YEAH I DID! KEEP TALKIN', CUZ YOU'RE TURNING ME ON!
I'M NOT JOKING AROUND!
CAN'T YOU SEE HOW UNHEALTHY IT WAS? I KNEW YOU LOVED ME AND I TOOK ADVANTAGE--I NEVER SAID IT BACK BECAUSE IT GAVE ME POWER OVER YOU.
BUT THAT'S ALL OVER. I'M THROUGH WITH BATMAN.
I WANT TO GIVE YOU THE VERSION OF ME YOU ALWAYS WANTED.
HAHA, NICE TRY! YOU MIGHT HAVE FOOLED THE COURTS, BUT YOU CAN'T FOOL ME!
PUDDIN', I'M SERIOUS.
WHUD!

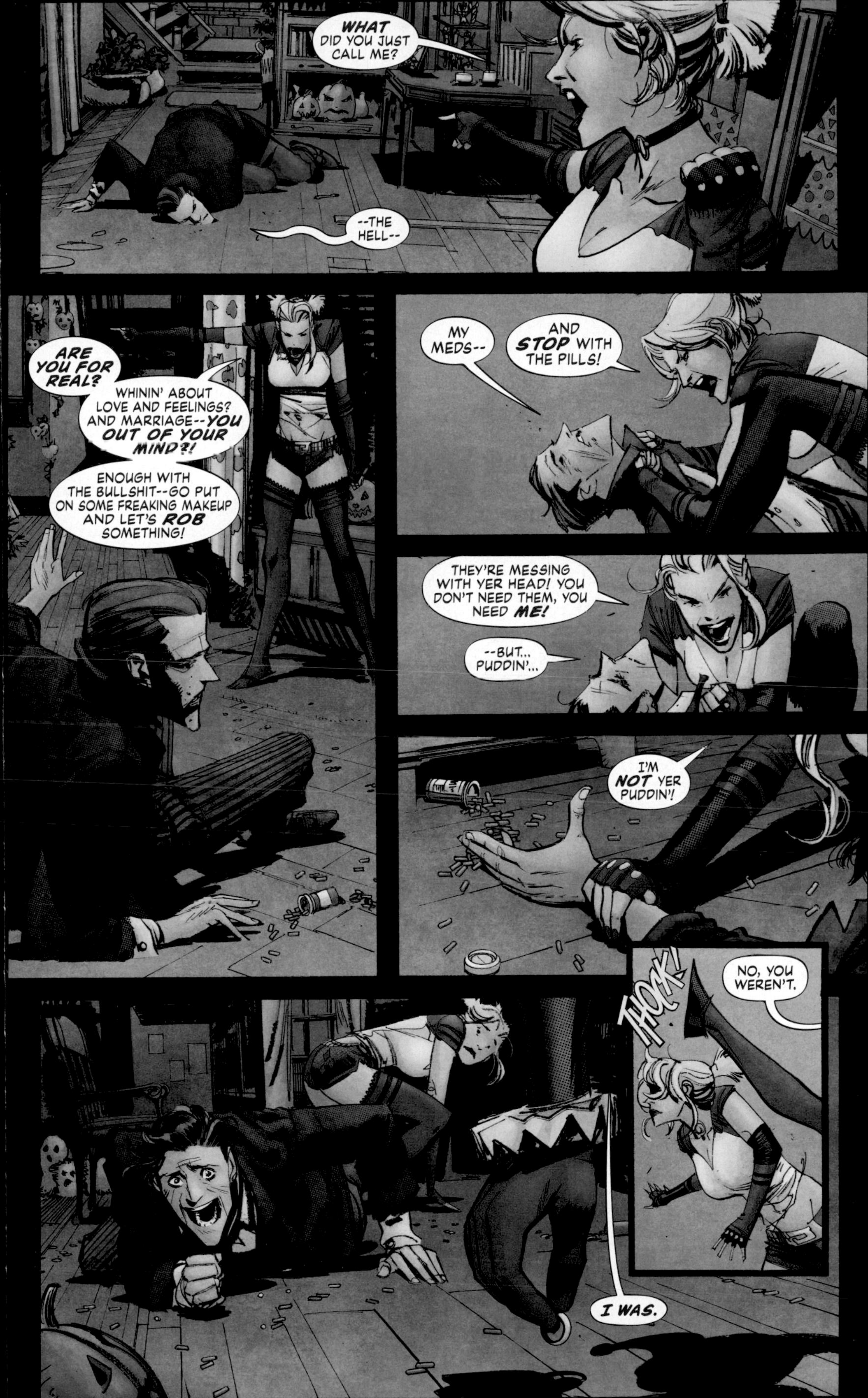
WHAT DID YOU JUST CALL ME?
--THE HELL--
ARE YOU FOR REAL?
WHININ' ABOUT LOVE AND FEELINGS? AND MARRIAGE--YOU OUT OF YOUR MIND?!
ENOUGH WITH THE BULLSHIT--GO PUT ON SOME FREAKING MAKEUP AND LET'S ROB SOMETHING!
MY MEDS--
AND STOP WITH THE PILLS!
THEY'RE MESSING WITH YER HEAD! YOU DON'T NEED THEM, YOU NEED ME!
--BUT... PUDDIN'...
I'M NOT YER PUDDIN'!
THOCK!
NO, YOU WEREN'T.
I WAS.

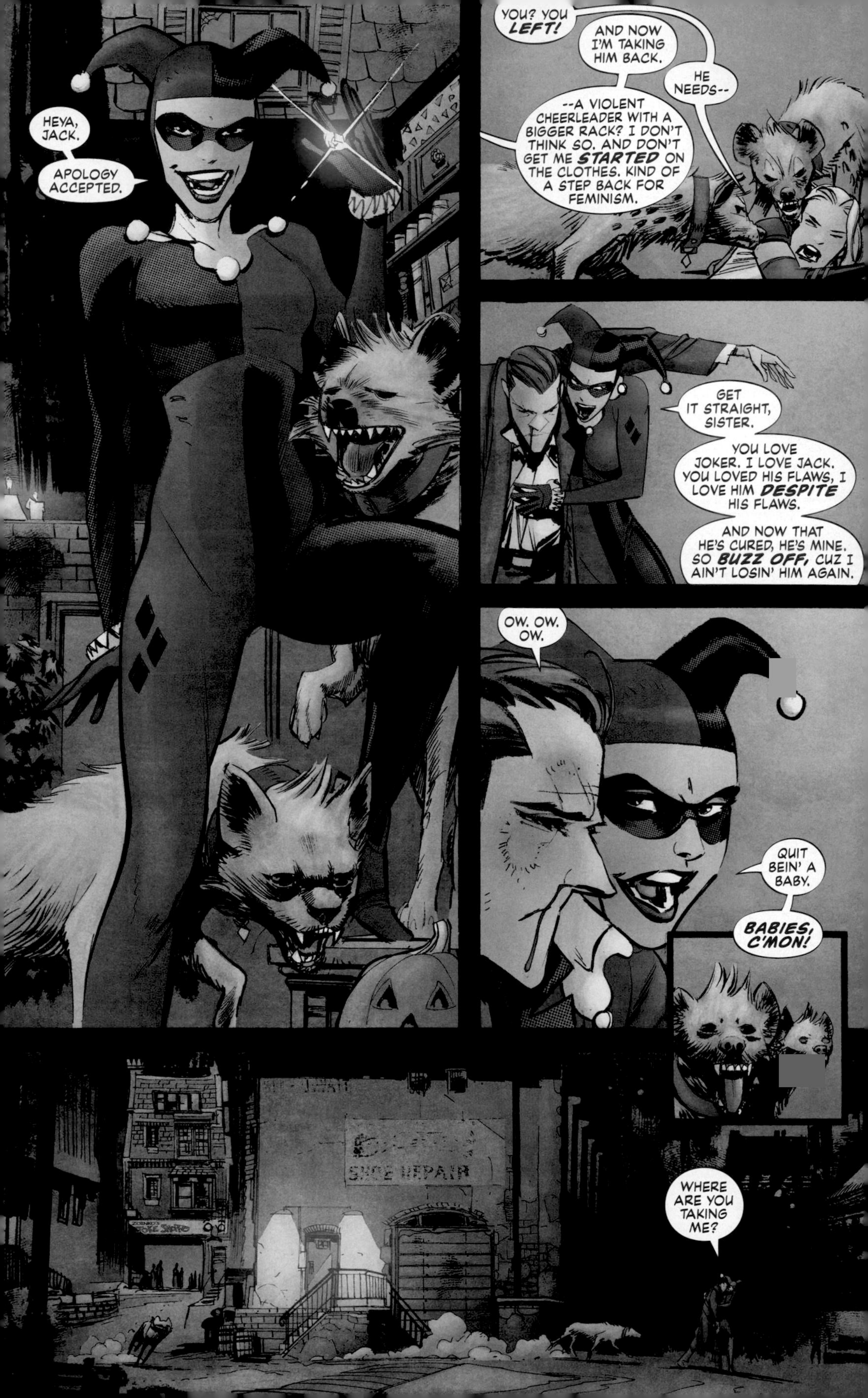
HEYA, JACK.
APOLOGY ACCEPTED.
YOU? YOU LEFT!
AND NOW I'M TAKING HIM BACK.
HE NEEDS--
--A VIOLENT CHEERLEADER WITH A BIGGER RACK? I DON'T THINK SO. AND DON'T GET ME STARTED ON THE CLOTHES. KIND OF A STEP BACK FOR FEMINISM.
GET IT STRAIGHT, SISTER.
YOU LOVE JOKER. I LOVE JACK. YOU LOVED HIS FLAWS, I LOVE HIM DESPITE HIS FLAWS.
AND NOW THAT HE'S CURED, HE'S MINE. SO BUZZ OFF, CUZ I AIN'T LOSIN' HIM AGAIN.
OW. OW. OW.
QUIT BEIN' A BABY.
BABIES, C'MON!
SHOE REPAIR
WHERE ARE YOU TAKING ME?

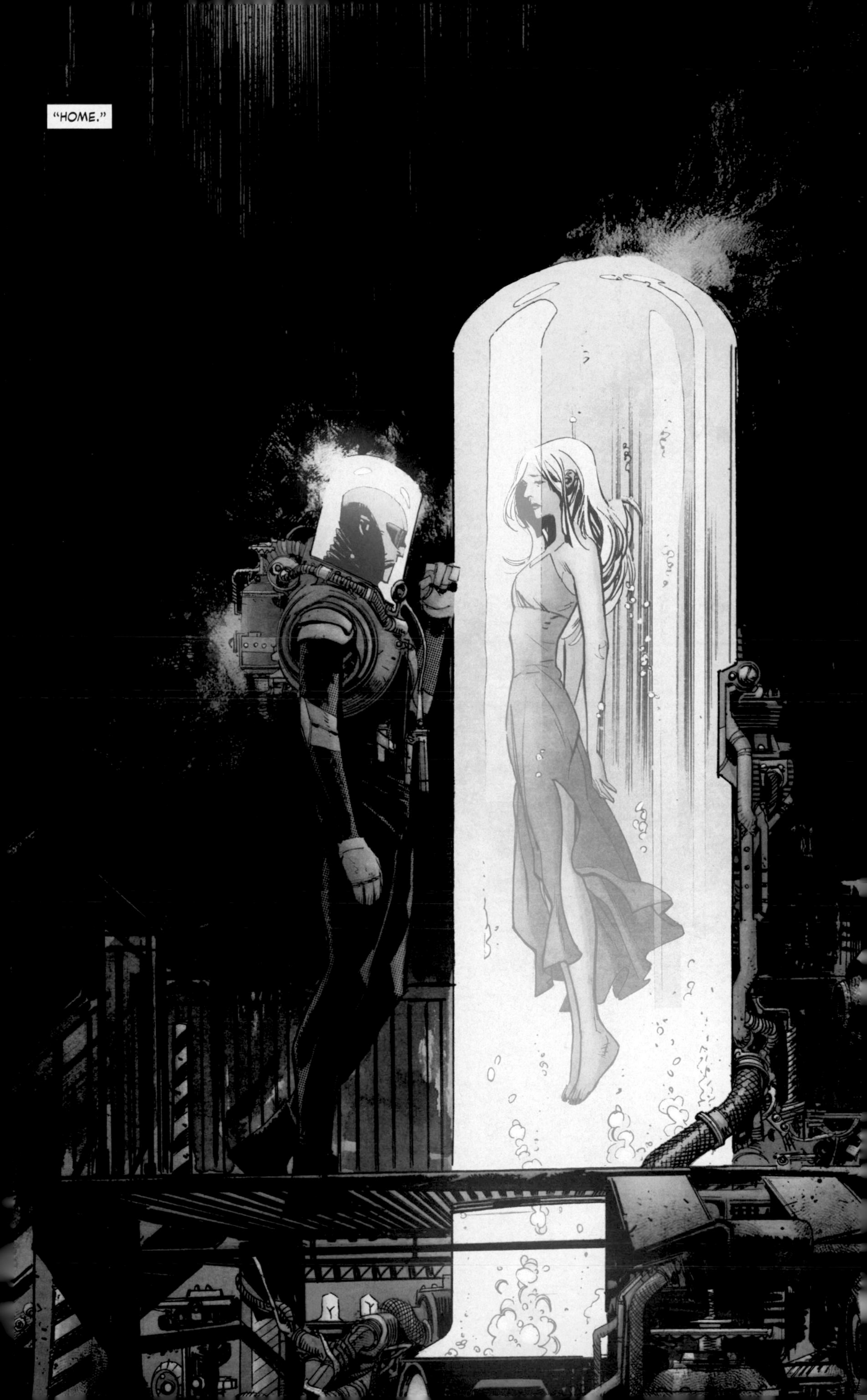
"HOME."

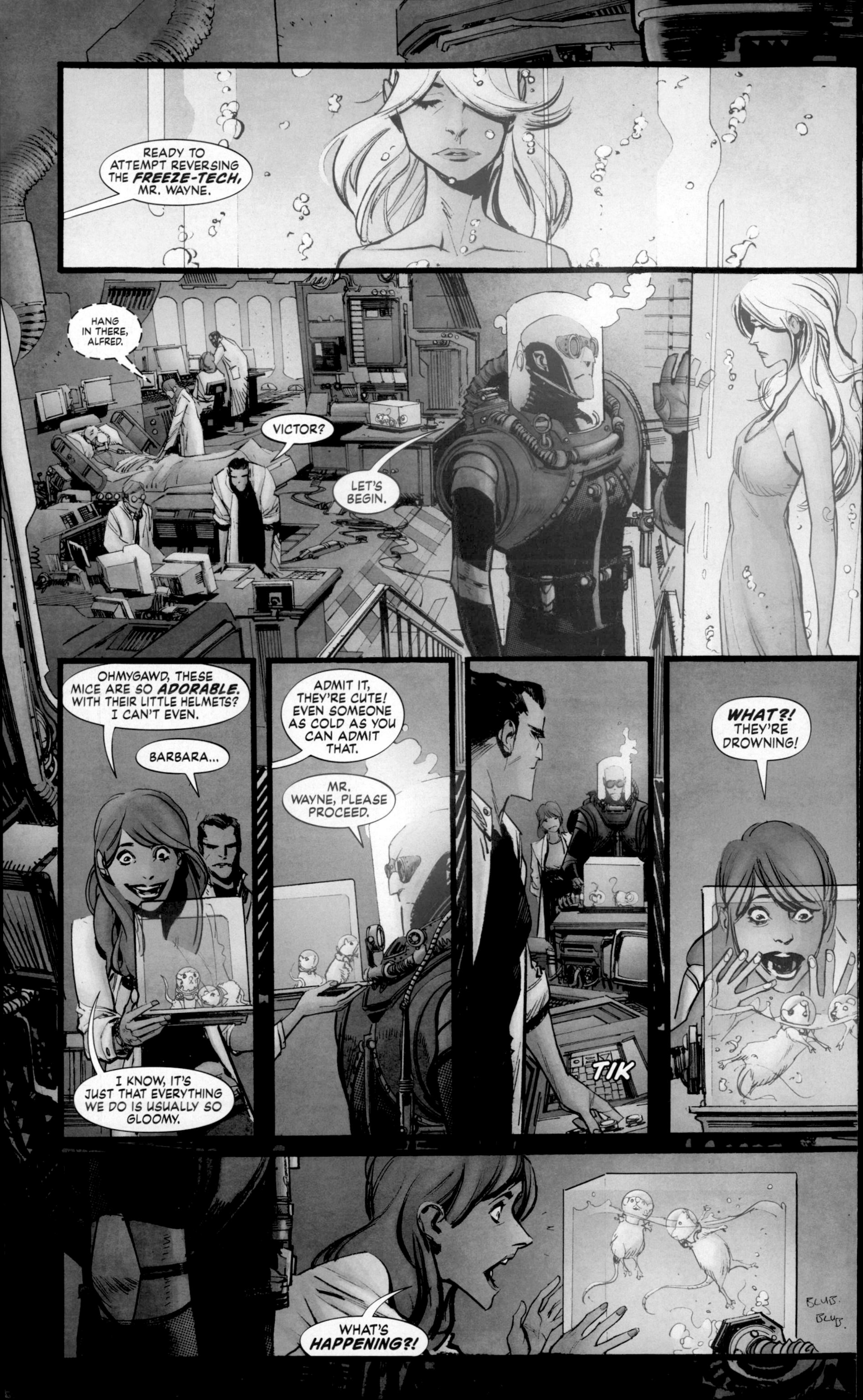
READY TO ATTEMPT REVERSING THE FREEZE-TECH, MR. WAYNE.
HANG IN THERE, ALFRED.
VICTOR?
LET'S BEGIN.
OHMYGAWD, THESE MICE ARE SO ADORABLE. WITH THEIR LITTLE HELMETS? I CAN'T EVEN.
BARBARA...
I KNOW, IT'S JUST THAT EVERYTHING WE DO IS USUALLY SO GLOOMY.
ADMIT IT, THEY'RE CUTE! EVEN SOMEONE AS COLD AS YOU CAN ADMIT THAT.
MR. WAYNE, PLEASE PROCEED.
TIK
WHAT?! THEY'RE DROWNING!
WHAT'S HAPPENING?!
BLUB. BLUB.

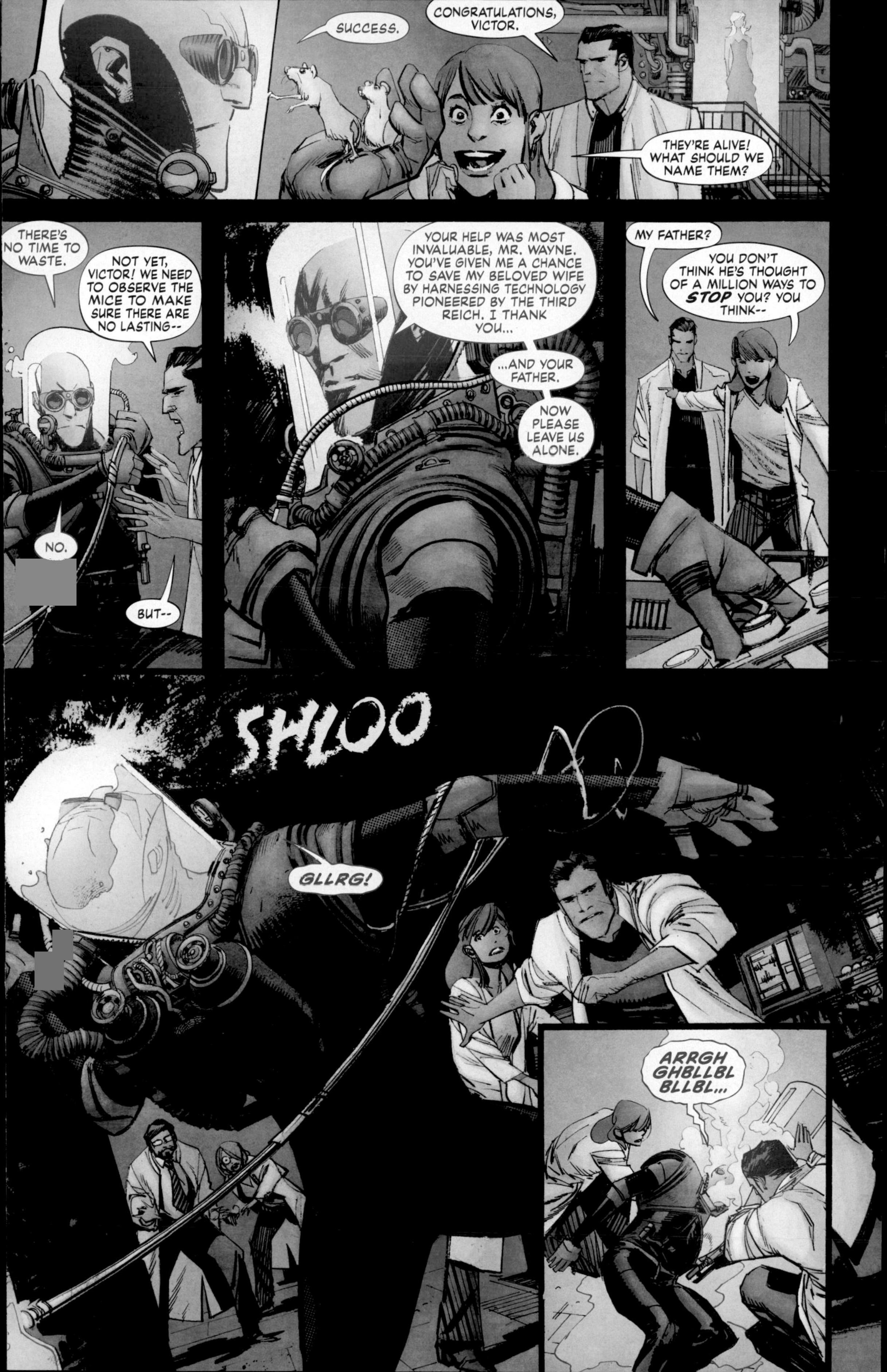
SUCCESS.
CONGRATULATIONS, VICTOR.
THEY'RE ALIVE! WHAT SHOULD WE NAME THEM?
THERE'S NO TIME TO WASTE.
NOT YET, VICTOR! WE NEED TO OBSERVE THE MICE TO MAKE SURE THERE ARE NO LASTING--
NO.
BUT--
YOUR HELP WAS MOST INVALUABLE, MR. WAYNE. YOU'VE GIVEN ME A CHANCE TO SAVE MY BELOVED WIFE BY HARNESSING TECHNOLOGY PIONEERED BY THE THIRD REICH. I THANK YOU...
...AND YOUR FATHER.
NOW PLEASE LEAVE US ALONE.
MY FATHER?
YOU DON'T THINK HE'S THOUGHT OF A MILLION WAYS TO STOP YOU? YOU THINK--
SHLOO
GLLRG!
ARRGH GHBLLBL BLLBL...

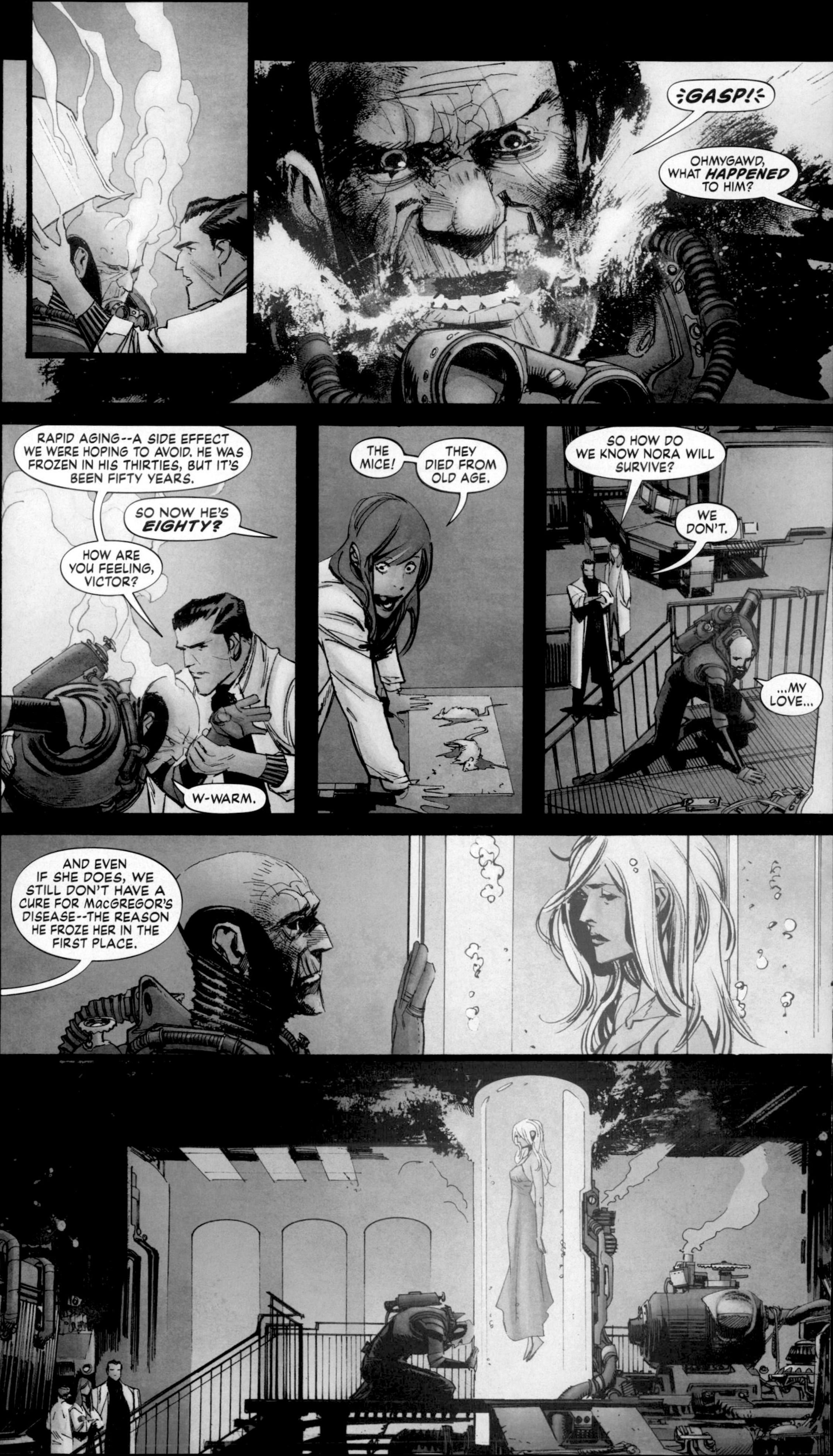

GASP!
OHMYGAWD, WHAT HAPPENED TO HIM?
RAPID AGING--A SIDE EFFECT WE WERE HOPING TO AVOID. HE WAS FROZEN IN HIS THIRTIES, BUT IT'S BEEN FIFTY YEARS.
SO NOW HE'S EIGHTY?
HOW ARE YOU FEELING, VICTOR?
W-WARM.
THE MICE!
THEY DIED FROM OLD AGE.
SO HOW DO WE KNOW NORA WILL SURVIVE?
WE DON'T.
...MY LOVE...
AND EVEN IF SHE DOES, WE STILL DON'T HAVE A CURE FOR MacGREGOR'S DISEASE--THE REASON HE FROZE HER IN THE FIRST PLACE.

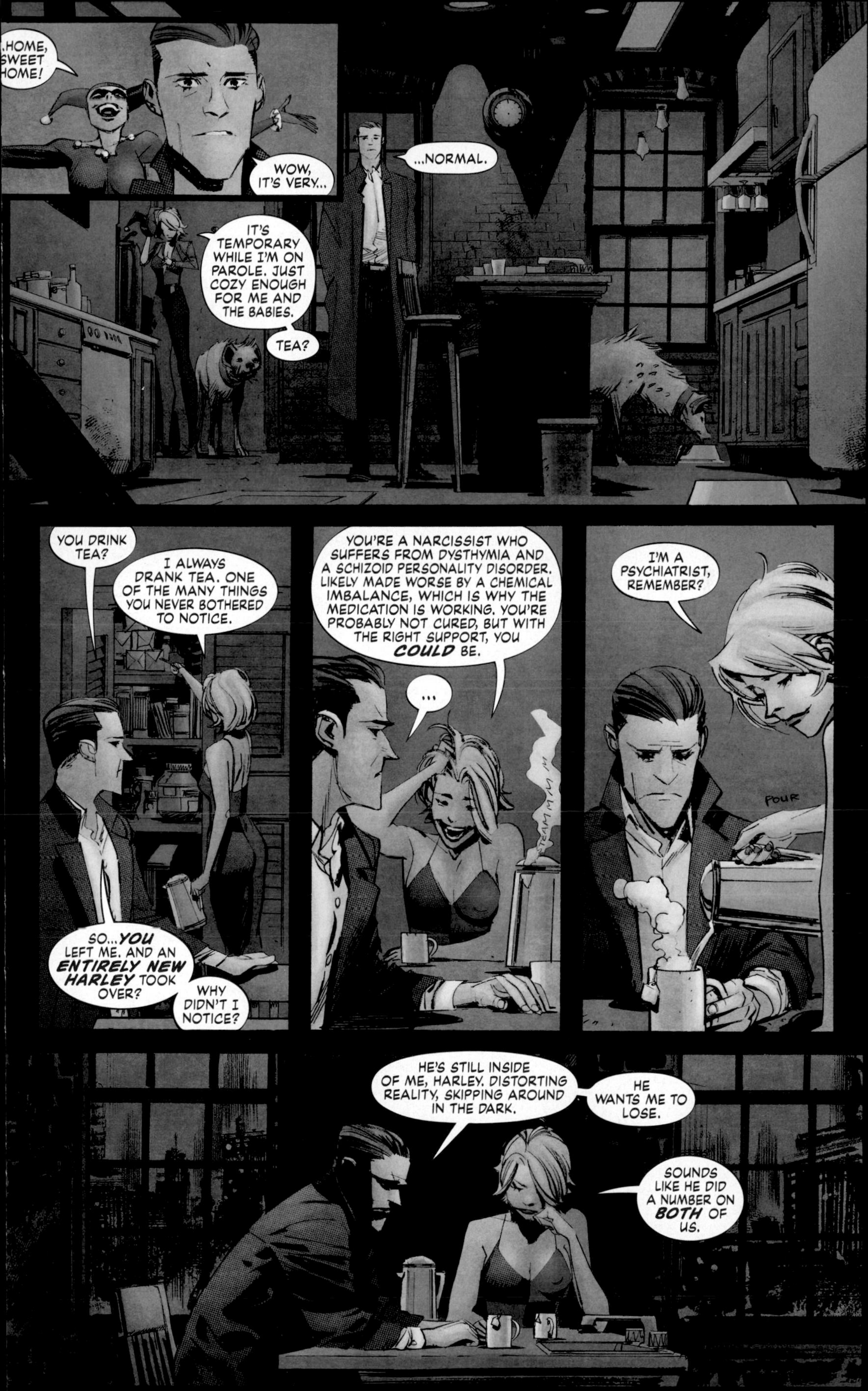
...HOME, SWEET HOME!
WOW, IT'S VERY...
...NORMAL.
IT'S TEMPORARY WHILE I'M ON PAROLE. JUST COZY ENOUGH FOR ME AND THE BABIES.
TEA?
YOU DRINK TEA?
I ALWAYS DRANK TEA. ONE OF THE MANY THINGS YOU NEVER BOTHERED TO NOTICE.
SO...YOU LEFT ME. AND AN ENTIRELY NEW HARLEY TOOK OVER?
WHY DIDN'T I NOTICE?
YOU'RE A NARCISSIST WHO SUFFERS FROM DYSTHYMIA AND A SCHIZOID PERSONALITY DISORDER. LIKELY MADE WORSE BY A CHEMICAL IMBALANCE, WHICH IS WHY THE MEDICATION IS WORKING. YOU'RE PROBABLY NOT CURED, BUT WITH THE RIGHT SUPPORT, YOU COULD BE.
...
STEAMMM
I'M A PSYCHIATRIST, REMEMBER?
POUR
HE'S STILL INSIDE OF ME, HARLEY. DISTORTING REALITY, SKIPPING AROUND IN THE DARK.
HE WANTS ME TO LOSE.
SOUNDS LIKE HE DID A NUMBER ON BOTH OF US.

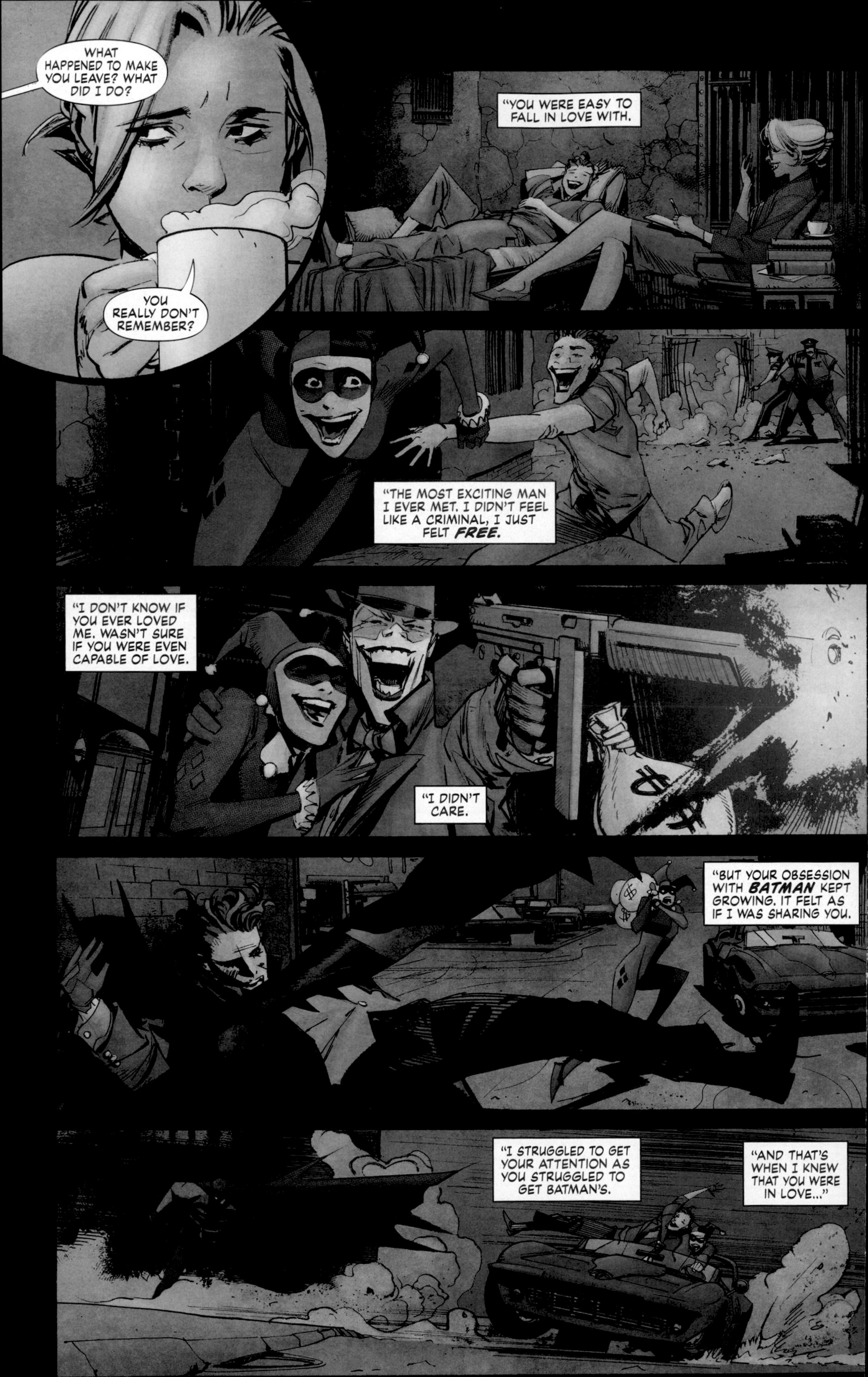
WHAT HAPPENED TO MAKE YOU LEAVE? WHAT DID I DO?
YOU REALLY DON'T REMEMBER?
"YOU WERE EASY TO FALL IN LOVE WITH.
"THE MOST EXCITING MAN I EVER MET. I DIDN'T FEEL LIKE A CRIMINAL, I JUST FELT FREE.
"I DON'T KNOW IF YOU EVER LOVED ME. WASN'T SURE IF YOU WERE EVEN CAPABLE OF LOVE.
"I DIDN'T CARE.
"BUT YOUR OBSESSION WITH BATMAN KEPT GROWING. IT FELT AS IF I WAS SHARING YOU.
"I STRUGGLED TO GET YOUR ATTENTION AS YOU STRUGGLED TO GET BATMAN'S.
"AND THAT'S WHEN I KNEW THAT YOU WERE IN LOVE..."

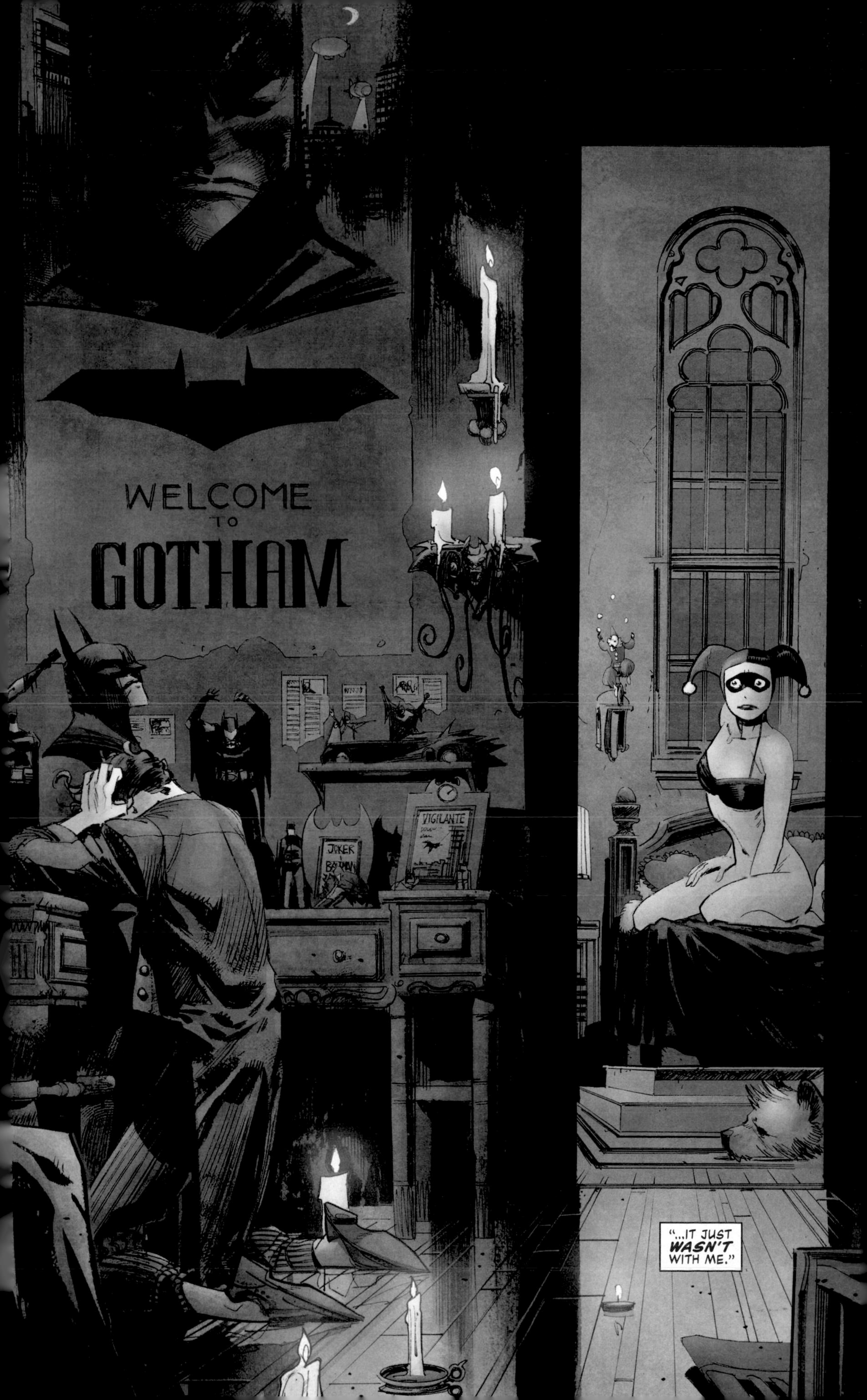
WELCOME
TO
GOTHAM
JOKER
VIGILANTE
"...IT JUST WASN'T WITH ME."

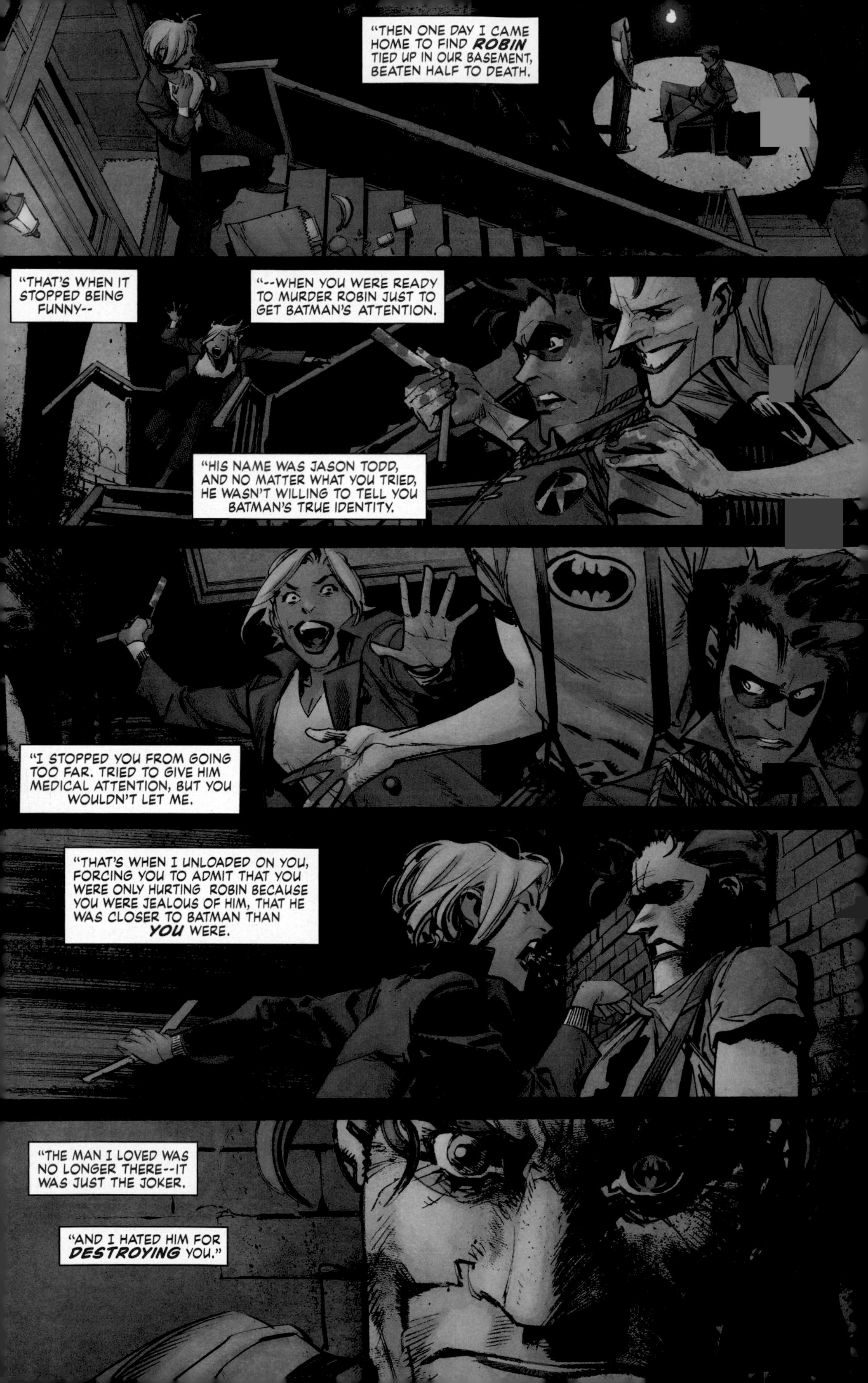
"THEN ONE DAY I CAME HOME TO FIND **ROBIN** TIED UP IN OUR BASEMENT, BEATEN HALF TO DEATH.
"THAT'S WHEN IT STOPPED BEING FUNNY--
"--WHEN YOU WERE READY TO MURDER ROBIN JUST TO GET BATMAN'S ATTENTION.
"HIS NAME WAS JASON TODD, AND NO MATTER WHAT YOU TRIED, HE WASN'T WILLING TO TELL YOU BATMAN'S TRUE IDENTITY.
"I STOPPED YOU FROM GOING TOO FAR. TRIED TO GIVE HIM MEDICAL ATTENTION, BUT YOU WOULDN'T LET ME.
"THAT'S WHEN I UNLOADED ON YOU, FORCING YOU TO ADMIT THAT YOU WERE ONLY HURTING ROBIN BECAUSE YOU WERE JEALOUS OF HIM, THAT HE WAS CLOSER TO BATMAN THAN ***YOU*** WERE.
"THE MAN I LOVED WAS NO LONGER THERE--IT WAS JUST THE JOKER.
"AND I HATED HIM FOR ***DESTROYING*** YOU."

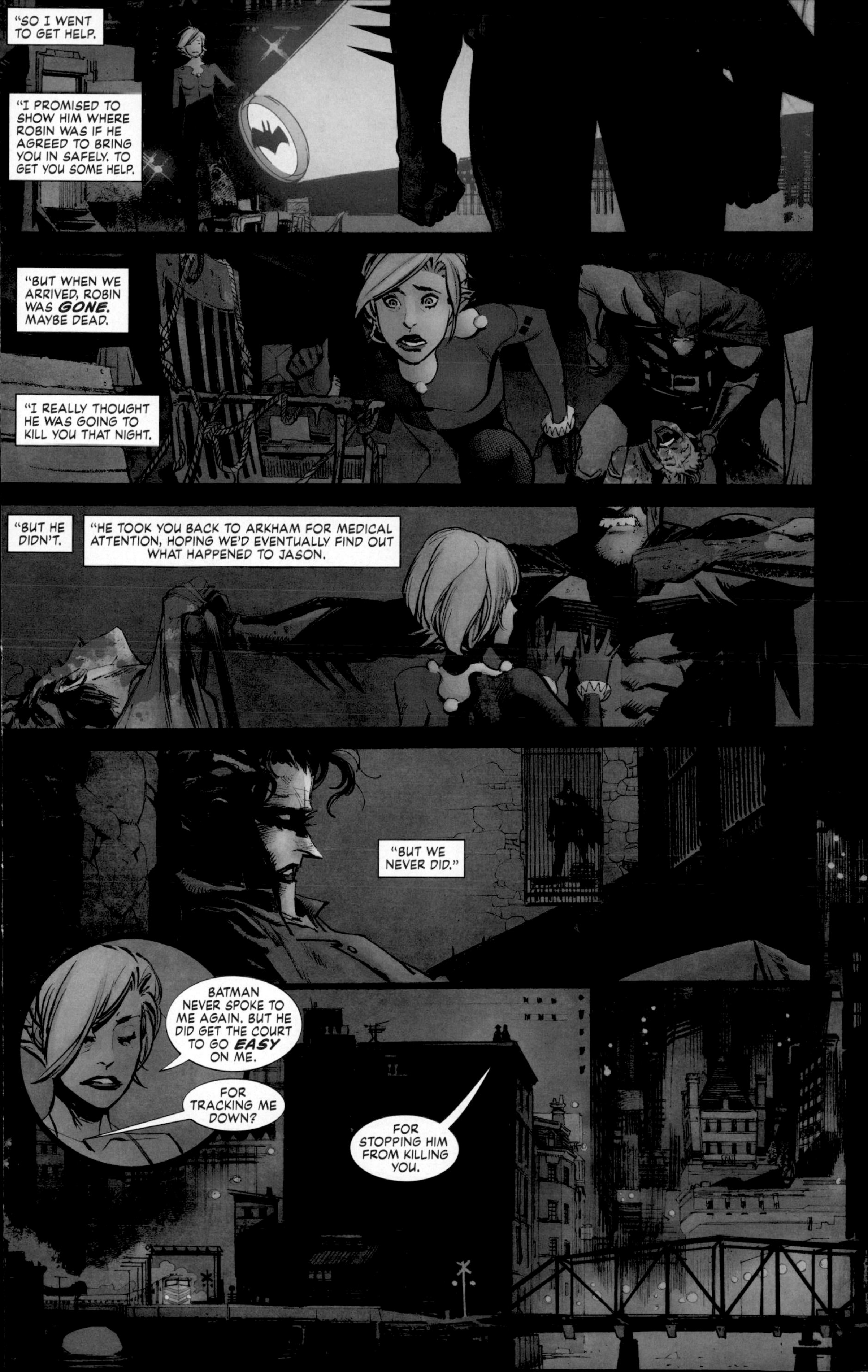
"SO I WENT TO GET HELP.
"I PROMISED TO SHOW HIM WHERE ROBIN WAS IF HE AGREED TO BRING YOU IN SAFELY. TO GET YOU SOME HELP.
"BUT WHEN WE ARRIVED, ROBIN WAS GONE. MAYBE DEAD.
"I REALLY THOUGHT HE WAS GOING TO KILL YOU THAT NIGHT.
"BUT HE DIDN'T.
"HE TOOK YOU BACK TO ARKHAM FOR MEDICAL ATTENTION, HOPING WE'D EVENTUALLY FIND OUT WHAT HAPPENED TO JASON.
"BUT WE NEVER DID."
BATMAN NEVER SPOKE TO ME AGAIN. BUT HE DID GET THE COURT TO GO EASY ON ME.
FOR TRACKING ME DOWN?
FOR STOPPING HIM FROM KILLING YOU.

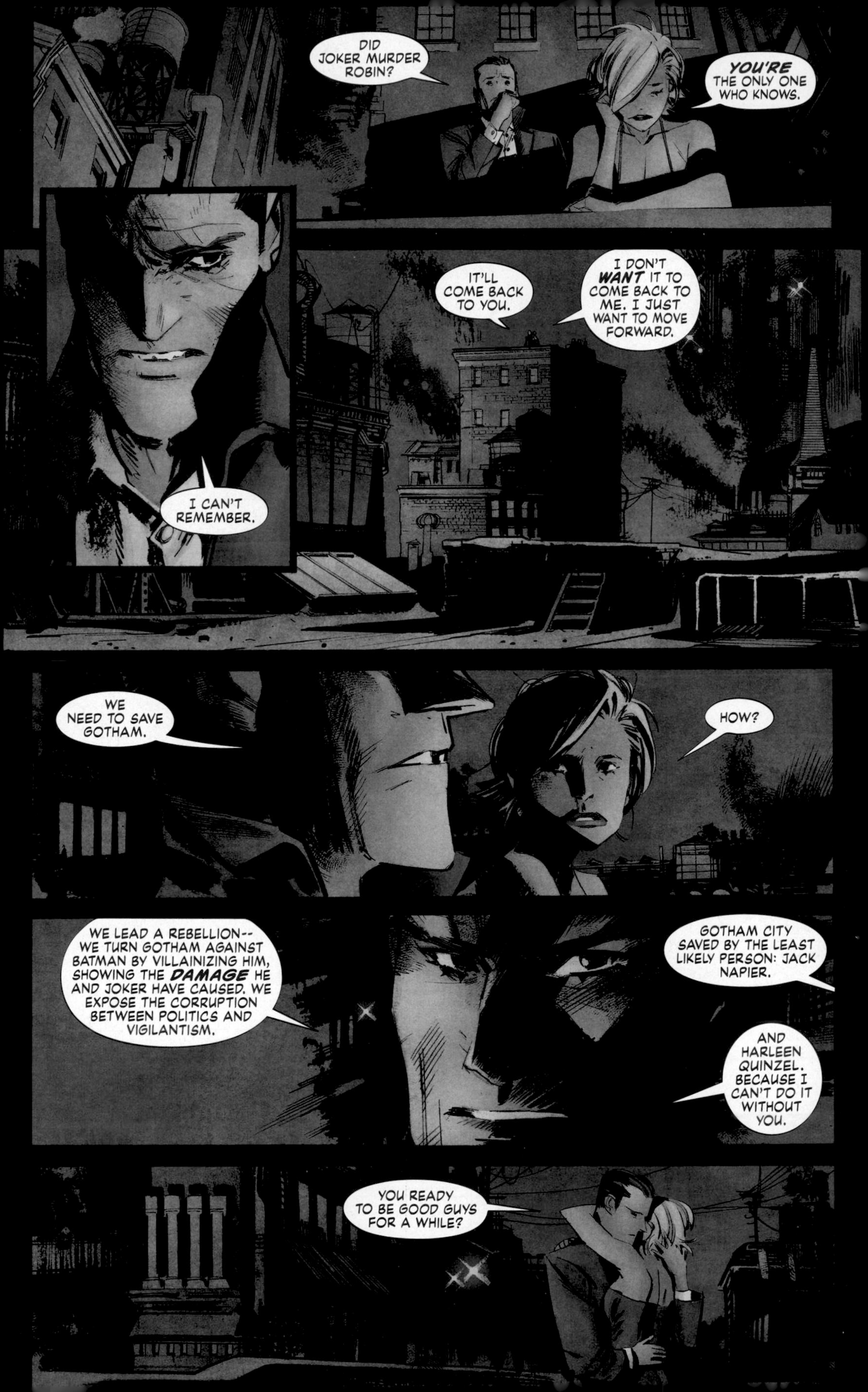
DID JOKER MURDER ROBIN?
YOU'RE THE ONLY ONE WHO KNOWS.
I CAN'T REMEMBER.
IT'LL COME BACK TO YOU.
I DON'T WANT IT TO COME BACK TO ME. I JUST WANT TO MOVE FORWARD.
WE NEED TO SAVE GOTHAM.
HOW?
WE LEAD A REBELLION-- WE TURN GOTHAM AGAINST BATMAN BY VILLAINIZING HIM, SHOWING THE DAMAGE HE AND JOKER HAVE CAUSED. WE EXPOSE THE CORRUPTION BETWEEN POLITICS AND VIGILANTISM.
GOTHAM CITY SAVED BY THE LEAST LIKELY PERSON: JACK NAPIER.
AND HARLEEN QUINZEL. BECAUSE I CAN'T DO IT WITHOUT YOU.
YOU READY TO BE GOOD GUYS FOR A WHILE?

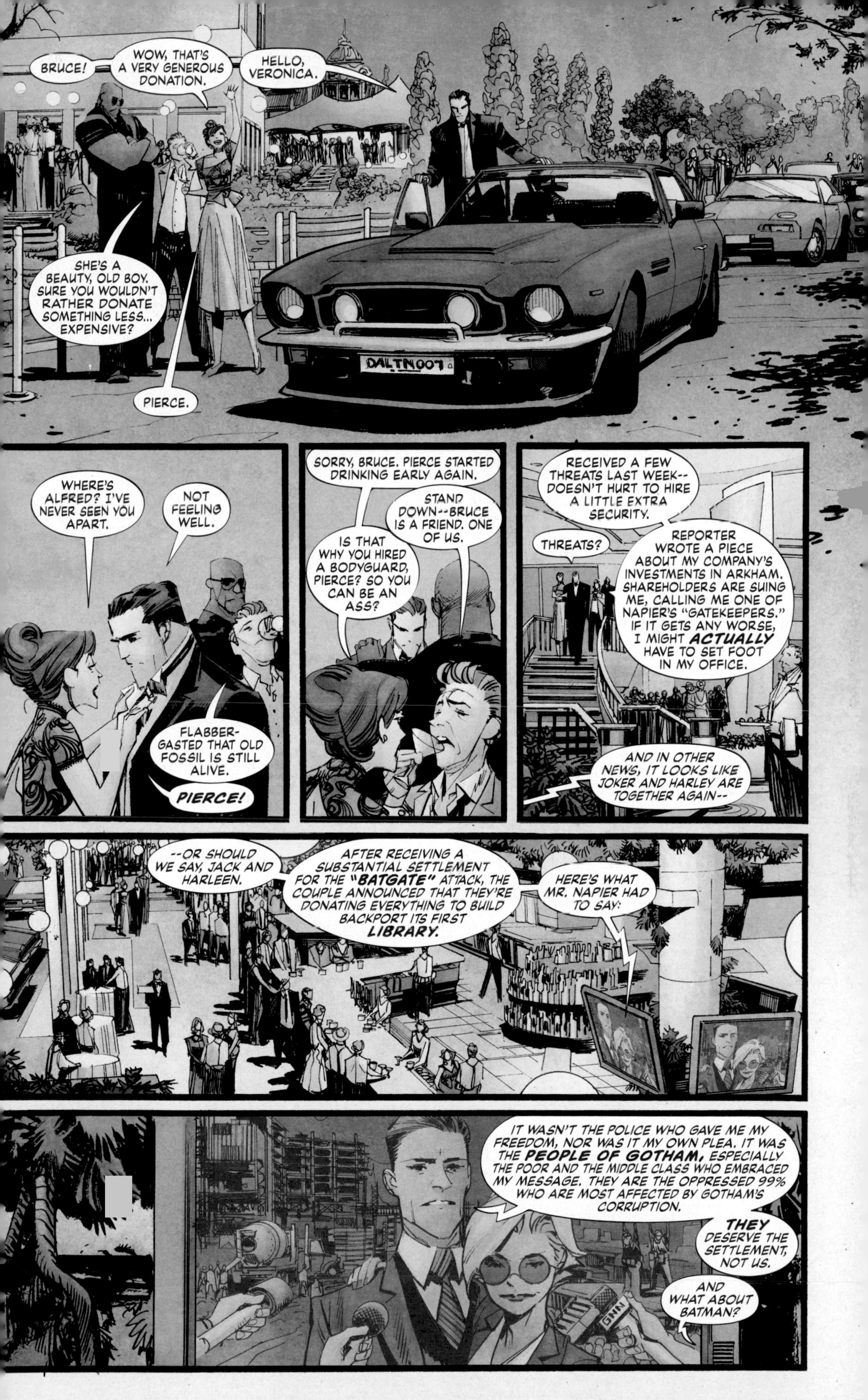
BRUCE!
WOW, THAT'S A VERY GENEROUS DONATION.
HELLO, VERONICA.
SHE'S A BEAUTY, OLD BOY. SURE YOU WOULDN'T RATHER DONATE SOMETHING LESS... EXPENSIVE?
PIERCE.
DALTN007
WHERE'S ALFRED? I'VE NEVER SEEN YOU APART.
NOT FEELING WELL.
FLABBERGASTED THAT OLD FOSSIL IS STILL ALIVE.
PIERCE!
SORRY, BRUCE. PIERCE STARTED DRINKING EARLY AGAIN.
IS THAT WHY YOU HIRED A BODYGUARD, PIERCE? SO YOU CAN BE AN ASS?
STAND DOWN--BRUCE IS A FRIEND. ONE OF US.
RECEIVED A FEW THREATS LAST WEEK--DOESN'T HURT TO HIRE A LITTLE EXTRA SECURITY.
THREATS?
REPORTER WROTE A PIECE ABOUT MY COMPANY'S INVESTMENTS IN ARKHAM. SHAREHOLDERS ARE SUING ME, CALLING ME ONE OF NAPIER'S "GATEKEEPERS." IF IT GETS ANY WORSE, I MIGHT ACTUALLY HAVE TO SET FOOT IN MY OFFICE.
AND IN OTHER NEWS, IT LOOKS LIKE JOKER AND HARLEY ARE TOGETHER AGAIN--
--OR SHOULD WE SAY, JACK AND HARLEEN.
AFTER RECEIVING A SUBSTANTIAL SETTLEMENT FOR THE "BATGATE" ATTACK, THE COUPLE ANNOUNCED THAT THEY'RE DONATING EVERYTHING TO BUILD BACKPORT ITS FIRST LIBRARY.
HERE'S WHAT MR. NAPIER HAD TO SAY:
IT WASN'T THE POLICE WHO GAVE ME MY FREEDOM, NOR WAS IT MY OWN PLEA. IT WAS THE PEOPLE OF GOTHAM, ESPECIALLY THE POOR AND THE MIDDLE CLASS WHO EMBRACED MY MESSAGE. THEY ARE THE OPPRESSED 99% WHO ARE MOST AFFECTED BY GOTHAM'S CORRUPTION.
THEY DESERVE THE SETTLEMENT, NOT US.
AND WHAT ABOUT BATMAN?
GNN

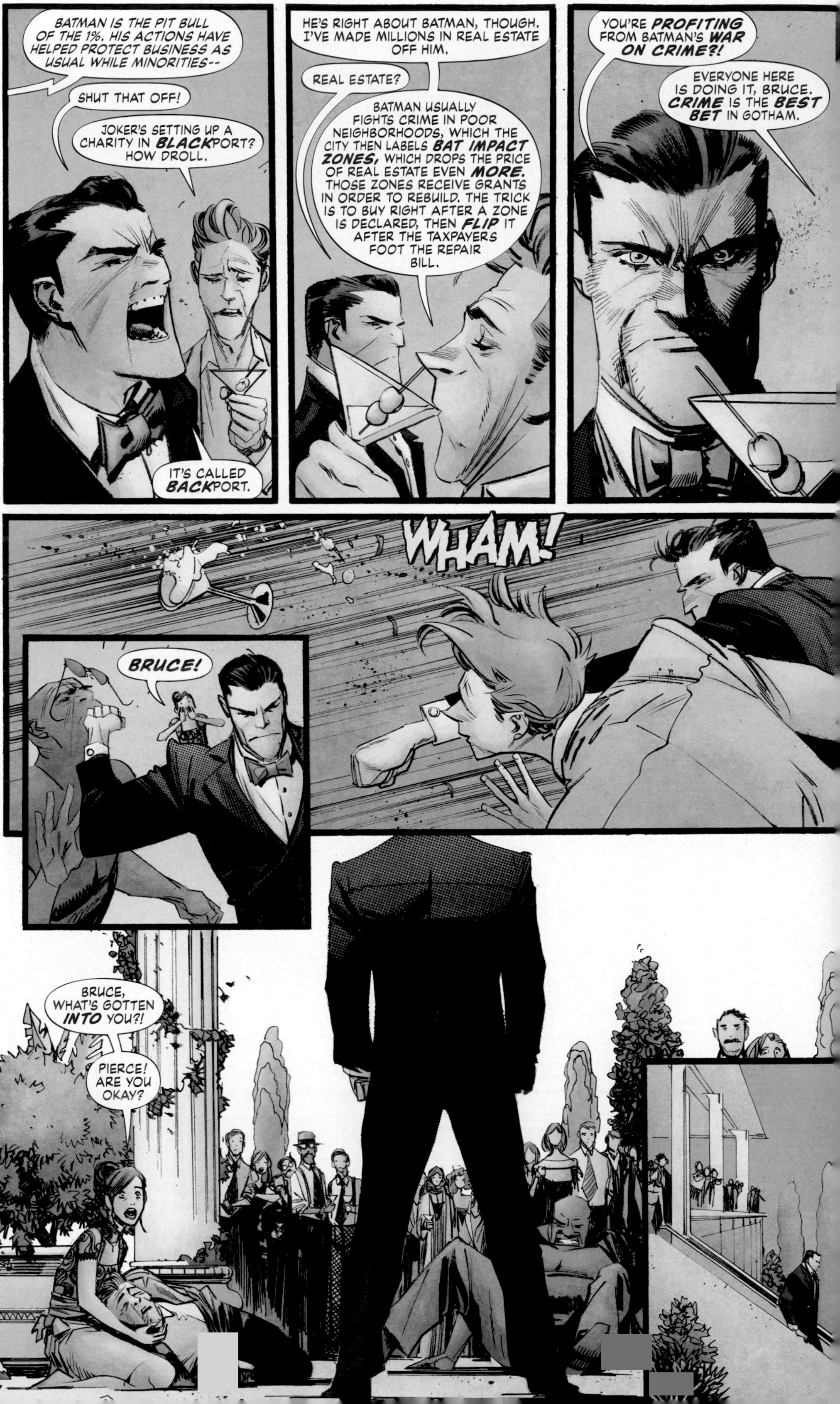
BATMAN IS THE PIT BULL OF THE 1%. HIS ACTIONS HAVE HELPED PROTECT BUSINESS AS USUAL WHILE MINORITIES--
SHUT THAT OFF!
JOKER'S SETTING UP A CHARITY IN BLACKPORT? HOW DROLL.
IT'S CALLED BACKPORT.
HE'S RIGHT ABOUT BATMAN, THOUGH. I'VE MADE MILLIONS IN REAL ESTATE OFF HIM.
REAL ESTATE?
BATMAN USUALLY FIGHTS CRIME IN POOR NEIGHBORHOODS, WHICH THE CITY THEN LABELS BAT IMPACT ZONES, WHICH DROPS THE PRICE OF REAL ESTATE EVEN MORE. THOSE ZONES RECEIVE GRANTS IN ORDER TO REBUILD. THE TRICK IS TO BUY RIGHT AFTER A ZONE IS DECLARED, THEN FLIP IT AFTER THE TAXPAYERS FOOT THE REPAIR BILL.
YOU'RE PROFITING FROM BATMAN'S WAR ON CRIME?!
EVERYONE HERE IS DOING IT, BRUCE. CRIME IS THE BEST BET IN GOTHAM.
WHAM!
BRUCE!
BRUCE, WHAT'S GOTTEN INTO YOU?!
PIERCE! ARE YOU OKAY?

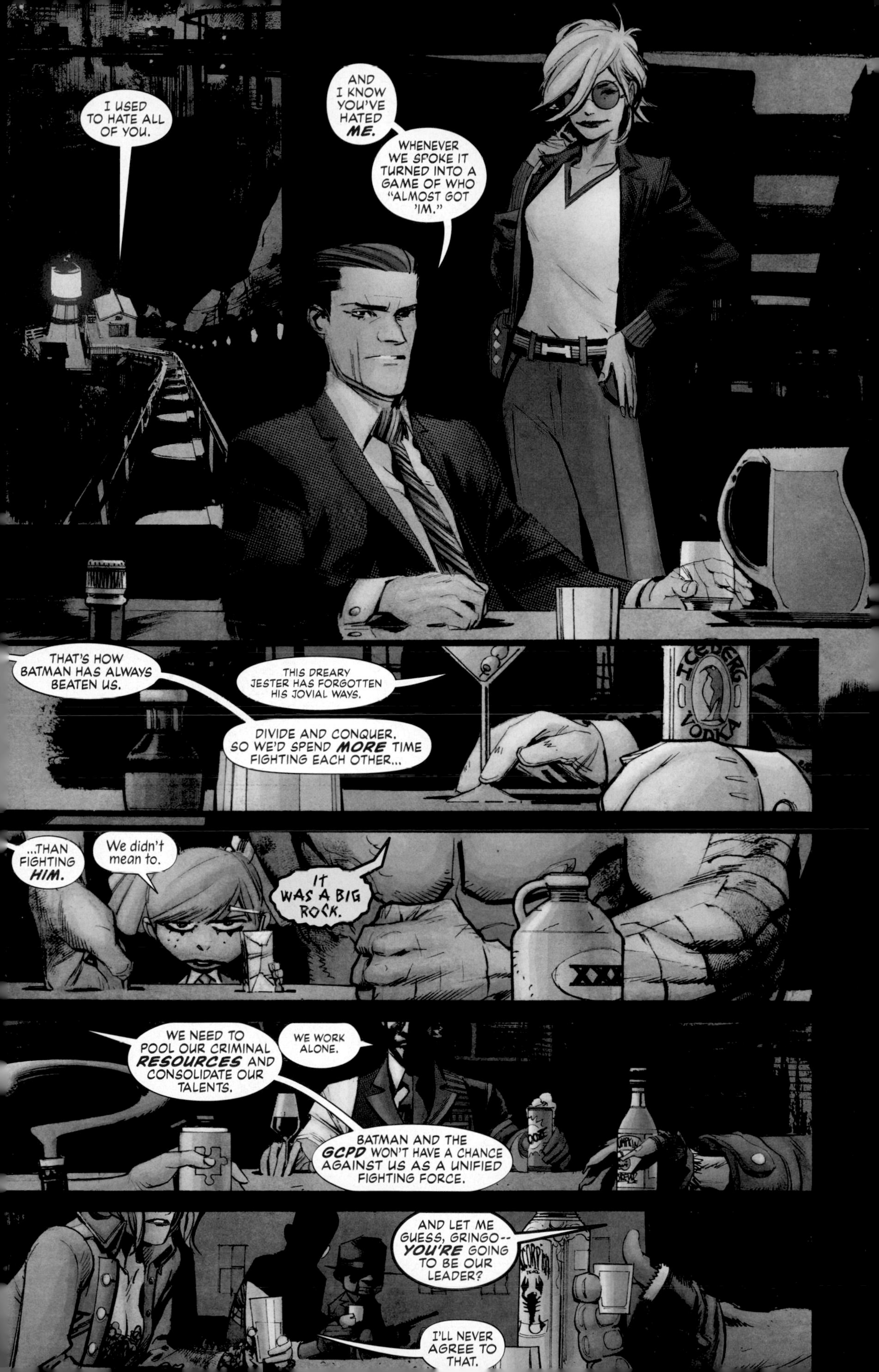
I USED TO HATE ALL OF YOU.
AND I KNOW YOU'VE HATED ME.
WHENEVER WE SPOKE IT TURNED INTO A GAME OF WHO "ALMOST GOT 'IM."
THAT'S HOW BATMAN HAS ALWAYS BEATEN US.
THIS DREARY JESTER HAS FORGOTTEN HIS JOVIAL WAYS.
DIVIDE AND CONQUER. SO WE'D SPEND MORE TIME FIGHTING EACH OTHER...
ICEBERG VODKA
...THAN FIGHTING HIM.
We didn't mean to.
IT WAS A BIG ROCK.
XXX
WE NEED TO POOL OUR CRIMINAL RESOURCES AND CONSOLIDATE OUR TALENTS.
WE WORK ALONE.
BATMAN AND THE GCPD WON'T HAVE A CHANCE AGAINST US AS A UNIFIED FIGHTING FORCE.
AND LET ME GUESS, GRINGO-- YOU'RE GOING TO BE OUR LEADER?
I'LL NEVER AGREE TO THAT.

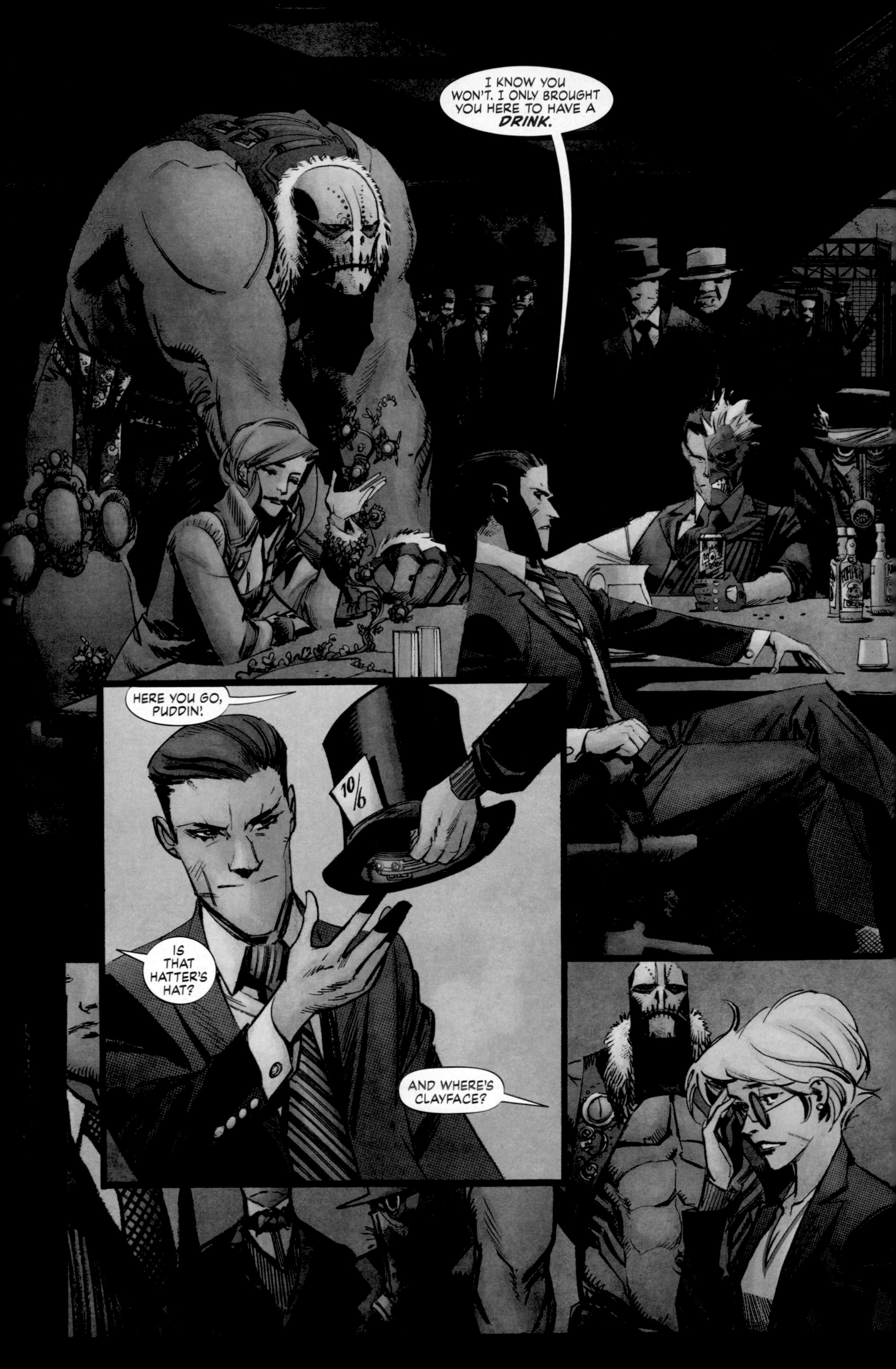
I KNOW YOU WON'T. I ONLY BROUGHT YOU HERE TO HAVE A DRINK.
HERE YOU GO, PUDDIN'.
10/6
IS THAT HATTER'S HAT?
AND WHERE'S CLAYFACE?

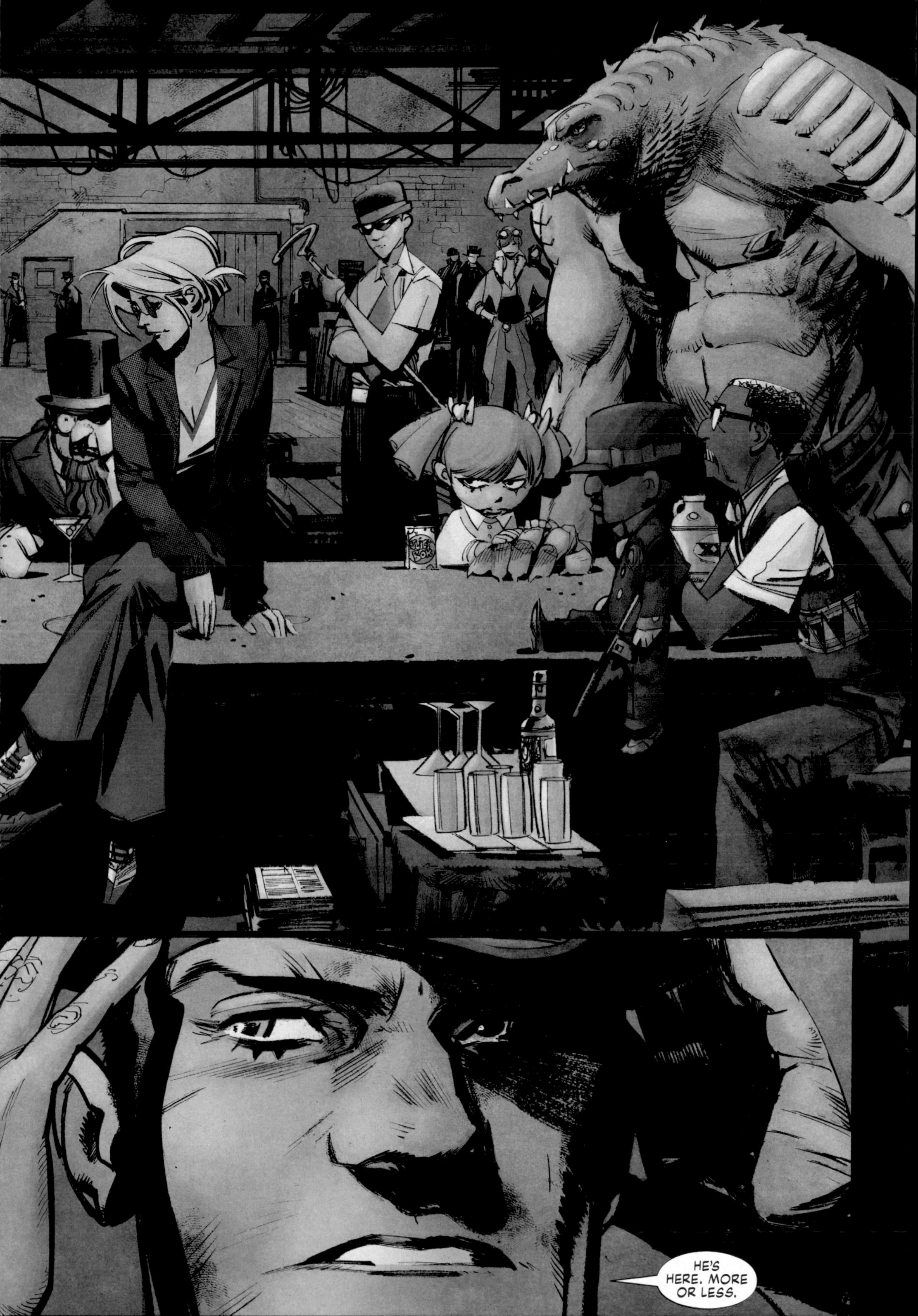

HE'S HERE. MORE OR LESS.

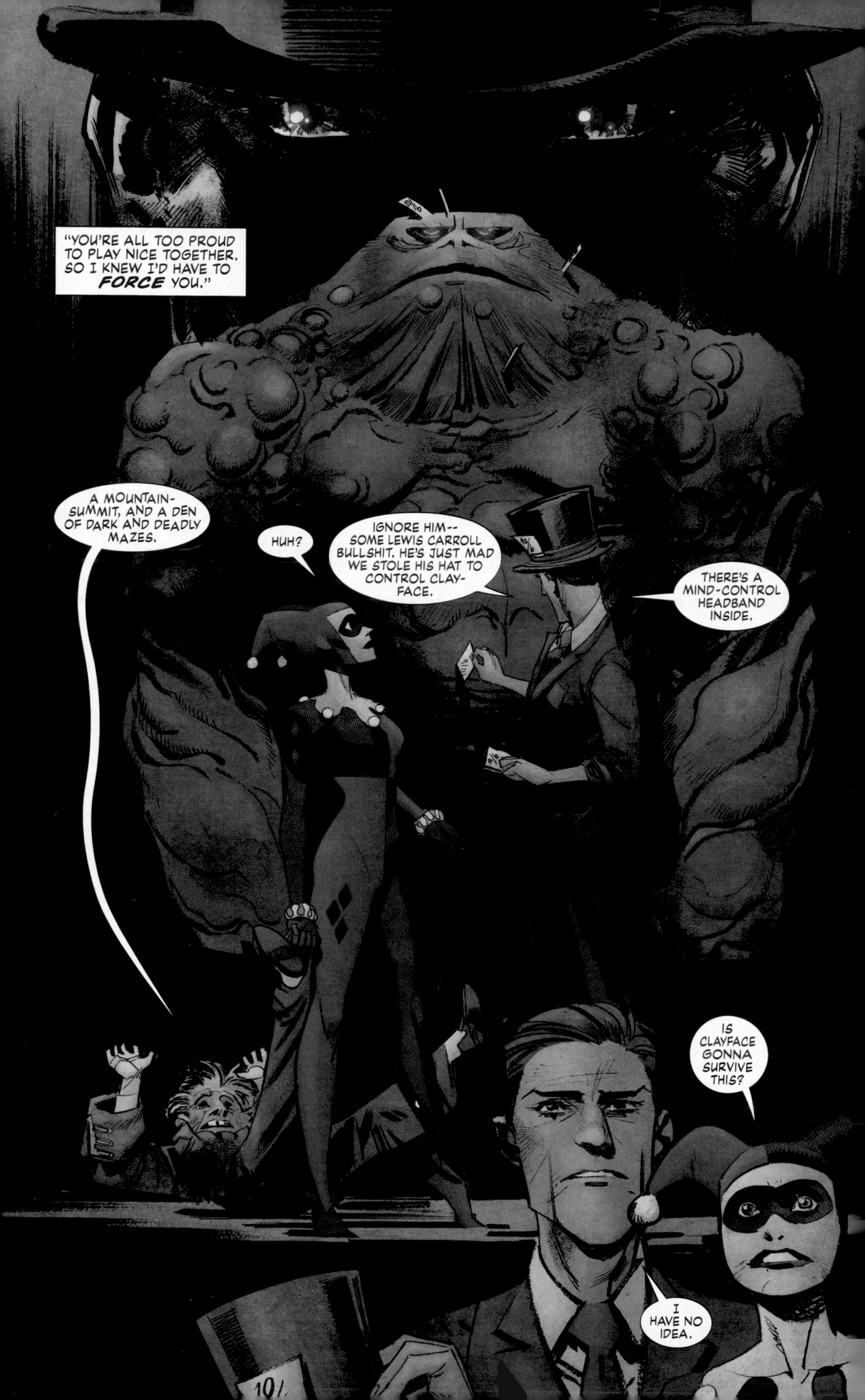
"YOU'RE ALL TOO PROUD TO PLAY NICE TOGETHER. SO I KNEW I'D HAVE TO FORCE YOU."
A MOUNTAIN-SUMMIT, AND A DEN OF DARK AND DEADLY MAZES.
HUH?
IGNORE HIM--SOME LEWIS CARROLL BULLSHIT. HE'S JUST MAD WE STOLE HIS HAT TO CONTROL CLAY-FACE.
THERE'S A MIND-CONTROL HEADBAND INSIDE.
IS CLAYFACE GONNA SURVIVE THIS?
I HAVE NO IDEA.

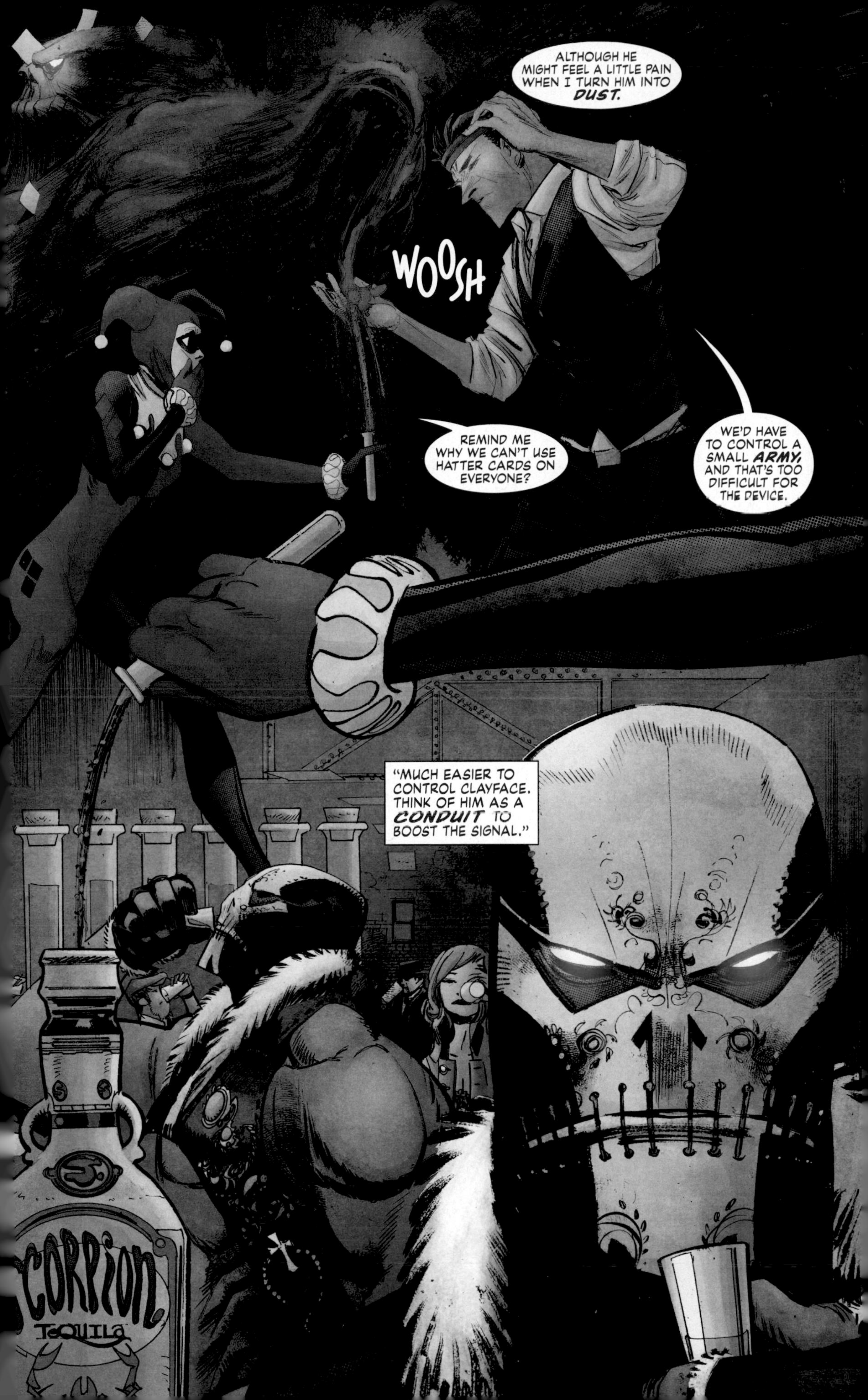

ALTHOUGH HE MIGHT FEEL A LITTLE PAIN WHEN I TURN HIM INTO DUST.
WOOSH
REMIND ME WHY WE CAN'T USE HATTER CARDS ON EVERYONE?
WE'D HAVE TO CONTROL A SMALL ARMY, AND THAT'S TOO DIFFICULT FOR THE DEVICE.
"MUCH EASIER TO CONTROL CLAYFACE. THINK OF HIM AS A CONDUIT TO BOOST THE SIGNAL."
CORPION
TEQUILA

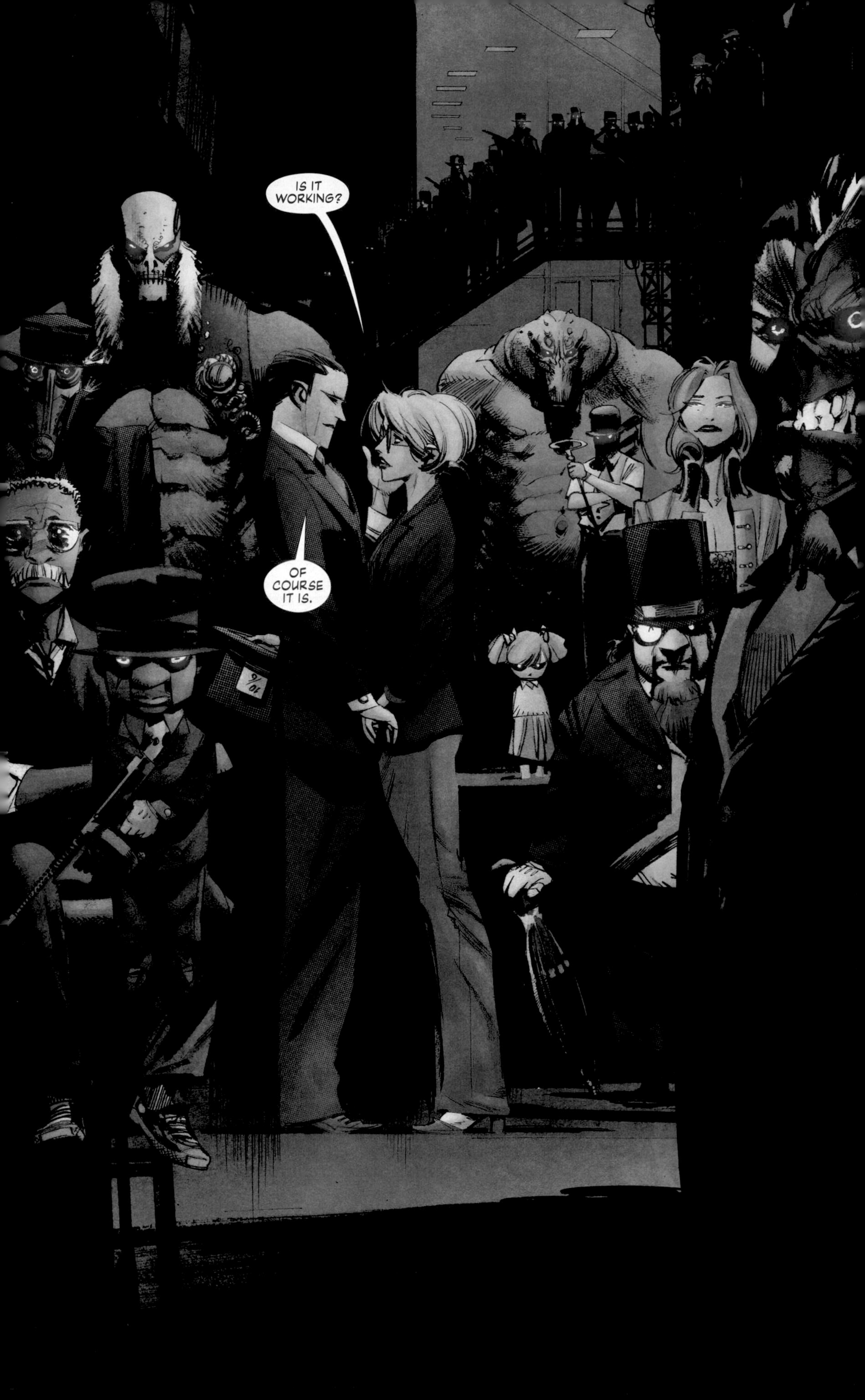
IS IT WORKING?
OF COURSE IT IS.

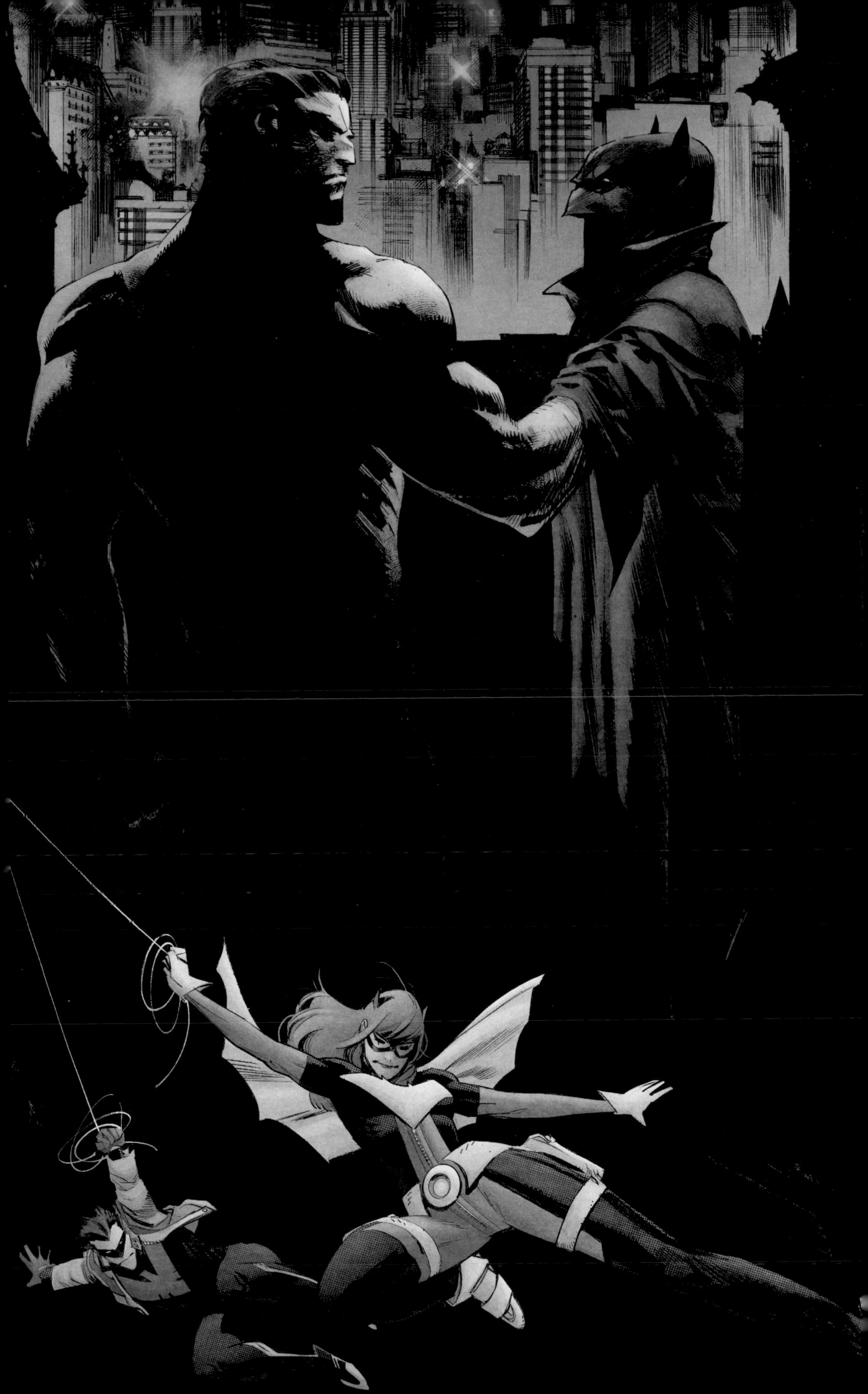

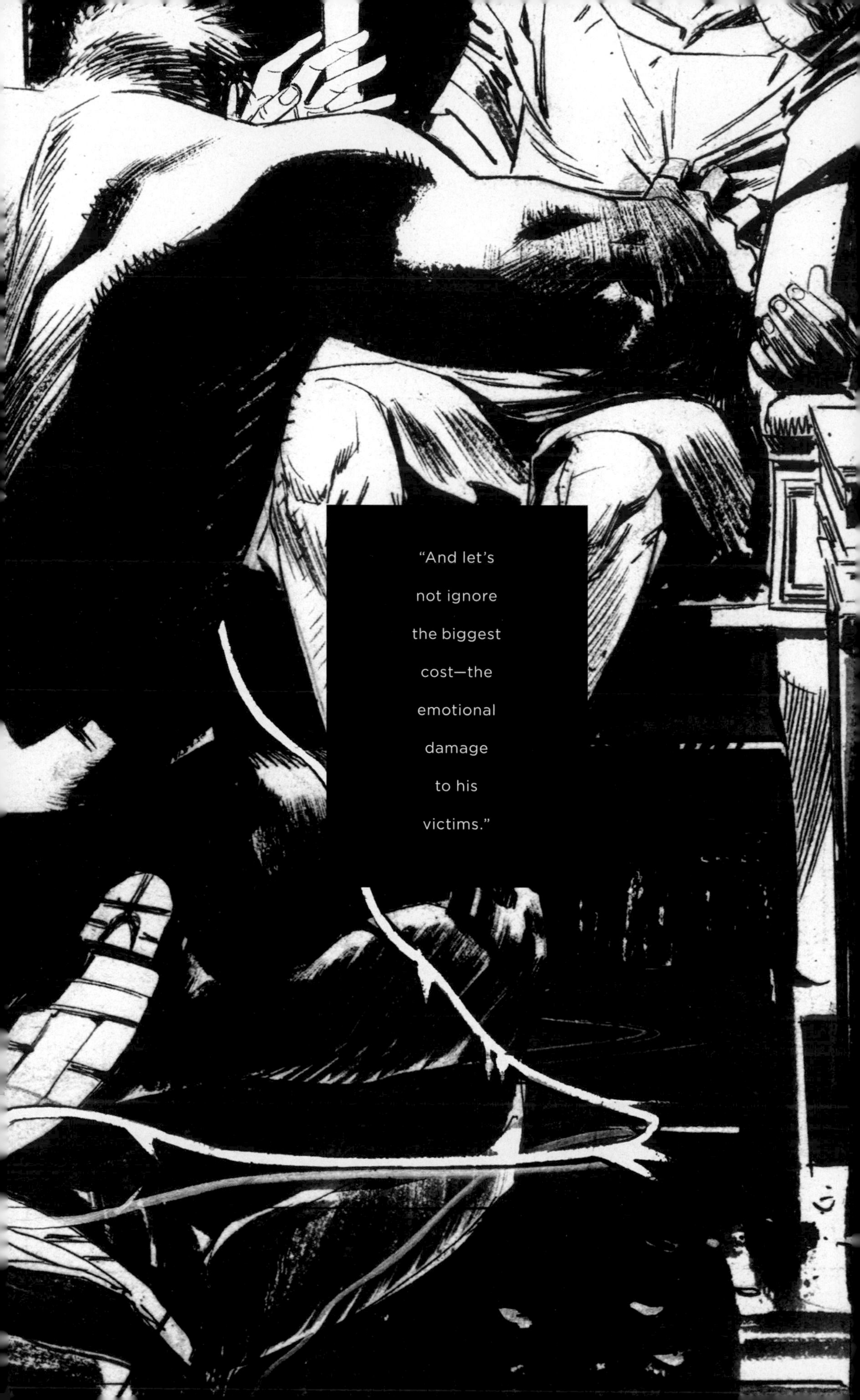
"And let's not ignore the biggest cost—the emotional damage to his victims."

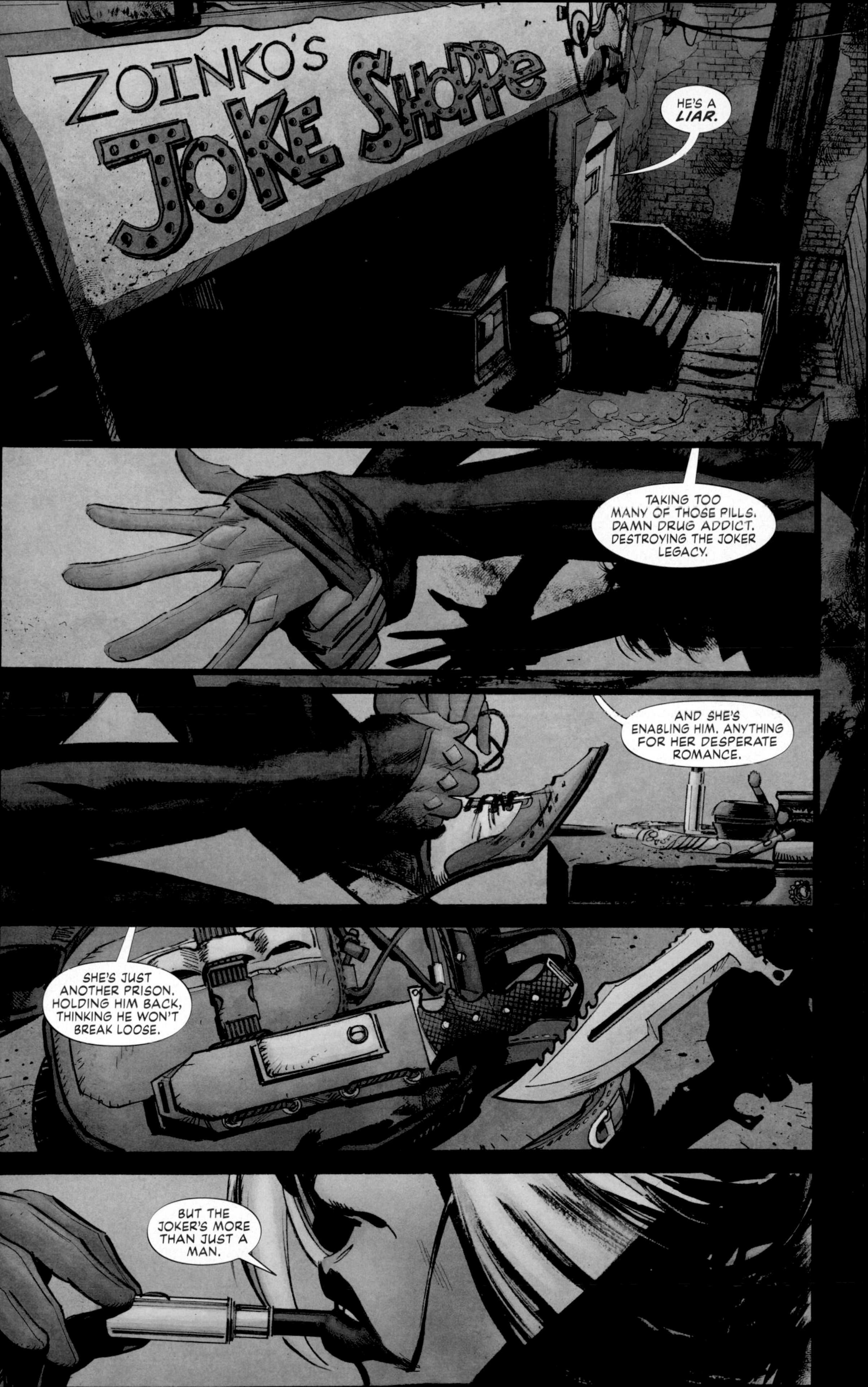
ZOINKO'S
JOKE SHOPPE
HE'S A **LIAR.**
TAKING TOO MANY OF THOSE PILLS. DAMN DRUG ADDICT. DESTROYING THE JOKER LEGACY.
AND SHE'S ENABLING HIM. ANYTHING FOR HER DESPERATE ROMANCE.
SHE'S JUST ANOTHER PRISON. HOLDING HIM BACK, THINKING HE WON'T BREAK LOOSE.
BUT THE JOKER'S MORE THAN JUST A MAN.

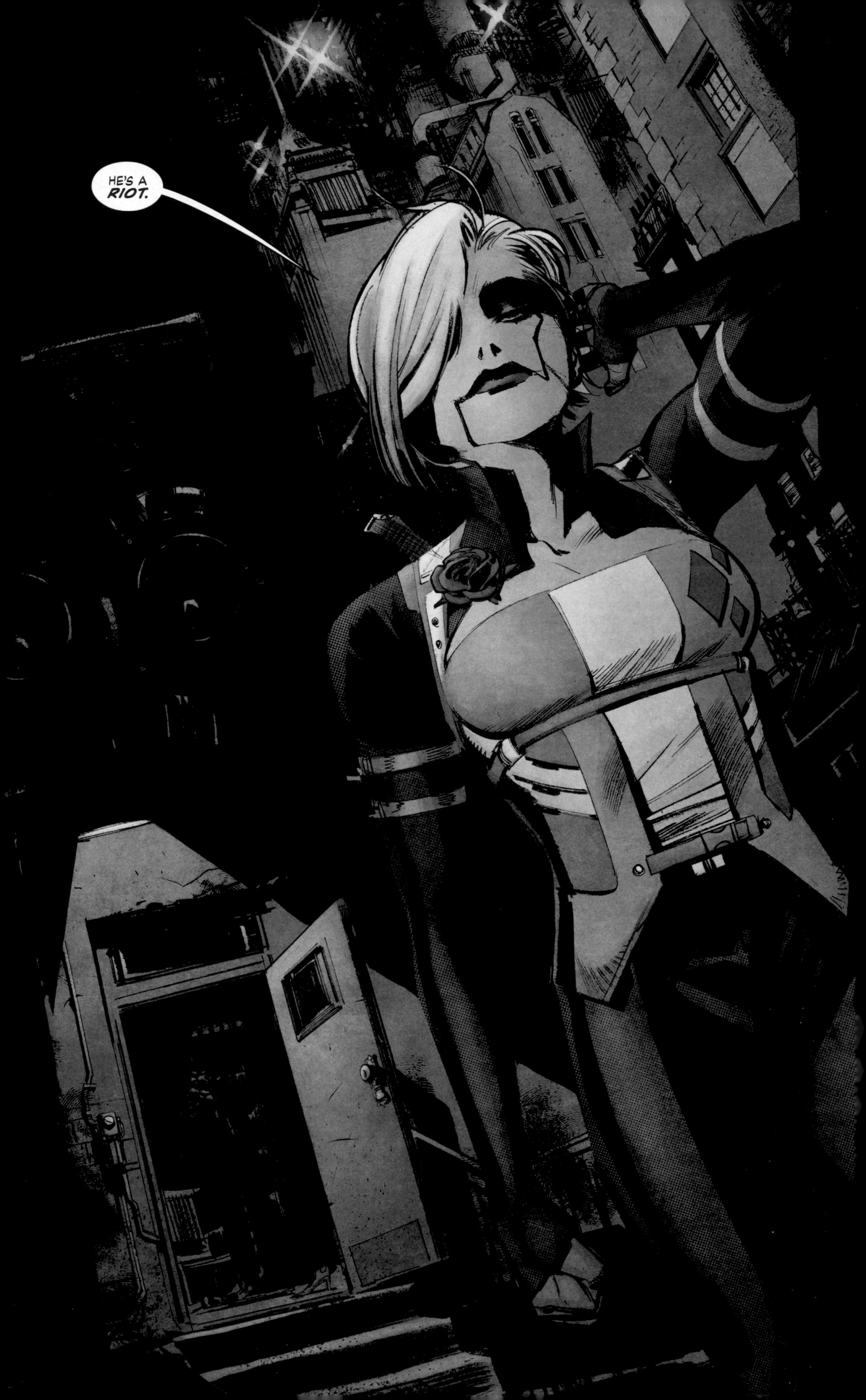
HE'S A RIOT.

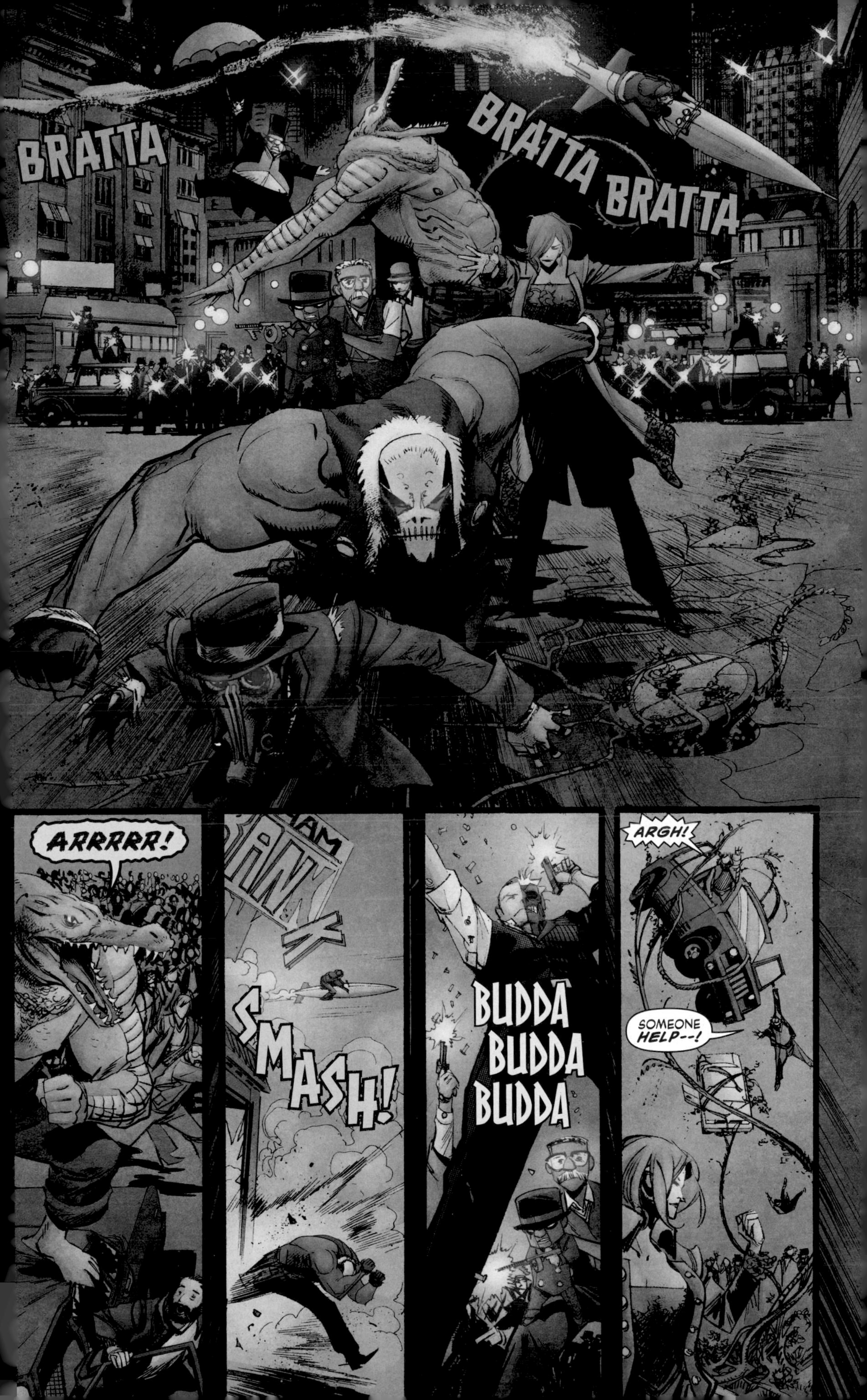
BRATTA
BRATTA BRATTA
ARRRRR!
SMASH!
BUDDA BUDDA BUDDA
ARGH!
SOMEONE HELP--!

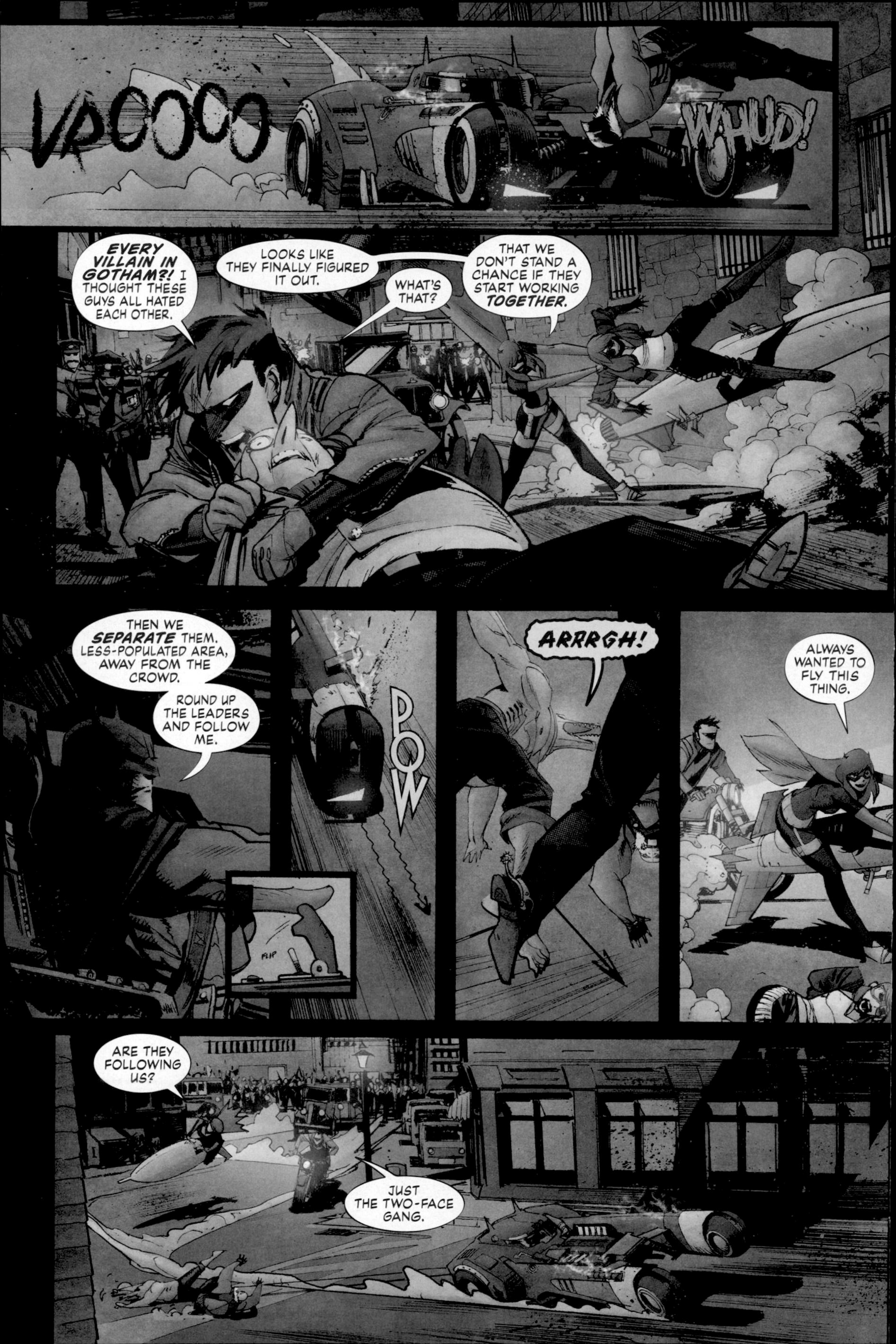

VROOOO
WHUD!
EVERY VILLAIN IN GOTHAM?! I THOUGHT THESE GUYS ALL HATED EACH OTHER.
LOOKS LIKE THEY FINALLY FIGURED IT OUT.
WHAT'S THAT?
THAT WE DON'T STAND A CHANCE IF THEY START WORKING TOGETHER.
THEN WE SEPARATE THEM. LESS-POPULATED AREA, AWAY FROM THE CROWD.
ROUND UP THE LEADERS AND FOLLOW ME.
POW
FLIP
ARRRGH!
ALWAYS WANTED TO FLY THIS THING.
ARE THEY FOLLOWING US?
JUST THE TWO-FACE GANG.

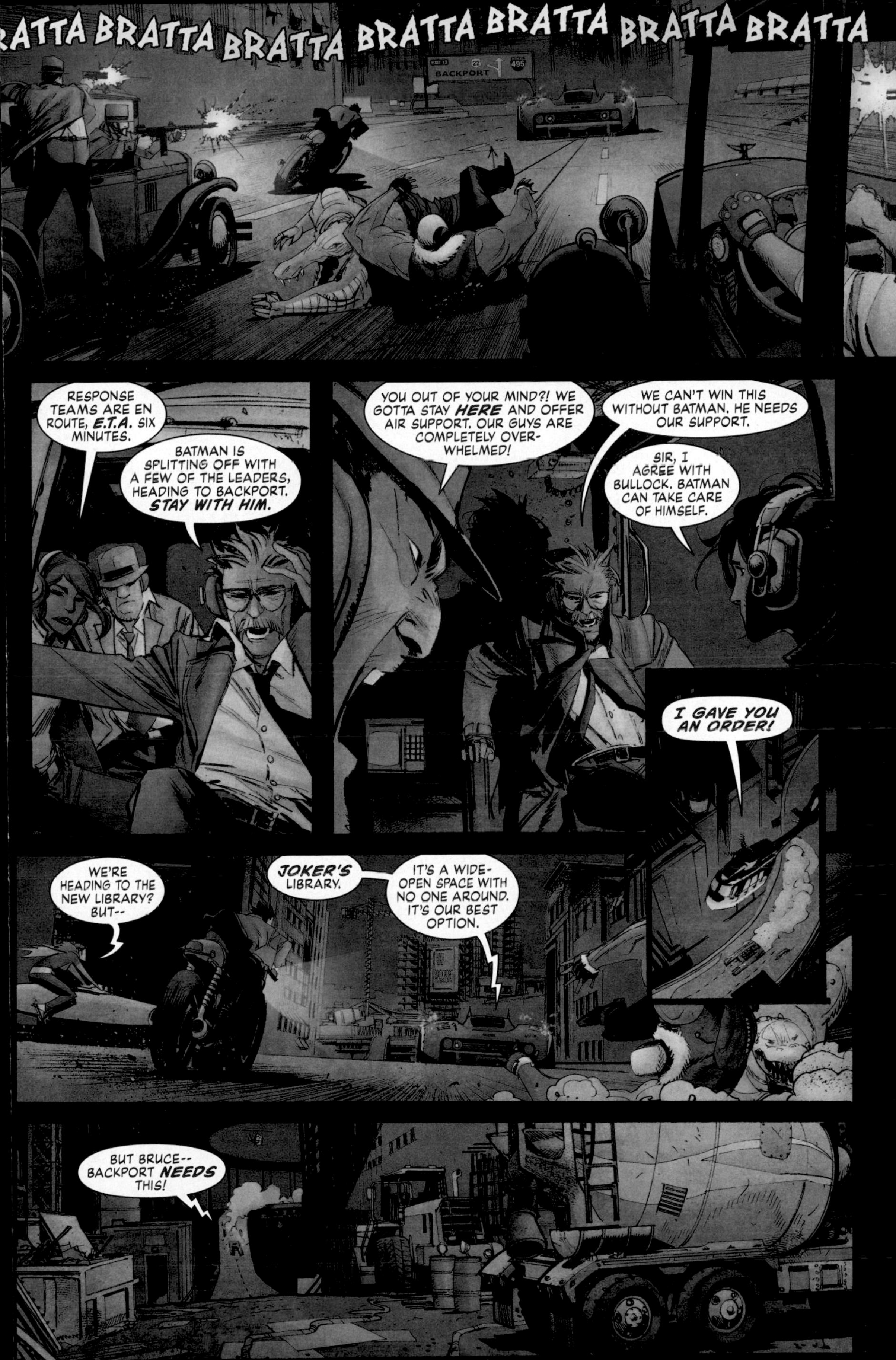

BRATTA BRATTA BRATTA BRATTA BRATTA BRATTA
EXIT 13 22 495 BACKPORT
RESPONSE TEAMS ARE EN ROUTE, E.T.A. SIX MINUTES.
BATMAN IS SPLITTING OFF WITH A FEW OF THE LEADERS, HEADING TO BACKPORT. STAY WITH HIM.
YOU OUT OF YOUR MIND?! WE GOTTA STAY HERE AND OFFER AIR SUPPORT. OUR GUYS ARE COMPLETELY OVER-WHELMED!
WE CAN'T WIN THIS WITHOUT BATMAN. HE NEEDS OUR SUPPORT.
SIR, I AGREE WITH BULLOCK. BATMAN CAN TAKE CARE OF HIMSELF.
I GAVE YOU AN ORDER!
WE'RE HEADING TO THE NEW LIBRARY? BUT--
JOKER'S LIBRARY.
IT'S A WIDE-OPEN SPACE WITH NO ONE AROUND. IT'S OUR BEST OPTION.
BUT BRUCE--BACKPORT NEEDS THIS!

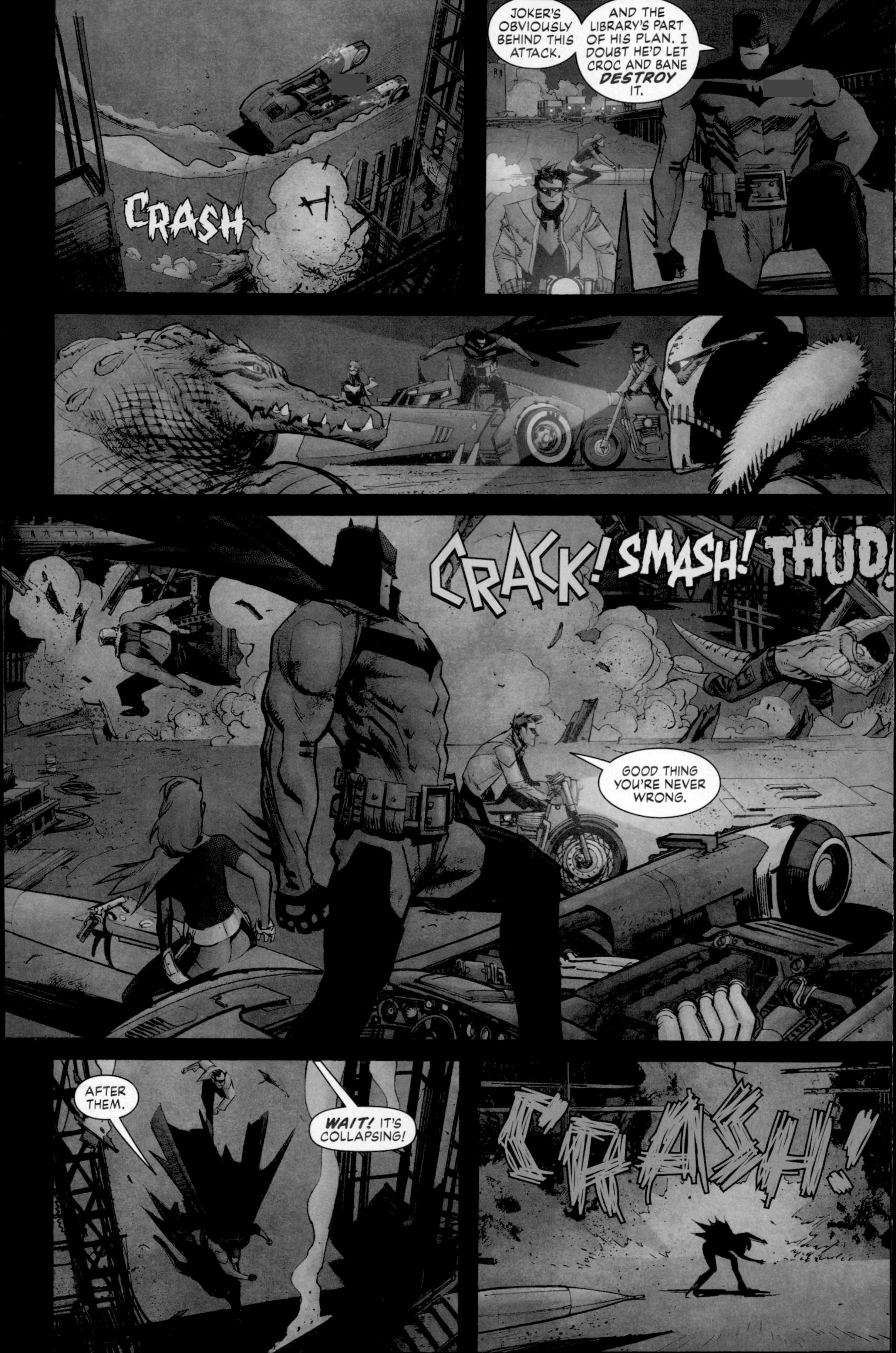
CRASH
JOKER'S OBVIOUSLY BEHIND THIS ATTACK.
AND THE LIBRARY'S PART OF HIS PLAN. I DOUBT HE'D LET CROC AND BANE **DESTROY** IT.
CRACK! SMASH! THUD!
GOOD THING YOU'RE NEVER WRONG.
AFTER THEM.
WAIT! IT'S COLLAPSING!
CRASH!

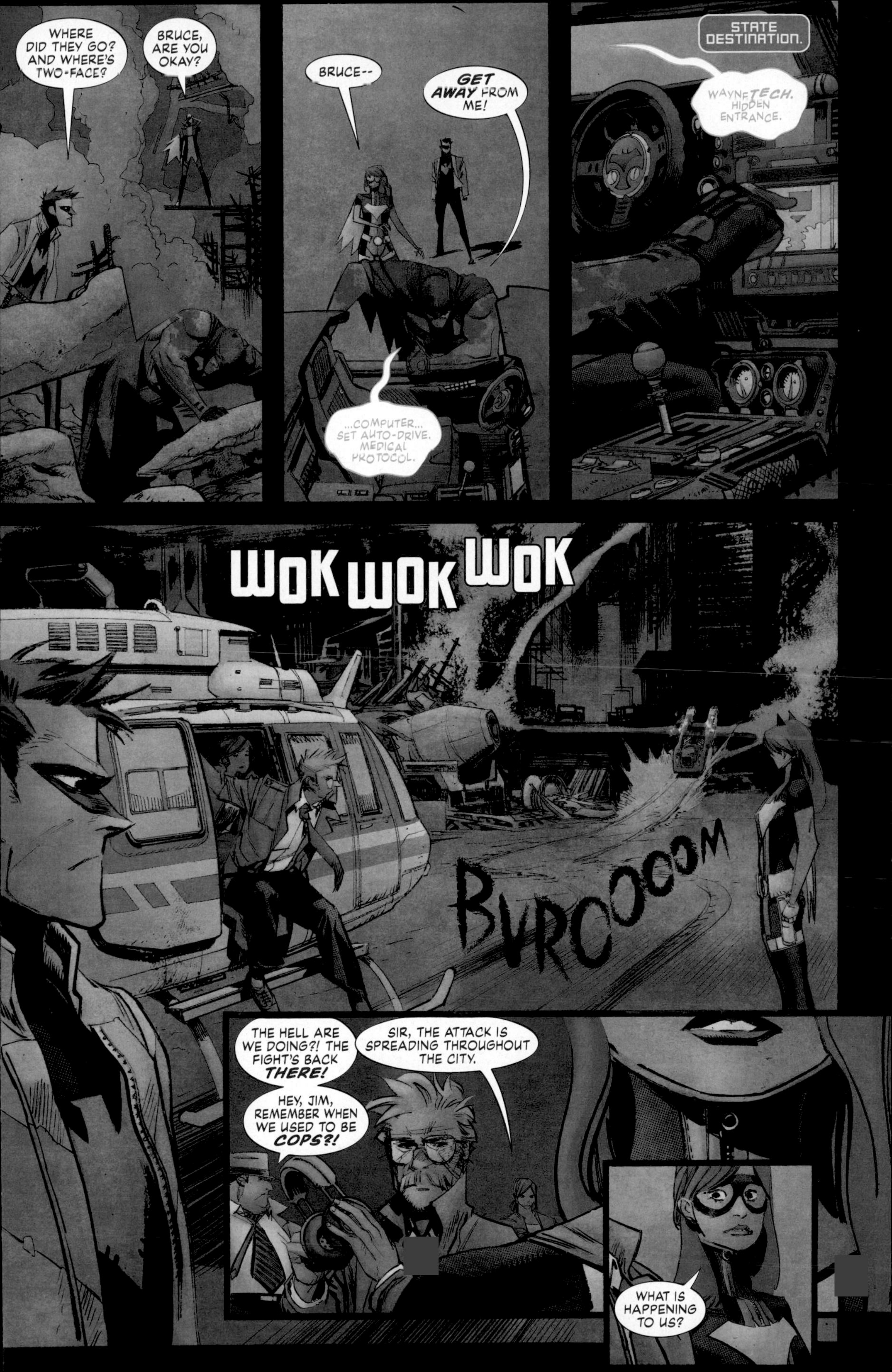
WHERE DID THEY GO? AND WHERE'S TWO-FACE?
BRUCE, ARE YOU OKAY?
BRUCE--
GET AWAY FROM ME!
...COMPUTER... SET AUTO-DRIVE. MEDICAL PROTOCOL.
STATE DESTINATION.
WAYNETECH. HIDDEN ENTRANCE.
WOK WOK WOK
BVRCOOOOM
THE HELL ARE WE DOING?! THE FIGHT'S BACK THERE!
SIR, THE ATTACK IS SPREADING THROUGHOUT THE CITY.
HEY, JIM, REMEMBER WHEN WE USED TO BE COPS?!
WHAT IS HAPPENING TO US?

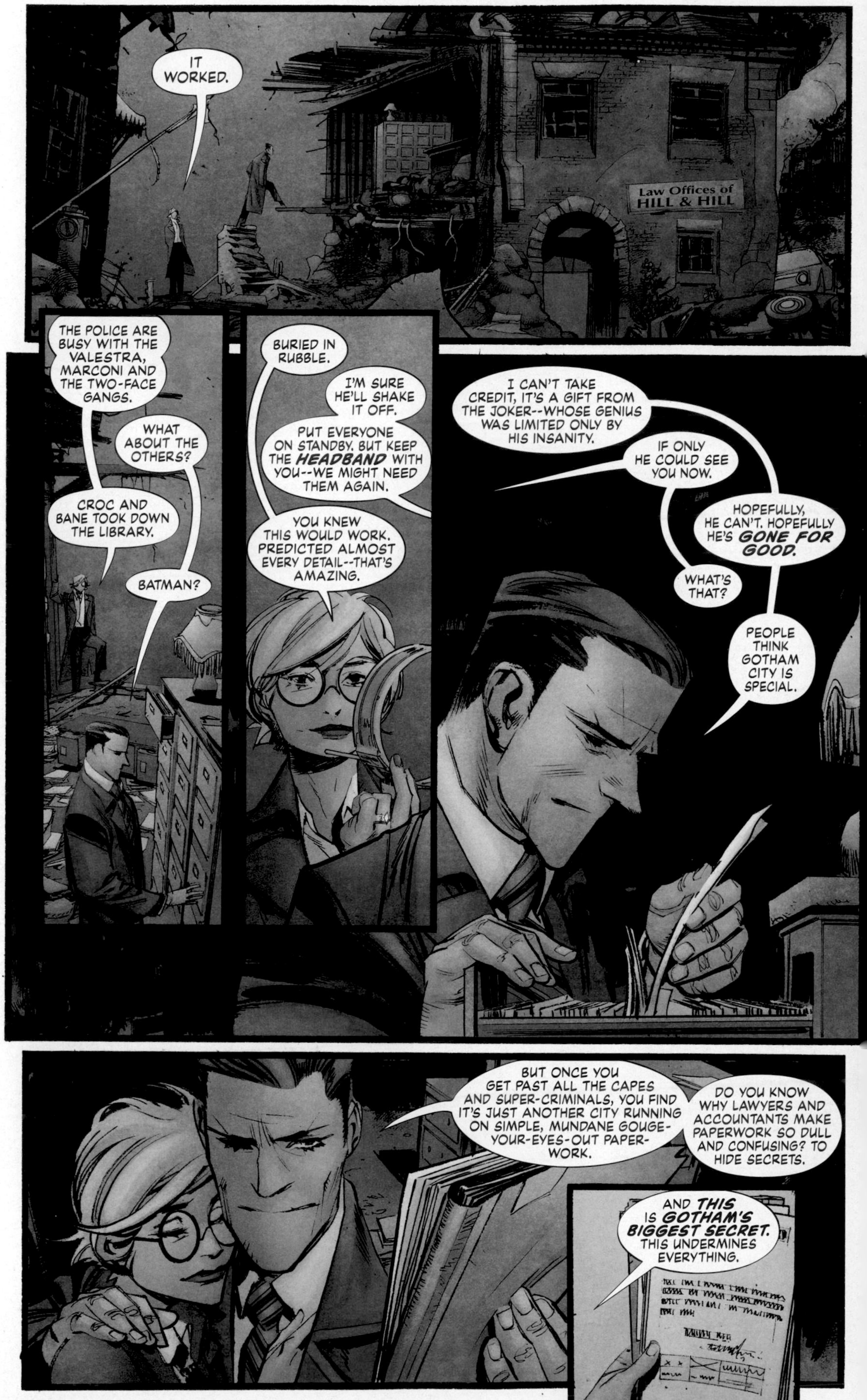
IT WORKED.
Law Offices of HILL & HILL
THE POLICE ARE BUSY WITH THE VALESTRA, MARCONI AND THE TWO-FACE GANGS.
WHAT ABOUT THE OTHERS?
CROC AND BANE TOOK DOWN THE LIBRARY.
BATMAN?
BURIED IN RUBBLE.
I'M SURE HE'LL SHAKE IT OFF.
PUT EVERYONE ON STANDBY. BUT KEEP THE HEADBAND WITH YOU--WE MIGHT NEED THEM AGAIN.
YOU KNEW THIS WOULD WORK. PREDICTED ALMOST EVERY DETAIL--THAT'S AMAZING.
I CAN'T TAKE CREDIT, IT'S A GIFT FROM THE JOKER--WHOSE GENIUS WAS LIMITED ONLY BY HIS INSANITY.
IF ONLY HE COULD SEE YOU NOW.
HOPEFULLY, HE CAN'T. HOPEFULLY HE'S GONE FOR GOOD.
WHAT'S THAT?
PEOPLE THINK GOTHAM CITY IS SPECIAL.
BUT ONCE YOU GET PAST ALL THE CAPES AND SUPER-CRIMINALS, YOU FIND IT'S JUST ANOTHER CITY RUNNING ON SIMPLE, MUNDANE GOUGE-YOUR-EYES-OUT PAPERWORK.
DO YOU KNOW WHY LAWYERS AND ACCOUNTANTS MAKE PAPERWORK SO DULL AND CONFUSING? TO HIDE SECRETS.
AND THIS IS GOTHAM'S BIGGEST SECRET. THIS UNDERMINES EVERYTHING.

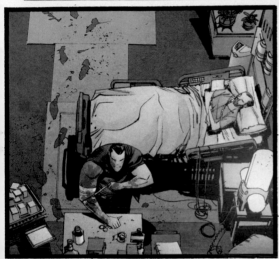

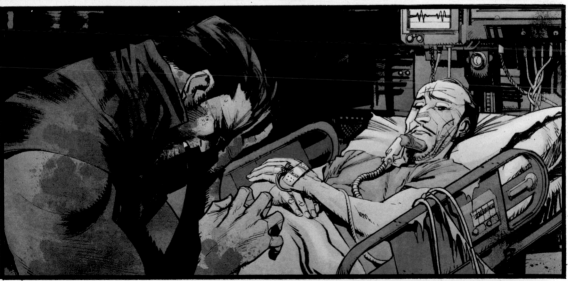

WHUD.

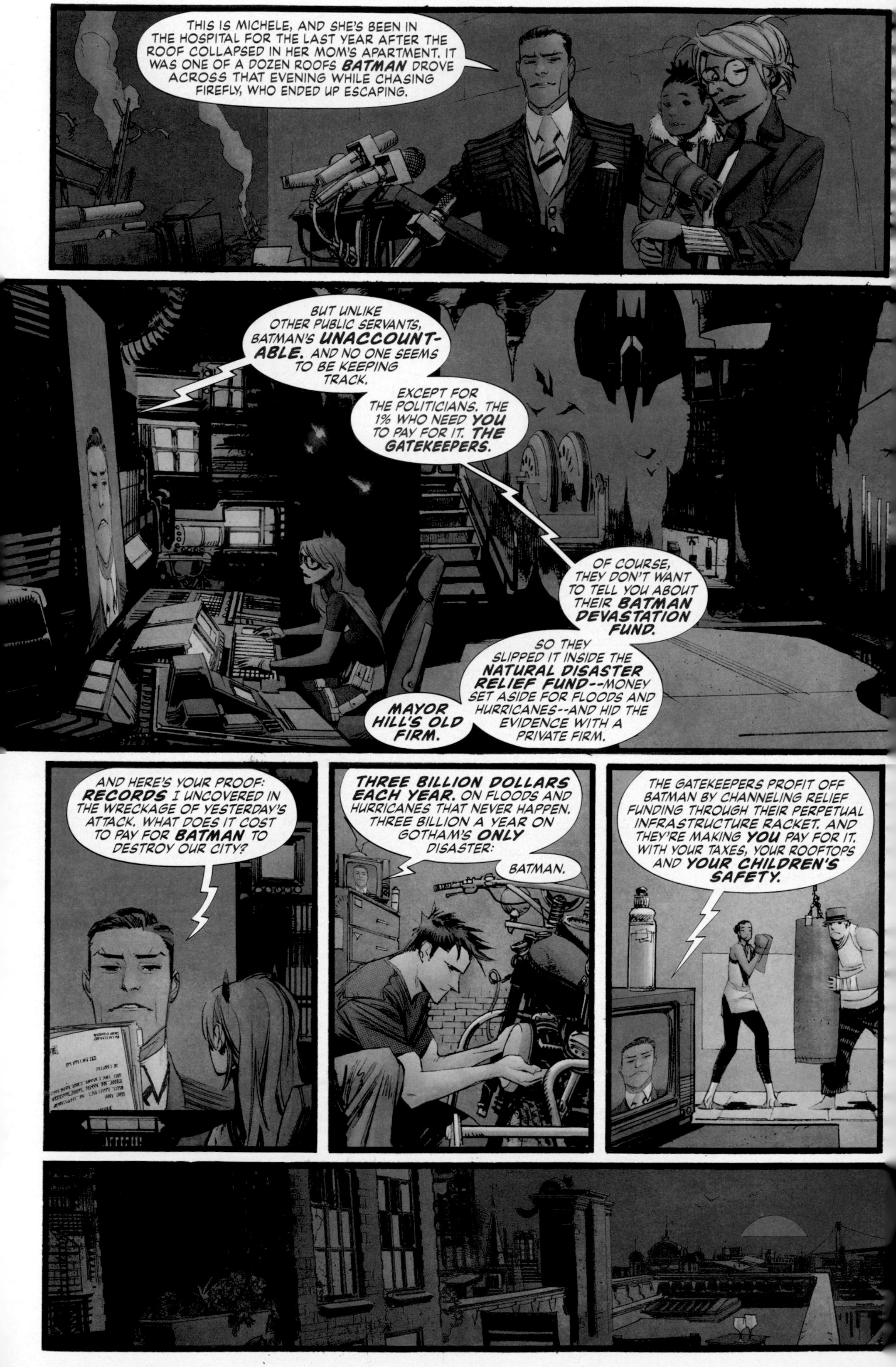

THIS IS MICHELE, AND SHE'S BEEN IN THE HOSPITAL FOR THE LAST YEAR AFTER THE ROOF COLLAPSED IN HER MOM'S APARTMENT. IT WAS ONE OF A DOZEN ROOFS BATMAN DROVE ACROSS THAT EVENING WHILE CHASING FIREFLY, WHO ENDED UP ESCAPING.
BUT UNLIKE OTHER PUBLIC SERVANTS, BATMAN'S UNACCOUNT-ABLE. AND NO ONE SEEMS TO BE KEEPING TRACK.
EXCEPT FOR THE POLITICIANS. THE 1% WHO NEED YOU TO PAY FOR IT. THE GATEKEEPERS.
OF COURSE, THEY DON'T WANT TO TELL YOU ABOUT THEIR BATMAN DEVASTATION FUND.
SO THEY SLIPPED IT INSIDE THE NATURAL DISASTER RELIEF FUND--MONEY SET ASIDE FOR FLOODS AND HURRICANES--AND HID THE EVIDENCE WITH A PRIVATE FIRM.
MAYOR HILL'S OLD FIRM.
AND HERE'S YOUR PROOF: RECORDS I UNCOVERED IN THE WRECKAGE OF YESTERDAY'S ATTACK. WHAT DOES IT COST TO PAY FOR BATMAN TO DESTROY OUR CITY?
THREE BILLION DOLLARS EACH YEAR. ON FLOODS AND HURRICANES THAT NEVER HAPPEN. THREE BILLION A YEAR ON GOTHAM'S ONLY DISASTER:
BATMAN.
THE GATEKEEPERS PROFIT OFF BATMAN BY CHANNELING RELIEF FUNDING THROUGH THEIR PERPETUAL INFRASTRUCTURE RACKET. AND THEY'RE MAKING YOU PAY FOR IT. WITH YOUR TAXES, YOUR ROOFTOPS AND YOUR CHILDREN'S SAFETY.

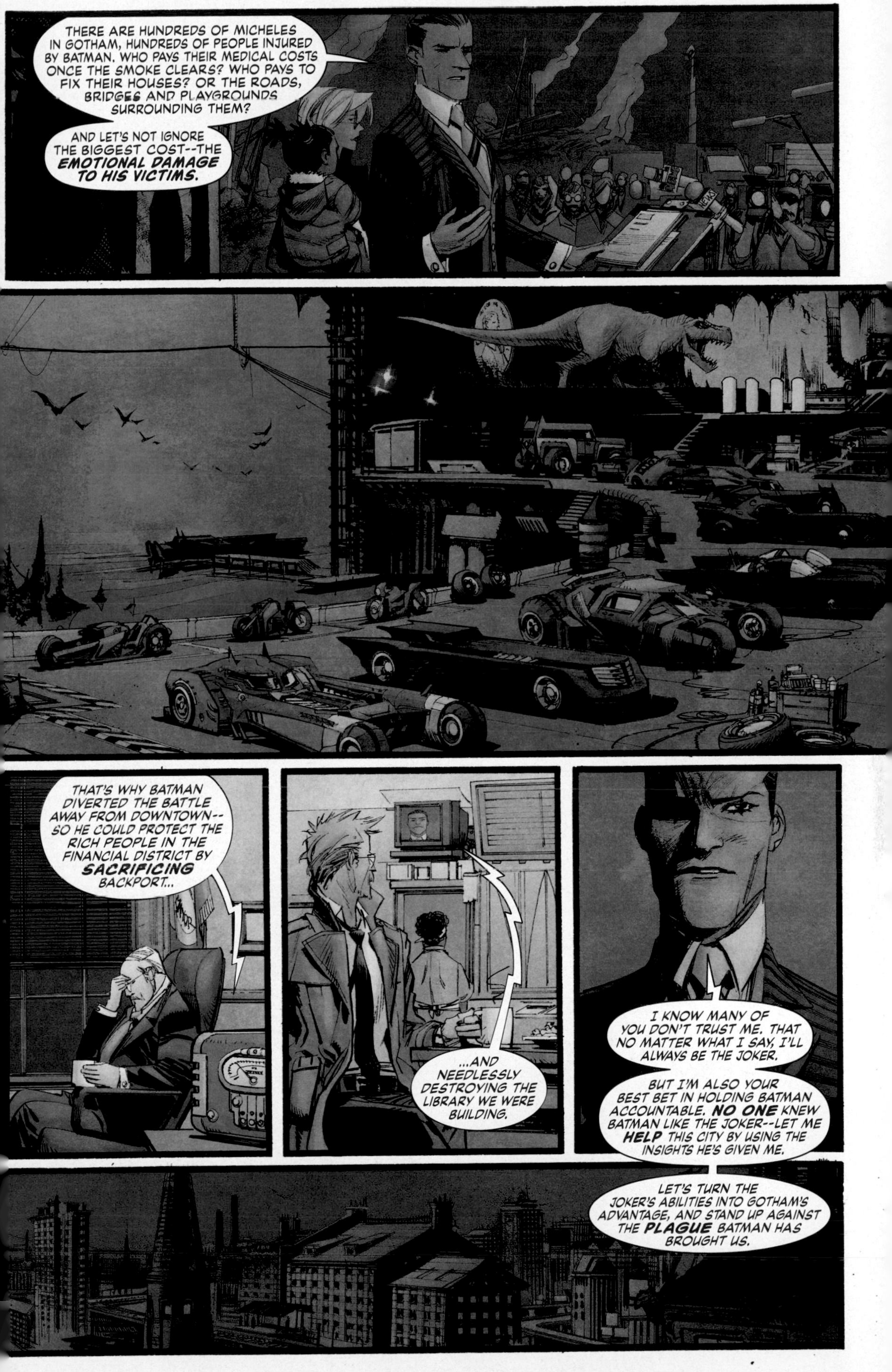
THERE ARE HUNDREDS OF MICHELES IN GOTHAM, HUNDREDS OF PEOPLE INJURED BY BATMAN. WHO PAYS THEIR MEDICAL COSTS ONCE THE SMOKE CLEARS? WHO PAYS TO FIX THEIR HOUSES? OR THE ROADS, BRIDGES AND PLAYGROUNDS SURROUNDING THEM?
AND LET'S NOT IGNORE THE BIGGEST COST--THE ***EMOTIONAL DAMAGE TO HIS VICTIMS.***
THAT'S WHY BATMAN DIVERTED THE BATTLE AWAY FROM DOWNTOWN--SO HE COULD PROTECT THE RICH PEOPLE IN THE FINANCIAL DISTRICT BY ***SACRIFICING*** BACKPORT...
...AND NEEDLESSLY DESTROYING THE LIBRARY WE WERE BUILDING.
I KNOW MANY OF YOU DON'T TRUST ME. THAT NO MATTER WHAT I SAY, I'LL ALWAYS BE THE JOKER.
BUT I'M ALSO YOUR BEST BET IN HOLDING BATMAN ACCOUNTABLE. ***NO ONE*** KNEW BATMAN LIKE THE JOKER--LET ME ***HELP*** THIS CITY BY USING THE INSIGHTS HE'S GIVEN ME.
LET'S TURN THE JOKER'S ABILITIES INTO GOTHAM'S ADVANTAGE, AND STAND UP AGAINST THE ***PLAGUE*** BATMAN HAS BROUGHT US.

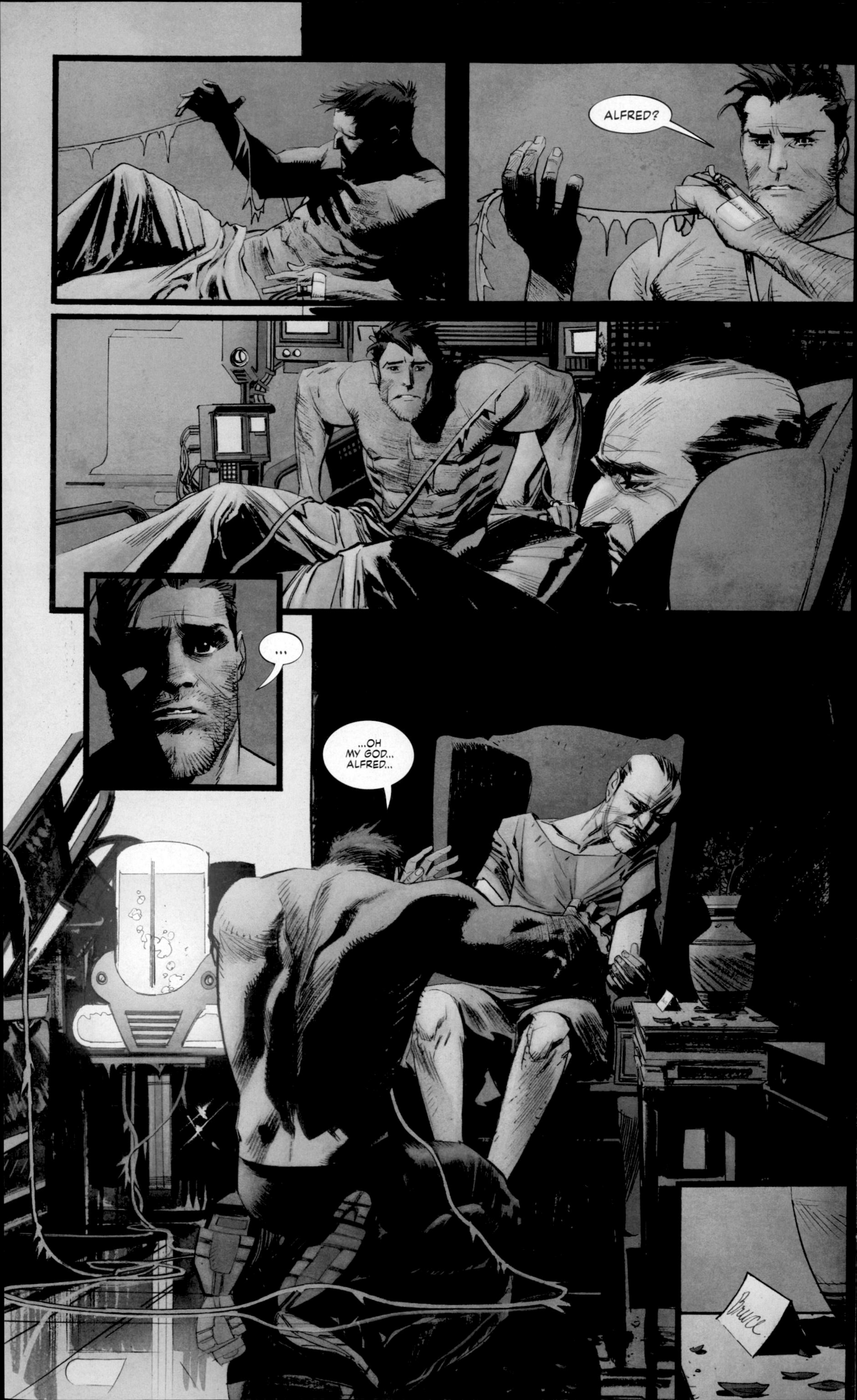
ALFRED?
...
...OH MY GOD... ALFRED...
Bruce

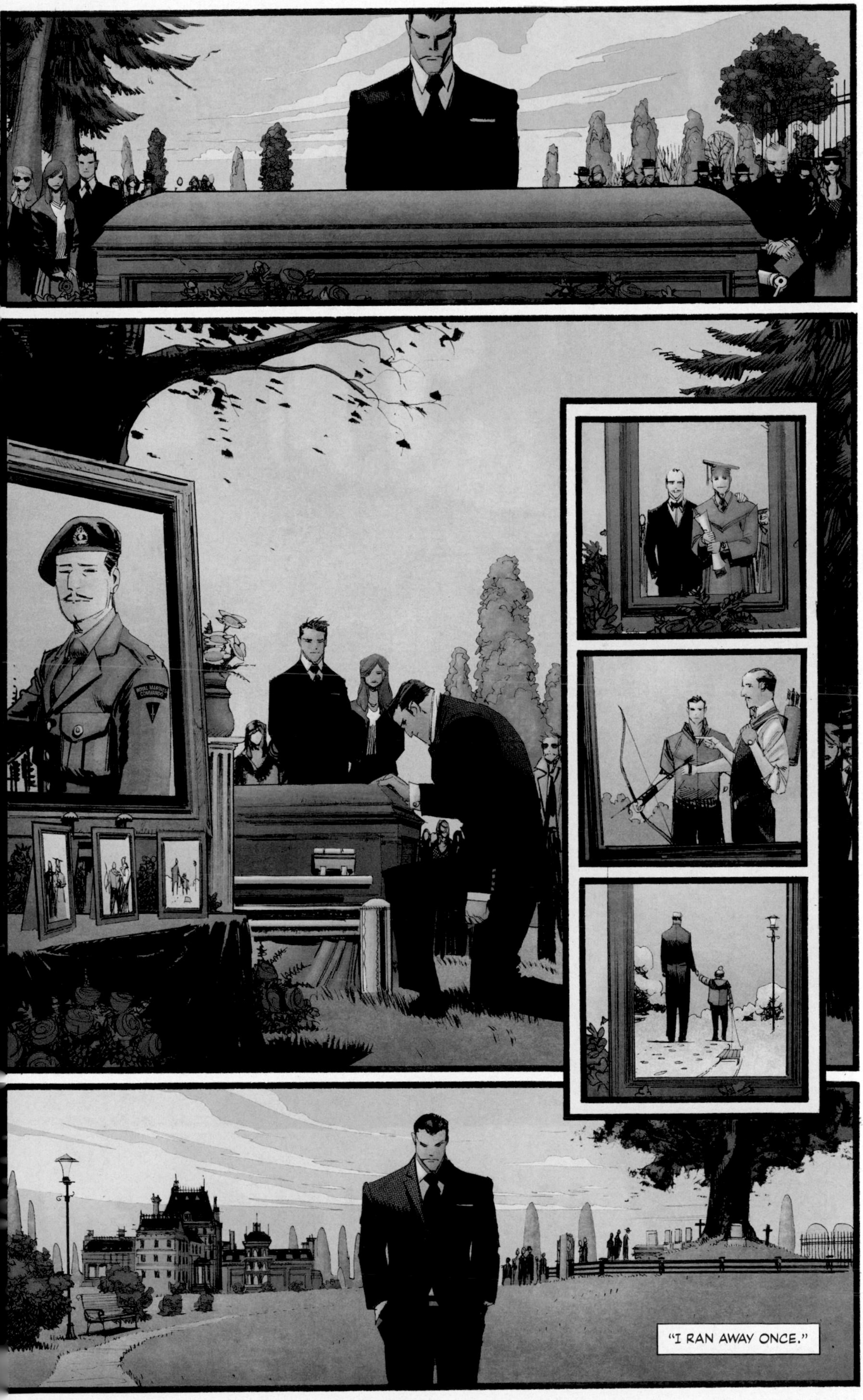
ROYAL MARINES COMMANDO
"I RAN AWAY ONCE."

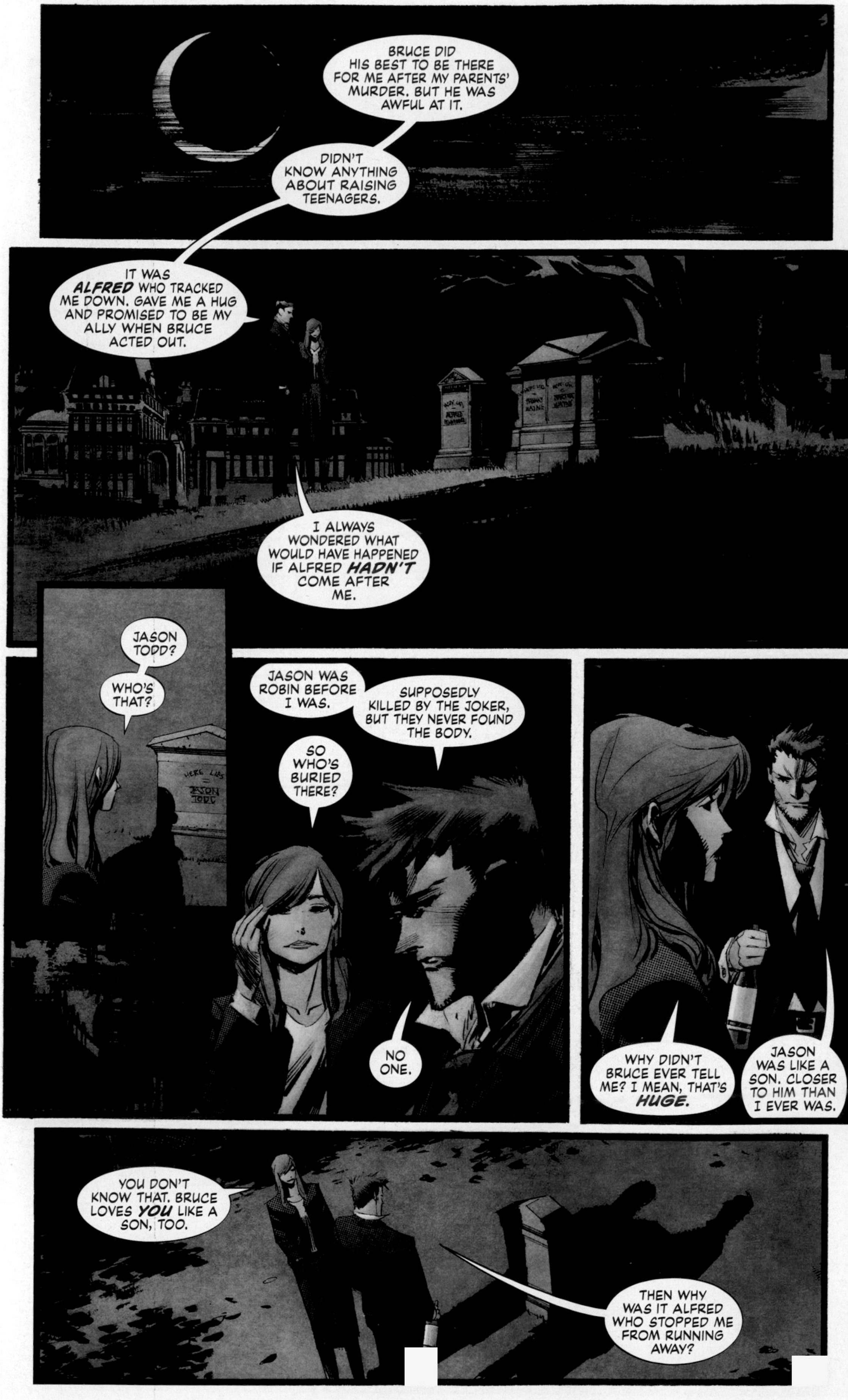
BRUCE DID HIS BEST TO BE THERE FOR ME AFTER MY PARENTS' MURDER. BUT HE WAS AWFUL AT IT.
DIDN'T KNOW ANYTHING ABOUT RAISING TEENAGERS.
IT WAS ALFRED WHO TRACKED ME DOWN. GAVE ME A HUG AND PROMISED TO BE MY ALLY WHEN BRUCE ACTED OUT.
I ALWAYS WONDERED WHAT WOULD HAVE HAPPENED IF ALFRED HADN'T COME AFTER ME.
JASON TODD?
WHO'S THAT?
HERE LIES JASON TODD
JASON WAS ROBIN BEFORE I WAS.
SUPPOSEDLY KILLED BY THE JOKER, BUT THEY NEVER FOUND THE BODY.
SO WHO'S BURIED THERE?
NO ONE.
WHY DIDN'T BRUCE EVER TELL ME? I MEAN, THAT'S HUGE.
JASON WAS LIKE A SON. CLOSER TO HIM THAN I EVER WAS.
YOU DON'T KNOW THAT. BRUCE LOVES YOU LIKE A SON, TOO.
THEN WHY WAS IT ALFRED WHO STOPPED ME FROM RUNNING AWAY?

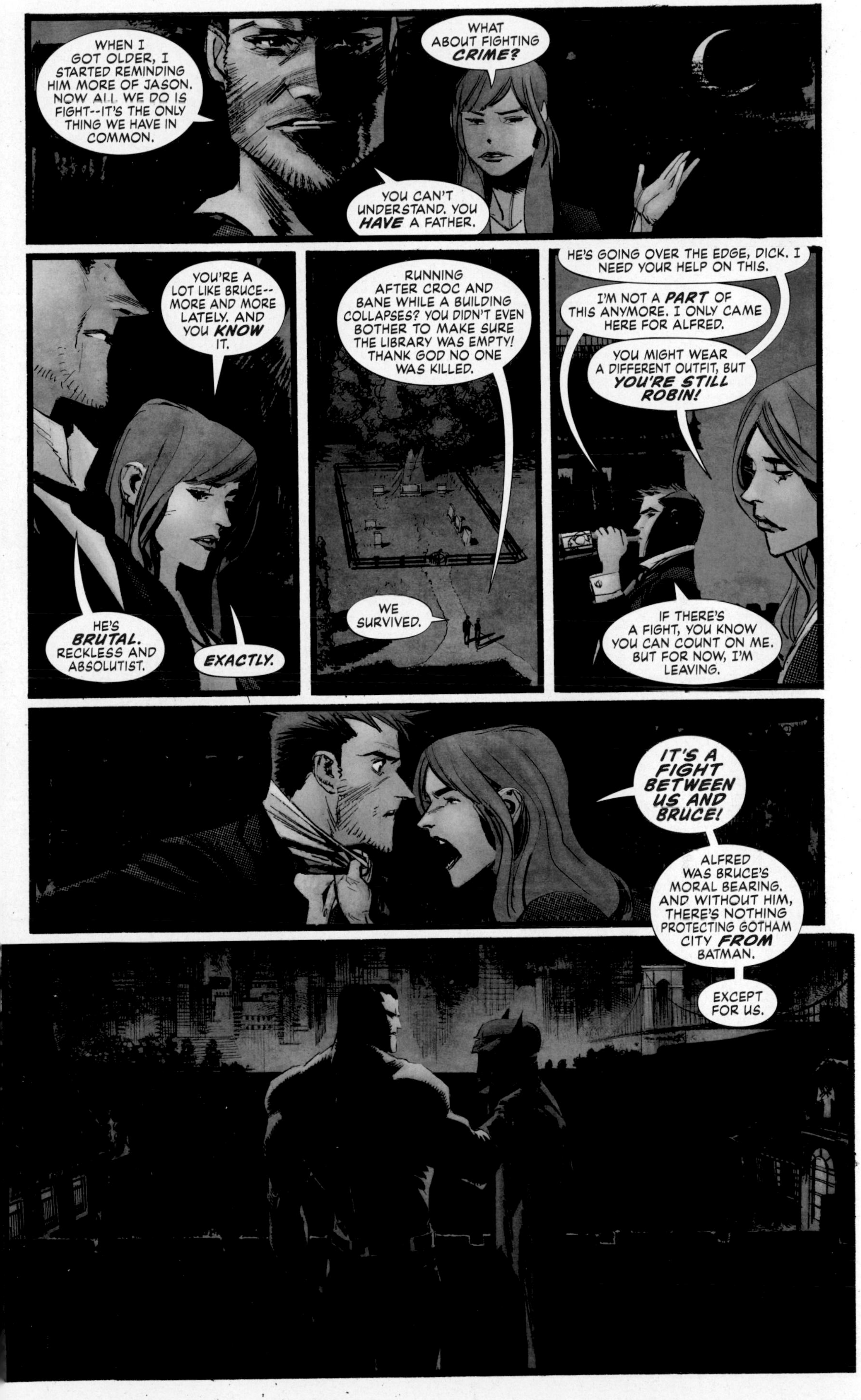
WHEN I GOT OLDER, I STARTED REMINDING HIM MORE OF JASON. NOW ALL WE DO IS FIGHT--IT'S THE ONLY THING WE HAVE IN COMMON.
WHAT ABOUT FIGHTING CRIME?
YOU CAN'T UNDERSTAND. YOU HAVE A FATHER.
YOU'RE A LOT LIKE BRUCE--MORE AND MORE LATELY. AND YOU KNOW IT.
HE'S BRUTAL. RECKLESS AND ABSOLUTIST.
EXACTLY.
RUNNING AFTER CROC AND BANE WHILE A BUILDING COLLAPSES? YOU DIDN'T EVEN BOTHER TO MAKE SURE THE LIBRARY WAS EMPTY! THANK GOD NO ONE WAS KILLED.
WE SURVIVED.
HE'S GOING OVER THE EDGE, DICK. I NEED YOUR HELP ON THIS.
I'M NOT A PART OF THIS ANYMORE. I ONLY CAME HERE FOR ALFRED.
YOU MIGHT WEAR A DIFFERENT OUTFIT, BUT YOU'RE STILL ROBIN!
IF THERE'S A FIGHT, YOU KNOW YOU CAN COUNT ON ME. BUT FOR NOW, I'M LEAVING.
IT'S A FIGHT BETWEEN US AND BRUCE!
ALFRED WAS BRUCE'S MORAL BEARING. AND WITHOUT HIM, THERE'S NOTHING PROTECTING GOTHAM CITY FROM BATMAN.
EXCEPT FOR US.

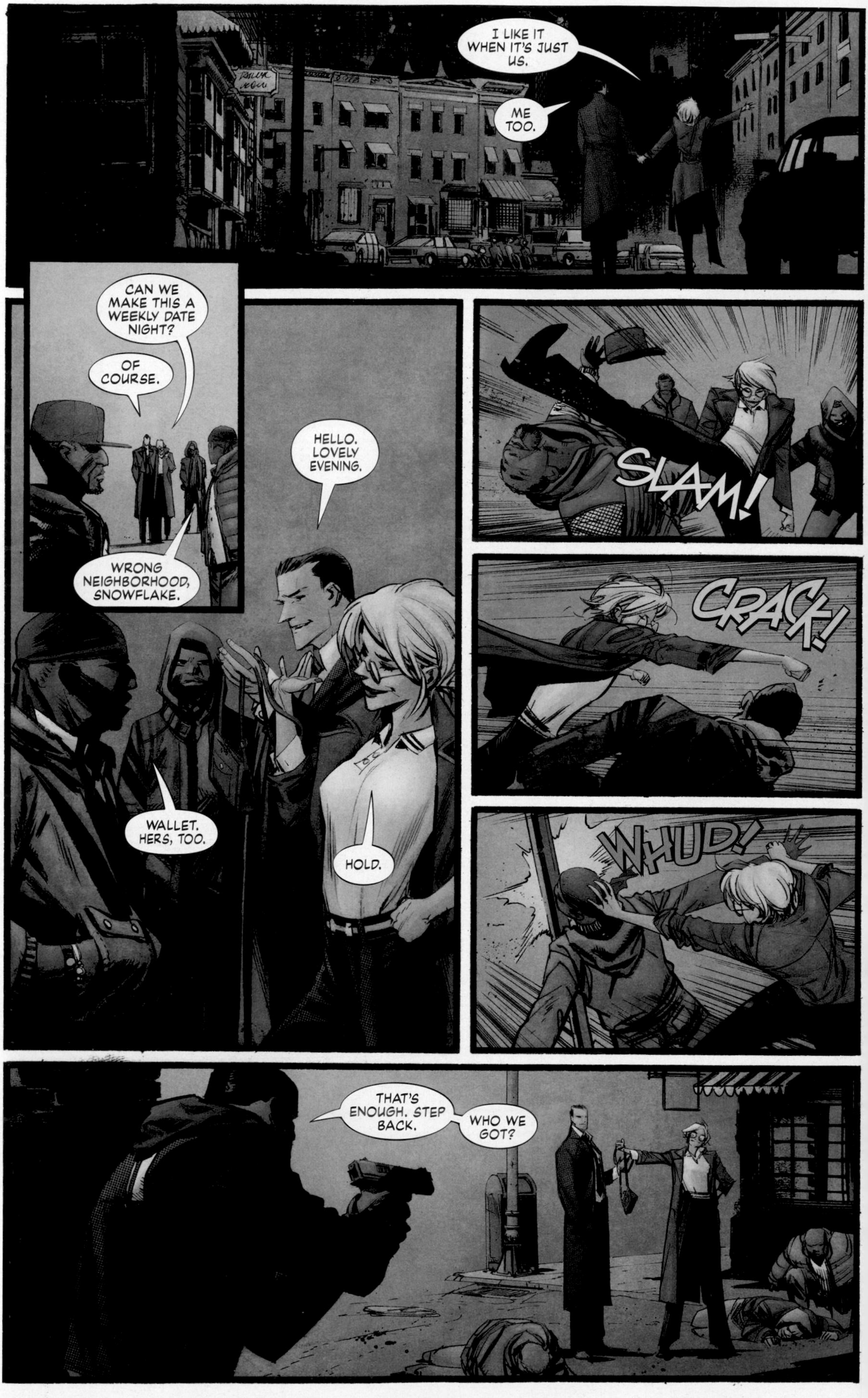

I LIKE IT WHEN IT'S JUST US.
ME TOO.
CAN WE MAKE THIS A WEEKLY DATE NIGHT?
OF COURSE.
WRONG NEIGHBORHOOD, SNOWFLAKE.
HELLO. LOVELY EVENING.
WALLET. HERS, TOO.
HOLD.
SLAM!
CRACK!
WHUD!
THAT'S ENOUGH. STEP BACK.
WHO WE GOT?

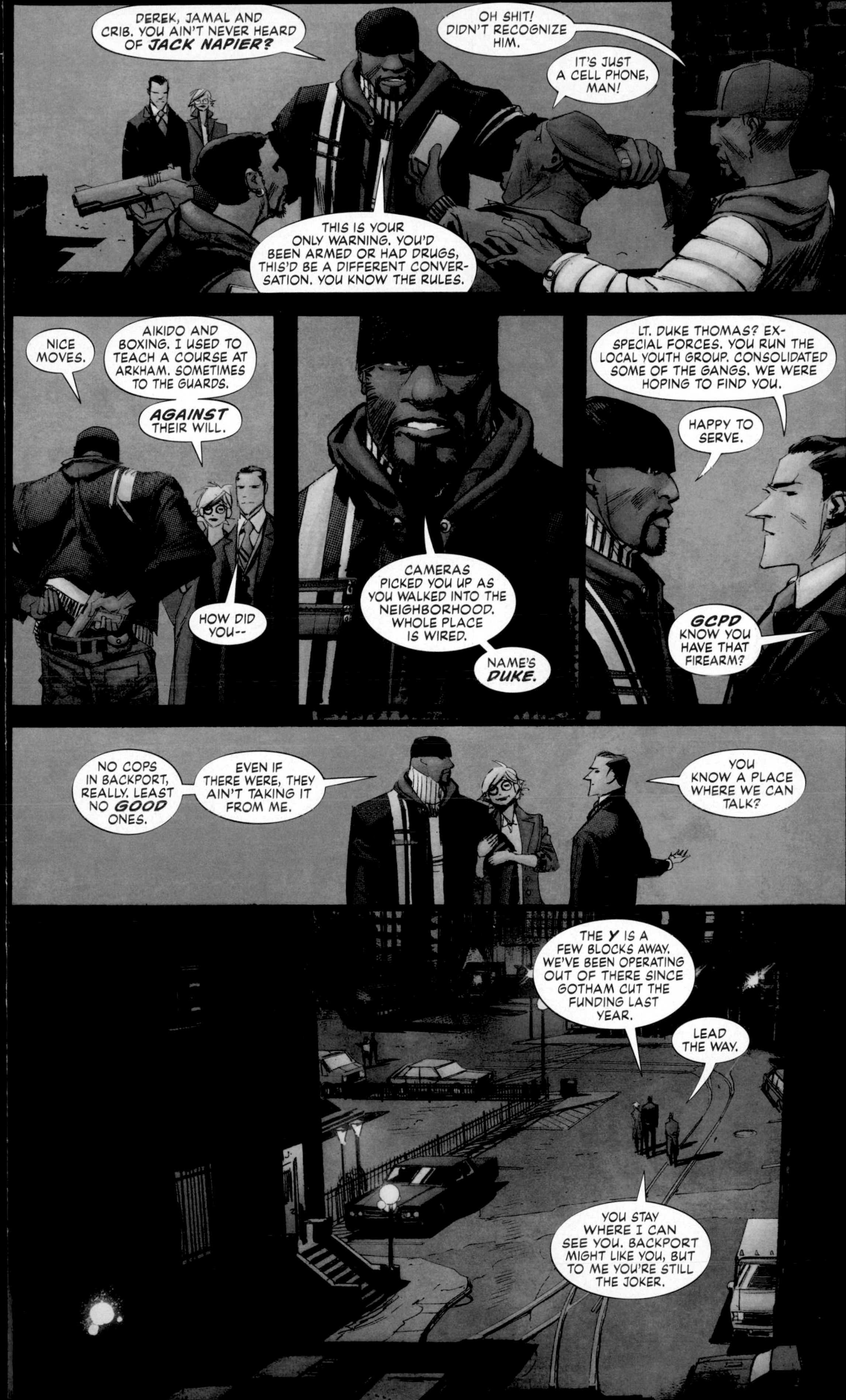
DEREK, JAMAL AND CRIB. YOU AIN'T NEVER HEARD OF JACK NAPIER?
OH SHIT! DIDN'T RECOGNIZE HIM.
IT'S JUST A CELL PHONE, MAN!
THIS IS YOUR ONLY WARNING. YOU'D BEEN ARMED OR HAD DRUGS, THIS'D BE A DIFFERENT CONVERSATION. YOU KNOW THE RULES.
NICE MOVES.
AIKIDO AND BOXING. I USED TO TEACH A COURSE AT ARKHAM. SOMETIMES TO THE GUARDS.
AGAINST THEIR WILL.
HOW DID YOU--
CAMERAS PICKED YOU UP AS YOU WALKED INTO THE NEIGHBORHOOD. WHOLE PLACE IS WIRED.
NAME'S DUKE.
LT. DUKE THOMAS? EX-SPECIAL FORCES. YOU RUN THE LOCAL YOUTH GROUP. CONSOLIDATED SOME OF THE GANGS. WE WERE HOPING TO FIND YOU.
HAPPY TO SERVE.
GCPD KNOW YOU HAVE THAT FIREARM?
NO COPS IN BACKPORT, REALLY. LEAST NO GOOD ONES.
EVEN IF THERE WERE, THEY AIN'T TAKING IT FROM ME.
YOU KNOW A PLACE WHERE WE CAN TALK?
THE Y IS A FEW BLOCKS AWAY. WE'VE BEEN OPERATING OUT OF THERE SINCE GOTHAM CUT THE FUNDING LAST YEAR.
LEAD THE WAY.
YOU STAY WHERE I CAN SEE YOU. BACKPORT MIGHT LIKE YOU, BUT TO ME YOU'RE STILL THE JOKER.

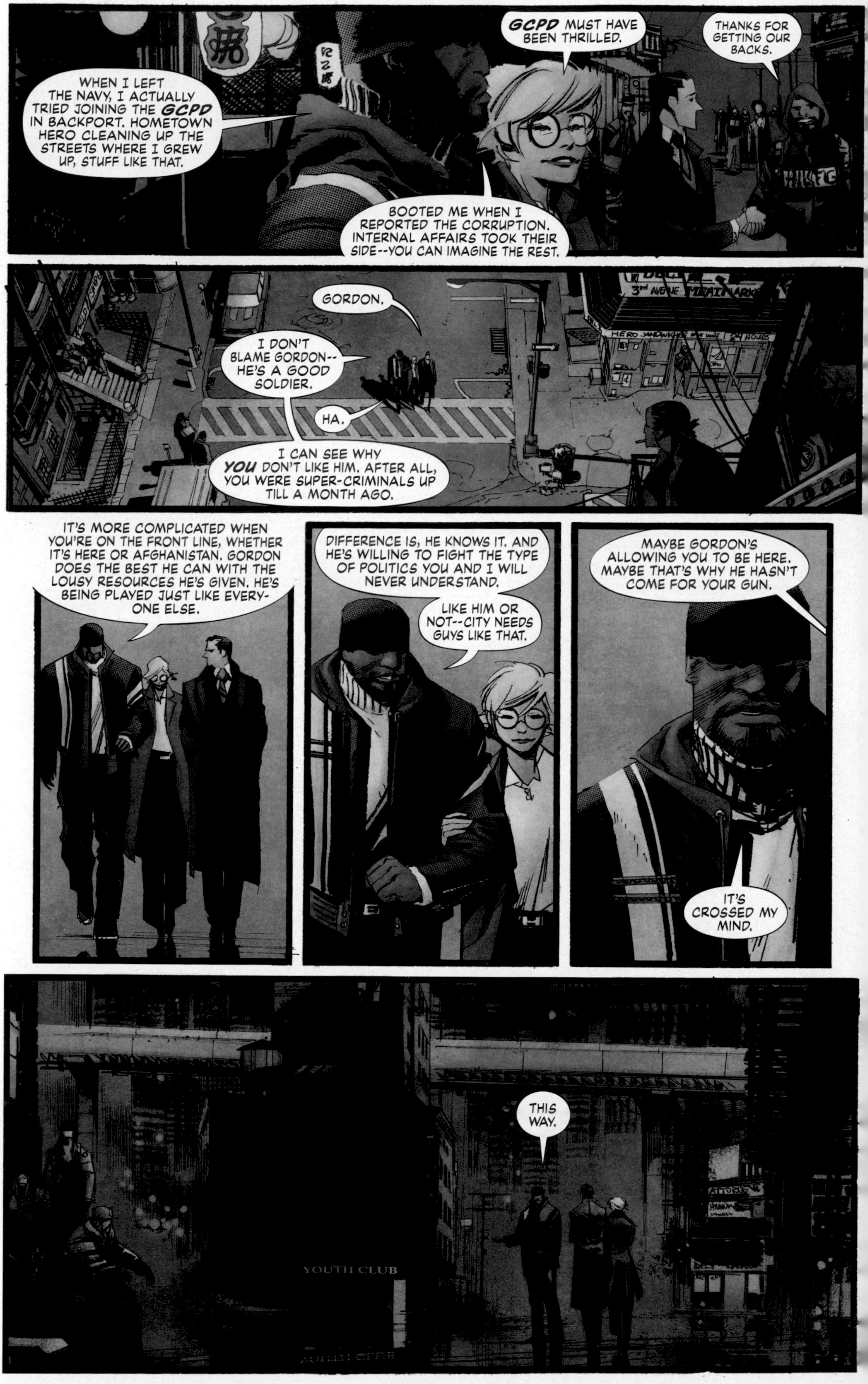
WHEN I LEFT THE NAVY, I ACTUALLY TRIED JOINING THE GCPD IN BACKPORT. HOMETOWN HERO CLEANING UP THE STREETS WHERE I GREW UP, STUFF LIKE THAT.
GCPD MUST HAVE BEEN THRILLED.
BOOTED ME WHEN I REPORTED THE CORRUPTION. INTERNAL AFFAIRS TOOK THEIR SIDE--YOU CAN IMAGINE THE REST.
THANKS FOR GETTING OUR BACKS.
GORDON.
I DON'T BLAME GORDON--HE'S A GOOD SOLDIER.
HA.
I CAN SEE WHY YOU DON'T LIKE HIM. AFTER ALL, YOU WERE SUPER-CRIMINALS UP TILL A MONTH AGO.
IT'S MORE COMPLICATED WHEN YOU'RE ON THE FRONT LINE, WHETHER IT'S HERE OR AFGHANISTAN. GORDON DOES THE BEST HE CAN WITH THE LOUSY RESOURCES HE'S GIVEN. HE'S BEING PLAYED JUST LIKE EVERY-ONE ELSE.
DIFFERENCE IS, HE KNOWS IT. AND HE'S WILLING TO FIGHT THE TYPE OF POLITICS YOU AND I WILL NEVER UNDERSTAND.
LIKE HIM OR NOT--CITY NEEDS GUYS LIKE THAT.
MAYBE GORDON'S ALLOWING YOU TO BE HERE. MAYBE THAT'S WHY HE HASN'T COME FOR YOUR GUN.
IT'S CROSSED MY MIND.
YOUTH CLUB
THIS WAY.

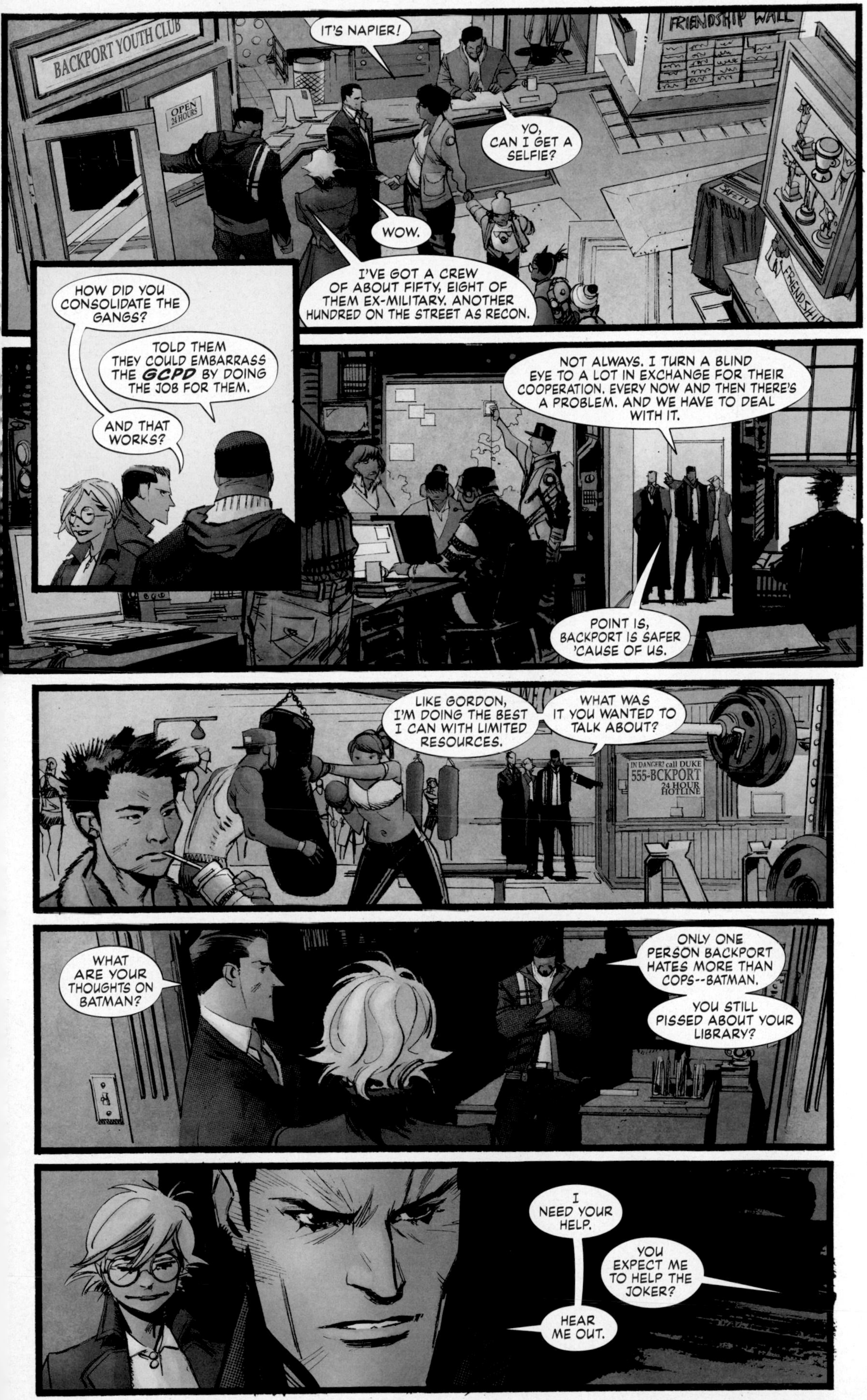
BACKPORT YOUTH CLUB
OPEN 24 HOURS
FRIENDSHIP WALL
IT'S NAPIER!
YO, CAN I GET A SELFIE?
WOW.
I'VE GOT A CREW OF ABOUT FIFTY, EIGHT OF THEM EX-MILITARY. ANOTHER HUNDRED ON THE STREET AS RECON.
HOW DID YOU CONSOLIDATE THE GANGS?
TOLD THEM THEY COULD EMBARRASS THE GCPD BY DOING THE JOB FOR THEM.
AND THAT WORKS?
NOT ALWAYS. I TURN A BLIND EYE TO A LOT IN EXCHANGE FOR THEIR COOPERATION. EVERY NOW AND THEN THERE'S A PROBLEM. AND WE HAVE TO DEAL WITH IT.
POINT IS, BACKPORT IS SAFER 'CAUSE OF US.
LIKE GORDON, I'M DOING THE BEST I CAN WITH LIMITED RESOURCES.
WHAT WAS IT YOU WANTED TO TALK ABOUT?
IN DANGER? call DUKE
555-BCKPORT
24 HOUR HOTLINE
WHAT ARE YOUR THOUGHTS ON BATMAN?
ONLY ONE PERSON BACKPORT HATES MORE THAN COPS--BATMAN.
YOU STILL PISSED ABOUT YOUR LIBRARY?
I NEED YOUR HELP.
YOU EXPECT ME TO HELP THE JOKER?
HEAR ME OUT.

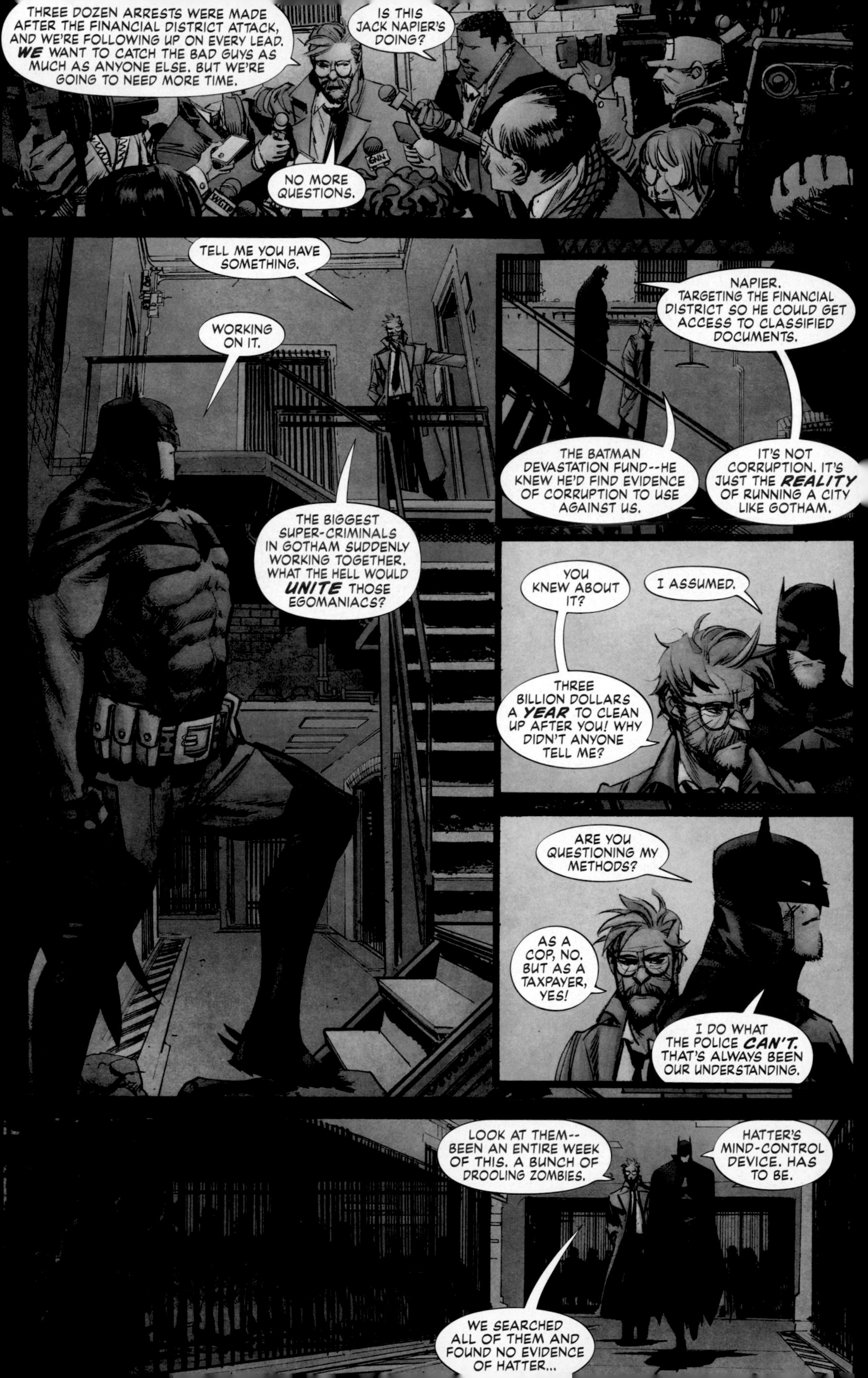
THREE DOZEN ARRESTS WERE MADE AFTER THE FINANCIAL DISTRICT ATTACK, AND WE'RE FOLLOWING UP ON EVERY LEAD. WE WANT TO CATCH THE BAD GUYS AS MUCH AS ANYONE ELSE. BUT WE'RE GOING TO NEED MORE TIME.
IS THIS JACK NAPIER'S DOING?
NO MORE QUESTIONS.
GNN
TELL ME YOU HAVE SOMETHING.
WORKING ON IT.
THE BIGGEST SUPER-CRIMINALS IN GOTHAM SUDDENLY WORKING TOGETHER. WHAT THE HELL WOULD UNITE THOSE EGOMANIACS?
NAPIER. TARGETING THE FINANCIAL DISTRICT SO HE COULD GET ACCESS TO CLASSIFIED DOCUMENTS.
THE BATMAN DEVASTATION FUND--HE KNEW HE'D FIND EVIDENCE OF CORRUPTION TO USE AGAINST US.
IT'S NOT CORRUPTION. IT'S JUST THE REALITY OF RUNNING A CITY LIKE GOTHAM.
YOU KNEW ABOUT IT?
I ASSUMED.
THREE BILLION DOLLARS A YEAR TO CLEAN UP AFTER YOU! WHY DIDN'T ANYONE TELL ME?
ARE YOU QUESTIONING MY METHODS?
AS A COP, NO. BUT AS A TAXPAYER, YES!
I DO WHAT THE POLICE CAN'T. THAT'S ALWAYS BEEN OUR UNDERSTANDING.
LOOK AT THEM--BEEN AN ENTIRE WEEK OF THIS. A BUNCH OF DROOLING ZOMBIES.
HATTER'S MIND-CONTROL DEVICE. HAS TO BE.
WE SEARCHED ALL OF THEM AND FOUND NO EVIDENCE OF HATTER...

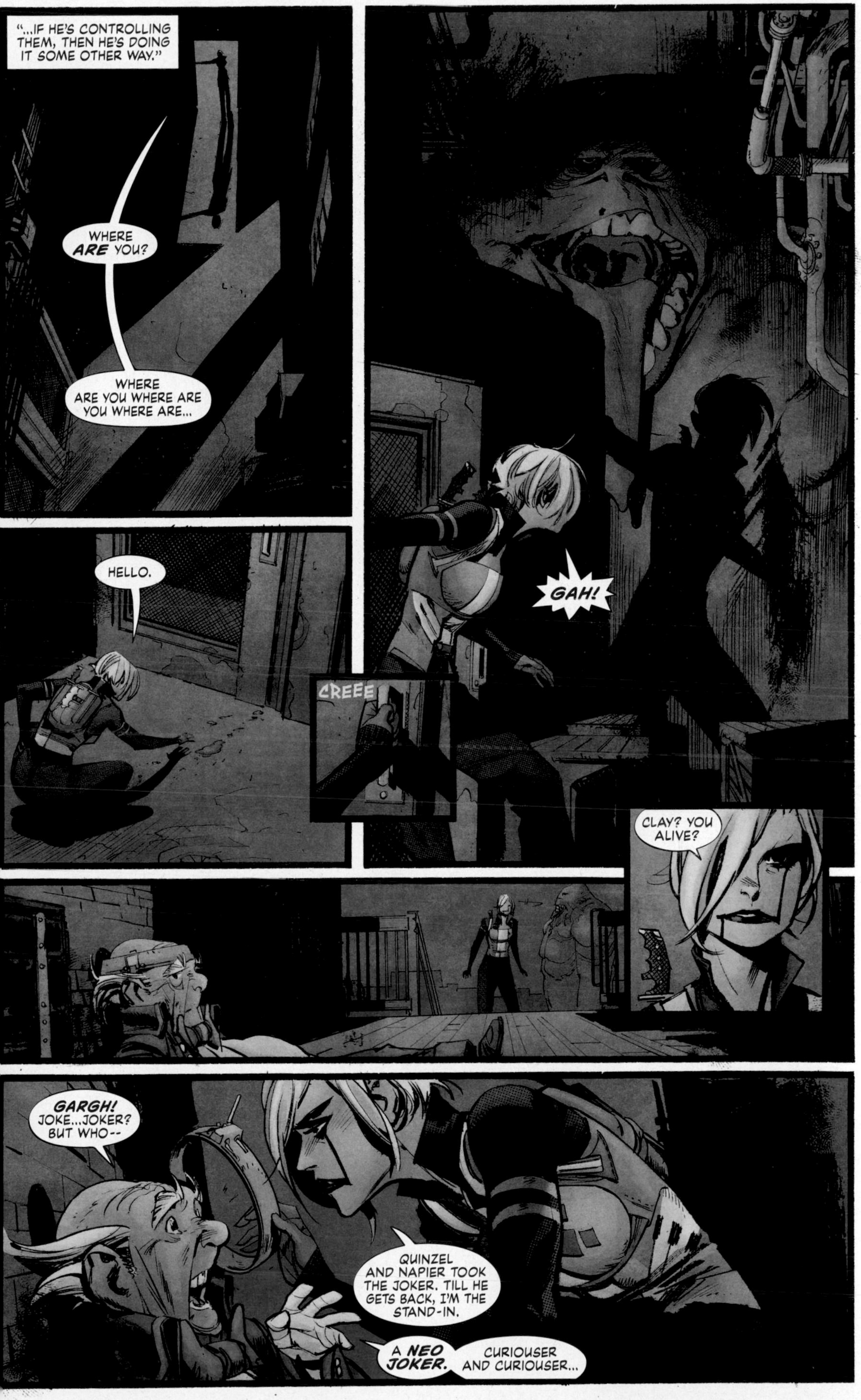
"...IF HE'S CONTROLLING THEM, THEN HE'S DOING IT SOME OTHER WAY."
WHERE *ARE* YOU?
WHERE ARE YOU WHERE ARE YOU WHERE ARE...
HELLO.
CREEE
GAH!
CLAY? YOU ALIVE?
GARGH! JOKE...JOKER? BUT WHO--
QUINZEL AND NAPIER TOOK THE JOKER. TILL HE GETS BACK, I'M THE STAND-IN.
A *NEO JOKER.*
CURIOUSER AND CURIOUSER...

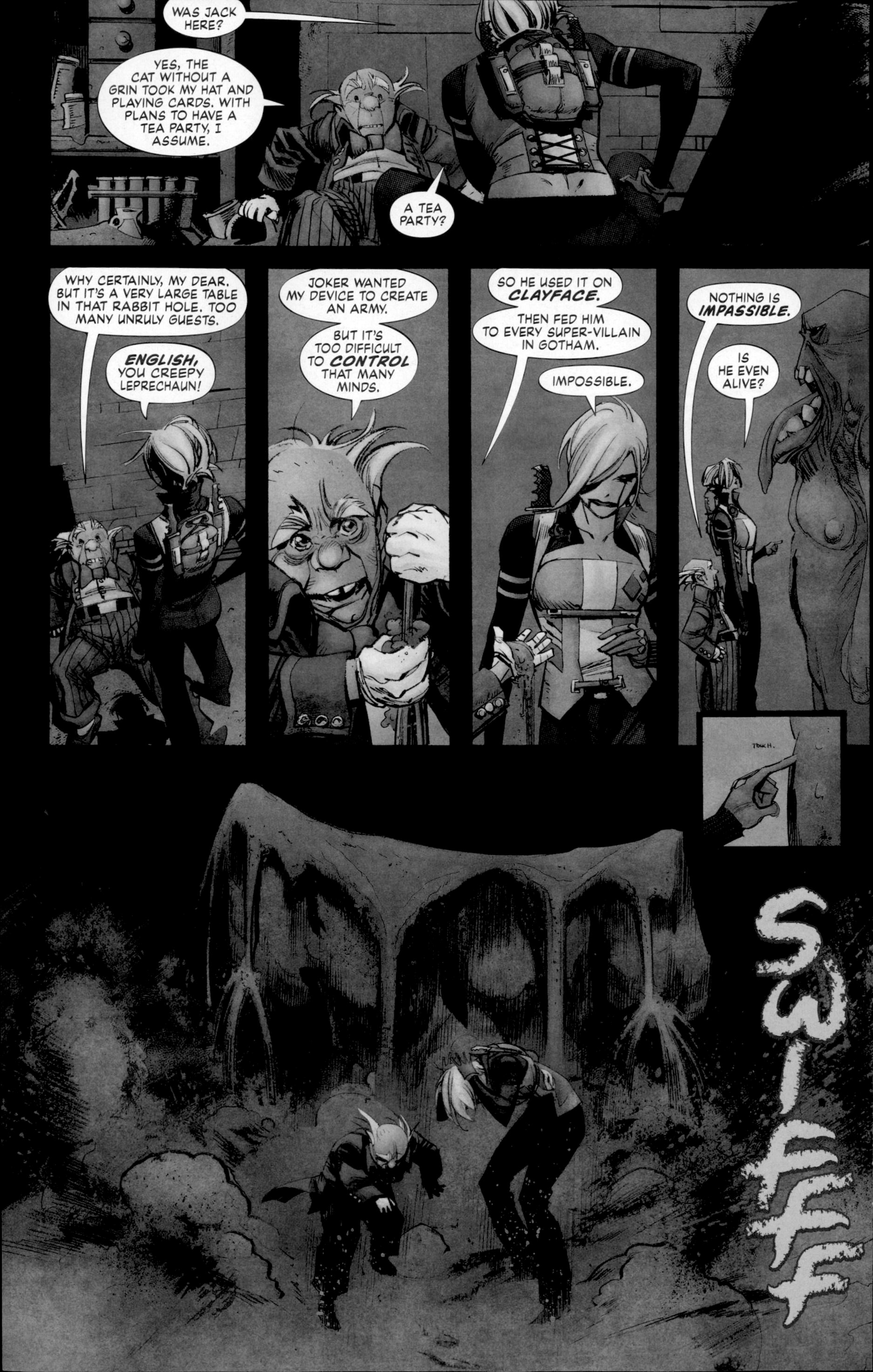
WAS JACK HERE?
YES, THE CAT WITHOUT A GRIN TOOK MY HAT AND PLAYING CARDS. WITH PLANS TO HAVE A TEA PARTY, I ASSUME.
A TEA PARTY?
WHY CERTAINLY, MY DEAR. BUT IT'S A VERY LARGE TABLE IN THAT RABBIT HOLE. TOO MANY UNRULY GUESTS.
ENGLISH, YOU CREEPY LEPRECHAUN!
JOKER WANTED MY DEVICE TO CREATE AN ARMY.
BUT IT'S TOO DIFFICULT TO CONTROL THAT MANY MINDS.
SO HE USED IT ON CLAYFACE.
THEN FED HIM TO EVERY SUPER-VILLAIN IN GOTHAM.
IMPOSSIBLE.
NOTHING IS IMPASSIBLE.
IS HE EVEN ALIVE?
TOUCH.
SHIFFT

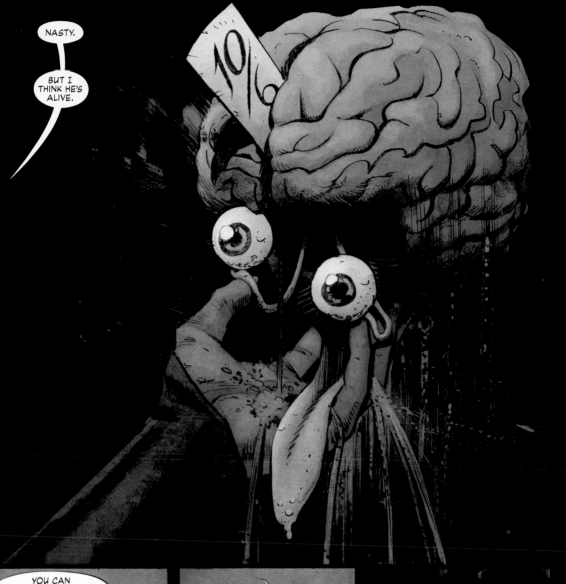

NASTY.

BUT I THINK HE'S ALIVE.

YOU CAN *OVERRIDE* NAPIER'S SIGNAL? WITH ANOTHER DEVICE?

YES, AS LONG AS I'M CLOSER TO CLAYFACE'S BRAIN THAN JOKER IS.

YOU HEAR THAT?

CURIOUSER AND --

YOU'RE WELCOME TO TAG ALONG, BUT *ENOUGH* WITH ALICE IN WONDER-LAND!

SHUFFLE

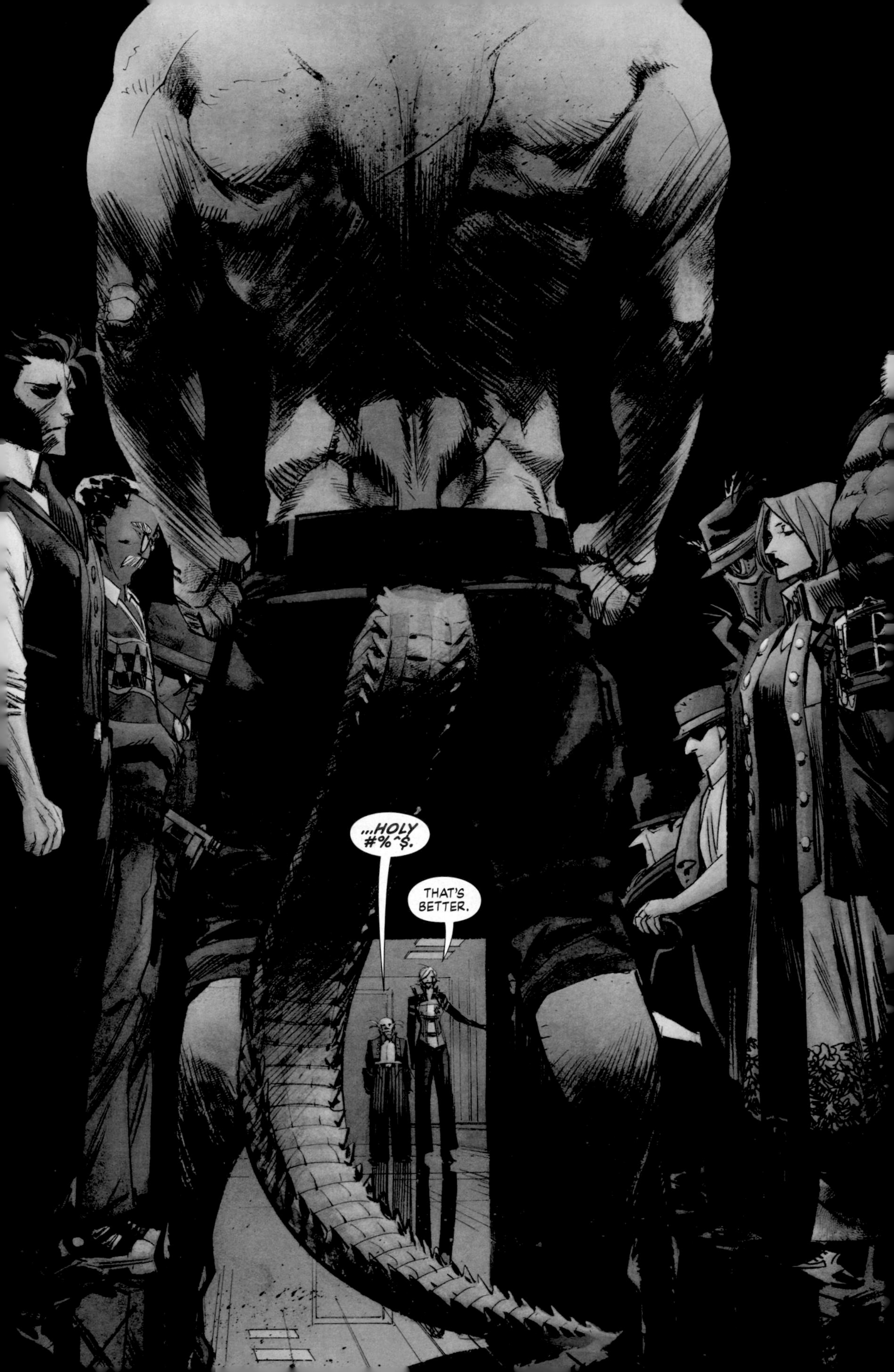
...HOLY #%^$.
THAT'S BETTER.

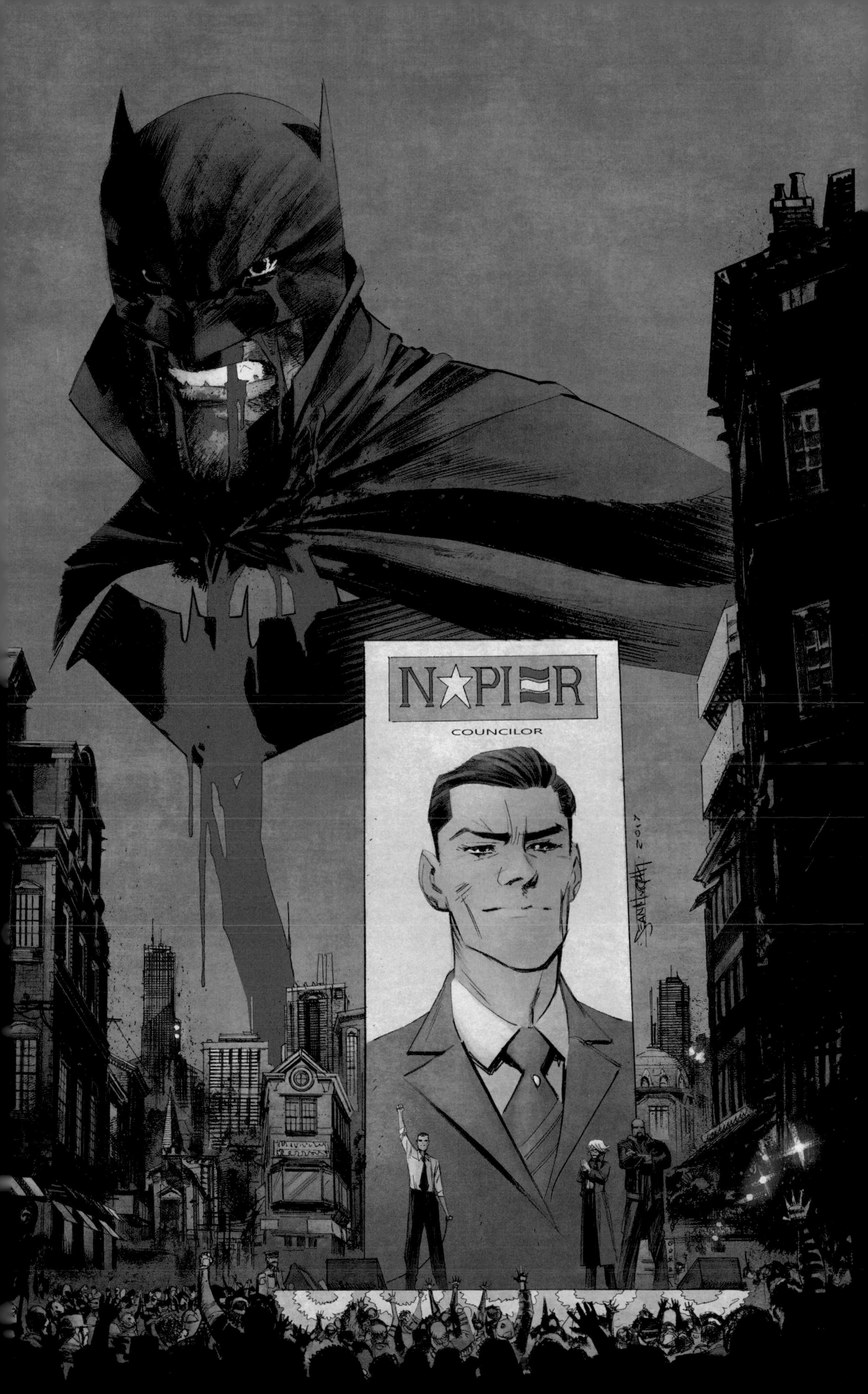
N★PIER
COUNCILOR

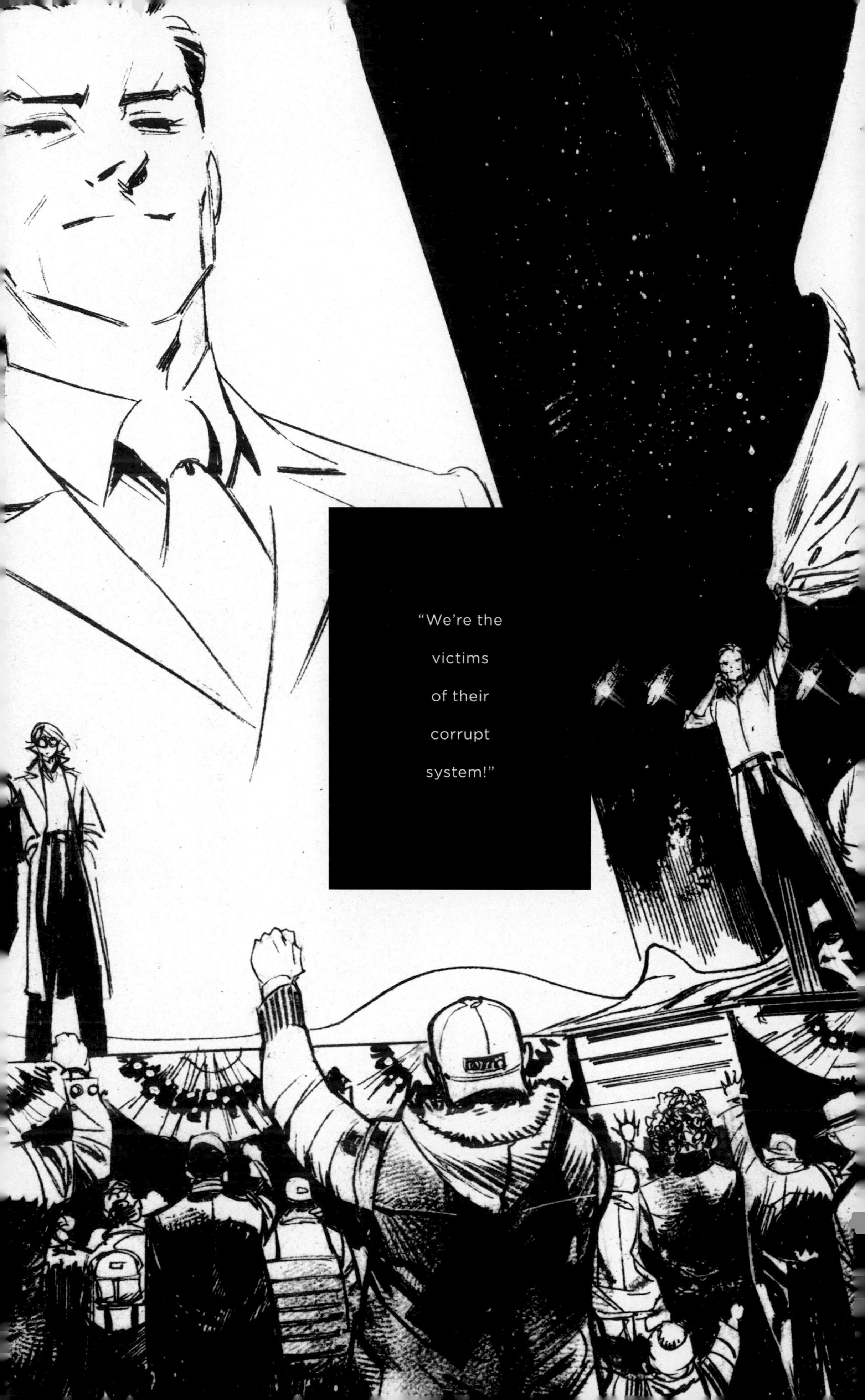
"We're the victims of their corrupt system!"

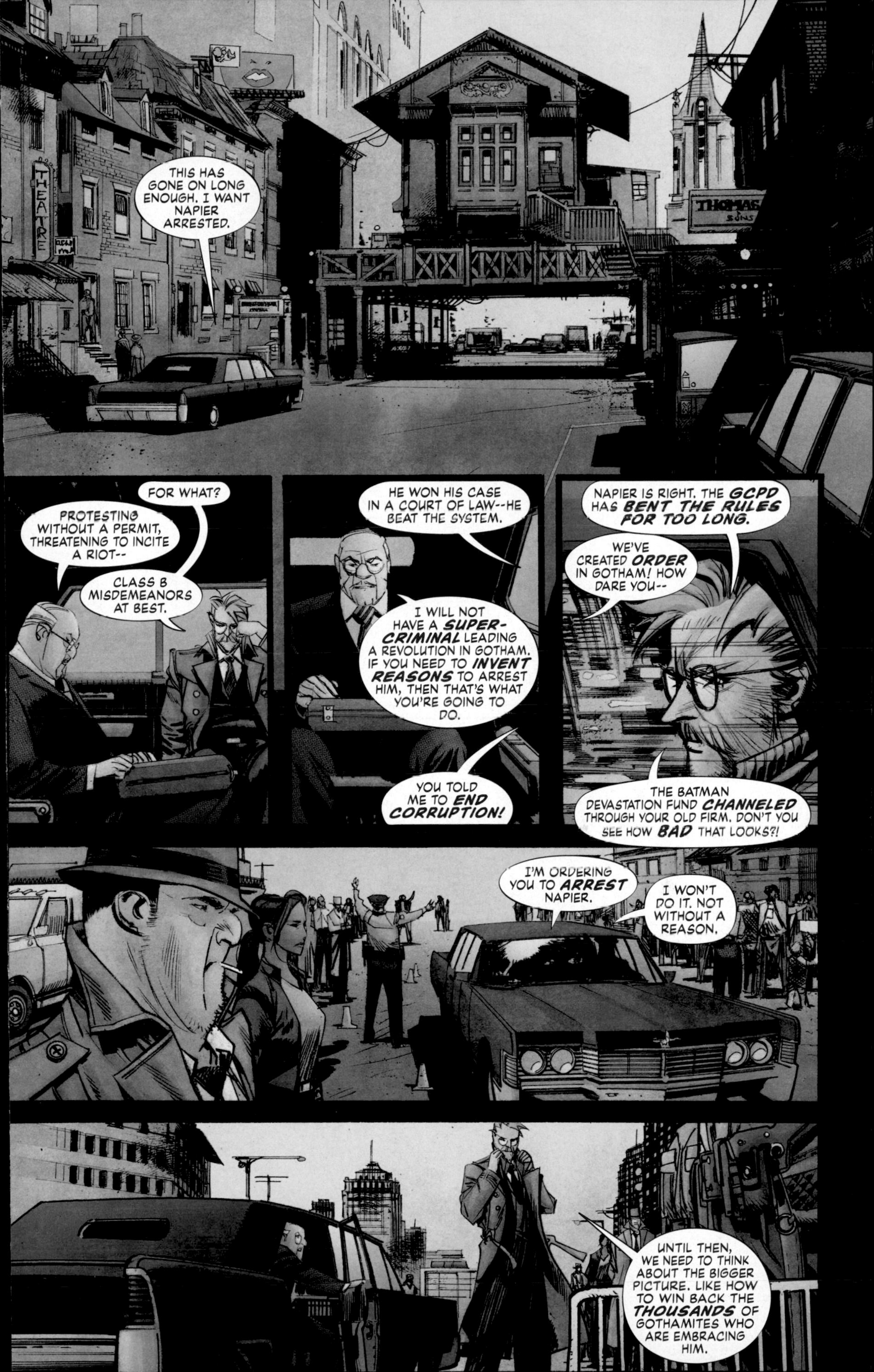

THEATRE
THOMAS & SONS
THIS HAS GONE ON LONG ENOUGH. I WANT NAPIER ARRESTED.
FOR WHAT?
PROTESTING WITHOUT A PERMIT, THREATENING TO INCITE A RIOT--
CLASS B MISDEMEANORS AT BEST.
HE WON HIS CASE IN A COURT OF LAW--HE BEAT THE SYSTEM.
I WILL NOT HAVE A SUPER-CRIMINAL LEADING A REVOLUTION IN GOTHAM. IF YOU NEED TO INVENT REASONS TO ARREST HIM, THEN THAT'S WHAT YOU'RE GOING TO DO.
YOU TOLD ME TO END CORRUPTION!
NAPIER IS RIGHT. THE GCPD HAS BENT THE RULES FOR TOO LONG.
WE'VE CREATED ORDER IN GOTHAM! HOW DARE YOU--
THE BATMAN DEVASTATION FUND CHANNELED THROUGH YOUR OLD FIRM. DON'T YOU SEE HOW BAD THAT LOOKS?!
I'M ORDERING YOU TO ARREST NAPIER.
I WON'T DO IT. NOT WITHOUT A REASON.
UNTIL THEN, WE NEED TO THINK ABOUT THE BIGGER PICTURE. LIKE HOW TO WIN BACK THE THOUSANDS OF GOTHAMITES WHO ARE EMBRACING HIM.

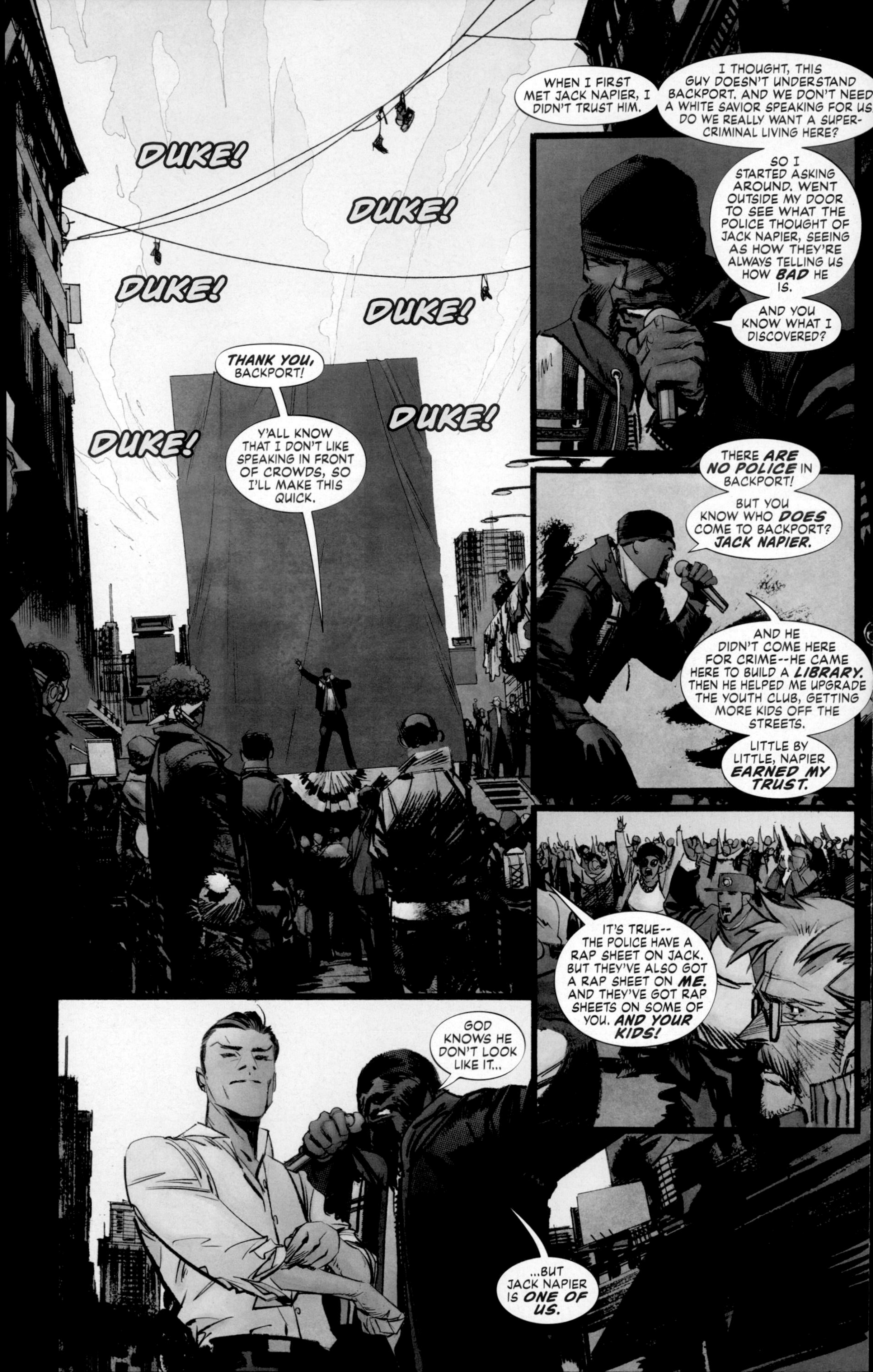
DUKE!
DUKE!
DUKE!
DUKE!
DUKE!
DUKE!
THANK YOU, BACKPORT!
Y'ALL KNOW THAT I DON'T LIKE SPEAKING IN FRONT OF CROWDS, SO I'LL MAKE THIS QUICK.
WHEN I FIRST MET JACK NAPIER, I DIDN'T TRUST HIM.
I THOUGHT, THIS GUY DOESN'T UNDERSTAND BACKPORT. AND WE DON'T NEED A WHITE SAVIOR SPEAKING FOR US. DO WE REALLY WANT A SUPER-CRIMINAL LIVING HERE?
SO I STARTED ASKING AROUND. WENT OUTSIDE MY DOOR TO SEE WHAT THE POLICE THOUGHT OF JACK NAPIER, SEEING AS HOW THEY'RE ALWAYS TELLING US HOW BAD HE IS.
AND YOU KNOW WHAT I DISCOVERED?
THERE ARE NO POLICE IN BACKPORT!
BUT YOU KNOW WHO DOES COME TO BACKPORT? JACK NAPIER.
AND HE DIDN'T COME HERE FOR CRIME--HE CAME HERE TO BUILD A LIBRARY. THEN HE HELPED ME UPGRADE THE YOUTH CLUB, GETTING MORE KIDS OFF THE STREETS.
LITTLE BY LITTLE, NAPIER EARNED MY TRUST.
IT'S TRUE-- THE POLICE HAVE A RAP SHEET ON JACK. BUT THEY'VE ALSO GOT A RAP SHEET ON ME. AND THEY'VE GOT RAP SHEETS ON SOME OF YOU. AND YOUR KIDS!
GOD KNOWS HE DON'T LOOK LIKE IT...
...BUT JACK NAPIER IS ONE OF US.

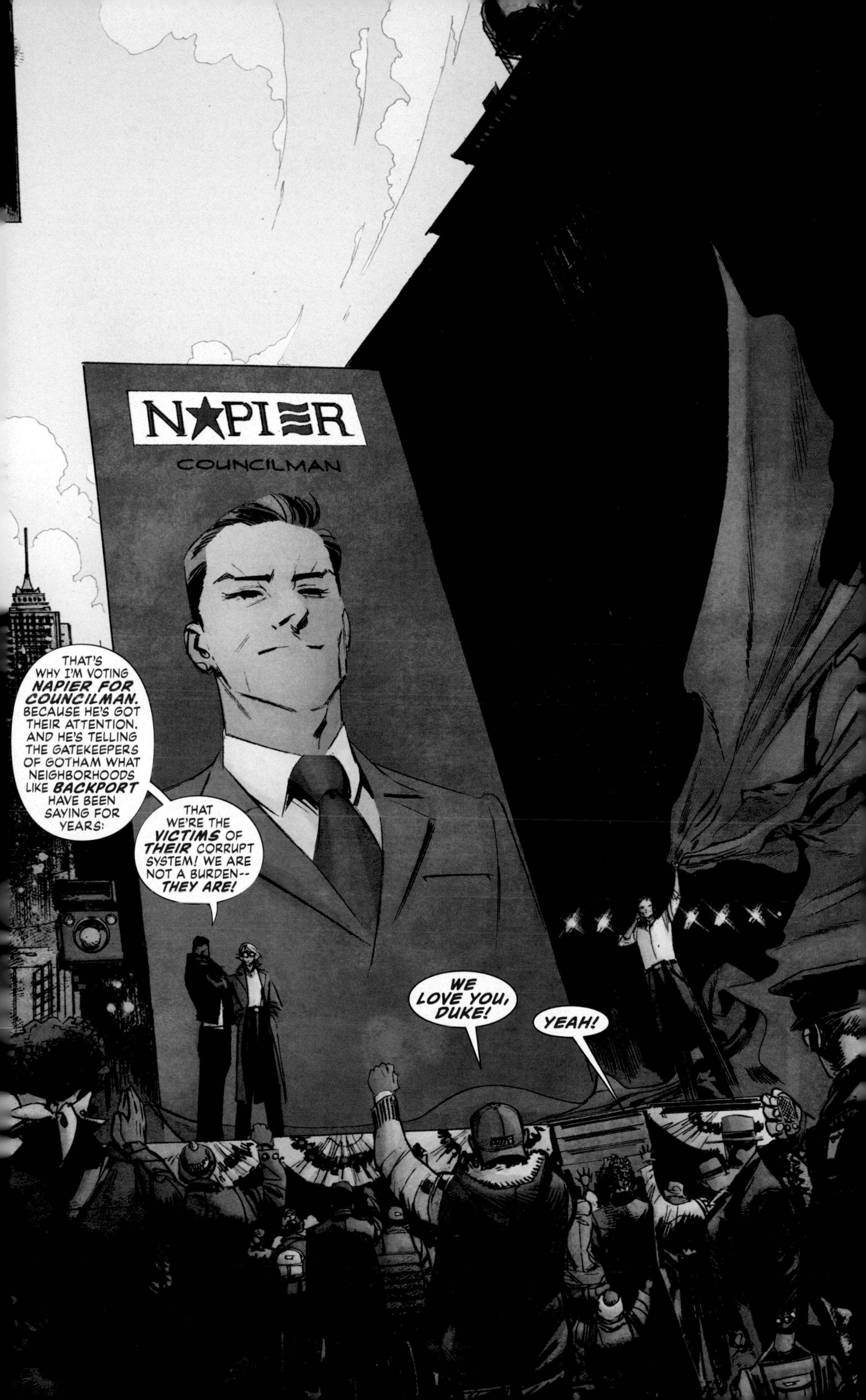
NAPIER
COUNCILMAN
THAT'S WHY I'M VOTING NAPIER FOR COUNCILMAN. BECAUSE HE'S GOT THEIR ATTENTION. AND HE'S TELLING THE GATEKEEPERS OF GOTHAM WHAT NEIGHBORHOODS LIKE BACKPORT HAVE BEEN SAYING FOR YEARS:
THAT WE'RE THE VICTIMS OF THEIR CORRUPT SYSTEM! WE ARE NOT A BURDEN-- THEY ARE!
WE LOVE YOU, DUKE!
YEAH!

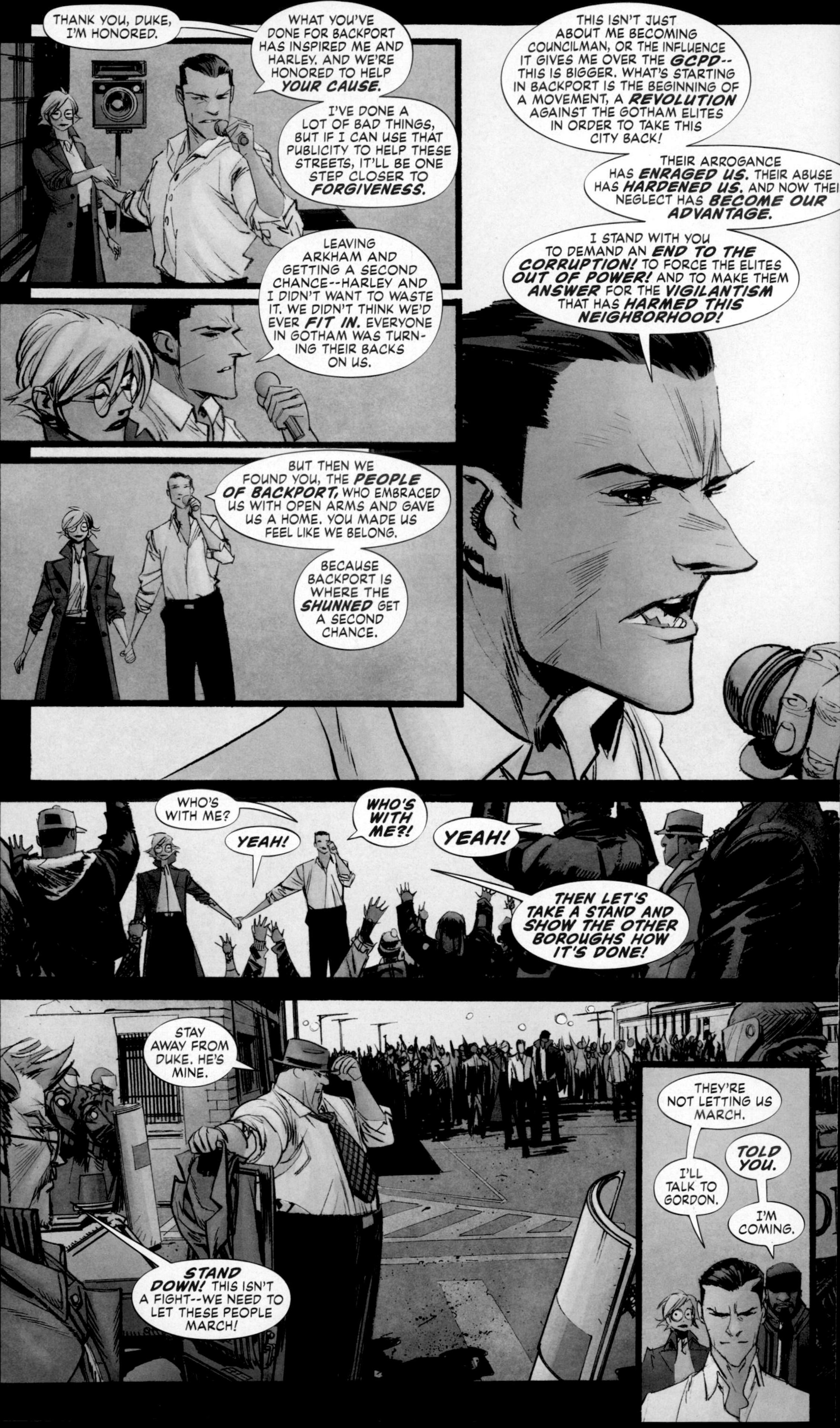
THANK YOU, DUKE, I'M HONORED.
WHAT YOU'VE DONE FOR BACKPORT HAS INSPIRED ME AND HARLEY. AND WE'RE HONORED TO HELP YOUR CAUSE.
I'VE DONE A LOT OF BAD THINGS, BUT IF I CAN USE THAT PUBLICITY TO HELP THESE STREETS, IT'LL BE ONE STEP CLOSER TO FORGIVENESS.
LEAVING ARKHAM AND GETTING A SECOND CHANCE--HARLEY AND I DIDN'T WANT TO WASTE IT. WE DIDN'T THINK WE'D EVER FIT IN. EVERYONE IN GOTHAM WAS TURNING THEIR BACKS ON US.
BUT THEN WE FOUND YOU, THE PEOPLE OF BACKPORT, WHO EMBRACED US WITH OPEN ARMS AND GAVE US A HOME. YOU MADE US FEEL LIKE WE BELONG.
BECAUSE BACKPORT IS WHERE THE SHUNNED GET A SECOND CHANCE.
THIS ISN'T JUST ABOUT ME BECOMING COUNCILMAN, OR THE INFLUENCE IT GIVES ME OVER THE GCPD-- THIS IS BIGGER. WHAT'S STARTING IN BACKPORT IS THE BEGINNING OF A MOVEMENT, A REVOLUTION AGAINST THE GOTHAM ELITES IN ORDER TO TAKE THIS CITY BACK!
THEIR ARROGANCE HAS ENRAGED US. THEIR ABUSE HAS HARDENED US. AND NOW THEI NEGLECT HAS BECOME OUR ADVANTAGE.
I STAND WITH YOU TO DEMAND AN END TO THE CORRUPTION! TO FORCE THE ELITES OUT OF POWER! AND TO MAKE THEM ANSWER FOR THE VIGILANTISM THAT HAS HARMED THIS NEIGHBORHOOD!
WHO'S WITH ME?
YEAH!
WHO'S WITH ME?!
YEAH!
THEN LET'S TAKE A STAND AND SHOW THE OTHER BOROUGHS HOW IT'S DONE!
STAY AWAY FROM DUKE. HE'S MINE.
STAND DOWN! THIS ISN'T A FIGHT--WE NEED TO LET THESE PEOPLE MARCH!
THEY'RE NOT LETTING US MARCH.
I'LL TALK TO GORDON.
TOLD YOU.
I'M COMING.

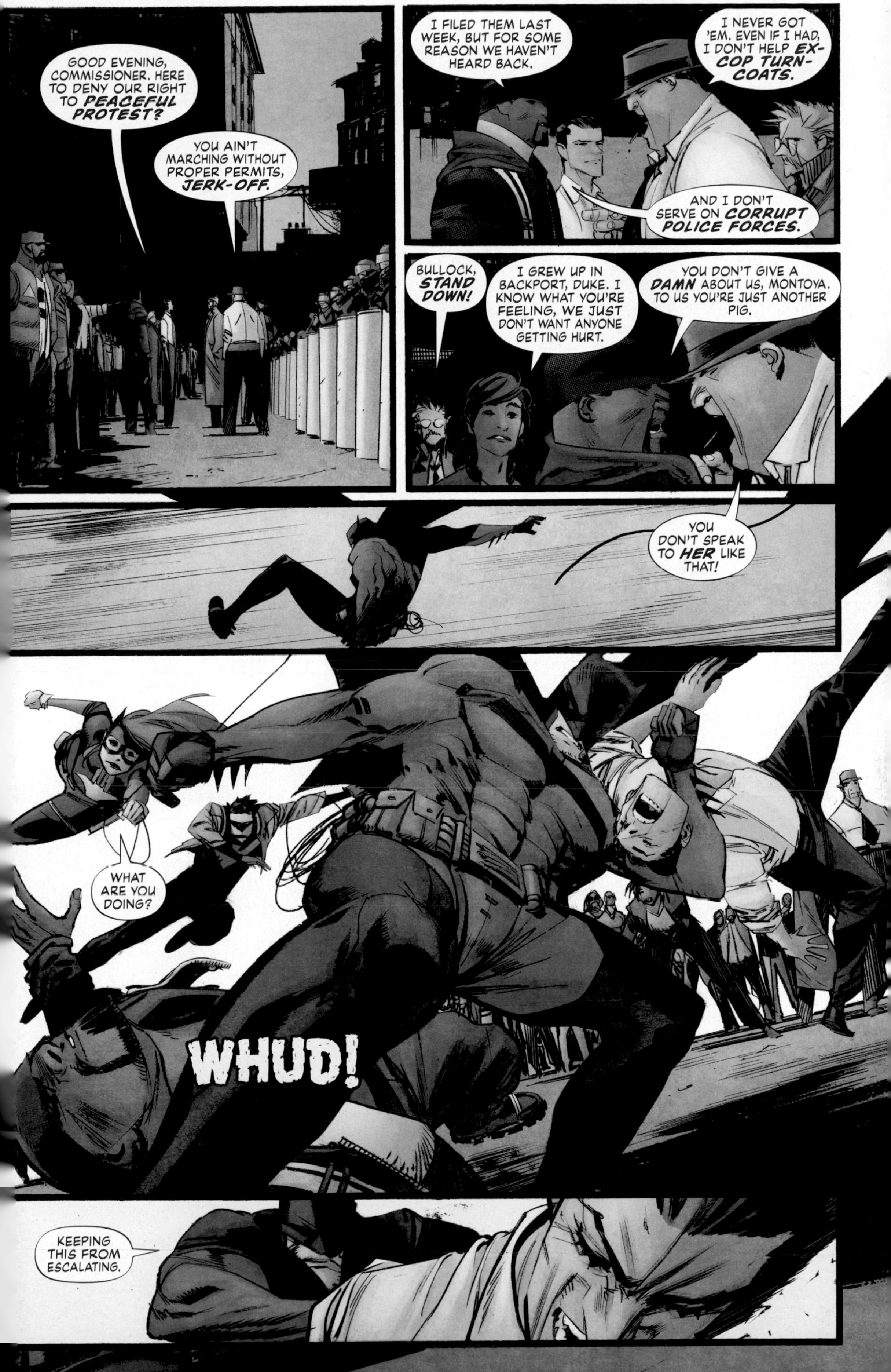
GOOD EVENING, COMMISSIONER. HERE TO DENY OUR RIGHT TO PEACEFUL PROTEST?
YOU AIN'T MARCHING WITHOUT PROPER PERMITS, JERK-OFF.
I FILED THEM LAST WEEK, BUT FOR SOME REASON WE HAVEN'T HEARD BACK.
I NEVER GOT 'EM. EVEN IF I HAD, I DON'T HELP EX-COP TURN-COATS.
AND I DON'T SERVE ON CORRUPT POLICE FORCES.
BULLOCK, STAND DOWN!
I GREW UP IN BACKPORT, DUKE. I KNOW WHAT YOU'RE FEELING, WE JUST DON'T WANT ANYONE GETTING HURT.
YOU DON'T GIVE A DAMN ABOUT US, MONTOYA. TO US YOU'RE JUST ANOTHER PIG.
YOU DON'T SPEAK TO HER LIKE THAT!
WHAT ARE YOU DOING?
WHUD!
KEEPING THIS FROM ESCALATING.

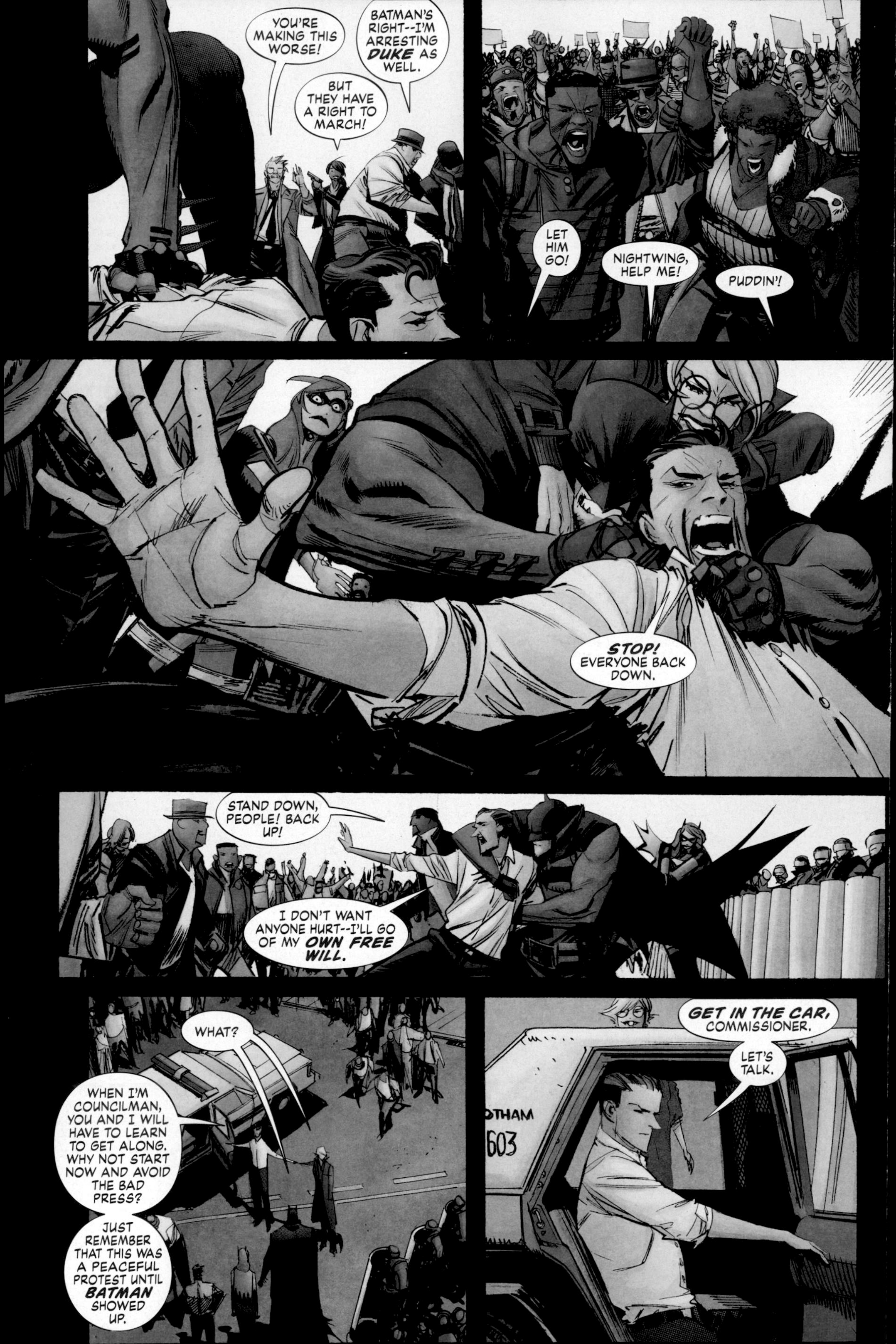
YOU'RE MAKING THIS WORSE!
BUT THEY HAVE A RIGHT TO MARCH!
BATMAN'S RIGHT--I'M ARRESTING DUKE AS WELL.
LET HIM GO!
NIGHTWING, HELP ME!
PUDDIN'!
STOP! EVERYONE BACK DOWN.
STAND DOWN, PEOPLE! BACK UP!
I DON'T WANT ANYONE HURT--I'LL GO OF MY OWN FREE WILL.
WHAT?
WHEN I'M COUNCILMAN, YOU AND I WILL HAVE TO LEARN TO GET ALONG. WHY NOT START NOW AND AVOID THE BAD PRESS?
JUST REMEMBER THAT THIS WAS A PEACEFUL PROTEST UNTIL BATMAN SHOWED UP.
GET IN THE CAR, COMMISSIONER.
LET'S TALK.

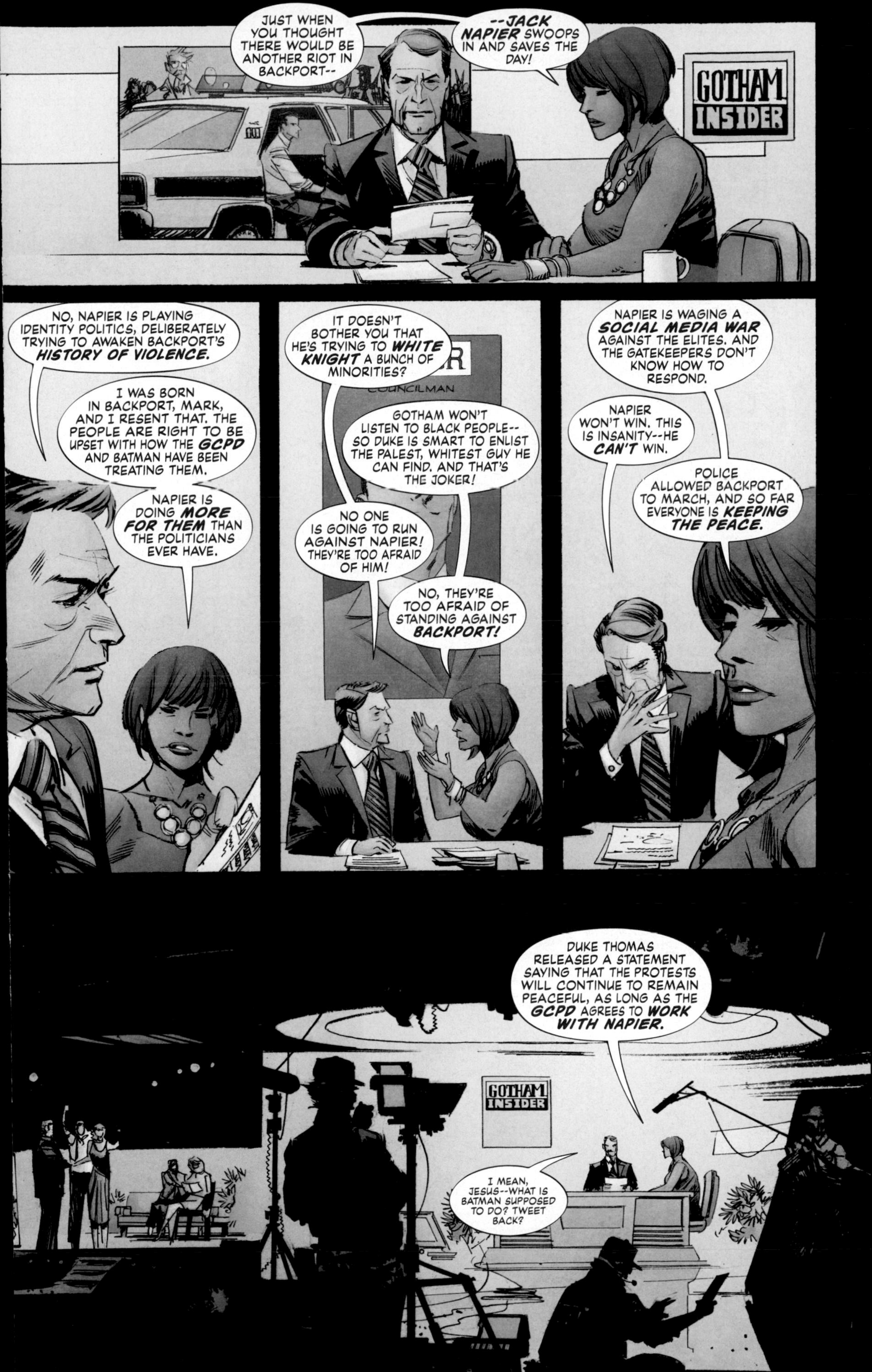
JUST WHEN YOU THOUGHT THERE WOULD BE ANOTHER RIOT IN BACKPORT--
--JACK NAPIER SWOOPS IN AND SAVES THE DAY!
GOTHAM INSIDER
NO, NAPIER IS PLAYING IDENTITY POLITICS, DELIBERATELY TRYING TO AWAKEN BACKPORT'S HISTORY OF VIOLENCE.
I WAS BORN IN BACKPORT, MARK, AND I RESENT THAT. THE PEOPLE ARE RIGHT TO BE UPSET WITH HOW THE GCPD AND BATMAN HAVE BEEN TREATING THEM.
NAPIER IS DOING MORE FOR THEM THAN THE POLITICIANS EVER HAVE.
IT DOESN'T BOTHER YOU THAT HE'S TRYING TO WHITE KNIGHT A BUNCH OF MINORITIES?
COUNCILMAN
GOTHAM WON'T LISTEN TO BLACK PEOPLE--SO DUKE IS SMART TO ENLIST THE PALEST, WHITEST GUY HE CAN FIND. AND THAT'S THE JOKER!
NO ONE IS GOING TO RUN AGAINST NAPIER! THEY'RE TOO AFRAID OF HIM!
NO, THEY'RE TOO AFRAID OF STANDING AGAINST BACKPORT!
NAPIER IS WAGING A SOCIAL MEDIA WAR AGAINST THE ELITES. AND THE GATEKEEPERS DON'T KNOW HOW TO RESPOND.
NAPIER WON'T WIN. THIS IS INSANITY--HE CAN'T WIN.
POLICE ALLOWED BACKPORT TO MARCH, AND SO FAR EVERYONE IS KEEPING THE PEACE.
DUKE THOMAS RELEASED A STATEMENT SAYING THAT THE PROTESTS WILL CONTINUE TO REMAIN PEACEFUL, AS LONG AS THE GCPD AGREES TO WORK WITH NAPIER.
GOTHAM INSIDER
I MEAN, JESUS--WHAT IS BATMAN SUPPOSED TO DO? TWEET BACK?

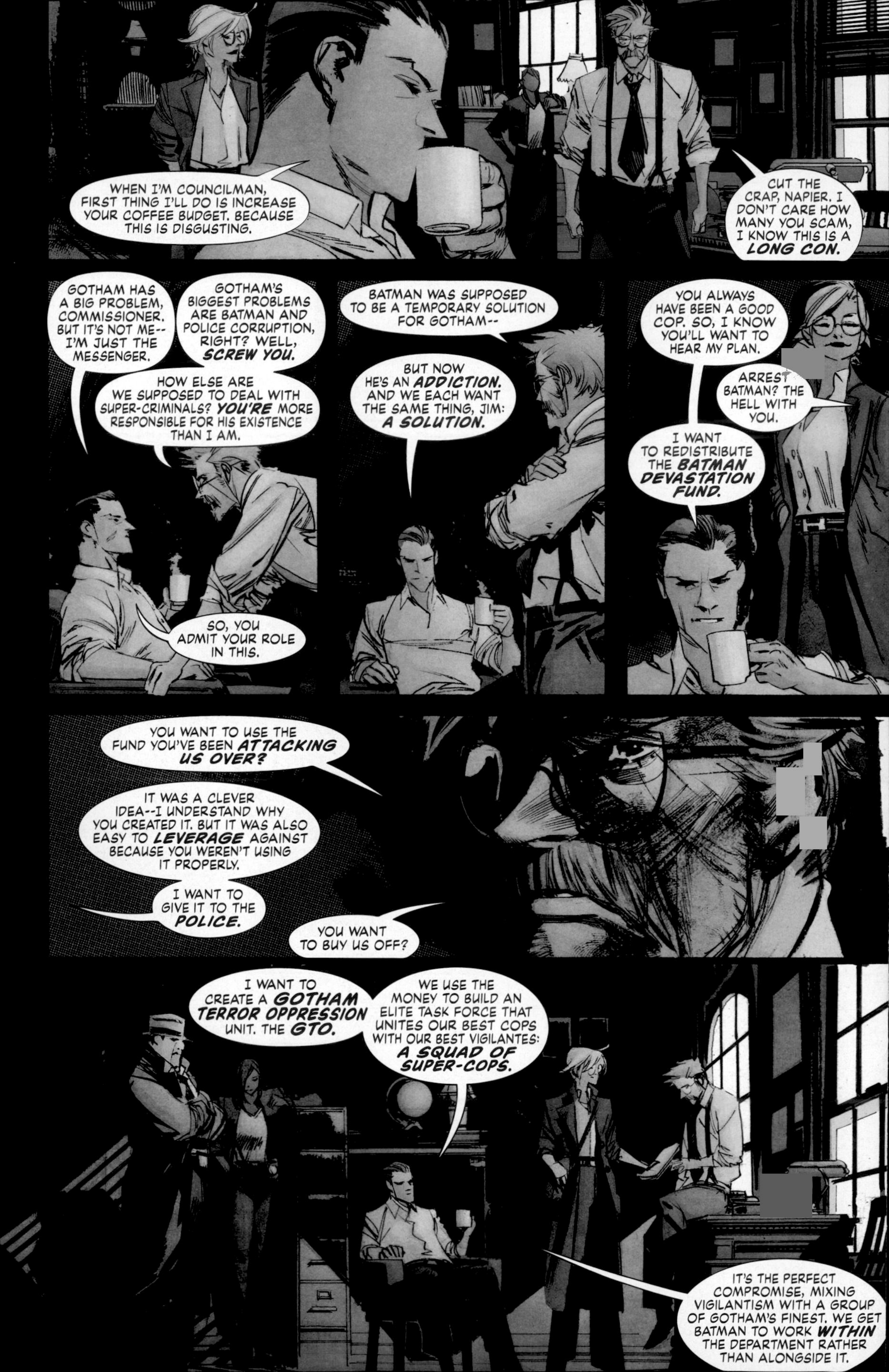
WHEN I'M COUNCILMAN, FIRST THING I'LL DO IS INCREASE YOUR COFFEE BUDGET. BECAUSE THIS IS DISGUSTING.
CUT THE CRAP, NAPIER. I DON'T CARE HOW MANY YOU SCAM, I KNOW THIS IS A LONG CON.
GOTHAM HAS A BIG PROBLEM, COMMISSIONER. BUT IT'S NOT ME--I'M JUST THE MESSENGER.
GOTHAM'S BIGGEST PROBLEMS ARE BATMAN AND POLICE CORRUPTION, RIGHT? WELL, SCREW YOU.
HOW ELSE ARE WE SUPPOSED TO DEAL WITH SUPER-CRIMINALS? YOU'RE MORE RESPONSIBLE FOR HIS EXISTENCE THAN I AM.
SO, YOU ADMIT YOUR ROLE IN THIS.
BATMAN WAS SUPPOSED TO BE A TEMPORARY SOLUTION FOR GOTHAM--
BUT NOW HE'S AN ADDICTION. AND WE EACH WANT THE SAME THING, JIM: A SOLUTION.
YOU ALWAYS HAVE BEEN A GOOD COP. SO, I KNOW YOU'LL WANT TO HEAR MY PLAN.
ARREST BATMAN? THE HELL WITH YOU.
I WANT TO REDISTRIBUTE THE BATMAN DEVASTATION FUND.
YOU WANT TO USE THE FUND YOU'VE BEEN ATTACKING US OVER?
IT WAS A CLEVER IDEA--I UNDERSTAND WHY YOU CREATED IT. BUT IT WAS ALSO EASY TO LEVERAGE AGAINST BECAUSE YOU WEREN'T USING IT PROPERLY.
I WANT TO GIVE IT TO THE POLICE.
YOU WANT TO BUY US OFF?
I WANT TO CREATE A GOTHAM TERROR OPPRESSION UNIT. THE GTO.
WE USE THE MONEY TO BUILD AN ELITE TASK FORCE THAT UNITES OUR BEST COPS WITH OUR BEST VIGILANTES: A SQUAD OF SUPER-COPS.
IT'S THE PERFECT COMPROMISE, MIXING VIGILANTISM WITH A GROUP OF GOTHAM'S FINEST. WE GET BATMAN TO WORK WITHIN THE DEPARTMENT RATHER THAN ALONGSIDE IT.

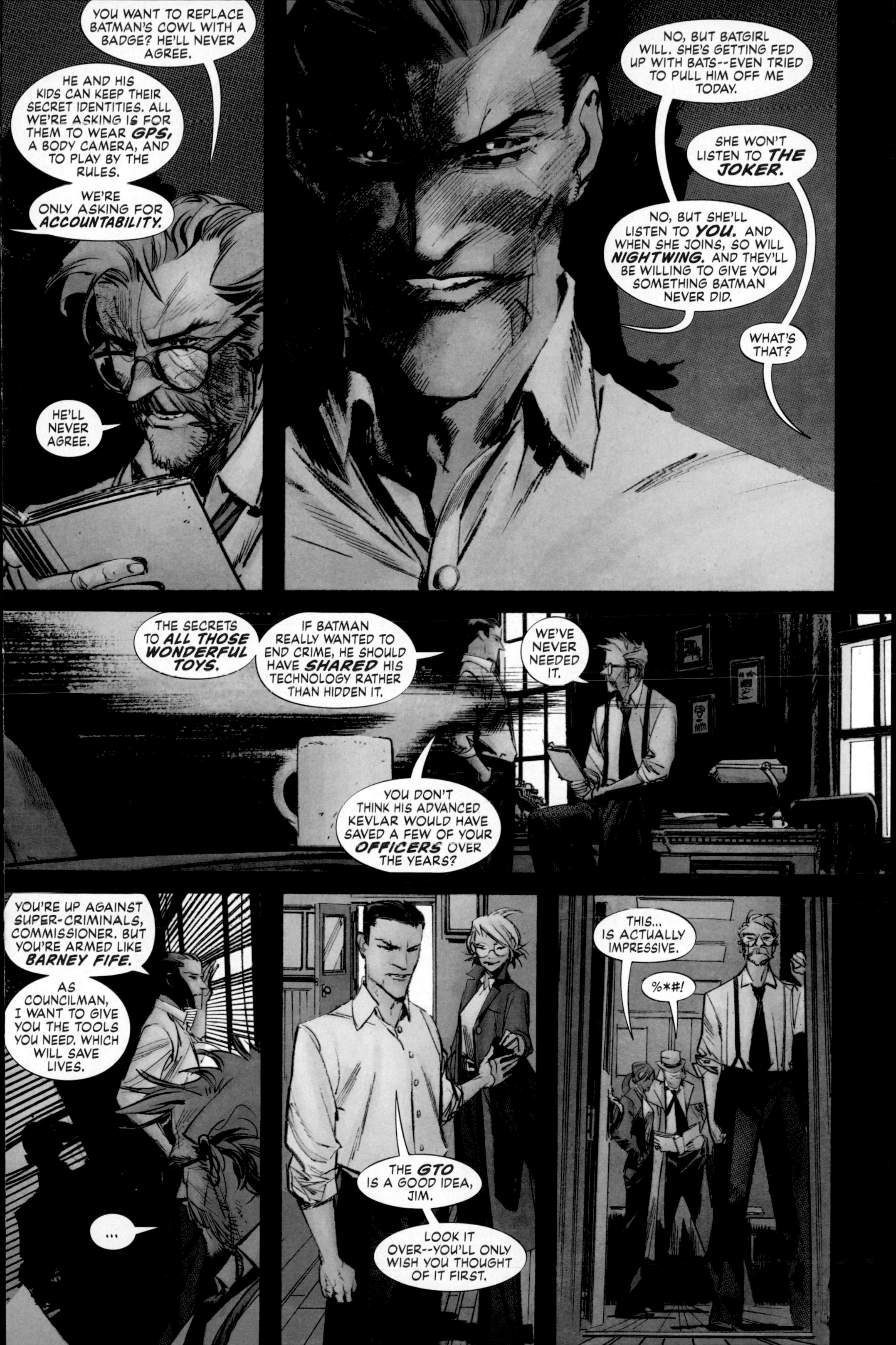
YOU WANT TO REPLACE BATMAN'S COWL WITH A BADGE? HE'LL NEVER AGREE.
HE AND HIS KIDS CAN KEEP THEIR SECRET IDENTITIES. ALL WE'RE ASKING IS FOR THEM TO WEAR GPS, A BODY CAMERA, AND TO PLAY BY THE RULES.
WE'RE ONLY ASKING FOR ACCOUNTABILITY.
HE'LL NEVER AGREE.
NO, BUT BATGIRL WILL. SHE'S GETTING FED UP WITH BATS--EVEN TRIED TO PULL HIM OFF ME TODAY.
SHE WON'T LISTEN TO THE JOKER.
NO, BUT SHE'LL LISTEN TO YOU. AND WHEN SHE JOINS, SO WILL NIGHTWING. AND THEY'LL BE WILLING TO GIVE YOU SOMETHING BATMAN NEVER DID.
WHAT'S THAT?
THE SECRETS TO ALL THOSE WONDERFUL TOYS.
IF BATMAN REALLY WANTED TO END CRIME, HE SHOULD HAVE SHARED HIS TECHNOLOGY RATHER THAN HIDDEN IT.
WE'VE NEVER NEEDED IT.
YOU DON'T THINK HIS ADVANCED KEVLAR WOULD HAVE SAVED A FEW OF YOUR OFFICERS OVER THE YEARS?
YOU'RE UP AGAINST SUPER-CRIMINALS, COMMISSIONER. BUT YOU'RE ARMED LIKE BARNEY FIFE.
AS COUNCILMAN, I WANT TO GIVE YOU THE TOOLS YOU NEED. WHICH WILL SAVE LIVES.
...
THE GTO IS A GOOD IDEA, JIM.
LOOK IT OVER--YOU'LL ONLY WISH YOU THOUGHT OF IT FIRST.
THIS... IS ACTUALLY IMPRESSIVE.
%*#!

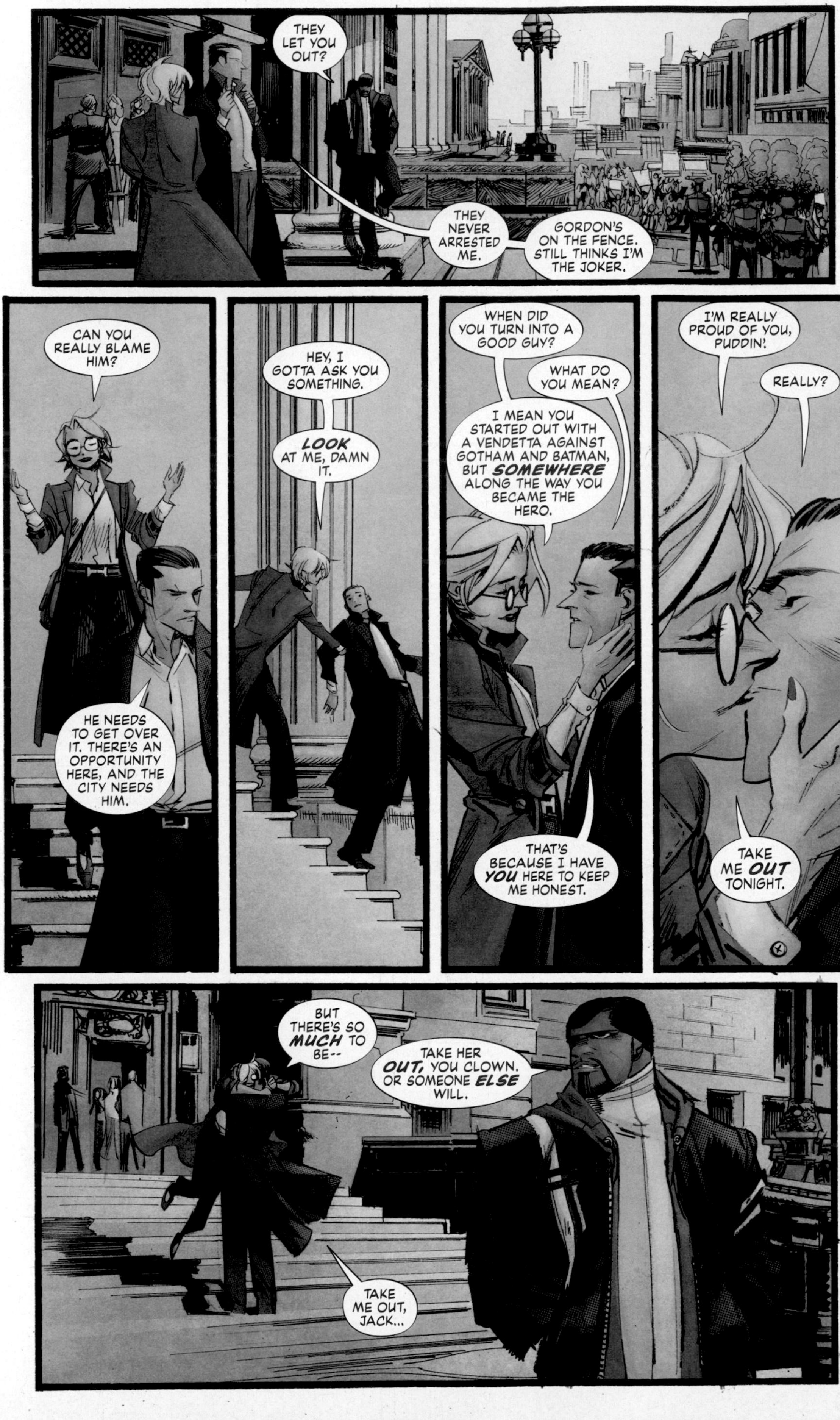

THEY LET YOU OUT?
THEY NEVER ARRESTED ME.
GORDON'S ON THE FENCE. STILL THINKS I'M THE JOKER.
CAN YOU REALLY BLAME HIM?
HE NEEDS TO GET OVER IT. THERE'S AN OPPORTUNITY HERE, AND THE CITY NEEDS HIM.
HEY, I GOTTA ASK YOU SOMETHING.
LOOK AT ME, DAMN IT.
WHEN DID YOU TURN INTO A GOOD GUY?
WHAT DO YOU MEAN?
I MEAN YOU STARTED OUT WITH A VENDETTA AGAINST GOTHAM AND BATMAN, BUT SOMEWHERE ALONG THE WAY YOU BECAME THE HERO.
THAT'S BECAUSE I HAVE YOU HERE TO KEEP ME HONEST.
I'M REALLY PROUD OF YOU, PUDDIN'.
REALLY?
TAKE ME OUT TONIGHT.
BUT THERE'S SO MUCH TO BE--
TAKE HER OUT, YOU CLOWN. OR SOMEONE ELSE WILL.
TAKE ME OUT, JACK...

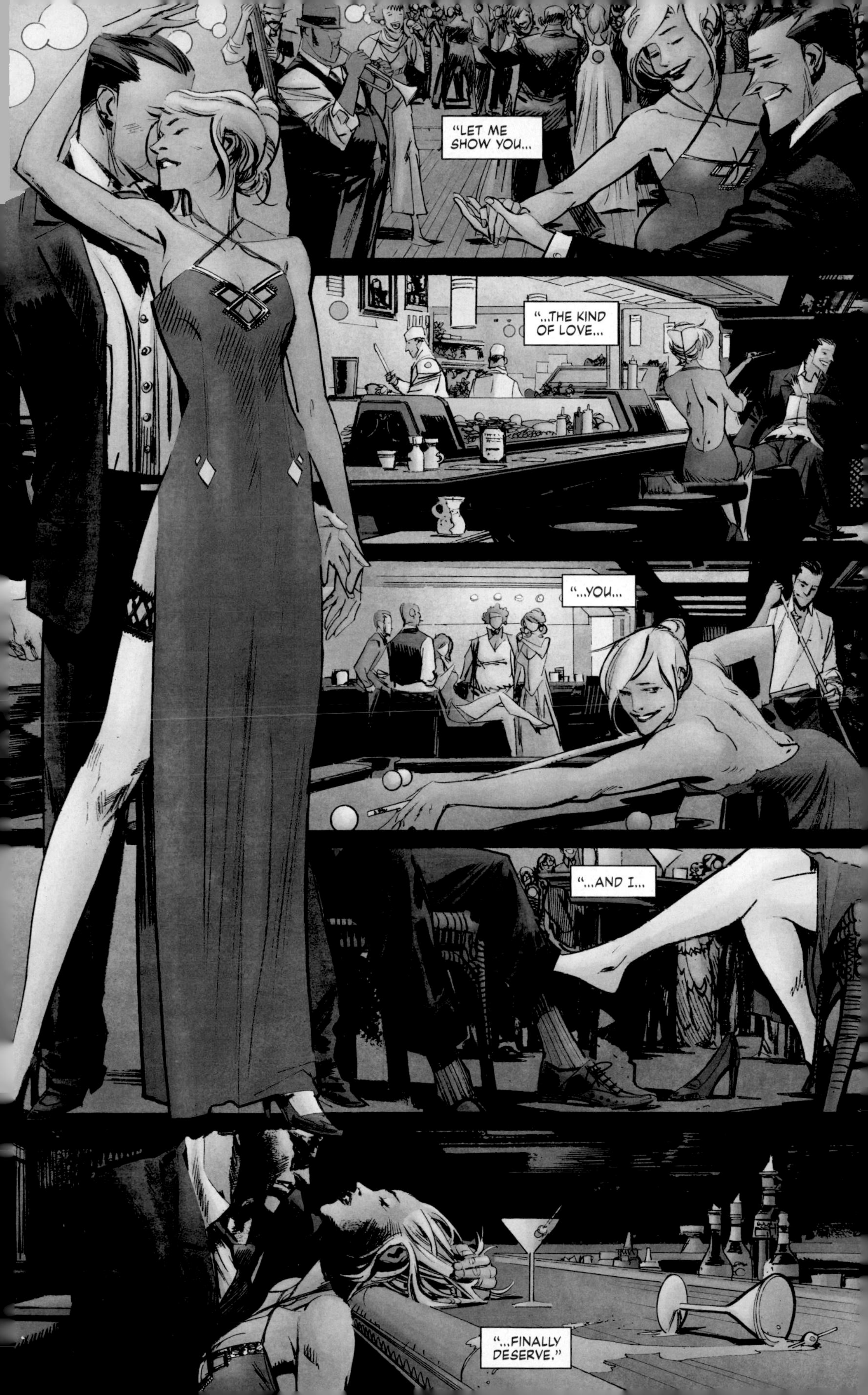
"LET ME SHOW YOU...
"...THE KIND OF LOVE...
"...YOU...
"...AND I...
"...FINALLY DESERVE."

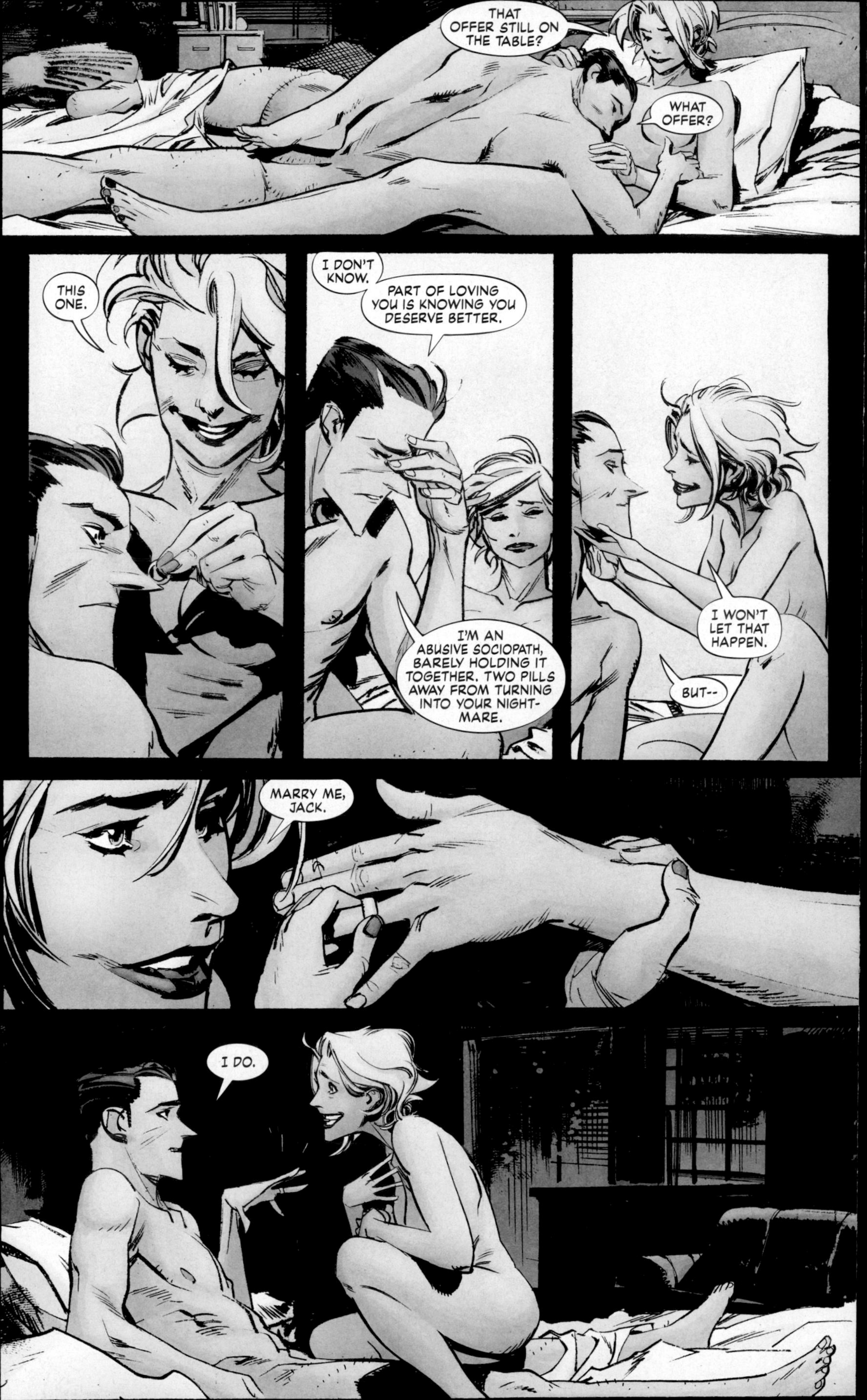
THAT OFFER STILL ON THE TABLE?
WHAT OFFER?
THIS ONE.
I DON'T KNOW.
PART OF LOVING YOU IS KNOWING YOU DESERVE BETTER.
I'M AN ABUSIVE SOCIOPATH, BARELY HOLDING IT TOGETHER. TWO PILLS AWAY FROM TURNING INTO YOUR NIGHT-MARE.
I WON'T LET THAT HAPPEN.
BUT--
MARRY ME, JACK.
I DO.

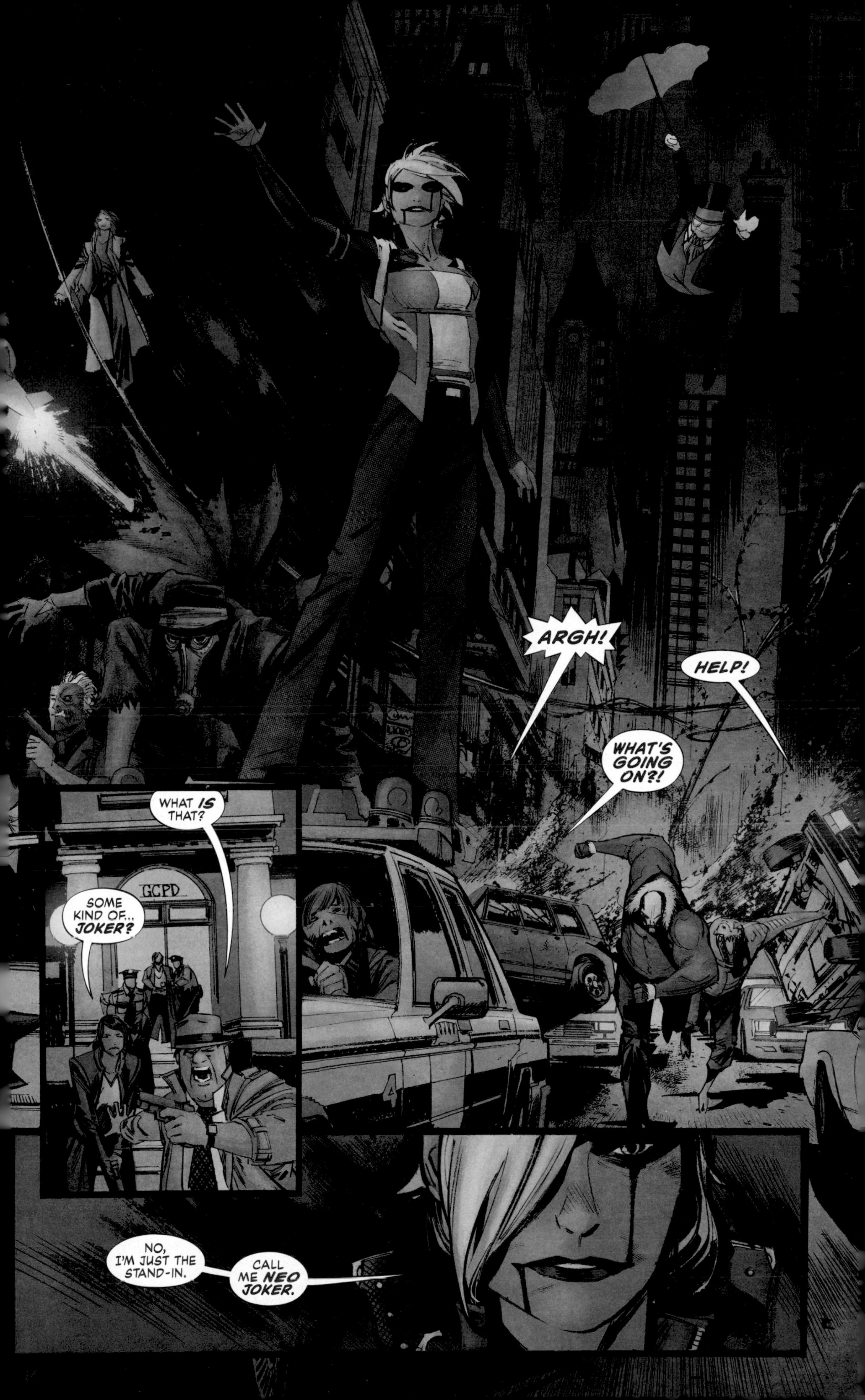

ARGH!
HELP!
WHAT'S GOING ON?!
WHAT *IS* THAT?
SOME KIND OF... *JOKER?*
GCPD
NO, I'M JUST THE STAND-IN.
CALL ME *NEO JOKER.*

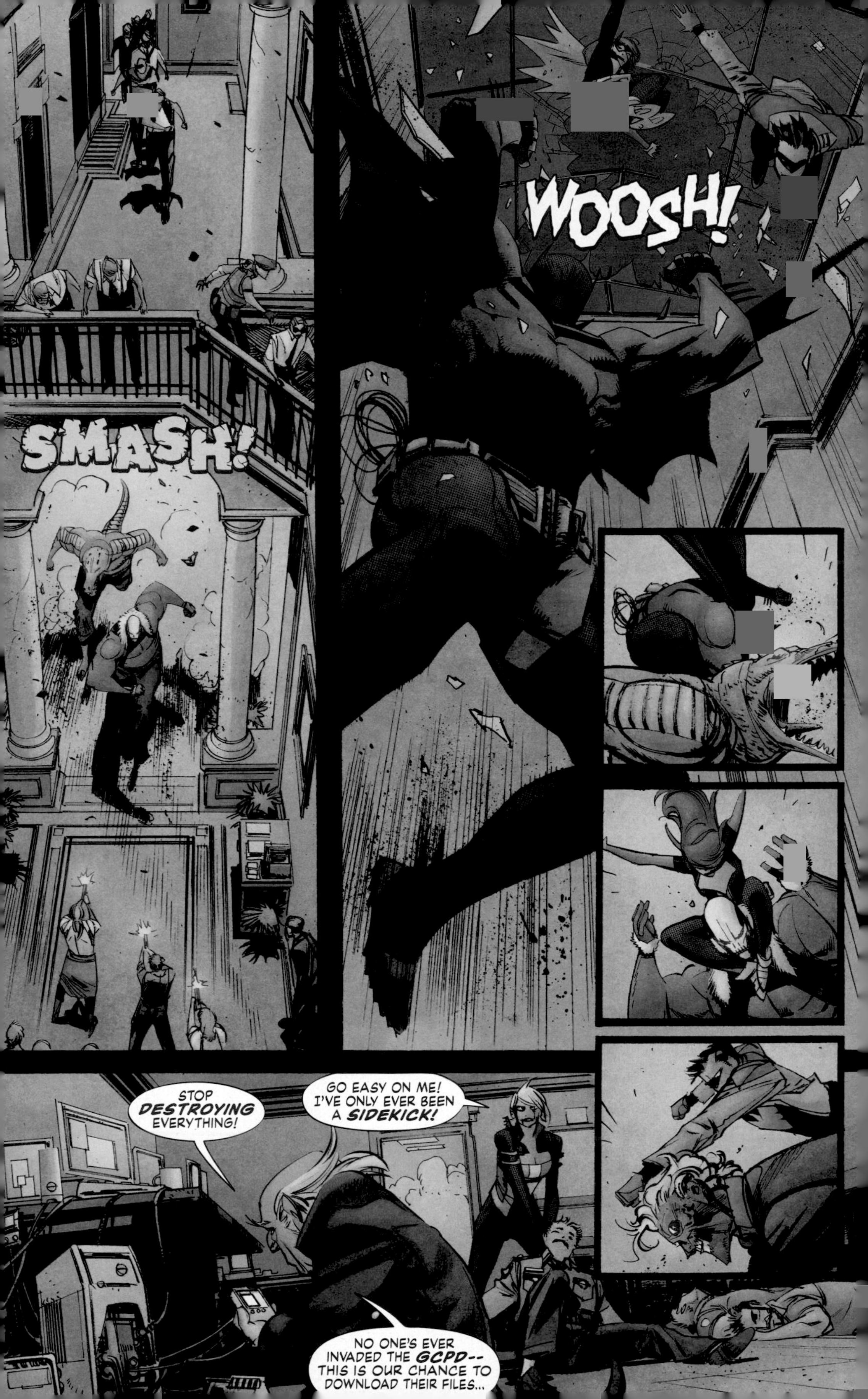
SMASH!
WOOSH!
STOP DESTROYING EVERYTHING!
GO EASY ON ME! I'VE ONLY EVER BEEN A SIDEKICK!
NO ONE'S EVER INVADED THE GCPD-- THIS IS OUR CHANCE TO DOWNLOAD THEIR FILES...

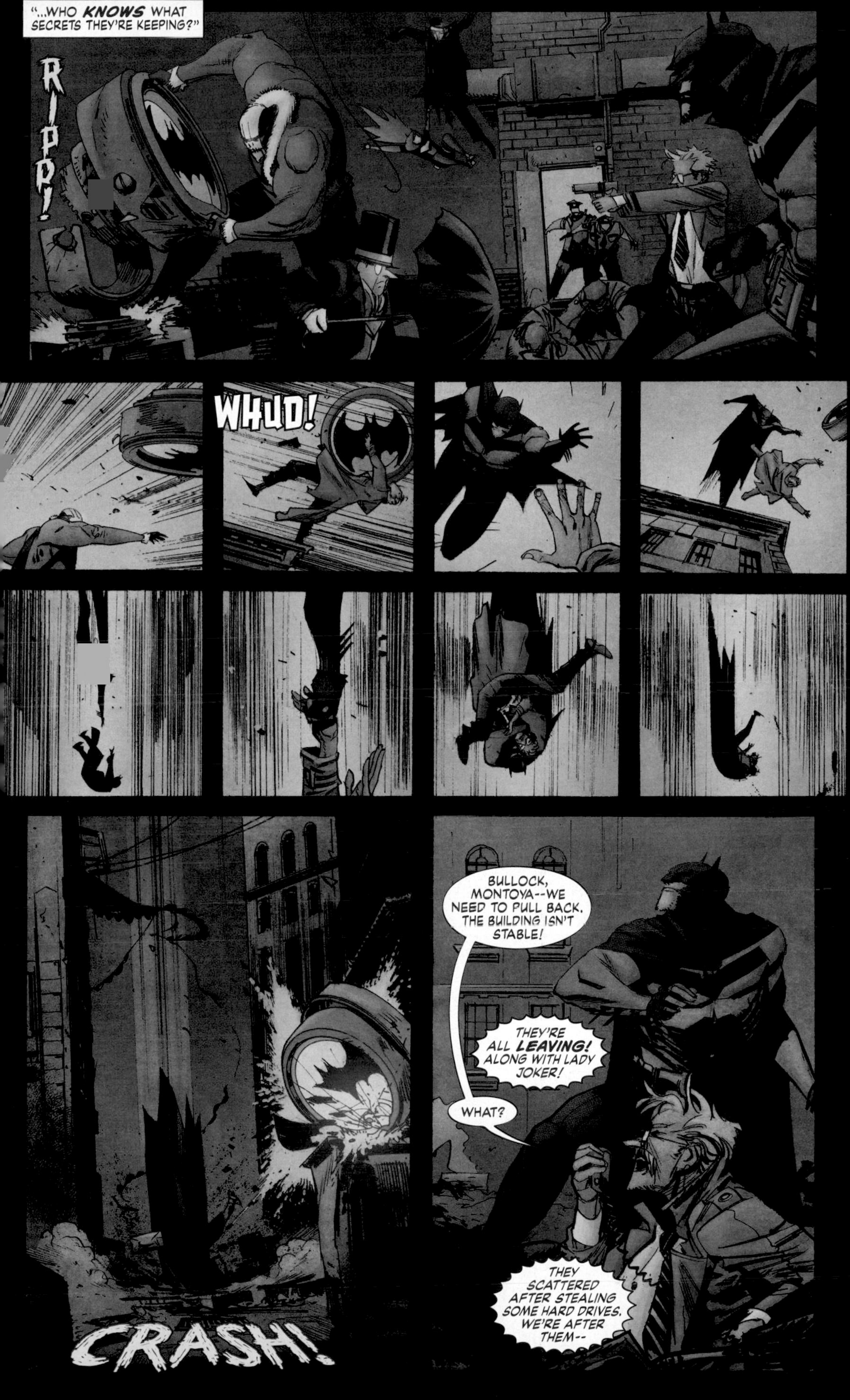
"...WHO **KNOWS** WHAT SECRETS THEY'RE KEEPING?"
RIPP!
WHUD!
CRASH!
BULLOCK, MONTOYA--WE NEED TO PULL BACK. THE BUILDING ISN'T STABLE!
THEY'RE ALL **LEAVING!** ALONG WITH LADY JOKER!
WHAT?
THEY SCATTERED AFTER STEALING SOME HARD DRIVES. WE'RE AFTER THEM--

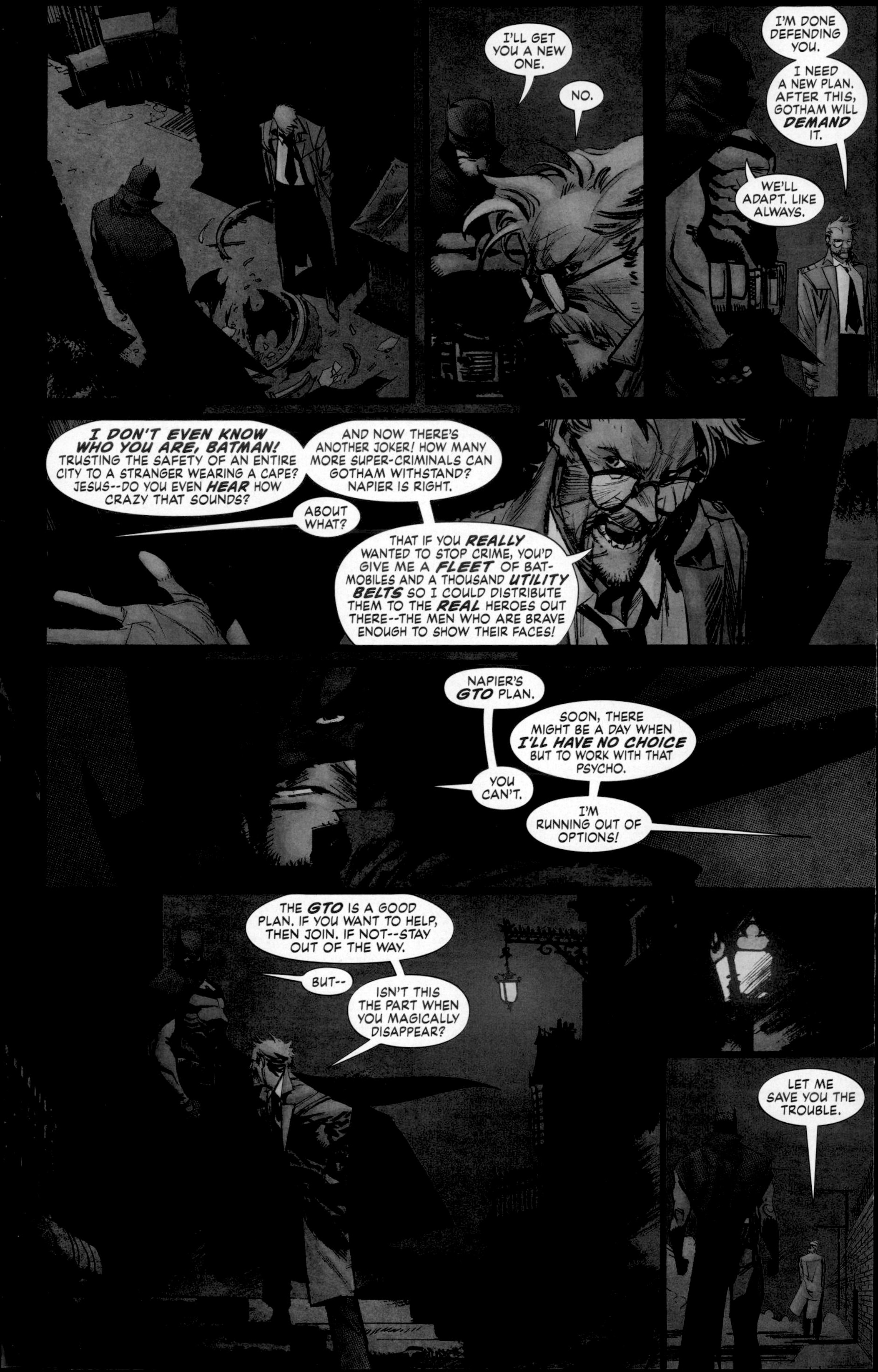
I'LL GET YOU A NEW ONE.
NO.
I'M DONE DEFENDING YOU.
I NEED A NEW PLAN. AFTER THIS, GOTHAM WILL DEMAND IT.
WE'LL ADAPT. LIKE ALWAYS.
I DON'T EVEN KNOW WHO YOU ARE, BATMAN! TRUSTING THE SAFETY OF AN ENTIRE CITY TO A STRANGER WEARING A CAPE? JESUS--DO YOU EVEN HEAR HOW CRAZY THAT SOUNDS?
AND NOW THERE'S ANOTHER JOKER! HOW MANY MORE SUPER-CRIMINALS CAN GOTHAM WITHSTAND? NAPIER IS RIGHT.
ABOUT WHAT?
THAT IF YOU REALLY WANTED TO STOP CRIME, YOU'D GIVE ME A FLEET OF BAT-MOBILES AND A THOUSAND UTILITY BELTS SO I COULD DISTRIBUTE THEM TO THE REAL HEROES OUT THERE--THE MEN WHO ARE BRAVE ENOUGH TO SHOW THEIR FACES!
NAPIER'S GTO PLAN.
YOU CAN'T.
SOON, THERE MIGHT BE A DAY WHEN I'LL HAVE NO CHOICE BUT TO WORK WITH THAT PSYCHO.
I'M RUNNING OUT OF OPTIONS!
THE GTO IS A GOOD PLAN. IF YOU WANT TO HELP, THEN JOIN. IF NOT--STAY OUT OF THE WAY.
BUT--
ISN'T THIS THE PART WHEN YOU MAGICALLY DISAPPEAR?
LET ME SAVE YOU THE TROUBLE.

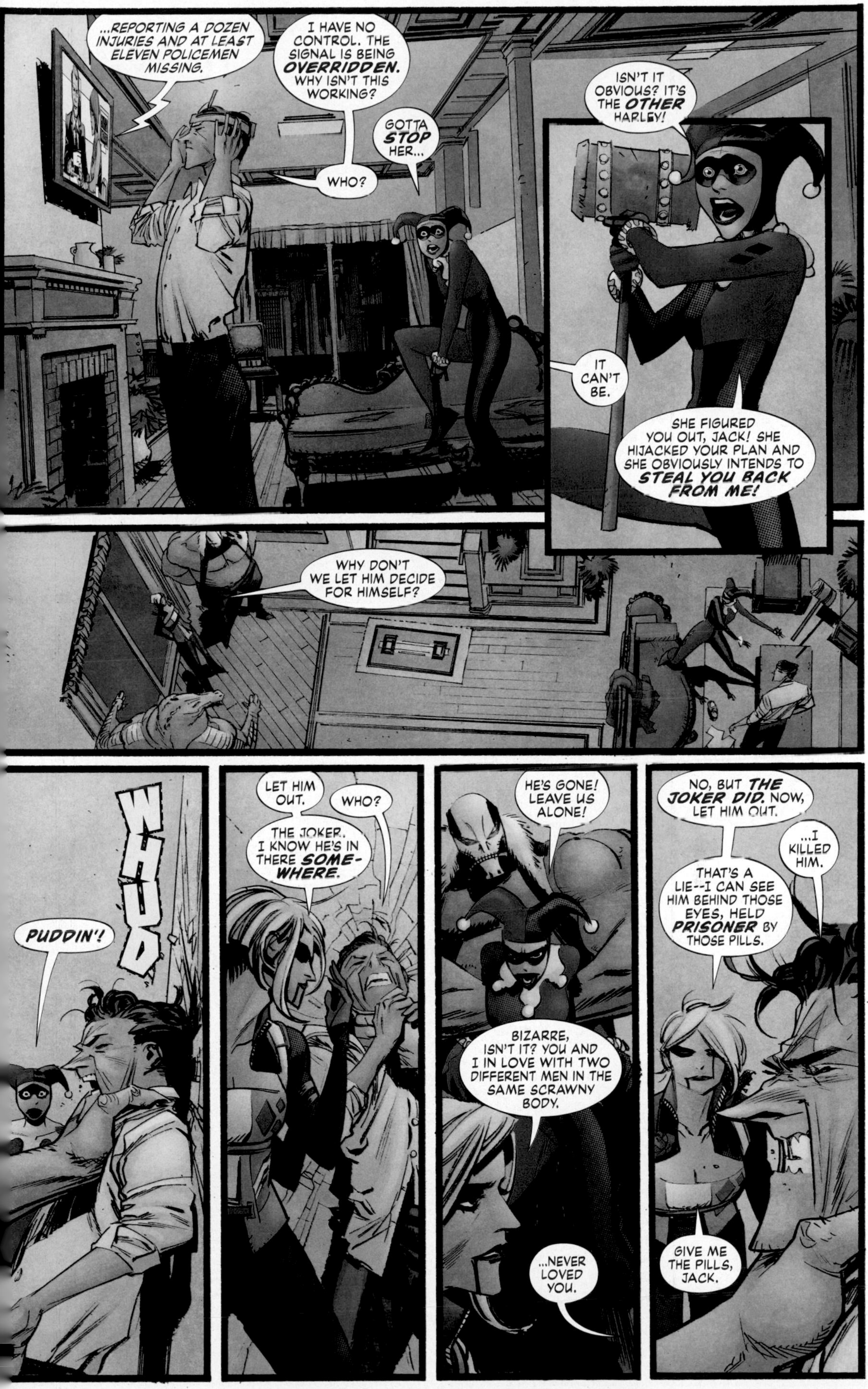

...REPORTING A DOZEN INJURIES AND AT LEAST ELEVEN POLICEMEN MISSING.
I HAVE NO CONTROL. THE SIGNAL IS BEING OVERRIDDEN. WHY ISN'T THIS WORKING?
WHO?
GOTTA STOP HER...
ISN'T IT OBVIOUS? IT'S THE OTHER HARLEY!
IT CAN'T BE.
SHE FIGURED YOU OUT, JACK! SHE HIJACKED YOUR PLAN AND SHE OBVIOUSLY INTENDS TO STEAL YOU BACK FROM ME!
WHY DON'T WE LET HIM DECIDE FOR HIMSELF?
WHUD
PUDDIN'!
LET HIM OUT.
WHO?
THE JOKER. I KNOW HE'S IN THERE SOME-WHERE.
HE'S GONE! LEAVE US ALONE!
BIZARRE, ISN'T IT? YOU AND I IN LOVE WITH TWO DIFFERENT MEN IN THE SAME SCRAWNY BODY.
...NEVER LOVED YOU.
NO, BUT THE JOKER DID. NOW, LET HIM OUT.
...I KILLED HIM.
THAT'S A LIE--I CAN SEE HIM BEHIND THOSE EYES, HELD PRISONER BY THOSE PILLS.
GIVE ME THE PILLS, JACK.

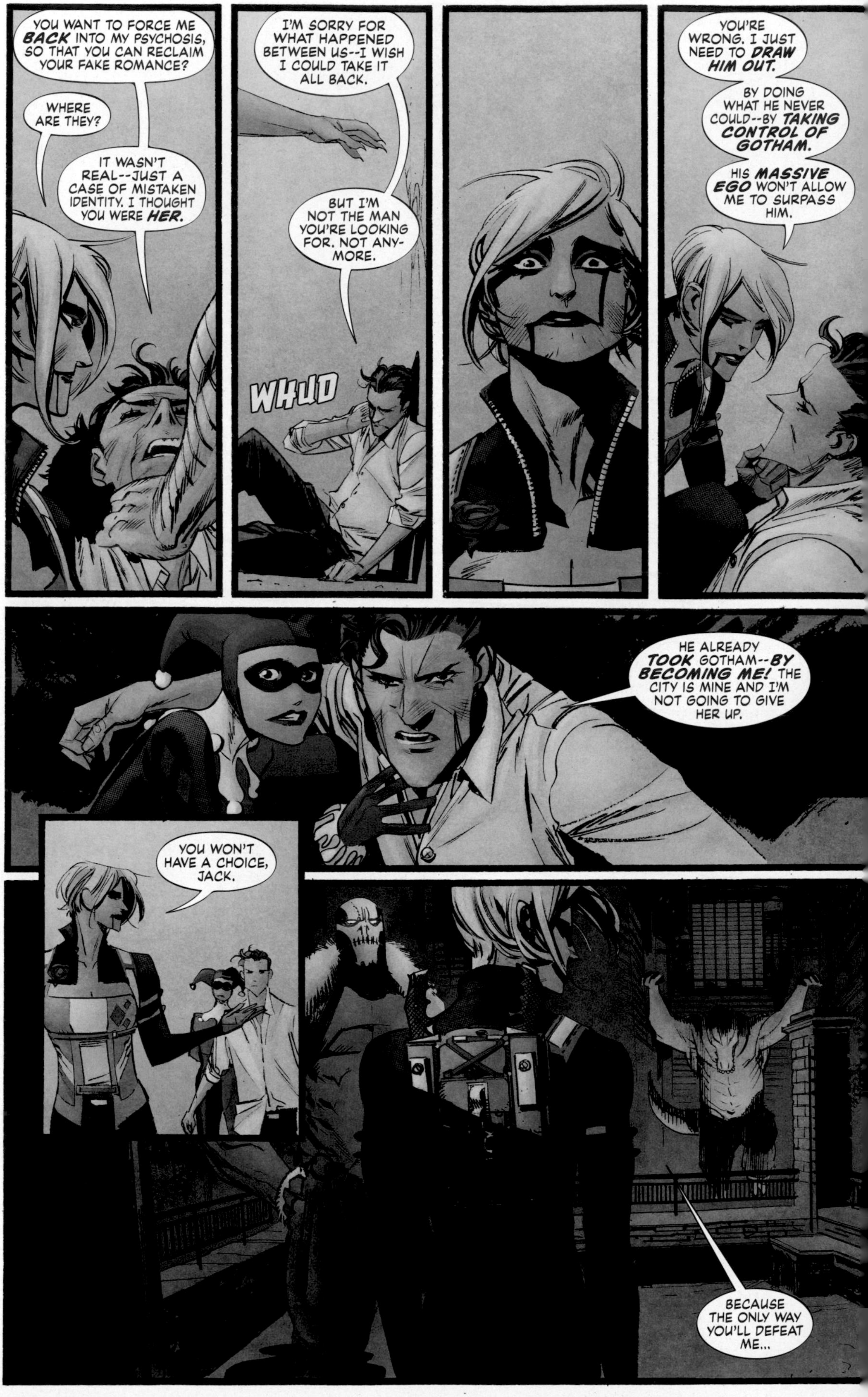
YOU WANT TO FORCE ME BACK INTO MY PSYCHOSIS, SO THAT YOU CAN RECLAIM YOUR FAKE ROMANCE?
WHERE ARE THEY?
IT WASN'T REAL--JUST A CASE OF MISTAKEN IDENTITY. I THOUGHT YOU WERE HER.
I'M SORRY FOR WHAT HAPPENED BETWEEN US--I WISH I COULD TAKE IT ALL BACK.
BUT I'M NOT THE MAN YOU'RE LOOKING FOR. NOT ANY-MORE.
WHUD
YOU'RE WRONG. I JUST NEED TO DRAW HIM OUT.
BY DOING WHAT HE NEVER COULD--BY TAKING CONTROL OF GOTHAM.
HIS MASSIVE EGO WON'T ALLOW ME TO SURPASS HIM.
HE ALREADY TOOK GOTHAM--BY BECOMING ME! THE CITY IS MINE AND I'M NOT GOING TO GIVE HER UP.
YOU WON'T HAVE A CHOICE, JACK.
BECAUSE THE ONLY WAY YOU'LL DEFEAT ME...

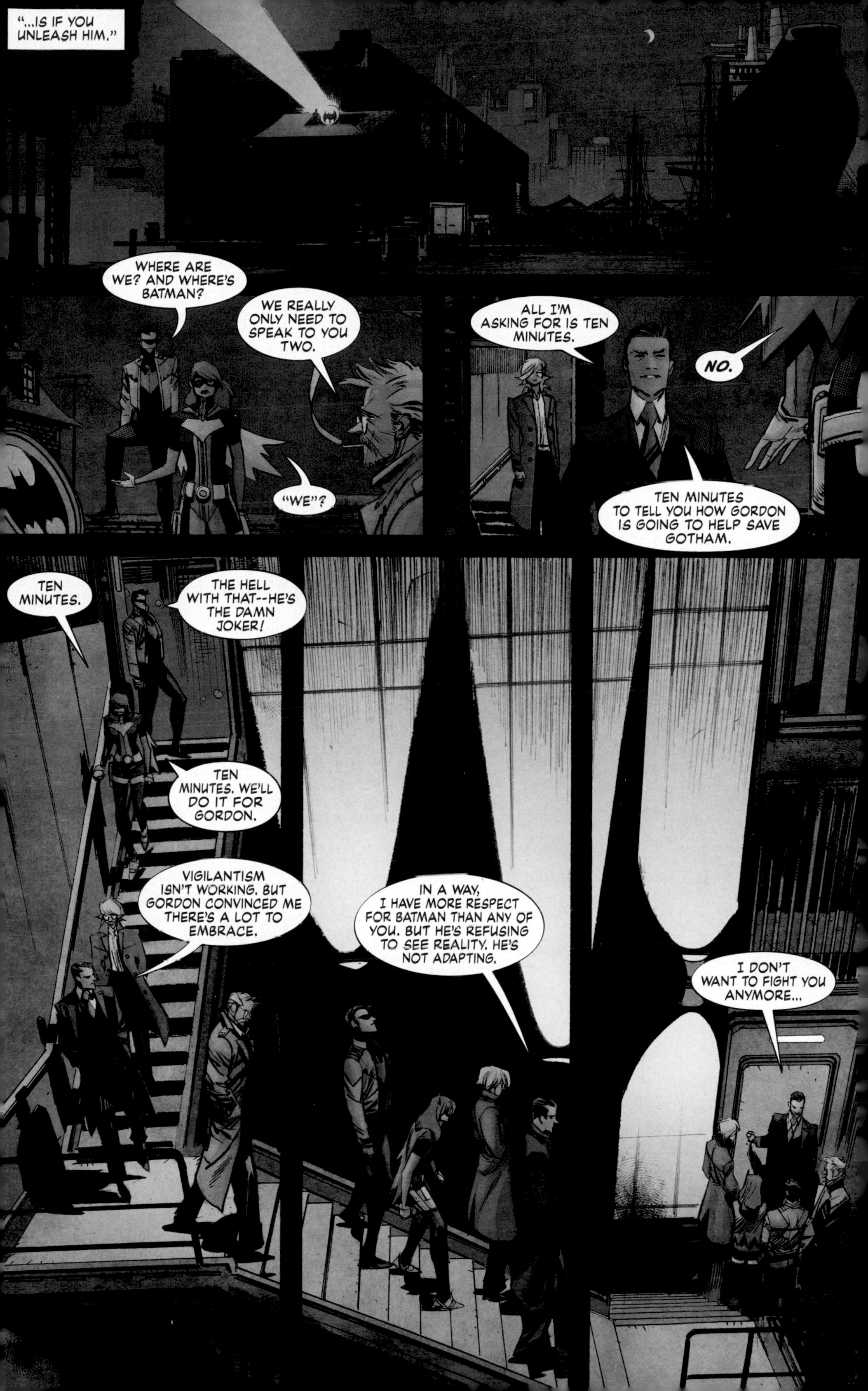
"...IS IF YOU UNLEASH HIM."
WHERE ARE WE? AND WHERE'S BATMAN?
WE REALLY ONLY NEED TO SPEAK TO YOU TWO.
"WE"?
ALL I'M ASKING FOR IS TEN MINUTES.
NO.
TEN MINUTES TO TELL YOU HOW GORDON IS GOING TO HELP SAVE GOTHAM.
TEN MINUTES.
THE HELL WITH THAT--HE'S THE DAMN JOKER!
TEN MINUTES. WE'LL DO IT FOR GORDON.
VIGILANTISM ISN'T WORKING. BUT GORDON CONVINCED ME THERE'S A LOT TO EMBRACE.
IN A WAY, I HAVE MORE RESPECT FOR BATMAN THAN ANY OF YOU. BUT HE'S REFUSING TO SEE REALITY. HE'S NOT ADAPTING.
I DON'T WANT TO FIGHT YOU ANYMORE...

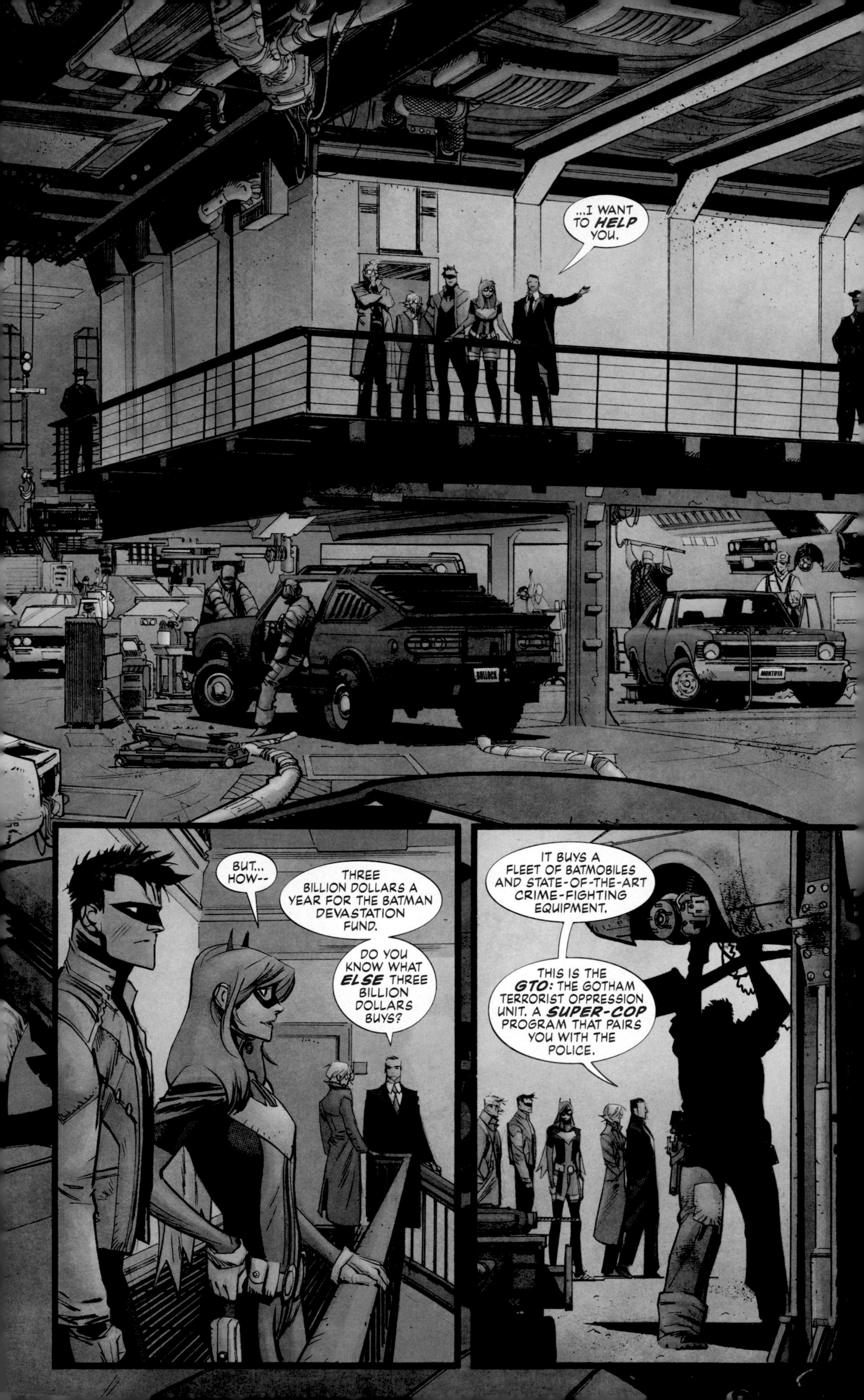
...I WANT TO HELP YOU.
BULLOCK
MONTOYA
BUT... HOW--
THREE BILLION DOLLARS A YEAR FOR THE BATMAN DEVASTATION FUND.
DO YOU KNOW WHAT ELSE THREE BILLION DOLLARS BUYS?
IT BUYS A FLEET OF BATMOBILES AND STATE-OF-THE-ART CRIME-FIGHTING EQUIPMENT.
THIS IS THE GTO: THE GOTHAM TERRORIST OPPRESSION UNIT. A SUPER-COP PROGRAM THAT PAIRS YOU WITH THE POLICE.

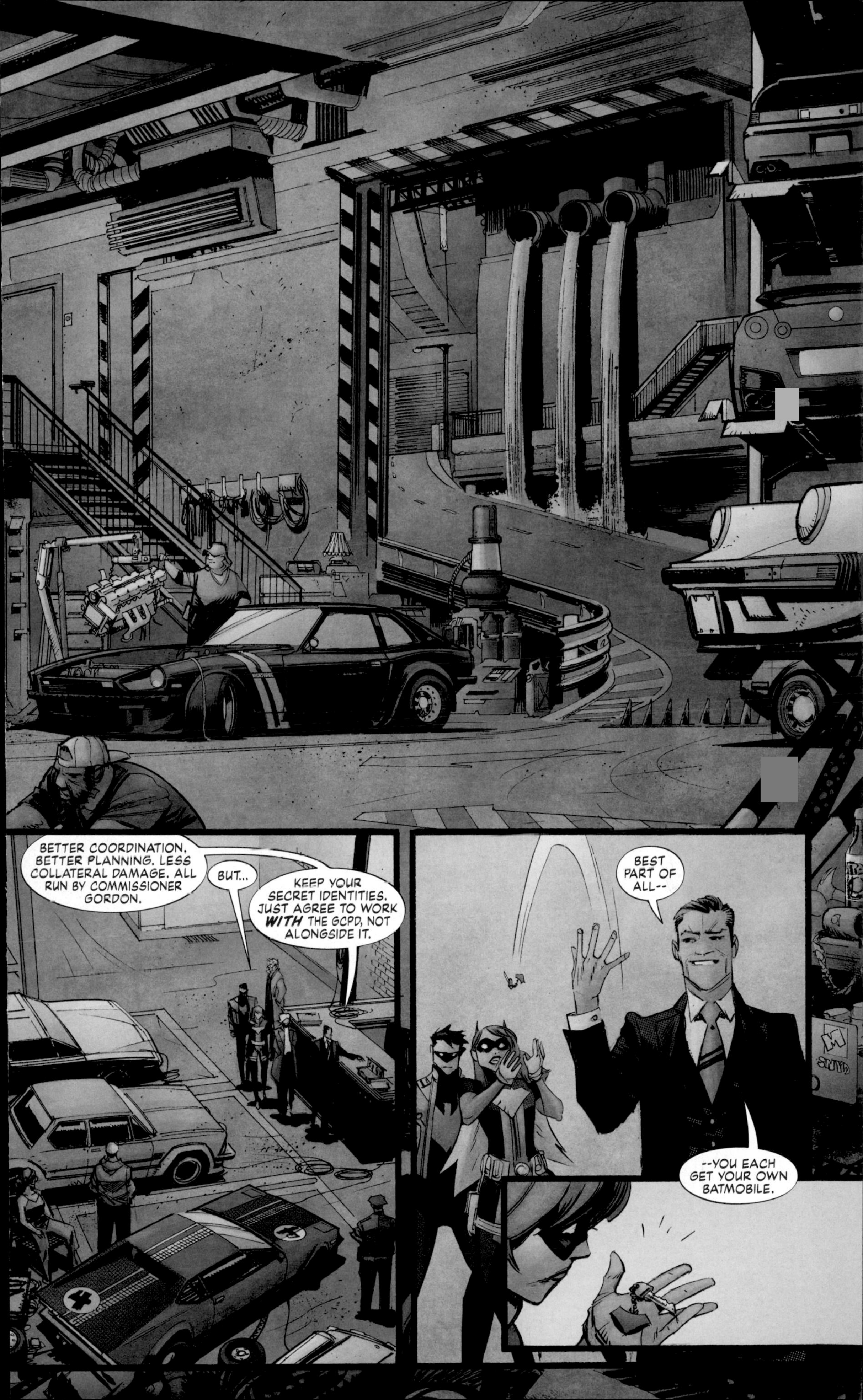
BETTER COORDINATION, BETTER PLANNING. LESS COLLATERAL DAMAGE. ALL RUN BY COMMISSIONER GORDON.
BUT...
KEEP YOUR SECRET IDENTITIES. JUST AGREE TO WORK *WITH* THE GCPD, NOT ALONGSIDE IT.
BEST PART OF ALL--
--YOU EACH GET YOUR OWN BATMOBILE.

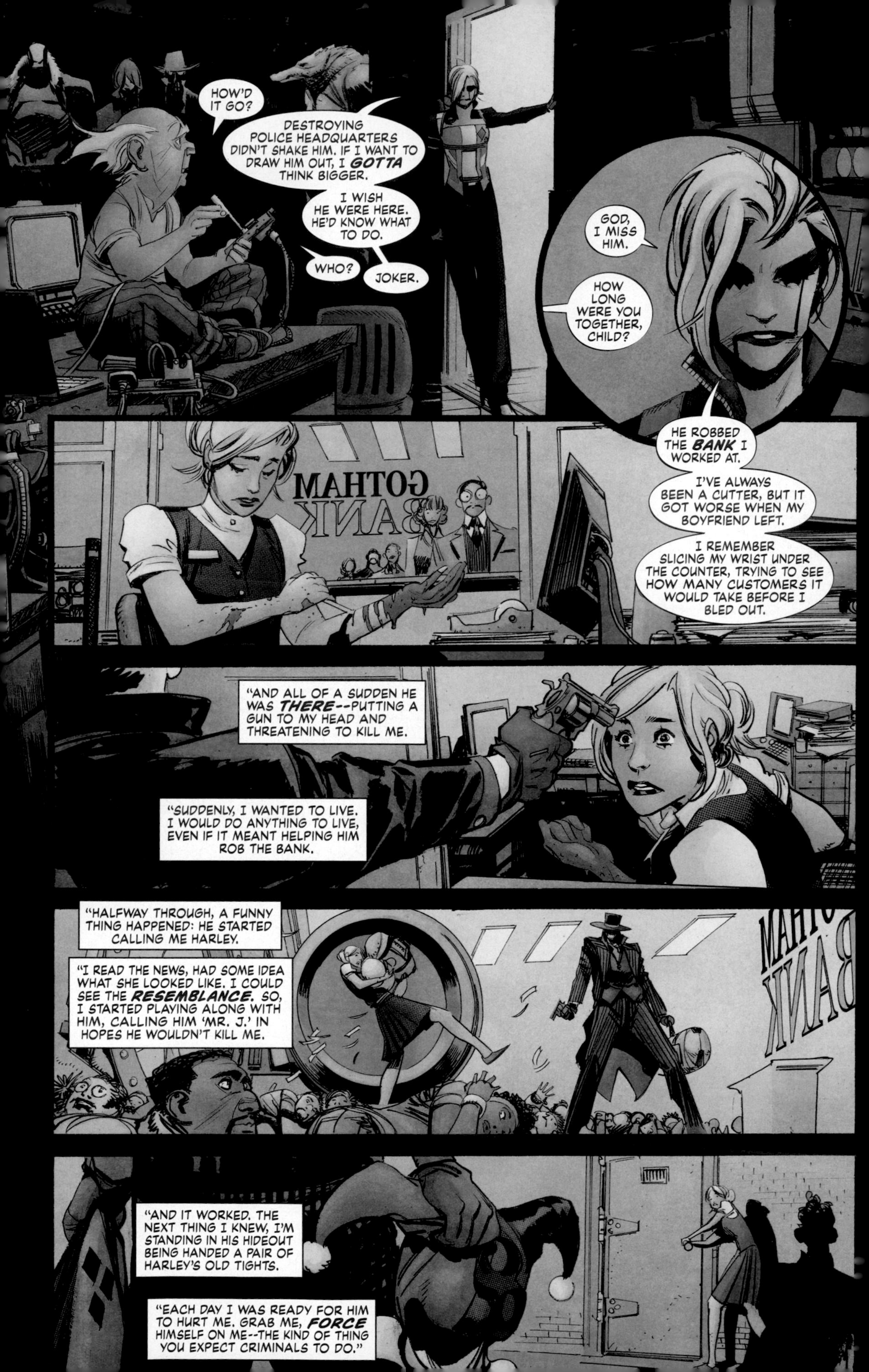
HOW'D IT GO?
DESTROYING POLICE HEADQUARTERS DIDN'T SHAKE HIM. IF I WANT TO DRAW HIM OUT, I GOTTA THINK BIGGER.
I WISH HE WERE HERE. HE'D KNOW WHAT TO DO.
WHO?
JOKER.
GOD, I MISS HIM.
HOW LONG WERE YOU TOGETHER, CHILD?
HE ROBBED THE BANK I WORKED AT.
I'VE ALWAYS BEEN A CUTTER, BUT IT GOT WORSE WHEN MY BOYFRIEND LEFT.
I REMEMBER SLICING MY WRIST UNDER THE COUNTER, TRYING TO SEE HOW MANY CUSTOMERS IT WOULD TAKE BEFORE I BLED OUT.
GOTHAM BANK
"AND ALL OF A SUDDEN HE WAS THERE--PUTTING A GUN TO MY HEAD AND THREATENING TO KILL ME.
"SUDDENLY, I WANTED TO LIVE. I WOULD DO ANYTHING TO LIVE, EVEN IF IT MEANT HELPING HIM ROB THE BANK.
"HALFWAY THROUGH, A FUNNY THING HAPPENED: HE STARTED CALLING ME HARLEY.
"I READ THE NEWS, HAD SOME IDEA WHAT SHE LOOKED LIKE. I COULD SEE THE RESEMBLANCE. SO, I STARTED PLAYING ALONG WITH HIM, CALLING HIM 'MR. J.' IN HOPES HE WOULDN'T KILL ME.
GOTHAM BANK
"AND IT WORKED. THE NEXT THING I KNEW, I'M STANDING IN HIS HIDEOUT BEING HANDED A PAIR OF HARLEY'S OLD TIGHTS.
"EACH DAY I WAS READY FOR HIM TO HURT ME. GRAB ME, FORCE HIMSELF ON ME--THE KIND OF THING YOU EXPECT CRIMINALS TO DO."

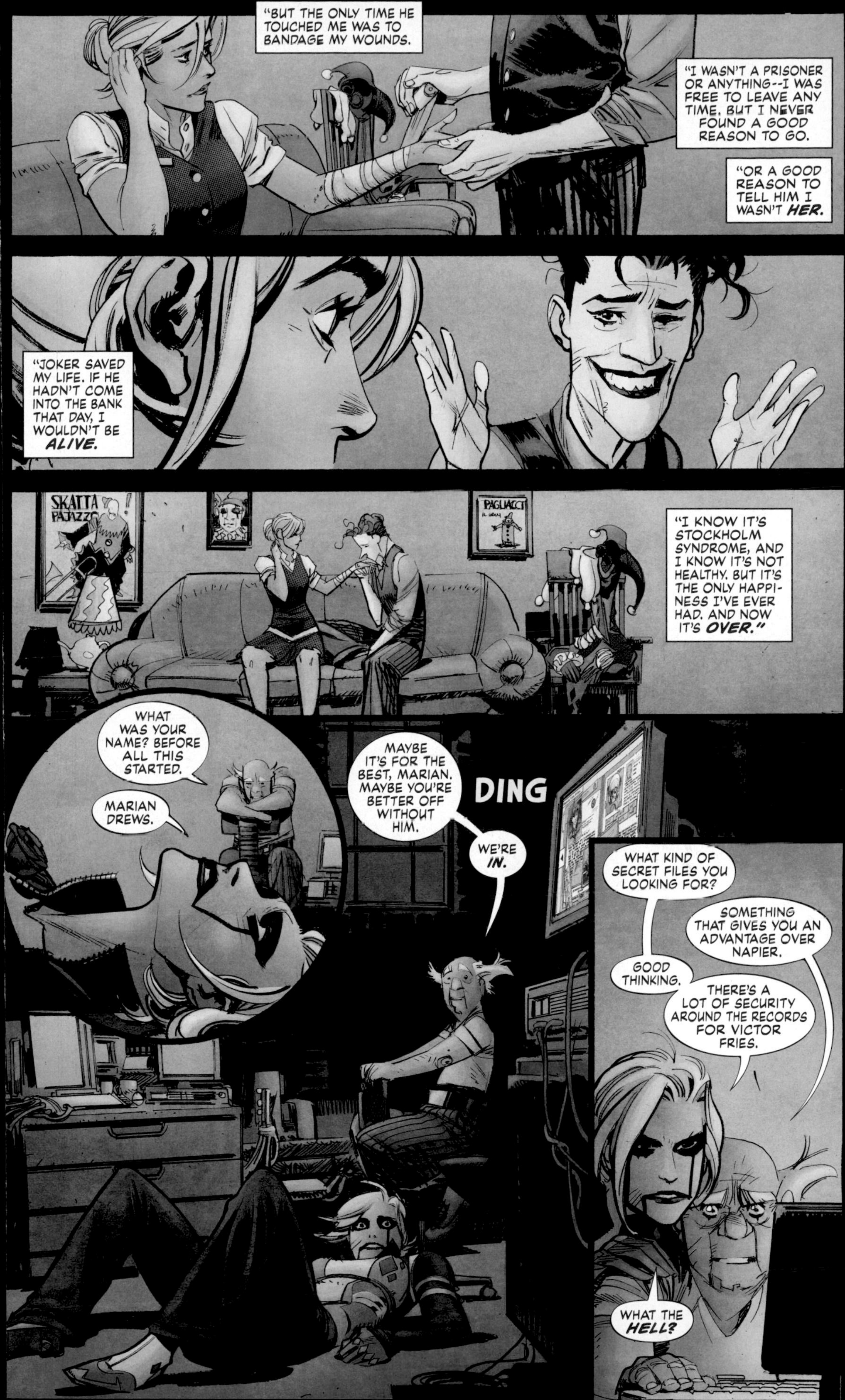
"BUT THE ONLY TIME HE TOUCHED ME WAS TO BANDAGE MY WOUNDS.
"I WASN'T A PRISONER OR ANYTHING--I WAS FREE TO LEAVE ANY TIME, BUT I NEVER FOUND A GOOD REASON TO GO.
"OR A GOOD REASON TO TELL HIM I WASN'T HER.
"JOKER SAVED MY LIFE. IF HE HADN'T COME INTO THE BANK THAT DAY, I WOULDN'T BE ALIVE.
SKATTA PAJAZZO
PAGLIACCI
"I KNOW IT'S STOCKHOLM SYNDROME, AND I KNOW IT'S NOT HEALTHY. BUT IT'S THE ONLY HAPPINESS I'VE EVER HAD. AND NOW IT'S OVER."
WHAT WAS YOUR NAME? BEFORE ALL THIS STARTED.
MARIAN DREWS.
MAYBE IT'S FOR THE BEST, MARIAN. MAYBE YOU'RE BETTER OFF WITHOUT HIM.
DING
WE'RE IN.
WHAT KIND OF SECRET FILES YOU LOOKING FOR?
SOMETHING THAT GIVES YOU AN ADVANTAGE OVER NAPIER.
GOOD THINKING.
THERE'S A LOT OF SECURITY AROUND THE RECORDS FOR VICTOR FRIES.
WHAT THE HELL?

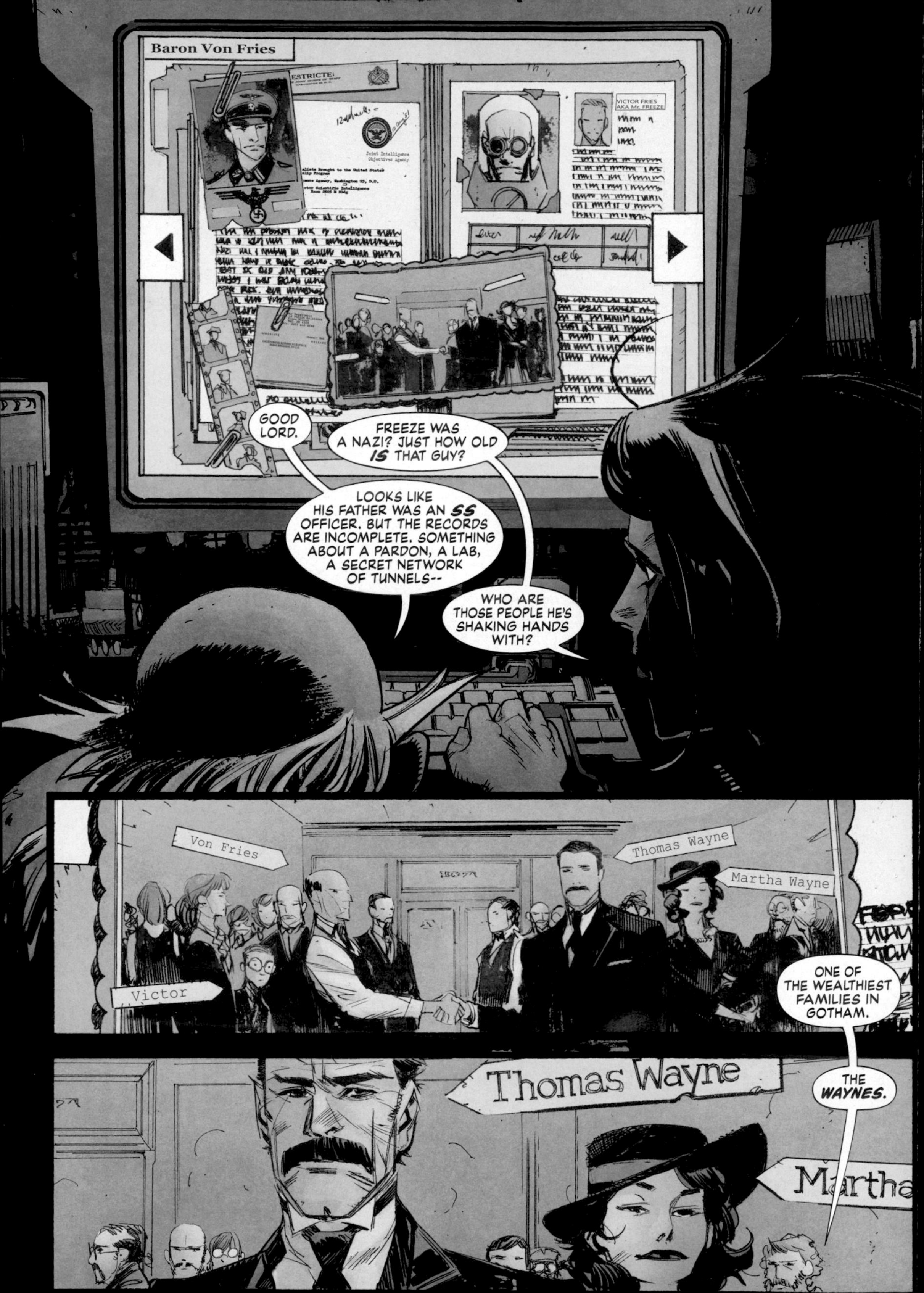

Baron Von Fries
RESTRICTED
Joint Intelligence Objectives Agency
VICTOR FRIES AKA Mr. FREEZE
GOOD LORD.
FREEZE WAS A NAZI? JUST HOW OLD *IS* THAT GUY?
LOOKS LIKE HIS FATHER WAS AN *SS* OFFICER. BUT THE RECORDS ARE INCOMPLETE. SOMETHING ABOUT A PARDON, A LAB, A SECRET NETWORK OF TUNNELS--
WHO ARE THOSE PEOPLE HE'S SHAKING HANDS WITH?
Von Fries
Thomas Wayne
Martha Wayne
Victor
ONE OF THE WEALTHIEST FAMILIES IN GOTHAM.
Thomas Wayne
Martha
THE *WAYNES.*

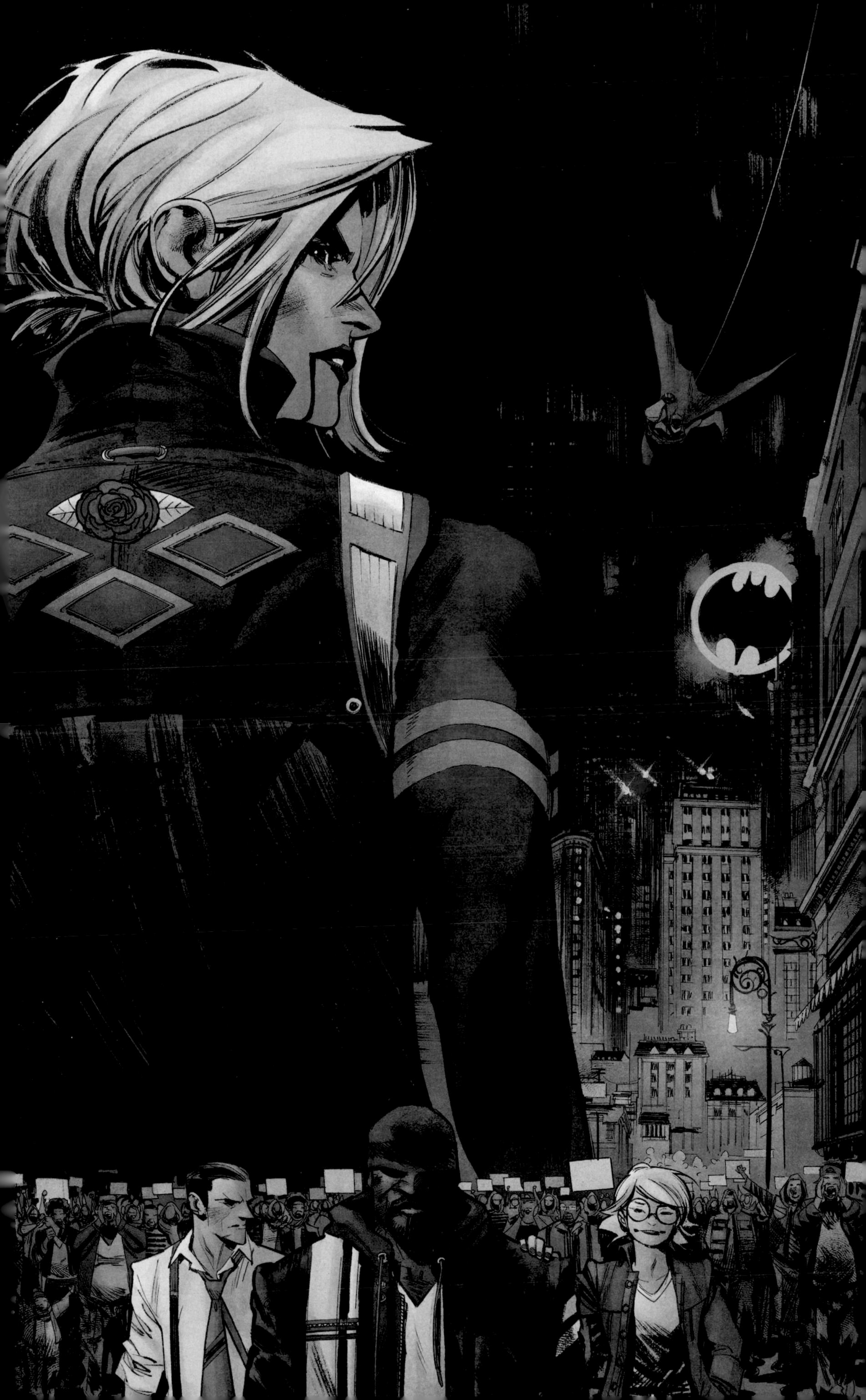

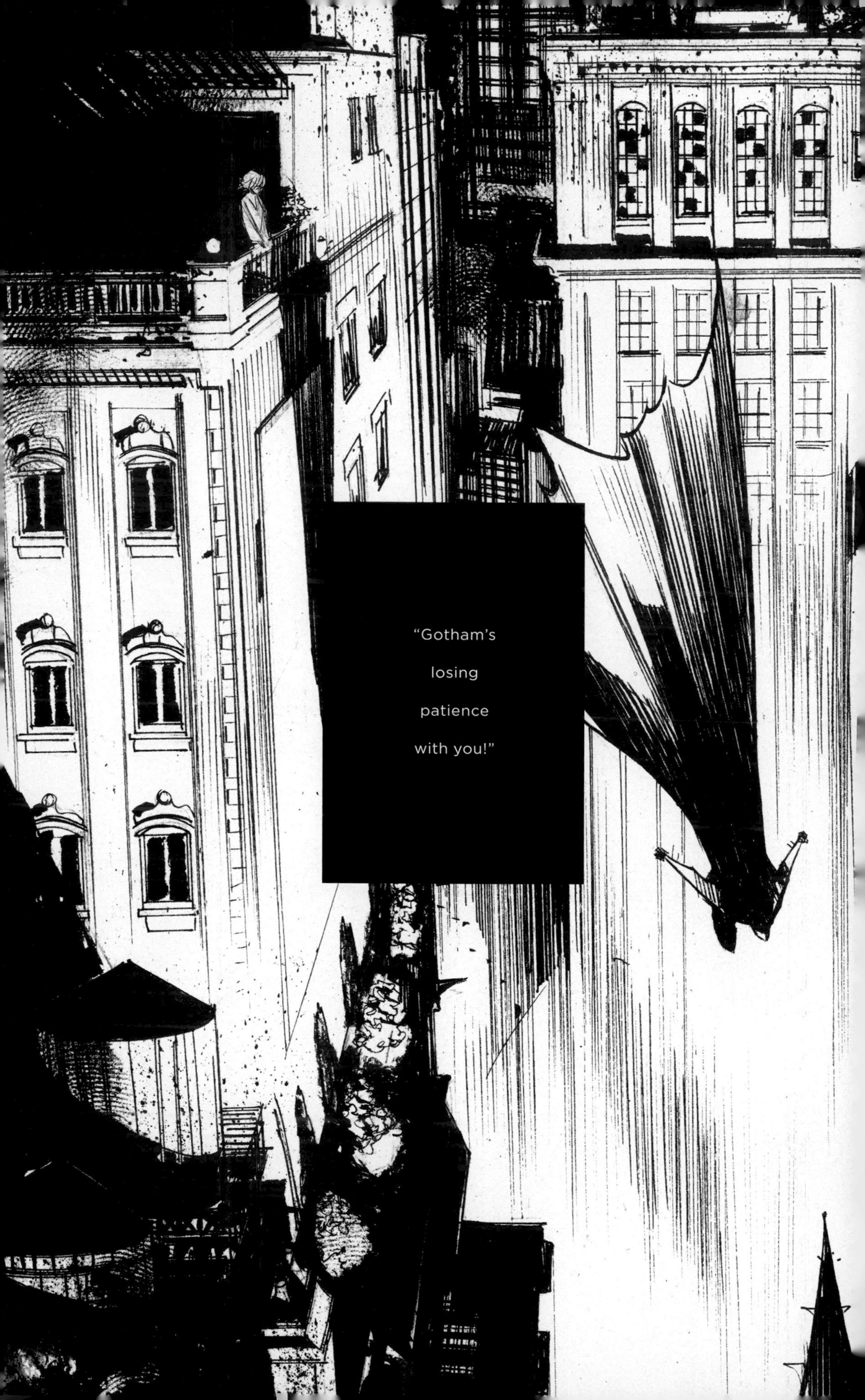
"Gotham's losing patience with you!"

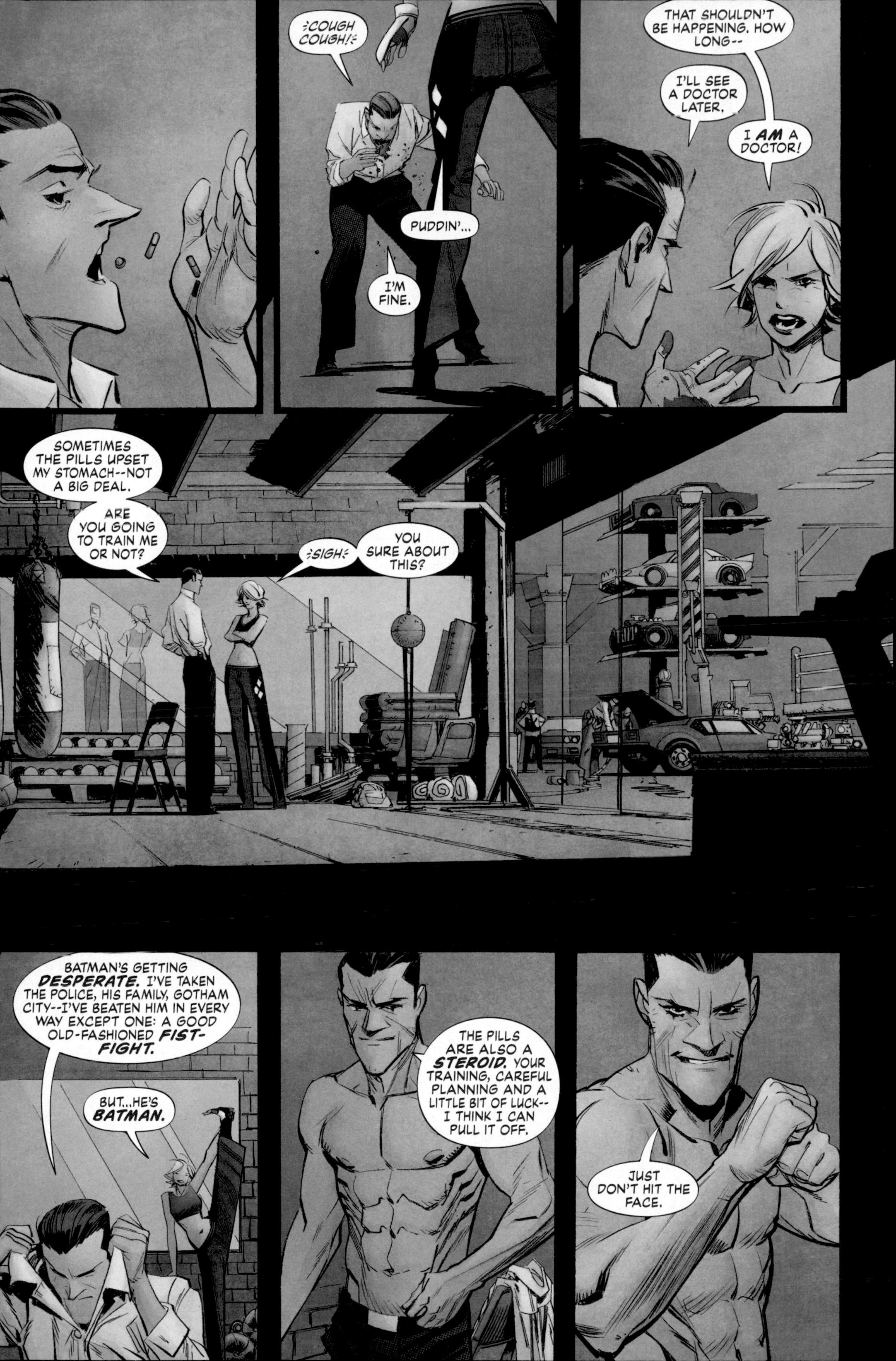

COUGH COUGH!
PUDDIN'...
I'M FINE.
THAT SHOULDN'T BE HAPPENING. HOW LONG--
I'LL SEE A DOCTOR LATER.
I AM A DOCTOR!
SOMETIMES THE PILLS UPSET MY STOMACH--NOT A BIG DEAL.
ARE YOU GOING TO TRAIN ME OR NOT?
SIGH
YOU SURE ABOUT THIS?
BATMAN'S GETTING DESPERATE. I'VE TAKEN THE POLICE, HIS FAMILY, GOTHAM CITY--I'VE BEATEN HIM IN EVERY WAY EXCEPT ONE: A GOOD OLD-FASHIONED FIST-FIGHT.
BUT...HE'S BATMAN.
THE PILLS ARE ALSO A STEROID. YOUR TRAINING, CAREFUL PLANNING AND A LITTLE BIT OF LUCK--I THINK I CAN PULL IT OFF.
JUST DON'T HIT THE FACE.

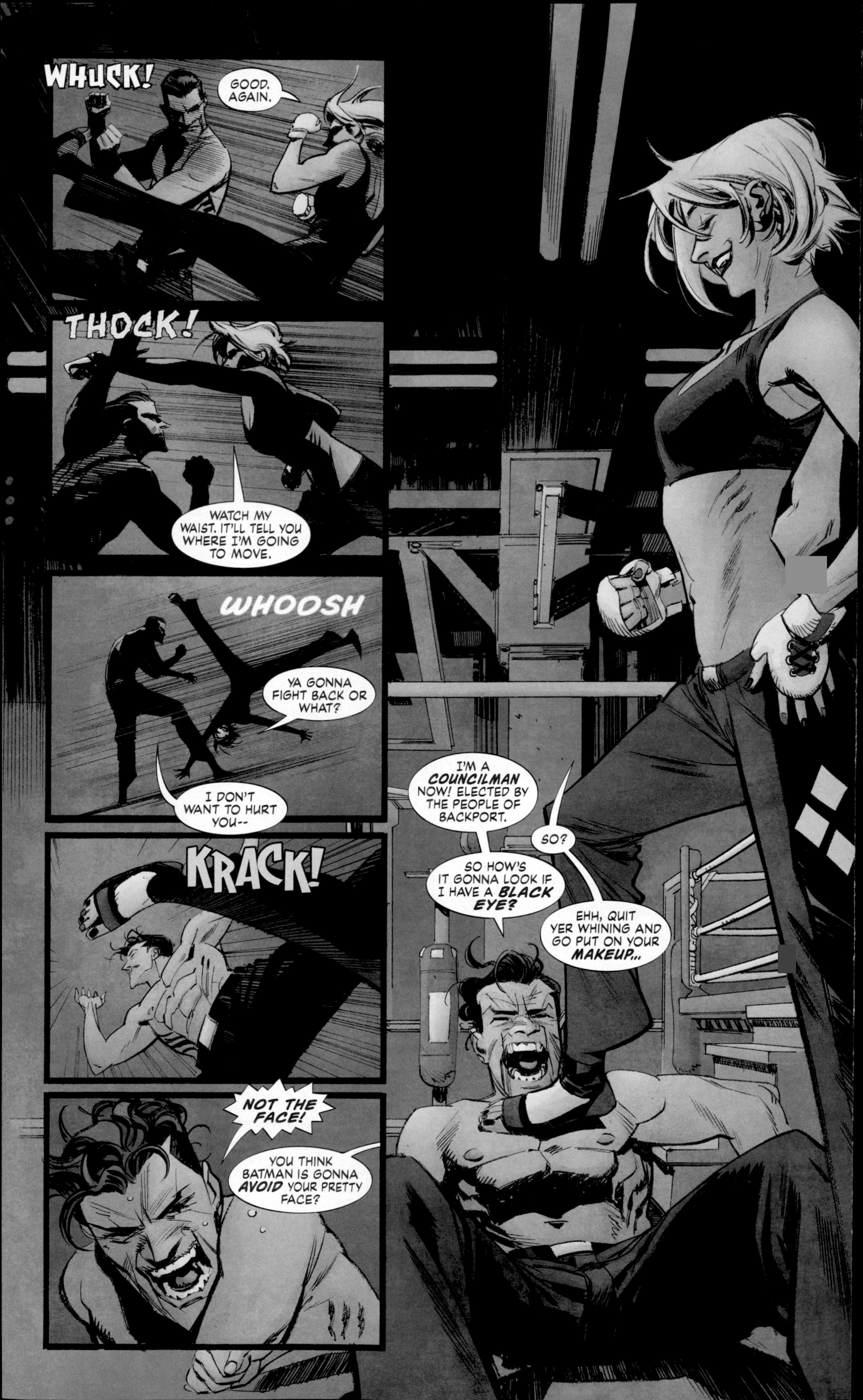
WHUCK!
GOOD. AGAIN.
THOCK!
WATCH MY WAIST. IT'LL TELL YOU WHERE I'M GOING TO MOVE.
WHOOSH
YA GONNA FIGHT BACK OR WHAT?
I DON'T WANT TO HURT YOU--
KRACK!
NOT THE FACE!
YOU THINK BATMAN IS GONNA AVOID YOUR PRETTY FACE?
I'M A COUNCILMAN NOW! ELECTED BY THE PEOPLE OF BACKPORT.
SO?
SO HOW'S IT GONNA LOOK IF I HAVE A BLACK EYE?
EHH, QUIT YER WHINING AND GO PUT ON YOUR MAKEUP...

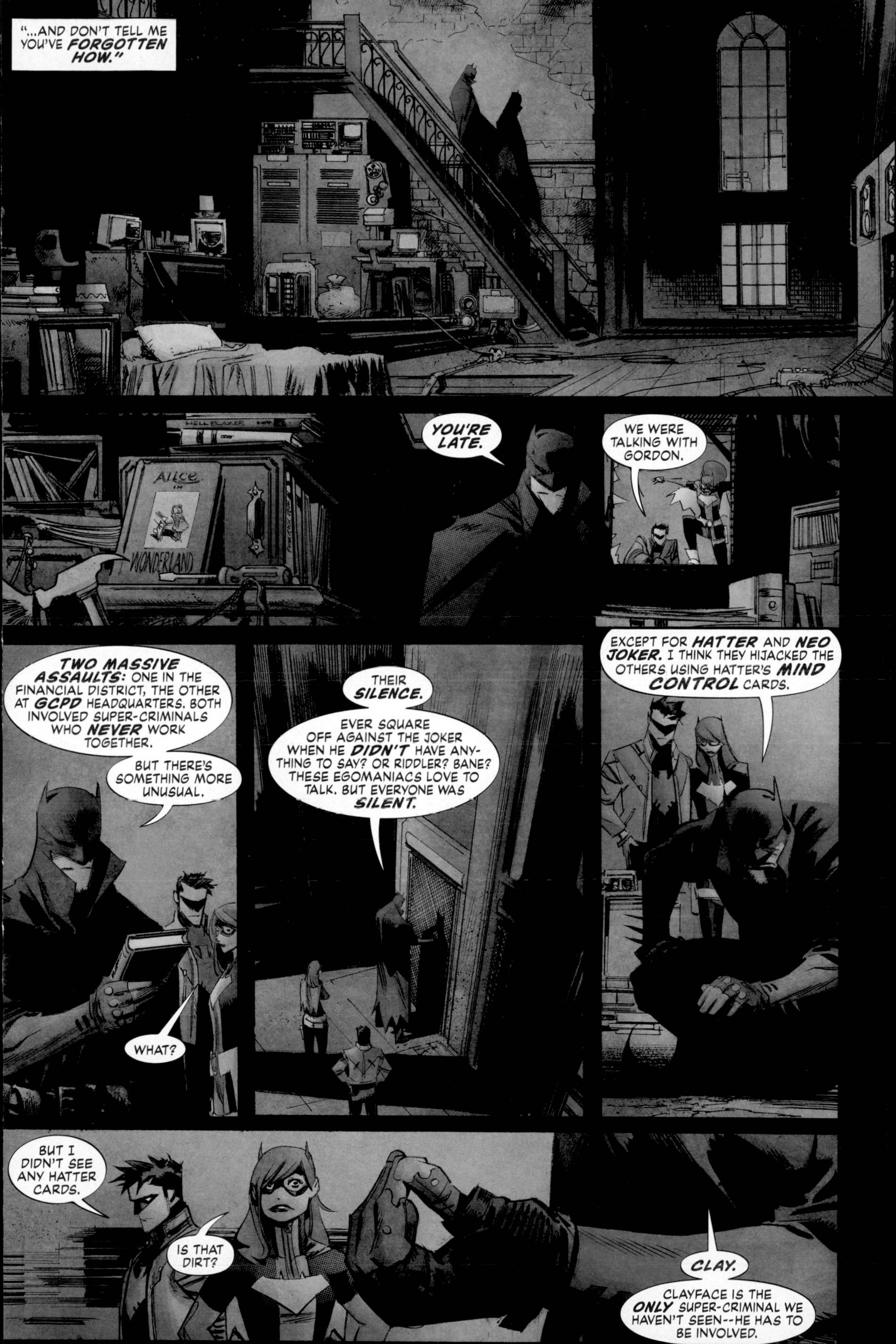
"...AND DON'T TELL ME YOU'VE FORGOTTEN HOW."
HELLBLAZER
ALICE IN WONDERLAND
YOU'RE LATE.
WE WERE TALKING WITH GORDON.
TWO MASSIVE ASSAULTS: ONE IN THE FINANCIAL DISTRICT, THE OTHER AT GCPD HEADQUARTERS. BOTH INVOLVED SUPER-CRIMINALS WHO NEVER WORK TOGETHER.
BUT THERE'S SOMETHING MORE UNUSUAL.
WHAT?
THEIR SILENCE.
EVER SQUARE OFF AGAINST THE JOKER WHEN HE DIDN'T HAVE ANYTHING TO SAY? OR RIDDLER? BANE? THESE EGOMANIACS LOVE TO TALK. BUT EVERYONE WAS SILENT.
EXCEPT FOR HATTER AND NEO JOKER. I THINK THEY HIJACKED THE OTHERS USING HATTER'S MIND CONTROL CARDS.
BUT I DIDN'T SEE ANY HATTER CARDS.
IS THAT DIRT?
CLAY.
CLAYFACE IS THE ONLY SUPER-CRIMINAL WE HAVEN'T SEEN--HE HAS TO BE INVOLVED.

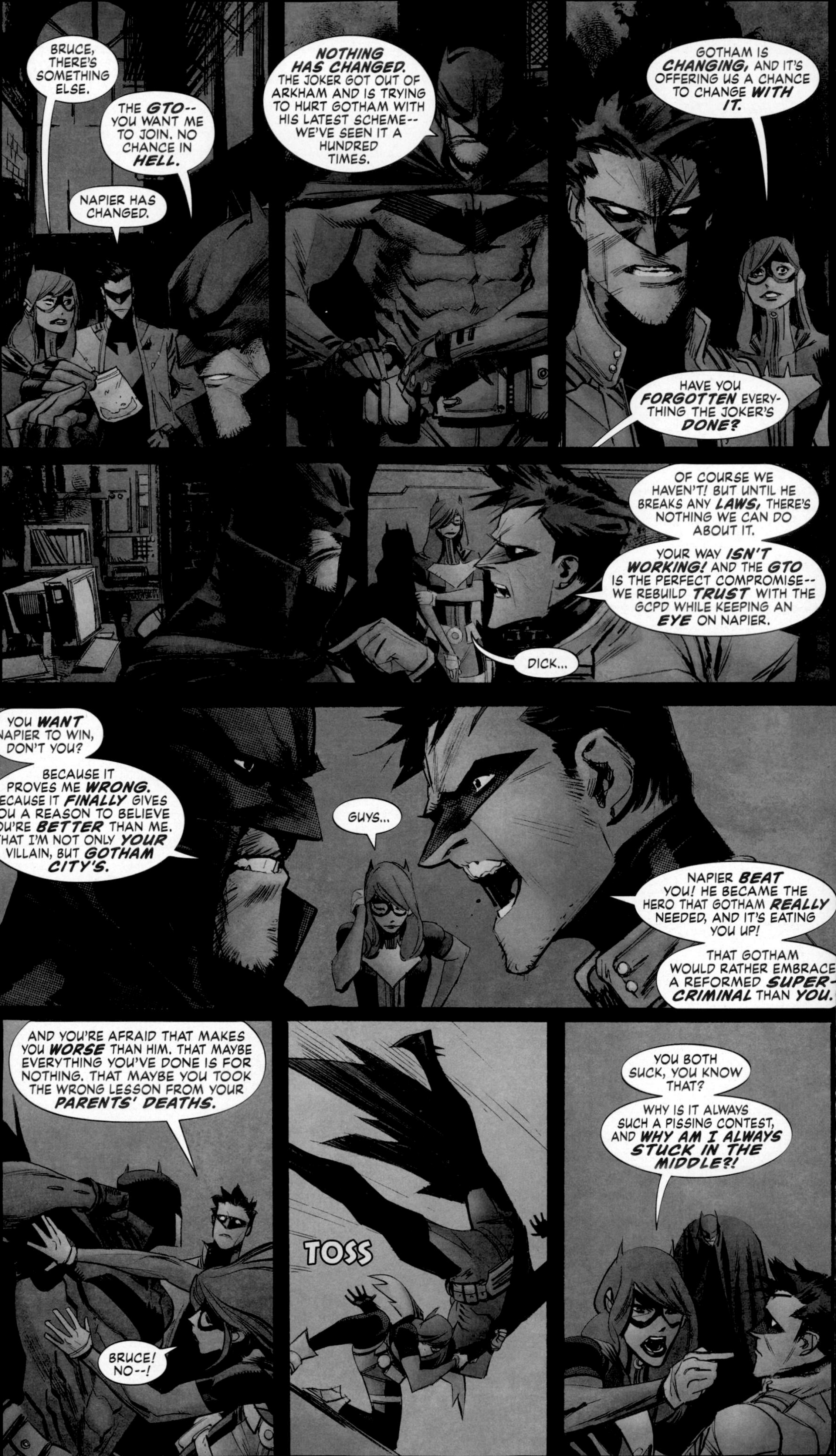
BRUCE, THERE'S SOMETHING ELSE.
NAPIER HAS CHANGED.
THE GTO-- YOU WANT ME TO JOIN. NO CHANCE IN HELL.
NOTHING HAS CHANGED. THE JOKER GOT OUT OF ARKHAM AND IS TRYING TO HURT GOTHAM WITH HIS LATEST SCHEME-- WE'VE SEEN IT A HUNDRED TIMES.
GOTHAM IS CHANGING, AND IT'S OFFERING US A CHANCE TO CHANGE WITH IT.
HAVE YOU FORGOTTEN EVERYTHING THE JOKER'S DONE?
OF COURSE WE HAVEN'T! BUT UNTIL HE BREAKS ANY LAWS, THERE'S NOTHING WE CAN DO ABOUT IT.
YOUR WAY ISN'T WORKING! AND THE GTO IS THE PERFECT COMPROMISE-- WE REBUILD TRUST WITH THE GCPD WHILE KEEPING AN EYE ON NAPIER.
DICK...
YOU WANT NAPIER TO WIN, DON'T YOU?
BECAUSE IT PROVES ME WRONG. BECAUSE IT FINALLY GIVES YOU A REASON TO BELIEVE YOU'RE BETTER THAN ME. THAT I'M NOT ONLY YOUR VILLAIN, BUT GOTHAM CITY'S.
GUYS...
NAPIER BEAT YOU! HE BECAME THE HERO THAT GOTHAM REALLY NEEDED, AND IT'S EATING YOU UP!
THAT GOTHAM WOULD RATHER EMBRACE A REFORMED SUPER-CRIMINAL THAN YOU.
AND YOU'RE AFRAID THAT MAKES YOU WORSE THAN HIM. THAT MAYBE EVERYTHING YOU'VE DONE IS FOR NOTHING. THAT MAYBE YOU TOOK THE WRONG LESSON FROM YOUR PARENTS' DEATHS.
BRUCE! NO--!
TOSS
YOU BOTH SUCK, YOU KNOW THAT?
WHY IS IT ALWAYS SUCH A PISSING CONTEST, AND WHY AM I ALWAYS STUCK IN THE MIDDLE?!

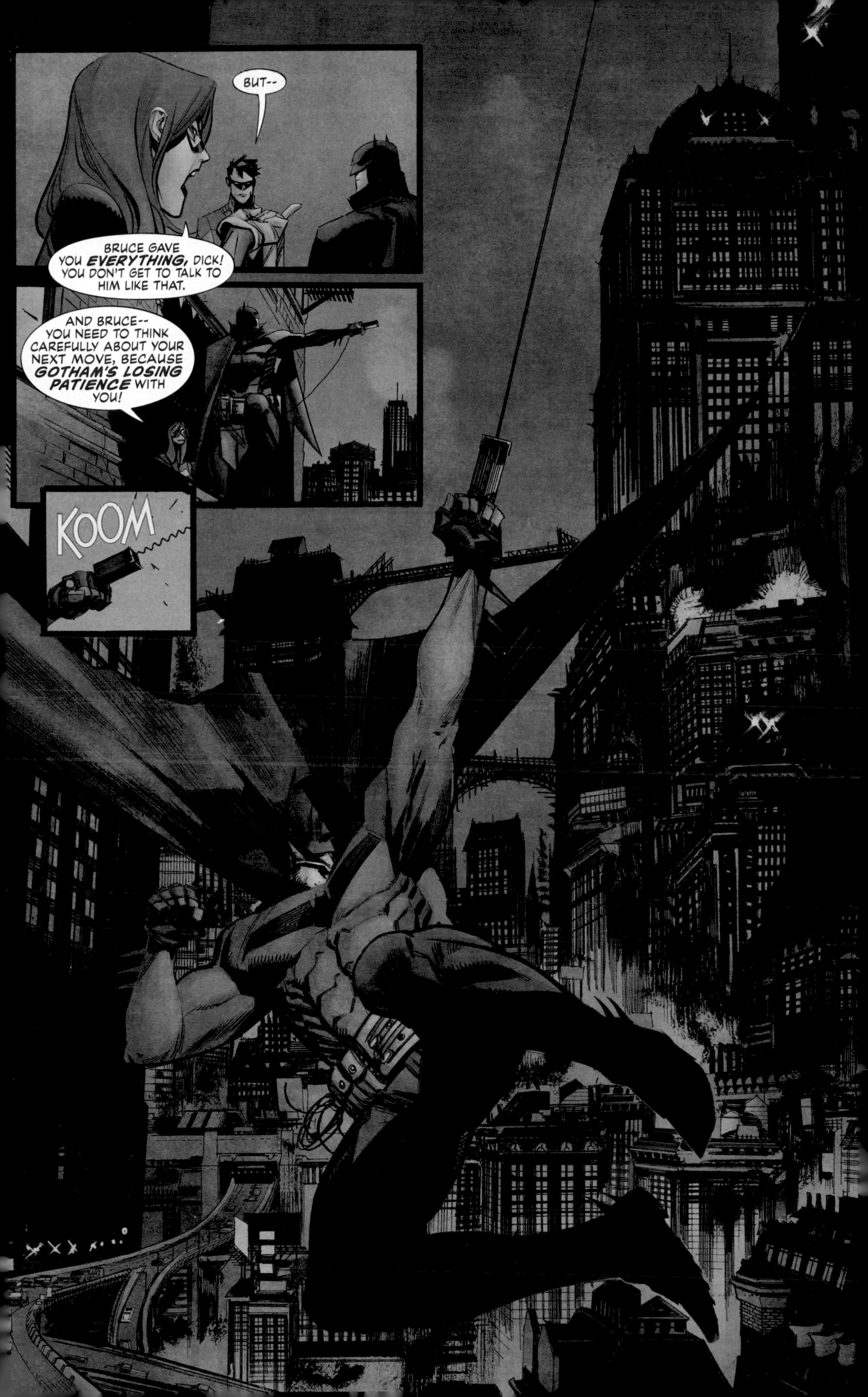
BUT--
BRUCE GAVE YOU EVERYTHING, DICK! YOU DON'T GET TO TALK TO HIM LIKE THAT.
AND BRUCE-- YOU NEED TO THINK CAREFULLY ABOUT YOUR NEXT MOVE, BECAUSE GOTHAM'S LOSING PATIENCE WITH YOU!
KOOM

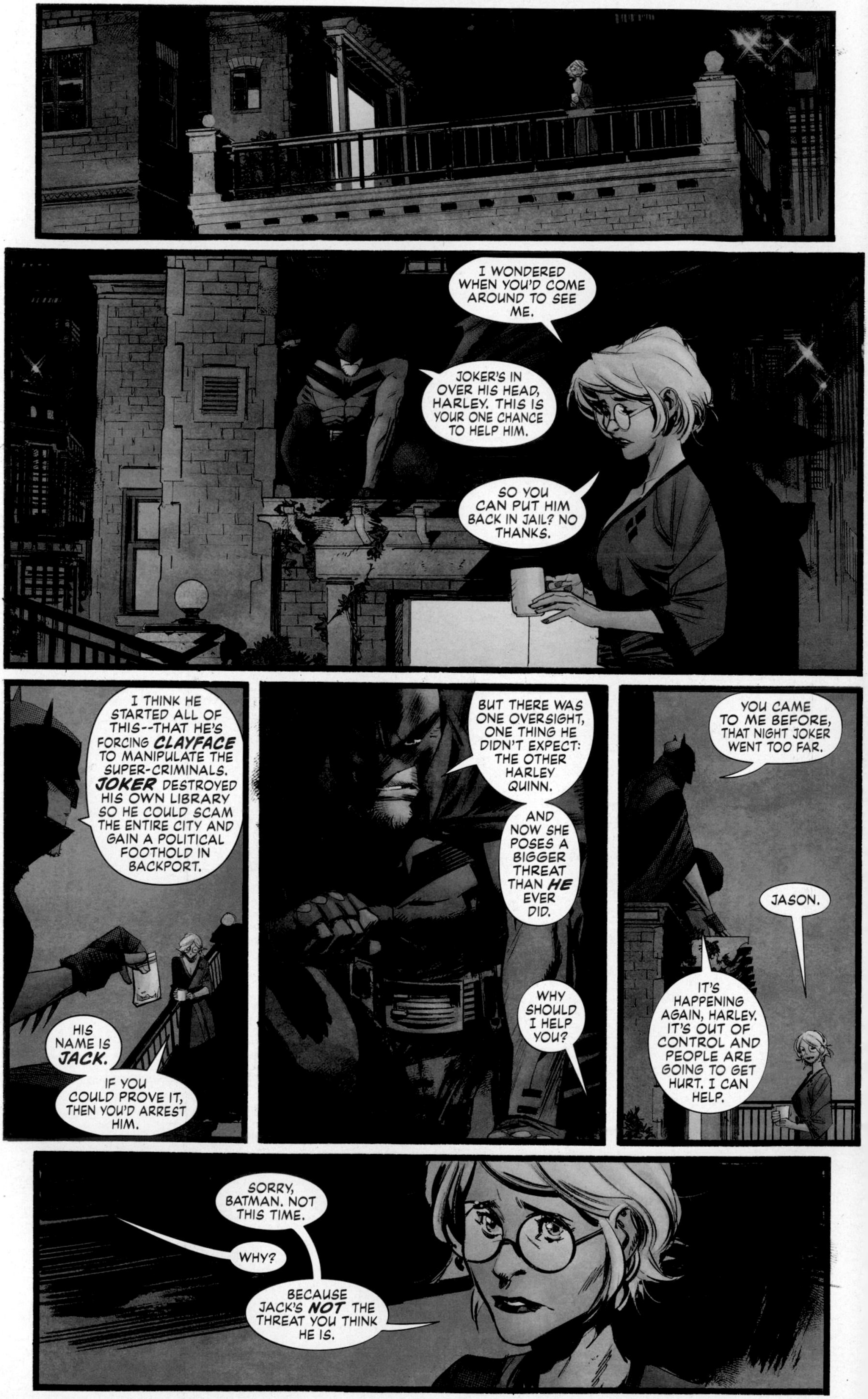
I WONDERED WHEN YOU'D COME AROUND TO SEE ME.
JOKER'S IN OVER HIS HEAD, HARLEY. THIS IS YOUR ONE CHANCE TO HELP HIM.
SO YOU CAN PUT HIM BACK IN JAIL? NO THANKS.
I THINK HE STARTED ALL OF THIS--THAT HE'S FORCING CLAYFACE TO MANIPULATE THE SUPER-CRIMINALS. JOKER DESTROYED HIS OWN LIBRARY SO HE COULD SCAM THE ENTIRE CITY AND GAIN A POLITICAL FOOTHOLD IN BACKPORT.
HIS NAME IS JACK.
IF YOU COULD PROVE IT, THEN YOU'D ARREST HIM.
BUT THERE WAS ONE OVERSIGHT, ONE THING HE DIDN'T EXPECT: THE OTHER HARLEY QUINN.
AND NOW SHE POSES A BIGGER THREAT THAN HE EVER DID.
WHY SHOULD I HELP YOU?
YOU CAME TO ME BEFORE, THAT NIGHT JOKER WENT TOO FAR.
JASON.
IT'S HAPPENING AGAIN, HARLEY. IT'S OUT OF CONTROL AND PEOPLE ARE GOING TO GET HURT. I CAN HELP.
SORRY, BATMAN. NOT THIS TIME.
WHY?
BECAUSE JACK'S NOT THE THREAT YOU THINK HE IS.

EVER WONDER WHY I WENT EASY ON YOU? WHY I NEVER TREATED YOU LIKE THE OTHERS? WHY YOU NEVER SPENT MUCH TIME IN ARKHAM?

BECAUSE I WANTED YOU WITH HIM. BECAUSE SOMETIMES YOU KEPT HIM *SANE.*

THAT'S WHAT CONNECTED US, HARLEY. BECAUSE AS *BAD* AS HE WAS--

--ONLY YOU AND I KNEW HOW BAD HE *WANTED* TO BE.

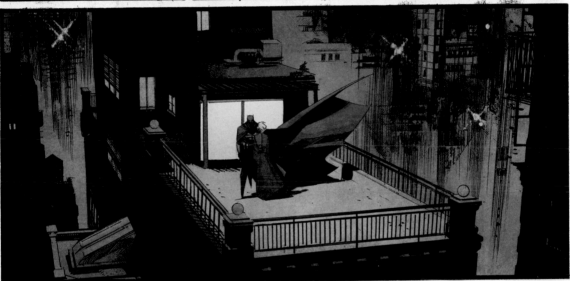

YOU BOUGHT ME A DRESS ONCE--THAT DAY I ALMOST BLEW MY OWN PAROLE WITH THE VREELAND INCIDENT, YOU STOOD BY ME.

I STILL HAVE THE DRESS.

EVEN WHEN I WAS LOSING JACK TO HIS OBSESSION WITH YOU, *EVEN* AFTER YOU PUT HIM IN THE HOSPITAL DOZENS OF TIMES, I NEVER *ONCE* GOT MAD AT YOU.

BECAUSE DEEP DOWN I KNOW YOU'RE A *GOOD GUY.*

BUT BEING A GOOD GUY DOESN'T MEAN YOU *ALWAYS* KNOW WHAT'S *BEST* FOR GOTHAM.

JACK IS *NOT* A VILLAIN ANYMORE.

AND WHATEVER HIS SINS, HE'S PUT THE CITY ON THE RIGHT TRACK.

I'M BEGGING YOU TO LET IT GO.

BEFORE IT'S TOO LATE FOR YOU.

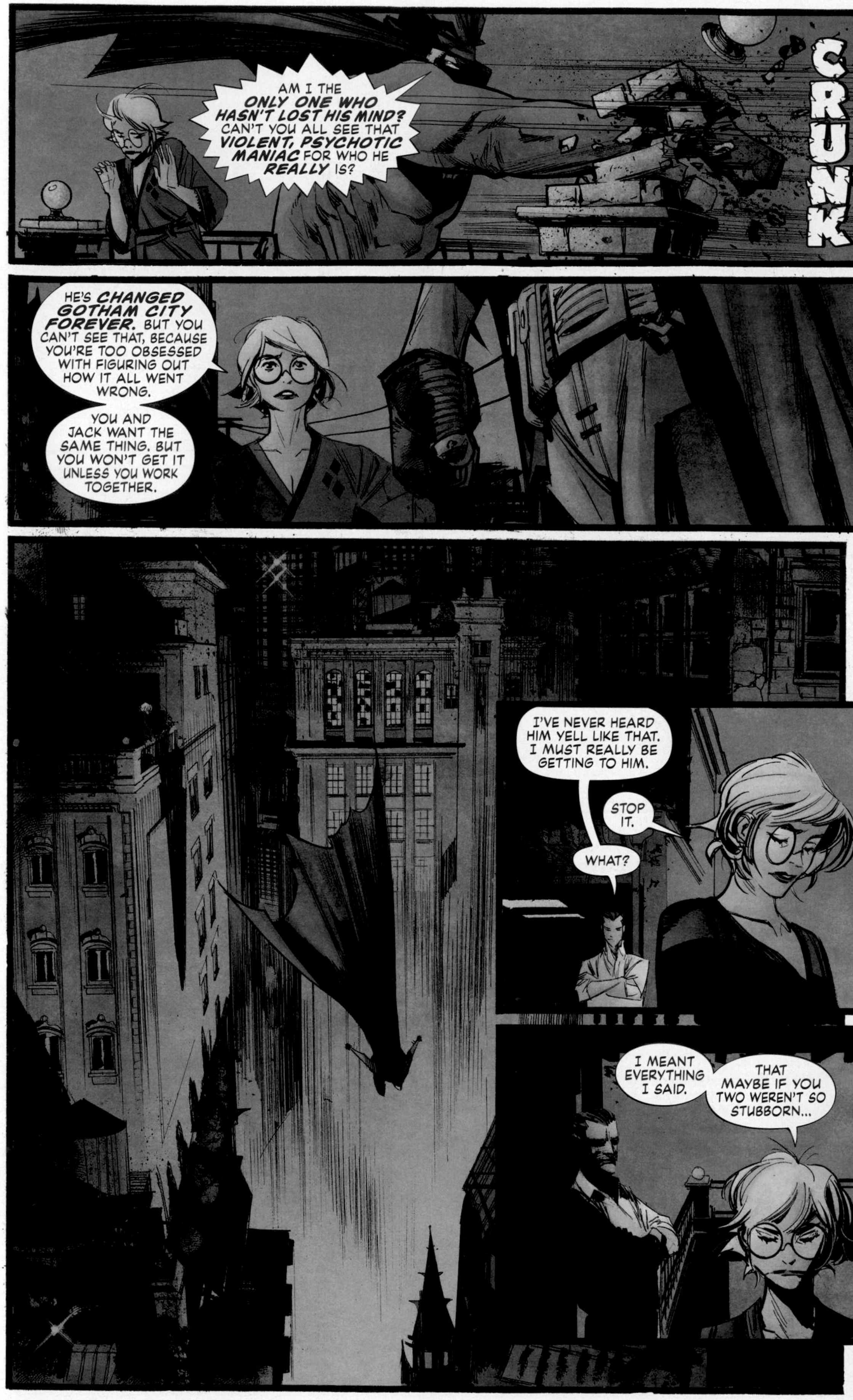

AM I THE ONLY ONE WHO HASN'T LOST HIS MIND? CAN'T YOU ALL SEE THAT VIOLENT, PSYCHOTIC MANIAC FOR WHO HE REALLY IS?
CRUNK
HE'S CHANGED GOTHAM CITY FOREVER. BUT YOU CAN'T SEE THAT, BECAUSE YOU'RE TOO OBSESSED WITH FIGURING OUT HOW IT ALL WENT WRONG.
YOU AND JACK WANT THE SAME THING. BUT YOU WON'T GET IT UNLESS YOU WORK TOGETHER.
I'VE NEVER HEARD HIM YELL LIKE THAT. I MUST REALLY BE GETTING TO HIM.
STOP IT.
WHAT?
I MEANT EVERYTHING I SAID.
THAT MAYBE IF YOU TWO WEREN'T SO STUBBORN...

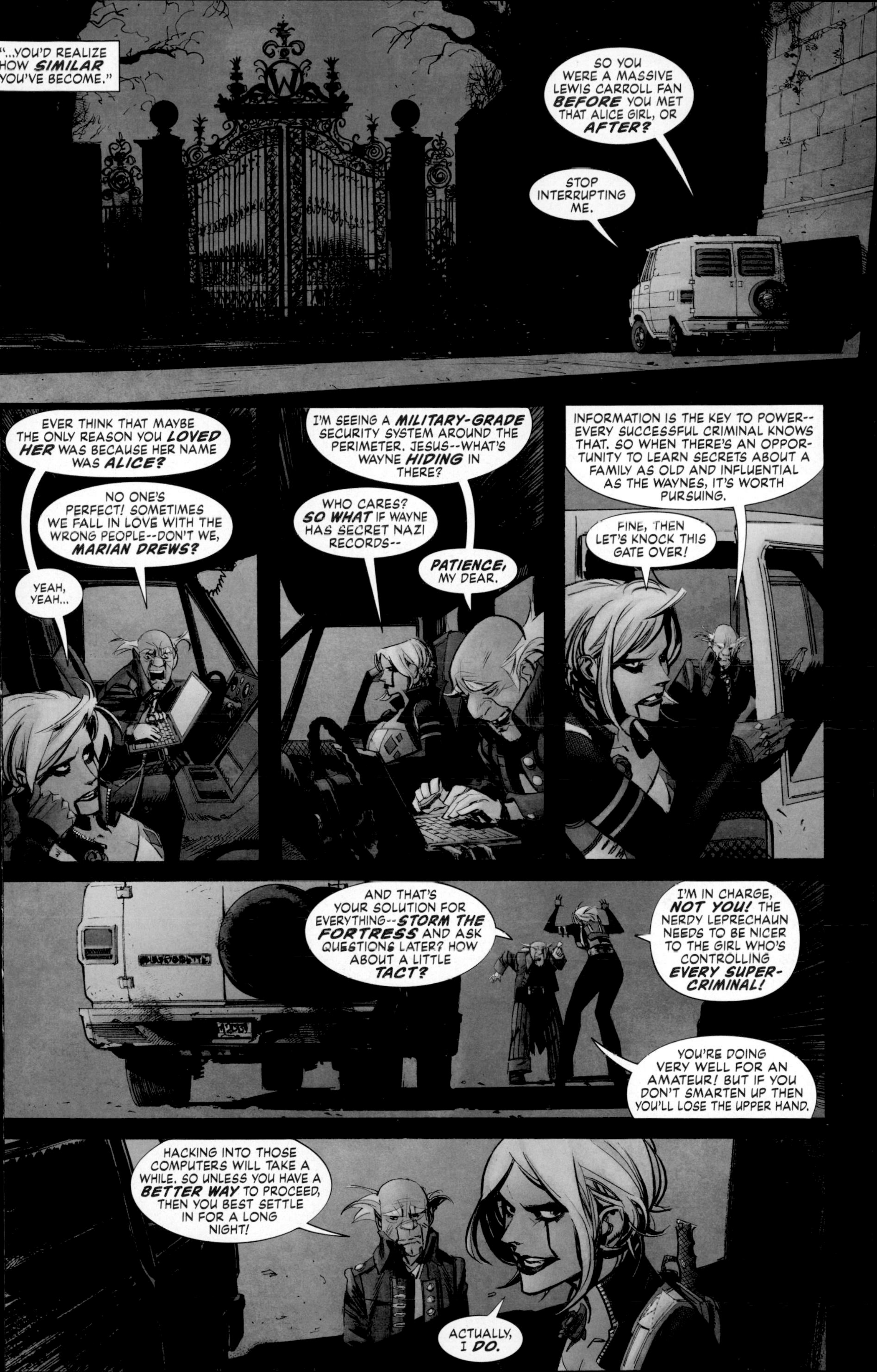
"...YOU'D REALIZE HOW SIMILAR YOU'VE BECOME."
SO YOU WERE A MASSIVE LEWIS CARROLL FAN BEFORE YOU MET THAT ALICE GIRL, OR AFTER?
STOP INTERRUPTING ME.
EVER THINK THAT MAYBE THE ONLY REASON YOU LOVED HER WAS BECAUSE HER NAME WAS ALICE?
NO ONE'S PERFECT! SOMETIMES WE FALL IN LOVE WITH THE WRONG PEOPLE--DON'T WE, MARIAN DREWS?
YEAH, YEAH...
I'M SEEING A MILITARY-GRADE SECURITY SYSTEM AROUND THE PERIMETER. JESUS--WHAT'S WAYNE HIDING IN THERE?
WHO CARES? SO WHAT IF WAYNE HAS SECRET NAZI RECORDS--
PATIENCE, MY DEAR.
INFORMATION IS THE KEY TO POWER-- EVERY SUCCESSFUL CRIMINAL KNOWS THAT. SO WHEN THERE'S AN OPPORTUNITY TO LEARN SECRETS ABOUT A FAMILY AS OLD AND INFLUENTIAL AS THE WAYNES, IT'S WORTH PURSUING.
FINE, THEN LET'S KNOCK THIS GATE OVER!
AND THAT'S YOUR SOLUTION FOR EVERYTHING--STORM THE FORTRESS AND ASK QUESTIONS LATER? HOW ABOUT A LITTLE TACT?
I'M IN CHARGE, NOT YOU! THE NERDY LEPRECHAUN NEEDS TO BE NICER TO THE GIRL WHO'S CONTROLLING EVERY SUPER-CRIMINAL!
YOU'RE DOING VERY WELL FOR AN AMATEUR! BUT IF YOU DON'T SMARTEN UP THEN YOU'LL LOSE THE UPPER HAND.
HACKING INTO THOSE COMPUTERS WILL TAKE A WHILE. SO UNLESS YOU HAVE A BETTER WAY TO PROCEED, THEN YOU BEST SETTLE IN FOR A LONG NIGHT!
ACTUALLY, I DO.

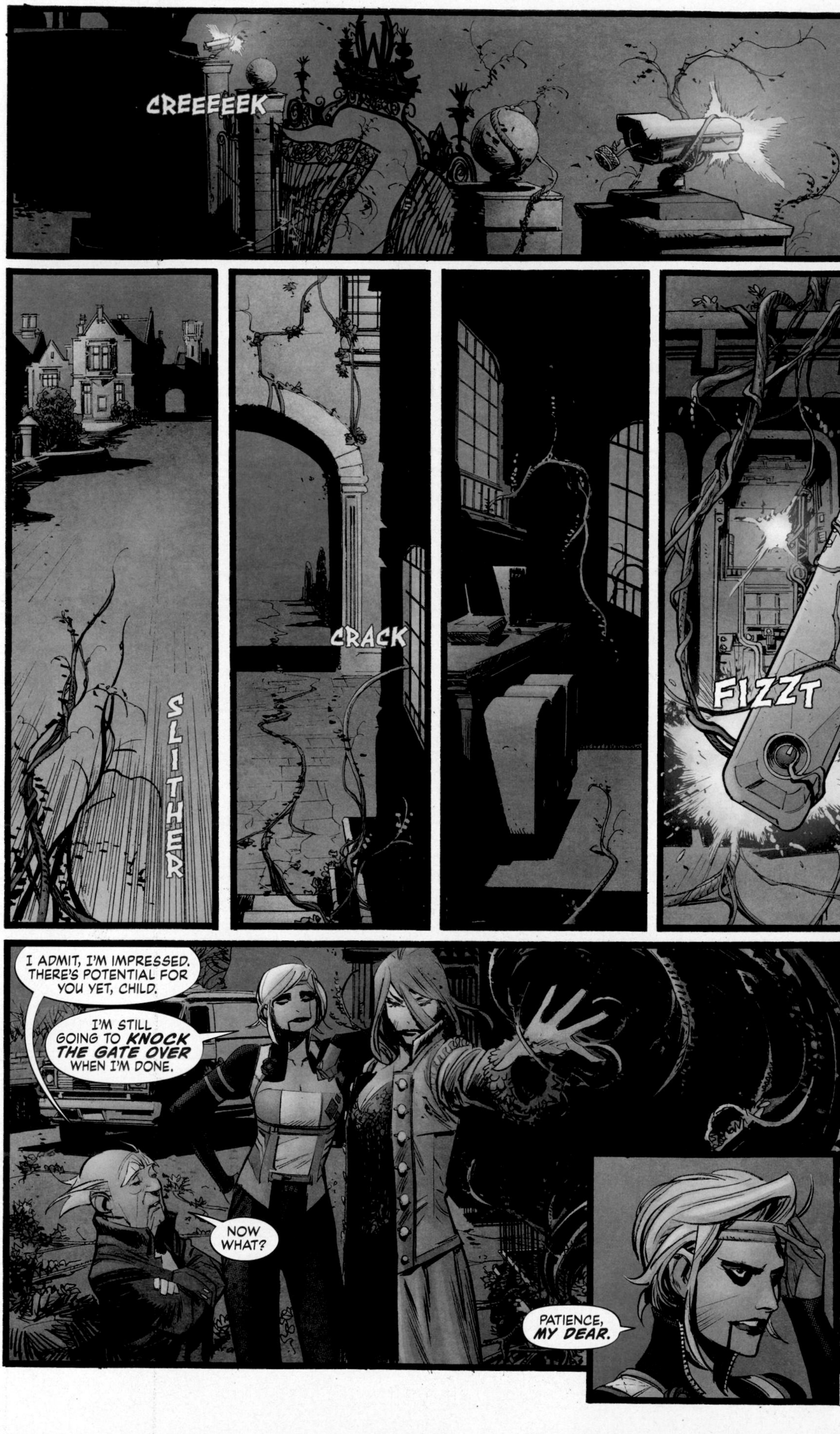
CREEEEEK
SLITHER
CRACK
FIZZT
I ADMIT, I'M IMPRESSED. THERE'S POTENTIAL FOR YOU YET, CHILD.
I'M STILL GOING TO **KNOCK THE GATE OVER** WHEN I'M DONE.
NOW WHAT?
PATIENCE, **MY DEAR.**

WOOSH!

WE'RE LOOKING FOR A *SECRET ROOM* OR SOME-THING?

YES-- SOMEPLACE YOU'D HIDE A DANGEROUS *FAMILY SECRET.*

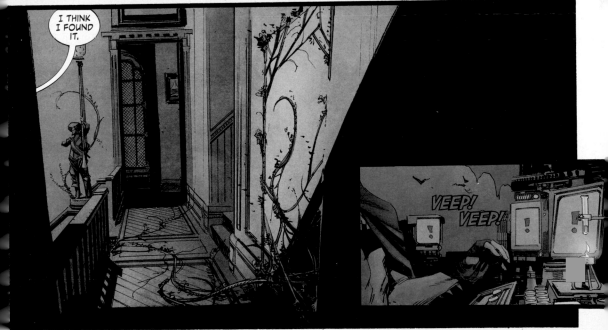

I THINK I FOUND IT.

VEEP! VEEP!

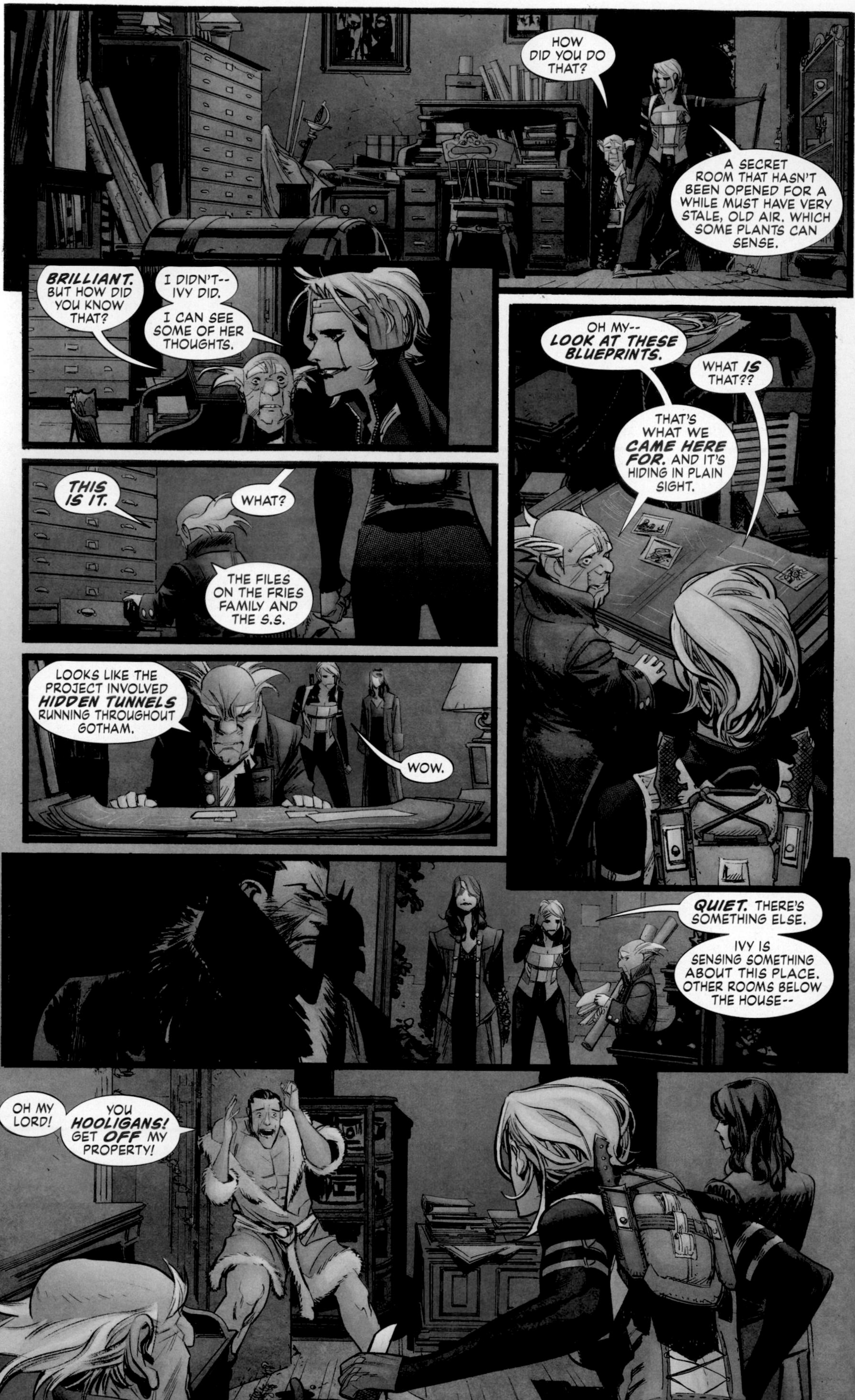
HOW DID YOU DO THAT?
A SECRET ROOM THAT HASN'T BEEN OPENED FOR A WHILE MUST HAVE VERY STALE, OLD AIR. WHICH SOME PLANTS CAN SENSE.
BRILLIANT. BUT HOW DID YOU KNOW THAT?
I DIDN'T-- IVY DID.
I CAN SEE SOME OF HER THOUGHTS.
THIS IS IT.
WHAT?
THE FILES ON THE FRIES FAMILY AND THE S.S.
LOOKS LIKE THE PROJECT INVOLVED HIDDEN TUNNELS RUNNING THROUGHOUT GOTHAM.
WOW.
OH MY-- LOOK AT THESE BLUEPRINTS.
WHAT IS THAT??
THAT'S WHAT WE CAME HERE FOR. AND IT'S HIDING IN PLAIN SIGHT.
QUIET. THERE'S SOMETHING ELSE.
IVY IS SENSING SOMETHING ABOUT THIS PLACE. OTHER ROOMS BELOW THE HOUSE--
OH MY LORD!
YOU HOOLIGANS! GET OFF MY PROPERTY!

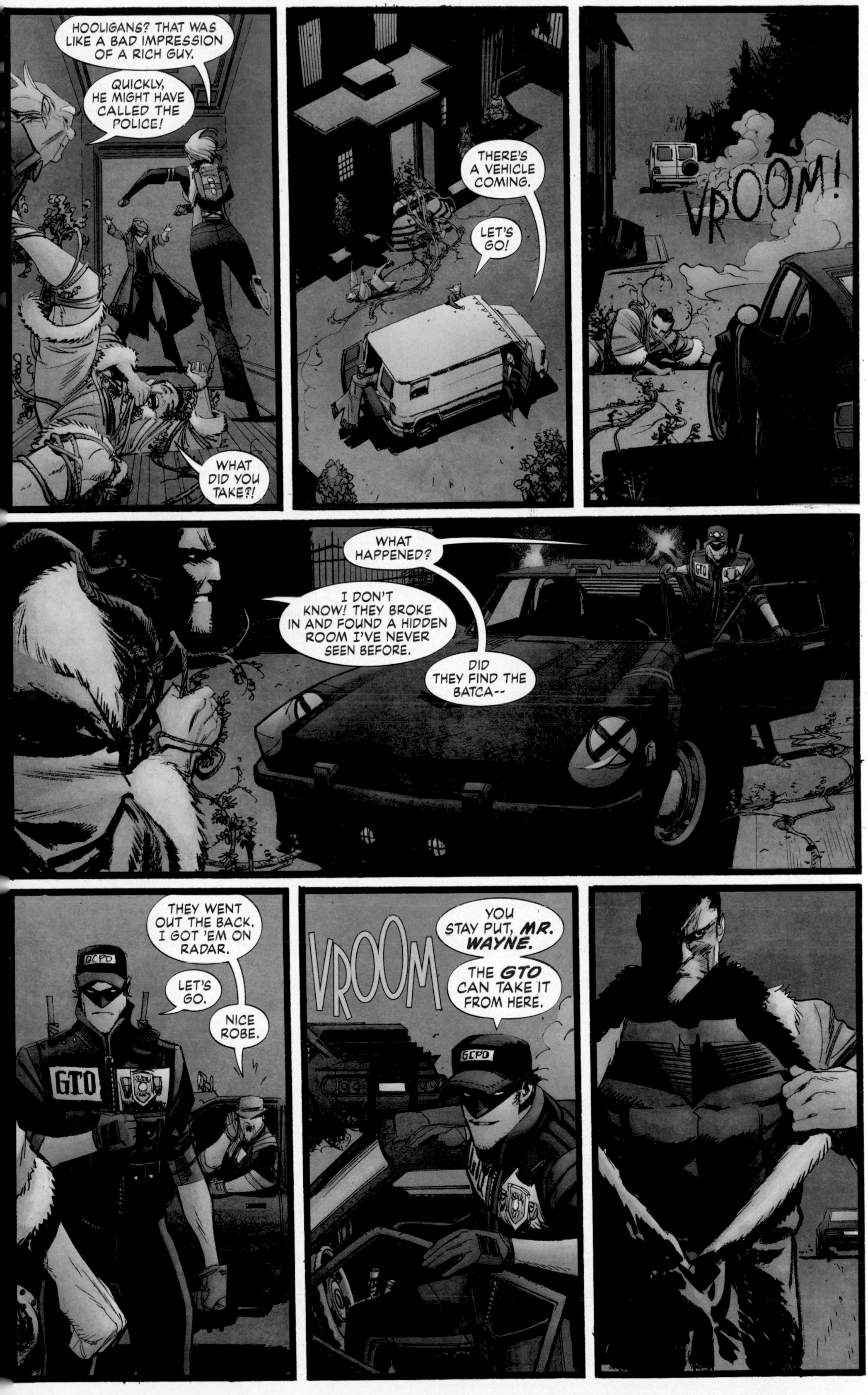
HOOLIGANS? THAT WAS LIKE A BAD IMPRESSION OF A RICH GUY.
QUICKLY, HE MIGHT HAVE CALLED THE POLICE!
WHAT DID YOU TAKE?!
THERE'S A VEHICLE COMING.
LET'S GO!
VROOM!
WHAT HAPPENED?
I DON'T KNOW! THEY BROKE IN AND FOUND A HIDDEN ROOM I'VE NEVER SEEN BEFORE.
DID THEY FIND THE BATCA--
THEY WENT OUT THE BACK. I GOT 'EM ON RADAR.
LET'S GO.
NICE ROBE.
VROOM
YOU STAY PUT, MR. WAYNE.
THE GTO CAN TAKE IT FROM HERE.

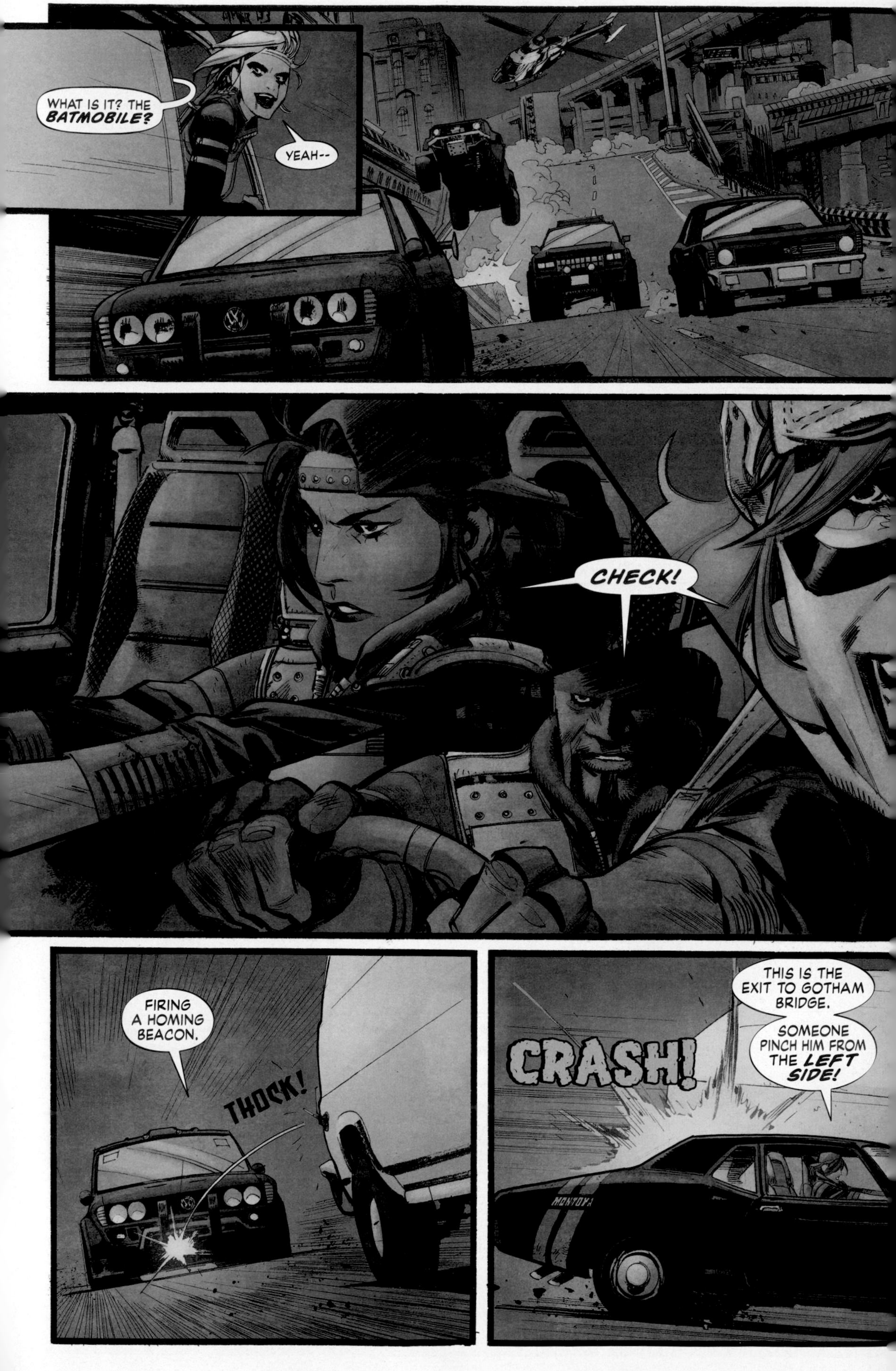
WHAT IS IT? THE *BATMOBILE?*
YEAH--
CHECK!
FIRING A HOMING BEACON.
THOCK!
CRASH!
THIS IS THE EXIT TO GOTHAM BRIDGE.
SOMEONE PINCH HIM FROM THE *LEFT SIDE!*

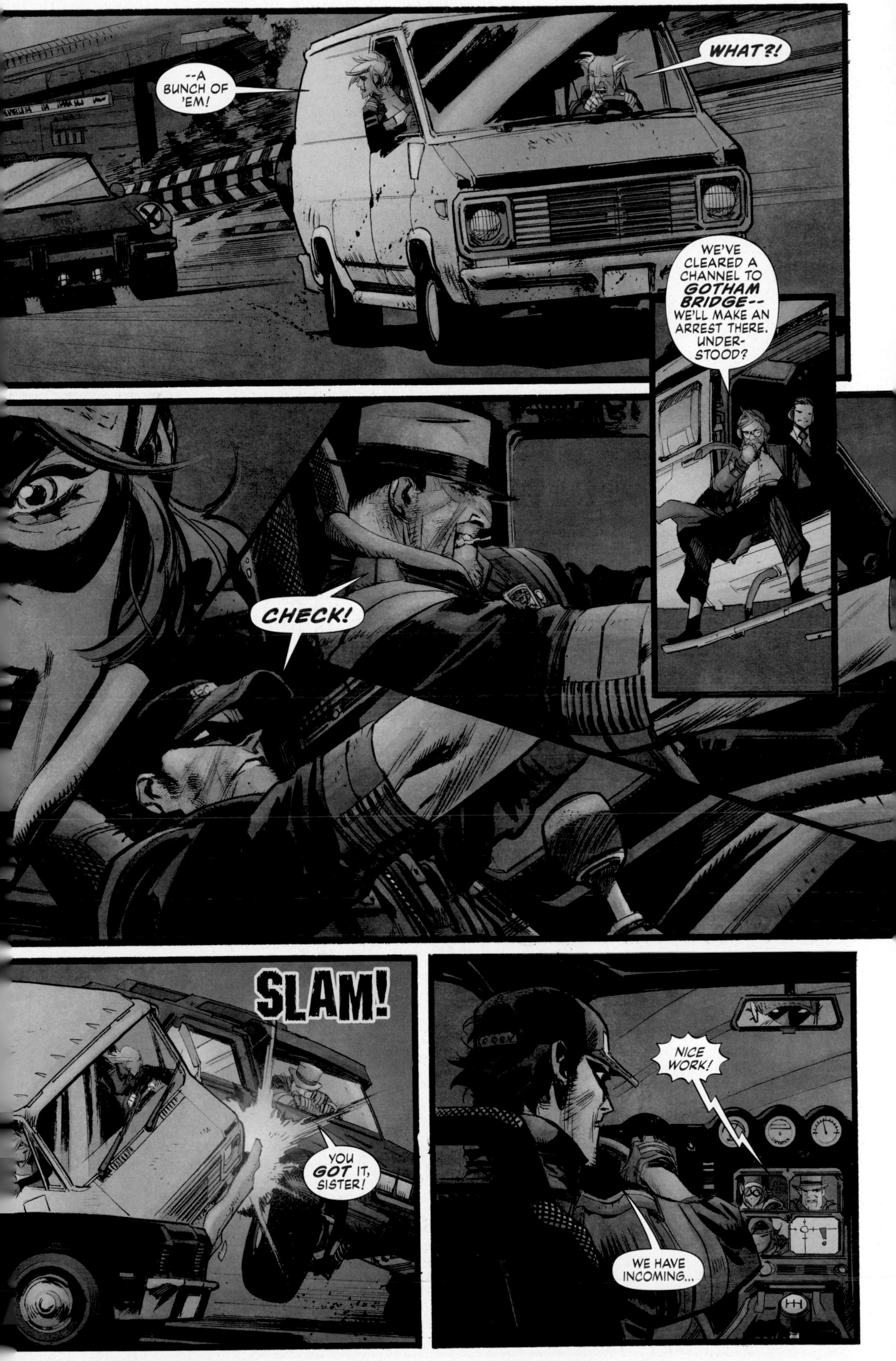
--A BUNCH OF 'EM!
WHAT?!
WE'VE CLEARED A CHANNEL TO GOTHAM BRIDGE-- WE'LL MAKE AN ARREST THERE. UNDERSTOOD?
CHECK!
SLAM!
YOU GOT IT, SISTER!
NICE WORK!
WE HAVE INCOMING...

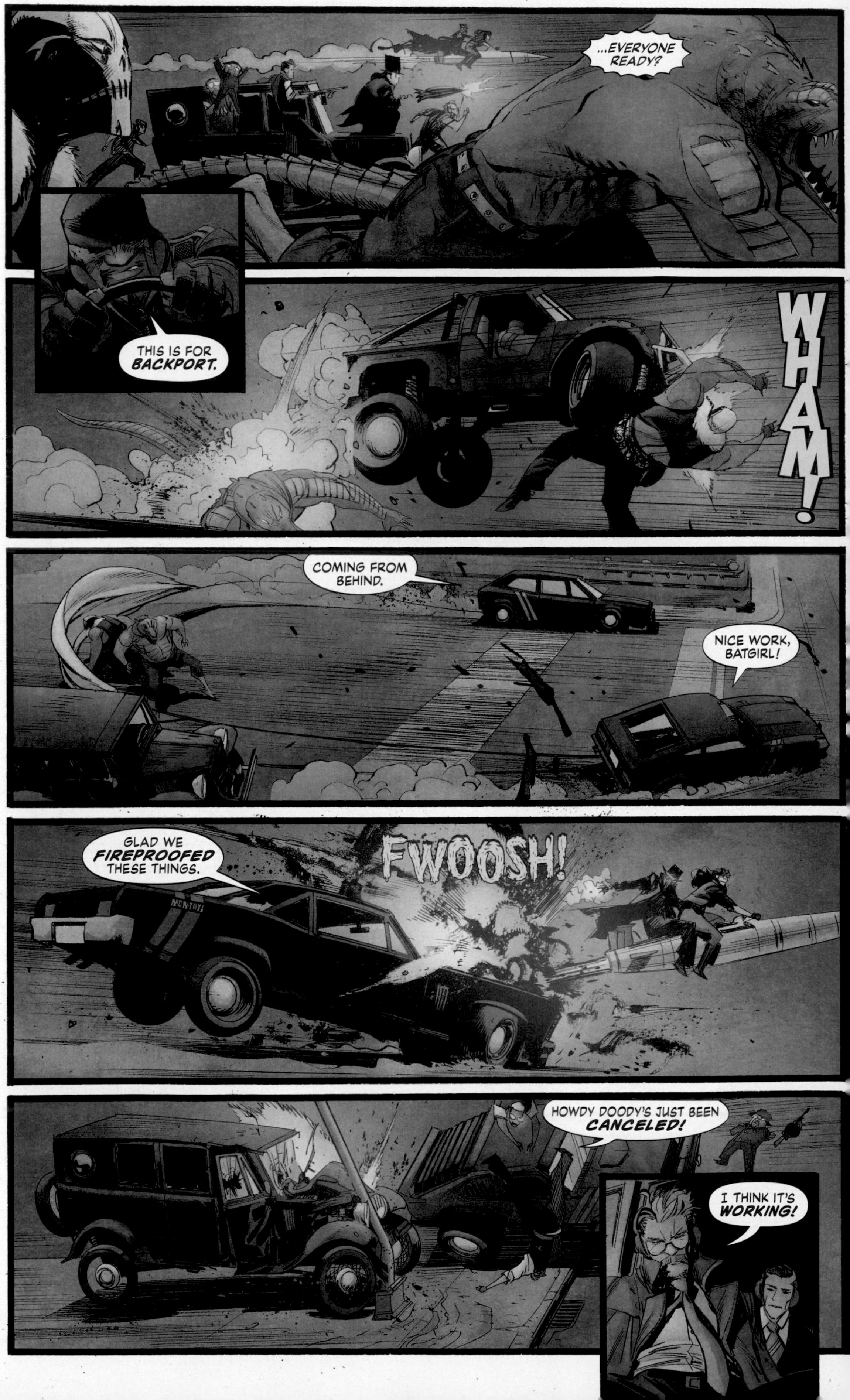
...EVERYONE READY?
THIS IS FOR BACKPORT.
WHAM!
COMING FROM BEHIND.
NICE WORK, BATGIRL!
GLAD WE FIREPROOFED THESE THINGS.
FWOOSH!
HOWDY DOODY'S JUST BEEN CANCELED!
I THINK IT'S WORKING!

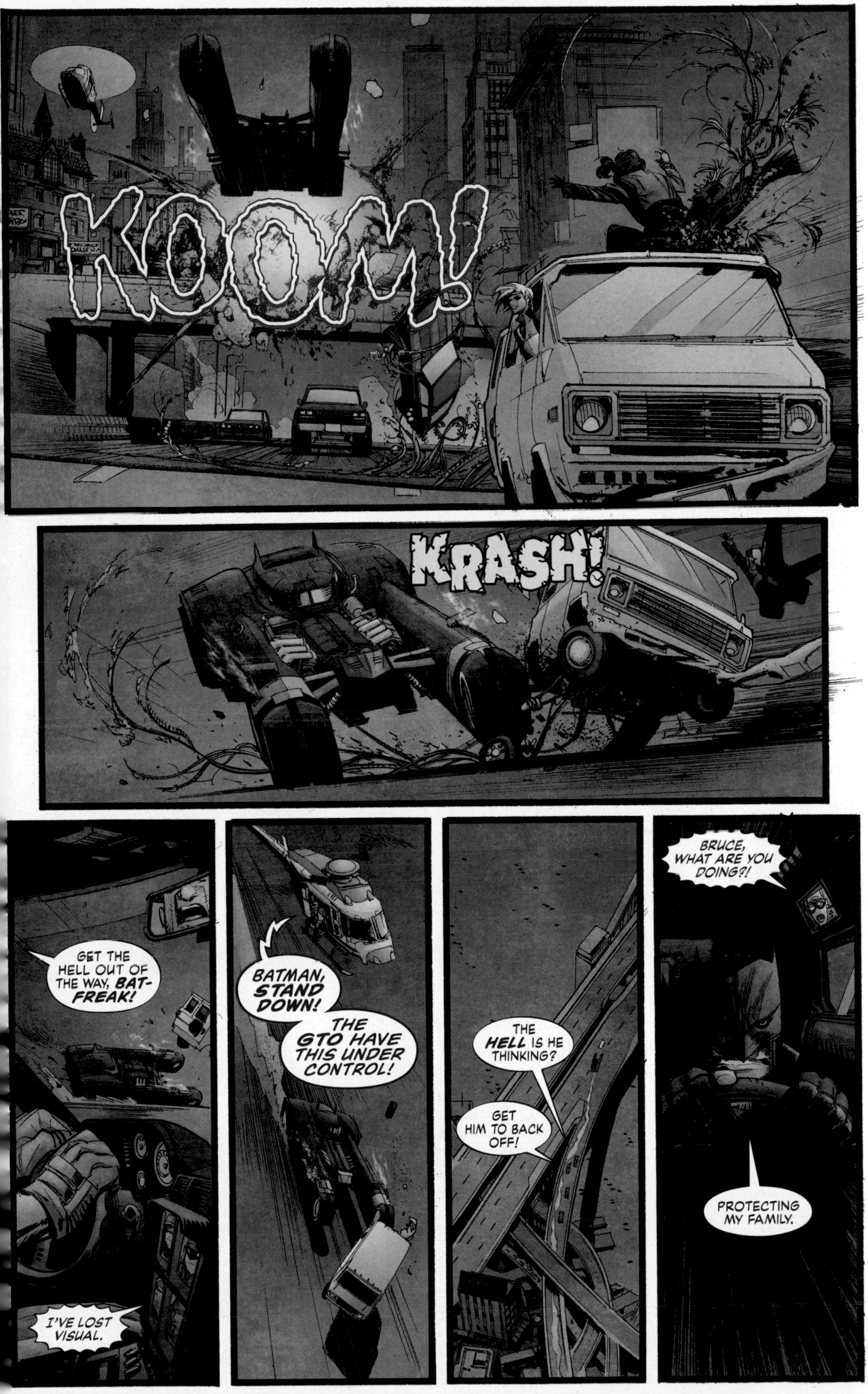
KOOM!
KRASH!
GET THE HELL OUT OF THE WAY, BAT-FREAK!
I'VE LOST VISUAL.
BATMAN, STAND DOWN!
THE GTO HAVE THIS UNDER CONTROL!
THE HELL IS HE THINKING?
GET HIM TO BACK OFF!
BRUCE, WHAT ARE YOU DOING?!
PROTECTING MY FAMILY.

KRASH!

THEY WENT OVER THE SIDE!

BOOM!

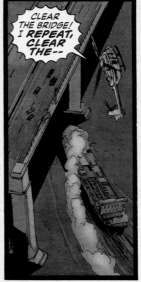

CLEAR THE BRIDGE! I REPEAT, CLEAR THE--

KRSSHHH

BATMAN'S IN THE WRECKAGE, HE'S GOT NEO JOKER--

THE BRIDGE IS COLLAPSING! WE NEED TO GO!

WHY WERE YOU AT THE WAYNES'?!

--WHAT IN??

RIPP!

WHACK!

HURRY! IT'S GOING TO--

VON FRIES

THOMAS WAYNE

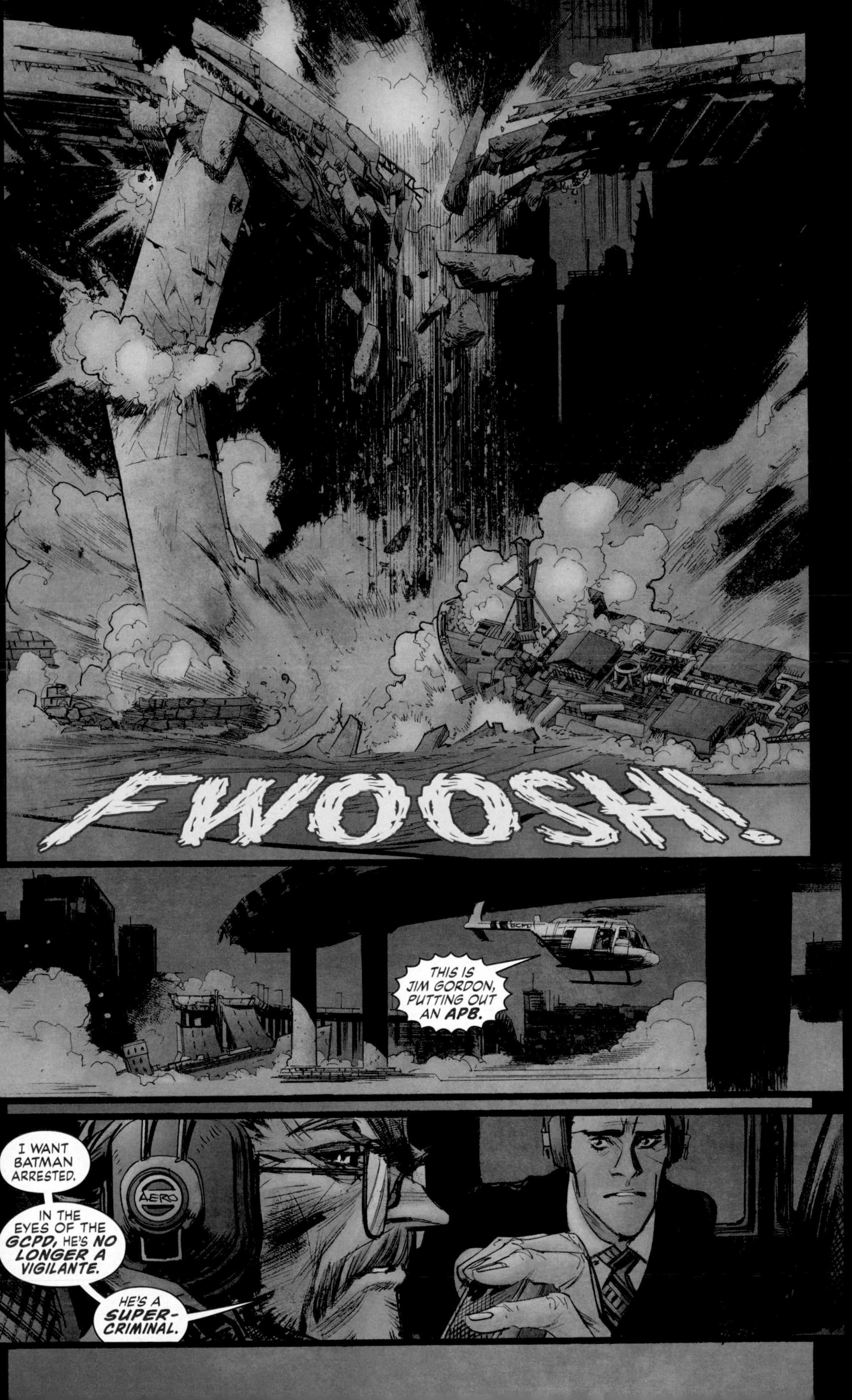
FWOOSH!
THIS IS JIM GORDON, PUTTING OUT AN APB.
I WANT BATMAN ARRESTED.
IN THE EYES OF THE GCPD, HE'S NO LONGER A VIGILANTE.
HE'S A SUPER-CRIMINAL.

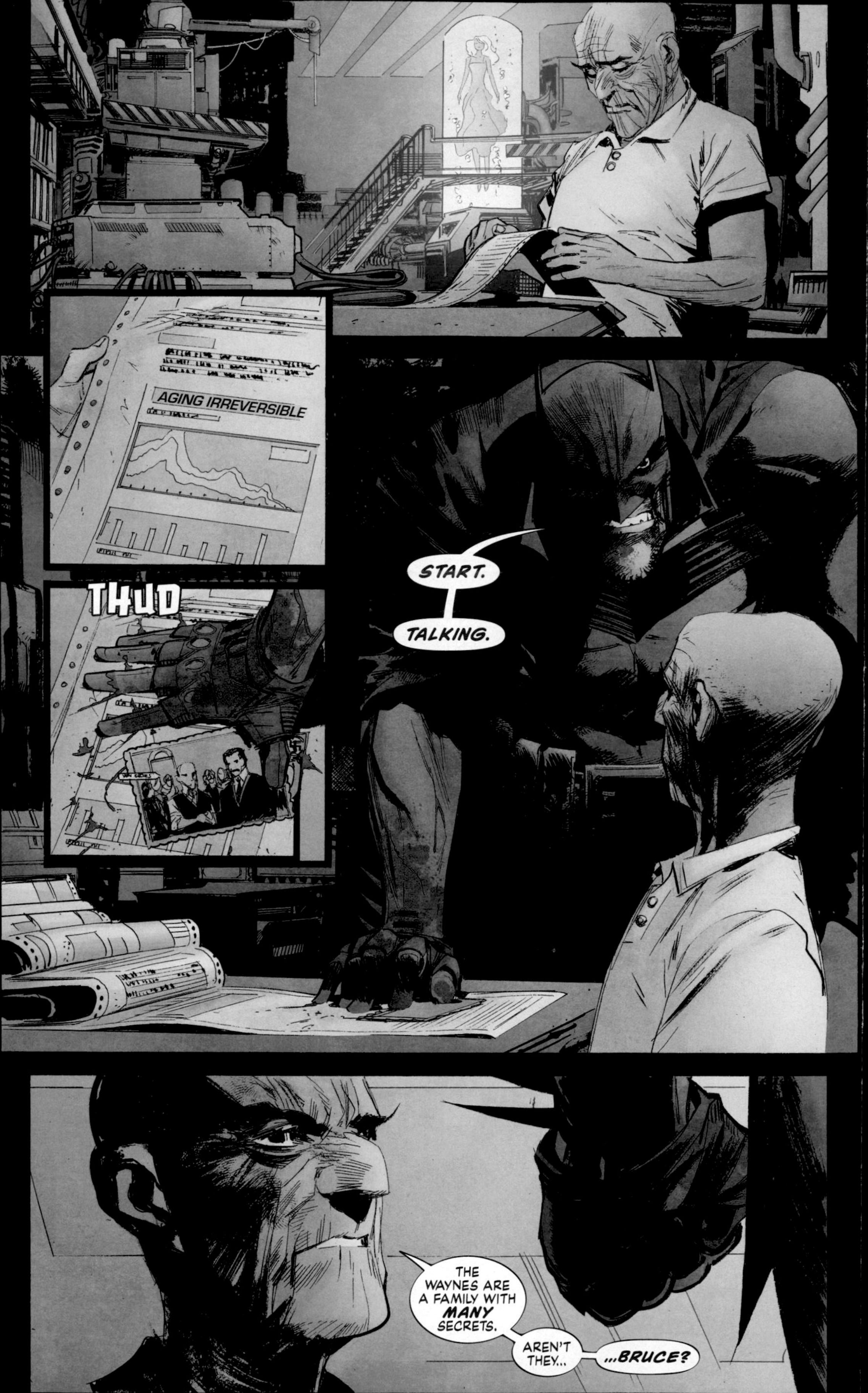
AGING IRREVERSIBLE
THUD
START.
TALKING.
THE WAYNES ARE A FAMILY WITH MANY SECRETS.
AREN'T THEY...
...BRUCE?

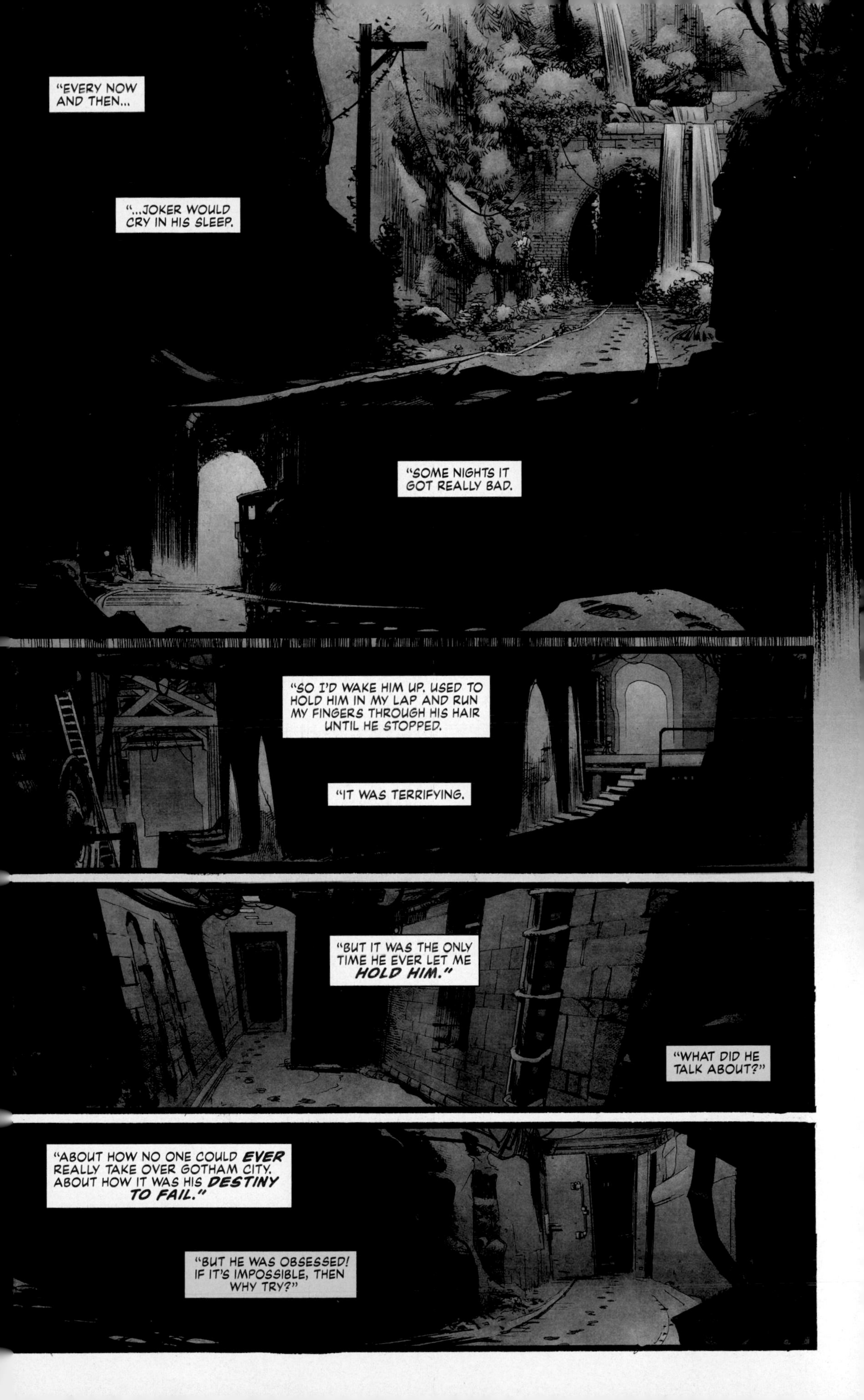
"EVERY NOW AND THEN...
"...JOKER WOULD CRY IN HIS SLEEP.
"SOME NIGHTS IT GOT REALLY BAD.
"SO I'D WAKE HIM UP. USED TO HOLD HIM IN MY LAP AND RUN MY FINGERS THROUGH HIS HAIR UNTIL HE STOPPED.
"IT WAS TERRIFYING.
"BUT IT WAS THE ONLY TIME HE EVER LET ME HOLD HIM."
"WHAT DID HE TALK ABOUT?"
"ABOUT HOW NO ONE COULD EVER REALLY TAKE OVER GOTHAM CITY. ABOUT HOW IT WAS HIS DESTINY TO FAIL."
"BUT HE WAS OBSESSED! IF IT'S IMPOSSIBLE, THEN WHY TRY?"

TO HIM, GOTHAM WAS A WARM, GLOWING LIGHT. AND ALL HE WANTED TO DO WAS HOLD IT TO HIS CHEST FOR A MOMENT...

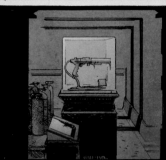

...LONG ENOUGH FOR *BATMAN* TO NOTICE...

...JUST SO HE COULD *GIVE IT BACK.*

THAT'S WHEN THE TWO OF THEM WERE CLOSEST.

THAT'S HOW I KNOW JOKER IS *STILL ALIVE.* HIS *METHODS* ARE DIFFERENT, BUT HIS *PLAN* IS THE SAME.

EVENTUALLY, HE'LL TRY TO *GIVE IT BACK.*

FLIP

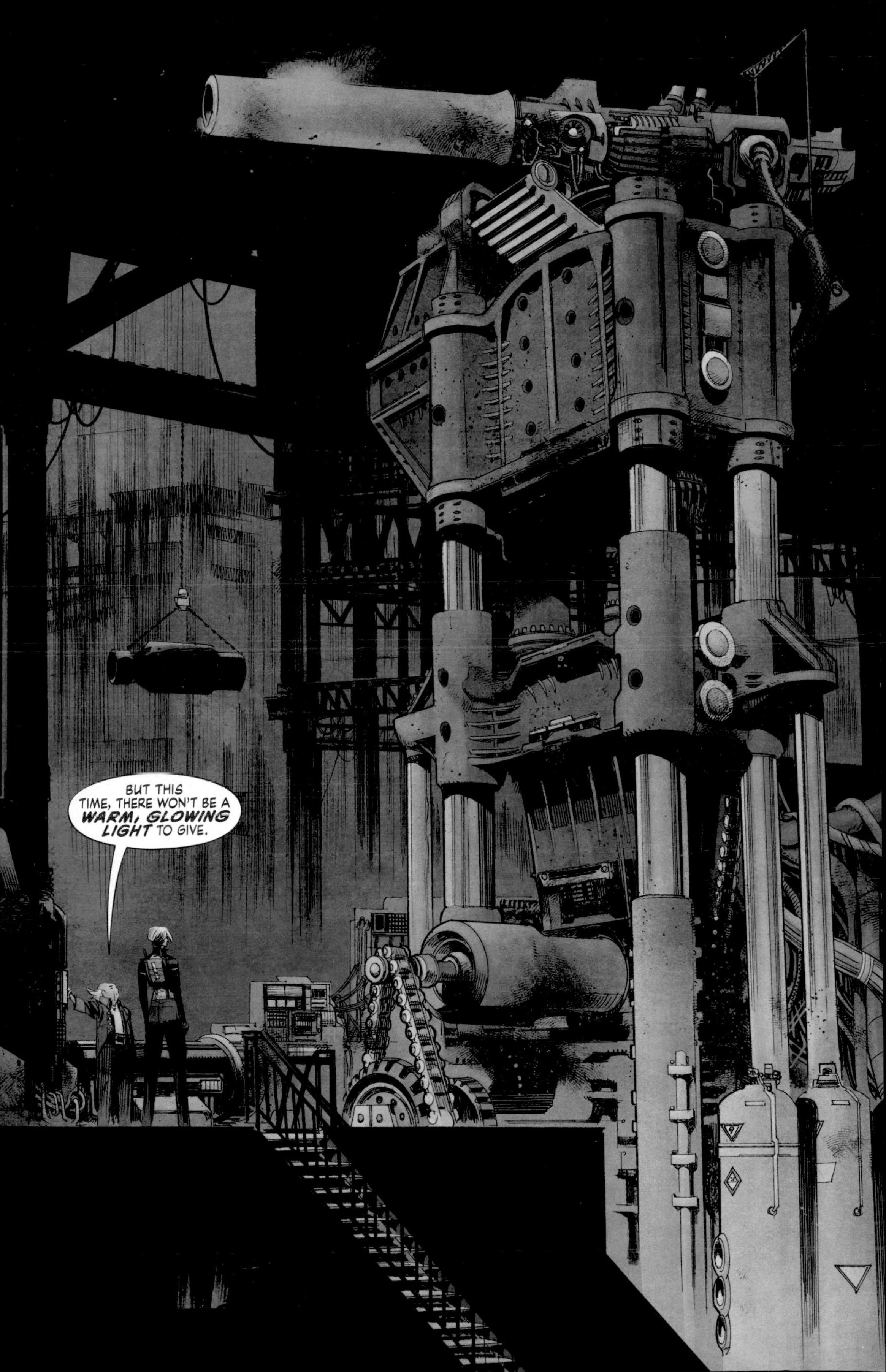
BUT THIS TIME, THERE WON'T BE A *WARM, GLOWING LIGHT* TO GIVE.

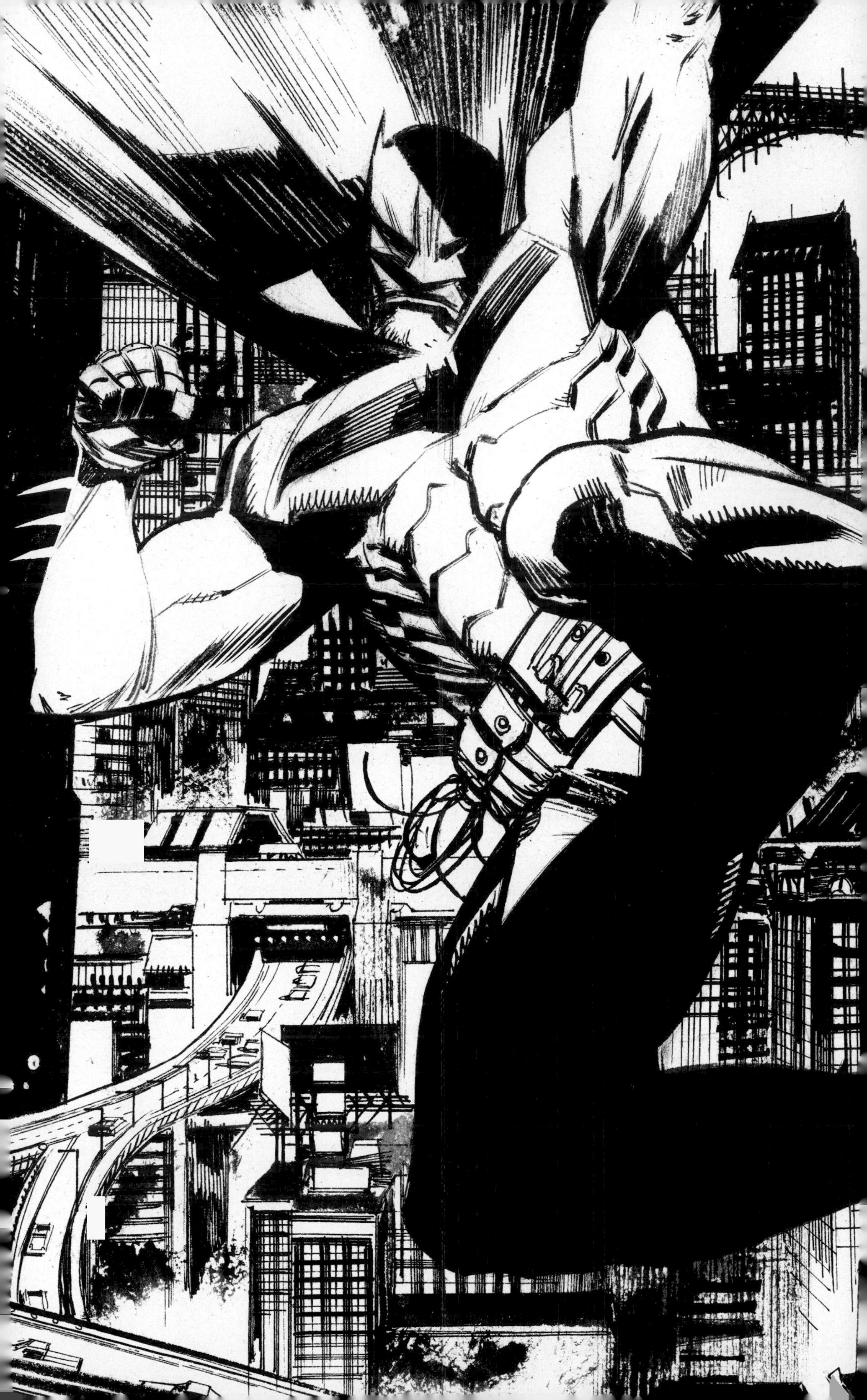

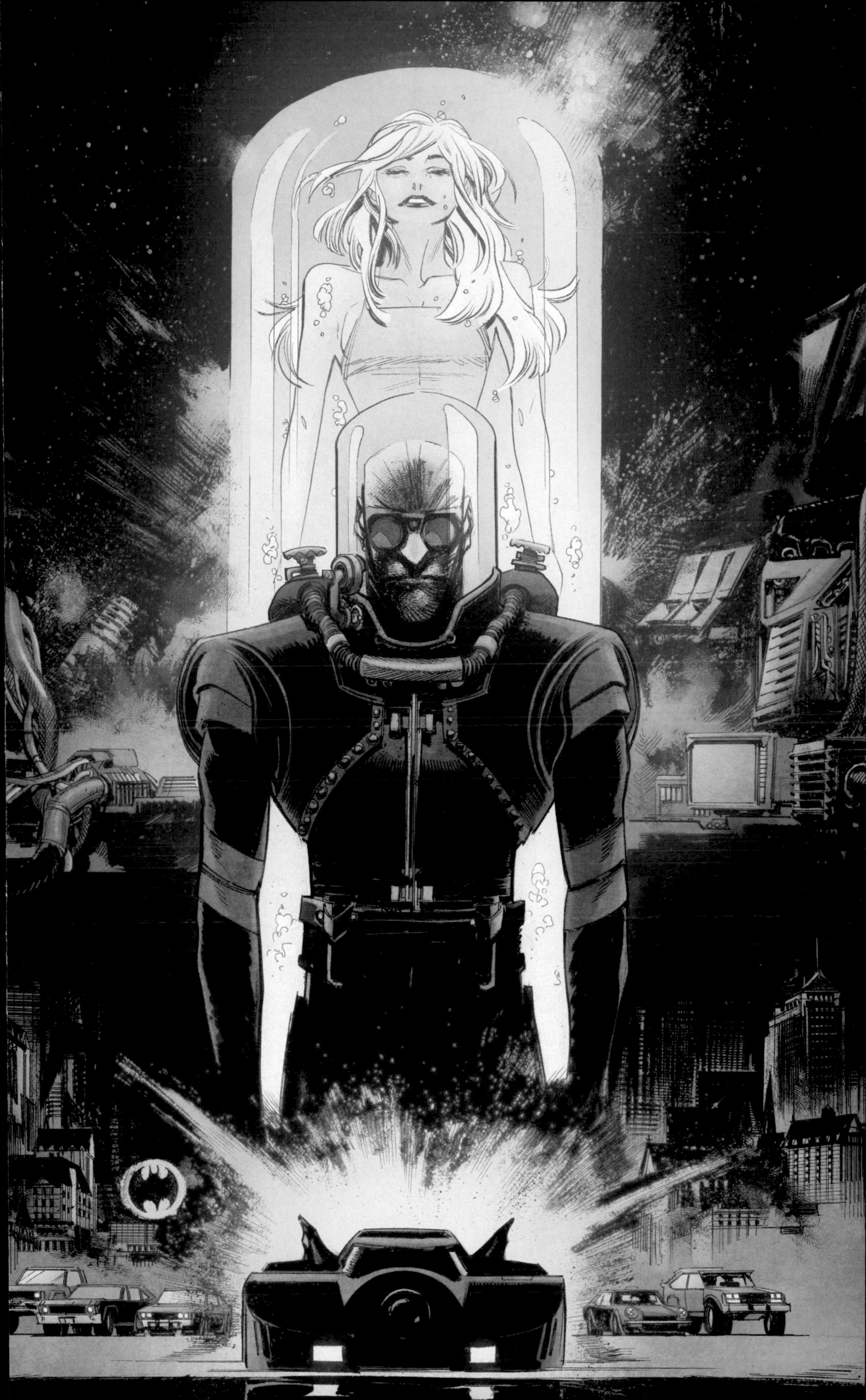

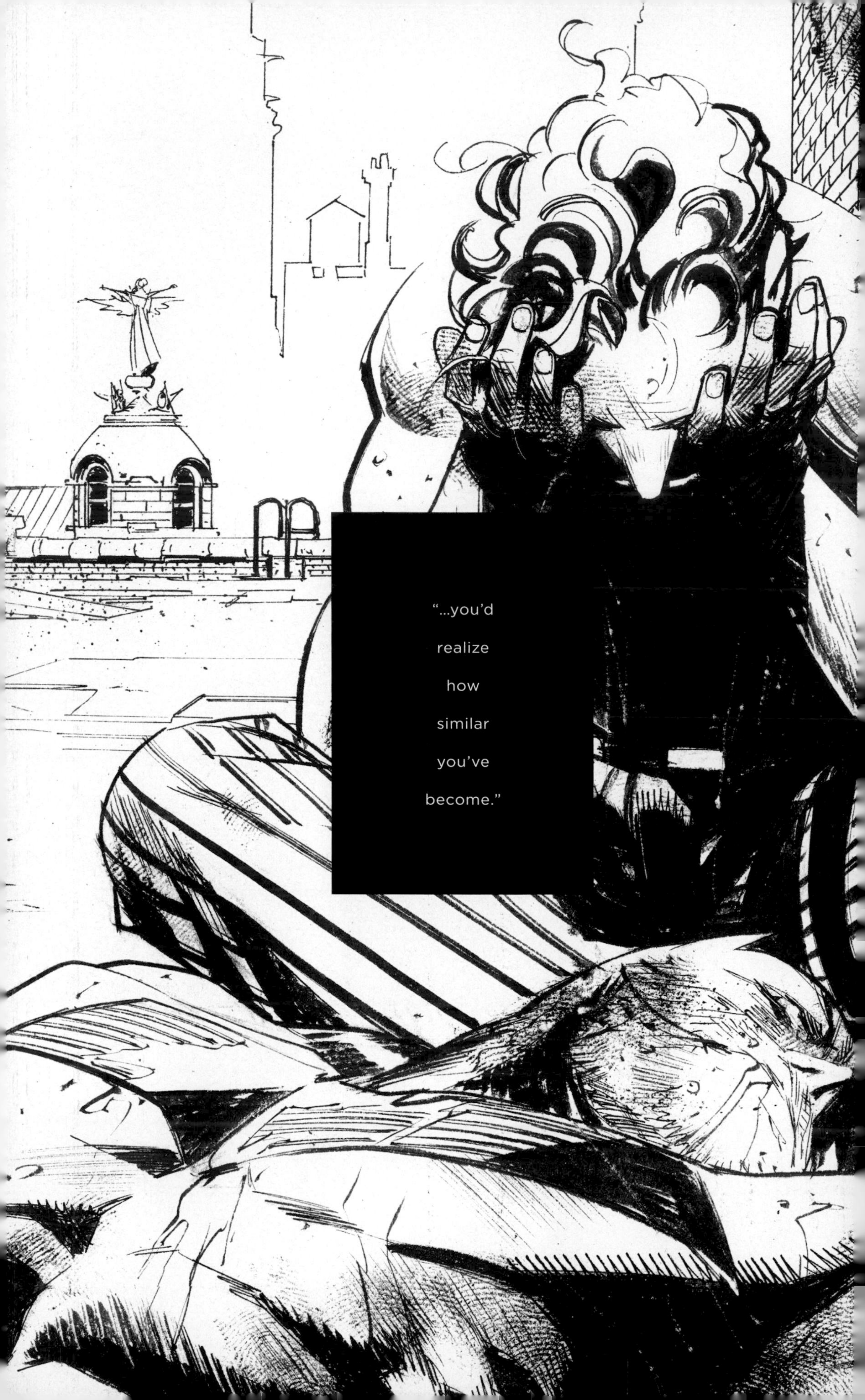
"...you'd realize how similar you've become."

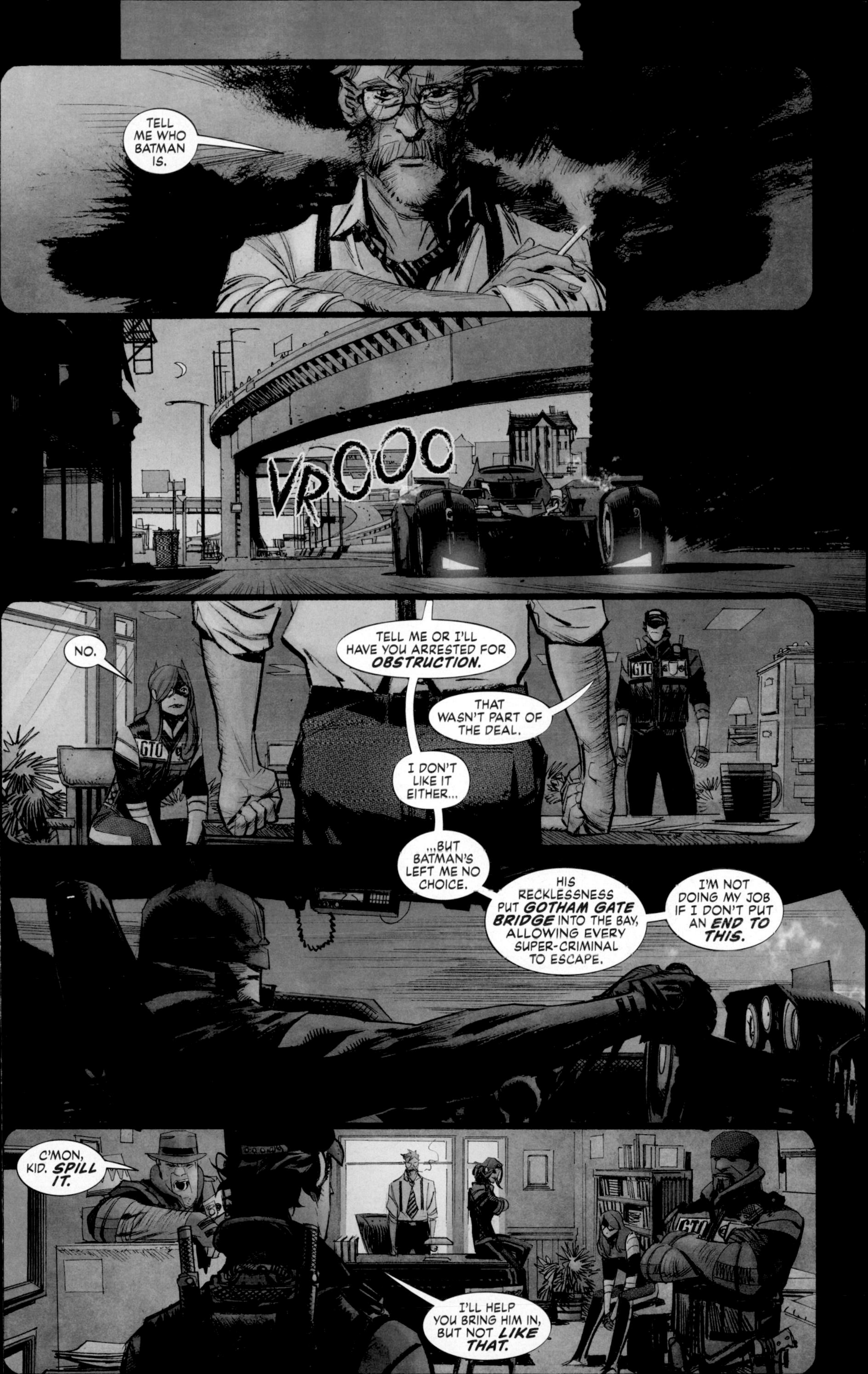
TELL ME WHO BATMAN IS.
VROOOO
NO.
TELL ME OR I'LL HAVE YOU ARRESTED FOR OBSTRUCTION.
THAT WASN'T PART OF THE DEAL.
I DON'T LIKE IT EITHER...
...BUT BATMAN'S LEFT ME NO CHOICE.
HIS RECKLESSNESS PUT GOTHAM GATE BRIDGE INTO THE BAY, ALLOWING EVERY SUPER-CRIMINAL TO ESCAPE.
I'M NOT DOING MY JOB IF I DON'T PUT AN END TO THIS.
C'MON, KID. SPILL IT.
I'LL HELP YOU BRING HIM IN, BUT NOT LIKE THAT.

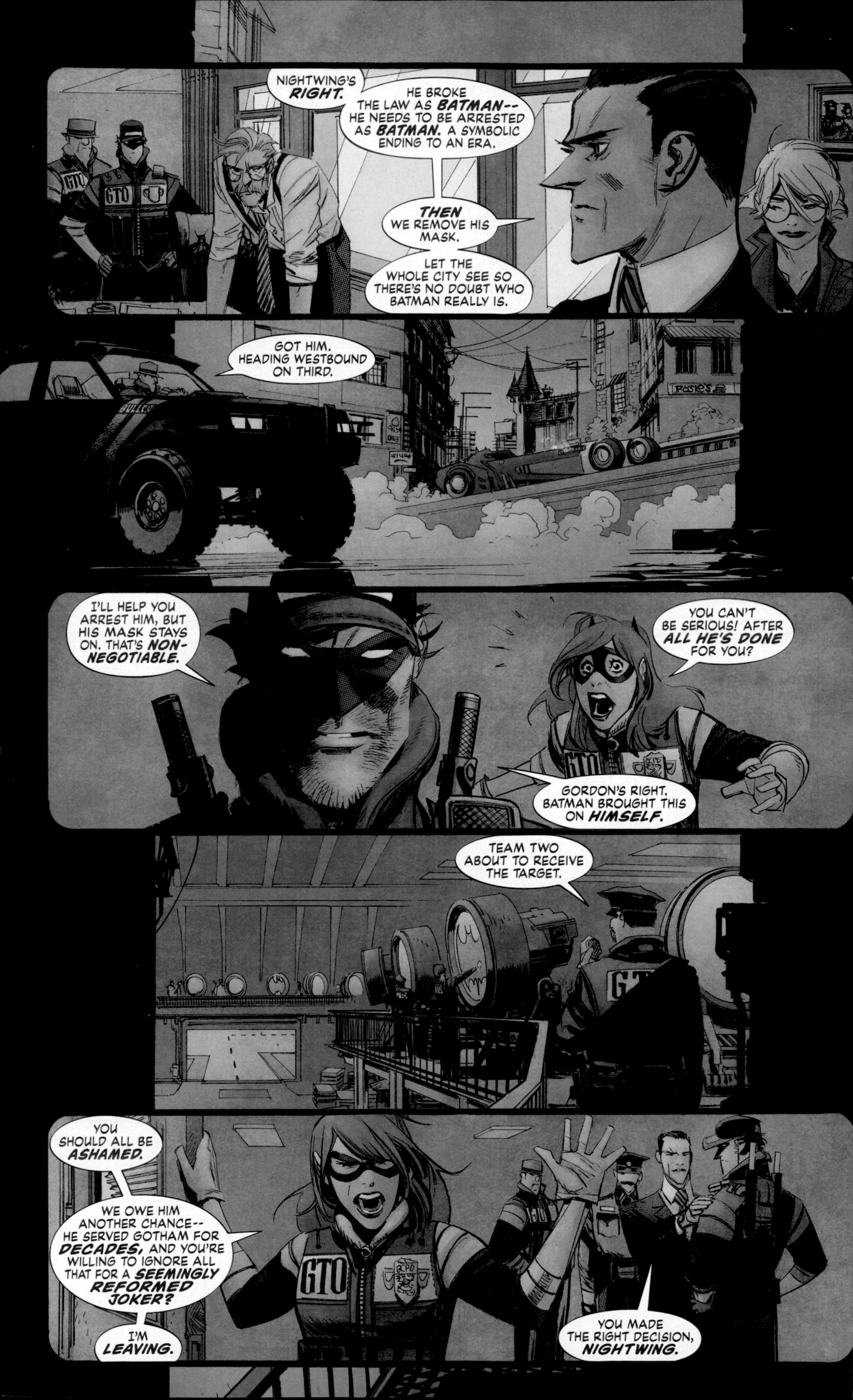
NIGHTWING'S RIGHT.
HE BROKE THE LAW AS BATMAN-- HE NEEDS TO BE ARRESTED AS BATMAN. A SYMBOLIC ENDING TO AN ERA.
THEN WE REMOVE HIS MASK.
LET THE WHOLE CITY SEE SO THERE'S NO DOUBT WHO BATMAN REALLY IS.
GOT HIM. HEADING WESTBOUND ON THIRD.
BULL
ROSIE'S
I'LL HELP YOU ARREST HIM, BUT HIS MASK STAYS ON. THAT'S NON-NEGOTIABLE.
YOU CAN'T BE SERIOUS! AFTER ALL HE'S DONE FOR YOU?
GTO
GORDON'S RIGHT. BATMAN BROUGHT THIS ON HIMSELF.
TEAM TWO ABOUT TO RECEIVE THE TARGET.
GTO
YOU SHOULD ALL BE ASHAMED.
WE OWE HIM ANOTHER CHANCE-- HE SERVED GOTHAM FOR DECADES, AND YOU'RE WILLING TO IGNORE ALL THAT FOR A SEEMINGLY REFORMED JOKER?
I'M LEAVING.
GTO
YOU MADE THE RIGHT DECISION, NIGHTWING.

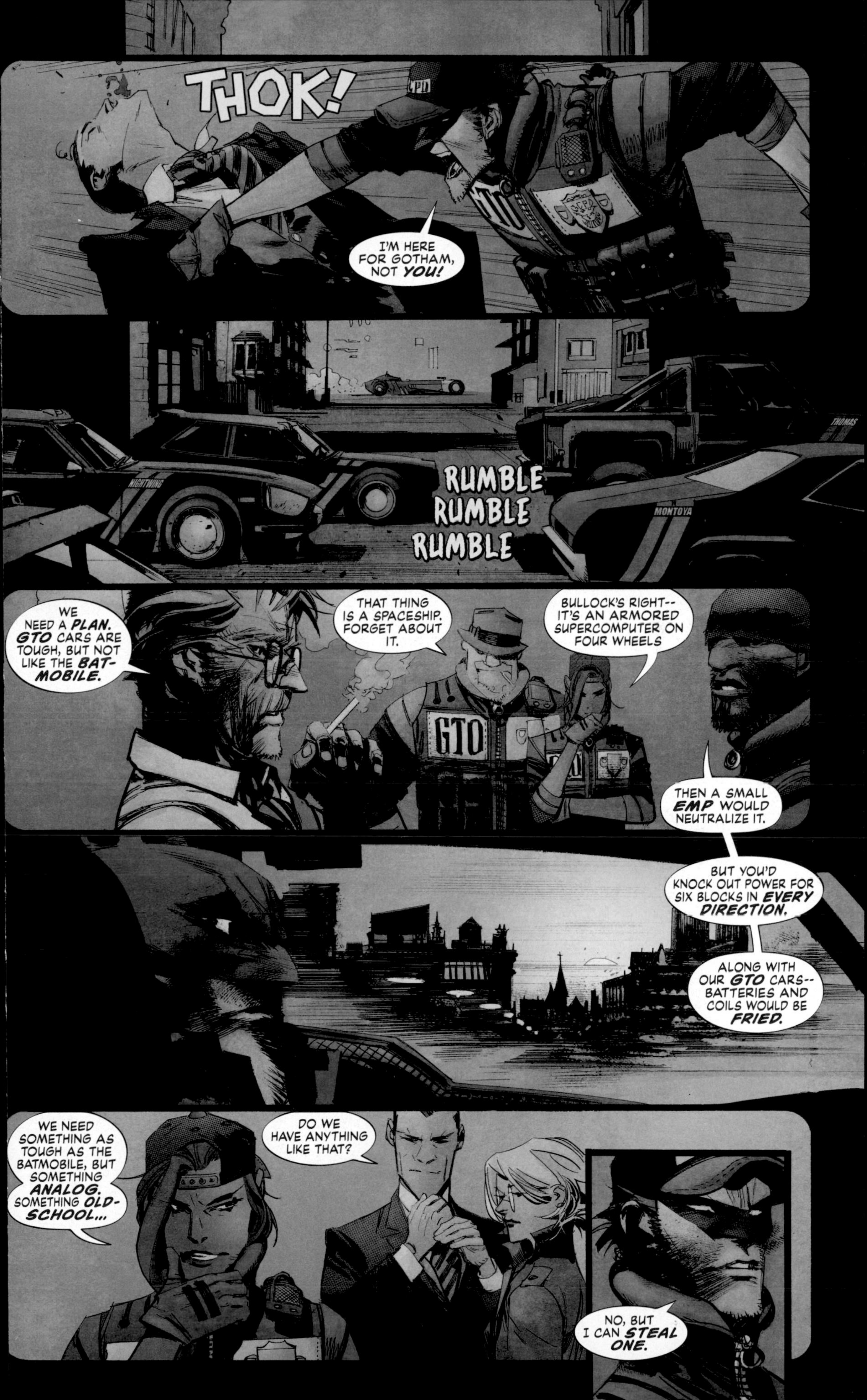
THOK!
I'M HERE FOR GOTHAM, NOT YOU!
RUMBLE RUMBLE RUMBLE
NIGHTWING
THOMAS
MONTOYA
WE NEED A PLAN. GTO CARS ARE TOUGH, BUT NOT LIKE THE BAT-MOBILE.
THAT THING IS A SPACESHIP. FORGET ABOUT IT.
BULLOCK'S RIGHT-- IT'S AN ARMORED SUPERCOMPUTER ON FOUR WHEELS
GTO
THEN A SMALL EMP WOULD NEUTRALIZE IT.
BUT YOU'D KNOCK OUT POWER FOR SIX BLOCKS IN EVERY DIRECTION.
ALONG WITH OUR GTO CARS-- BATTERIES AND COILS WOULD BE FRIED.
WE NEED SOMETHING AS TOUGH AS THE BATMOBILE, BUT SOMETHING ANALOG. SOMETHING OLD-SCHOOL...
DO WE HAVE ANYTHING LIKE THAT?
NO, BUT I CAN STEAL ONE.

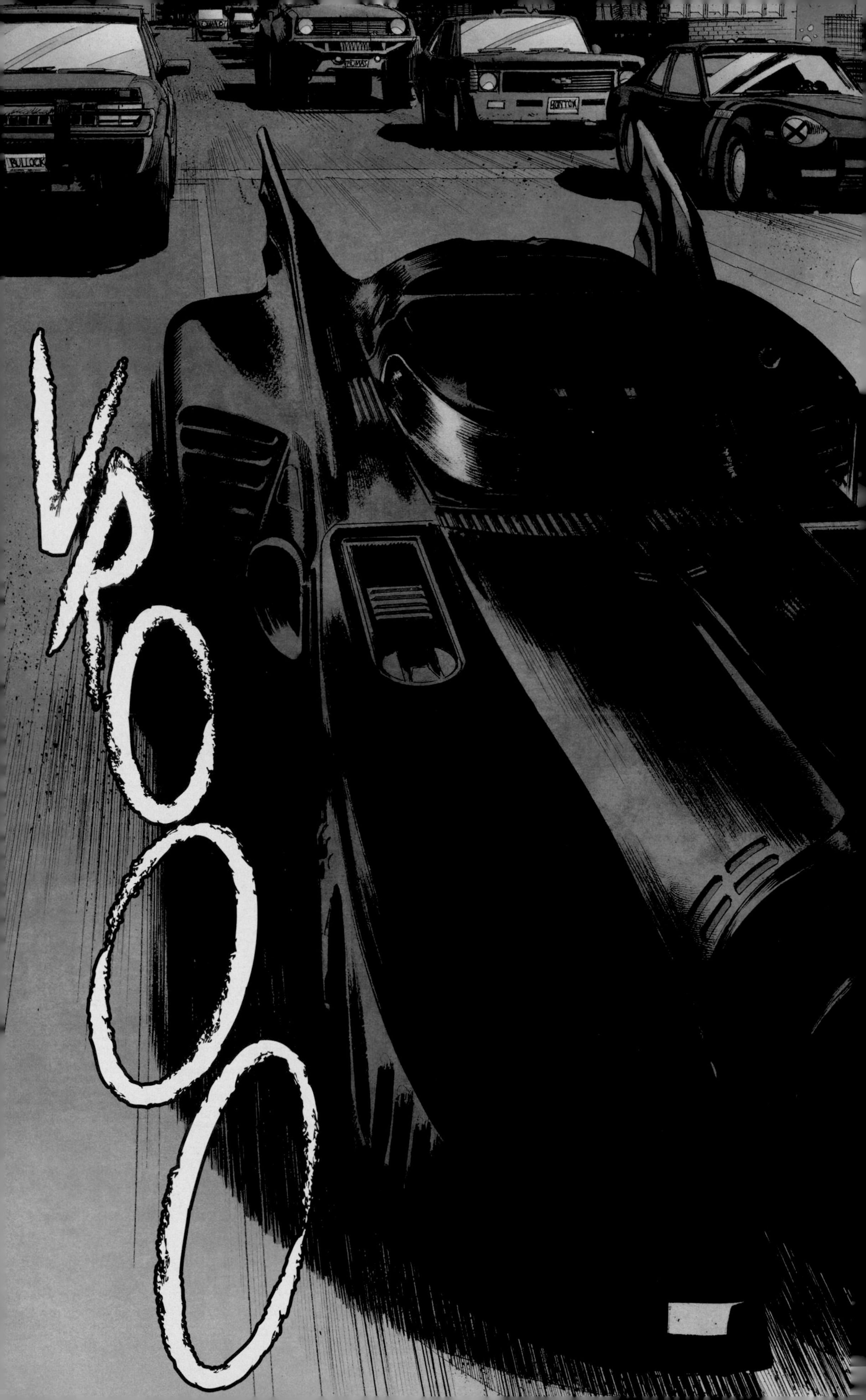
VROOO
BULLOCK

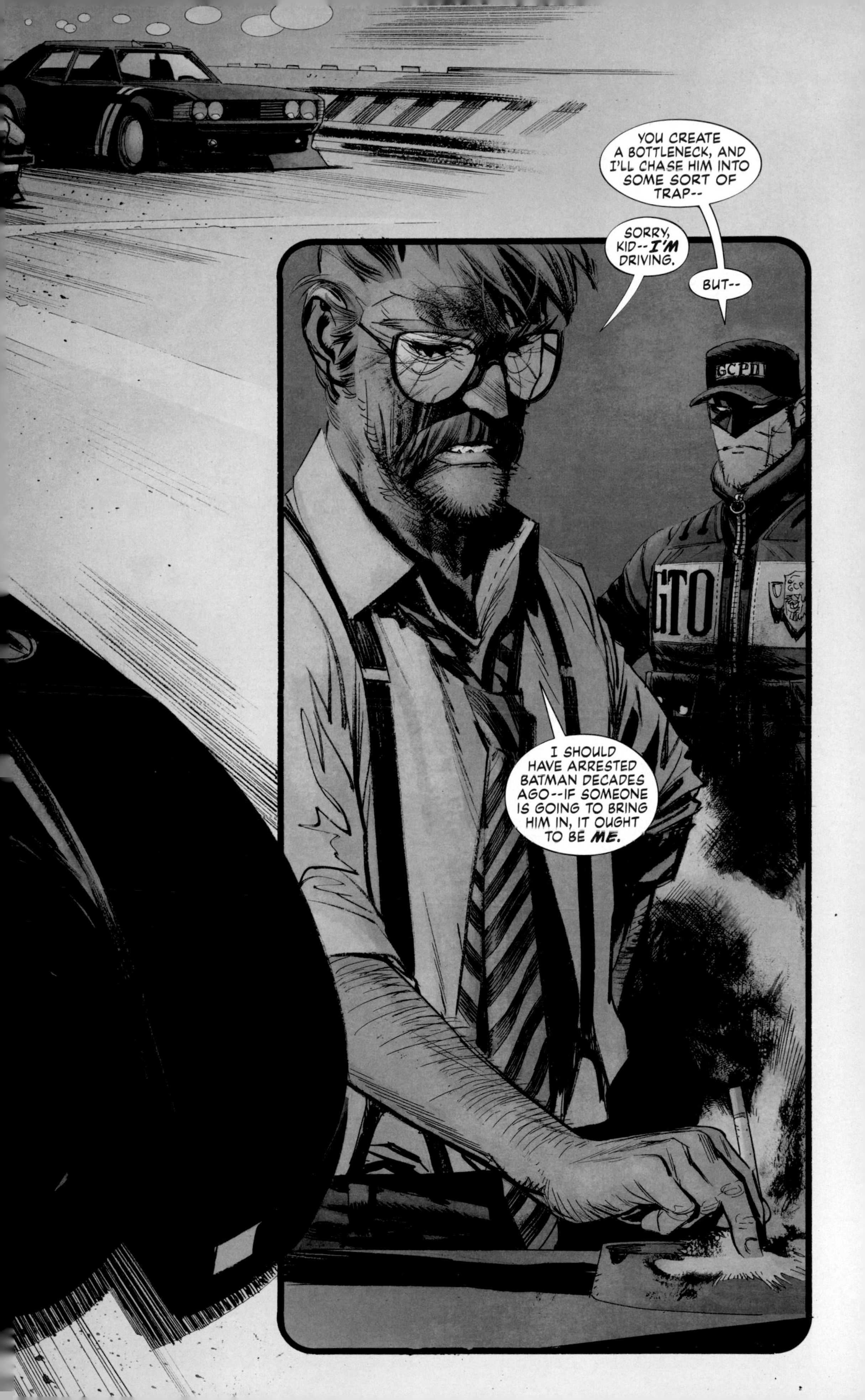

YOU CREATE A BOTTLENECK, AND I'LL CHASE HIM INTO SOME SORT OF TRAP--
SORRY, KID--*I'M* DRIVING.
BUT--
I SHOULD HAVE ARRESTED BATMAN DECADES AGO--IF SOMEONE IS GOING TO BRING HIM IN, IT OUGHT TO BE *ME.*

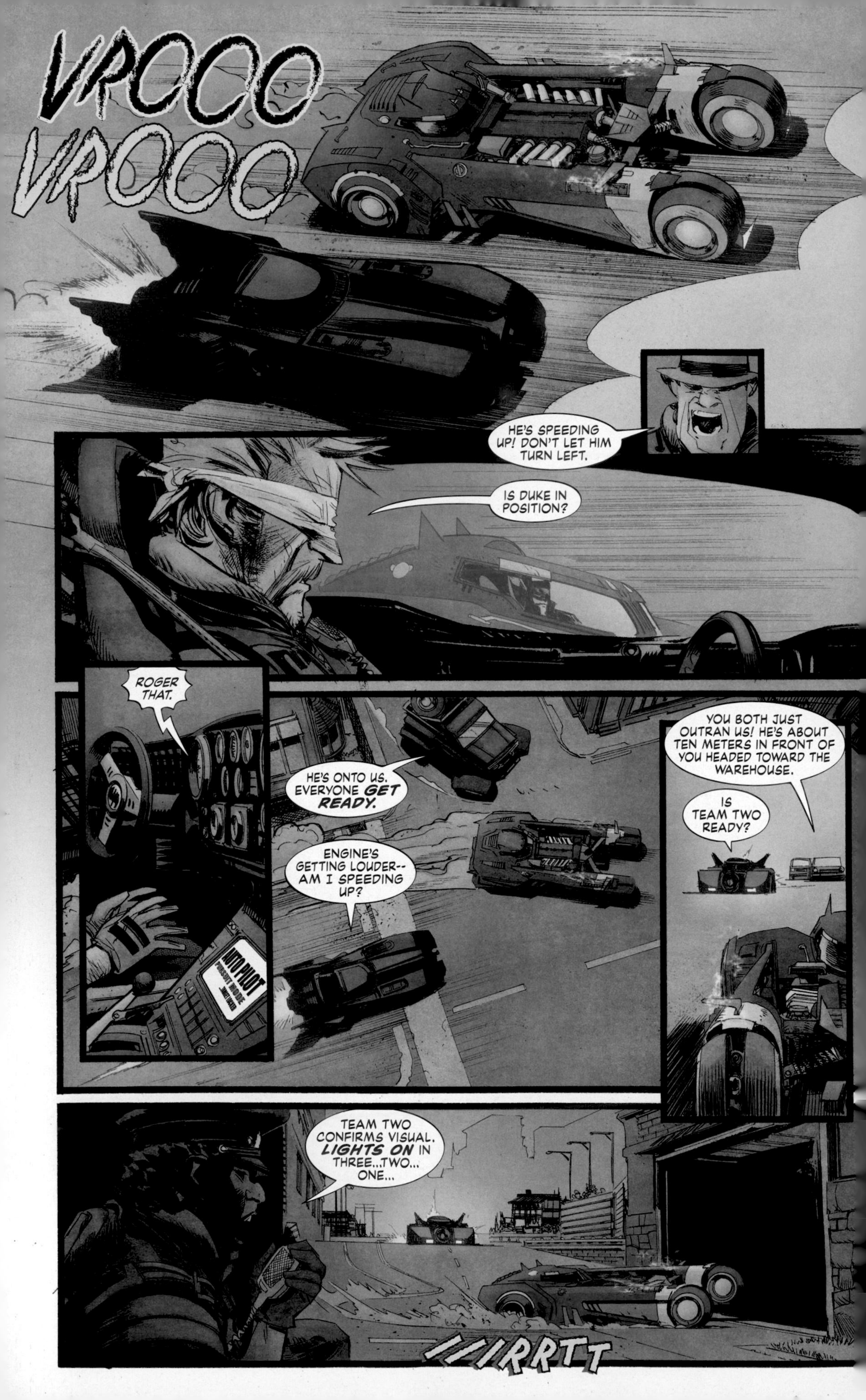
VROOO VROOO
HE'S SPEEDING UP! DON'T LET HIM TURN LEFT.
IS DUKE IN POSITION?
ROGER THAT.
HE'S ONTO US. EVERYONE GET READY.
ENGINE'S GETTING LOUDER-- AM I SPEEDING UP?
YOU BOTH JUST OUTRAN US! HE'S ABOUT TEN METERS IN FRONT OF YOU HEADED TOWARD THE WAREHOUSE.
IS TEAM TWO READY?
TEAM TWO CONFIRMS VISUAL. LIGHTS ON IN THREE...TWO... ONE...
IIIRRTT

LIGHT 'EM UP!

FWOOSH

ARGH!

GORDON, WE'RE ABOUT TO GO BLACK.

BLINDFOLD'S WORKING-- I SHOULD STILL BE DILATED.

YOU'RE CLOSE TO THE END ZONE. EMP IN THREE...

...TWO...

I'M IN NEUTRAL.

...ONE...

ENGINE OFF--I'M COASTING!

NOW!

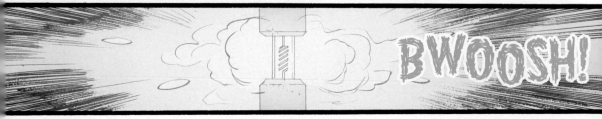

BWOOSH!

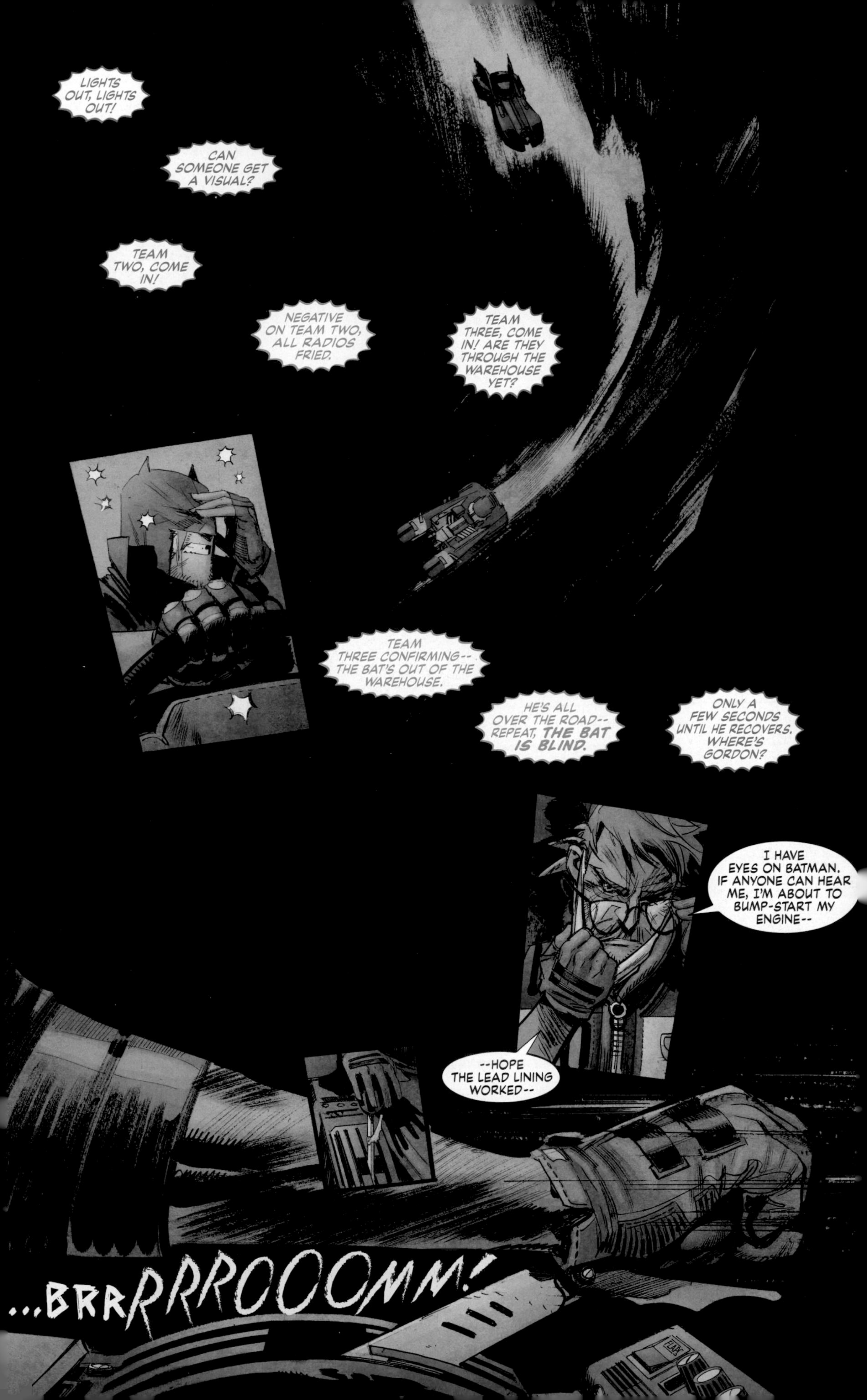
LIGHTS OUT, LIGHTS OUT!
CAN SOMEONE GET A VISUAL?
TEAM TWO, COME IN!
NEGATIVE ON TEAM TWO, ALL RADIOS FRIED.
TEAM THREE, COME IN! ARE THEY THROUGH THE WAREHOUSE YET?
TEAM THREE CONFIRMING-- THE BAT'S OUT OF THE WAREHOUSE.
HE'S ALL OVER THE ROAD-- REPEAT, **THE BAT IS BLIND.**
ONLY A FEW SECONDS UNTIL HE RECOVERS. WHERE'S GORDON?
I HAVE EYES ON BATMAN. IF ANYONE CAN HEAR ME, I'M ABOUT TO BUMP-START MY ENGINE--
--HOPE THE LEAD LINING WORKED--
...BRRRRROOOOMM!

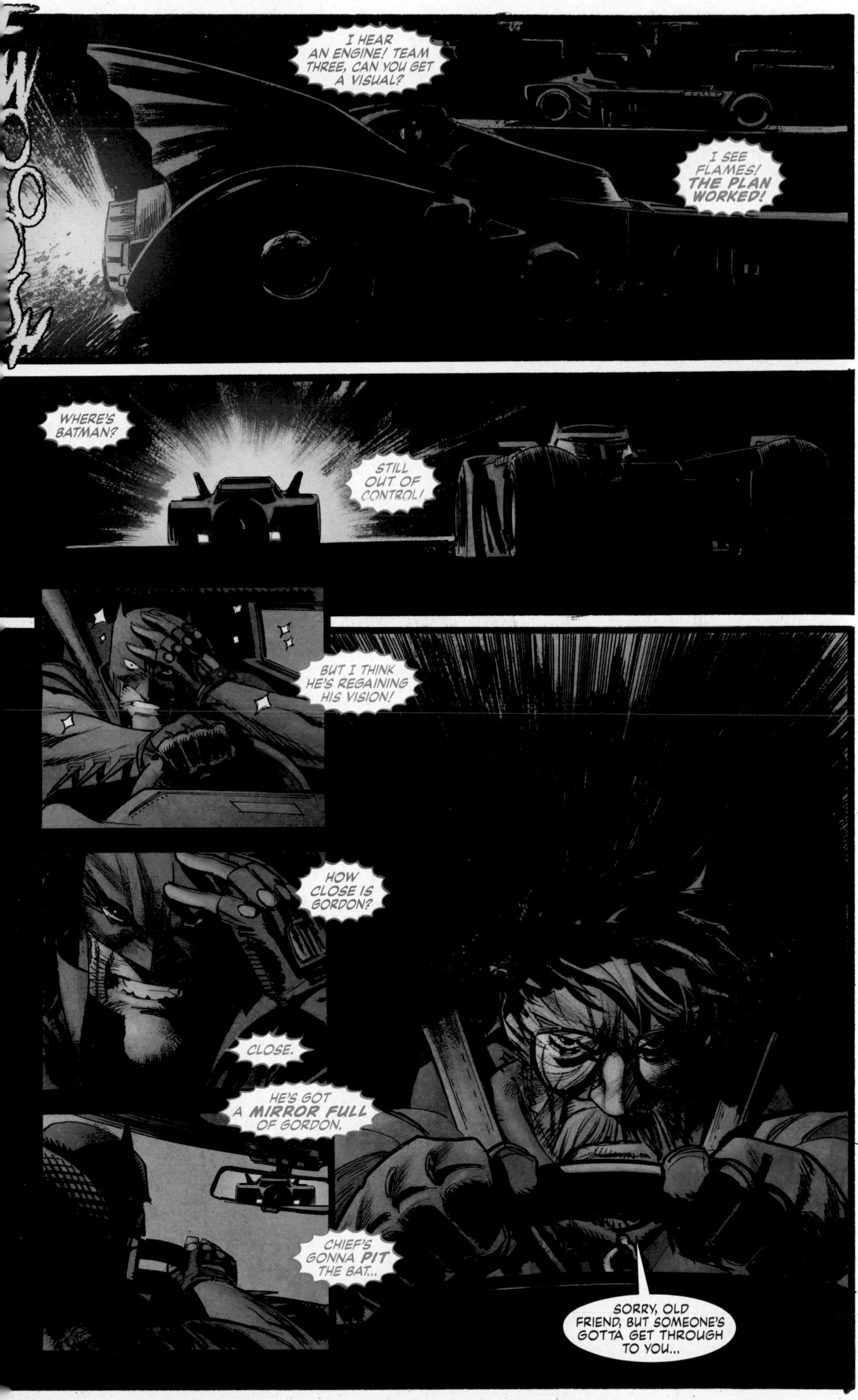

I HEAR AN ENGINE! TEAM THREE, CAN YOU GET A VISUAL?
I SEE FLAMES! THE PLAN WORKED!
WHERE'S BATMAN?
STILL OUT OF CONTROL!
BUT I THINK HE'S REGAINING HIS VISION!
HOW CLOSE IS GORDON?
CLOSE.
HE'S GOT A MIRROR FULL OF GORDON.
CHIEF'S GONNA PIT THE BAT...
SORRY, OLD FRIEND, BUT SOMEONE'S GOTTA GET THROUGH TO YOU...

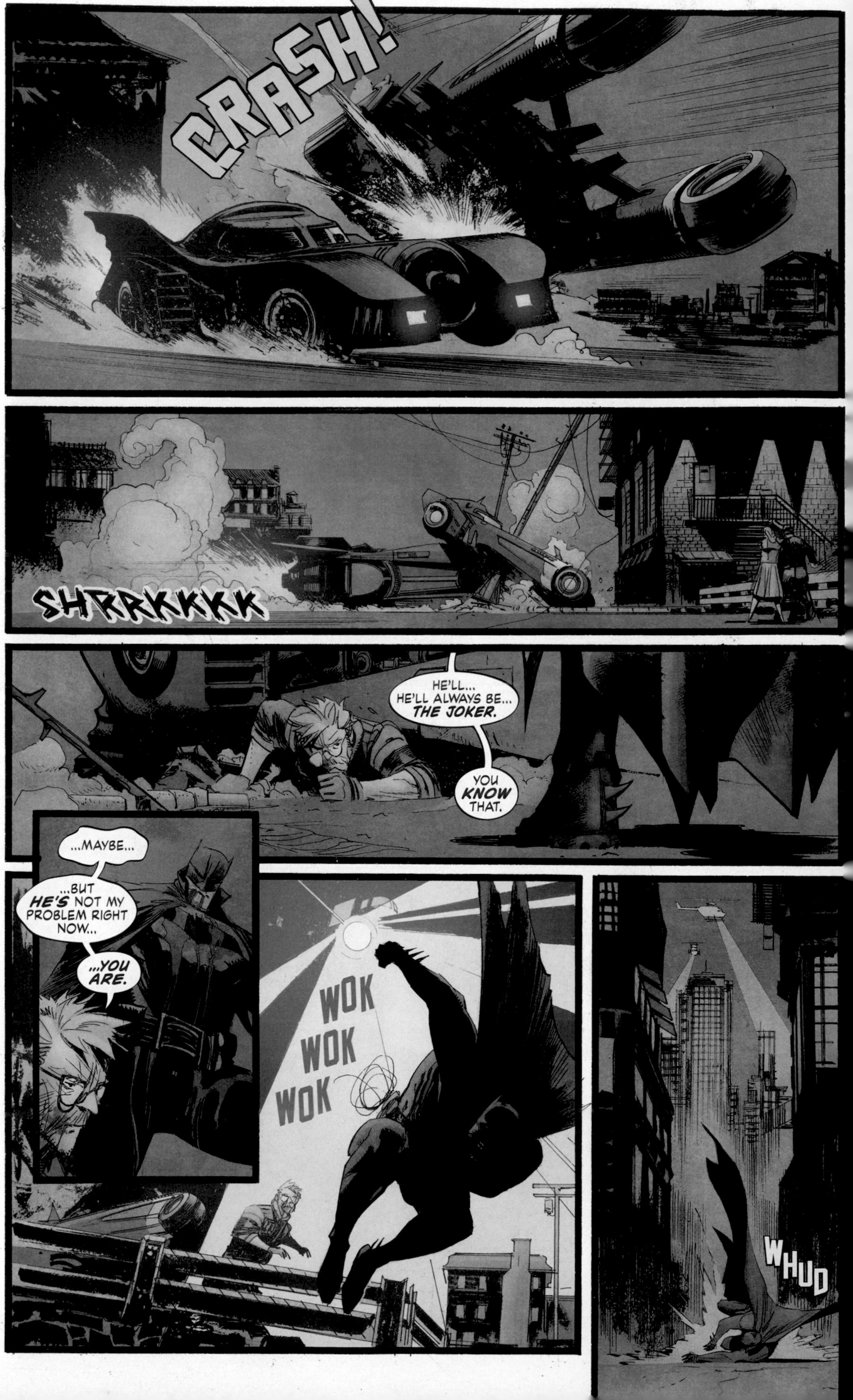
CRASH!
SHRRKKKK
HE'LL... HE'LL ALWAYS BE... THE JOKER.
YOU KNOW THAT.
...MAYBE...
...BUT HE'S NOT MY PROBLEM RIGHT NOW...
...YOU ARE.
WOK WOK WOK
WHUD

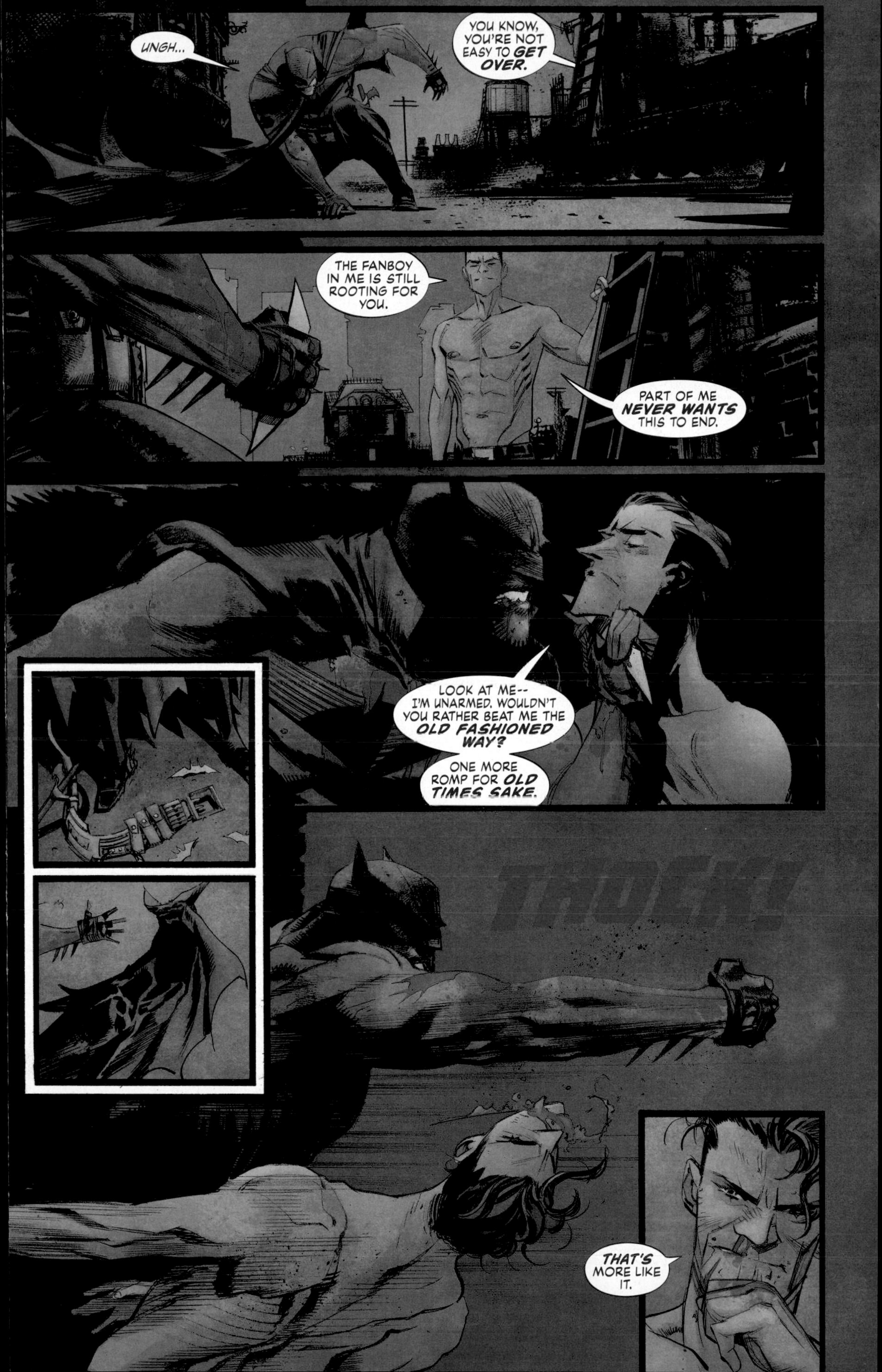
UNGH...
YOU KNOW, YOU'RE NOT EASY TO GET OVER.
THE FANBOY IN ME IS STILL ROOTING FOR YOU.
PART OF ME NEVER WANTS THIS TO END.
LOOK AT ME-- I'M UNARMED. WOULDN'T YOU RATHER BEAT ME THE OLD FASHIONED WAY?
ONE MORE ROMP FOR OLD TIMES SAKE.
THAT'S MORE LIKE IT.

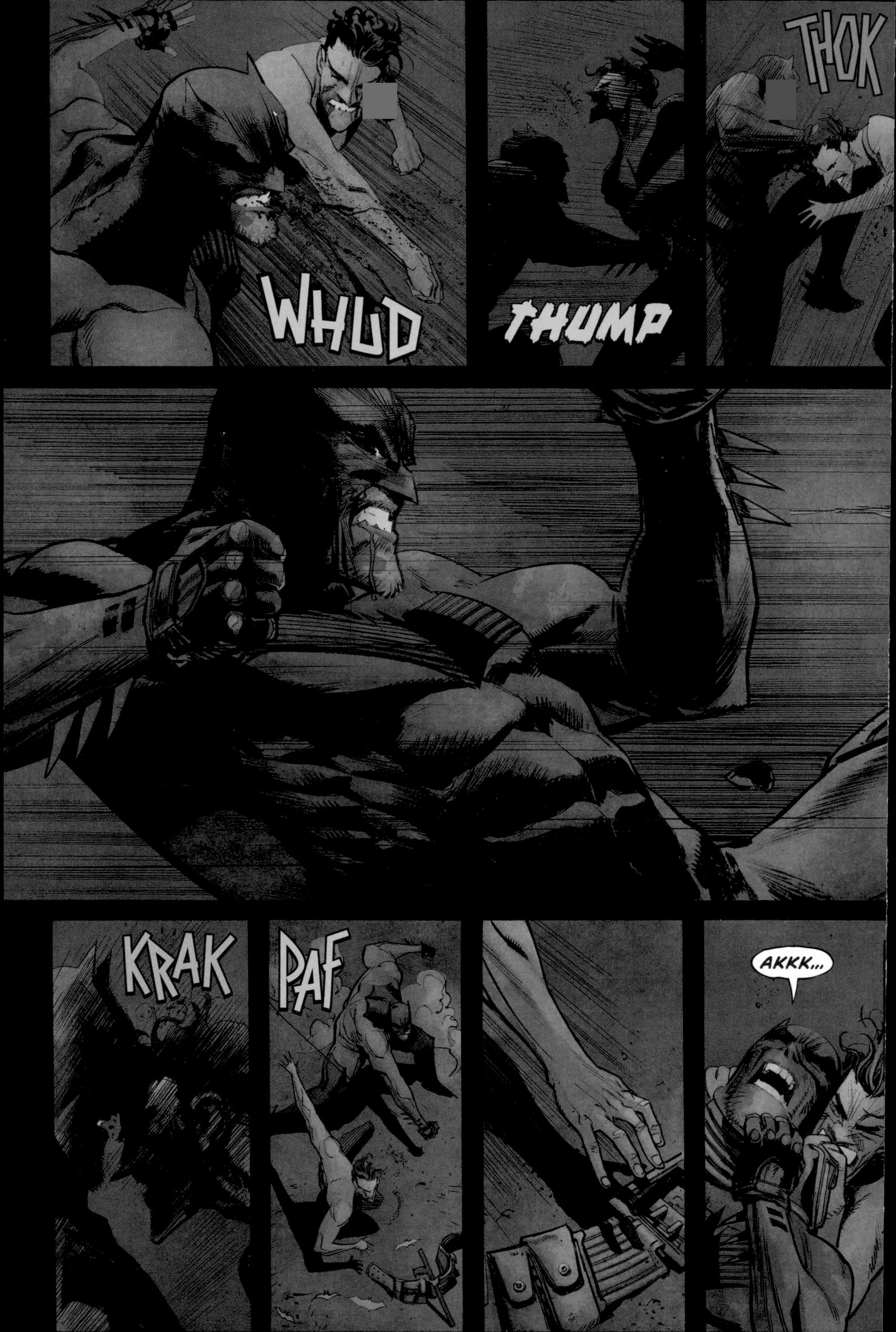
WHUD
THUMP
THOK
KRAK
PAF
AKKK...

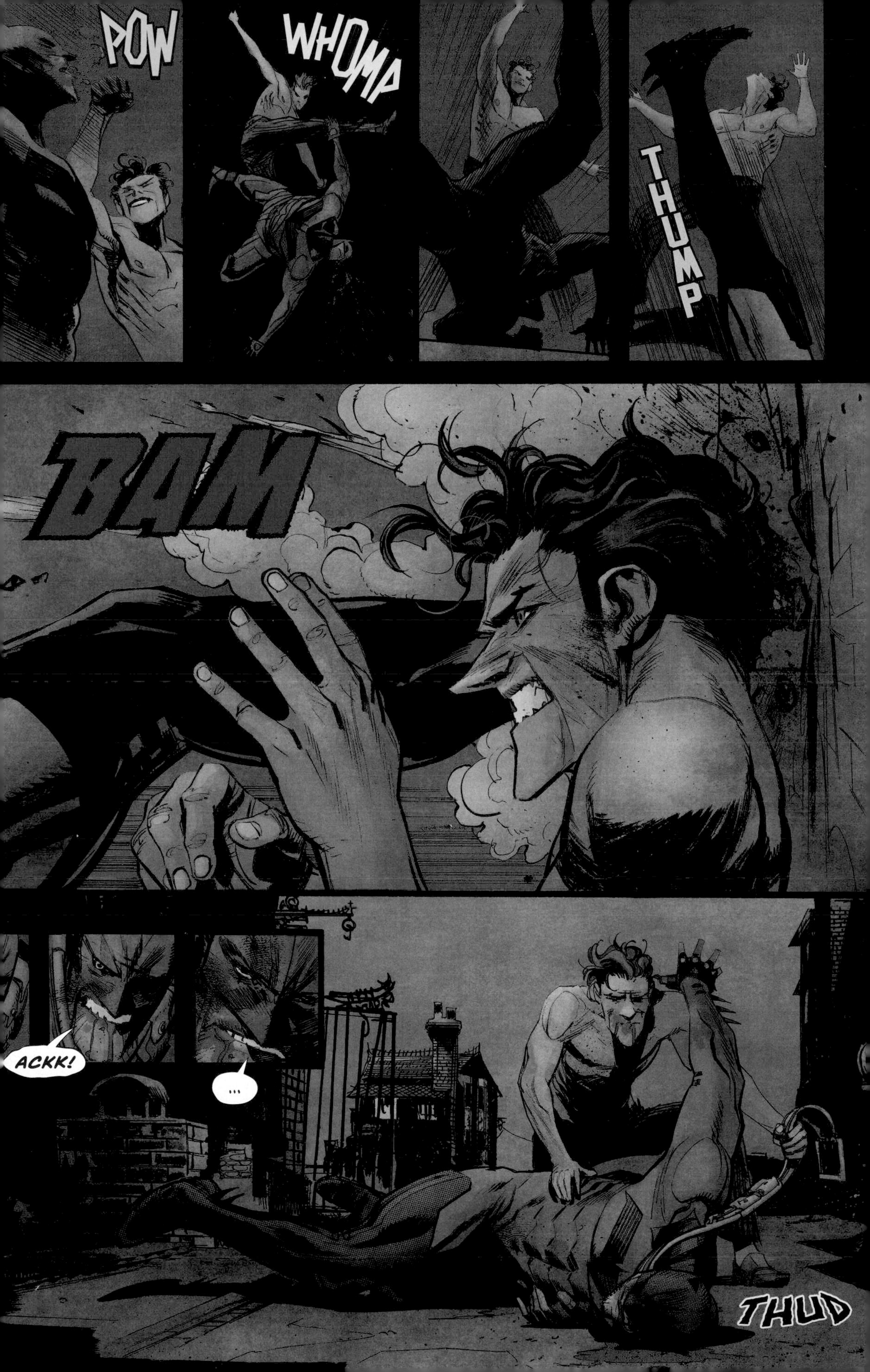
POW
WHOMP
THUMP
BAM
ACKK!
...
THUD

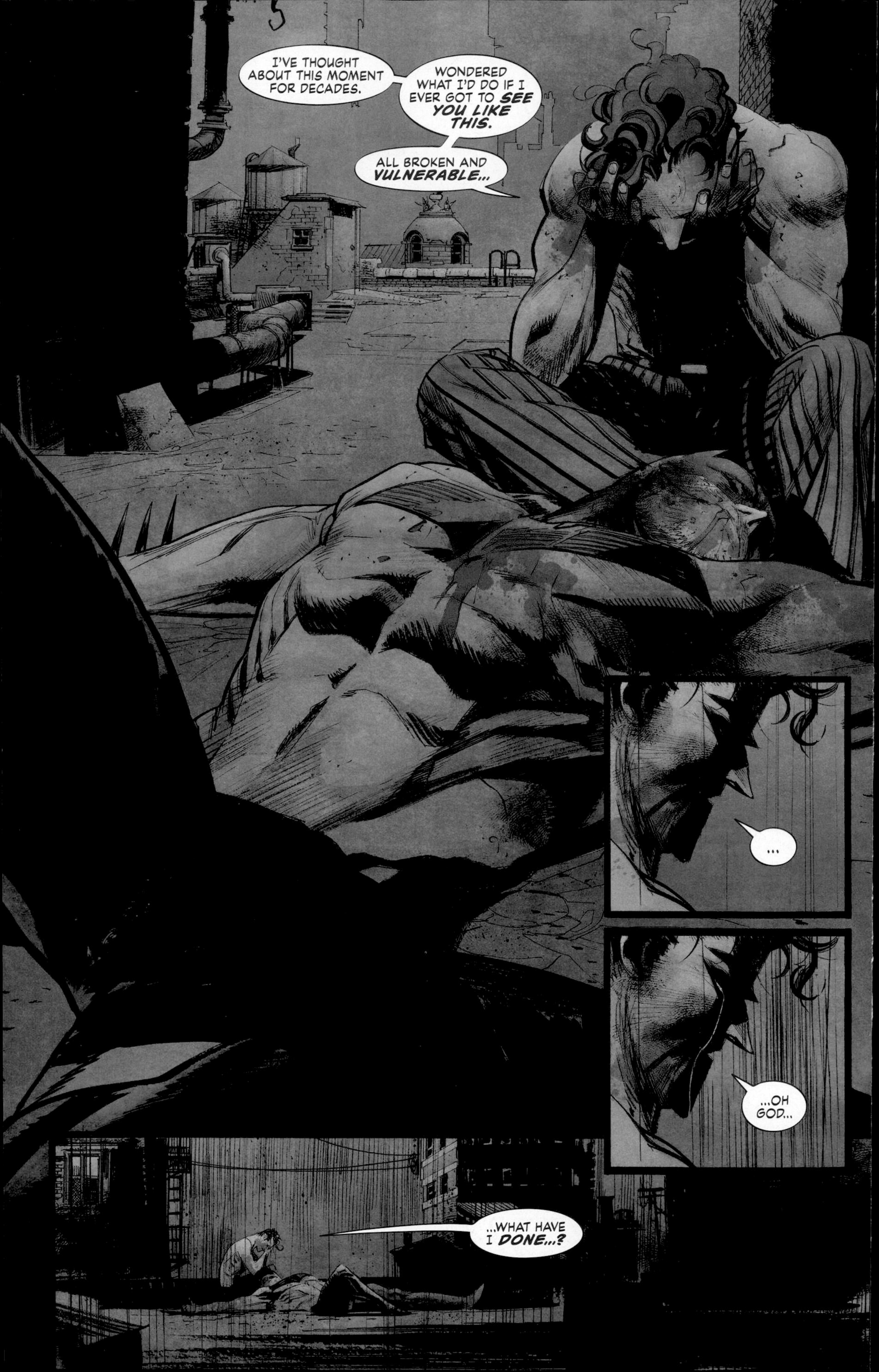
I'VE THOUGHT ABOUT THIS MOMENT FOR DECADES.
WONDERED WHAT I'D DO IF I EVER GOT TO SEE YOU LIKE THIS.
ALL BROKEN AND VULNERABLE...
...
...OH GOD...
...WHAT HAVE I DONE...?

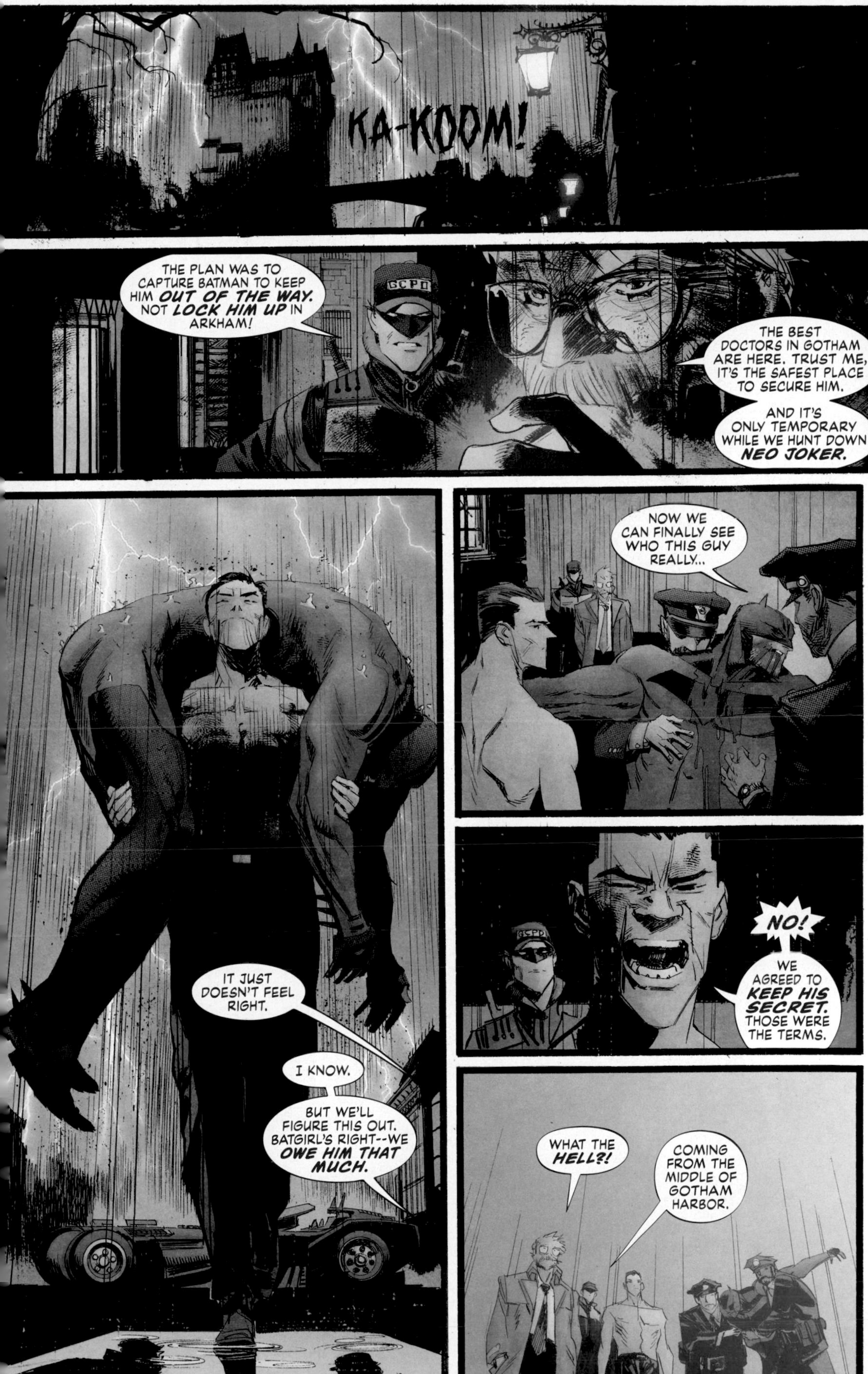
KA-KOOM!
THE PLAN WAS TO CAPTURE BATMAN TO KEEP HIM OUT OF THE WAY. NOT LOCK HIM UP IN ARKHAM!
THE BEST DOCTORS IN GOTHAM ARE HERE. TRUST ME, IT'S THE SAFEST PLACE TO SECURE HIM.
AND IT'S ONLY TEMPORARY WHILE WE HUNT DOWN NEO JOKER.
IT JUST DOESN'T FEEL RIGHT.
I KNOW.
BUT WE'LL FIGURE THIS OUT. BATGIRL'S RIGHT--WE OWE HIM THAT MUCH.
NOW WE CAN FINALLY SEE WHO THIS GUY REALLY...
NO!
WE AGREED TO KEEP HIS SECRET. THOSE WERE THE TERMS.
WHAT THE HELL?!
COMING FROM THE MIDDLE OF GOTHAM HARBOR.

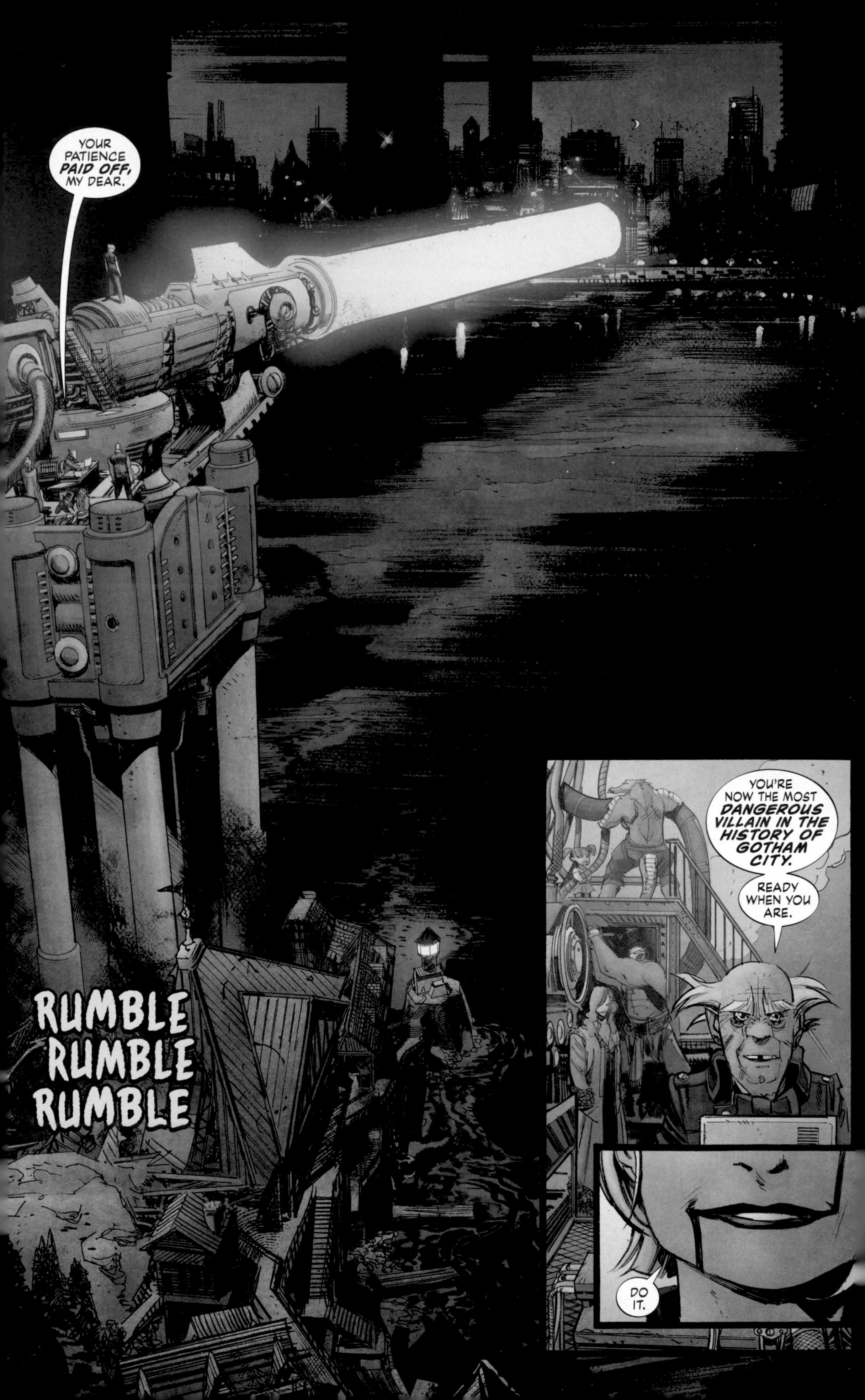
YOUR PATIENCE PAID OFF, MY DEAR.
RUMBLE RUMBLE RUMBLE
YOU'RE NOW THE MOST DANGEROUS VILLAIN IN THE HISTORY OF GOTHAM CITY.
READY WHEN YOU ARE.
DO IT.

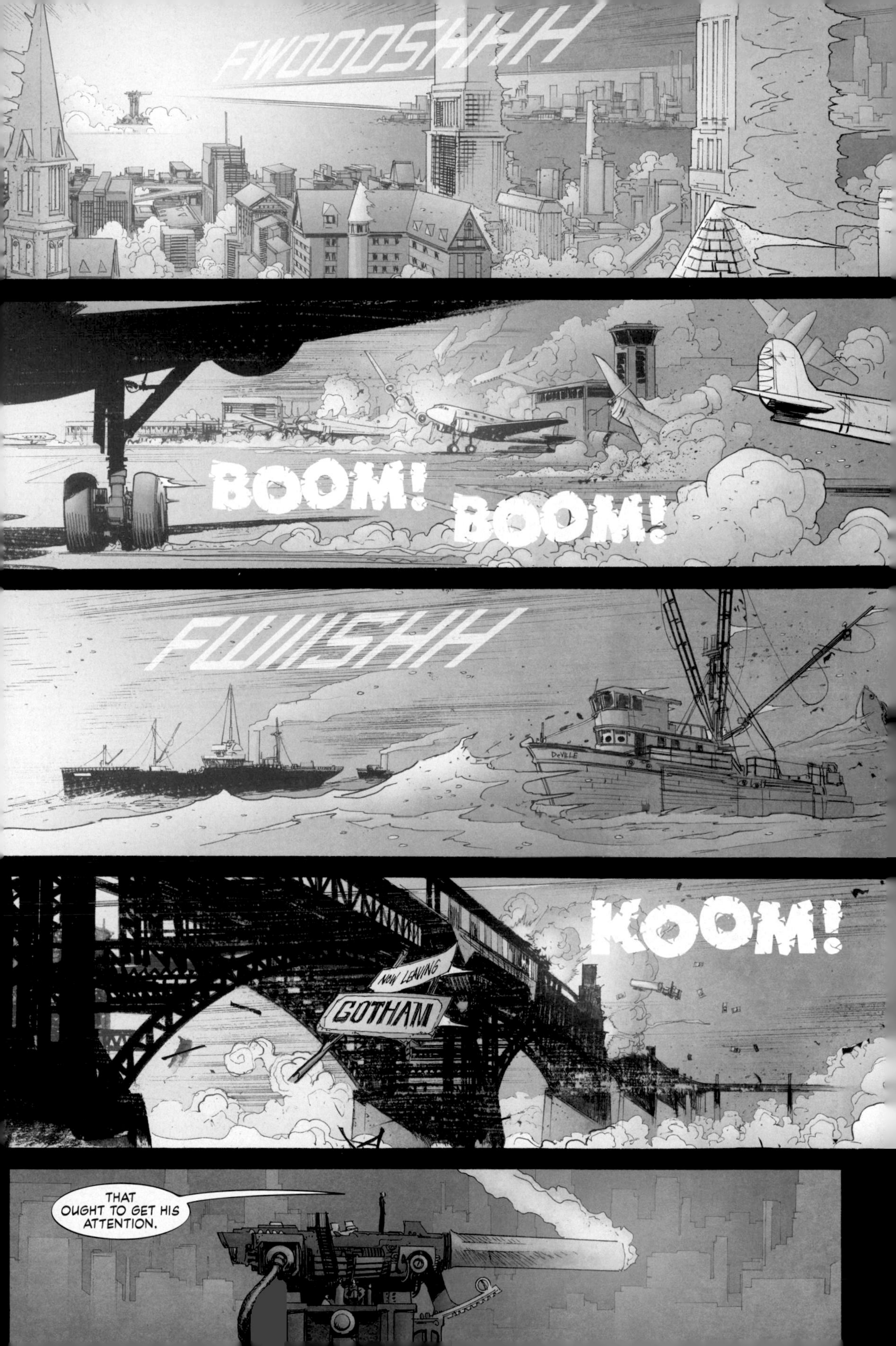
FWOOOSHHH
BOOM!
BOOM!
FWIISHH
DeVILLE
KOOM!
NOW LEAVING
GOTHAM
THAT OUGHT TO GET HIS ATTENTION.

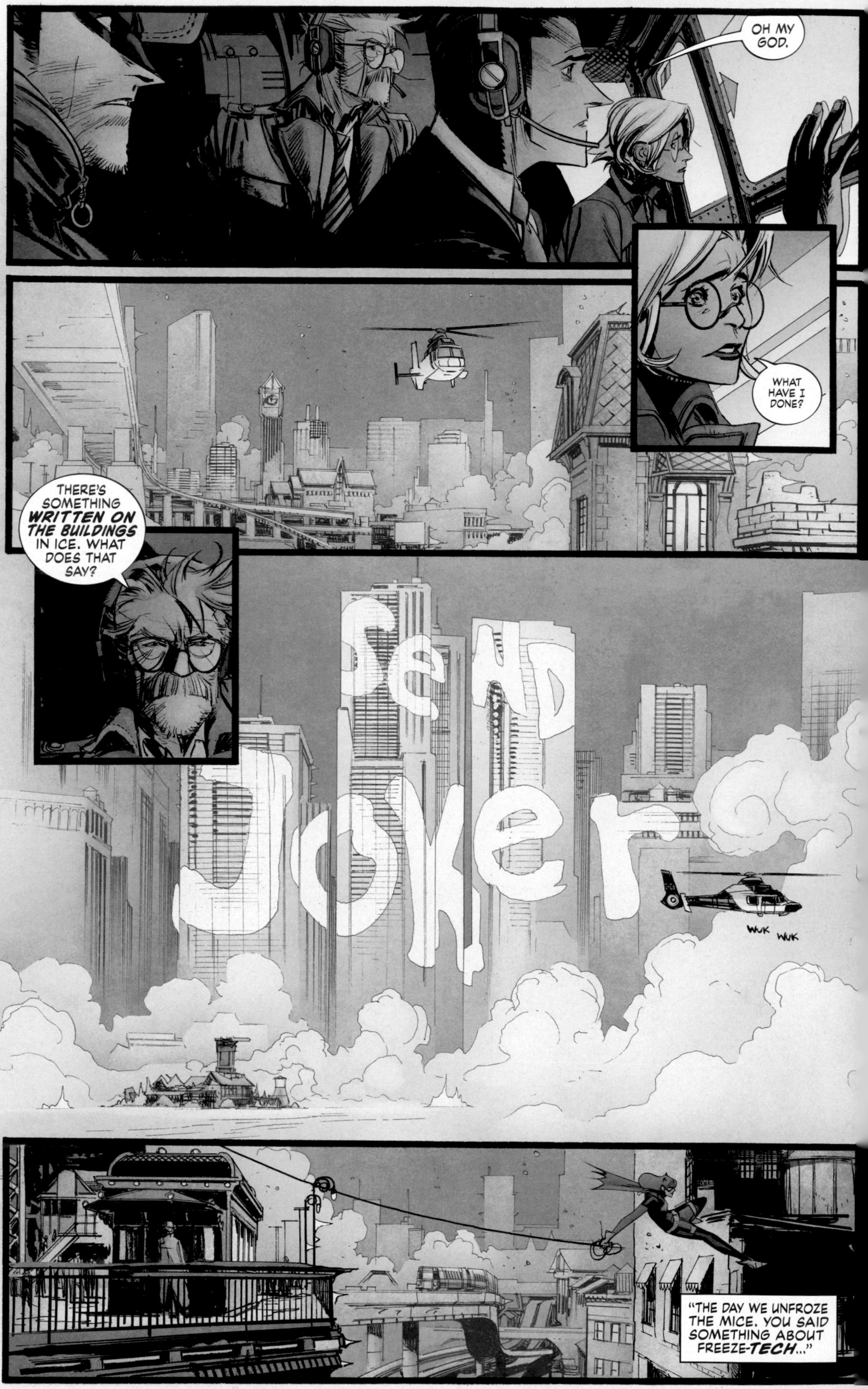

OH MY GOD.
WHAT HAVE I DONE?
THERE'S SOMETHING **WRITTEN ON THE BUILDINGS** IN ICE. WHAT DOES THAT SAY?
SEND JOKER
WUK WUK
"THE DAY WE UNFROZE THE MICE. YOU SAID SOMETHING ABOUT FREEZE-***TECH***..."

"...TECHNOLOGY PIONEERED IN THE FINAL DAYS OF THE *THIRD REICH*."

IS THAT GIANT CANNON IN THE MIDDLE OF GOTHAM HARBOR *YOURS*?

SOME KIND OF SECRET *NAZI ICE-GUN* YOU BUILT BENEATH THE OLD GERMAN EMBASSY?

I ASSUME YOU'RE THE LAB ASSISTANT.

THE YOUNG WOMAN HELPING MR. WAYNE IN THE LAB THAT DAY?

OH *CRAP*, I'M STILL WEARING MY COSTUME.

I'M ALREADY AWARE OF WHO MR. WAYNE *IS*. YOUR SECRETS ARE SAFE.

HOW DID YOU FIND OUT?

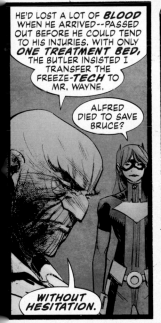

HE'D LOST A LOT OF *BLOOD* WHEN HE ARRIVED--PASSED OUT BEFORE HE COULD TEND TO HIS INJURIES. WITH ONLY *ONE TREATMENT BED*, THE BUTLER INSISTED I TRANSFER THE FREEZE-*TECH* TO MR. WAYNE.

ALFRED DIED TO SAVE BRUCE?

WITHOUT HESITATION.

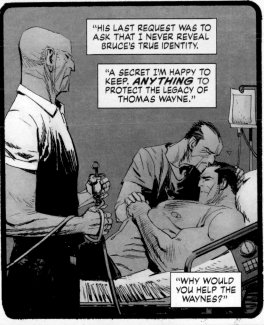

"HIS LAST REQUEST WAS TO ASK THAT I NEVER REVEAL BRUCE'S TRUE IDENTITY.

"A SECRET I'M HAPPY TO KEEP. *ANYTHING* TO PROTECT THE LEGACY OF THOMAS WAYNE."

"WHY WOULD YOU HELP THE WAYNES?"

I FIRST MET THOMAS WHEN I WAS A BOY, BACK DURING WORLD WAR TWO. HE WORKED WITH THE ALLIES TO CREATE A SECRET PROGRAM THAT UTILIZED VALUABLE NAZI ASSETS--

--HIGH-RANKING PRISONERS LIKE MY FATHER, BARON VON FRIES.

THOMAS CONVINCED THE WAR DEPARTMENT TO LET MY FATHER *CONTINUE WORKING* ON THE FREEZE-*TECH* SO IT MIGHT AID THE ALLIES. THEY AGREED TO GIVE HIM CUSTODY OF THE FRIES FAMILY ON ONE CONDITION:

THE ENTIRE PROJECT HAD TO BE KEPT *OFF* U.S. SOIL.

SO WAYNE BUILT YOU A WEAPONS LAB BENEATH THE GERMAN EMBASSY?

IT WAS A *MEDICAL LAB.* THOMAS WAS ONLY INTERESTED IN THE FREEZE-TECH'S HEALING ABILITIES.

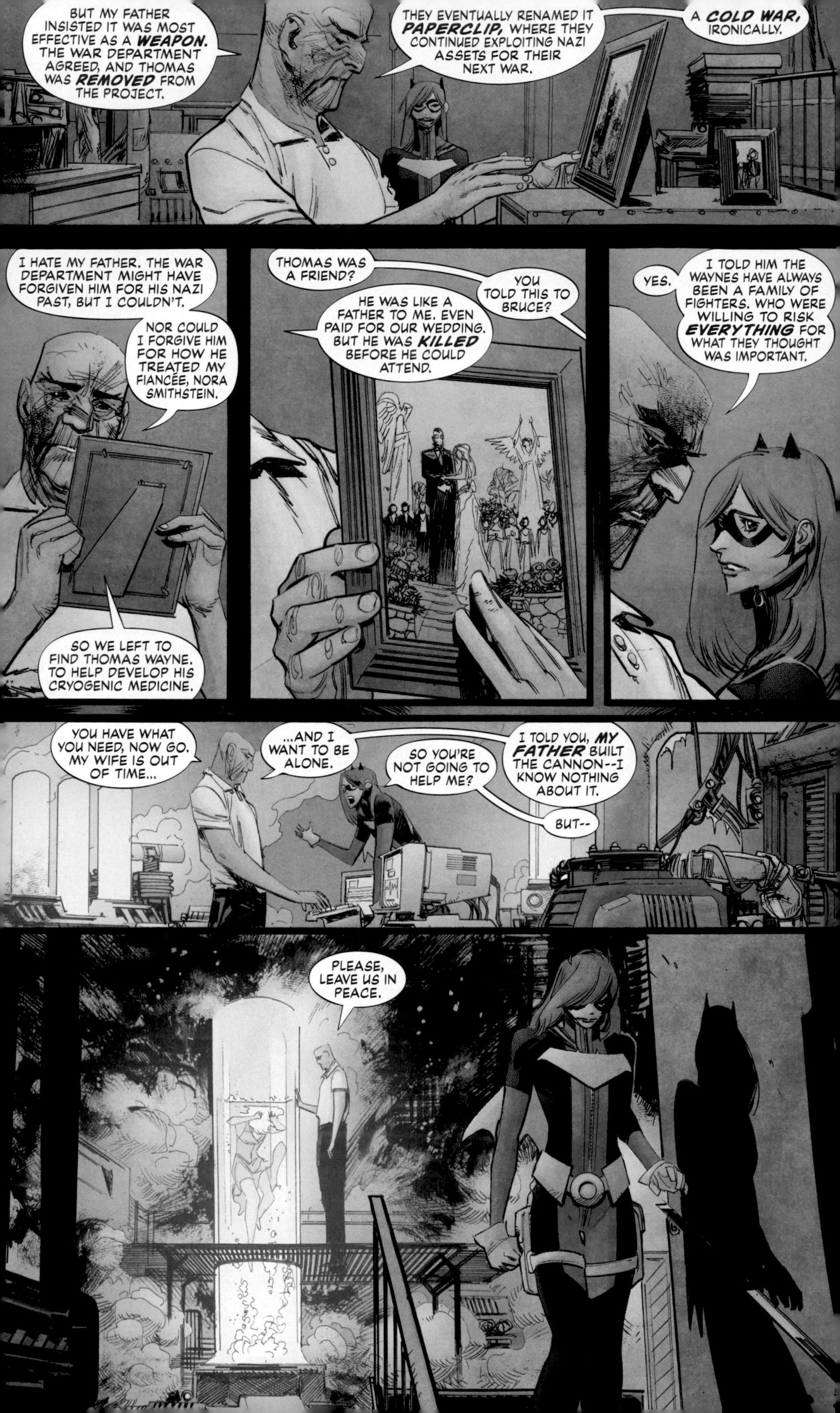
BUT MY FATHER INSISTED IT WAS MOST EFFECTIVE AS A **WEAPON**. THE WAR DEPARTMENT AGREED, AND THOMAS WAS **REMOVED** FROM THE PROJECT.
THEY EVENTUALLY RENAMED IT **PAPERCLIP**, WHERE THEY CONTINUED EXPLOITING NAZI ASSETS FOR THEIR NEXT WAR.
A **COLD WAR**, IRONICALLY.
I HATE MY FATHER. THE WAR DEPARTMENT MIGHT HAVE FORGIVEN HIM FOR HIS NAZI PAST, BUT I COULDN'T.
NOR COULD I FORGIVE HIM FOR HOW HE TREATED MY FIANCÉE, NORA SMITHSTEIN.
SO WE LEFT TO FIND THOMAS WAYNE. TO HELP DEVELOP HIS CRYOGENIC MEDICINE.
THOMAS WAS A FRIEND?
HE WAS LIKE A FATHER TO ME. EVEN PAID FOR OUR WEDDING. BUT HE WAS **KILLED** BEFORE HE COULD ATTEND.
YOU TOLD THIS TO BRUCE?
YES.
I TOLD HIM THE WAYNES HAVE ALWAYS BEEN A FAMILY OF FIGHTERS. WHO WERE WILLING TO RISK **EVERYTHING** FOR WHAT THEY THOUGHT WAS IMPORTANT.
YOU HAVE WHAT YOU NEED, NOW GO. MY WIFE IS OUT OF TIME...
...AND I WANT TO BE ALONE.
SO YOU'RE NOT GOING TO HELP ME?
I TOLD YOU, **MY FATHER** BUILT THE CANNON--I KNOW NOTHING ABOUT IT.
BUT--
PLEASE, LEAVE US IN PEACE.

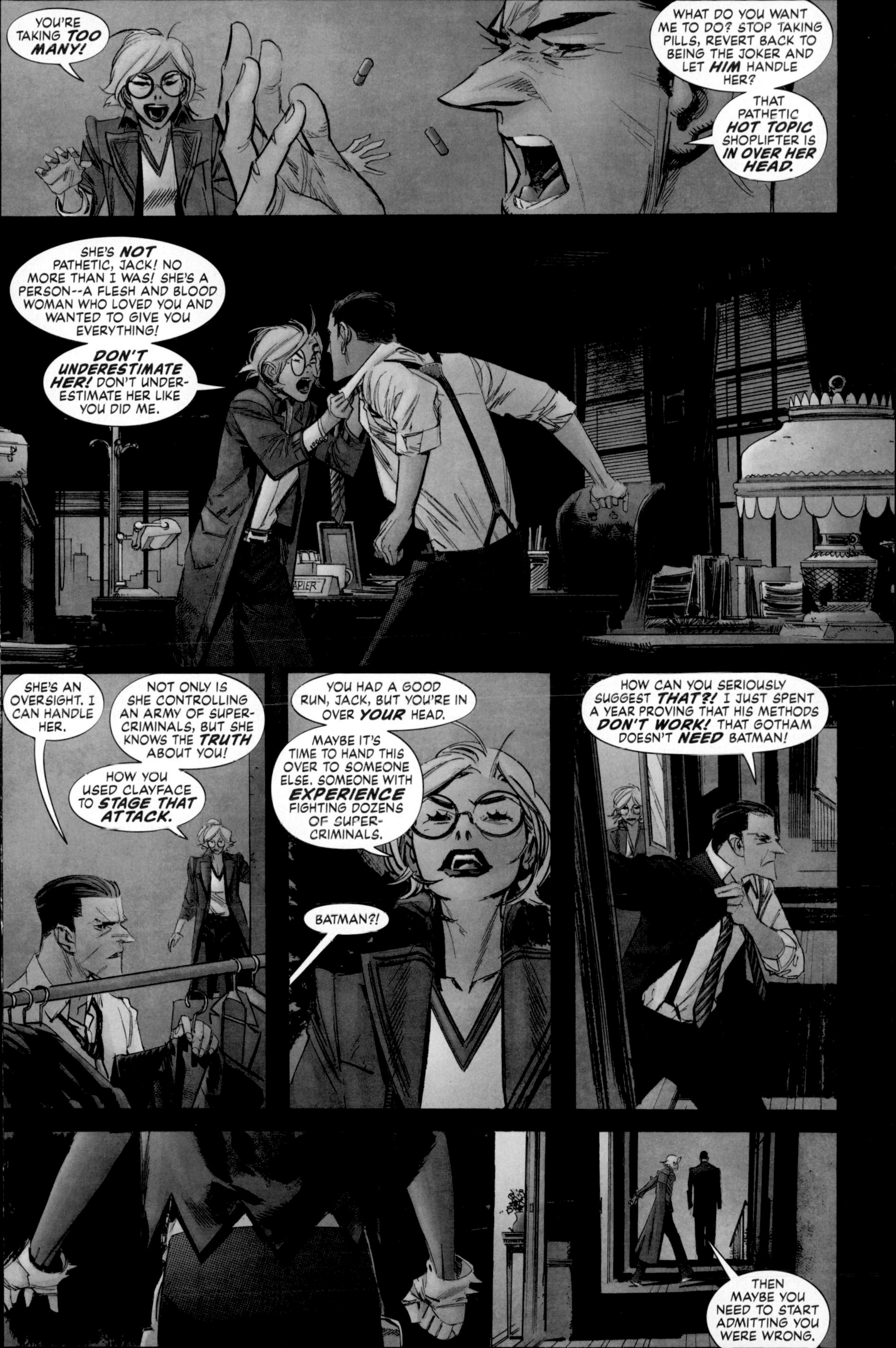
YOU'RE TAKING TOO MANY!
WHAT DO YOU WANT ME TO DO? STOP TAKING PILLS, REVERT BACK TO BEING THE JOKER AND LET HIM HANDLE HER?
THAT PATHETIC HOT TOPIC SHOPLIFTER IS IN OVER HER HEAD.
SHE'S NOT PATHETIC, JACK! NO MORE THAN I WAS! SHE'S A PERSON--A FLESH AND BLOOD WOMAN WHO LOVED YOU AND WANTED TO GIVE YOU EVERYTHING!
DON'T UNDERESTIMATE HER! DON'T UNDER-ESTIMATE HER LIKE YOU DID ME.
SHE'S AN OVERSIGHT. I CAN HANDLE HER.
NOT ONLY IS SHE CONTROLLING AN ARMY OF SUPER-CRIMINALS, BUT SHE KNOWS THE TRUTH ABOUT YOU!
HOW YOU USED CLAYFACE TO STAGE THAT ATTACK.
YOU HAD A GOOD RUN, JACK, BUT YOU'RE IN OVER YOUR HEAD.
MAYBE IT'S TIME TO HAND THIS OVER TO SOMEONE ELSE. SOMEONE WITH EXPERIENCE FIGHTING DOZENS OF SUPER-CRIMINALS.
BATMAN?!
HOW CAN YOU SERIOUSLY SUGGEST THAT?! I JUST SPENT A YEAR PROVING THAT HIS METHODS DON'T WORK! THAT GOTHAM DOESN'T NEED BATMAN!
THEN MAYBE YOU NEED TO START ADMITTING YOU WERE WRONG.

THOUSANDS OF GOTHAMITES ARE *FROZEN* IN THE STREETS, WHILE THE REST ARE STUCK *IN THEIR HOMES!* AND BOTH BRIDGES ARE OUT, SO THERE'S *NO LEAVING* GOTHAM.

IF WE ATTACK FROM THE AIR WE'LL BE *SHOT OUT OF THE SKY.* AND A FROZEN HARBOR NEGATES A WATERBORNE ASSAULT.

SO WHAT DO WE DO?

THE WHITE HOUSE JUST DECLARED A STATE OF EMERGENCY IN GOTHAM, AND THEY CONSIDER NEO JOKER TO BE A NATIONAL THREAT. THEY'LL BE HERE WITHIN A FEW HOURS.

NO! WE DON'T NEED THEIR HELP--THIS IS *GOTHAM CITY,* WE CAN HANDLE THIS *OURSELVES!*

THERE'S NO *TIME*-- NEO JOKER IS DEMANDING TO SEE NAPIER *NOW.*

ALL WE CAN DO IS STALL UNTIL THE MILITARY GETS HERE.

HOW?

HA HA HA HA HA HA HA HA HA HA HA HA HA HA HA HA HA HA HA HA

HA HA HA HA HA HA HAHAHA HA

WE'LL GIVE HER WHAT SHE WANTS.

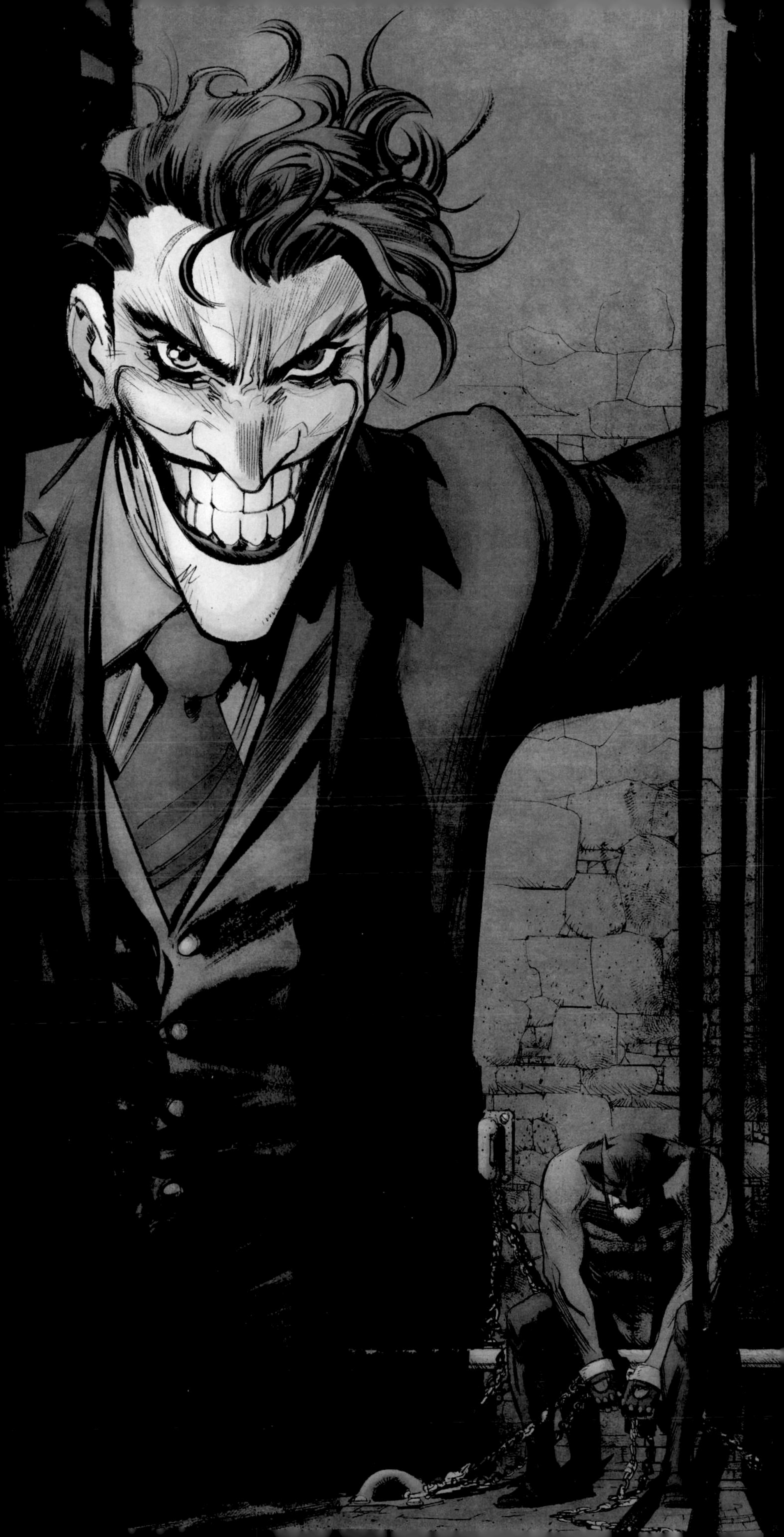

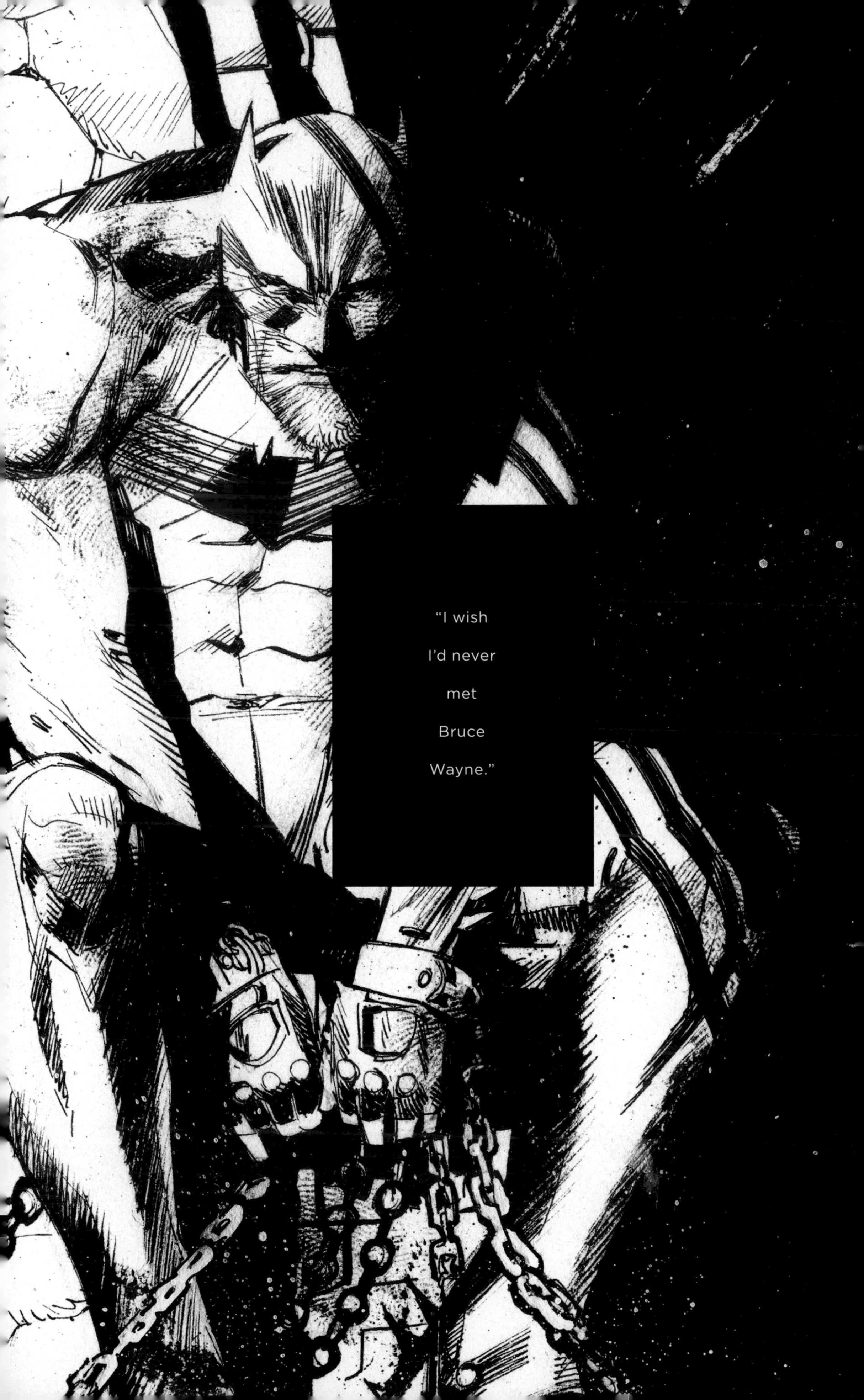
"I wish
I'd never
met
Bruce
Wayne."

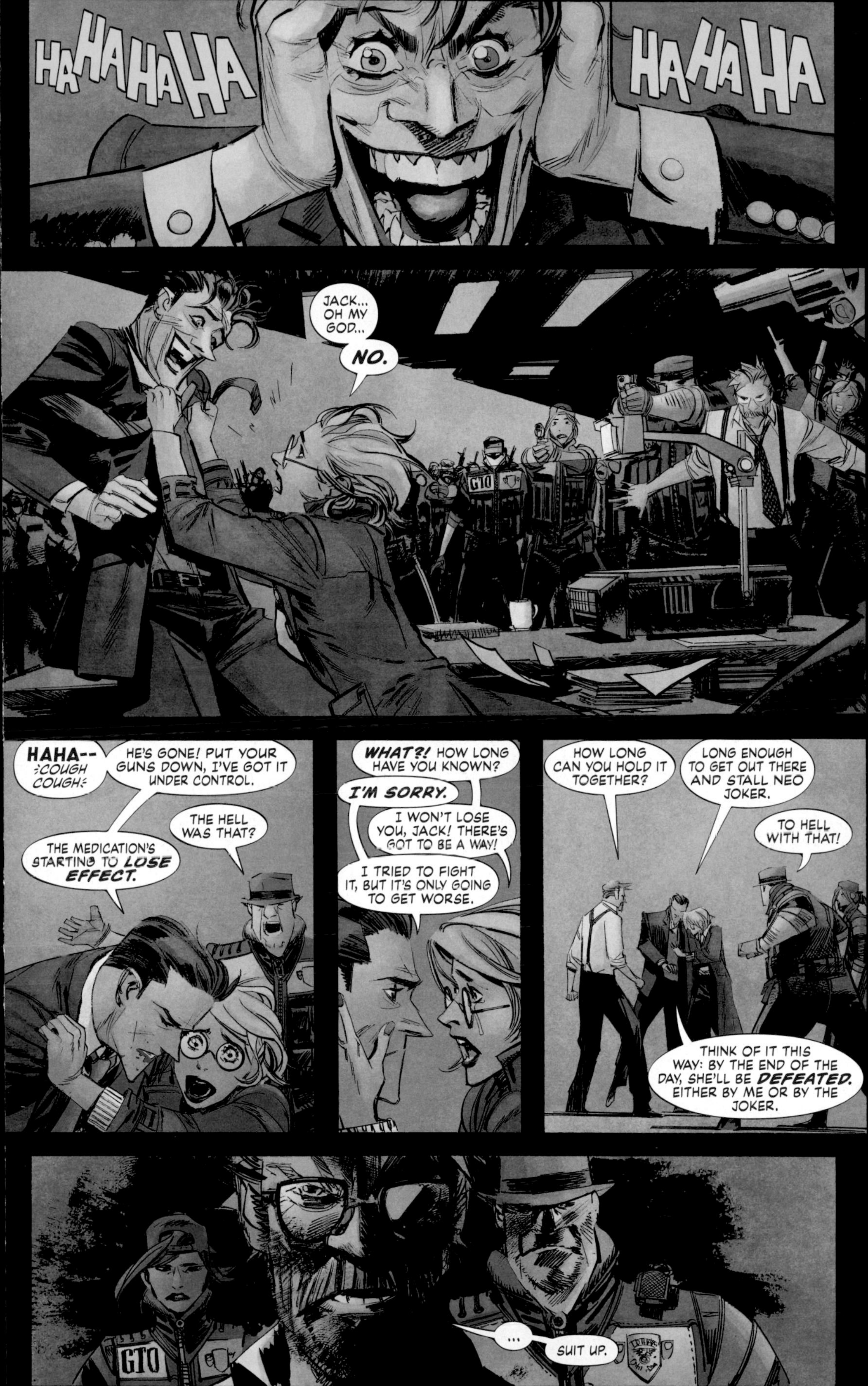

HAHAHAHAHA
HAHAHAHA
JACK... OH MY GOD... NO.
HAHA-- COUGH COUGH
HE'S GONE! PUT YOUR GUNS DOWN, I'VE GOT IT UNDER CONTROL.
THE HELL WAS THAT?
THE MEDICATION'S STARTING TO LOSE EFFECT.
WHAT?! HOW LONG HAVE YOU KNOWN?
I'M SORRY.
I WON'T LOSE YOU, JACK! THERE'S GOT TO BE A WAY!
I TRIED TO FIGHT IT, BUT IT'S ONLY GOING TO GET WORSE.
HOW LONG CAN YOU HOLD IT TOGETHER?
LONG ENOUGH TO GET OUT THERE AND STALL NEO JOKER.
TO HELL WITH THAT!
THINK OF IT THIS WAY: BY THE END OF THE DAY, SHE'LL BE DEFEATED. EITHER BY ME OR BY THE JOKER.
...
SUIT UP.

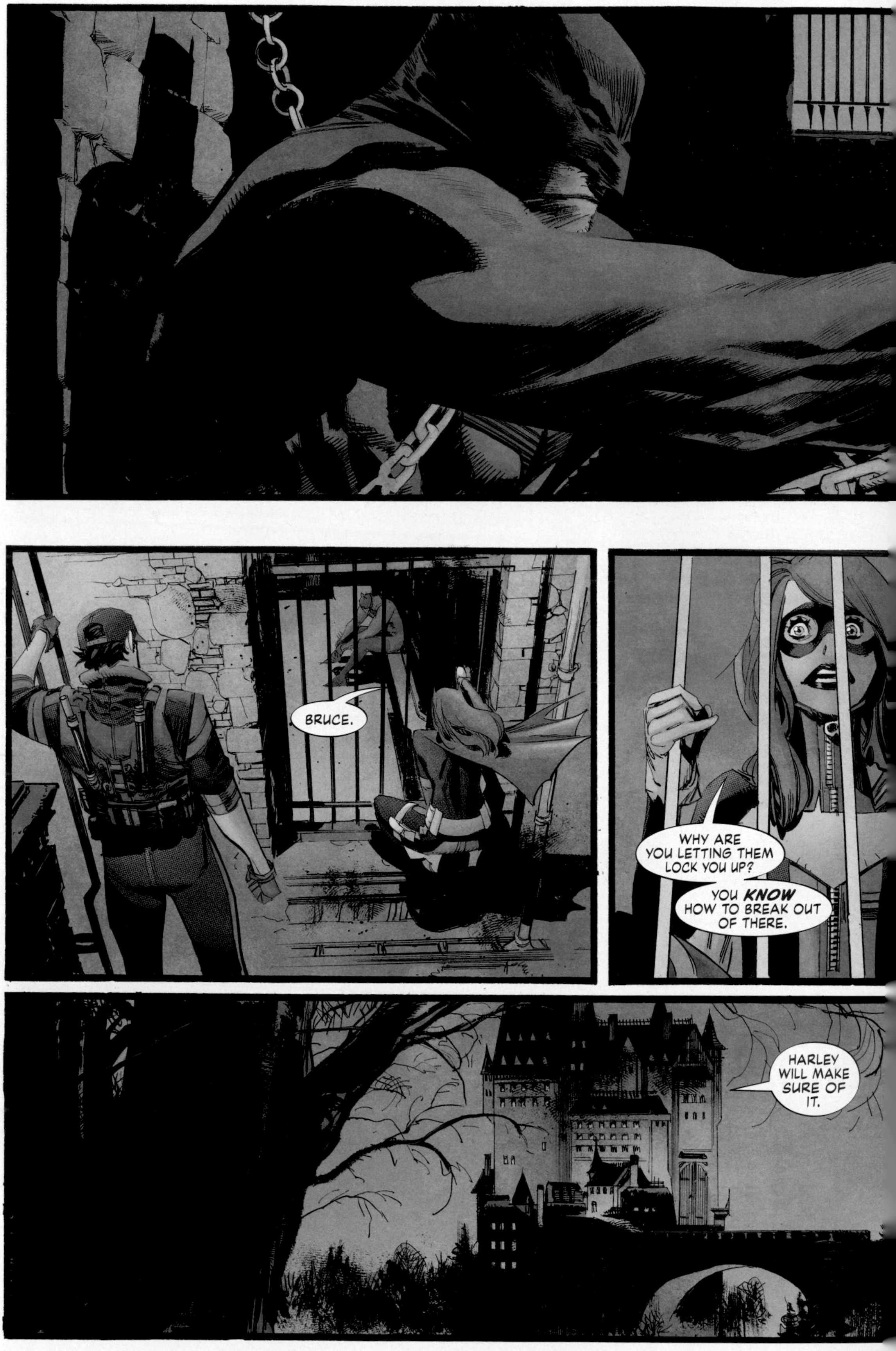
BRUCE.
WHY ARE YOU LETTING THEM LOCK YOU UP?
YOU KNOW HOW TO BREAK OUT OF THERE.
HARLEY WILL MAKE SURE OF IT.

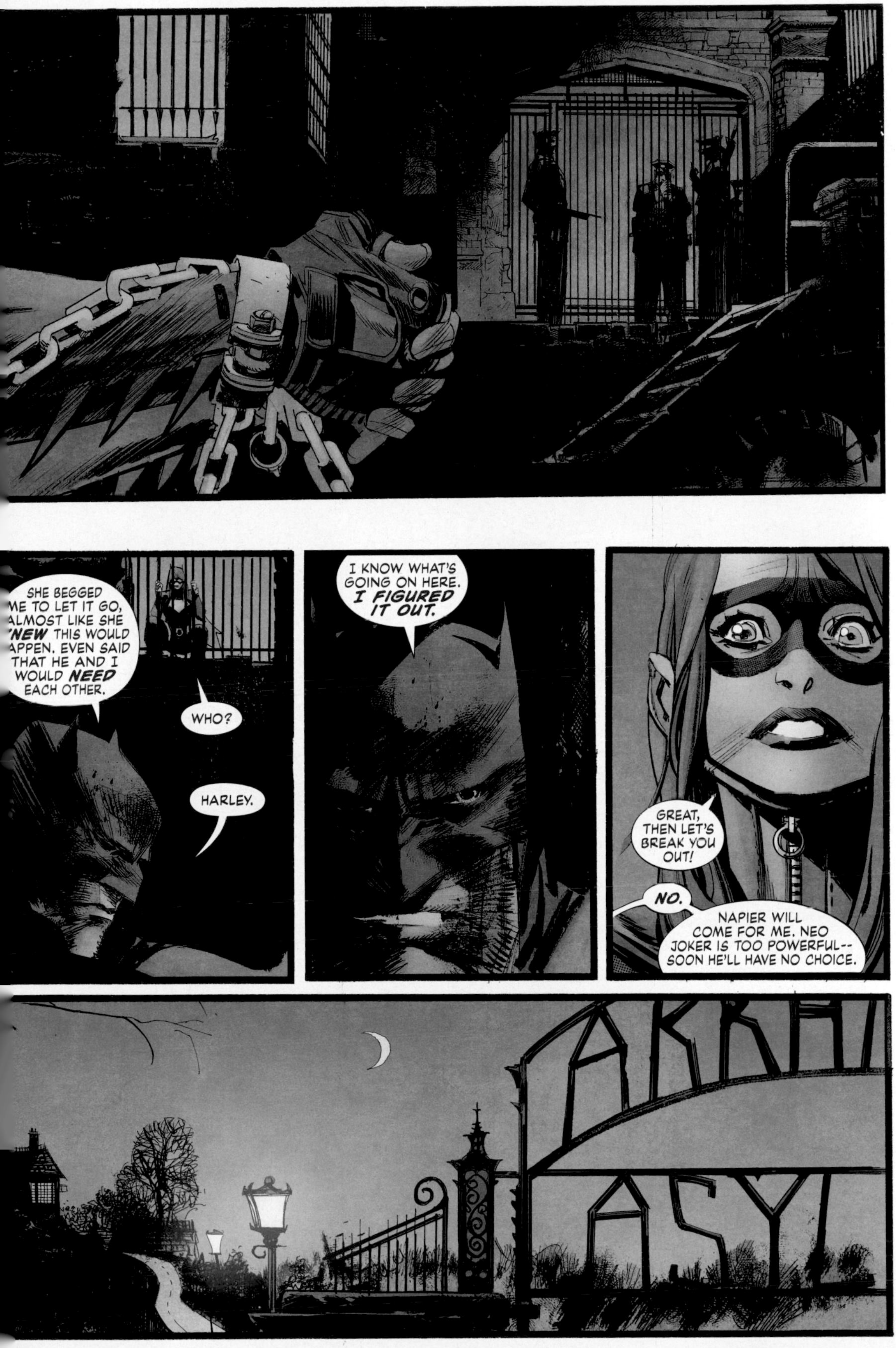
SHE BEGGED ME TO LET IT GO, ALMOST LIKE SHE NEW THIS WOULD APPEN. EVEN SAID THAT HE AND I WOULD NEED EACH OTHER.
WHO?
HARLEY.
I KNOW WHAT'S GOING ON HERE. I FIGURED IT OUT.
GREAT, THEN LET'S BREAK YOU OUT!
NO.
NAPIER WILL COME FOR ME. NEO JOKER IS TOO POWERFUL-- SOON HE'LL HAVE NO CHOICE.

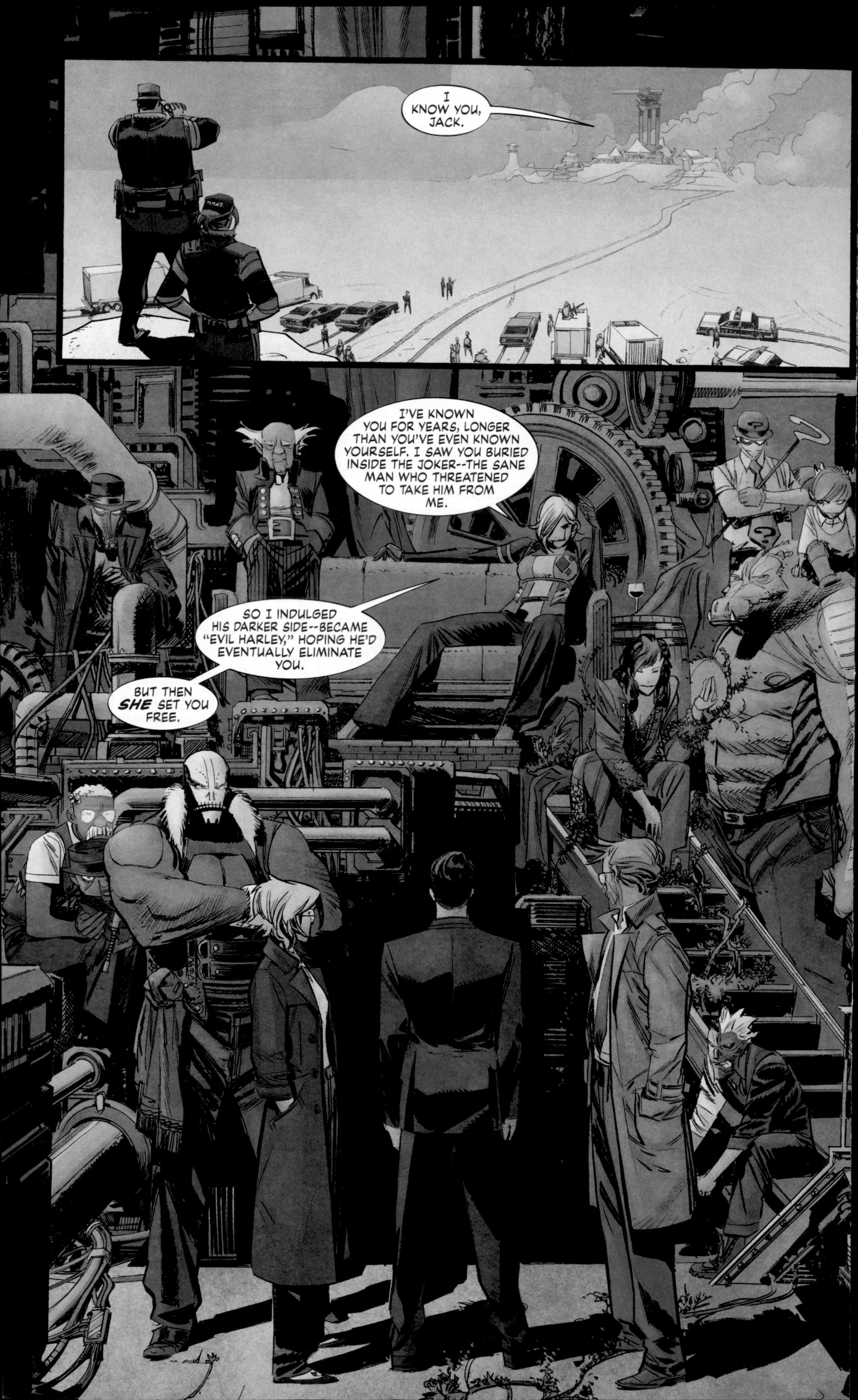
I KNOW YOU, JACK.
I'VE KNOWN YOU FOR YEARS, LONGER THAN YOU'VE EVEN KNOWN YOURSELF. I SAW YOU BURIED INSIDE THE JOKER--THE SANE MAN WHO THREATENED TO TAKE HIM FROM ME.
SO I INDULGED HIS DARKER SIDE--BECAME "EVIL HARLEY," HOPING HE'D EVENTUALLY ELIMINATE YOU.
BUT THEN SHE SET YOU FREE.

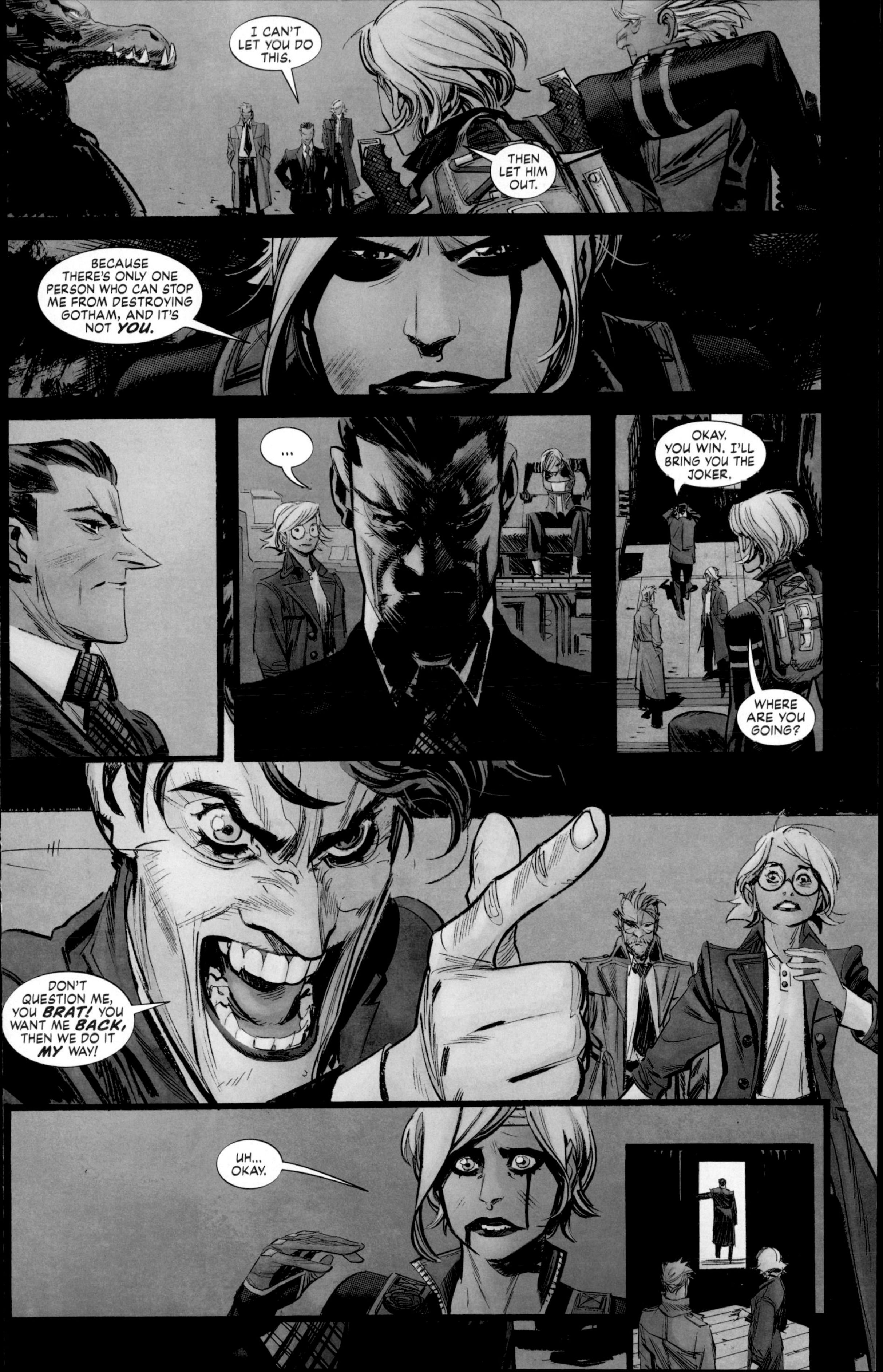
I CAN'T LET YOU DO THIS.
THEN LET HIM OUT.
BECAUSE THERE'S ONLY ONE PERSON WHO CAN STOP ME FROM DESTROYING GOTHAM, AND IT'S NOT ***YOU.***
...
OKAY. YOU WIN. I'LL BRING YOU THE JOKER.
WHERE ARE YOU GOING?
DON'T QUESTION ME, YOU ***BRAT!*** YOU WANT ME ***BACK,*** THEN WE DO IT ***MY*** WAY!
UH... OKAY.

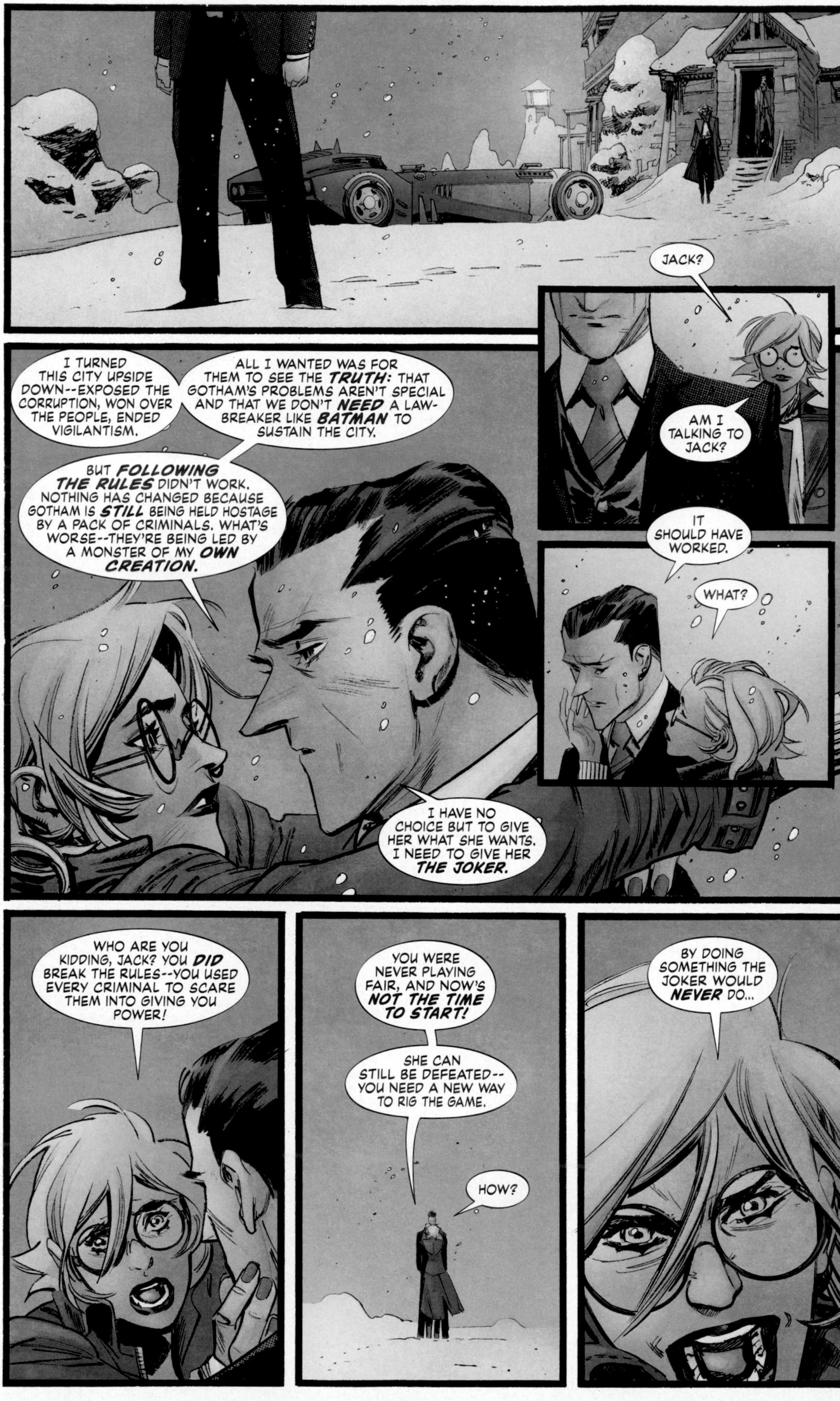
JACK?
AM I TALKING TO JACK?
I TURNED THIS CITY UPSIDE DOWN--EXPOSED THE CORRUPTION, WON OVER THE PEOPLE, ENDED VIGILANTISM.
ALL I WANTED WAS FOR THEM TO SEE THE TRUTH: THAT GOTHAM'S PROBLEMS AREN'T SPECIAL AND THAT WE DON'T NEED A LAW-BREAKER LIKE BATMAN TO SUSTAIN THE CITY.
BUT FOLLOWING THE RULES DIDN'T WORK. NOTHING HAS CHANGED BECAUSE GOTHAM IS STILL BEING HELD HOSTAGE BY A PACK OF CRIMINALS. WHAT'S WORSE--THEY'RE BEING LED BY A MONSTER OF MY OWN CREATION.
IT SHOULD HAVE WORKED.
WHAT?
I HAVE NO CHOICE BUT TO GIVE HER WHAT SHE WANTS. I NEED TO GIVE HER THE JOKER.
WHO ARE YOU KIDDING, JACK? YOU DID BREAK THE RULES--YOU USED EVERY CRIMINAL TO SCARE THEM INTO GIVING YOU POWER!
YOU WERE NEVER PLAYING FAIR, AND NOW'S NOT THE TIME TO START!
SHE CAN STILL BE DEFEATED--YOU NEED A NEW WAY TO RIG THE GAME.
HOW?
BY DOING SOMETHING THE JOKER WOULD NEVER DO...

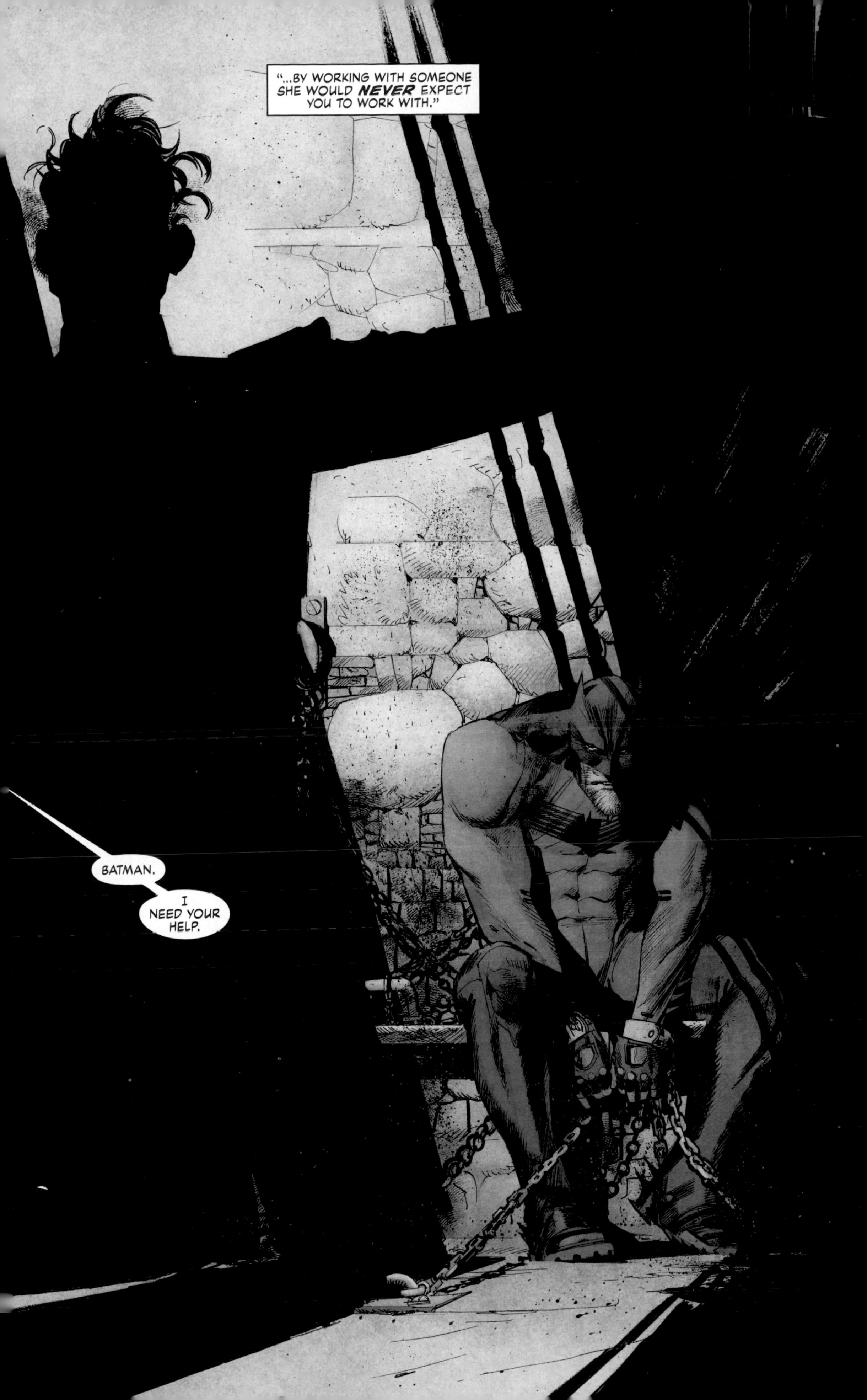
"...BY WORKING WITH SOMEONE SHE WOULD NEVER EXPECT YOU TO WORK WITH."
BATMAN.
I NEED YOUR HELP.

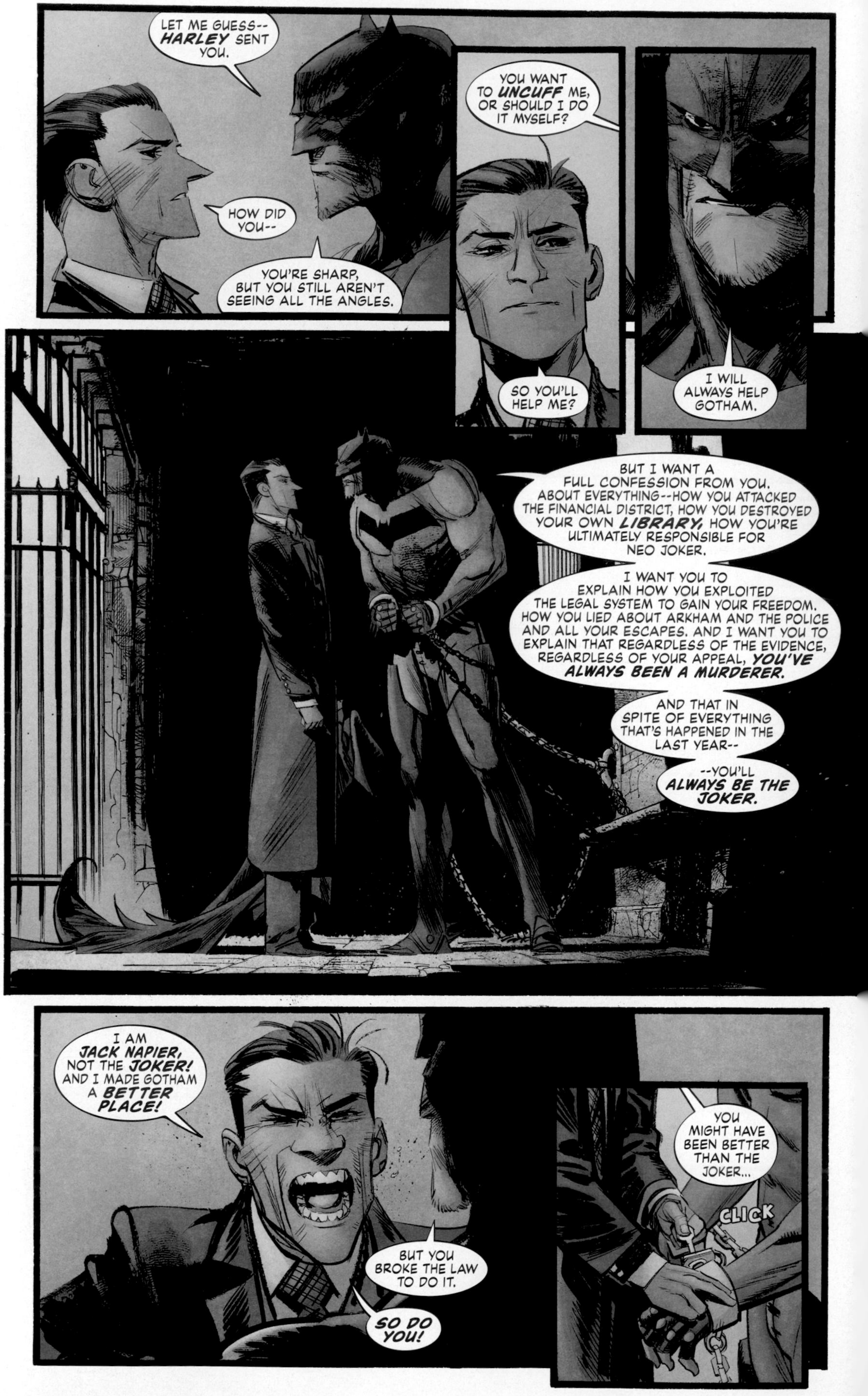
LET ME GUESS-- HARLEY SENT YOU.
HOW DID YOU--
YOU'RE SHARP, BUT YOU STILL AREN'T SEEING ALL THE ANGLES.
YOU WANT TO UNCUFF ME, OR SHOULD I DO IT MYSELF?
SO YOU'LL HELP ME?
I WILL ALWAYS HELP GOTHAM.
BUT I WANT A FULL CONFESSION FROM YOU. ABOUT EVERYTHING--HOW YOU ATTACKED THE FINANCIAL DISTRICT, HOW YOU DESTROYED YOUR OWN LIBRARY, HOW YOU'RE ULTIMATELY RESPONSIBLE FOR NEO JOKER.
I WANT YOU TO EXPLAIN HOW YOU EXPLOITED THE LEGAL SYSTEM TO GAIN YOUR FREEDOM. HOW YOU LIED ABOUT ARKHAM AND THE POLICE AND ALL YOUR ESCAPES. AND I WANT YOU TO EXPLAIN THAT REGARDLESS OF THE EVIDENCE, REGARDLESS OF YOUR APPEAL, YOU'VE ALWAYS BEEN A MURDERER.
AND THAT IN SPITE OF EVERYTHING THAT'S HAPPENED IN THE LAST YEAR--
--YOU'LL ALWAYS BE THE JOKER.
I AM JACK NAPIER, NOT THE JOKER! AND I MADE GOTHAM A BETTER PLACE!
BUT YOU BROKE THE LAW TO DO IT.
SO DO YOU!
YOU MIGHT HAVE BEEN BETTER THAN THE JOKER...
CLICK

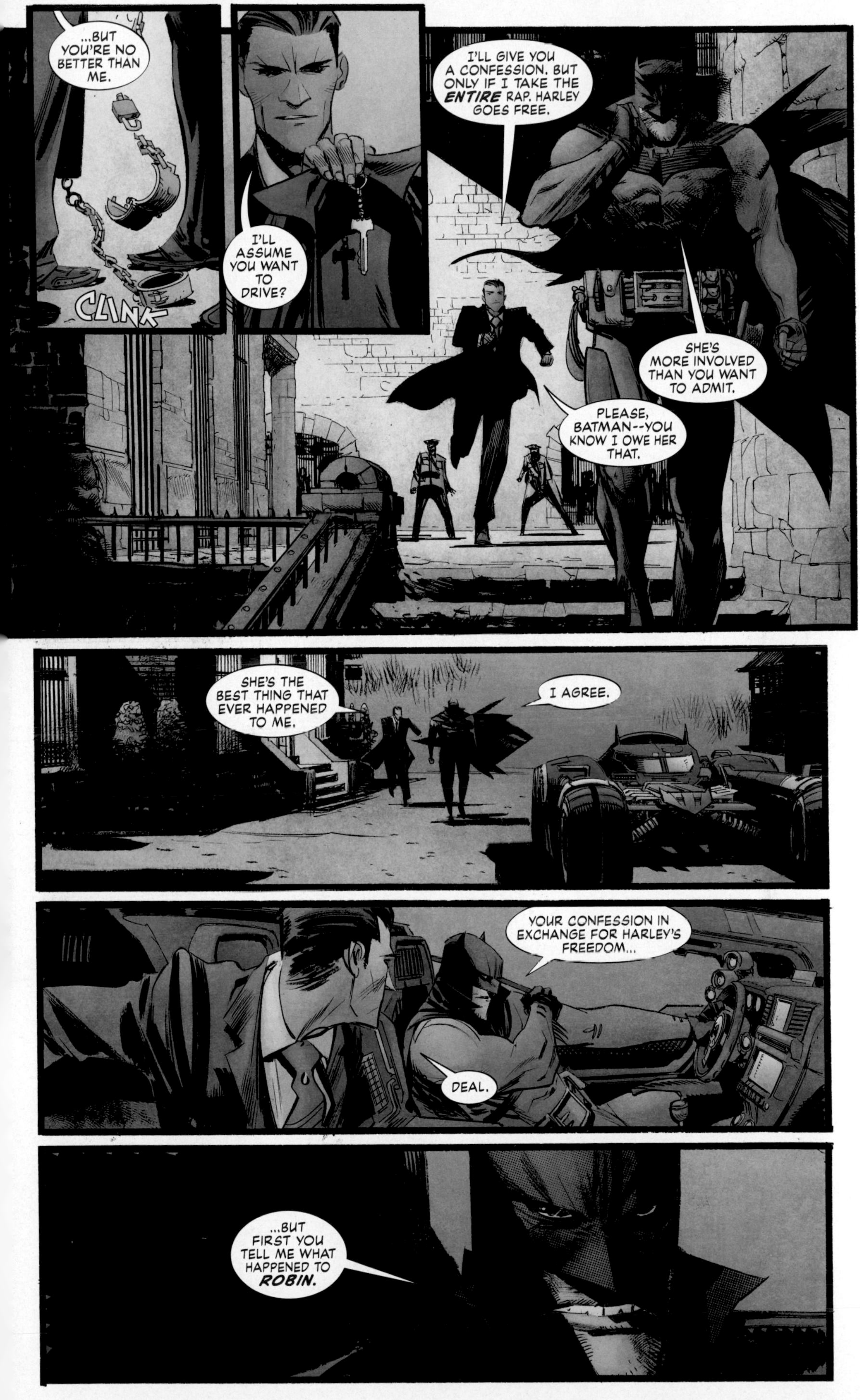
...BUT YOU'RE NO BETTER THAN ME.
CLINK
I'LL ASSUME YOU WANT TO DRIVE?
I'LL GIVE YOU A CONFESSION. BUT ONLY IF I TAKE THE ENTIRE RAP. HARLEY GOES FREE.
SHE'S MORE INVOLVED THAN YOU WANT TO ADMIT.
PLEASE, BATMAN--YOU KNOW I OWE HER THAT.
SHE'S THE BEST THING THAT EVER HAPPENED TO ME.
I AGREE.
YOUR CONFESSION IN EXCHANGE FOR HARLEY'S FREEDOM...
DEAL.
...BUT FIRST YOU TELL ME WHAT HAPPENED TO ROBIN.

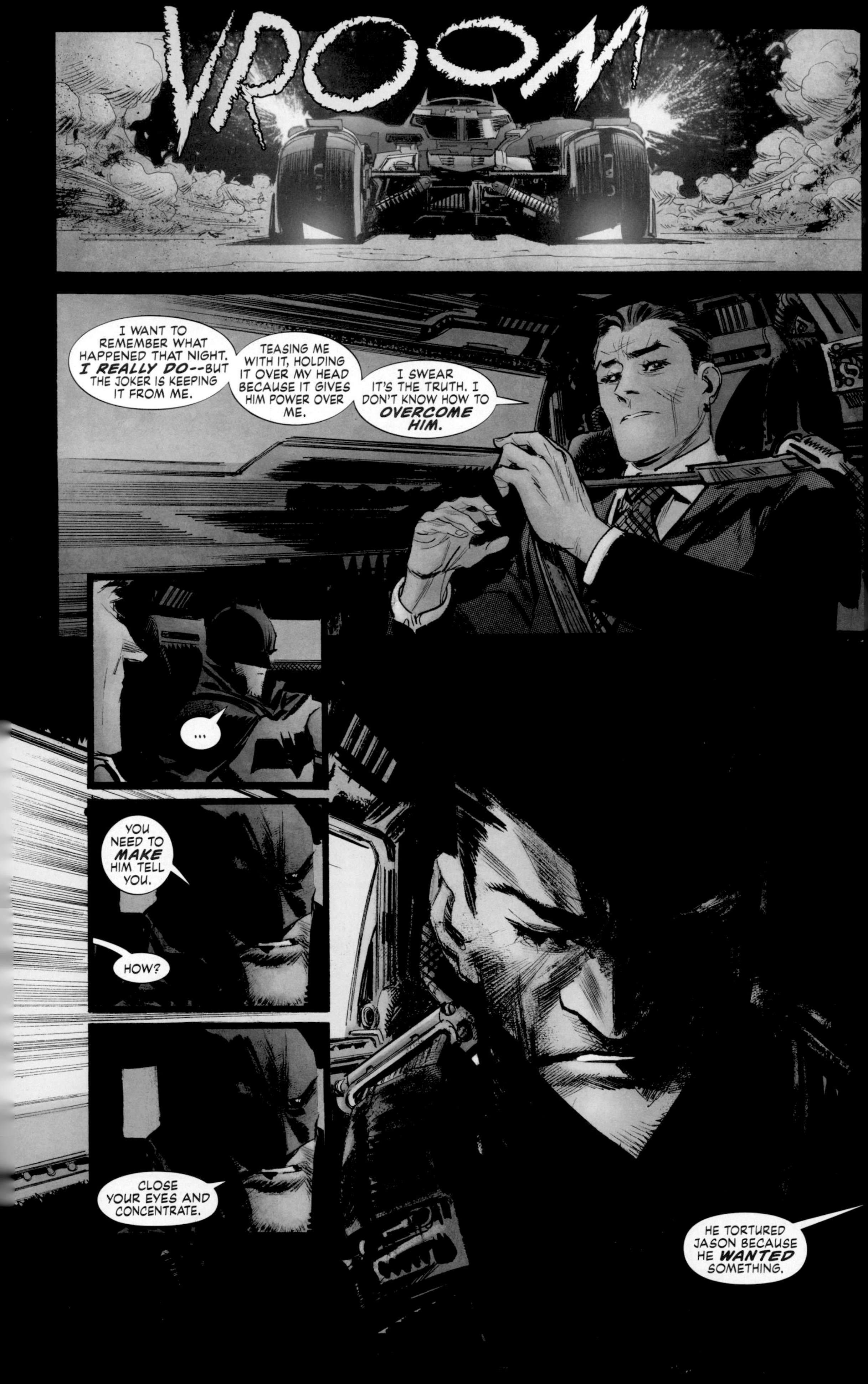
VROOM
I WANT TO REMEMBER WHAT HAPPENED THAT NIGHT. I REALLY DO--BUT THE JOKER IS KEEPING IT FROM ME.
TEASING ME WITH IT, HOLDING IT OVER MY HEAD BECAUSE IT GIVES HIM POWER OVER ME.
I SWEAR IT'S THE TRUTH. I DON'T KNOW HOW TO OVERCOME HIM.
...
YOU NEED TO MAKE HIM TELL YOU.
HOW?
CLOSE YOUR EYES AND CONCENTRATE.
HE TORTURED JASON BECAUSE HE WANTED SOMETHING.

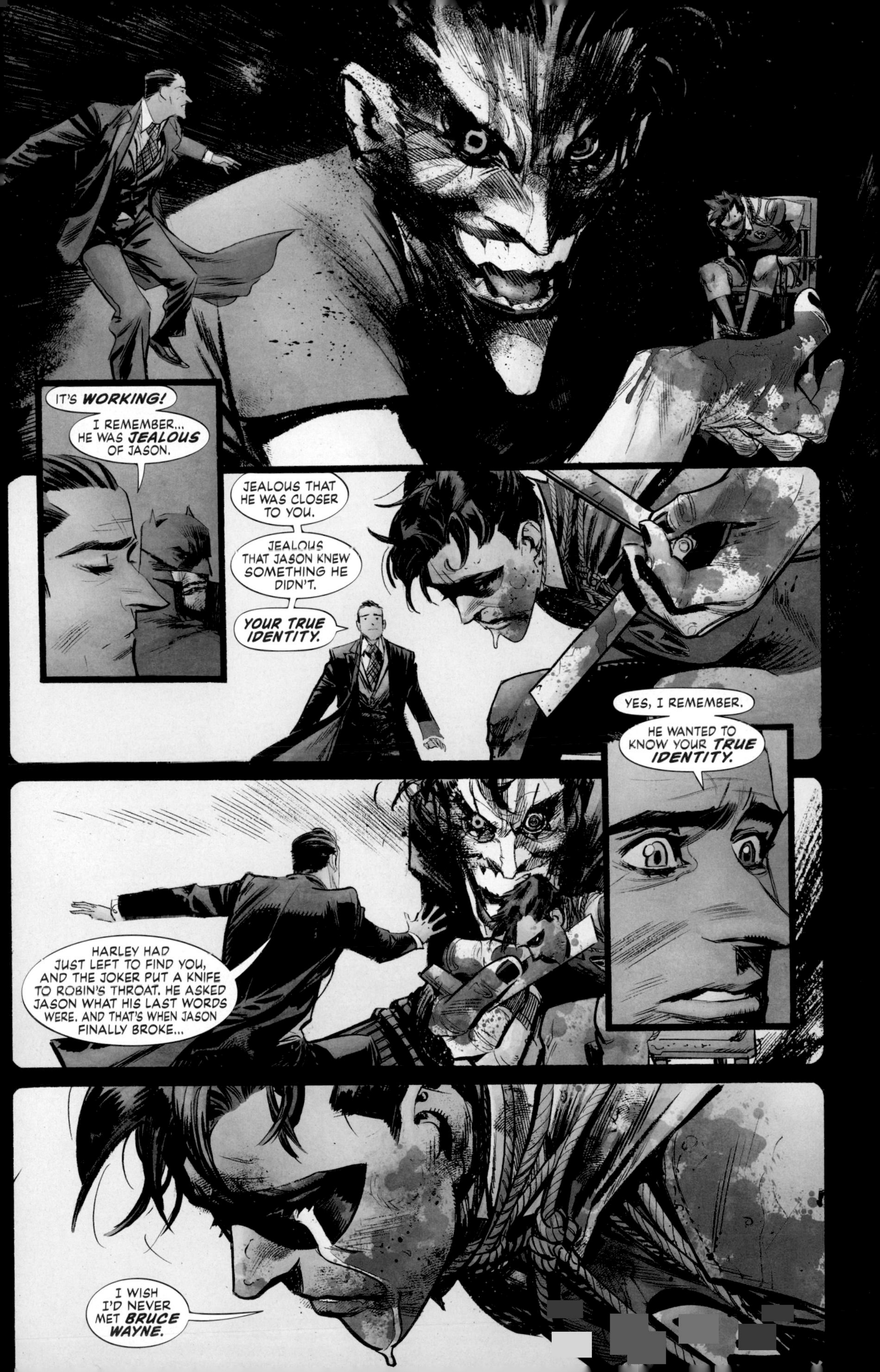
IT'S WORKING!
I REMEMBER... HE WAS JEALOUS OF JASON.
JEALOUS THAT HE WAS CLOSER TO YOU.
JEALOUS THAT JASON KNEW SOMETHING HE DIDN'T.
YOUR TRUE IDENTITY.
YES, I REMEMBER.
HE WANTED TO KNOW YOUR TRUE IDENTITY.
HARLEY HAD JUST LEFT TO FIND YOU, AND THE JOKER PUT A KNIFE TO ROBIN'S THROAT. HE ASKED JASON WHAT HIS LAST WORDS WERE. AND THAT'S WHEN JASON FINALLY BROKE...
I WISH I'D NEVER MET BRUCE WAYNE.

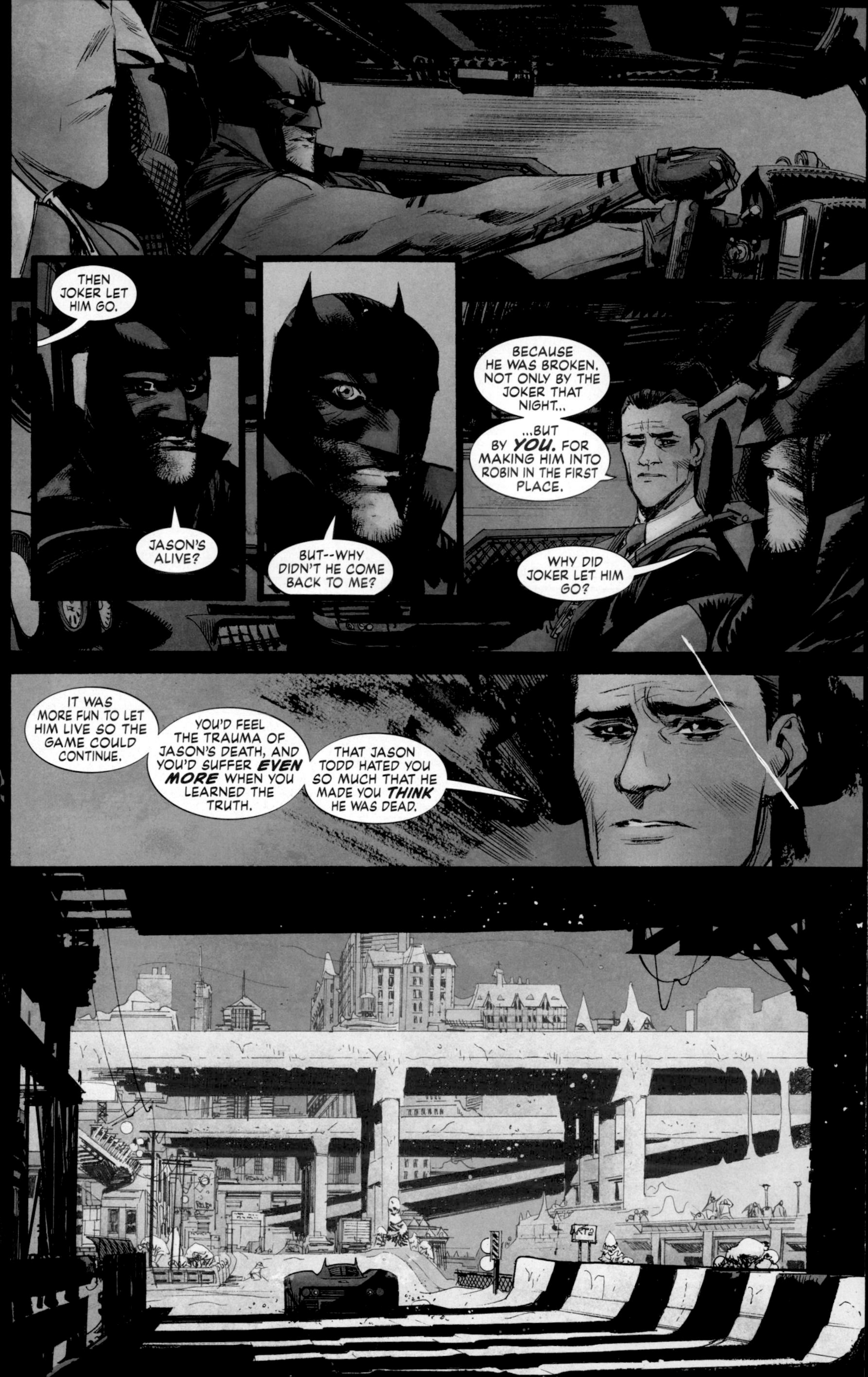
THEN JOKER LET HIM GO.
JASON'S ALIVE?
BUT--WHY DIDN'T HE COME BACK TO ME?
BECAUSE HE WAS BROKEN. NOT ONLY BY THE JOKER THAT NIGHT...
...BUT BY *YOU.* FOR MAKING HIM INTO ROBIN IN THE FIRST PLACE.
WHY DID JOKER LET HIM GO?
IT WAS MORE FUN TO LET HIM LIVE SO THE GAME COULD CONTINUE.
YOU'D FEEL THE TRAUMA OF JASON'S DEATH, AND YOU'D SUFFER *EVEN MORE* WHEN YOU LEARNED THE TRUTH.
THAT JASON TODD HATED YOU SO MUCH THAT HE MADE YOU *THINK* HE WAS DEAD.

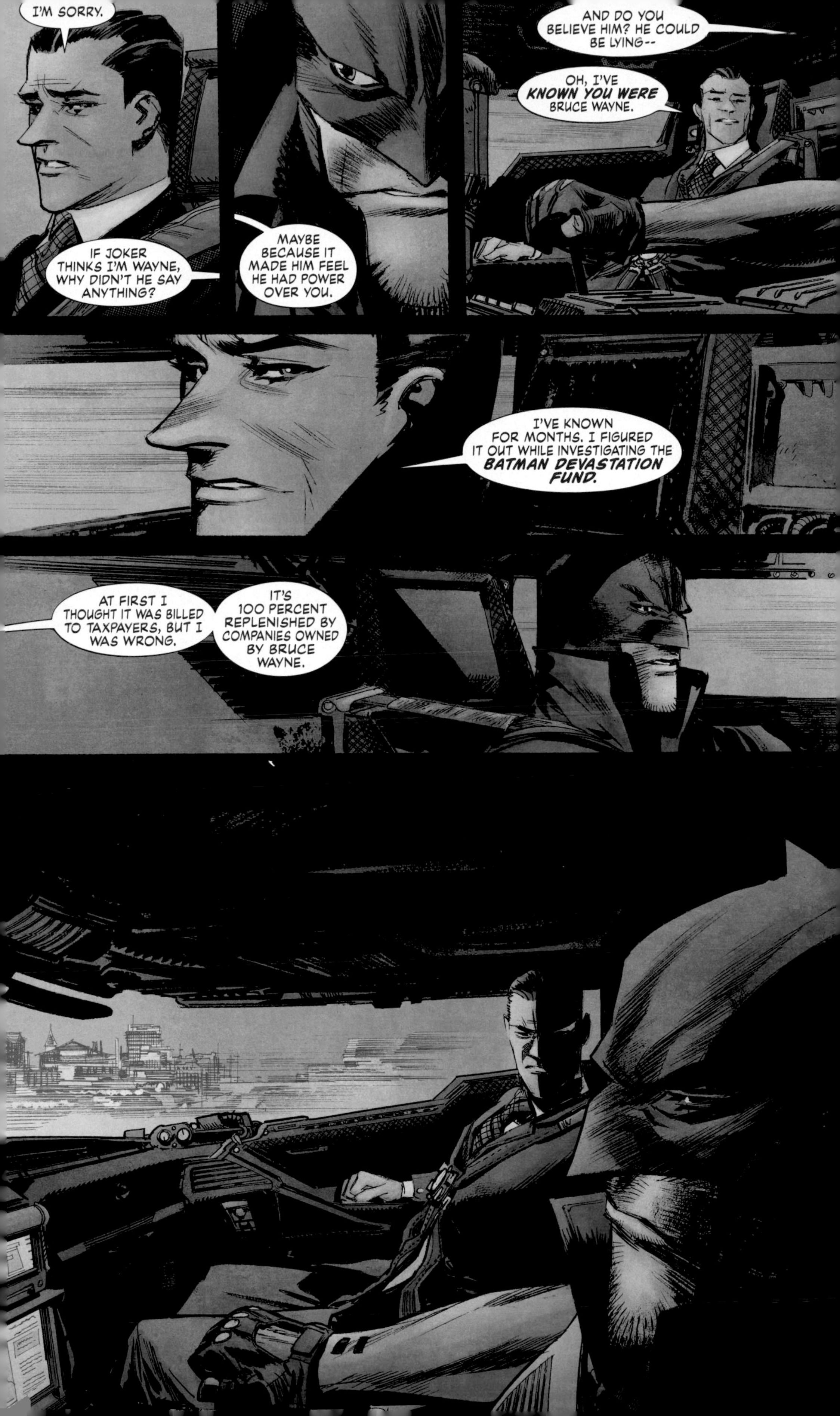
I'M SORRY.
IF JOKER THINKS I'M WAYNE, WHY DIDN'T HE SAY ANYTHING?
MAYBE BECAUSE IT MADE HIM FEEL HE HAD POWER OVER YOU.
AND DO YOU BELIEVE HIM? HE COULD BE LYING--
OH, I'VE KNOWN YOU WERE BRUCE WAYNE.
I'VE KNOWN FOR MONTHS. I FIGURED IT OUT WHILE INVESTIGATING THE BATMAN DEVASTATION FUND.
AT FIRST I THOUGHT IT WAS BILLED TO TAXPAYERS, BUT I WAS WRONG.
IT'S 100 PERCENT REPLENISHED BY COMPANIES OWNED BY BRUCE WAYNE.

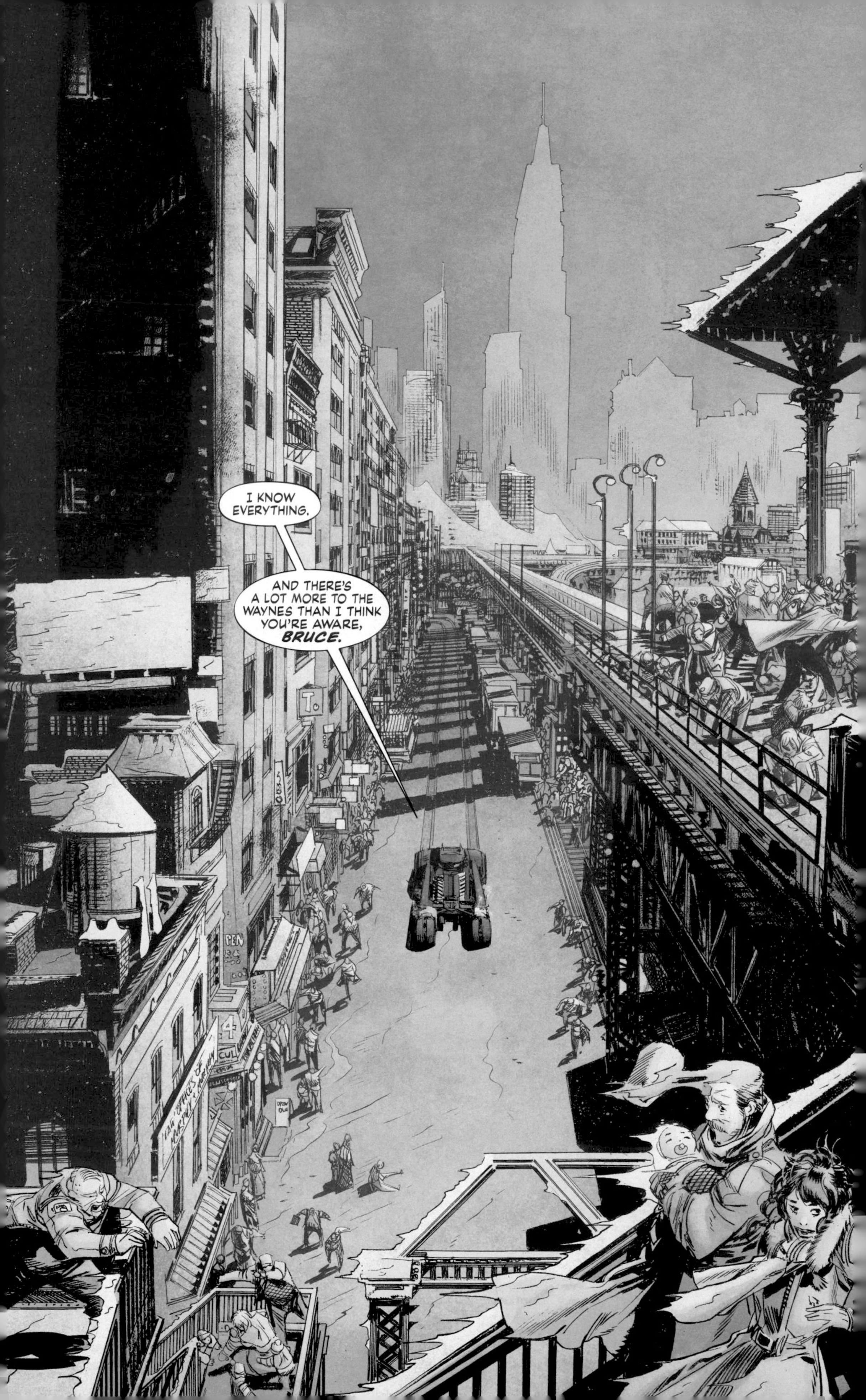
I KNOW EVERYTHING.
AND THERE'S A LOT MORE TO THE WAYNES THAN I THINK YOU'RE AWARE, **BRUCE.**

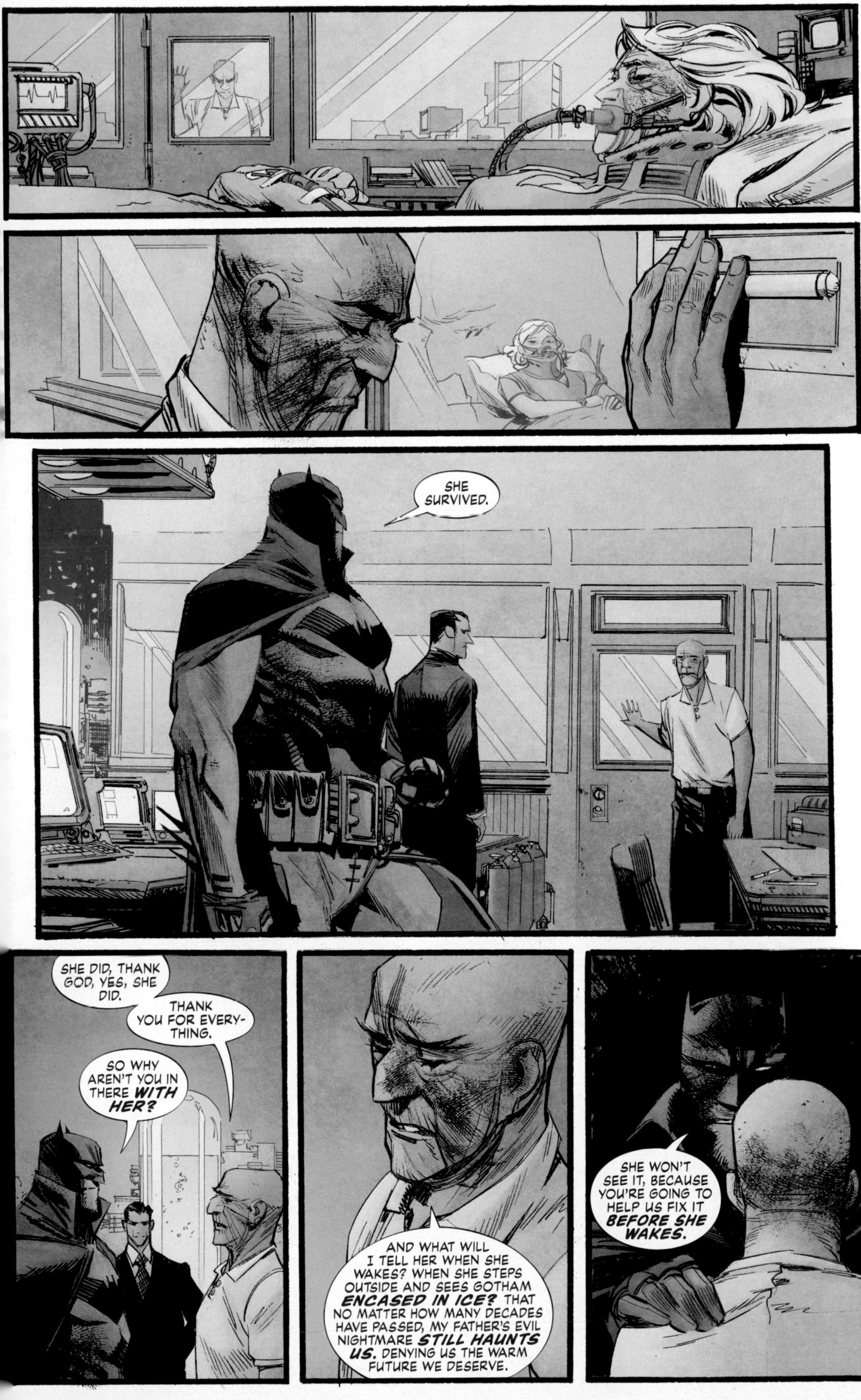
SHE SURVIVED.
SHE DID, THANK GOD, YES, SHE DID.
THANK YOU FOR EVERY-THING.
SO WHY AREN'T YOU IN THERE WITH HER?
AND WHAT WILL I TELL HER WHEN SHE WAKES? WHEN SHE STEPS OUTSIDE AND SEES GOTHAM ENCASED IN ICE? THAT NO MATTER HOW MANY DECADES HAVE PASSED, MY FATHER'S EVIL NIGHTMARE STILL HAUNTS US. DENYING US THE WARM FUTURE WE DESERVE.
SHE WON'T SEE IT, BECAUSE YOU'RE GOING TO HELP US FIX IT BEFORE SHE WAKES.

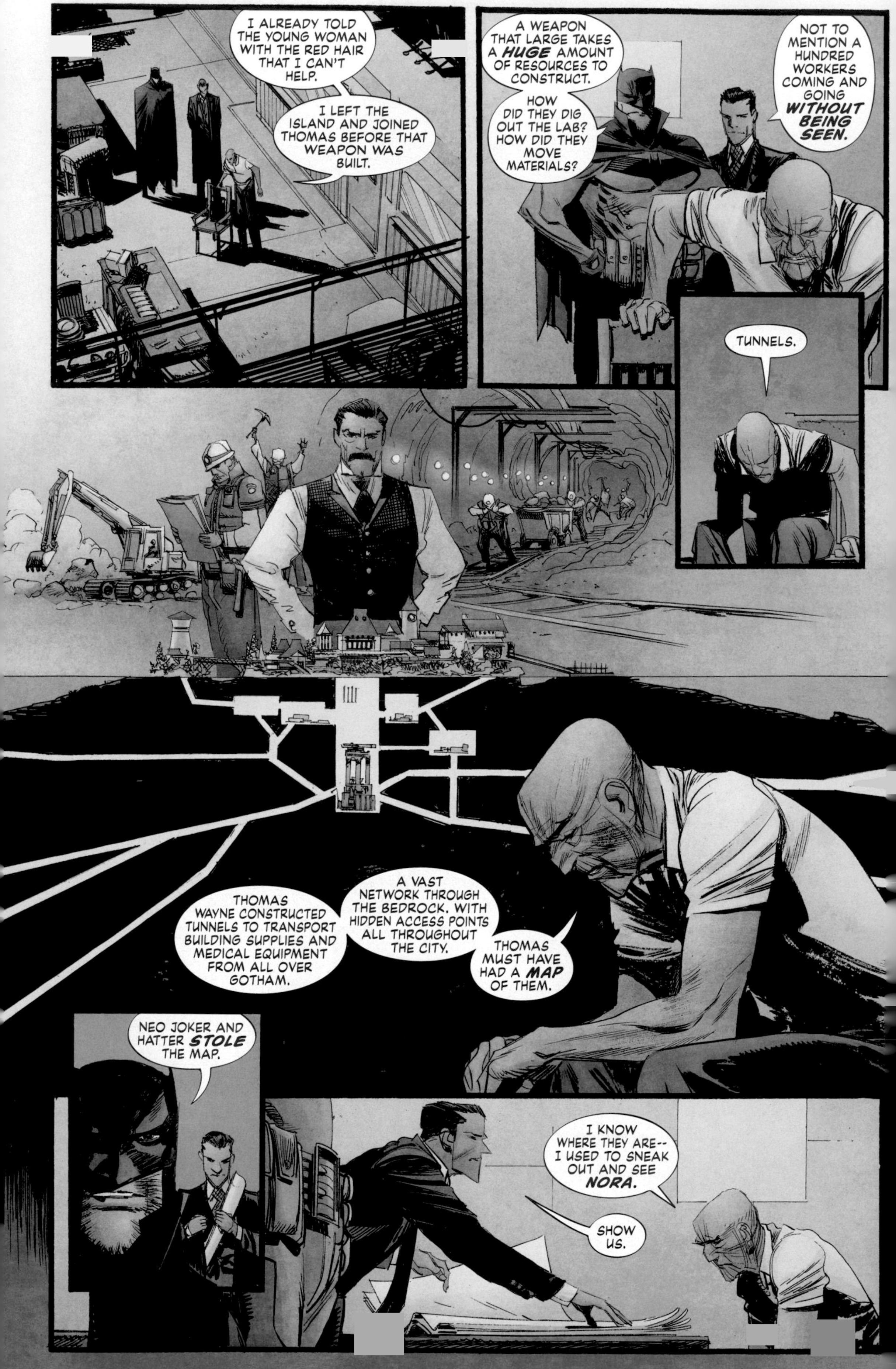
I ALREADY TOLD THE YOUNG WOMAN WITH THE RED HAIR THAT I CAN'T HELP.
I LEFT THE ISLAND AND JOINED THOMAS BEFORE THAT WEAPON WAS BUILT.
A WEAPON THAT LARGE TAKES A HUGE AMOUNT OF RESOURCES TO CONSTRUCT.
HOW DID THEY DIG OUT THE LAB? HOW DID THEY MOVE MATERIALS?
NOT TO MENTION A HUNDRED WORKERS COMING AND GOING WITHOUT BEING SEEN.
TUNNELS.
THOMAS WAYNE CONSTRUCTED TUNNELS TO TRANSPORT BUILDING SUPPLIES AND MEDICAL EQUIPMENT FROM ALL OVER GOTHAM.
A VAST NETWORK THROUGH THE BEDROCK. WITH HIDDEN ACCESS POINTS ALL THROUGHOUT THE CITY.
THOMAS MUST HAVE HAD A MAP OF THEM.
NEO JOKER AND HATTER STOLE THE MAP.
I KNOW WHERE THEY ARE-- I USED TO SNEAK OUT AND SEE NORA.
SHOW US.

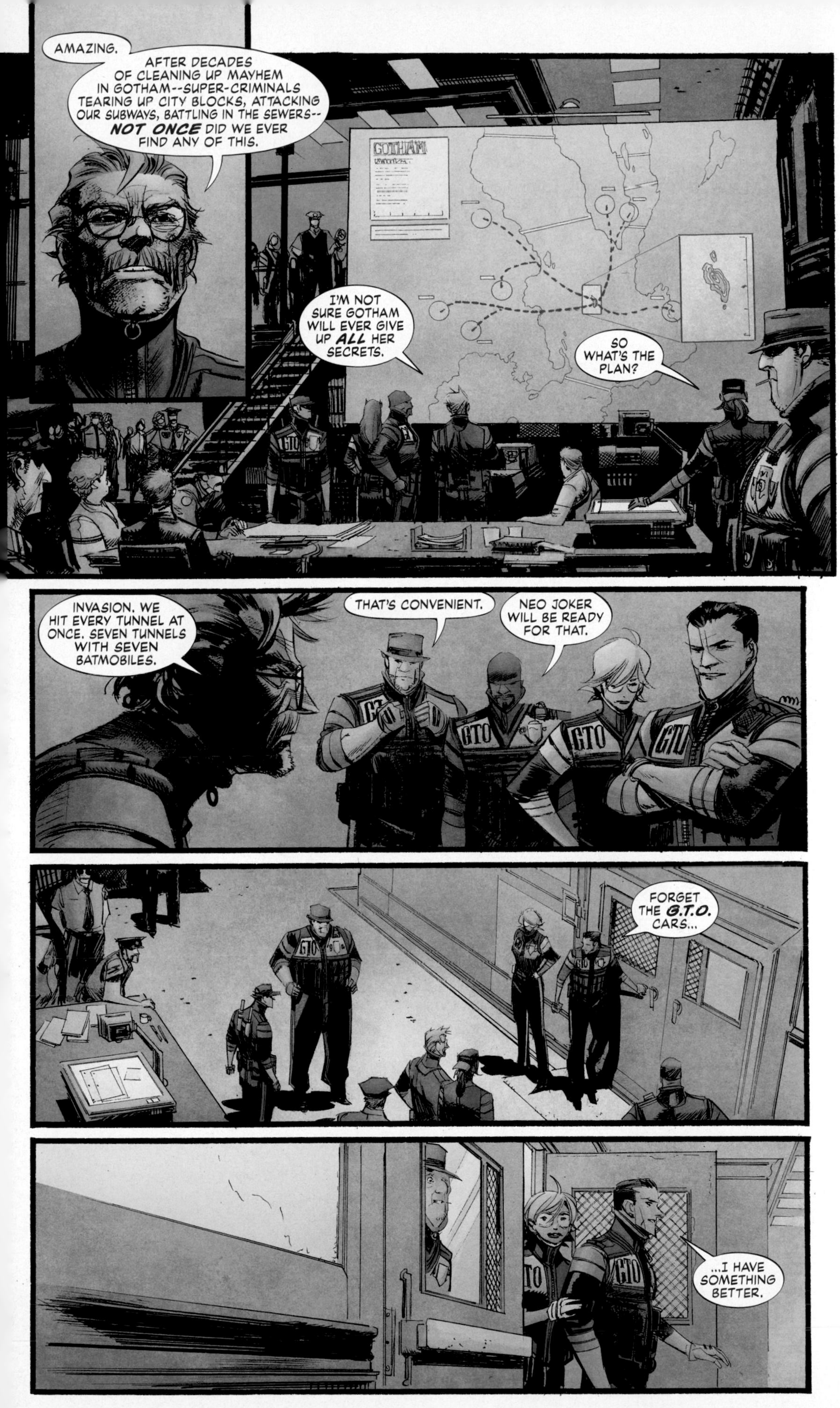
AMAZING.
AFTER DECADES OF CLEANING UP MAYHEM IN GOTHAM--SUPER-CRIMINALS TEARING UP CITY BLOCKS, ATTACKING OUR SUBWAYS, BATTLING IN THE SEWERS-- NOT ONCE DID WE EVER FIND ANY OF THIS.
GOTHAM
I'M NOT SURE GOTHAM WILL EVER GIVE UP ALL HER SECRETS.
SO WHAT'S THE PLAN?
INVASION. WE HIT EVERY TUNNEL AT ONCE. SEVEN TUNNELS WITH SEVEN BATMOBILES.
THAT'S CONVENIENT.
NEO JOKER WILL BE READY FOR THAT.
FORGET THE G.T.O. CARS...
...I HAVE SOMETHING BETTER.

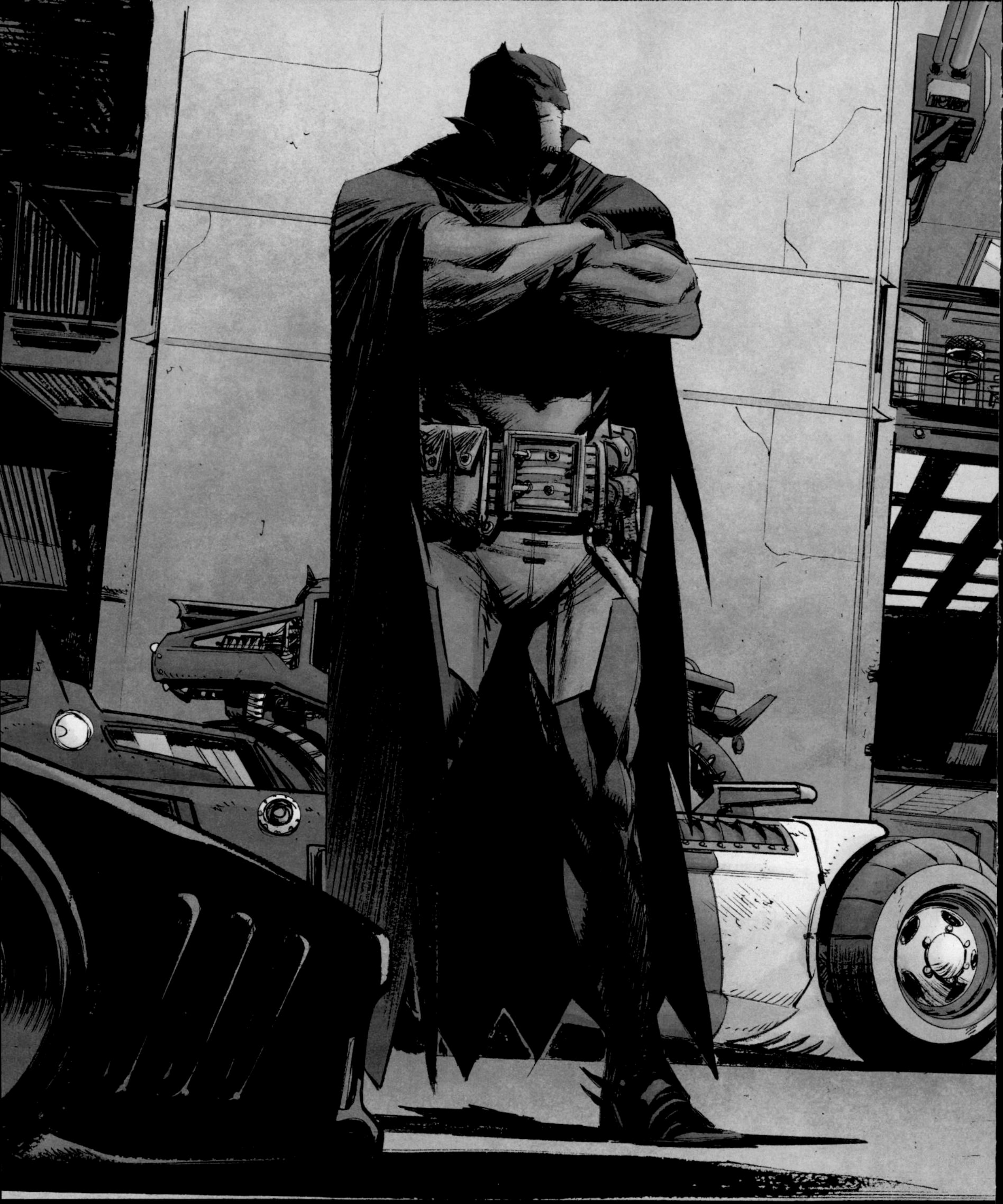

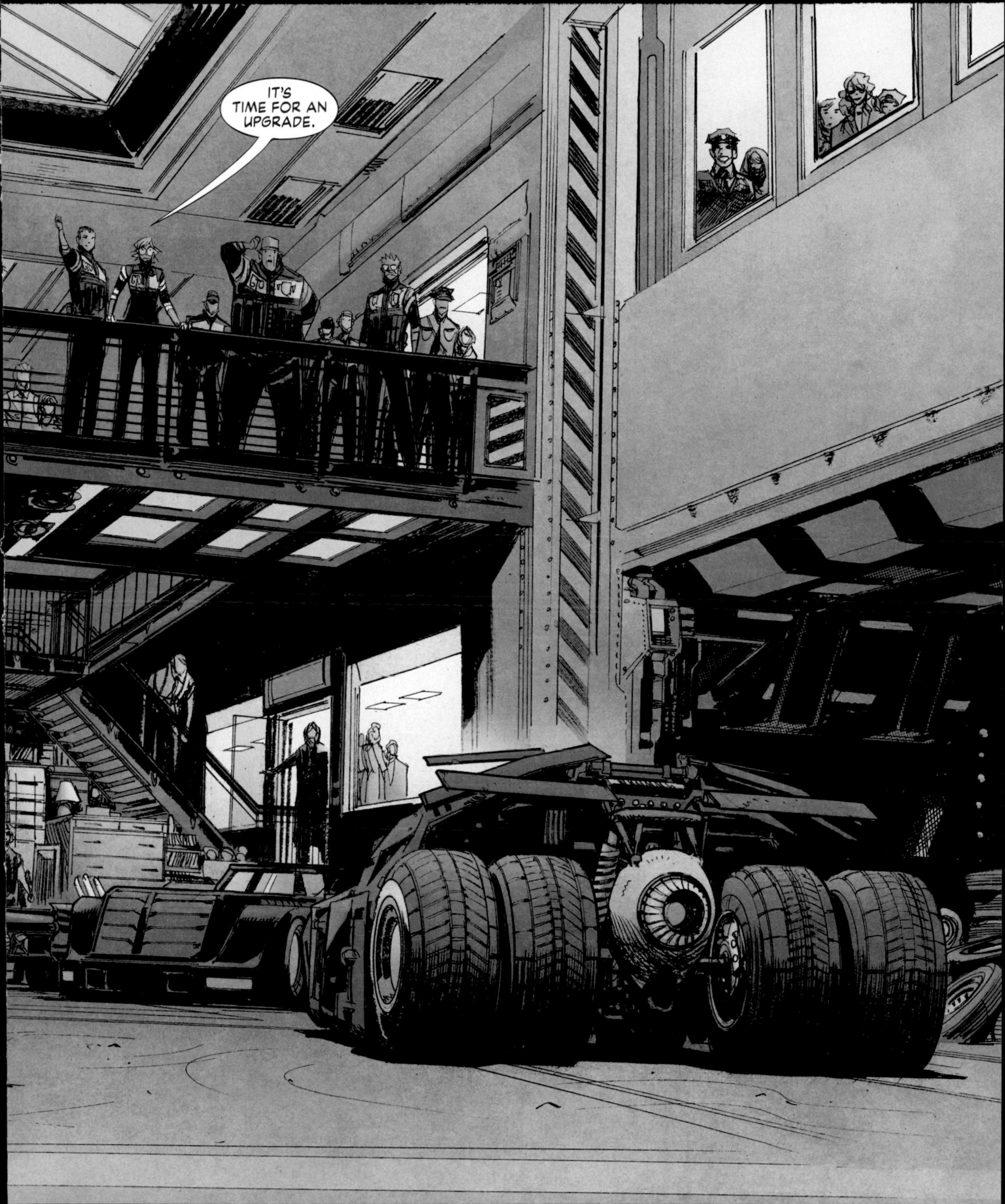
IT'S TIME FOR AN UPGRADE.

BATMAN AND I WORKING TOGETHER-- IT'S THE *LAST* THING SHE'LL EXPECT.

HA HA HA HA! HA HA! HA HA! HA HA HA! HA HA! HA HA! HA! HA! HA! HA!

SHE THINKS SHE CAN WIN...

...BUT SHE'LL *NEVER BE A JOKER!*

HAHA HAHAHA HAHA!

GLIRK

PUDDIN', I NEED YOU TO COME *BACK* TO ME. BREATHE!

OKAY. I'M OKAY.

I'M BACK. IT'S UNDER CONTROL.

HE RIDES WITH ME.

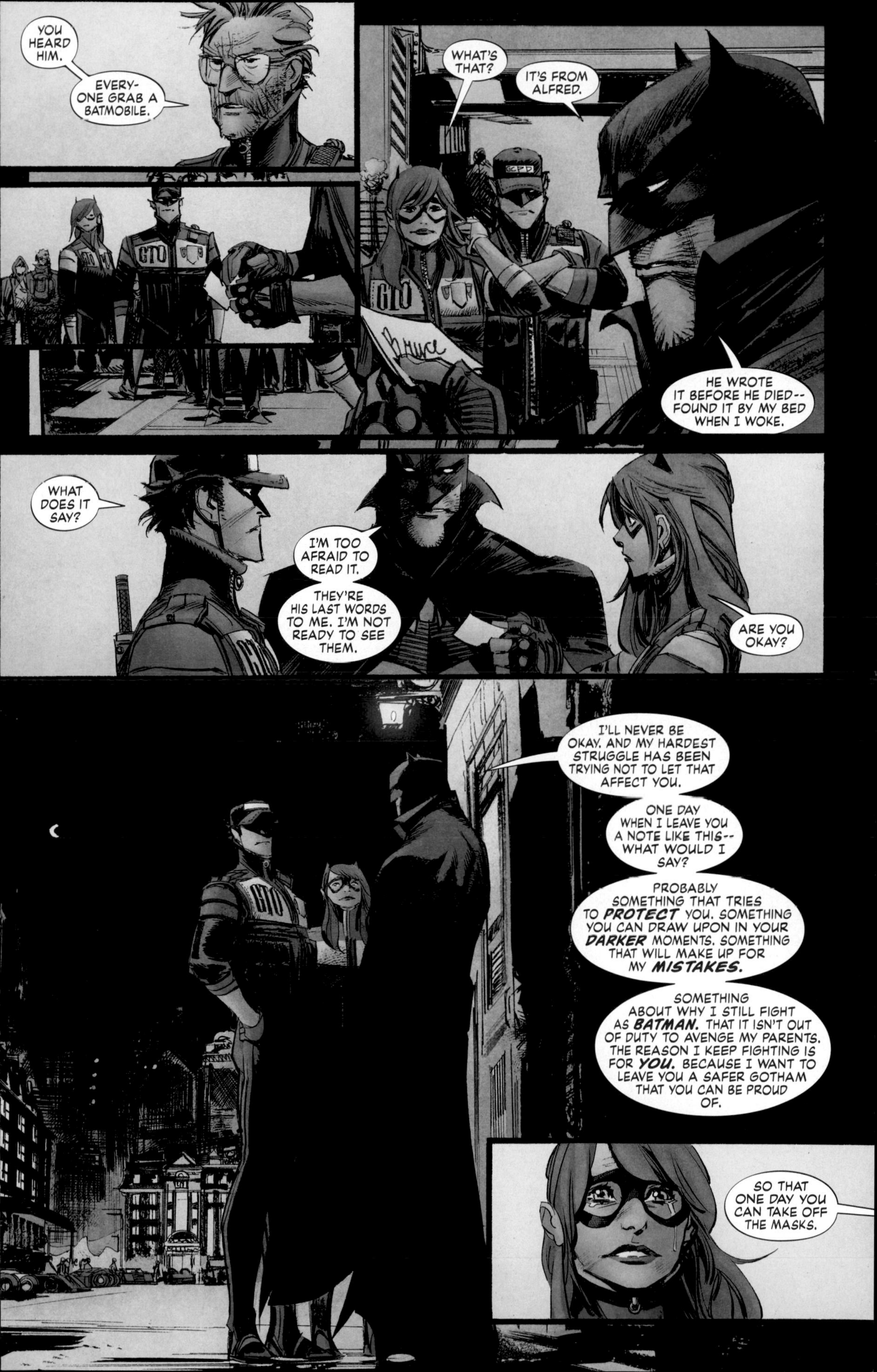

YOU HEARD HIM.
EVERY-ONE GRAB A BATMOBILE.
WHAT'S THAT?
IT'S FROM ALFRED.
Bruce
HE WROTE IT BEFORE HE DIED-- FOUND IT BY MY BED WHEN I WOKE.
WHAT DOES IT SAY?
I'M TOO AFRAID TO READ IT.
THEY'RE HIS LAST WORDS TO ME. I'M NOT READY TO SEE THEM.
ARE YOU OKAY?
I'LL NEVER BE OKAY. AND MY HARDEST STRUGGLE HAS BEEN TRYING NOT TO LET THAT AFFECT YOU.
ONE DAY WHEN I LEAVE YOU A NOTE LIKE THIS-- WHAT WOULD I SAY?
PROBABLY SOMETHING THAT TRIES TO **PROTECT** YOU. SOMETHING YOU CAN DRAW UPON IN YOUR **DARKER** MOMENTS. SOMETHING THAT WILL MAKE UP FOR MY **MISTAKES.**
SOMETHING ABOUT WHY I STILL FIGHT AS **BATMAN.** THAT IT ISN'T OUT OF DUTY TO AVENGE MY PARENTS. THE REASON I KEEP FIGHTING IS FOR **YOU.** BECAUSE I WANT TO LEAVE YOU A SAFER GOTHAM THAT YOU CAN BE PROUD OF.
SO THAT ONE DAY YOU CAN TAKE OFF THE MASKS.

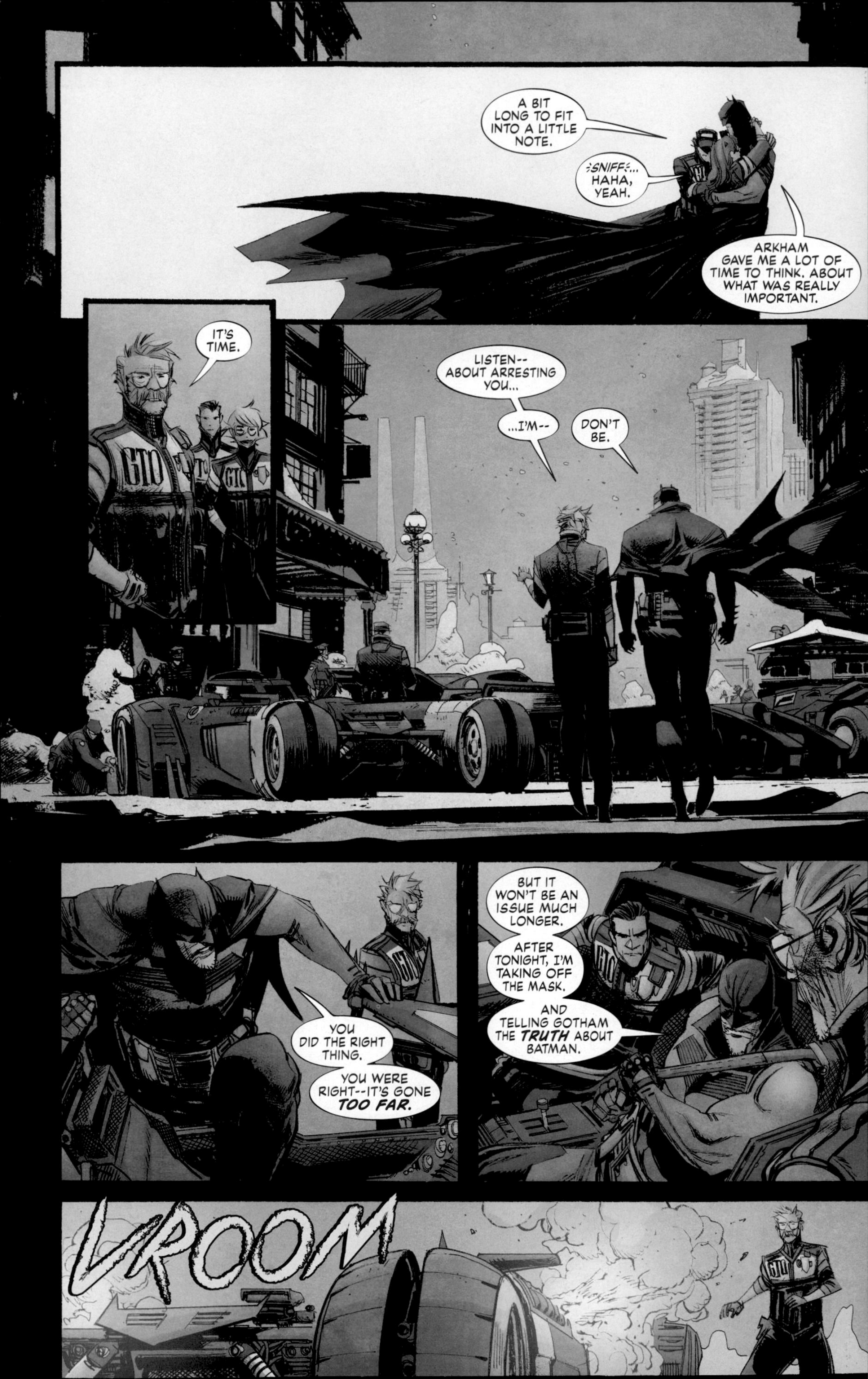
A BIT LONG TO FIT INTO A LITTLE NOTE.
SNIFF... HAHA, YEAH.
ARKHAM GAVE ME A LOT OF TIME TO THINK. ABOUT WHAT WAS REALLY IMPORTANT.
IT'S TIME.
LISTEN-- ABOUT ARRESTING YOU...
...I'M--
DON'T BE.
YOU DID THE RIGHT THING.
YOU WERE RIGHT--IT'S GONE TOO FAR.
BUT IT WON'T BE AN ISSUE MUCH LONGER.
AFTER TONIGHT, I'M TAKING OFF THE MASK.
AND TELLING GOTHAM THE TRUTH ABOUT BATMAN.
VROOM

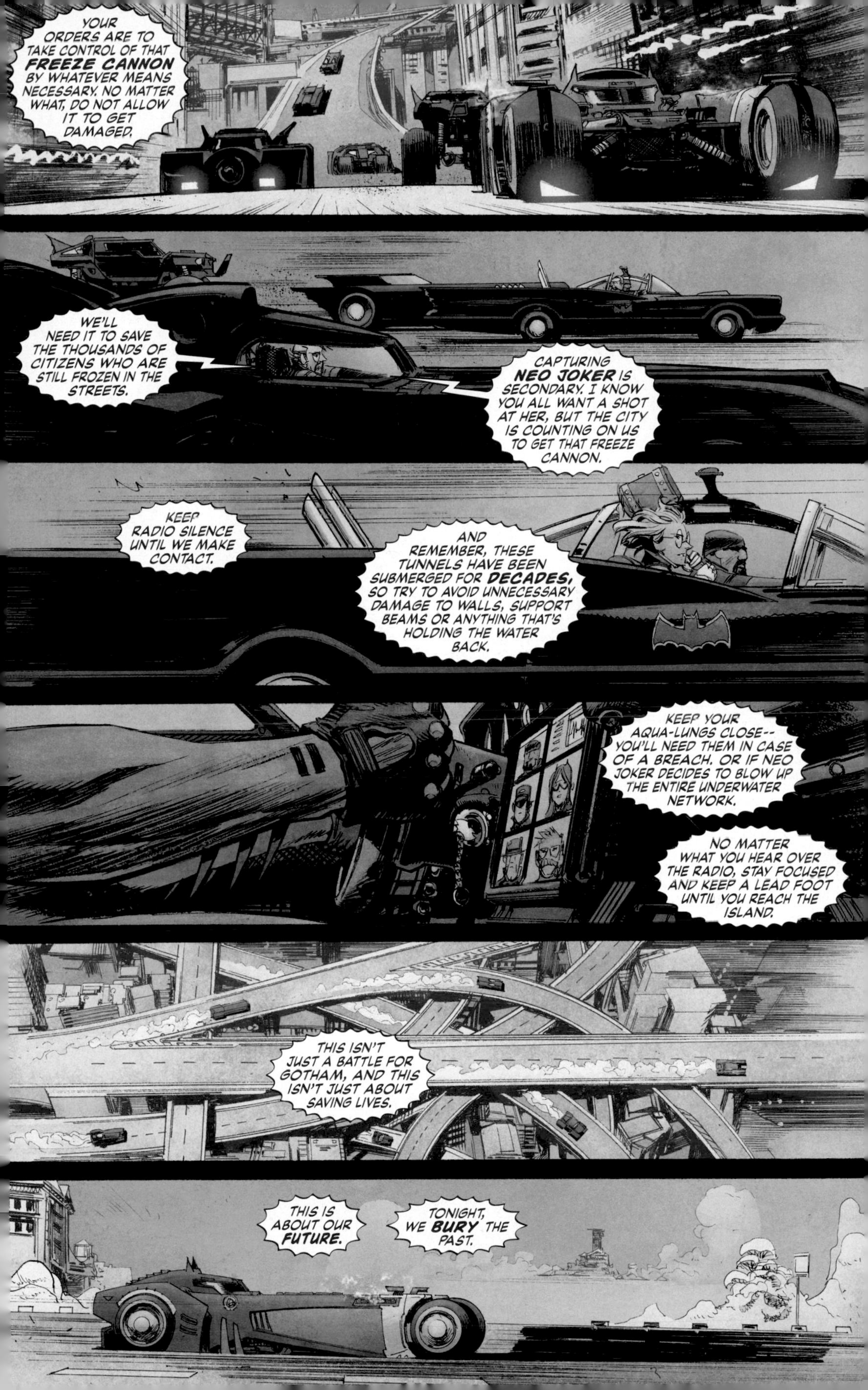

YOUR ORDERS ARE TO TAKE CONTROL OF THAT **FREEZE CANNON** BY WHATEVER MEANS NECESSARY. NO MATTER WHAT, DO NOT ALLOW IT TO GET DAMAGED.
WE'LL NEED IT TO SAVE THE THOUSANDS OF CITIZENS WHO ARE STILL FROZEN IN THE STREETS.
CAPTURING **NEO JOKER** IS SECONDARY. I KNOW YOU ALL WANT A SHOT AT HER, BUT THE CITY IS COUNTING ON US TO GET THAT FREEZE CANNON.
KEEP RADIO SILENCE UNTIL WE MAKE CONTACT.
AND REMEMBER, THESE TUNNELS HAVE BEEN SUBMERGED FOR **DECADES,** SO TRY TO AVOID UNNECESSARY DAMAGE TO WALLS, SUPPORT BEAMS OR ANYTHING THAT'S HOLDING THE WATER BACK.
KEEP YOUR AQUA-LUNGS CLOSE-- YOU'LL NEED THEM IN CASE OF A BREACH. OR IF NEO JOKER DECIDES TO BLOW UP THE ENTIRE UNDERWATER NETWORK.
NO MATTER WHAT YOU HEAR OVER THE RADIO, STAY FOCUSED AND KEEP A LEAD FOOT UNTIL YOU REACH THE ISLAND.
THIS ISN'T JUST A BATTLE FOR GOTHAM, AND THIS ISN'T JUST ABOUT SAVING LIVES.
THIS IS ABOUT OUR **FUTURE.**
TONIGHT, WE **BURY** THE PAST.

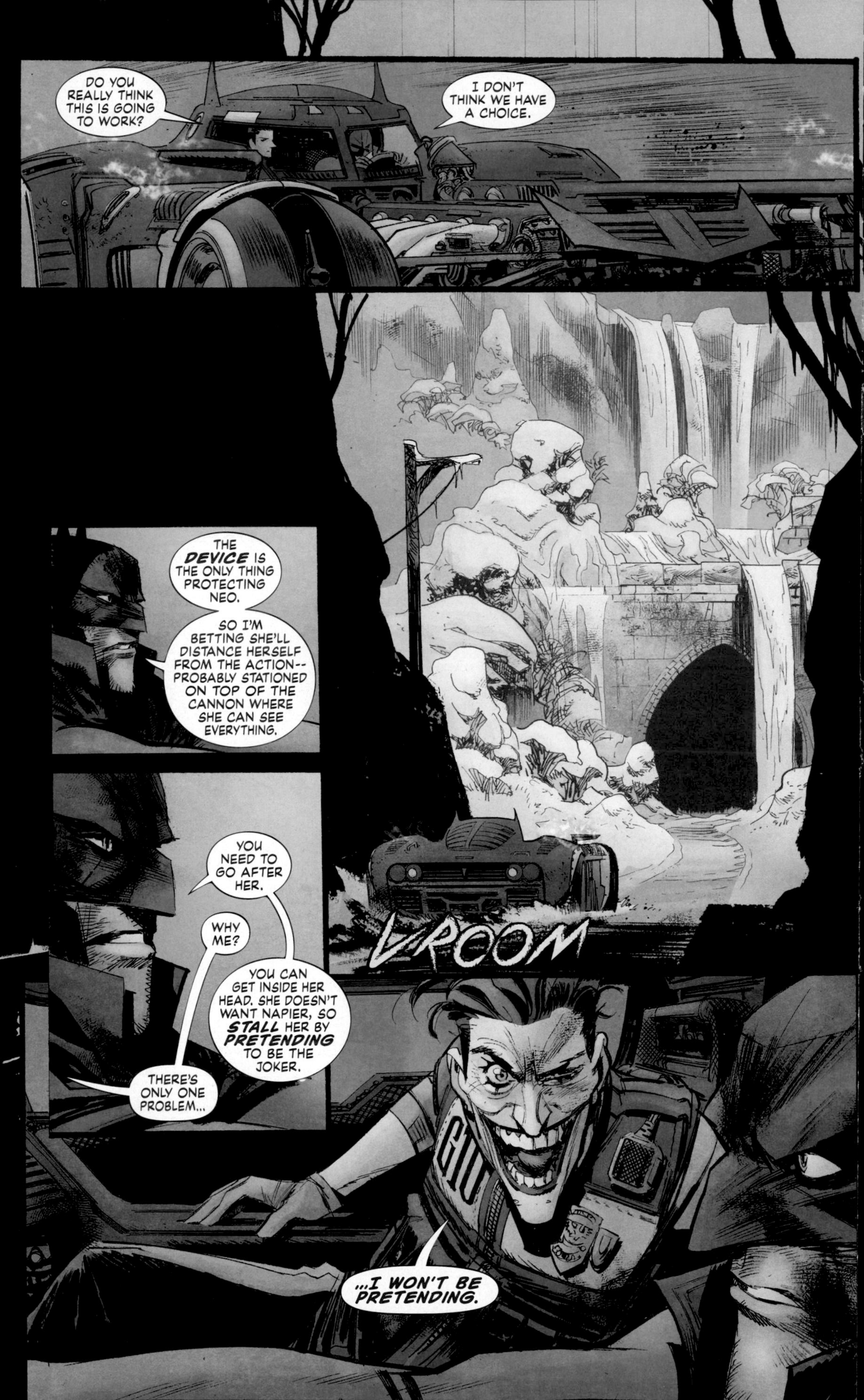
DO YOU REALLY THINK THIS IS GOING TO WORK?
I DON'T THINK WE HAVE A CHOICE.
THE DEVICE IS THE ONLY THING PROTECTING NEO.
SO I'M BETTING SHE'LL DISTANCE HERSELF FROM THE ACTION--PROBABLY STATIONED ON TOP OF THE CANNON WHERE SHE CAN SEE EVERYTHING.
VROOM
YOU NEED TO GO AFTER HER.
WHY ME?
YOU CAN GET INSIDE HER HEAD. SHE DOESN'T WANT NAPIER, SO STALL HER BY PRETENDING TO BE THE JOKER.
THERE'S ONLY ONE PROBLEM...
...I WON'T BE PRETENDING.

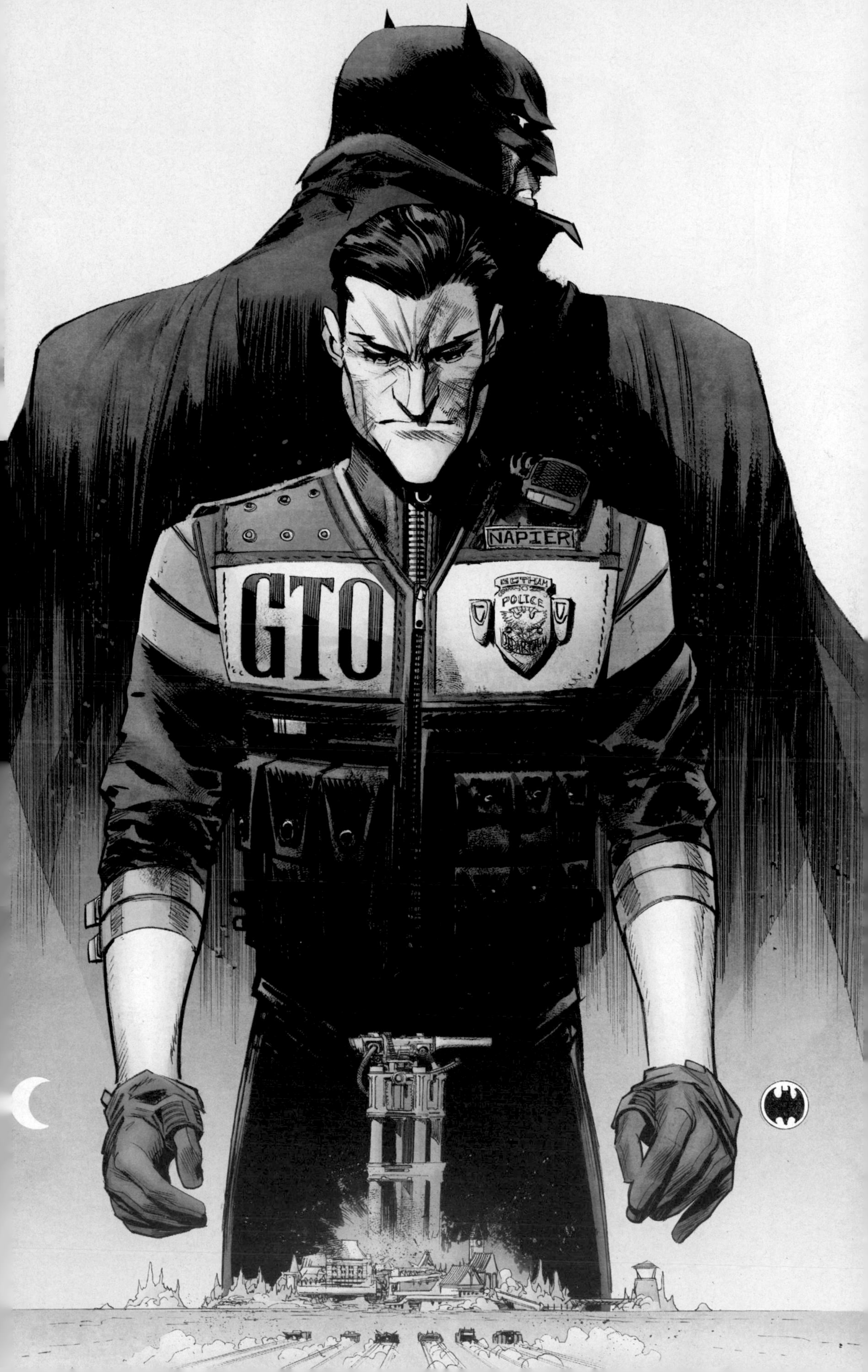
NAPIER
GTO
POLICE

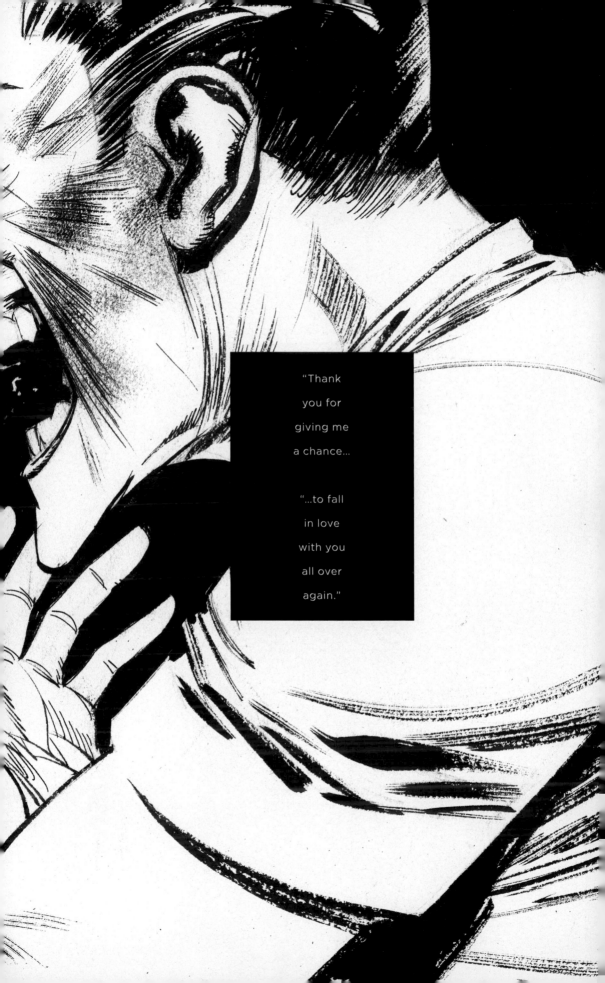

"Thank
you for
giving me
a chance...

"...to fall
in love
with you
all over
again."

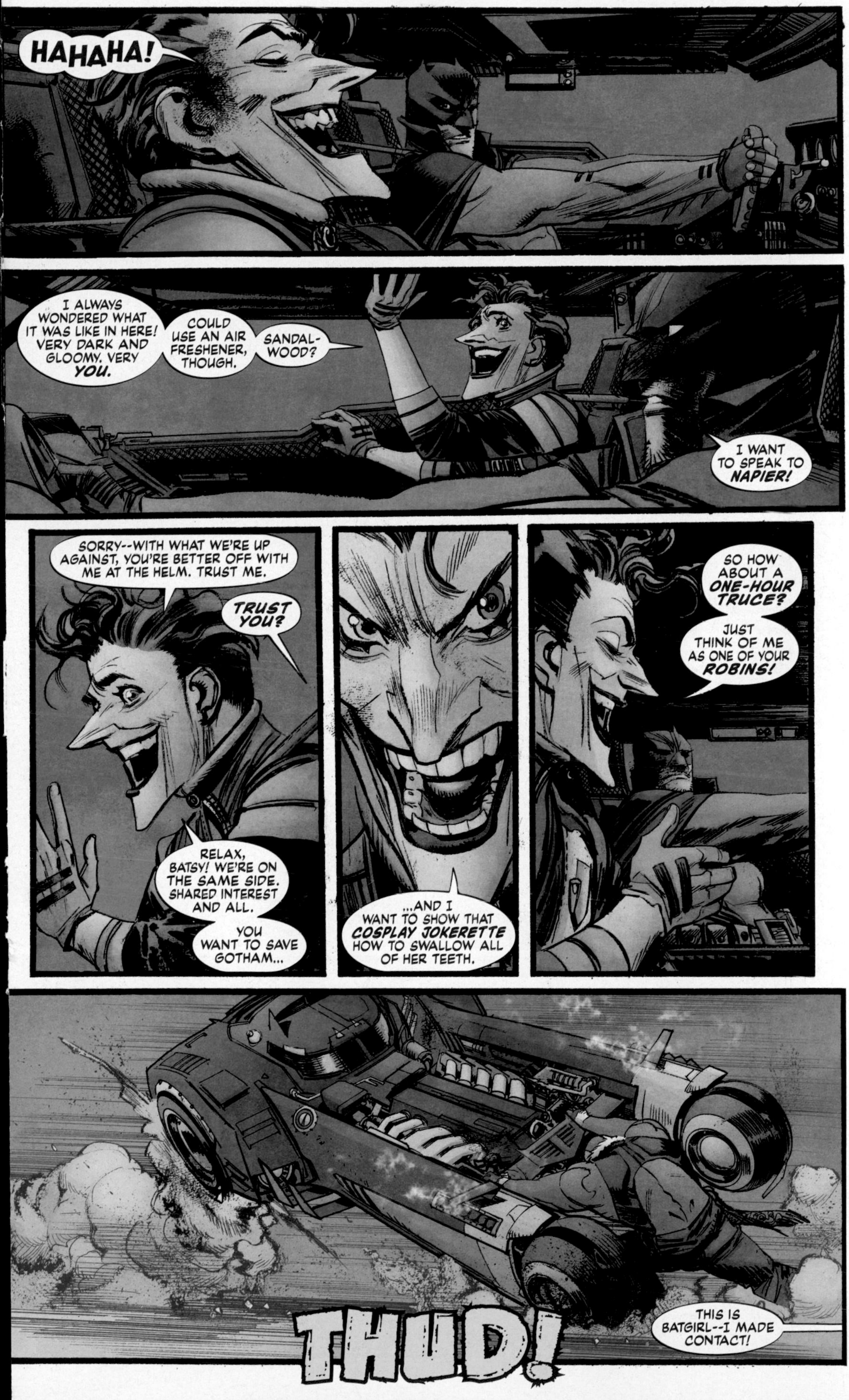
HAHAHA!
I ALWAYS WONDERED WHAT IT WAS LIKE IN HERE! VERY DARK AND GLOOMY. VERY YOU.
COULD USE AN AIR FRESHENER, THOUGH.
SANDAL-WOOD?
I WANT TO SPEAK TO NAPIER!
SORRY--WITH WHAT WE'RE UP AGAINST, YOU'RE BETTER OFF WITH ME AT THE HELM. TRUST ME.
TRUST YOU?
RELAX, BATSY! WE'RE ON THE SAME SIDE. SHARED INTEREST AND ALL.
YOU WANT TO SAVE GOTHAM...
...AND I WANT TO SHOW THAT COSPLAY JOKERETTE HOW TO SWALLOW ALL OF HER TEETH.
SO HOW ABOUT A ONE-HOUR TRUCE?
JUST THINK OF ME AS ONE OF YOUR ROBINS!
THUD!
THIS IS BATGIRL--I MADE CONTACT!

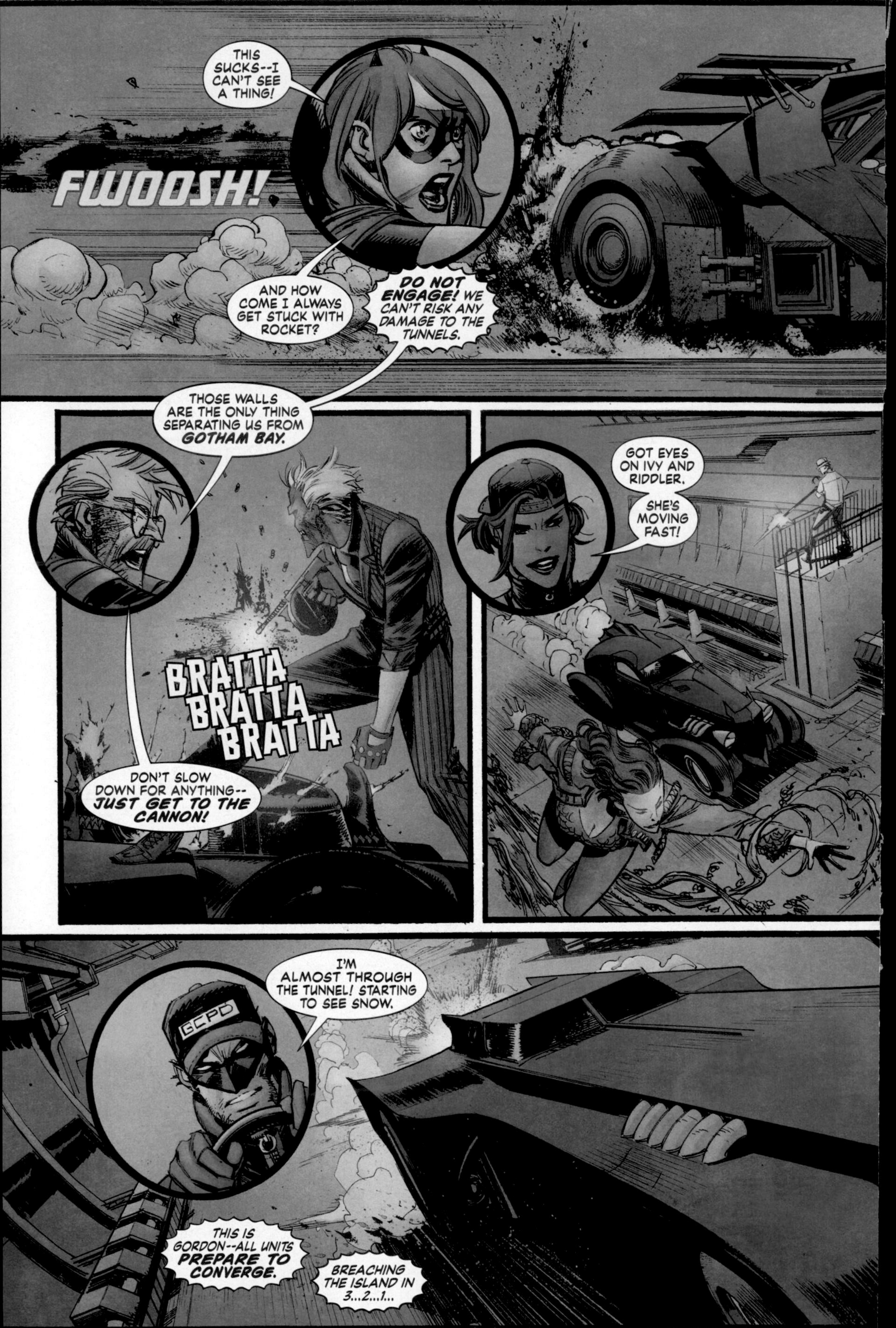
FWOOSH!
THIS SUCKS--I CAN'T SEE A THING!
AND HOW COME I ALWAYS GET STUCK WITH ROCKET?
DO NOT ENGAGE! WE CAN'T RISK ANY DAMAGE TO THE TUNNELS.
THOSE WALLS ARE THE ONLY THING SEPARATING US FROM GOTHAM BAY.
BRATTA BRATTA BRATTA
DON'T SLOW DOWN FOR ANYTHING-- JUST GET TO THE CANNON!
GOT EYES ON IVY AND RIDDLER.
SHE'S MOVING FAST!
I'M ALMOST THROUGH THE TUNNEL! STARTING TO SEE SNOW.
GCPD
THIS IS GORDON--ALL UNITS PREPARE TO CONVERGE.
BREACHING THE ISLAND IN 3...2...1...

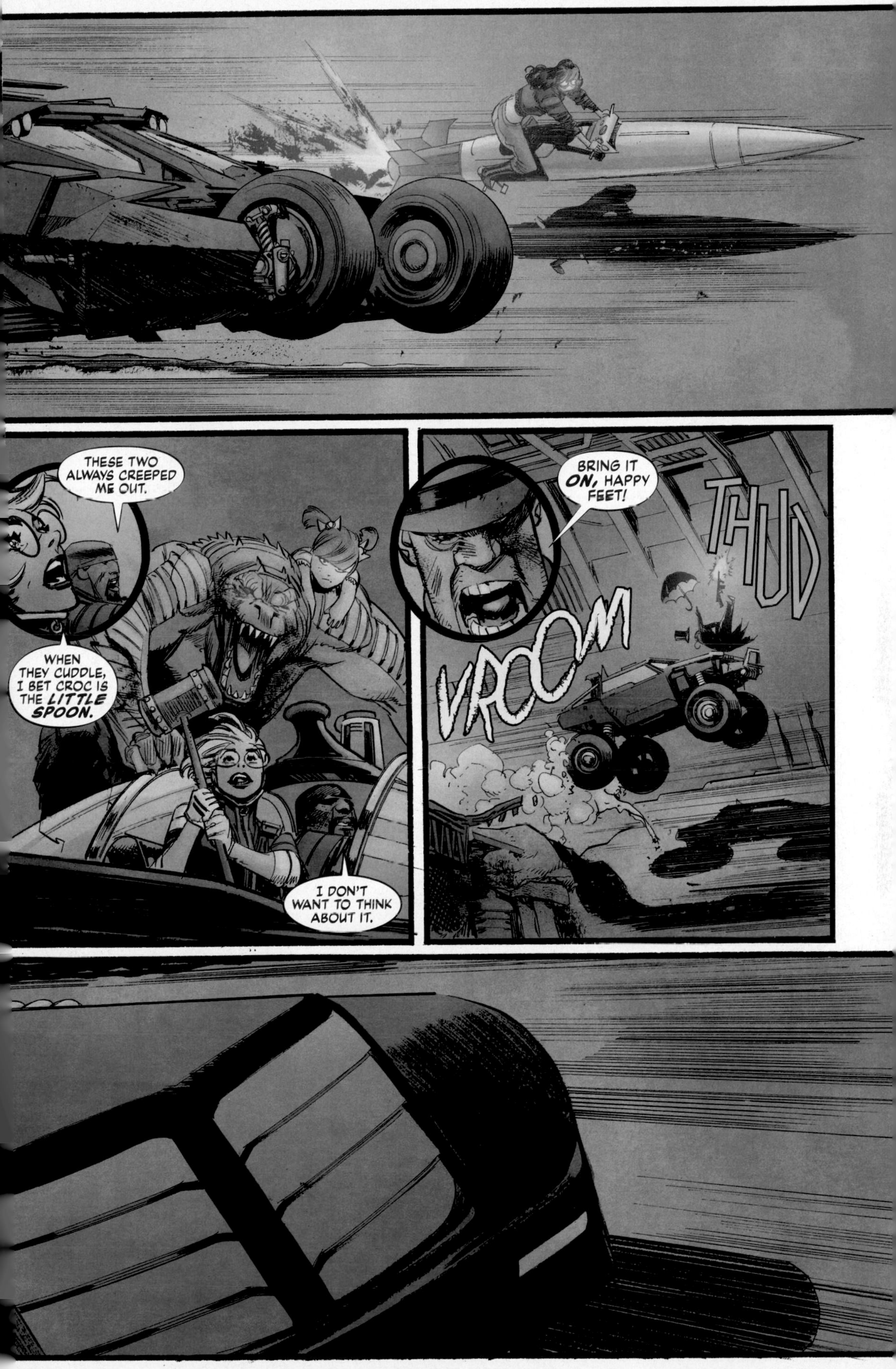
THESE TWO ALWAYS CREEPED ME OUT.
WHEN THEY CUDDLE, I BET CROC IS THE *LITTLE SPOON.*
I DON'T WANT TO THINK ABOUT IT.
BRING IT *ON,* HAPPY FEET!
THUD
VROOM

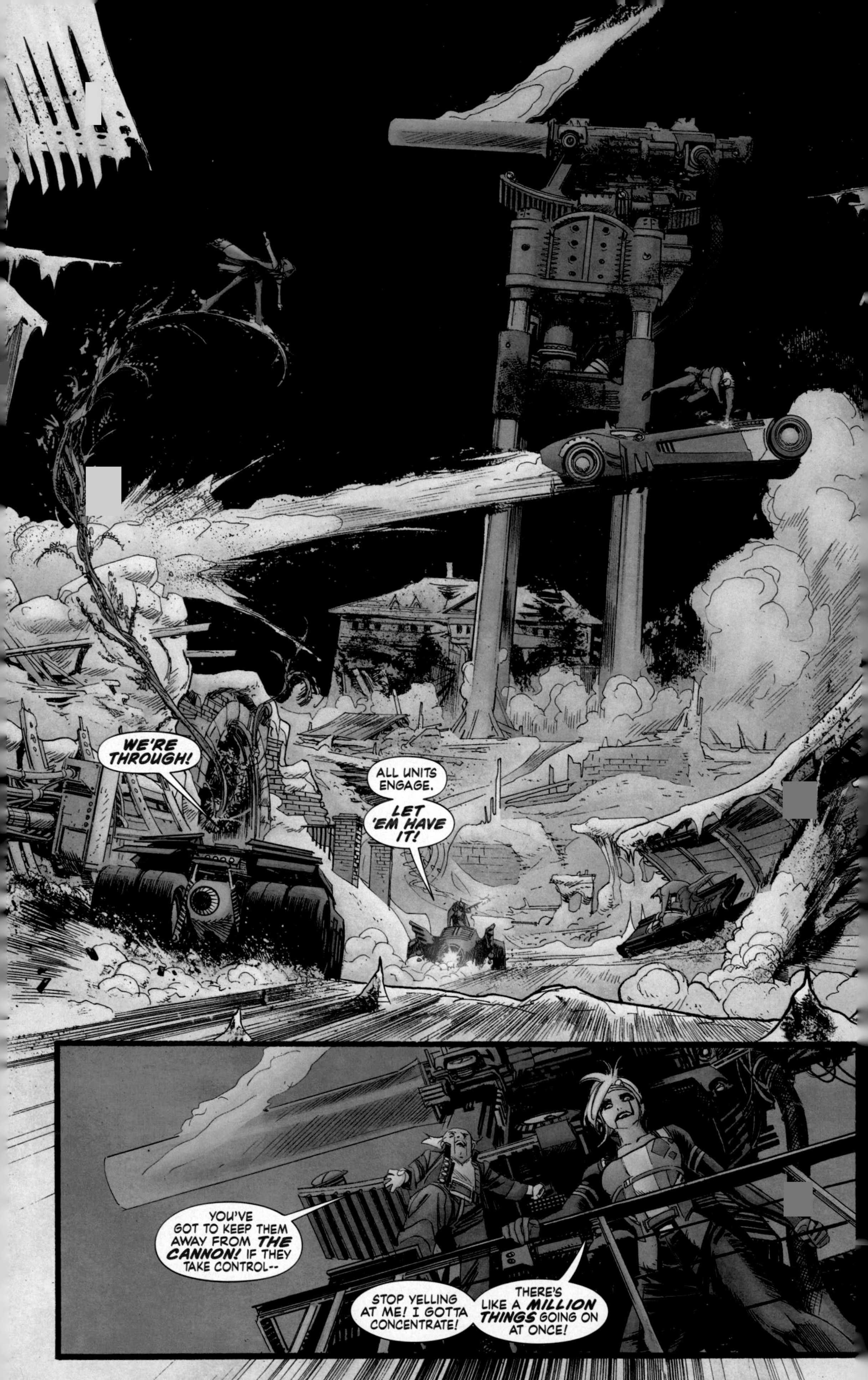
WE'RE THROUGH!
ALL UNITS ENGAGE.
LET 'EM HAVE IT!
YOU'VE GOT TO KEEP THEM AWAY FROM THE CANNON! IF THEY TAKE CONTROL--
STOP YELLING AT ME! I GOTTA CONCENTRATE!
THERE'S LIKE A MILLION THINGS GOING ON AT ONCE!

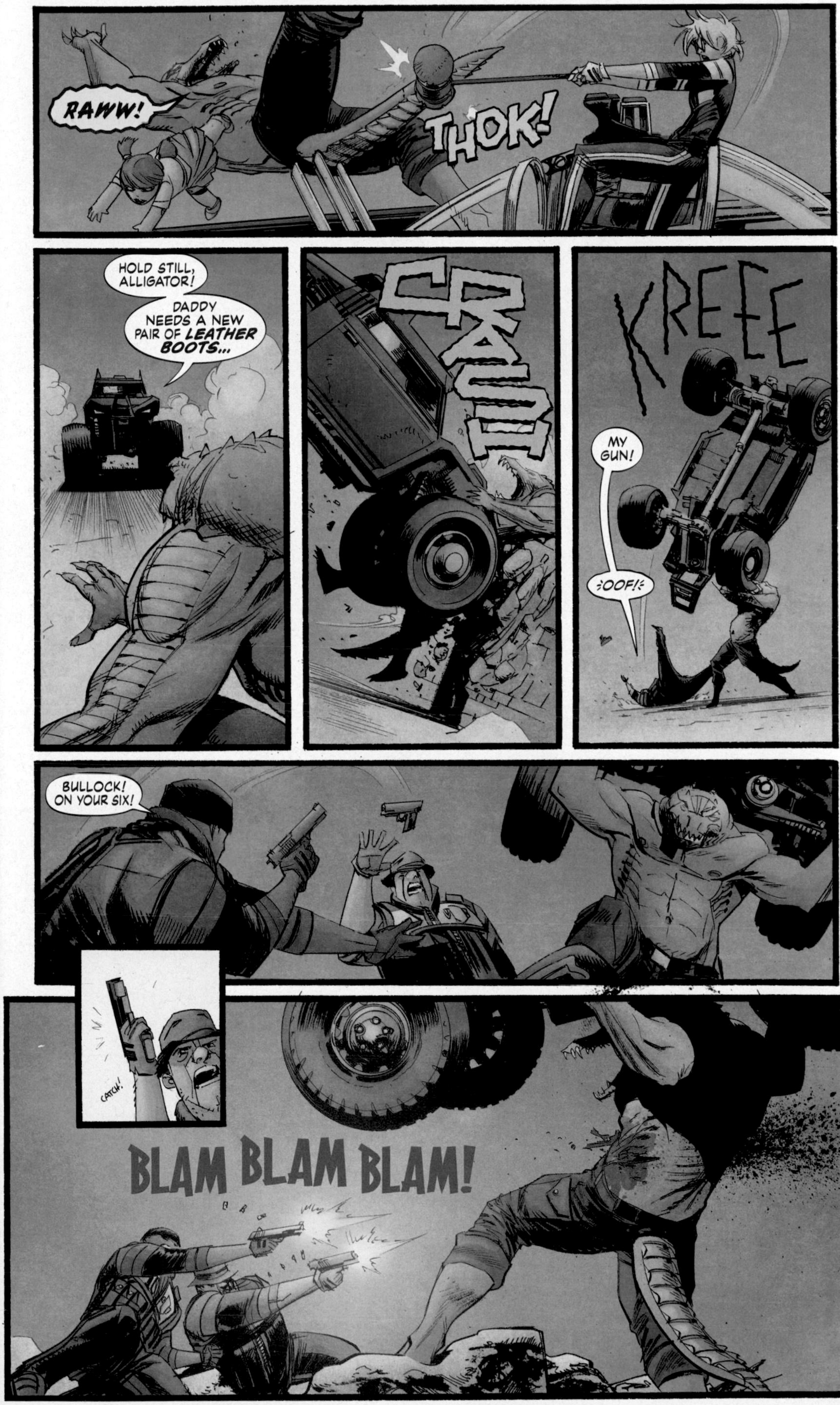
RAWW!
THOK!
HOLD STILL, ALLIGATOR!
DADDY NEEDS A NEW PAIR OF LEATHER BOOTS...
CRASH
KREEE
MY GUN!
OOF!
BULLOCK! ON YOUR SIX!
CATCH!
BLAM BLAM BLAM!

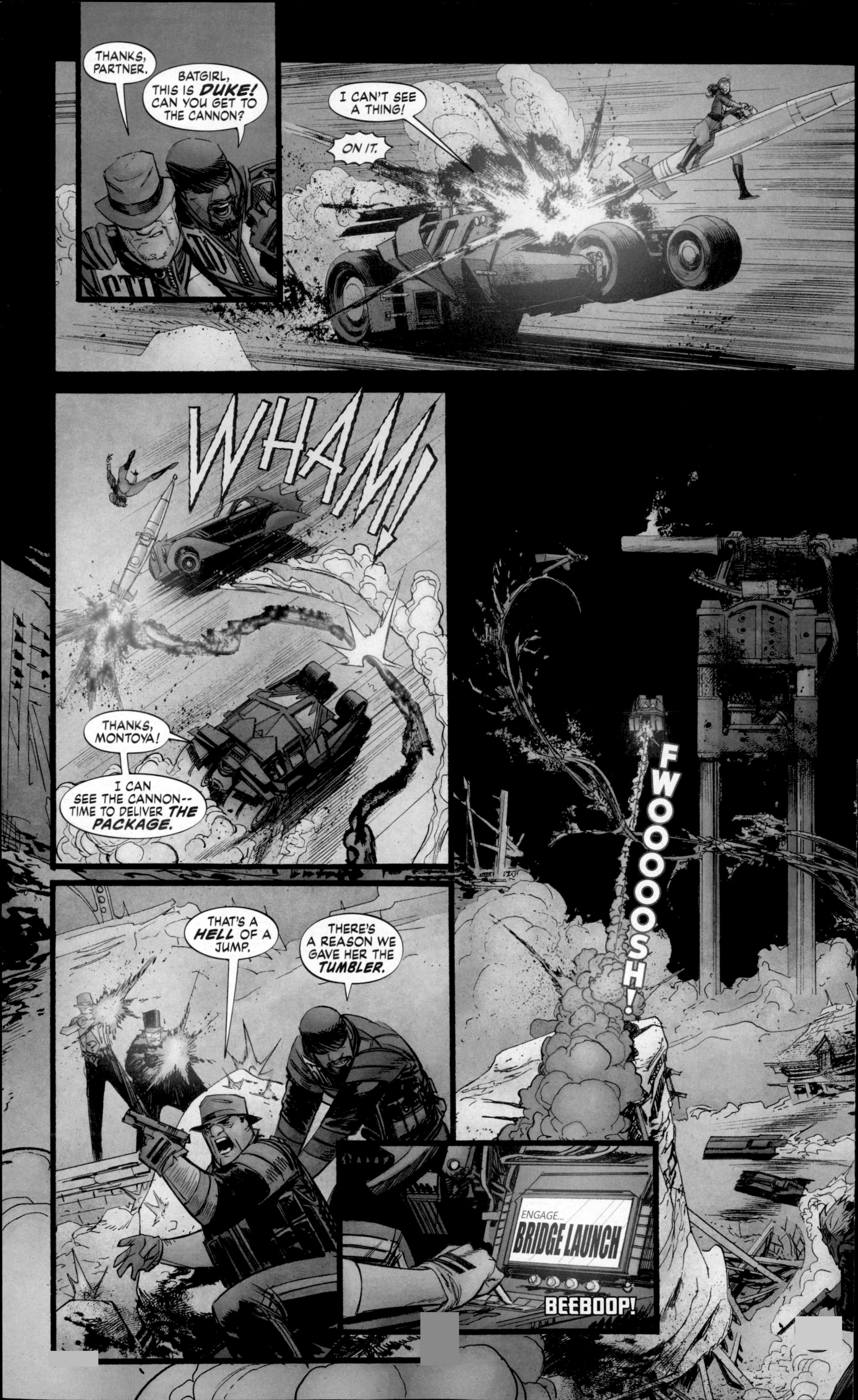
THANKS, PARTNER.
BATGIRL, THIS IS DUKE! CAN YOU GET TO THE CANNON?
I CAN'T SEE A THING!
ON IT.
WHAM!
THANKS, MONTOYA!
I CAN SEE THE CANNON-- TIME TO DELIVER THE PACKAGE.
FWOOOOOOSH!
THAT'S A HELL OF A JUMP.
THERE'S A REASON WE GAVE HER THE TUMBLER.
ENGAGE...
BRIDGE LAUNCH
BEEBOOP!

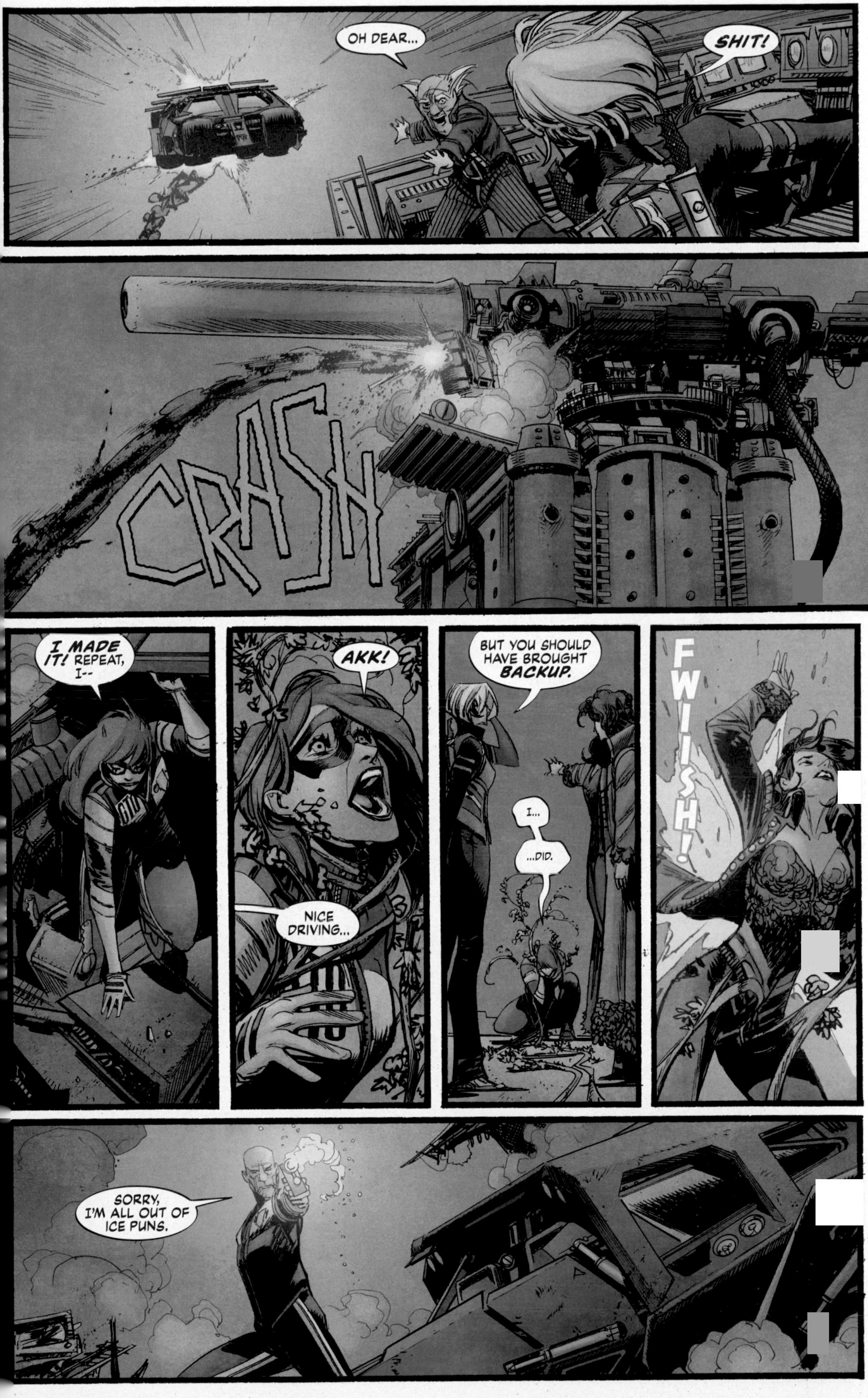
OH DEAR...
SHIT!
CRASH
I MADE IT! REPEAT, I--
AKK!
NICE DRIVING...
BUT YOU SHOULD HAVE BROUGHT BACKUP.
I...
...DID.
FWISH!
SORRY, I'M ALL OUT OF ICE PUNS.

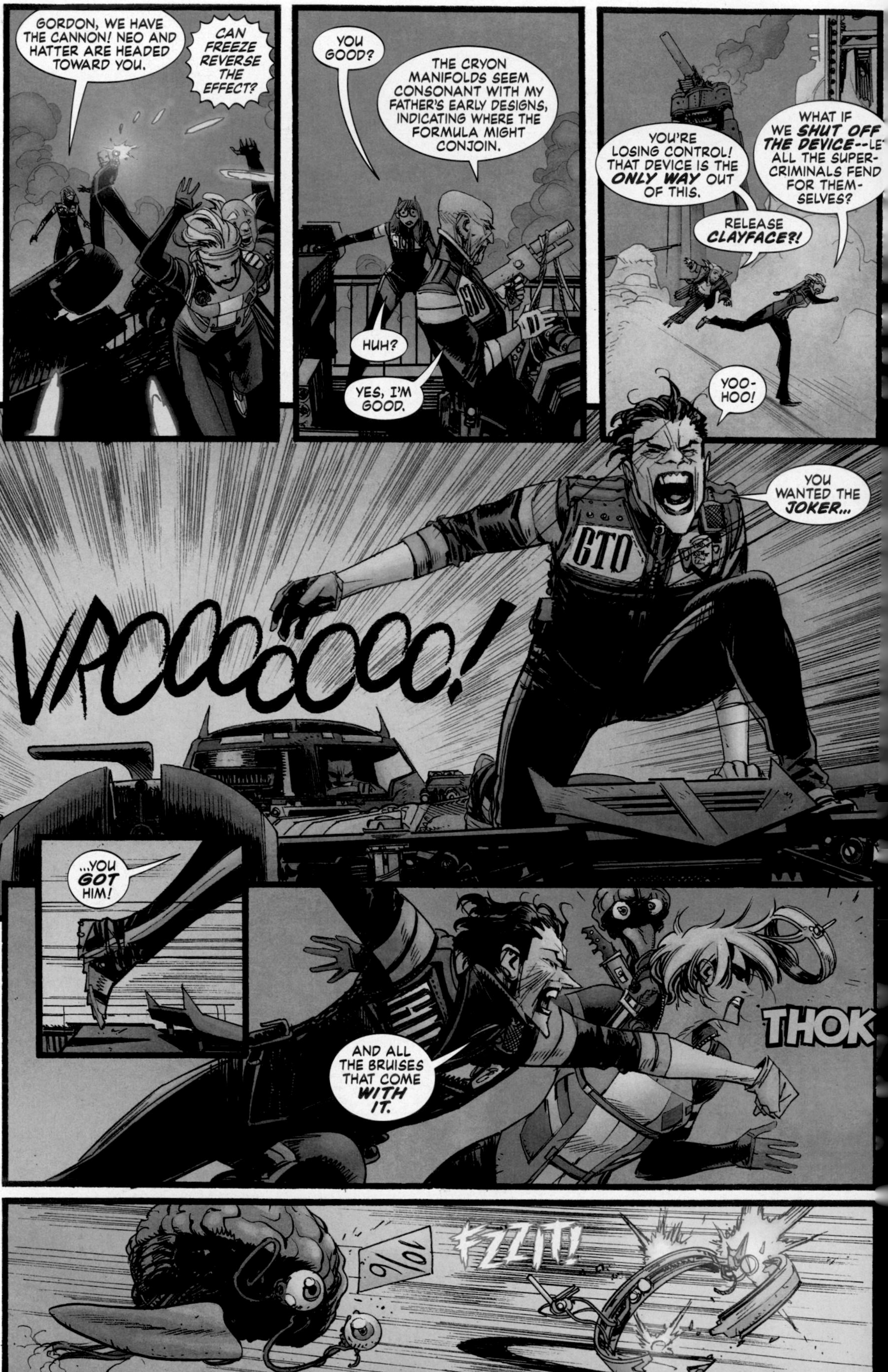
GORDON, WE HAVE THE CANNON! NEO AND HATTER ARE HEADED TOWARD YOU.
CAN FREEZE REVERSE THE EFFECT?
YOU GOOD?
THE CRYON MANIFOLDS SEEM CONSONANT WITH MY FATHER'S EARLY DESIGNS, INDICATING WHERE THE FORMULA MIGHT CONJOIN.
HUH?
YES, I'M GOOD.
YOU'RE LOSING CONTROL! THAT DEVICE IS THE ONLY WAY OUT OF THIS.
WHAT IF WE SHUT OFF THE DEVICE--LET ALL THE SUPER-CRIMINALS FEND FOR THEM-SELVES?
RELEASE CLAYFACE?!
YOO-HOO!
YOU WANTED THE JOKER...
VROOOOOOOO!
...YOU GOT HIM!
AND ALL THE BRUISES THAT COME WITH IT.
THOK
10/6
FZZIT!

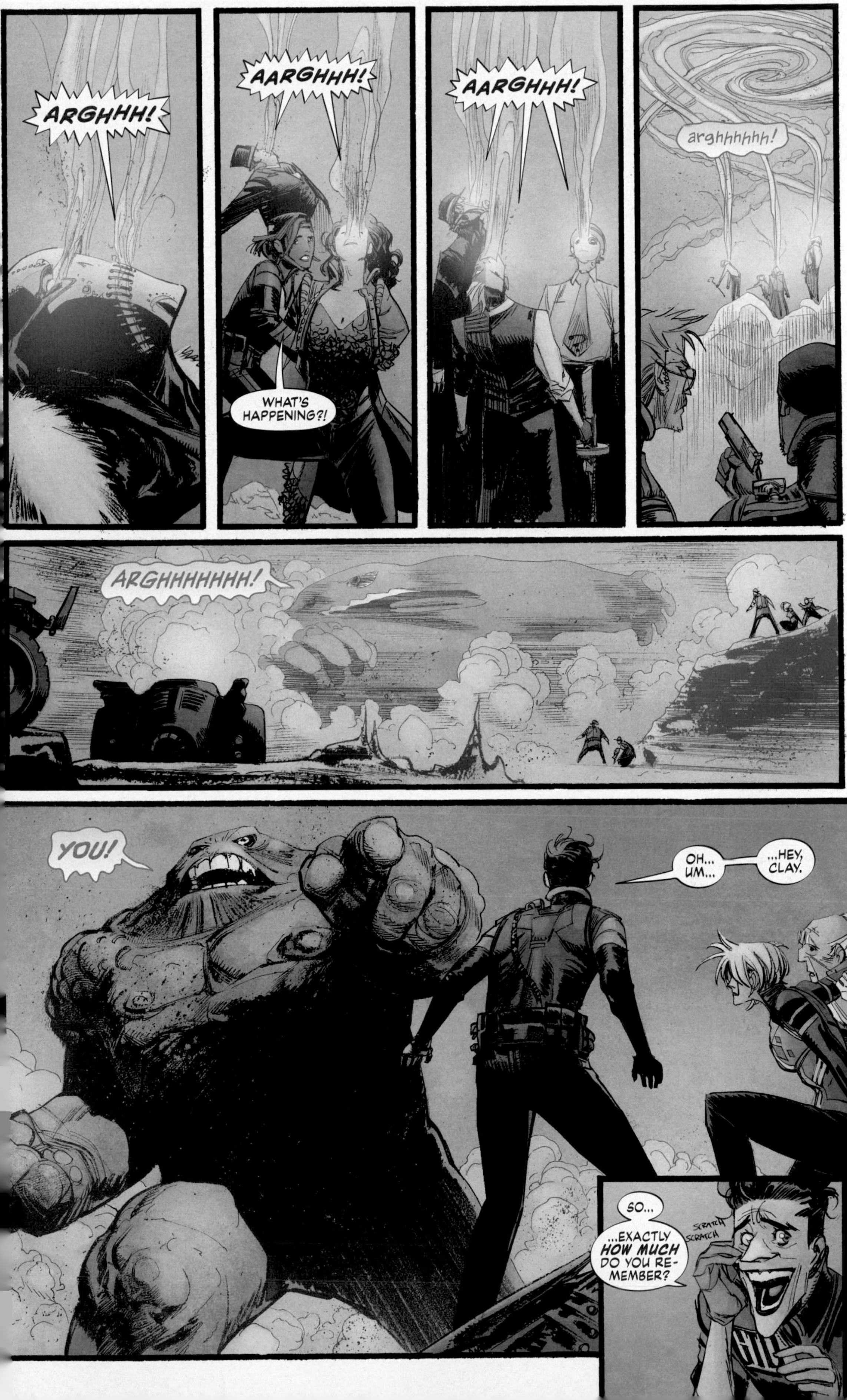
ARGHHH!
AARGHHH!
WHAT'S HAPPENING?!
AARGHHH!
arghhhhhh!
ARGHHHHHHH!
YOU!
OH... UM...
...HEY, CLAY.
SO...
...EXACTLY HOW MUCH DO YOU REMEMBER?
SCRATCH SCRATCH

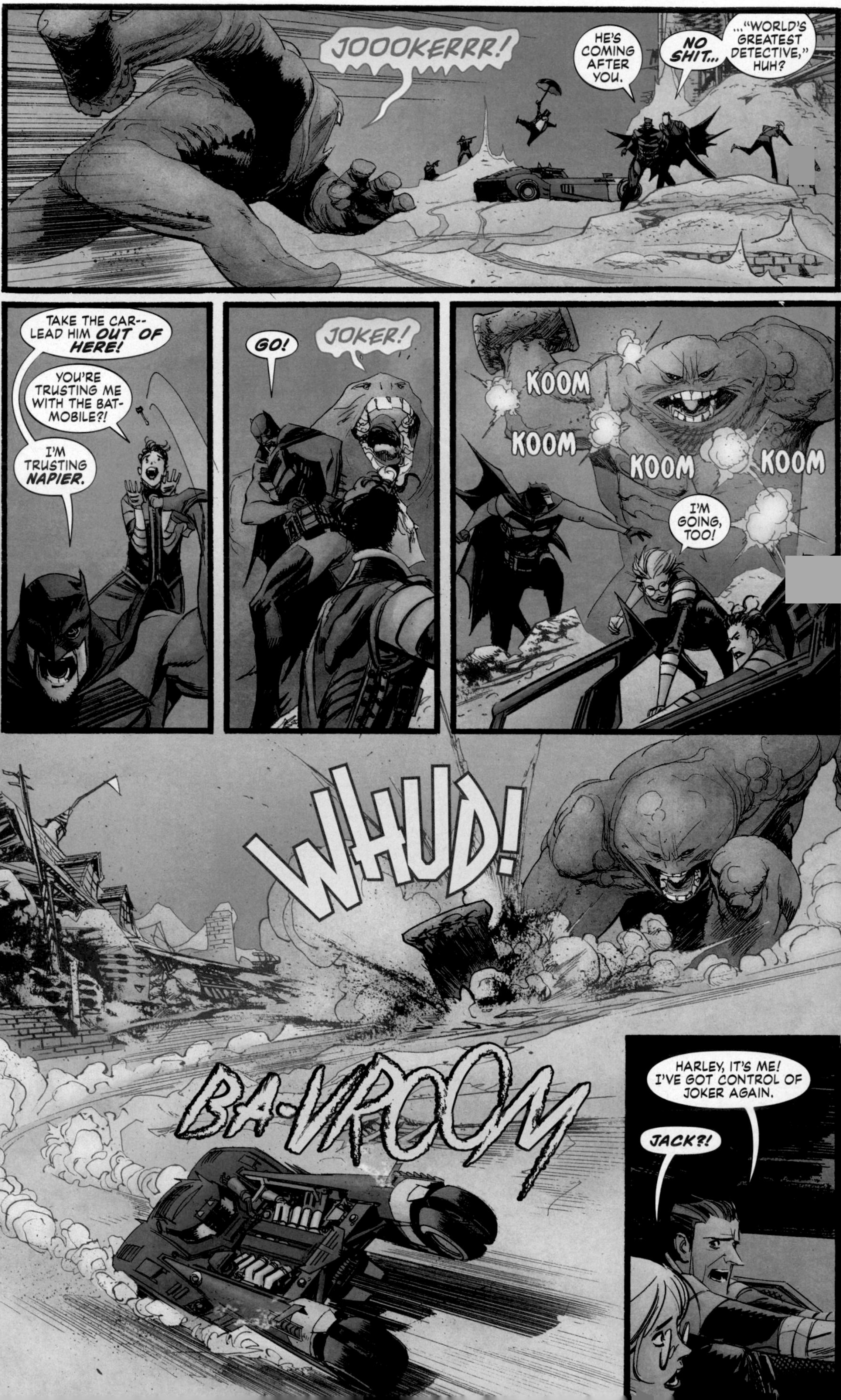
JOOOKERRR!
HE'S COMING AFTER YOU.
NO SHIT...
..."WORLD'S GREATEST DETECTIVE," HUH?
TAKE THE CAR-- LEAD HIM OUT OF HERE!
YOU'RE TRUSTING ME WITH THE BAT-MOBILE?!
I'M TRUSTING NAPIER.
GO!
JOKER!
KOOM
KOOM
KOOM
KOOM
I'M GOING, TOO!
WHUD!
BA-VROOM
HARLEY, IT'S ME! I'VE GOT CONTROL OF JOKER AGAIN.
JACK?!

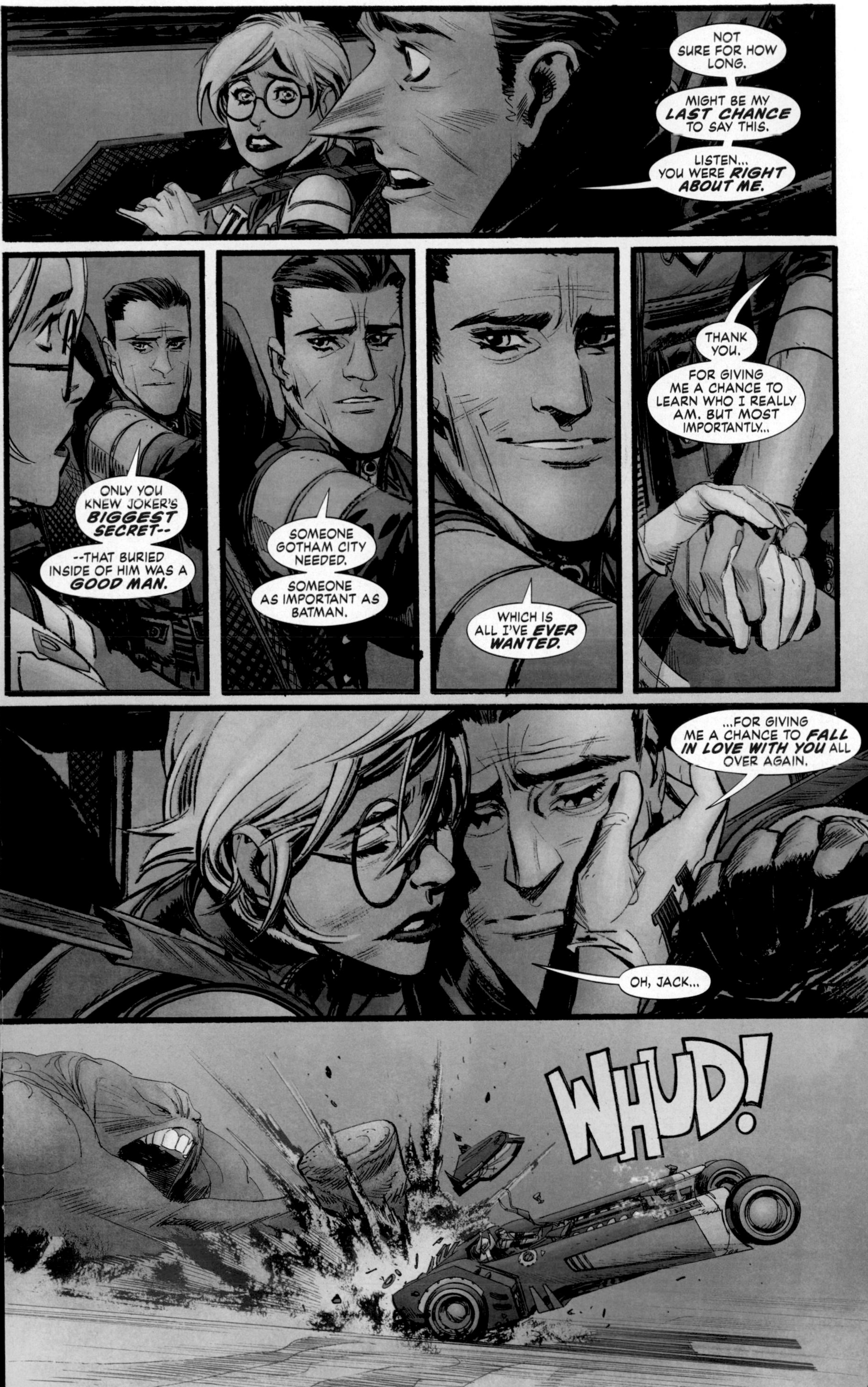
NOT SURE FOR HOW LONG.
MIGHT BE MY LAST CHANCE TO SAY THIS.
LISTEN... YOU WERE RIGHT ABOUT ME.
ONLY YOU KNEW JOKER'S BIGGEST SECRET--
--THAT BURIED INSIDE OF HIM WAS A GOOD MAN.
SOMEONE GOTHAM CITY NEEDED.
SOMEONE AS IMPORTANT AS BATMAN.
WHICH IS ALL I'VE EVER WANTED.
THANK YOU.
FOR GIVING ME A CHANCE TO LEARN WHO I REALLY AM. BUT MOST IMPORTANTLY...
...FOR GIVING ME A CHANCE TO FALL IN LOVE WITH YOU ALL OVER AGAIN.
OH, JACK...
WHUD!

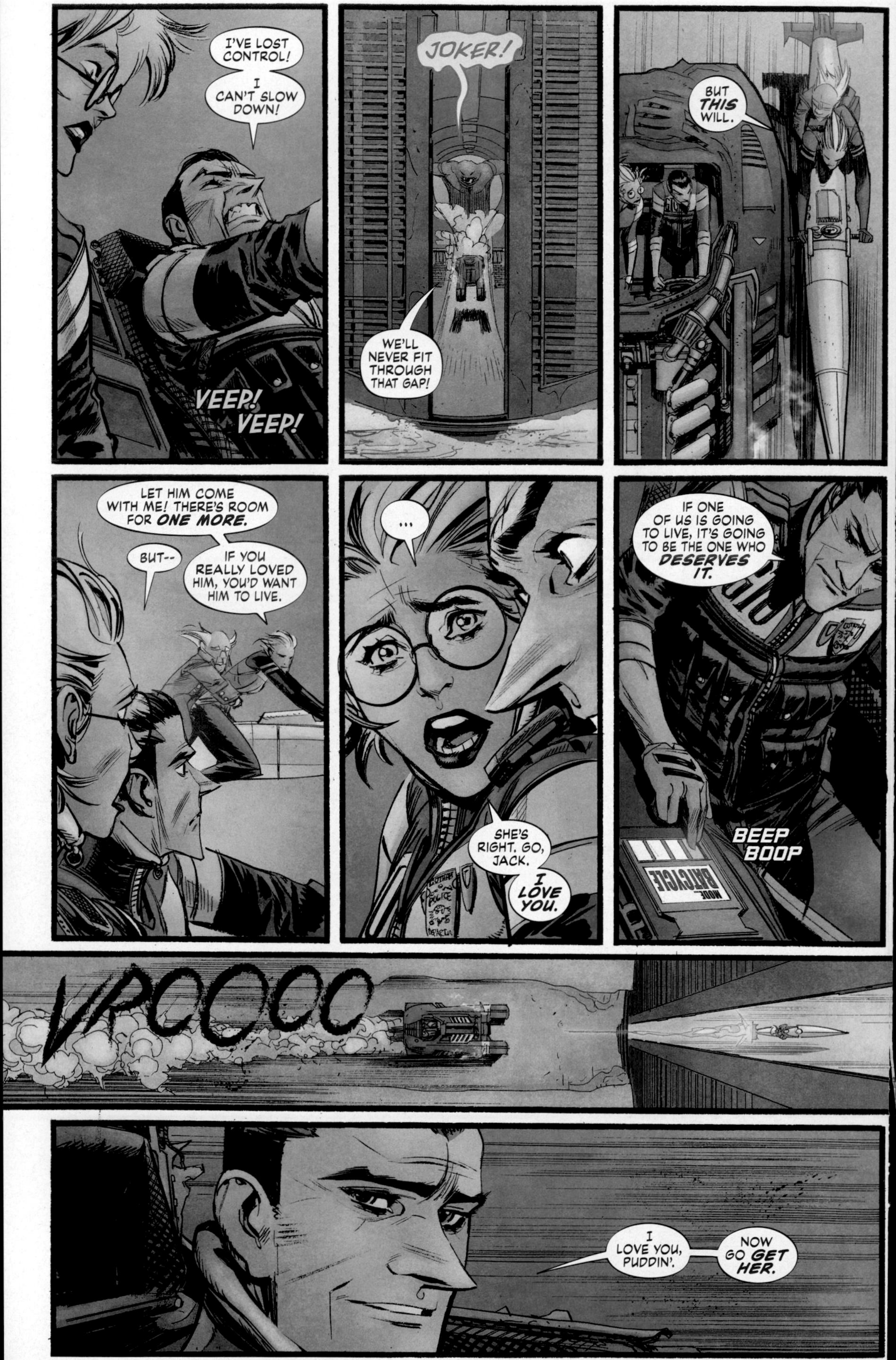
I'VE LOST CONTROL!
I CAN'T SLOW DOWN!
VEEP! VEEP!
JOKER!
WE'LL NEVER FIT THROUGH THAT GAP!
BUT THIS WILL.
LET HIM COME WITH ME! THERE'S ROOM FOR ONE MORE.
BUT--
IF YOU REALLY LOVED HIM, YOU'D WANT HIM TO LIVE.
...
SHE'S RIGHT. GO, JACK.
I LOVE YOU.
IF ONE OF US IS GOING TO LIVE, IT'S GOING TO BE THE ONE WHO DESERVES IT.
BATCYCLE MODE
BEEP BOOP
VROOOOO
I LOVE YOU, PUDDIN'.
NOW GO GET HER.

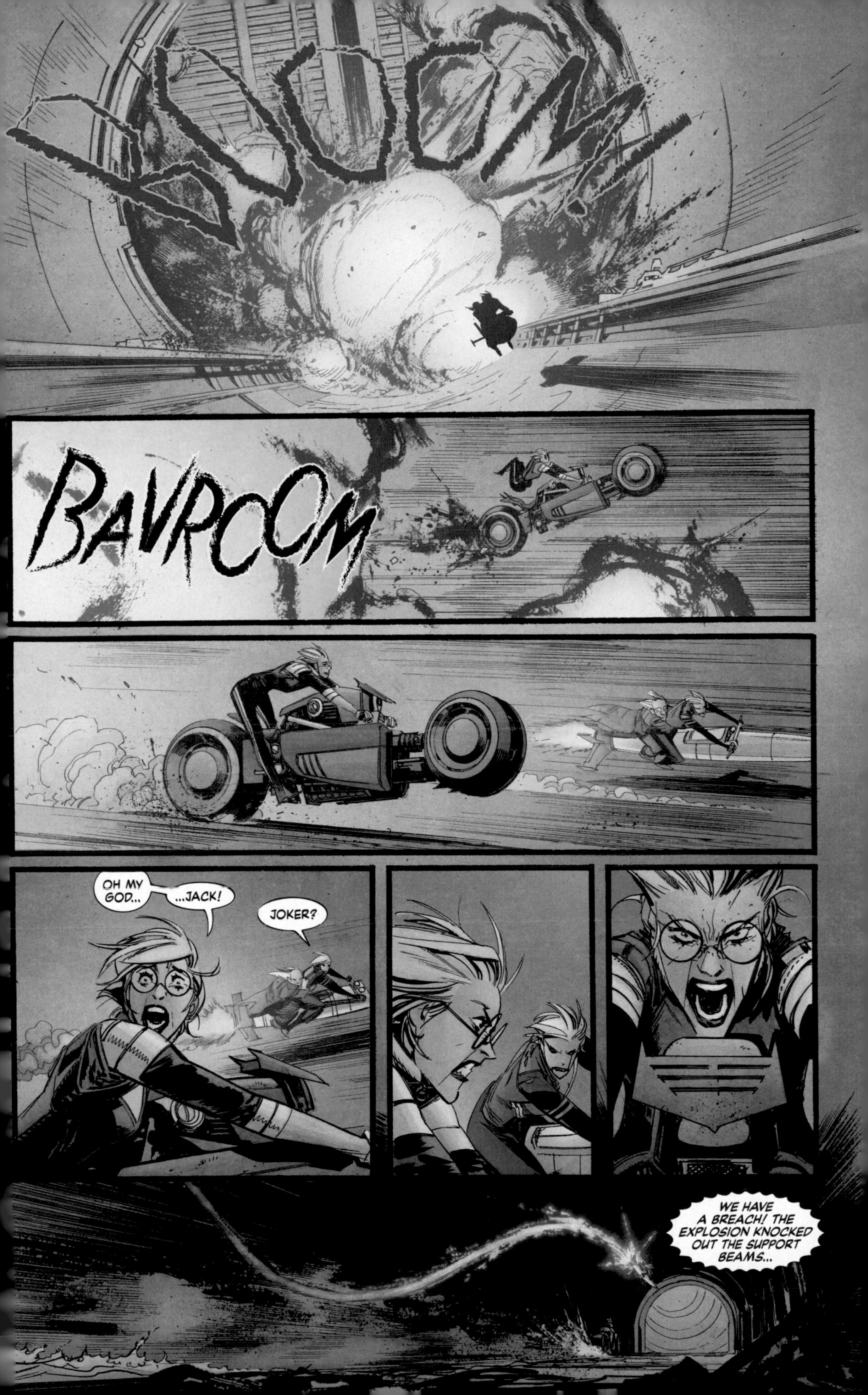

KROOM
BAVROOM
OH MY GOD...
...JACK!
JOKER?
WE HAVE A BREACH! THE EXPLOSION KNOCKED OUT THE SUPPORT BEAMS...

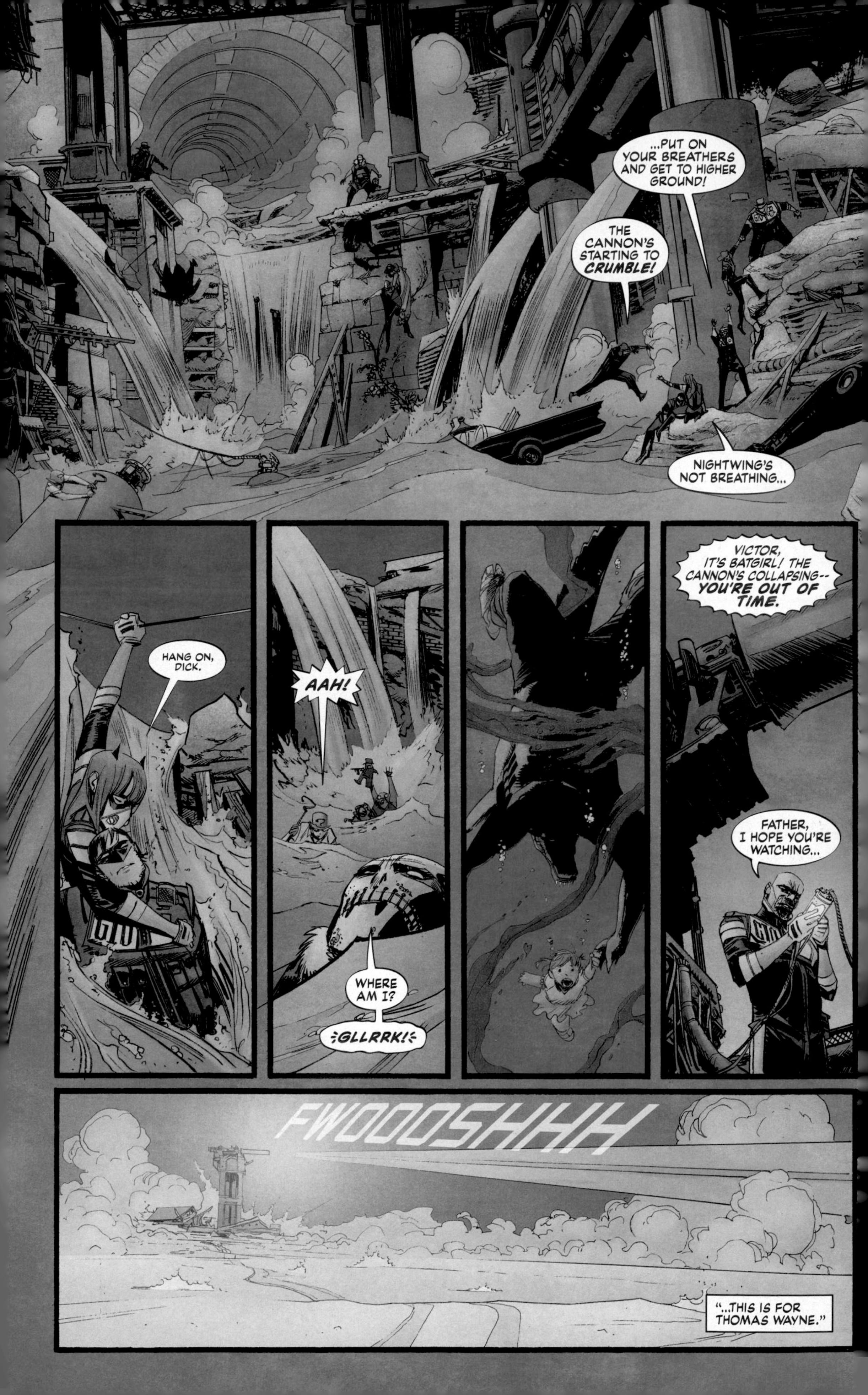
...PUT ON YOUR BREATHERS AND GET TO HIGHER GROUND!
THE CANNON'S STARTING TO CRUMBLE!
NIGHTWING'S NOT BREATHING...
HANG ON, DICK.
AAH!
WHERE AM I?
GLLRRK!
VICTOR, IT'S BATGIRL! THE CANNON'S COLLAPSING-- YOU'RE OUT OF TIME.
FATHER, I HOPE YOU'RE WATCHING...
FWOOOSHHH
"...THIS IS FOR THOMAS WAYNE."

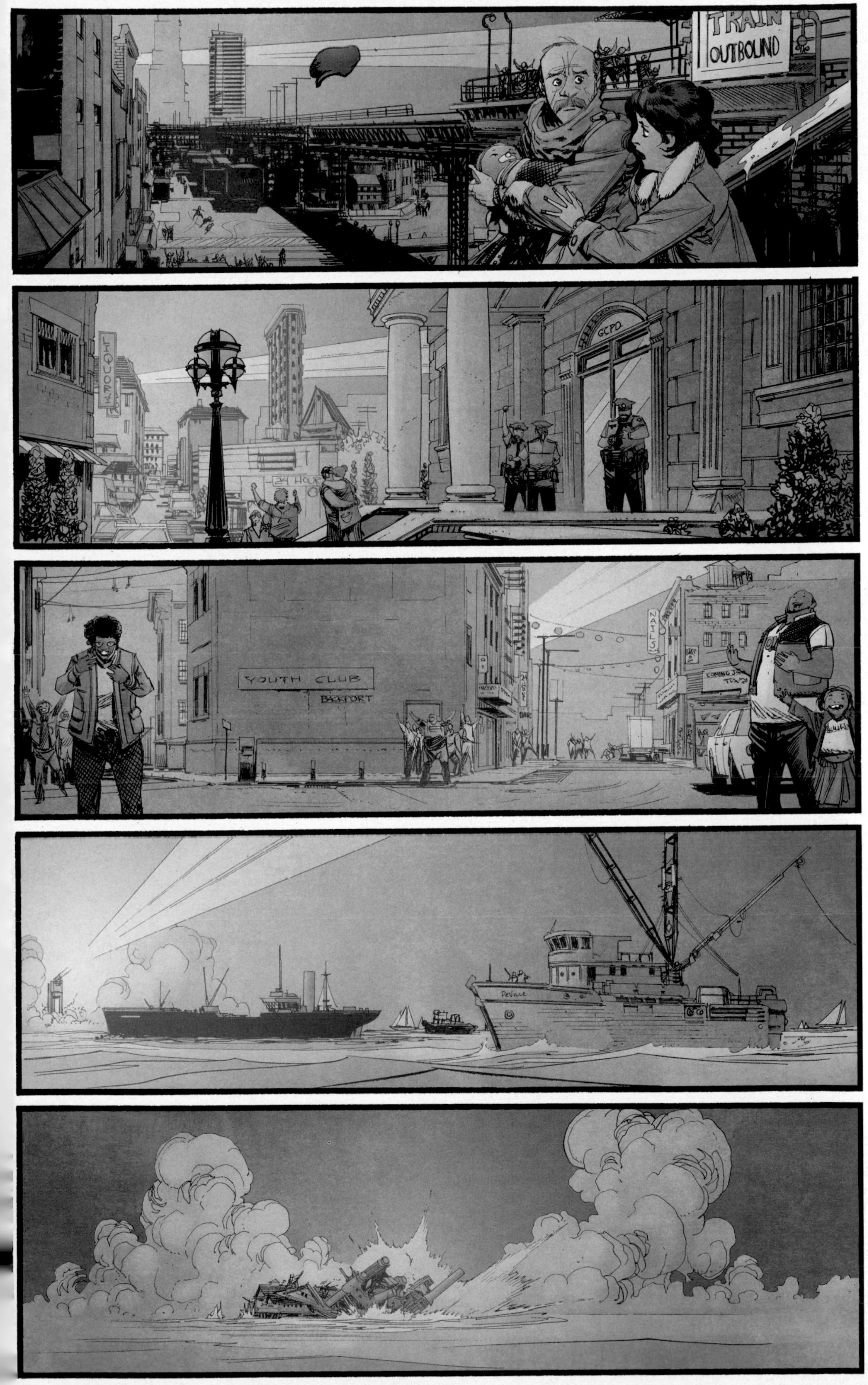
TRAIN
OUTBOUND
LIQUOR
GCPD
24 HOUR
YOUTH CLUB
BACKPORT
NAILS

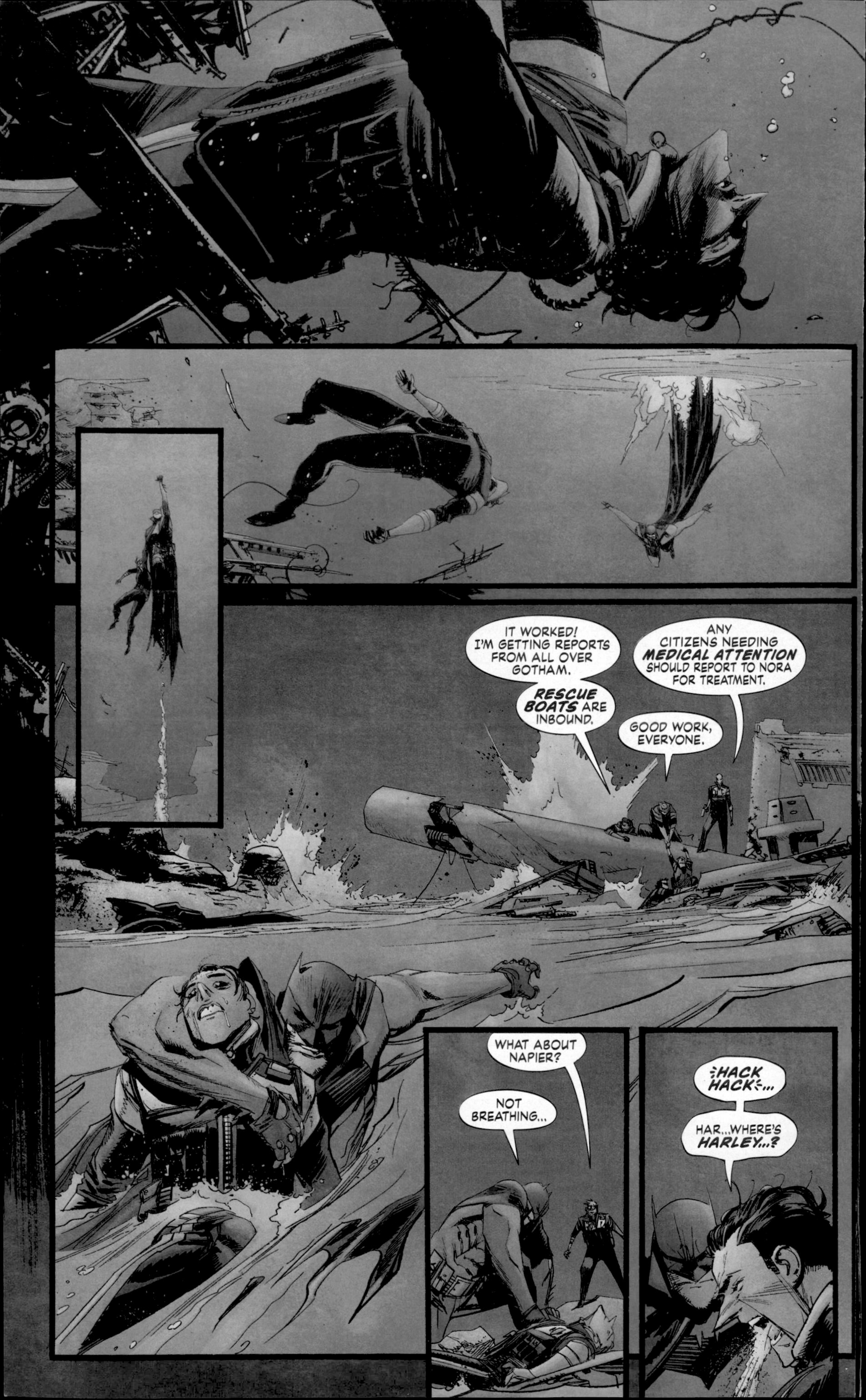
IT WORKED! I'M GETTING REPORTS FROM ALL OVER GOTHAM.
RESCUE BOATS ARE INBOUND.
ANY CITIZENS NEEDING MEDICAL ATTENTION SHOULD REPORT TO NORA FOR TREATMENT.
GOOD WORK, EVERYONE.
WHAT ABOUT NAPIER?
NOT BREATHING...
HACK HACK...
HAR...WHERE'S HARLEY...?

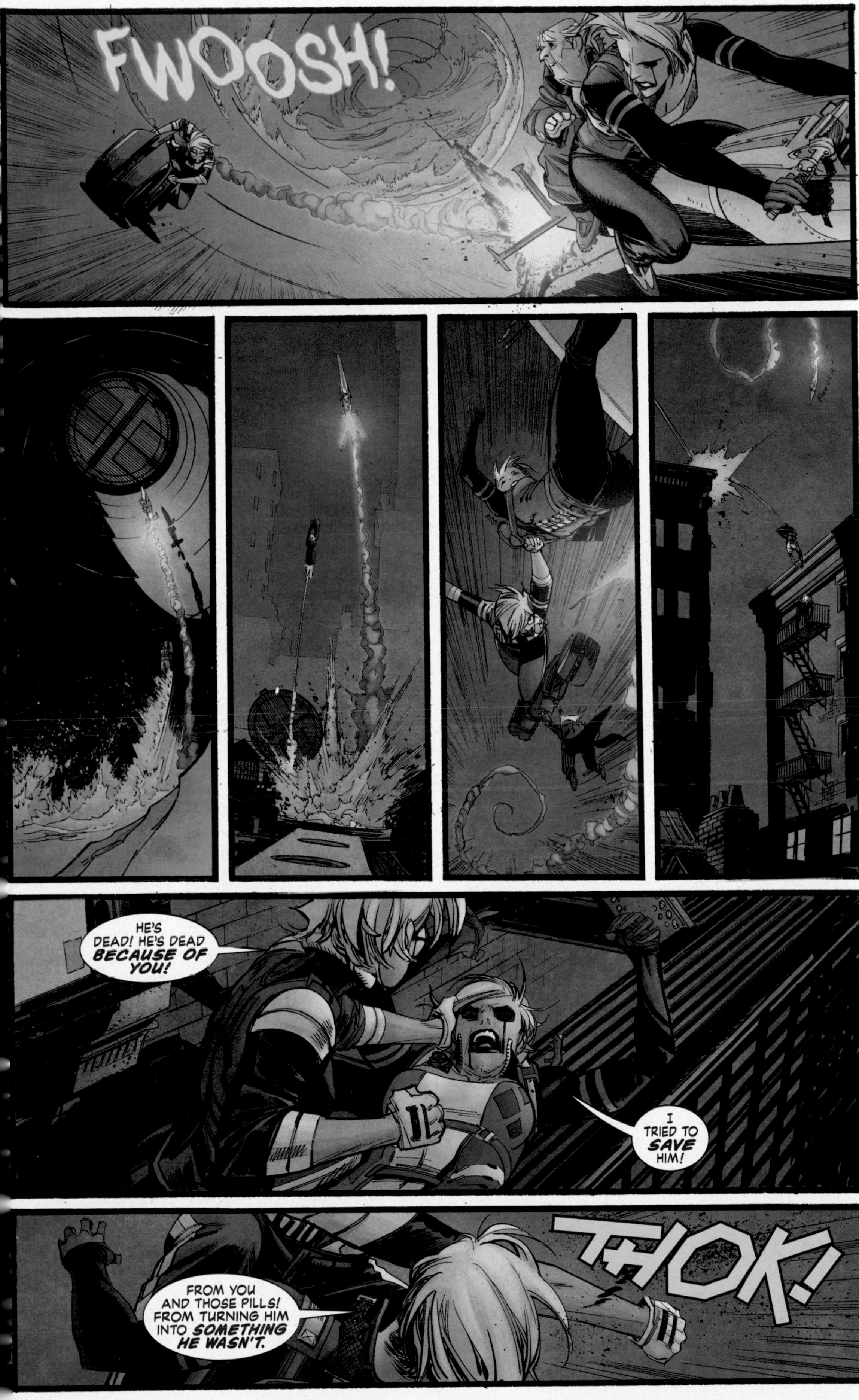
FWOOSH!
HE'S DEAD! HE'S DEAD *BECAUSE OF YOU!*
I TRIED TO *SAVE* HIM!
FROM YOU AND THOSE PILLS! FROM TURNING HIM INTO *SOMETHING HE WASN'T.*
THOK!

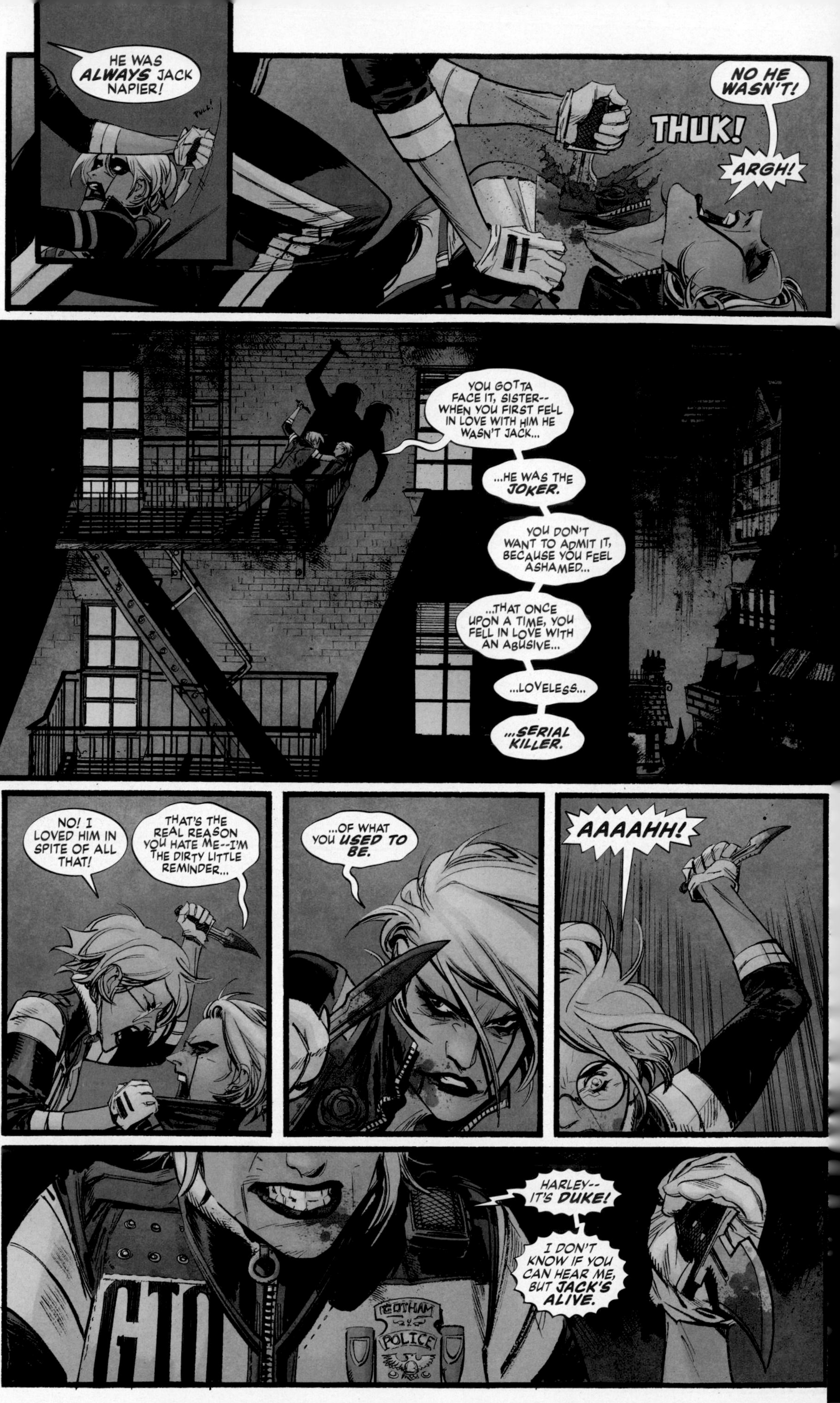
HE WAS ALWAYS JACK NAPIER!
NO HE WASN'T!
THUK!
ARGH!
YOU GOTTA FACE IT, SISTER-- WHEN YOU FIRST FELL IN LOVE WITH HIM HE WASN'T JACK...
...HE WAS THE JOKER.
YOU DON'T WANT TO ADMIT IT, BECAUSE YOU FEEL ASHAMED...
...THAT ONCE UPON A TIME, YOU FELL IN LOVE WITH AN ABUSIVE...
...LOVELESS...
...SERIAL KILLER.
NO! I LOVED HIM IN SPITE OF ALL THAT!
THAT'S THE REAL REASON YOU HATE ME--I'M THE DIRTY LITTLE REMINDER...
...OF WHAT YOU USED TO BE.
AAAAHH!
HARLEY-- IT'S DUKE!
I DON'T KNOW IF YOU CAN HEAR ME, BUT JACK'S ALIVE.
GTO
GOTHAM POLICE

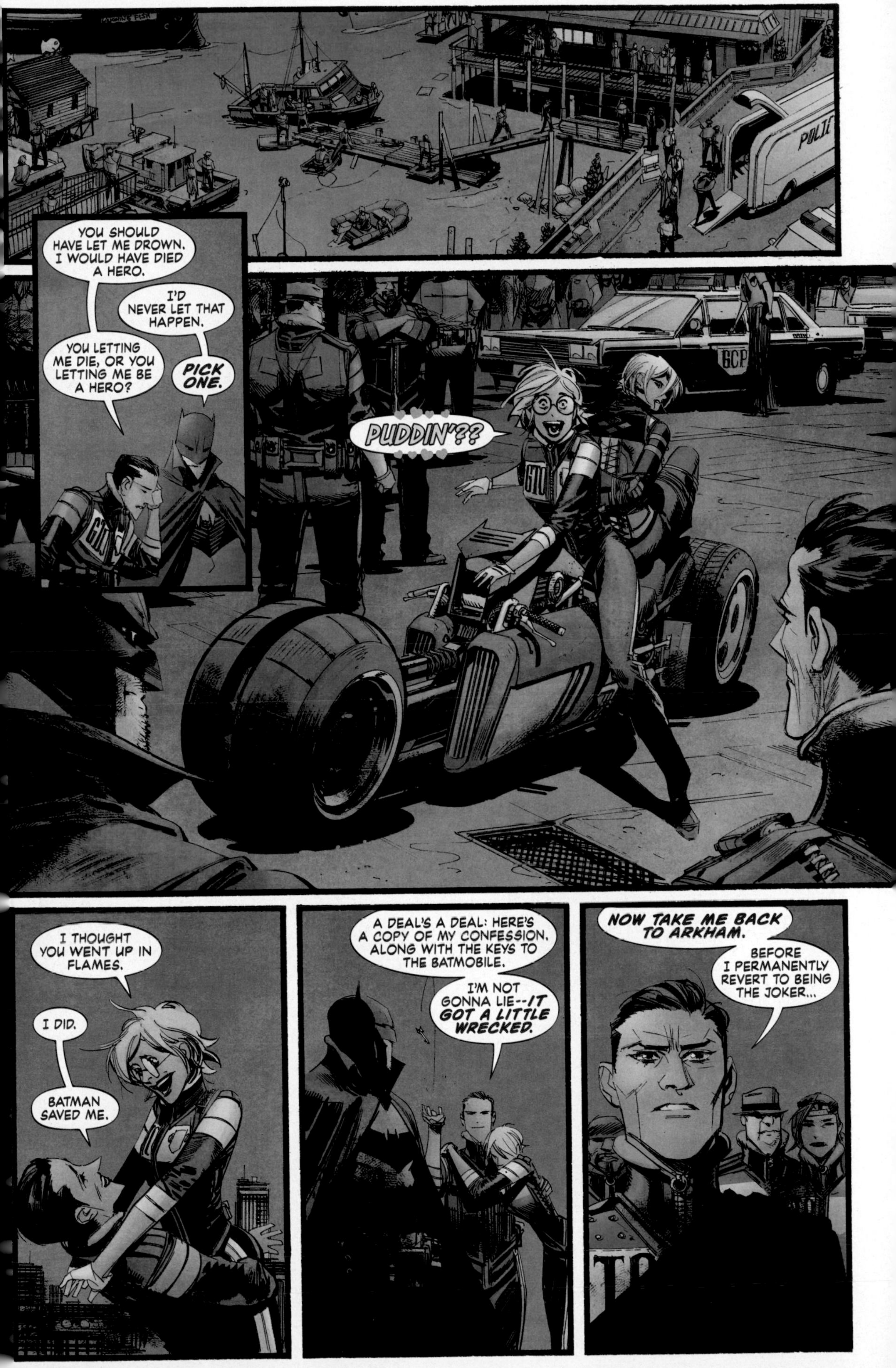

YOU SHOULD HAVE LET ME DROWN. I WOULD HAVE DIED A HERO.
I'D NEVER LET THAT HAPPEN.
YOU LETTING ME DIE, OR YOU LETTING ME BE A HERO?
PICK ONE.
PUDDIN'??
I THOUGHT YOU WENT UP IN FLAMES.
I DID.
BATMAN SAVED ME.
A DEAL'S A DEAL: HERE'S A COPY OF MY CONFESSION, ALONG WITH THE KEYS TO THE BATMOBILE.
I'M NOT GONNA LIE--IT GOT A LITTLE WRECKED.
NOW TAKE ME BACK TO ARKHAM.
BEFORE I PERMANENTLY REVERT TO BEING THE JOKER...

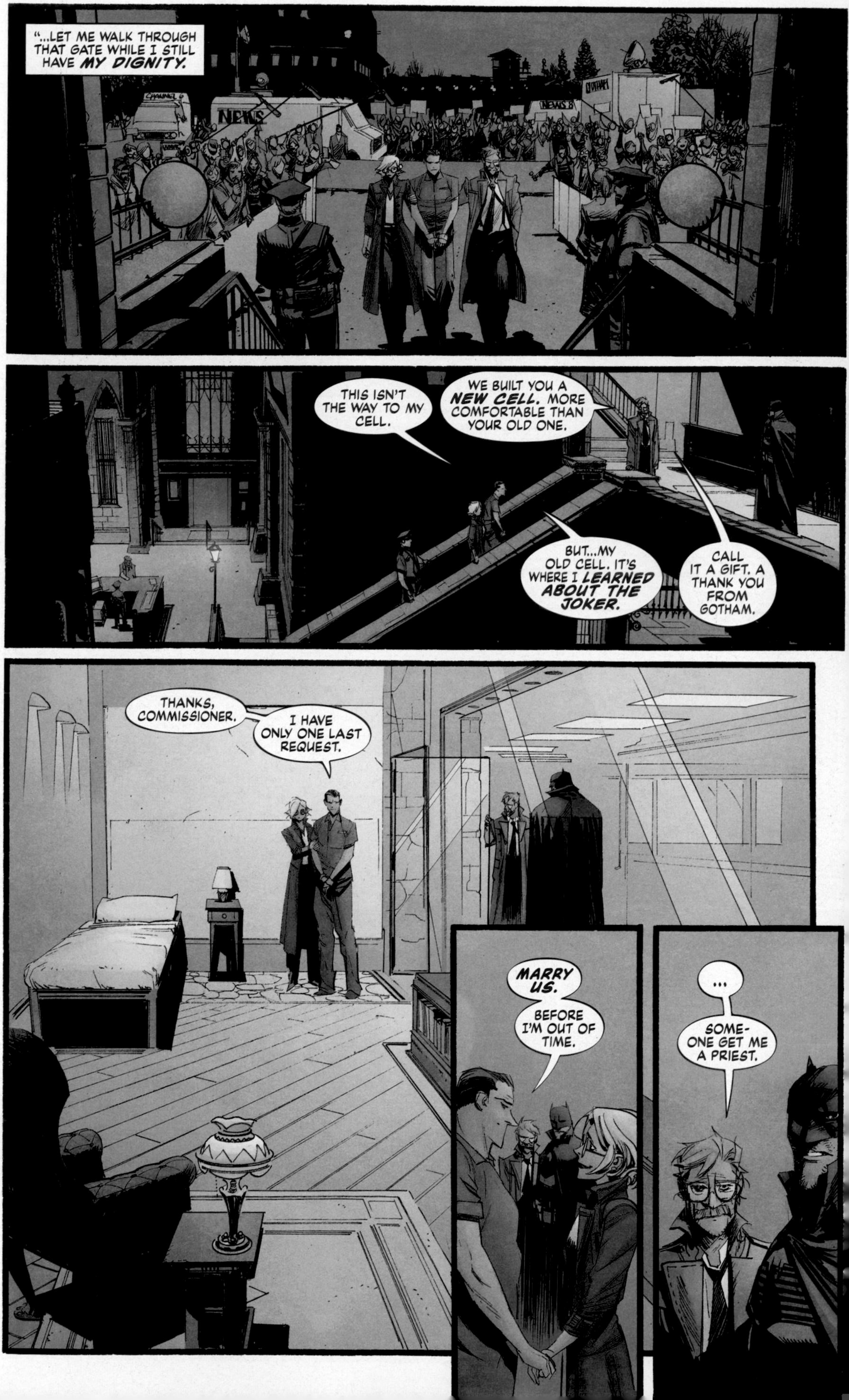
"...LET ME WALK THROUGH THAT GATE WHILE I STILL HAVE MY DIGNITY.
NEWS
NEWS 8
GOTHAM
THIS ISN'T THE WAY TO MY CELL.
WE BUILT YOU A NEW CELL. MORE COMFORTABLE THAN YOUR OLD ONE.
BUT...MY OLD CELL. IT'S WHERE I LEARNED ABOUT THE JOKER.
CALL IT A GIFT. A THANK YOU FROM GOTHAM.
THANKS, COMMISSIONER.
I HAVE ONLY ONE LAST REQUEST.
MARRY US.
BEFORE I'M OUT OF TIME.
...
SOME-ONE GET ME A PRIEST.

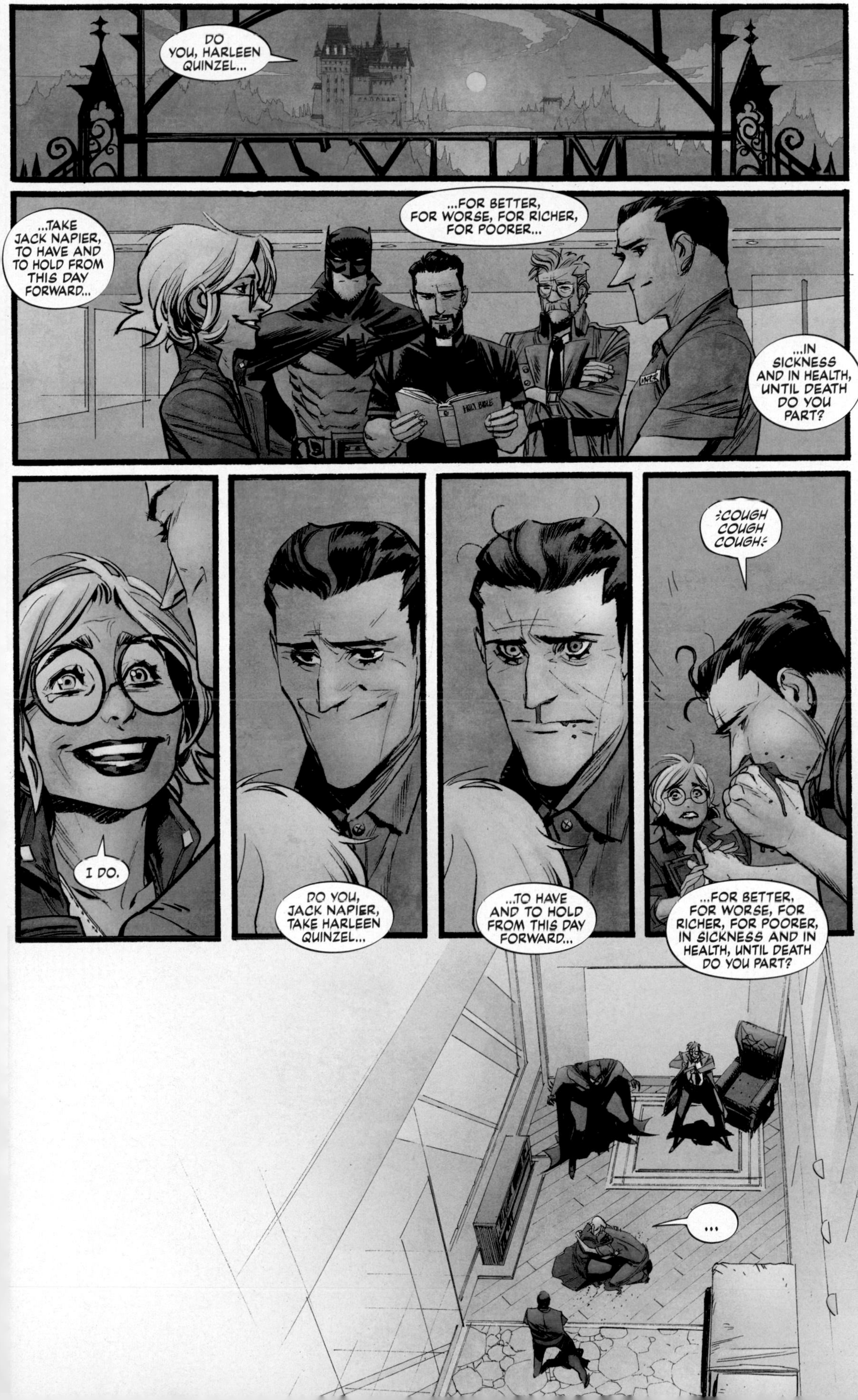
DO YOU, HARLEEN QUINZEL...
...TAKE JACK NAPIER, TO HAVE AND TO HOLD FROM THIS DAY FORWARD...
...FOR BETTER, FOR WORSE, FOR RICHER, FOR POORER...
...IN SICKNESS AND IN HEALTH, UNTIL DEATH DO YOU PART?
I DO.
DO YOU, JACK NAPIER, TAKE HARLEEN QUINZEL...
...TO HAVE AND TO HOLD FROM THIS DAY FORWARD...
COUGH COUGH COUGH
...FOR BETTER, FOR WORSE, FOR RICHER, FOR POORER, IN SICKNESS AND IN HEALTH, UNTIL DEATH DO YOU PART?
...

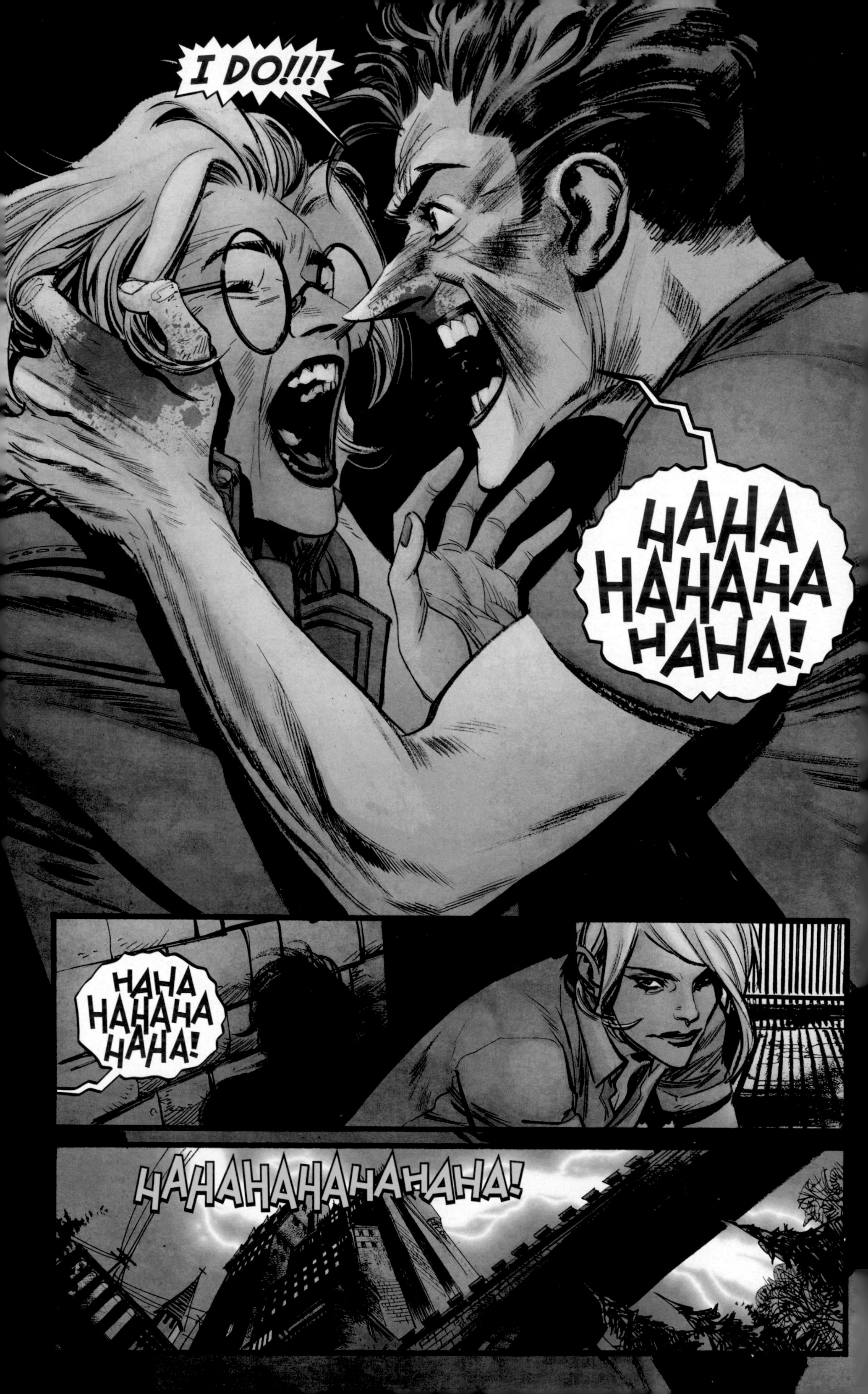
I DO!!!
HAHA HAHAHA HAHA!
HAHA HAHAHA HAHA!
HAHAHAHAHAHAHAHA!

DICK.

BARBARA.

THANKS FOR WAITING.

I THOUGHT WE COULD READ THIS TOGETHER.

I JUST...

...

I KNOW. IT'S OKAY.

Bruce,

I know you waited as long as possible before reading this. Because you're too frightened to let me go, and because you don't know how to say good-bye.

No doubt my death made you feel more alone than ever, causing you to retreat into that dark place where you think no one can find you. And you probably tried to push everyone away, convinced that only the isolation could give you the strength to return. But you were wrong. And that's always been hard for you to understand.

That there's no strength in being alone.

I'm happy you're finally reading this, because it means you now understand. It means Barbara and Richard are there with you, as I doubt you could have read this without them. It means you understand how their love is essential to moving forward.

But most importantly, it means you're ready to say good-bye. Good-bye, my son.

Alfred

PS: Check the loose floorboard in my quarters. There's something there you're ready to see.

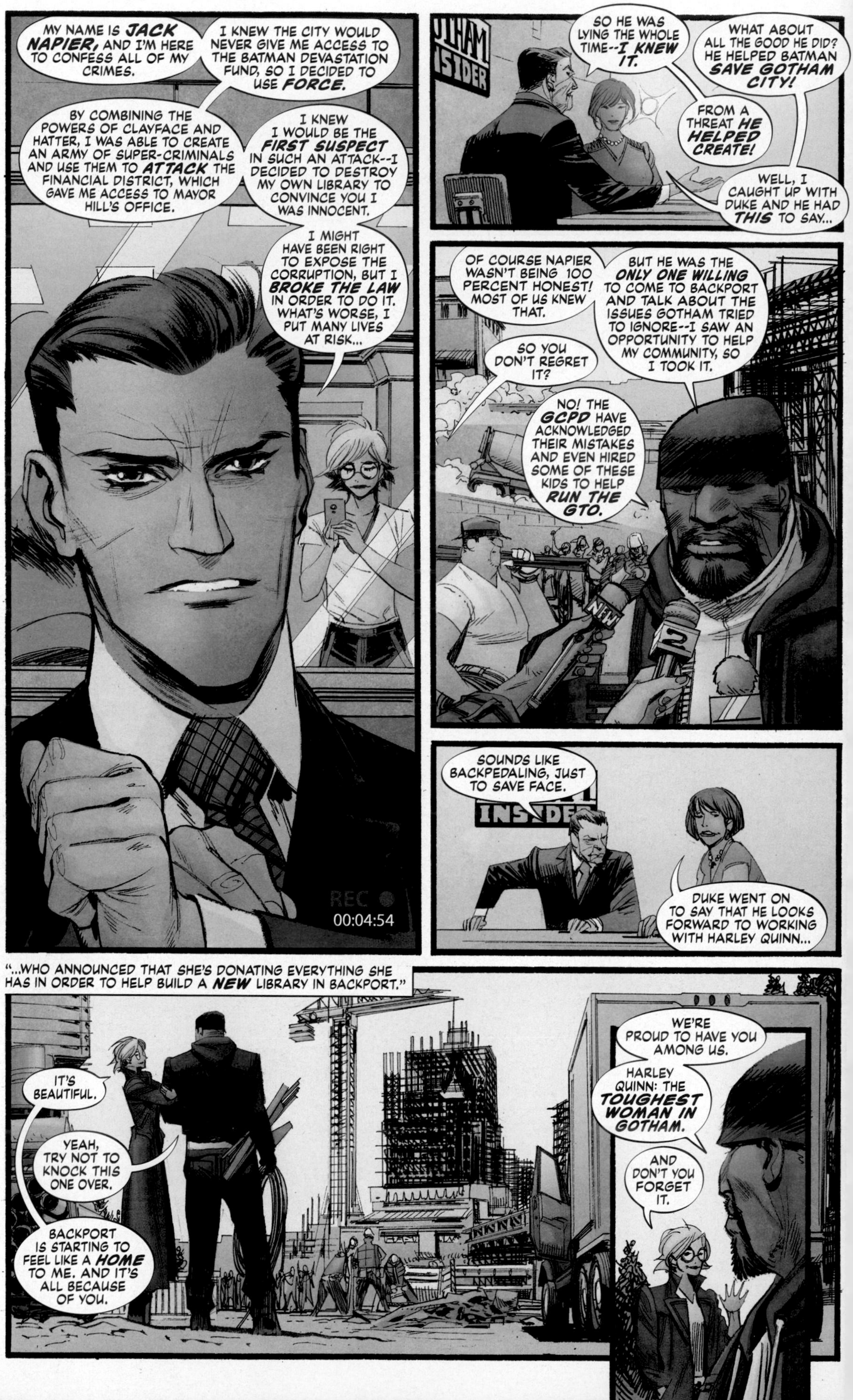

MY NAME IS JACK NAPIER, AND I'M HERE TO CONFESS ALL OF MY CRIMES.
I KNEW THE CITY WOULD NEVER GIVE ME ACCESS TO THE BATMAN DEVASTATION FUND, SO I DECIDED TO USE FORCE.
BY COMBINING THE POWERS OF CLAYFACE AND HATTER, I WAS ABLE TO CREATE AN ARMY OF SUPER-CRIMINALS AND USE THEM TO ATTACK THE FINANCIAL DISTRICT, WHICH GAVE ME ACCESS TO MAYOR HILL'S OFFICE.
I KNEW I WOULD BE THE FIRST SUSPECT IN SUCH AN ATTACK--I DECIDED TO DESTROY MY OWN LIBRARY TO CONVINCE YOU I WAS INNOCENT.
I MIGHT HAVE BEEN RIGHT TO EXPOSE THE CORRUPTION, BUT I BROKE THE LAW IN ORDER TO DO IT. WHAT'S WORSE, I PUT MANY LIVES AT RISK...
REC
00:04:54
SO HE WAS LYING THE WHOLE TIME--I KNEW IT.
WHAT ABOUT ALL THE GOOD HE DID? HE HELPED BATMAN SAVE GOTHAM CITY!
FROM A THREAT HE HELPED CREATE!
WELL, I CAUGHT UP WITH DUKE AND HE HAD THIS TO SAY...
OF COURSE NAPIER WASN'T BEING 100 PERCENT HONEST! MOST OF US KNEW THAT.
BUT HE WAS THE ONLY ONE WILLING TO COME TO BACKPORT AND TALK ABOUT THE ISSUES GOTHAM TRIED TO IGNORE--I SAW AN OPPORTUNITY TO HELP MY COMMUNITY, SO I TOOK IT.
SO YOU DON'T REGRET IT?
NO! THE GCPD HAVE ACKNOWLEDGED THEIR MISTAKES AND EVEN HIRED SOME OF THESE KIDS TO HELP RUN THE GTO.
SOUNDS LIKE BACKPEDALING, JUST TO SAVE FACE.
INSIDE
DUKE WENT ON TO SAY THAT HE LOOKS FORWARD TO WORKING WITH HARLEY QUINN...
"...WHO ANNOUNCED THAT SHE'S DONATING EVERYTHING SHE HAS IN ORDER TO HELP BUILD A NEW LIBRARY IN BACKPORT."
IT'S BEAUTIFUL.
YEAH, TRY NOT TO KNOCK THIS ONE OVER.
BACKPORT IS STARTING TO FEEL LIKE A HOME TO ME. AND IT'S ALL BECAUSE OF YOU.
WE'RE PROUD TO HAVE YOU AMONG US.
HARLEY QUINN: THE TOUGHEST WOMAN IN GOTHAM.
AND DON'T YOU FORGET IT.

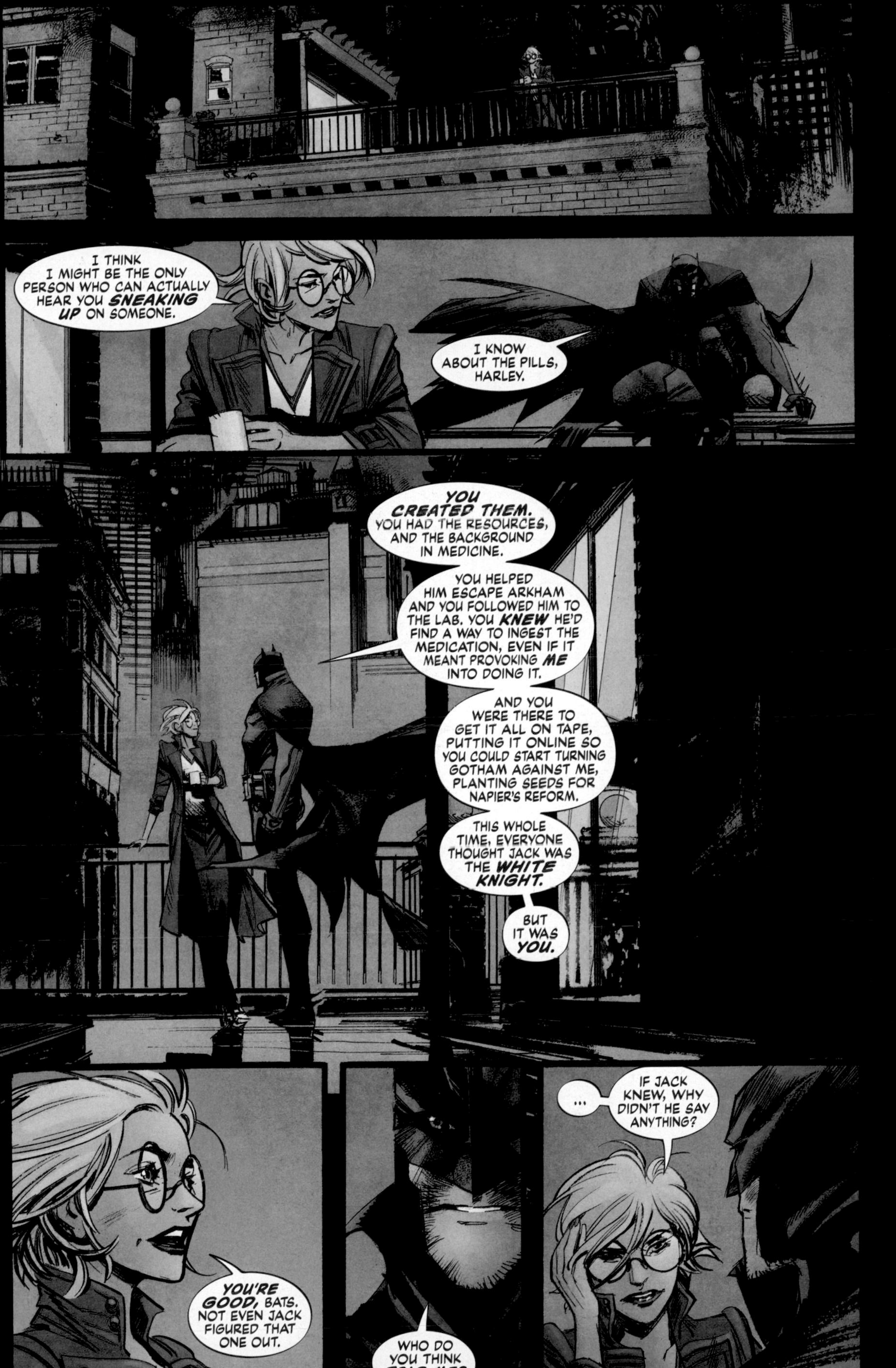
I THINK I MIGHT BE THE ONLY PERSON WHO CAN ACTUALLY HEAR YOU SNEAKING UP ON SOMEONE.
I KNOW ABOUT THE PILLS, HARLEY.
YOU CREATED THEM. YOU HAD THE RESOURCES, AND THE BACKGROUND IN MEDICINE.
YOU HELPED HIM ESCAPE ARKHAM AND YOU FOLLOWED HIM TO THE LAB. YOU KNEW HE'D FIND A WAY TO INGEST THE MEDICATION, EVEN IF IT MEANT PROVOKING ME INTO DOING IT.
AND YOU WERE THERE TO GET IT ALL ON TAPE, PUTTING IT ONLINE SO YOU COULD START TURNING GOTHAM AGAINST ME, PLANTING SEEDS FOR NAPIER'S REFORM.
THIS WHOLE TIME, EVERYONE THOUGHT JACK WAS THE WHITE KNIGHT.
BUT IT WAS YOU.
YOU'RE GOOD, BATS. NOT EVEN JACK FIGURED THAT ONE OUT.
WHO DO YOU THINK TOLD ME?
...
IF JACK KNEW, WHY DIDN'T HE SAY ANYTHING?

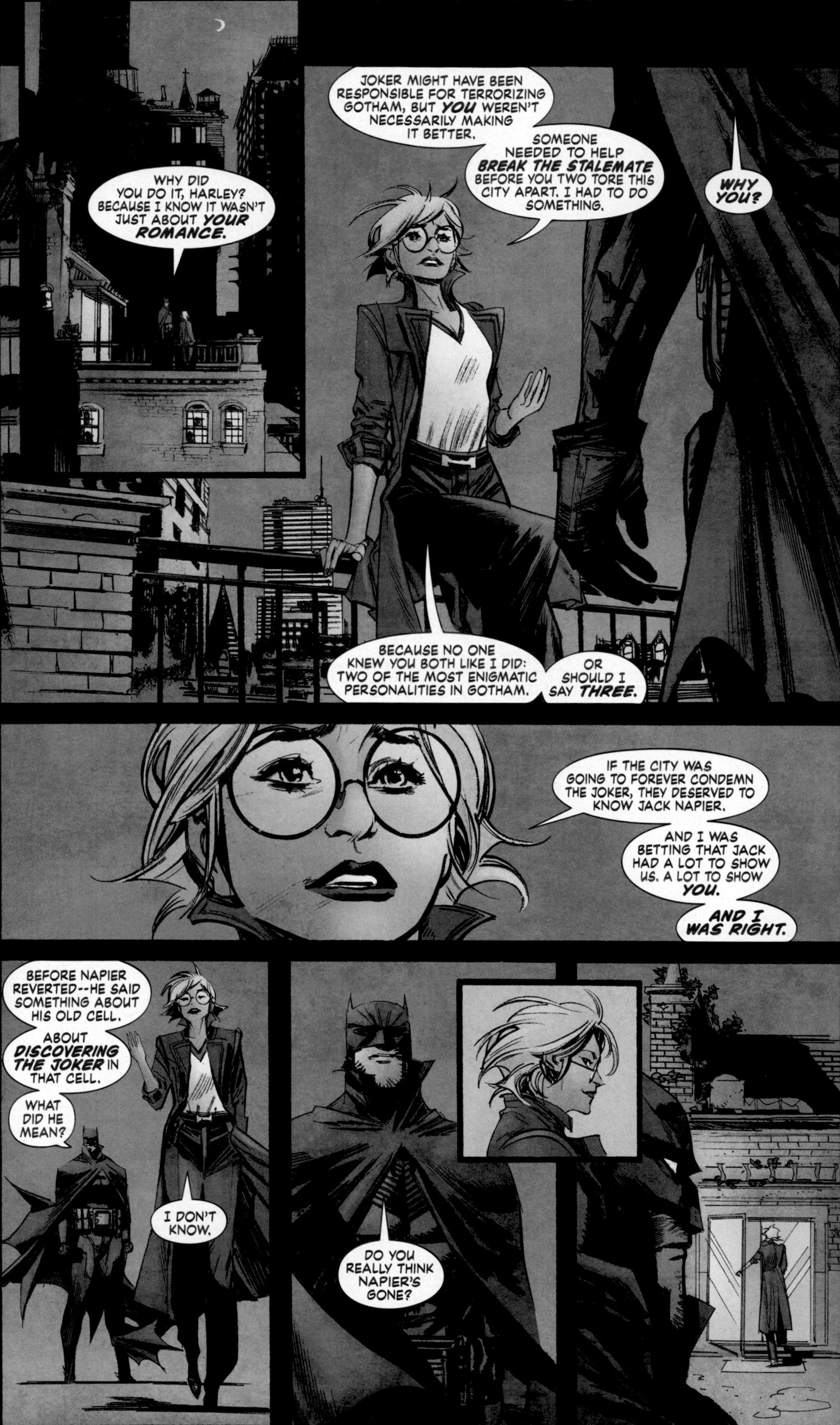
WHY DID YOU DO IT, HARLEY? BECAUSE I KNOW IT WASN'T JUST ABOUT YOUR ROMANCE.
JOKER MIGHT HAVE BEEN RESPONSIBLE FOR TERRORIZING GOTHAM, BUT YOU WEREN'T NECESSARILY MAKING IT BETTER.
SOMEONE NEEDED TO HELP BREAK THE STALEMATE BEFORE YOU TWO TORE THIS CITY APART. I HAD TO DO SOMETHING.
WHY YOU?
BECAUSE NO ONE KNEW YOU BOTH LIKE I DID: TWO OF THE MOST ENIGMATIC PERSONALITIES IN GOTHAM.
OR SHOULD I SAY THREE.
IF THE CITY WAS GOING TO FOREVER CONDEMN THE JOKER, THEY DESERVED TO KNOW JACK NAPIER.
AND I WAS BETTING THAT JACK HAD A LOT TO SHOW US. A LOT TO SHOW YOU.
AND I WAS RIGHT.
BEFORE NAPIER REVERTED--HE SAID SOMETHING ABOUT HIS OLD CELL.
ABOUT DISCOVERING THE JOKER IN THAT CELL.
WHAT DID HE MEAN?
I DON'T KNOW.
DO YOU REALLY THINK NAPIER'S GONE?

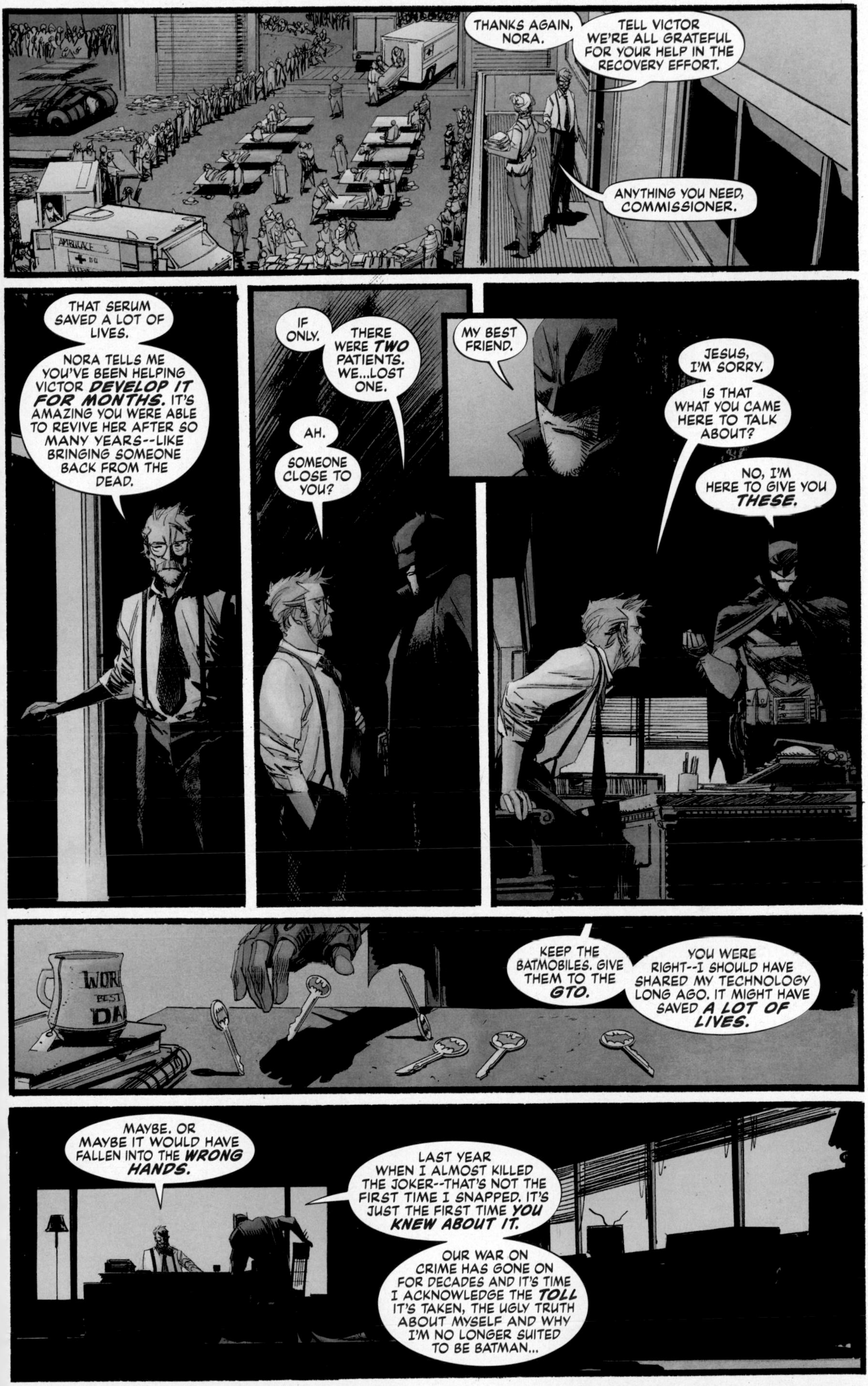
THANKS AGAIN, NORA.
TELL VICTOR WE'RE ALL GRATEFUL FOR YOUR HELP IN THE RECOVERY EFFORT.
ANYTHING YOU NEED, COMMISSIONER.
THAT SERUM SAVED A LOT OF LIVES.
NORA TELLS ME YOU'VE BEEN HELPING VICTOR DEVELOP IT FOR MONTHS. IT'S AMAZING YOU WERE ABLE TO REVIVE HER AFTER SO MANY YEARS--LIKE BRINGING SOMEONE BACK FROM THE DEAD.
IF ONLY.
THERE WERE TWO PATIENTS. WE...LOST ONE.
AH.
SOMEONE CLOSE TO YOU?
MY BEST FRIEND.
JESUS, I'M SORRY.
IS THAT WHAT YOU CAME HERE TO TALK ABOUT?
NO, I'M HERE TO GIVE YOU THESE.
WORLD'S BEST DAD
KEEP THE BATMOBILES. GIVE THEM TO THE GTO.
YOU WERE RIGHT--I SHOULD HAVE SHARED MY TECHNOLOGY LONG AGO. IT MIGHT HAVE SAVED A LOT OF LIVES.
MAYBE. OR MAYBE IT WOULD HAVE FALLEN INTO THE WRONG HANDS.
LAST YEAR WHEN I ALMOST KILLED THE JOKER--THAT'S NOT THE FIRST TIME I SNAPPED. IT'S JUST THE FIRST TIME YOU KNEW ABOUT IT.
OUR WAR ON CRIME HAS GONE ON FOR DECADES AND IT'S TIME I ACKNOWLEDGE THE TOLL IT'S TAKEN, THE UGLY TRUTH ABOUT MYSELF AND WHY I'M NO LONGER SUITED TO BE BATMAN...

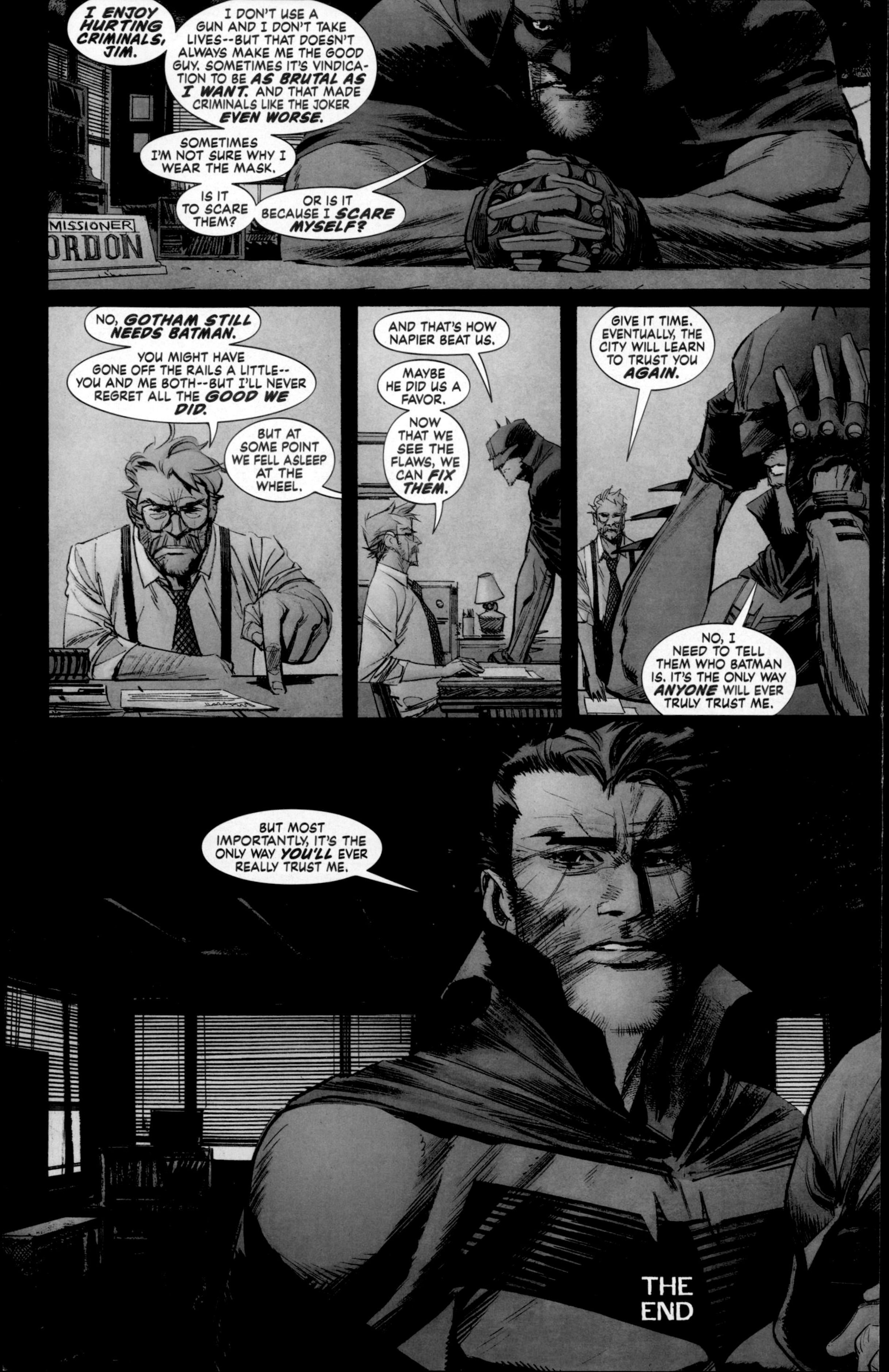
I ENJOY HURTING CRIMINALS, JIM.
I DON'T USE A GUN AND I DON'T TAKE LIVES--BUT THAT DOESN'T ALWAYS MAKE ME THE GOOD GUY. SOMETIMES IT'S VINDICATION TO BE AS BRUTAL AS I WANT. AND THAT MADE CRIMINALS LIKE THE JOKER EVEN WORSE.
SOMETIMES I'M NOT SURE WHY I WEAR THE MASK.
IS IT TO SCARE THEM?
OR IS IT BECAUSE I SCARE MYSELF?
MISSIONER ORDON
NO, GOTHAM STILL NEEDS BATMAN.
YOU MIGHT HAVE GONE OFF THE RAILS A LITTLE-- YOU AND ME BOTH--BUT I'LL NEVER REGRET ALL THE GOOD WE DID.
BUT AT SOME POINT WE FELL ASLEEP AT THE WHEEL.
AND THAT'S HOW NAPIER BEAT US.
MAYBE HE DID US A FAVOR.
NOW THAT WE SEE THE FLAWS, WE CAN FIX THEM.
GIVE IT TIME. EVENTUALLY, THE CITY WILL LEARN TO TRUST YOU AGAIN.
NO, I NEED TO TELL THEM WHO BATMAN IS. IT'S THE ONLY WAY ANYONE WILL EVER TRULY TRUST ME.
BUT MOST IMPORTANTLY, IT'S THE ONLY WAY YOU'LL EVER REALLY TRUST ME.
THE END

VARIANT COVER GALLERY

by SEAN MURPHY

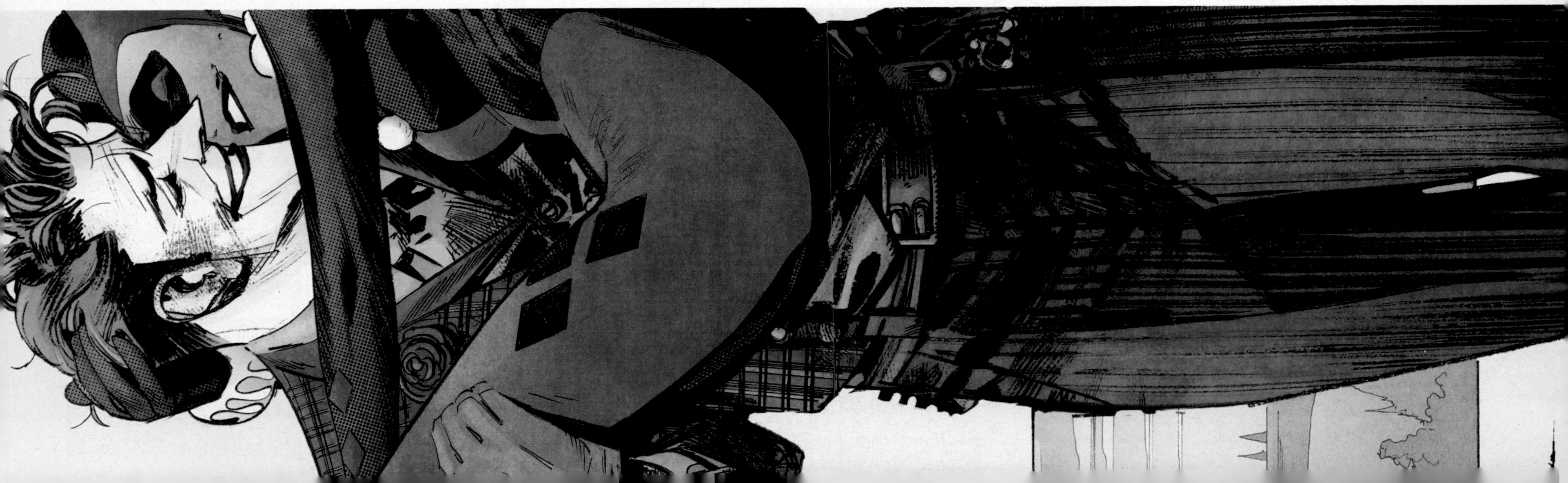

Issue №1 variant cover one
BATMAN
WHITE KNIGHT
Sean Murphy 2017
ARKHAM
ASYLUM

Issue №1 variant cover two

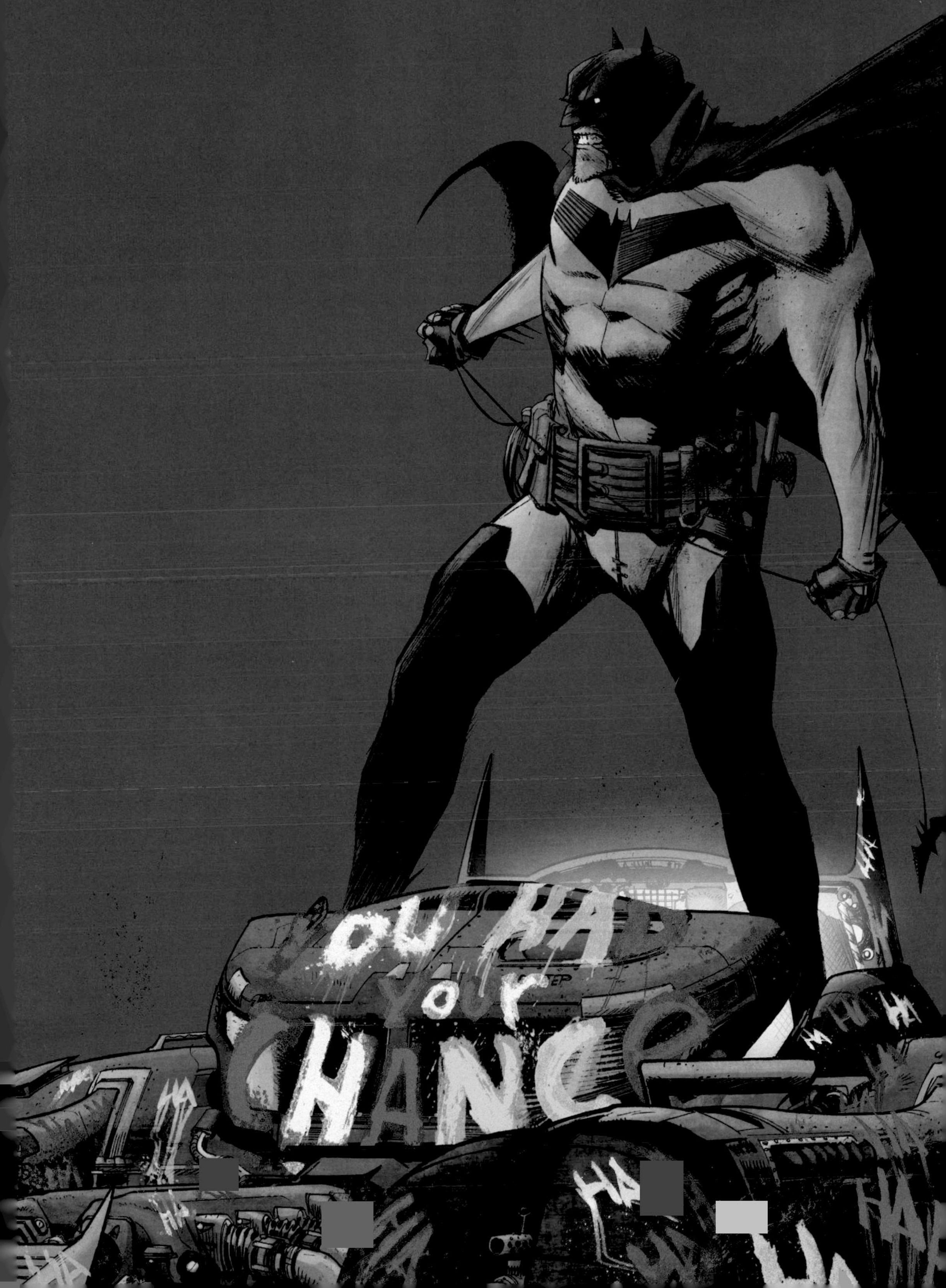
OU HAD
your
HANC
HA

Issue №2 variant cover

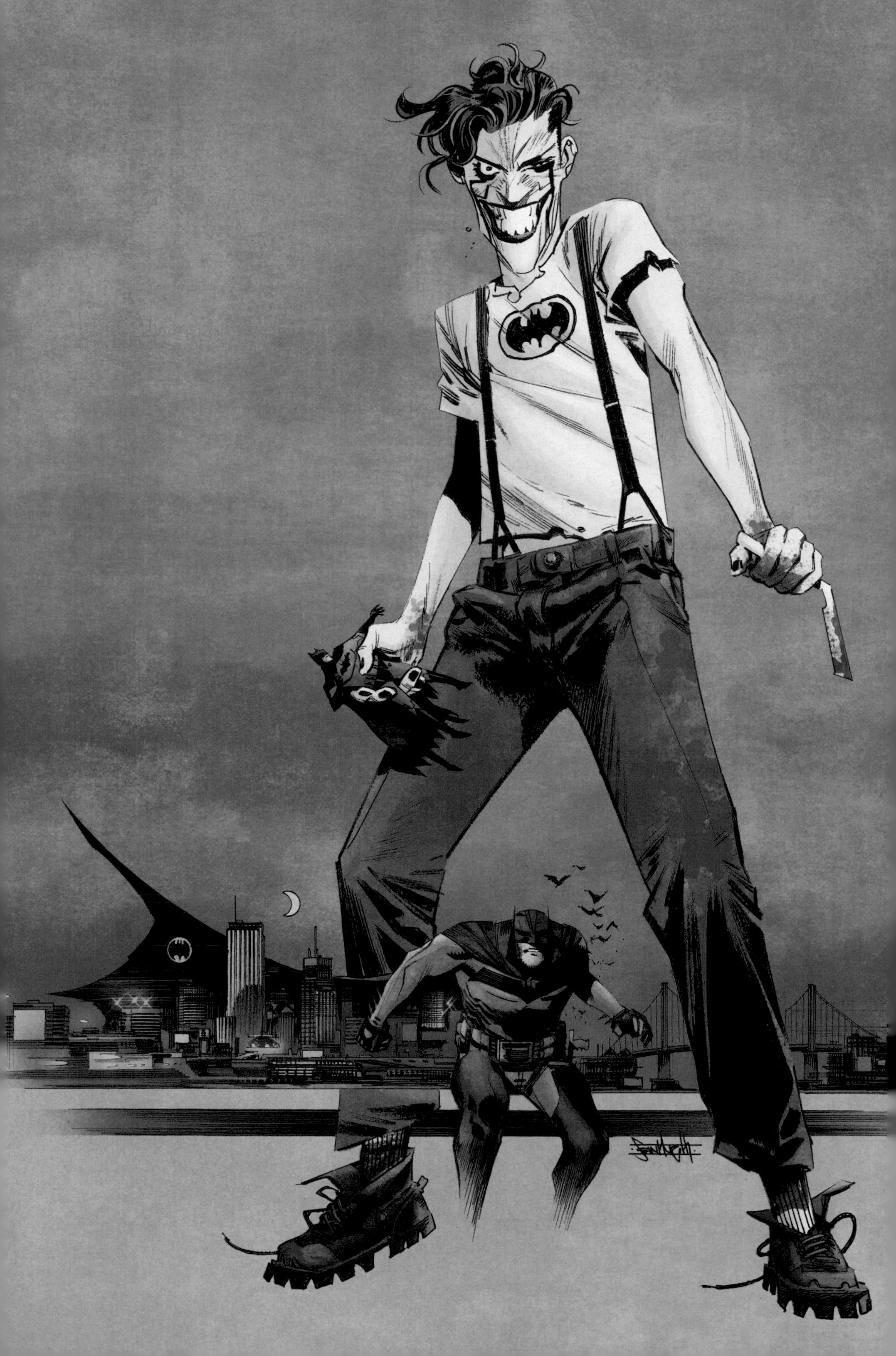

Issue №3 variant cover

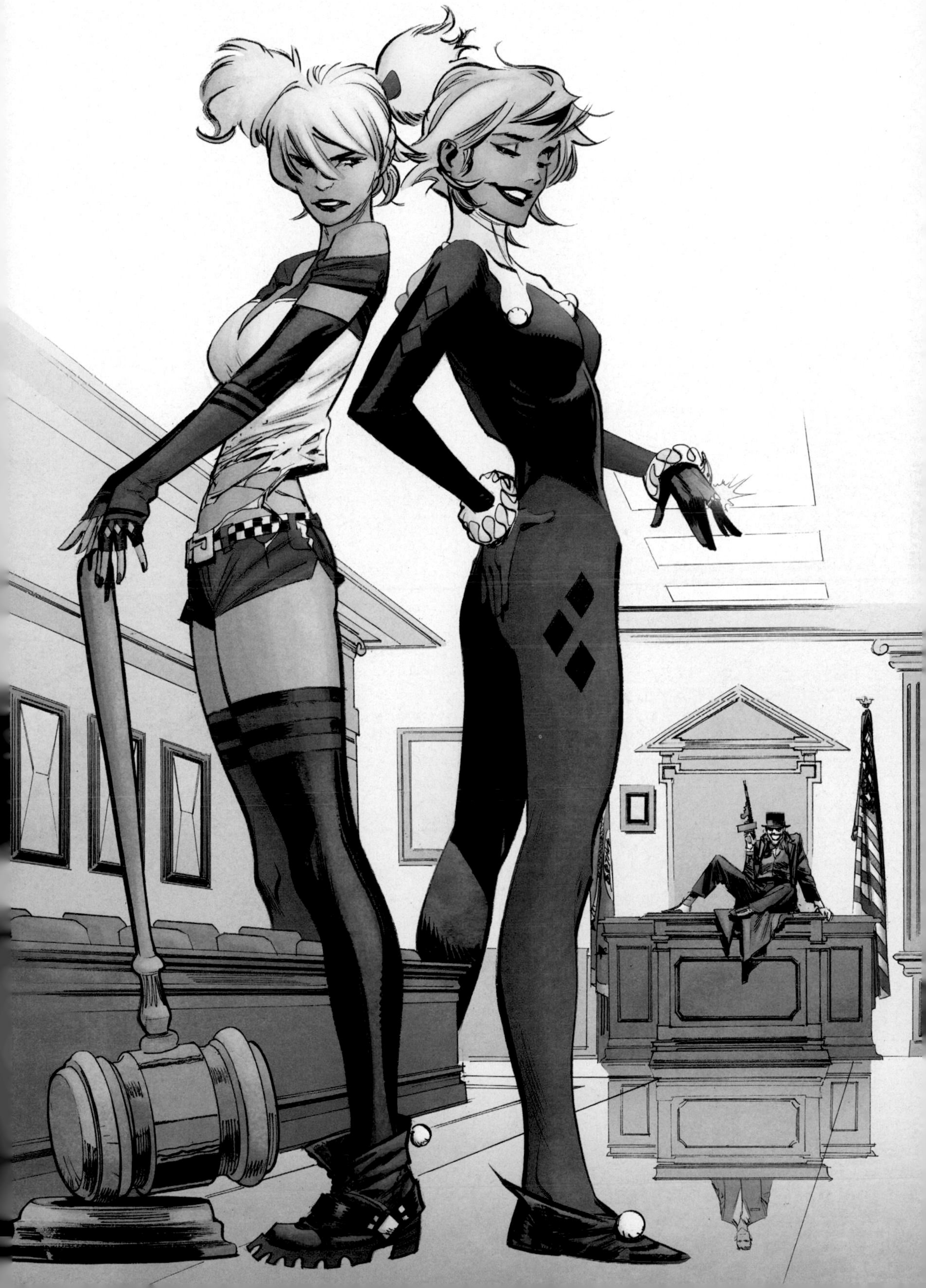

Issue №4 variant cover

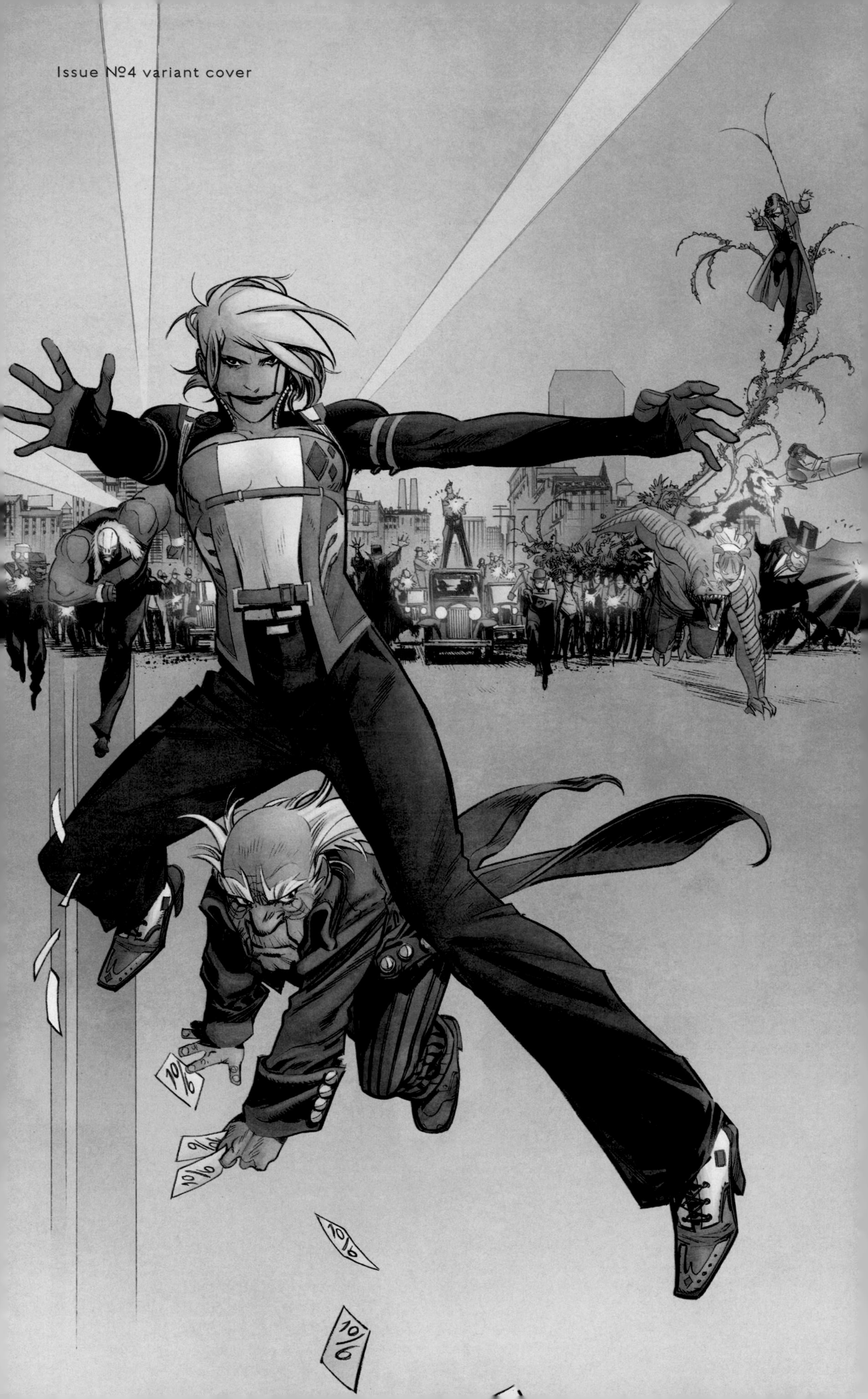
10/6

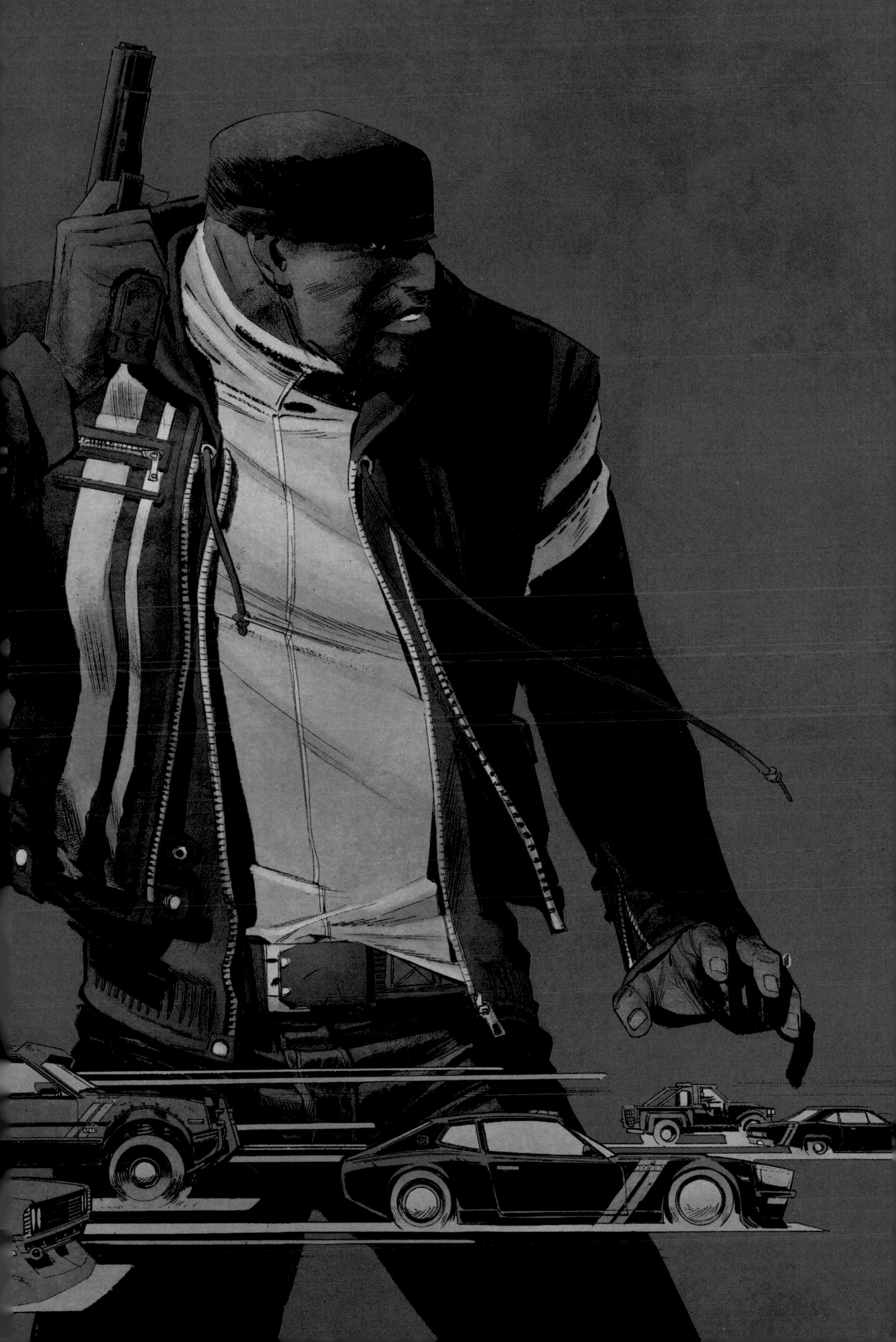

Issue №5 variant cover

Issue №6 variant cover

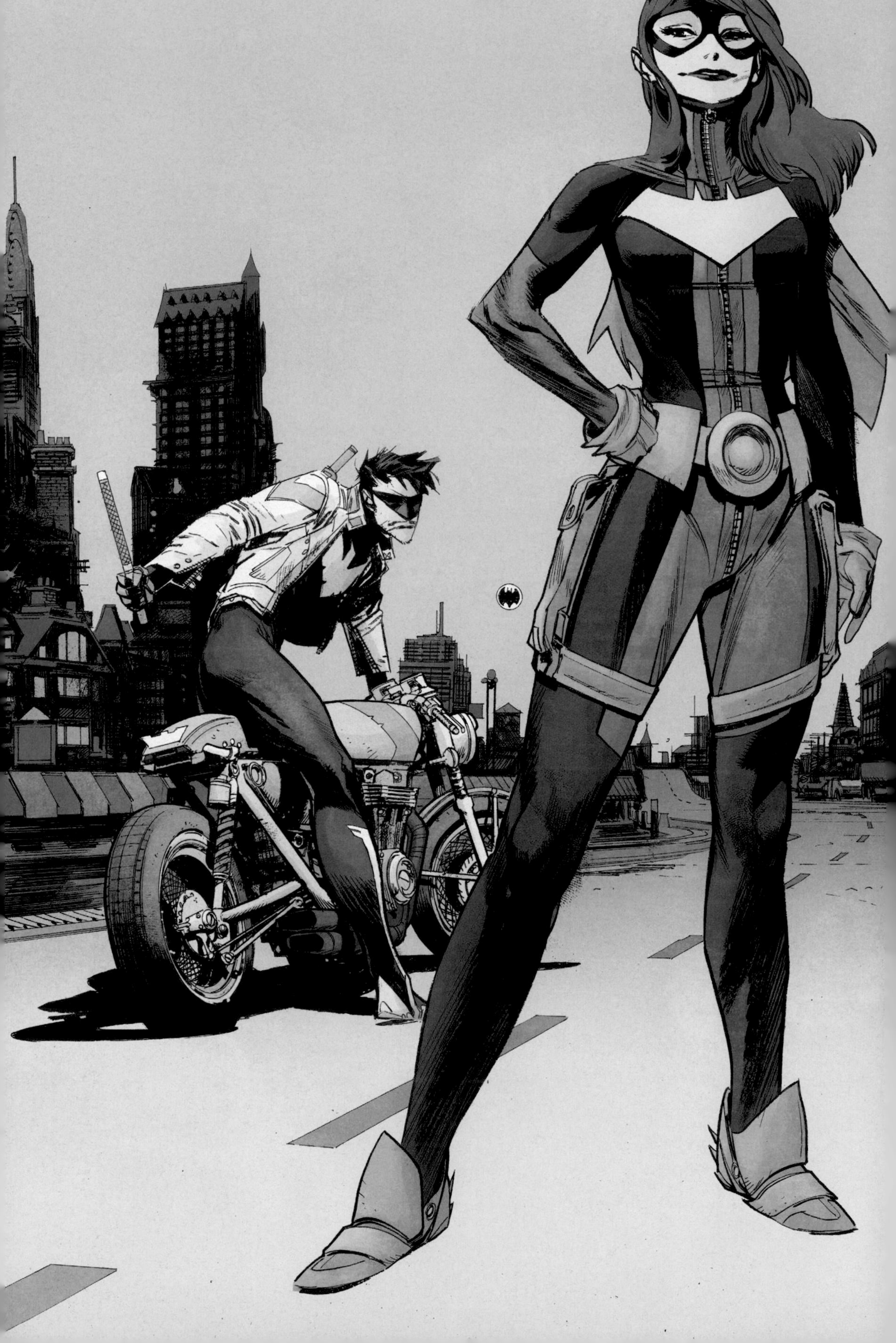

Issue №7 variant cover

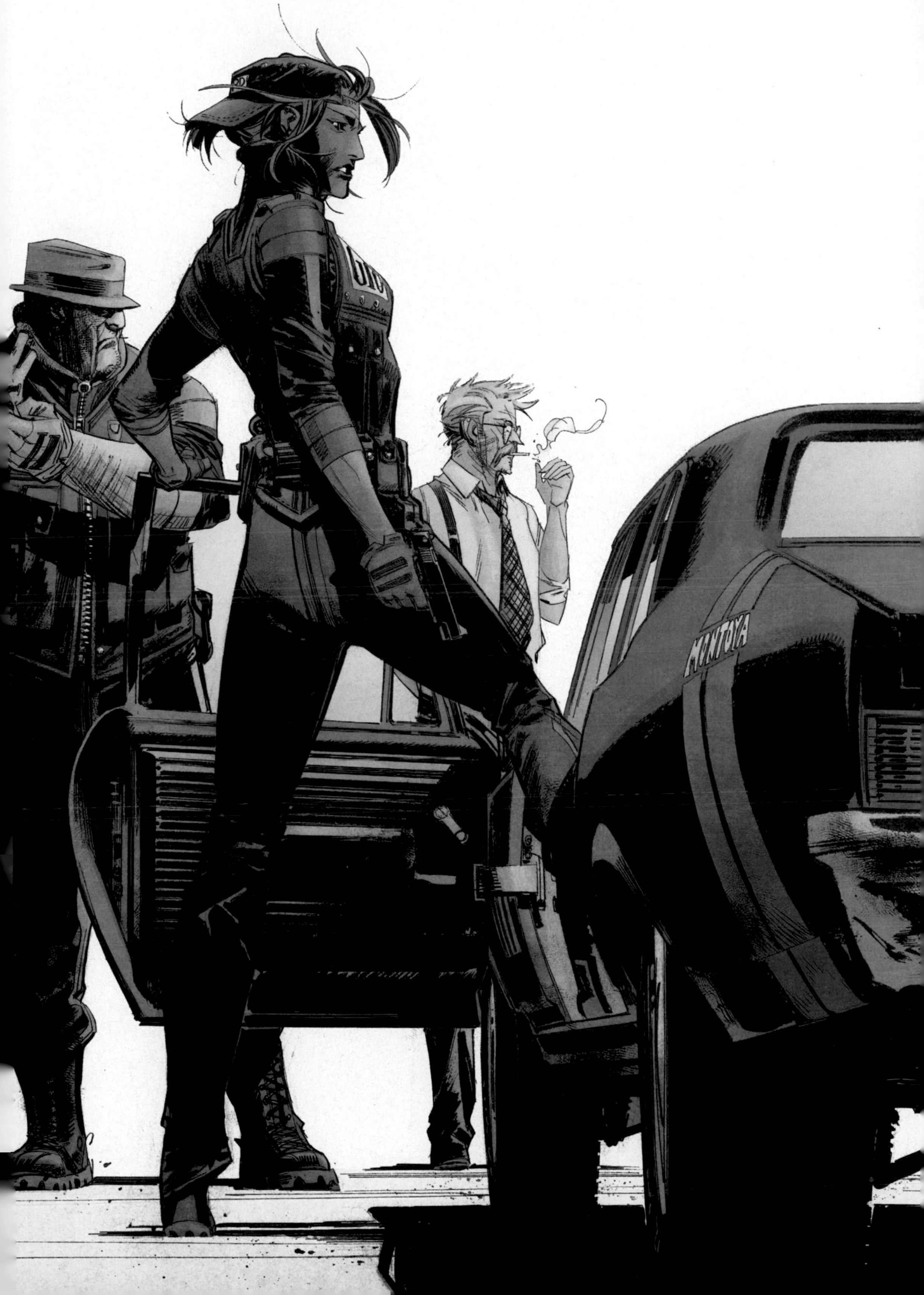
MONTOYA

Issue №8 variant cover

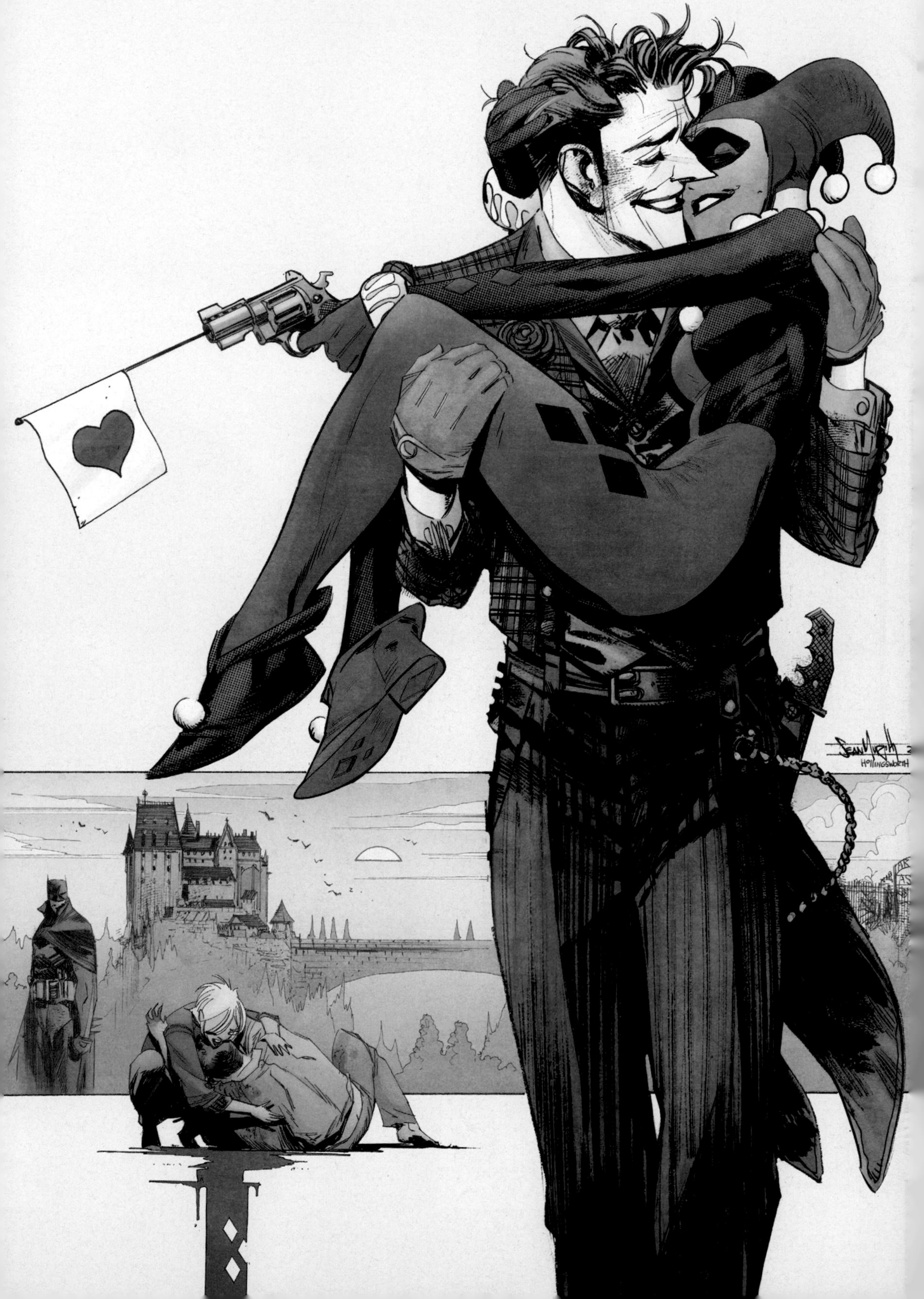

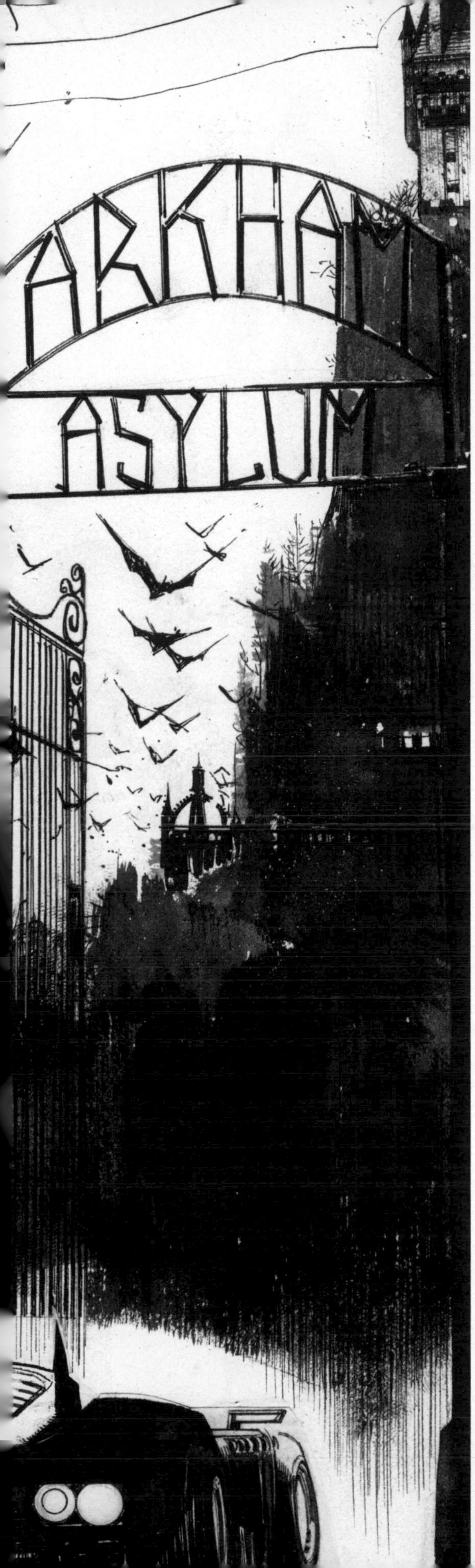
ARKHAM
ASYLUM

SHADES OF GRAY

character designs
and preliminary artwork
by SEAN MURPHY

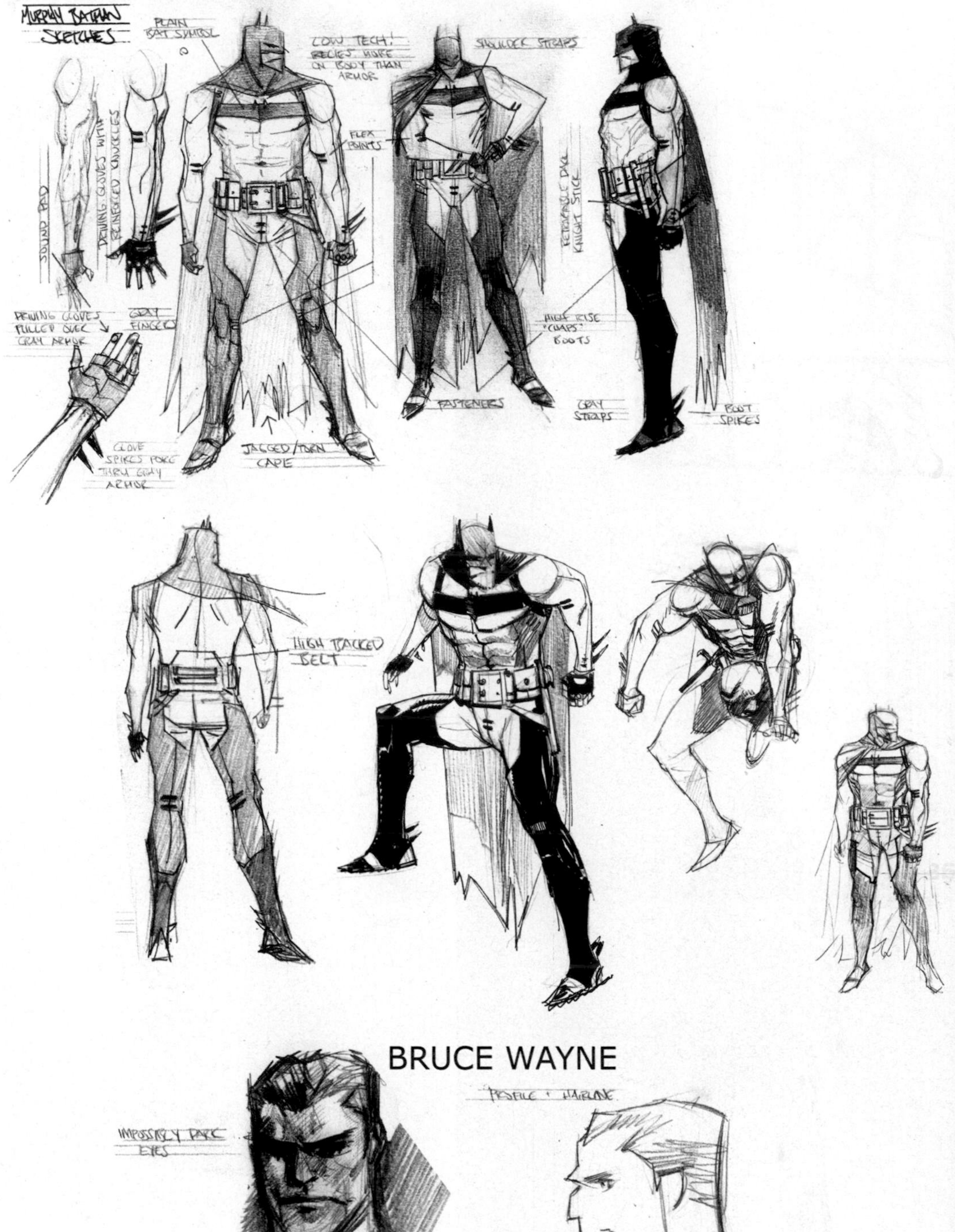
MURPHY BATMAN
SKETCHES
PLAIN BAT SYMBOL
LOW TECH! RELIES MORE ON BODY THAN ARMOR
SHOULDER STRAPS
SOUND PAD
DRIVING GLOVES WITH REINFORCED KNUCKLES
FLEX POINTS
RETRACTABLE DAGGER KNIGHT STICK
DRIVING GLOVES PULLED OVER GRAY ARMOR
GRAY FINGERS
HIGH RISE "CHAPS" BOOTS
FASTENERS
GRAY STRAPS
BOOT SPIKES
GLOVE SPIKES FORCE THRU GRAY ARMOR
JAGGED/TORN CAPE
HIGH BACKED BELT

BRUCE WAYNE

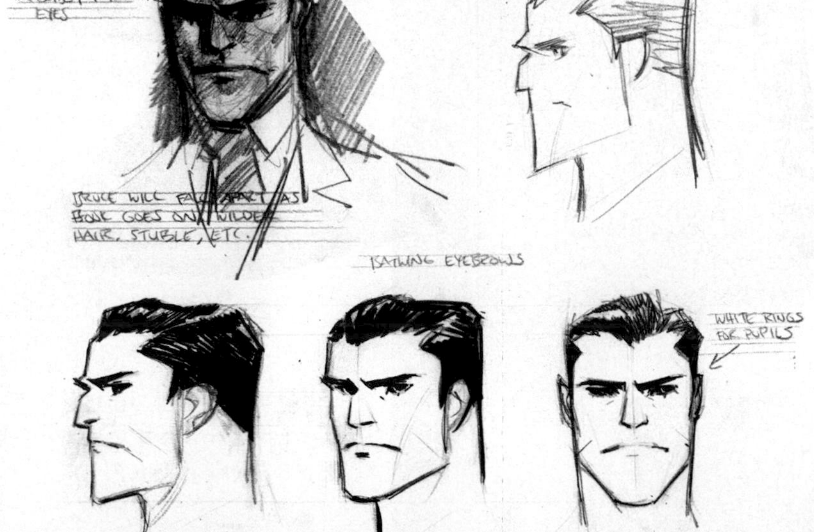
PROFILE + HAIRLINE
IMPOSSIBLY DARK EYES
BRUCE WILL FALL APART AS BOOK GOES ON. WILDER HAIR, STUBLE, ETC.
BATWING EYEBROWS
WHITE RINGS FOR PUPILS

JOKER
before and after

JACK
NAPIER

EYE MAKEUP
ALWAYS RUNNING
DOWN FACE
FROM LAUGHTER

HARLEY

Harley will be without custom
for most of the book, as will
Jack.

HARLEY WANTS TO HELP DEFEAT
BATMAN SO JOKER WILL
GET OVER HIM.

JOKER
starts
as psycho

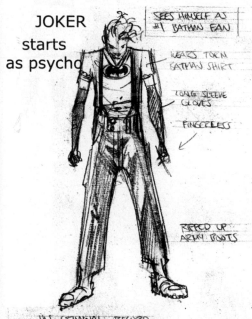

SEES HIMSELF AS
#1 BATMAN FAN

WEARS TORN
BATMAN SHIRT

LONG SLEEVE
GLOVES

FINGERLESS

RIPPED UP
ARMY BOOTS

HIS CRIMINAL RECORD
IS DUE TO HIS OBSESSION +
LOVE AFFAIR WITH BATMAN.

JOKER BECOMES
DON DRAPER

NAPIER

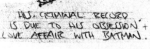

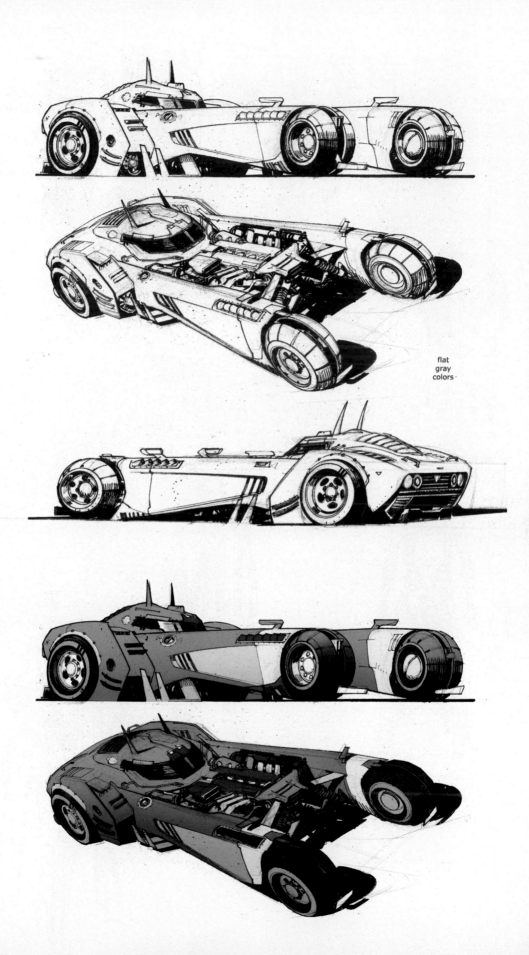

flat
gray
colors

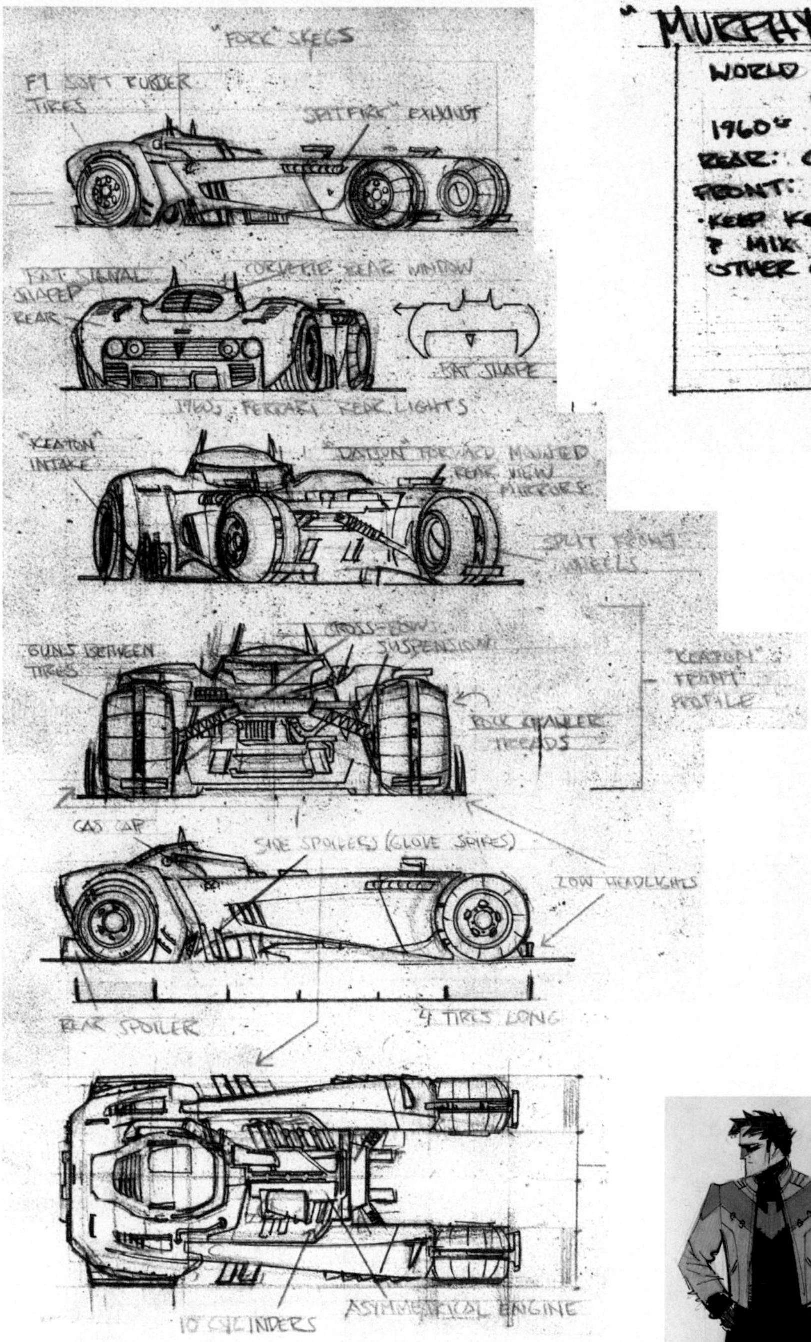
"FORK" SKEGS
F1 SOFT RUBBER TIRES
"SPITFIRE" EXHAUST
BAT SIGNAL SHAPED REAR
CORVETTE REAR WINDOW
BAT SHAPE
1960s FERRARI REAR LIGHTS
"KEATON" INTAKE
"DATSUN" FORWARD MOUNTED REAR VIEW MIRRORS
SPLIT FRONT WHEELS
GUNS BETWEEN TIRES
CROSS-BOW SUSPENSION
ROCK CRAWLER TREADS
"KEATON" FRONT PROFILE
GAS CAP
SIDE SPOILERS (GLOVE SPIKES)
LOW HEADLIGHTS
REAR SPOILER
4 TIRES LONG
10 CYLINDERS
ASYMMETRICAL ENGINE

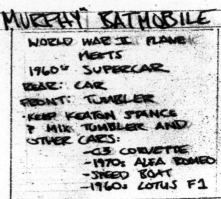

"MURPHY" BATMOBILE

WORLD WAR II PLANE
MEETS
1960s SUPERCAR
REAR: CAR
FRONT: TUMBLER
• KEEP KEATON STANCE
& MIX TUMBLER AND
OTHER CARS:
- C3 CORVETTE
- 1970s ALFA ROMEO
- SPEED BOAT
- 1960s LOTUS F1

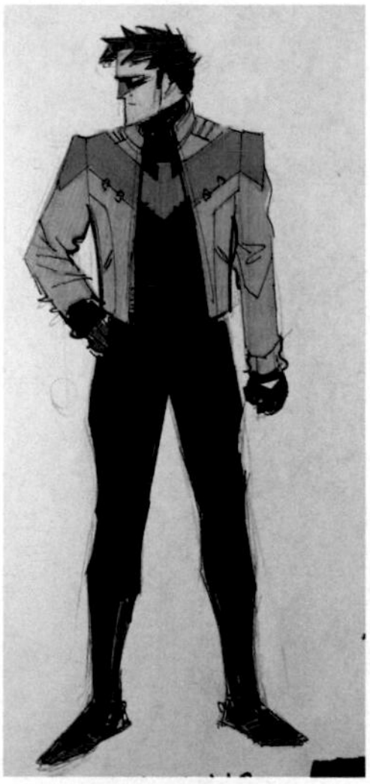

DUKE
(ROBIN)

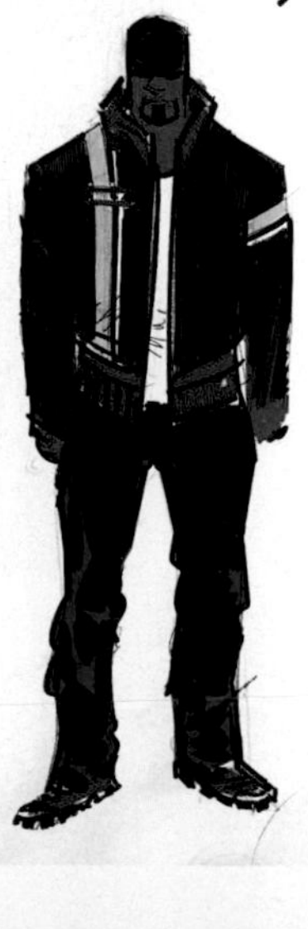

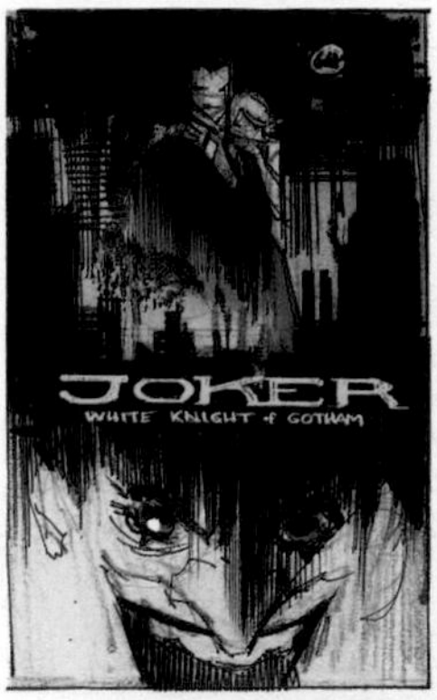
JOKER
WHITE KNIGHT of GOTHAM

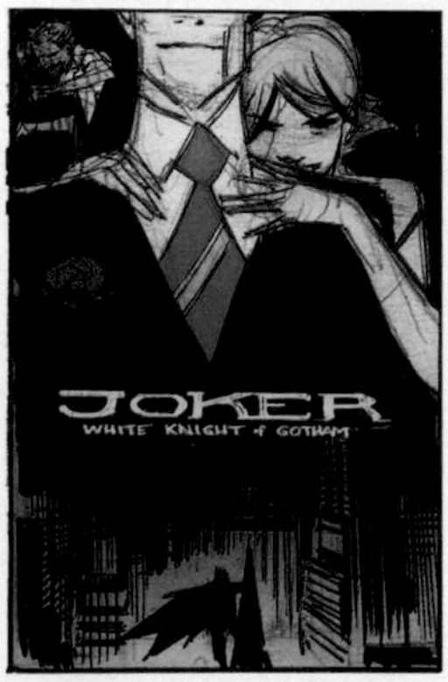
JOKER
WHITE KNIGHT of GOTHAM

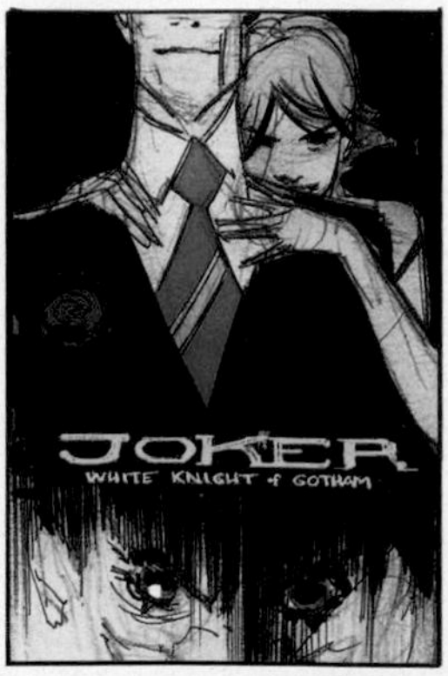
JOKER
WHITE KNIGHT of GOTHAM

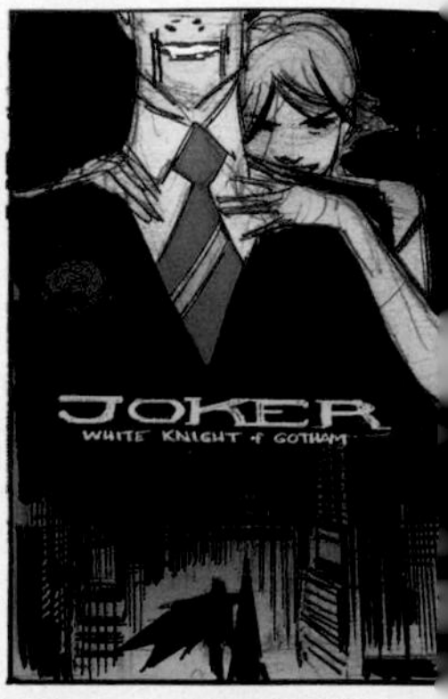
JOKER
WHITE KNIGHT of GOTHAM

WK cover 5

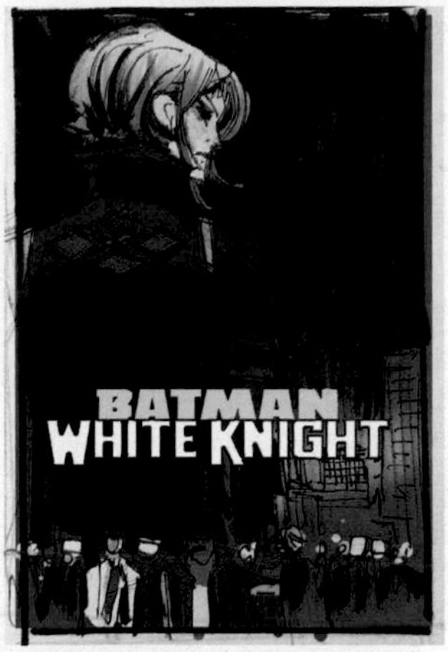
BATMAN
WHITE KNIGHT

Neo Joker wearing her logo: 3 Harley diamonds with a Joker rose.

Duke, Jack and Harley at a BLM protest in Backport at the bottom.

WK variant 5

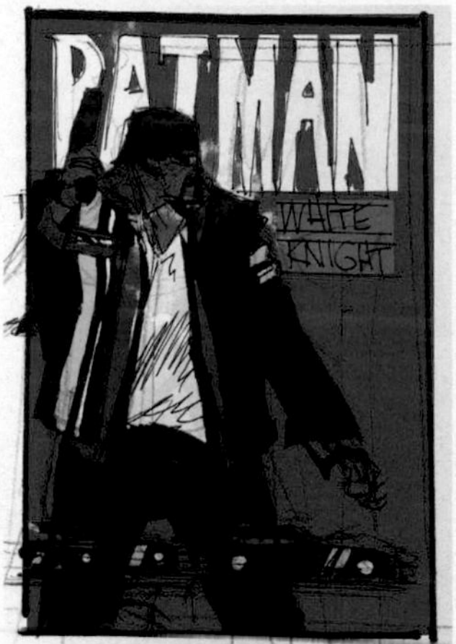
BATMAN
WHITE KNIGHT

Duke with Robin colors, holding his gun. The GTO cars racing by underneath him.

6

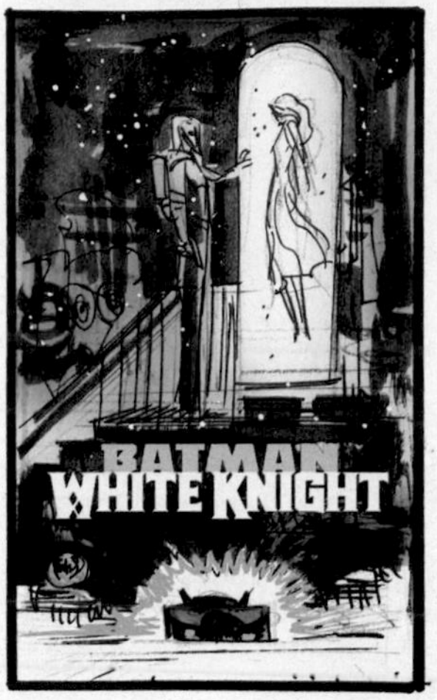
BATMAN
WHITE KNIGHT

2

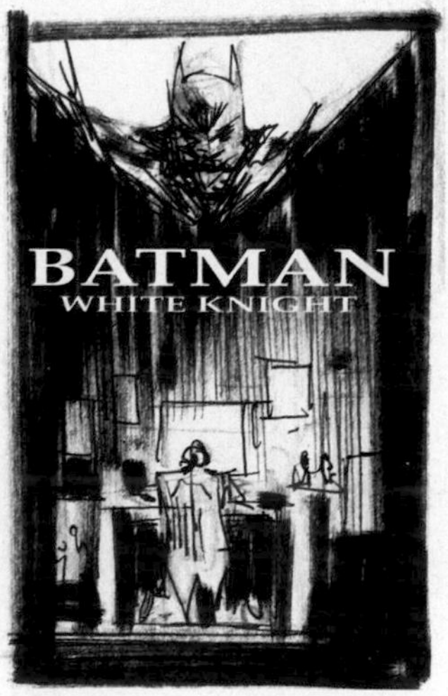
BATMAN
WHITE KNIGHT

3

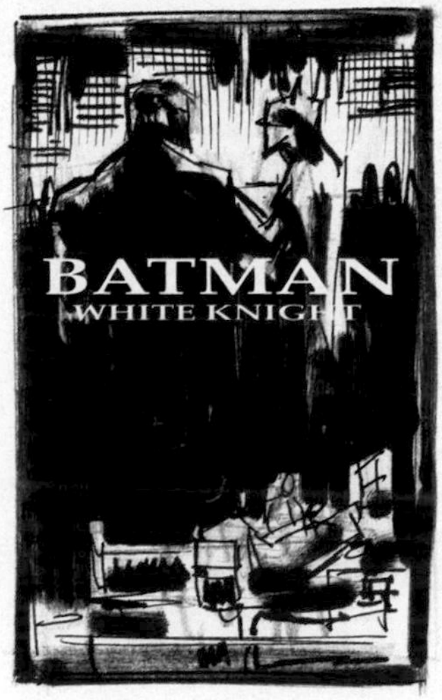
BATMAN
WHITE KNIGHT

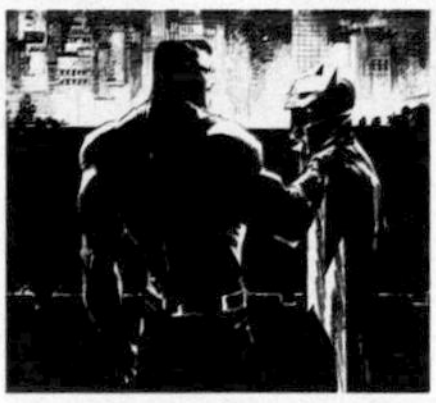

Cover based on this panel.Bottom half Alfred in bed, Batgirl and Nightwing by his side.

1

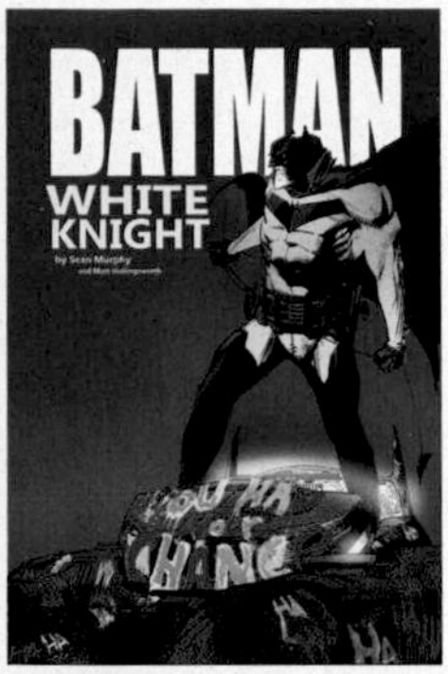
BATMAN
WHITE
KNIGHT

2

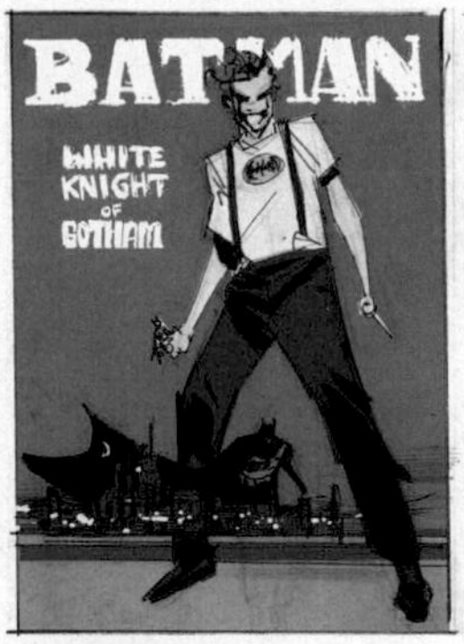
BATMAN
WHITE
KNIGHT
OF
GOTHAM

3

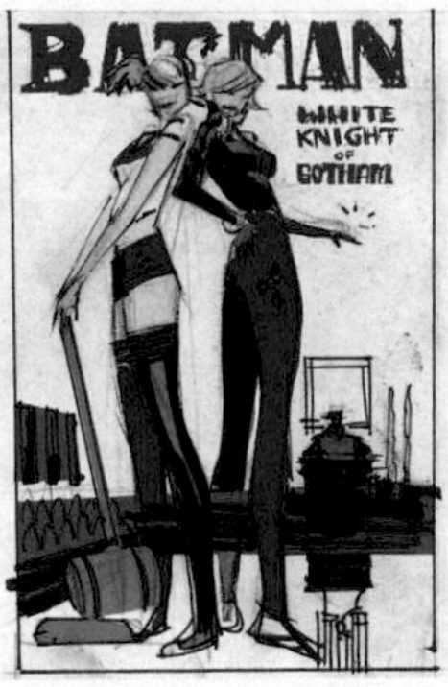
BATMAN
WHITE
KNIGHT
OF
GOTHAM

4

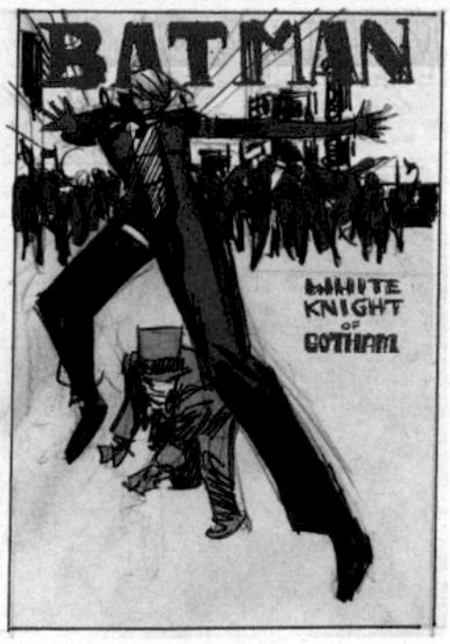
BATMAN
WHITE
KNIGHT
OF
GOTHAM

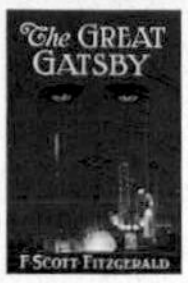
The GREAT
GATSBY
F. SCOTT FITZGERALD

Matt: please match this Gatsby cover even better than I did.

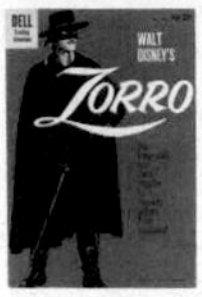
DELL
WALT DISNEY'S
ZORRO

Variant covers for White Knight based on classic Dell Four Color covers

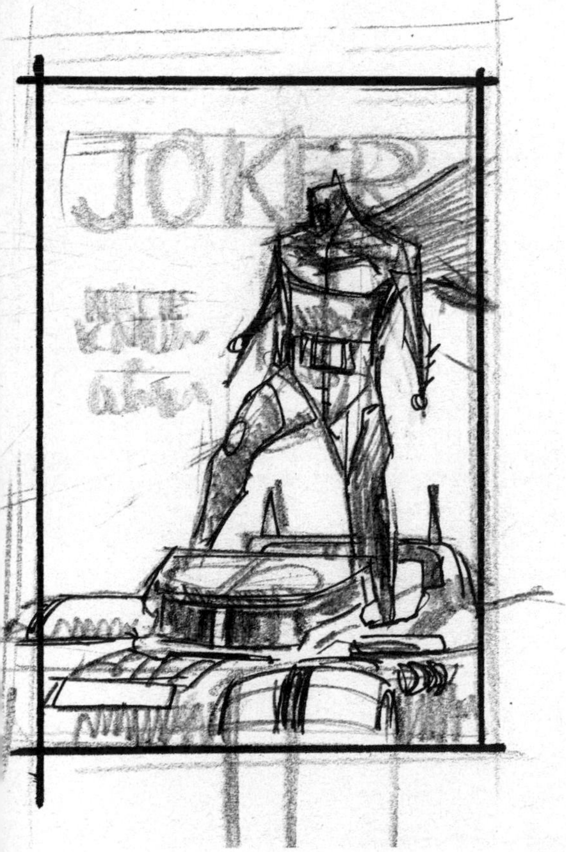
JOKER

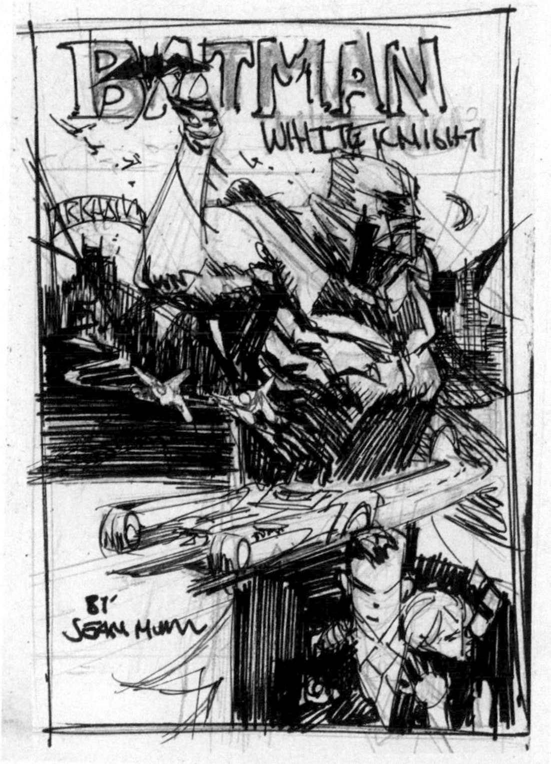
BATMAN
WHITE KNIGHT

Uncolored Toppi style cover.

Photo by Colleen Katana

After breaking into the industry at a young age, Sean Murphy made a name for himself in the world of indie comics before joining up with DC. In his tenure, he has worked on such titles as BATMAN/SCARECROW: YEAR ONE, TEEN TITANS, HELLBLAZER, JOE THE BARBARIAN and the critically acclaimed miniseries AMERICAN VAMPIRE: SURVIVAL OF THE FITTEST and THE WAKE with Scott Snyder. Murphy also wrote and illustrated the original graphic novel *Off Road* and the popular miniseries PUNK ROCK JESUS.